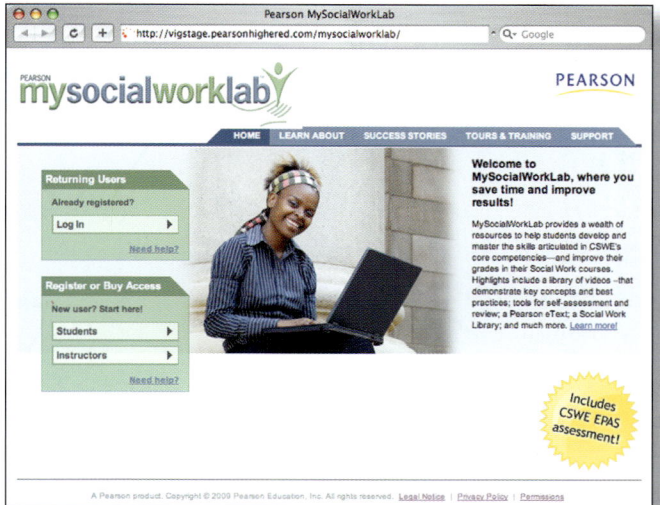

MySocialWorkLab offers:

- A complete **Pearson eText** of the book
- A wealth of engaging **videos**
  - **Brand-new videos**—organized around the competencies and accompanied by interactive assessment—that demonstrate key concepts and practices
  - **Career Exploration videos** that contain interviews with a wide range of social workers
- Tools for **self-assessment and review**—chapter specific quizzes tied to the core competencies, many written in the same format students will find on the licensing exam
- A **Gradebook** that reports progress of students and the class as a whole
- **MySocialWorkLibrary**—a compendium of articles and case studies in social work, searchable by course, topic, author, and title
- **MySearchLab**—a collection of tools that aid students in mastering research assignments and papers
- And much more!

Save time and improve results!

MySocialWorkLab is a dynamic website that provides a wealth of resources geared to help students develop and master the skills articulated in CSWE's core competencies—and improve their grades in their social work courses.

MySocialWorkLab is available at no extra cost when bundled with any text in the **Connecting Core Competencies Series.** Visit **www.mysocialworklab.com** to learn more.

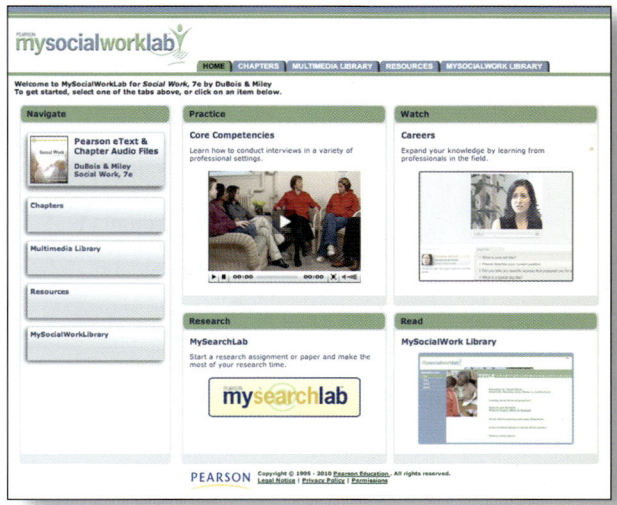

"I would require [MySocialWorkLab]—especially if there were a way to harvest the results for program assessment."

—Jane Peller, *Northeastern Illinois University*

CONNECTING CORE COMPETENCIES SERIES

In recent years, many Social Work departments have been focusing on the CSWE Educational Policy and Accreditation Standards (EPAS) to guide their accreditation process. The current standards, issued in 2008, focus on mastery of the CSWE's ten core competencies and practice behaviors. Each of the ten core competencies now contains specific knowledge, values, skills, and the resulting practice behaviors as guidance for the curriculum and assessment methods of Social Work programs.

In writing this text, we have used the CSWE core competency standards and assessment recommendations as guidelines for structuring content and integrating the pedagogy. For details on the CSWE core competencies, please see www.cswe.org.

For the core competencies highlighted in this text, see page iv.

CSWE EPAS 2008 Core Competencies

Professional Identity

2.1.1 Identify as a professional social worker and conduct oneself accordingly.

Necessary Knowledge, Values, Skills	Operational Practice Behaviors
• Social workers serve as representatives of the profession, its mission, and its core values. • Social workers know the profession's history. • Social workers commit themselves to the profession's enhancement and to their own professional conduct and growth.	• Social workers advocate for client access to the services of social work; • Social workers practice personal reflection and self-correction to assure continual professional development; • Social workers attend to professional roles and boundaries; • Social workers demonstrate professional demeanor in behavior, appearance, and communication; • Social workers engage in career-long learning; and • Social workers use supervision and consultation.

Ethical Practice

2.1.2 Apply social work ethical principles to guide professional practice.

Necessary Knowledge, Values, Skills	Operational Practice Behaviors
• Social workers have an obligation to conduct themselves ethically and engage in ethical decision-making. • Social workers are knowledgeable about the value base of the profession, its ethical standards, and relevant law.	• Social workers recognize and manage personal values in a way that allows professional values to guide practice; • Social workers make ethical decisions by applying standards of the National Association of Social Workers Code of Ethics and, as applicable, of the International Federation of Social Workers/International Association of Schools of Social Work Ethics in Social Work, Statement of Principles; • Social workers tolerate ambiguity in resolving ethical conflicts; and • Social workers apply strategies of ethical reasoning to arrive at principled decisions.

Critical Thinking

2.1.3 Apply critical thinking to inform and communicate professional judgments.

Necessary Knowledge, Values, Skills	Operational Practice Behaviors
• Social workers are knowledgeable about the principles of logic, scientific inquiry, and reasoned discernment. • They use critical thinking augmented by creativity and curiosity. • Critical thinking also requires the synthesis and communication of relevant information.	• Social workers distinguish, appraise, and integrate multiple sources of knowledge, including research-based knowledge, and practice wisdom; • Social workers analyze models of assessment, prevention, intervention, and evaluation; and • Social workers demonstrate effective oral and written communication in working with individuals, families, groups, organizations, communities, and colleagues.

Adapted with the permission of Council on Social Work Education

CSWE EPAS 2008 Core Competencies *(continued)*

Diversity in Practice
2.1.4 Engage diversity and difference in practice.

Necessary Knowledge, Values, Skills

- Social workers understand how diversity characterizes and shapes the human experience and is critical to the formation of identity.
- The dimensions of diversity are understood as the intersectionality of multiple factors including age, class, color, culture, disability, ethnicity, gender, gender identity and expression, immigration status, political ideology, race, religion, sex, and sexual orientation.
- Social workers appreciate that, as a consequence of difference, a person's life experiences may include oppression, poverty, marginalization, and alienation as well as privilege, power, and acclaim.

Operational Practice Behaviors

- Social workers recognize the extent to which a culture's structures and values may oppress, marginalize, alienate, or create or enhance privilege and power;
- Social workers gain sufficient self-awareness to eliminate the influence of personal biases and values in working with diverse groups;
- Social workers recognize and communicate their understanding of the importance of difference in shaping life experiences; and
- Social workers view themselves as learners and engage those with whom they work as informants.

Human Rights & Justice
2.1.5 Advance human rights and social and economic justice.

Necessary Knowledge, Values, Skills

- Each person, regardless of position in society, has basic human rights, such as freedom, safety, privacy, an adequate standard of living, health care, and education.
- Social workers recognize the global interconnections of oppression and are knowledgeable about theories of justice and strategies to promote human and civil rights.
- Social work incorporates social justice practices in organizations, institutions, and society to ensure that these basic human rights are distributed equitably and without prejudice.

Operational Practice Behaviors

- Social workers understand the forms and mechanisms of oppression and discrimination;
- Social workers advocate for human rights and social and economic justice; and
- Social workers engage in practices that advance social and economic justice.

Research Based Practice
2.1.6 Engage in research-informed practice and practice-informed research.

Necessary Knowledge, Values, Skills

- Social workers use practice experience to inform research, employ evidence-based interventions, evaluate their own practice, and use research findings to improve practice, policy, and social service delivery.
- Social workers comprehend quantitative and qualitative research and understand scientific and ethical approaches to building knowledge.

Operational Practice Behaviors

- Social workers use practice experience to inform scientific inquiry; and
- Social workers use research evidence to inform practice.

Human Behavior
2.1.7 Apply knowledge of human behavior and the social environment.

Necessary Knowledge, Values, Skills

- Social workers are knowledgeable about human behavior across the life course; the range of social systems in which people live; and the ways social systems promote or deter people in maintaining or achieving health and well-being.
- Social workers apply theories and knowledge from the liberal arts to understand biological, social, cultural, psychological, and spiritual development.

Operational Practice Behaviors

- Social workers utilize conceptual frameworks to guide the processes of assessment, intervention, and evaluation; and
- Social workers critique and apply knowledge to understand person and environment.

CSWE EPAS 2008 Core Competencies (continued)

Policy Practice
2.1.8 Engage in policy practice to advance social and economic well-being and to deliver effective social work services.

Necessary Knowledge, Values, Skills
- Social work practitioners understand that policy affects service delivery and they actively engage in policy practice.
- Social workers know the history and current structures of social policies and services; the role of policy in service delivery; and the role of practice in policy development.

Operational Practice Behaviors
- Social workers analyze, formulate, and advocate for policies that advance social well-being; and
- Social workers collaborate with colleagues and clients for effective policy action.

Practice Contexts
2.1.9 Respond to contexts that shape practice.

Necessary Knowledge, Values, Skills
- Social workers are informed, resourceful, and proactive in responding to evolving organizational, community, and societal contexts at all levels of practice.
- Social workers recognize that the context of practice is dynamic, and use knowledge and skill to respond proactively.

Operational Practice Behaviors
- Social workers continuously discover, appraise, and attend to changing locales, populations, scientific and technological developments, and emerging societal trends to provide relevant services; and
- Social workers provide leadership in promoting sustainable changes in service delivery and practice to improve the quality of social services.

Engage, Assess, Intervene, Evaluate
2.1.10 Engage, assess, intervene, and evaluate with individuals, families, groups, organizations, and communities.

Necessary Knowledge, Values, Skills
- Professional practice involves the dynamic and interactive processes of engagement, assessment, intervention, and evaluation at multiple levels.
- Social workers have the knowledge and skills to practice with individuals, families, groups, organizations, and communities.
- Practice knowledge includes
  - identifying, analyzing, and implementing evidence-based interventions designed to achieve client goals;
  - using research and technological advances;
  - evaluating program outcomes and practice effectiveness;
  - developing, analyzing, advocating, and providing leadership for policies and services; and
  - promoting social and economic justice.

Operational Practice Behaviors

(a) Engagement
- Social workers substantively and affectively prepare for action with individuals, families, groups, organizations, and communities;
- Social workers use empathy and other interpersonal skills; and
- Social workers develop a mutually agreed-on focus of work and desired outcomes.

(b) Assessment
- Social workers collect, organize, and interpret client data;
- Social workers assess client strengths and limitations;
- Social workers develop mutually agreed-on intervention goals and objectives; and
- Social workers select appropriate intervention strategies.

(c) Intervention
- Social workers initiate actions to achieve organizational goals;
- Social workers implement prevention interventions that enhance client capacities;
- Social workers help clients resolve problems;
- Social workers negotiate, mediate, and advocate for clients; and
- Social workers facilitate transitions and endings.

(d) Evaluation
- Social workers critically analyze, monitor, and evaluate interventions.

CONNECTING CORE COMPETENCIES Chapter-by-Chapter Matrix

Chapter	Professional Identity	Ethical Practice	Critical Thinking	Diversity in Practice	Human Rights & Justice	Research Based Practice	Human Behavior	Policy Practice	Practice Contexts	Engage Assess Intervene Evaluate
1	✔			✔	✔			✔		
2				✔	✔		✔		✔	
3			✔		✔			✔	✔	
4	✔	✔		✔		✔				
5			✔	✔	✔				✔	
6	✔	✔					✔		✔	
7			✔		✔			✔	✔	
8					✔		✔	✔		✔
9		✔	✔						✔	
10				✔	✔		✔		✔	
11	✔			✔	✔				✔	
12			✔					✔		✔
13			✔		✔	✔		✔		
14		✔					✔		✔	✔
15	✔						✔	✔	✔	
16					✔			✔	✔	
Total Chapters	5	4	6	6	10	2	6	8	11	3

Social Work and Social Welfare

An Introduction

Jerry D. Marx
University of New Hampshire

C. Anne Broussard
University of New Hampshire

Fleur A. Hopper
Bowdoin College

David Worster
University of New Hampshire

Allyn & Bacon

Boston Columbus Indianapolis New York San Francisco Upper Saddle River
Amsterdam Cape Town Dubai London Madrid Milan Munich Paris Montreal Toronto
Delhi Mexico City São Paulo Sydney Hong Kong Seoul Singapore Taipei Tokyo

Editor in Chief: Dickson Musslewhite
Executive Editor: Ashley Dodge
Editorial Project Manager: Carly Czech
Executive Marketing Manager: Jeanette Koskinas
Senior Marketing Manager: Wendy Albert
Marketing Assistant: Patrick M. Walsh
Production Manager: Kathy Sleys
Associate Production Project Manager: Maggie Brobeck
Editorial Production and Composition Service: Aparna Yellai/PreMediaGlobal
Photo Researcher: Martha Shethar
Cover Designer: Kristina Mose-Libon/ Suzanne Duda
Cover Image: Ana Abejon/iStockphoto
Creative Director: Jayne Conte
Printer/Binder: Edwards Brothers
Cover Printer: Lehigh-Phoenix

Credits appear on page 397, which constitutes an extension of the copyright page.

Copyright © 2011 Pearson Education, Inc., publishing as Allyn & Bacon, 75 Arlington St., Suite 300, Boston, MA 02116. All rights reserved. Manufactured in the United States of America. This publication is protected by Copyright, and permission should be obtained from the publisher prior to any prohibited reproduction, storage in a retrieval system, or transmission in any form or by any means, electronic, mechanical, photocopying, recording, or likewise. To obtain permission(s) to use material from this work, please submit a written request to Pearson Higher Education, Rights and Contracts Department, 501 Boylston Street, Suite 900, Boston, MA 02116, or fax your request to 617-671-3447.

Many of the designations by manufacturers and sellers to distinguish their products are claimed as trademarks. Where those designations appear in this book, and the publisher was aware of a trademark claim, the designations have been printed in initial caps or all caps.

Library of Congress Cataloging-in-Publication Data

Social work and social welfare : an introduction / Jerry D. Mark . . . [et al.]. — 1st ed.
  p. cm.
  Includes bibliographical references and index.
  ISBN-13: 978-0-205-50229-5
  ISBN-10: 0-205-50229-6
 1. Social service—United States. 2. Public welfare—United States.
 I. Mark, Jerry D.
  HV91.S6244 2011
  361.30973—dc22

2010029068

10 9 8 7 6 5 4 3 2 1 EB 14 13 12 11 10

Allyn & Bacon
is an imprint of

www.pearsonhighered.com

ISBN 10: 0-205-50229-6
ISBN 13: 978-0-205-50229-5

Contents

Preface   xvii

1. Social Work as a Profession   1

A Profession Defined   2
  Would You Enjoy a Career in Social Work?   2
  Social Work Defined   2
  Social Work in Relation to Social Welfare   4

Possible Careers in Social Work   5
  Social Work with Individuals   5
  Social Work with Families   6
  Social Work with Groups   7
  Social Work with Communities   8
  Social Workers in Administration   9
  Social Workers in Policy Practice   10
  Social Workers in Research   11
  Social Work in Relation to Other Professions   11

Social Work: A Values-Based Profession   14
  Values   14
  Ethics   15
  Competence in Relation to Diversity and Individual Dignity   18
  Social Justice and Human Rights   20
  Strengths and Empowerment   21

Baccalaureate Social Work Education   22

The Future of Social Work   25

Summary   26

PRACTICE TEST   27

MySocialWorkLab   27

2. Theoretical and Conceptual Models of Social Work   28

The Complexity of Social Work Theory and Practice   29

Human Behavior and the Social Environment   30
  Multidimensional View: The Biopsychosocial Model of HBSE   31
  Biological Domain   32
  Psychological Domain   33
  Social Domain   37
  Expanding Our Perspective: The Spiritual and Physical Domains   40

Systems Theory and Social Work Practice   42
    The Ecosystems Perspective   43

The Strengths Perspective in Social Work Practice   45

Summary   46

PRACTICE TEST   48

MySocialWorkLab   48

3. Basic Concepts in Social Welfare   49

Social Welfare: A Conceptualization   50
    Ideological Input   51
    Economic Institutions   53
    Political Institutions   54
    Social Institutions   57
    Outcome: Societal Well-Being   59

Summary   60

PRACTICE TEST   61

MySocialWorkLab   61

4. Generalist Social Work Practice   62

Roles and Functions of Social Work   63

The Nature of Helping Relationships   64

Diversity and Cultural Competency   65

Engagement   66

Data Collection and Assessment   68
    Family Assessments   69
    Group Assessments   70
    Organization and Community Assessment   70

Planning and Contracting   72

Intervention in Generalist Social Work   73
    Generalist Social Work with Individuals   74
    Generalist Social Work with Families   75
    Generalist Social Work with Groups   76
    Generalist Social Work with Organizations and Communities   77

Evaluation   78

Termination   80

Summary   83

PRACTICE TEST   85

MySocialWorkLab   85

5. Social Work and Social Justice: Diversity, Difference, and Oppression   86

Human Difference and Diversity   87

Diverse Peoples of the United States   90
- *Major Social Groups in the United States   90*

Organizing Principles of Diversity and Difference in Society   98
- *Social Groups   98*
- *Inequality: Discrimination and Prejudice   99*
- *Inequality: Domination and Subordination   99*
- *Identity   100*
- *Oppression, Power, and Privilege   102*

The Lived Experience of Oppression: "The Isms"   104
- *Racism   104*
- *Ethnocentrism   104*
- *Xenophobia   105*
- *Classism   105*
- *Sexism   106*
- *Homophobia and Heterosexism   107*
- *Ableism   108*

Social Work and Social Justice   109
- *Empowering Practices: Social Justice in Action   109*
- *Practice Focus: Strengths-Based Practice   109*

Summary   111

PRACTICE TEST   113

MySocialWorkLab   113

6. History of Social Work and Social Welfare   114

The Beginnings of a U.S. Social Welfare System   115
- *Caring for the Poor: Poverty and the Workhouse   115*
- *The Central Role of Organized Religion and the First Amendment   116*
- *The Influence of American Philanthropy   117*

Industrialization of America   117
- *The Poor Laborer   117*
- *The Antipauper Movement   117*
- *The Growth of Private Nonprofit Agencies for the Poor   118*
- *The Development of Charity Organization Societies   118*
- *The Progressive Era   119*
- *The Social Advocacy of Women and the Settlement Houses   121*
- *Business Charitable Contributions: The Growth of Community Chests and Service Clubs   123*

The Great Depression and Creation of a National Social Welfare System   124
- *The Great Depression   124*
- *The New Deal   125*

The Role of Social Work in the New Deal   127
Successes and Failures of the New Deal   128

Lyndon B. Johnson and the Great Society   129
The Great Society   129

Nixon and the Federal Social Welfare Partnership   131

The Women's Movement   132
Impact of the Civil Rights and Women's Movements on Professional Social Work   133

Reagan and New Federalism   134
The First President Bush: George H. W. Bush   135
Bill Clinton and Welfare Reform   135
Developments in Social Work   136
Social Welfare Developments: George W. Bush–Barak H. Obama   137

Summary   137

PRACTICE TEST   138

MySocialWorkLab   138

7. Poverty and Social Welfare   139

Introduction to Poverty   140

Definition and Causes of Poverty   140
Defining and Measuring Poverty   140
Federal Poverty Thresholds and Guidelines   141
Current Federal Poverty Thresholds: Problems and Alternatives   142
Who Are the Poor?   143
Demographic Trends in Poverty   144

Causes of Poverty   145
Economic System Factors: Work, Income, and the Labor Market   146
Wage Inequality   148
Education and "Human Capital"   149
Oppression and Discrimination   150
The Impact of Changing Family Structures   151
The "Culture of Poverty"   152

Publicly Funded Services to the Poor   154

Social Insurance Programs   155

Public Assistance Programs   156
Current Issues in Public Assistance: A Critical Analysis of Welfare Reform   158

Food and Shelter Programs   158
Food Stamps   158
The Special Supplemental Food Program for Women, Infants, and Children (WIC)   159
Public Housing and Section 8 Housing Assistance   159
Contributions of Business and the Private Nonprofit Sector to Housing   160

Current Shelter Issues: The Homeless   161
Other Publicly Funded Programs in American Social Welfare   163

Summary   163

PRACTICE TEST   164

**MySocialWorkLab   164**

---

8. Health, Health Care, and Medical Social Work   165

Social Workers in the Healthcare Profession   166

Major Health Problems   166
Heart Disease   166
Cancer   167
Obesity   168
Asthma   169
AIDS   170

Socioeconomic Aspects of Illness   170

Health Services   171
Medicare and Medicaid   172
Private Insurance and Managed Care   173
Problems in the Healthcare System   174
Problems with Managed Care   175
Uninsured and Underinsured   175
Why Don't People Have Health Insurance?   175
The Un-Covered Middle Class   176
Prescription Drugs   176
Innovations and Proposed Solutions   177
Policy Proposal: Health Care Reform in the United States   178

Social Work in a Medical Setting   180
Hospital Social Work   180
Community Health Clinics   181
Hospice   182
Health Promotion and Prevention   182

Interprofessional Collaboration: Social Work and Healthcare Professionals   184

Summary   186

PRACTICE TEST   187

MySocialWorkLab   187

---

9. Emotional and Behavioral Problems and Social Work Treatment   188

Mental Health in the United States   189

Mental Health and "Illness": Conceptualizations of Mental Disorder   189
The Medical Model   190
Developmental Models   191
Sociological Theories and the "Myth of Mental Illness"   193
The Diagnostic and Statistical Manual of Mental Disorders (DSM)   194

Mental Disorders 195
  Disorders Usually First Diagnosed in Infancy, Childhood, or Adolescence 196
  Delirium, Dementia, Amnesic, and Other Cognitive Disorders 196
  Schizophrenia and Other Psychotic Disorders 196
  Mood Disorders 197
  Anxiety Disorders 197
  Sexual and Gender Identity Disorders 198
  Eating Disorders 198
  Personality Disorders 199
  Culture-Bound Syndromes 200

Social Work and Mental Health Services 200
  Micro Practice: Services to Individuals 200
  Mezzo Practice: Practice with Groups and Families 203
  Macro Practice: Policy, Administration, and Advocacy 205
  Practice Settings 205

Challenges and Trends in Mental Health and Social Work Practice 208
  Racial Disparities in Mental Health Care 208
  Managed Care 209
  Evidence-Based Treatment 210

Interprofessional Collaboration in Assertive Community Treatment (ACT) 210

Summary 212

PRACTICE TEST 213

MySocialWorkLab 213

10. Children, Youth, Family Problems, and Services 214

Families in the United States: Decades of Change 215
  Demographic Changes in the Family 215
  Changes in Functions of the Family 216
  Diverse Family Forms 216
  Monica McGoldrick and the Family Life Cycle 217

Major Challenges Facing Children, Youth, and Families 219
  Divorce 219
  Single-Parent Families 220
  Blended Families 221
  Family Violence 222
  Partner Abuse 223
  Sexual Violence 224
  Child Abuse and Neglect 225
  Types of Abuse 225
  Child Sexual Abuse and Incest 226

The Family-(Un)friendly Workplace 227

Major Services to Children, Youth, and Families 228

Child Welfare and Child Protection 228
Family Intervention 229
Out-of-Home Placements and Foster Care 229
The Removal vs. Reunification Debate 230
Adoption Services 231
Parenting Support Services and Education 232
Self-Help: Parents Anonymous 233
Adolescent Pregnancy and Parenting 233
Family Planning Services 234
Family Violence Services 234
Services to Survivors 234
Services to Batterers 235
Services to Families in an Educational Setting 235
Head Start and Early Head Start 235
School Social Work 236
Alternative Education Programs 237
Child, Couple, and Family Therapy 237
Therapeutic Work with Children: Play Therapy 238
Couples Counseling, Marital Therapy, and Family Therapy 238
Child Abuse and Family Violence Prevention 239
Adolescent Pregnancy Prevention 240

Summary 240

PRACTICE TEST 241

MySocialWorkLab 241

11. Physical and Developmental Disabilities 242

Defining Disability 243
Physical Disabilities 244
Developmental Disabilities 245
Cognitive Disabilities 248
Disabling Illness: Stroke, ALS 251

Social Response to Individuals with Disabilities 252
Historical Perspective 252
Current Trends 254

Major Services to Individuals with Disabilities 256
Publicly Funded Services 256
Rehabilitation and Vocational Services 259
Residential Services 260
In-Home Services 261
Special Education 263

Interprofessional Collaboration: Social Workers and Occupational Therapists, Physical Therapists, Speech Therapists 265

Summary 266

PRACTICE TEST 267

MySocialWorkLab 267

12. Substance Abuse and Social Work   268

Substance Use and Abuse Defined   269
- *What Is Substance Abuse?*   269

Current Issues in Substance Use and Abuse   271
- *Preventing Youth Smoking*   272
- *Youth, Drugs, and Alcohol*   273
- *The Debate over the Legalization of Marijuana*   275
- *Crystal Methamphetamine Abuse: An Emerging National Epidemic?*   275
- *Status of the Federal "War on Drugs"*   276

Models of Addiction   277
- *The Biopsychosocial Model of Addiction*   278
- *Sociocultural Models of Addiction*   278
- *Psychological Models of Addiction*   279
- *The Disease Model*   280

Substance Abuse Intervention   280
- *Self-Help: Twelve-Step Support Groups*   280
- *Professional Treatment Programs and Services*   282
- *Treatment Facilities*   283
- *Needle Exchange Programs*   284
- *Drug Courts*   286
- *Future Challenges in Drug Treatment: Dual Diagnosis*   286
- *Substance Abuse Prevention*   288

Summary   289

PRACTICE TEST   290

MySocialWorkLab   290

13. Crime and Social Work Intervention   291

Defining Crime   292
- *Categories of Criminal Behavior*   292

Theories of Crime and Criminal Behavior   293

Trends in Crime and Incarceration   294
- *Racism, Crime, and Incarceration*   295

The Adult Criminal Justice System   296
- *Law Enforcement*   296
- *Courts*   296
- *Corrections*   299

Youth Offenders and Juvenile Crime   299
- *Juvenile Justice System*   299
- *Juvenile and Family Court*   300
- *Recent Developments and Trends*   300
- *Prevention and Diversion Programs*   300
- *Restorative Justice and Juvenile Justice*   301
- *Girls and Juvenile Justice*   302

Social Work and Criminal Justice   303
    Correctional Social Workers and Services to Inmates   303
    Post-Release and Rehabilitation Services   306
    Probation and Parole   307
    Criminal Justice Reform   309

Crime Prevention   310
    Reducing Recidivism   310
    Crime Prevention Programs   311

Interprofessional Collaboration   312

Summary   314

PRACTICE TEST   316

MySocialWorkLab   316

14. Aging and Gerontological Social Work   317

Who Are Older Americans?   318
    Young-Old, Old-Old, and Oldest-Old   318
    The Graying of America   319

Social and Economic Challenges   319
    Ageism   319
    Declines in Private Pensions   320
    Health Care and Prescription Drugs   321
    Transportation Alternatives   322
    Remaining at Home   323

Elder Abuse   324

Lifecycle Challenges   325
    Loss and Grief   325
    Death and Dying   326
    Finding Meaning in Later Life   327

Services for Older Americans   328
    Social Security   328
    Medicare   328
    In-Home Care and Assistance Services   329
    Residential Care and Assisted Living   329
    Senior Centers   330
    Hospice Care   330

Advocacy and Collaboration for Older Americans   332

Summary   334

PRACTICE TEST   335

MySocialWorkLab   335

15. Globalization and International Social Work   336

The Global Economy   337
    Globalization Defined   337
    A Brief History of Globalization   337

The Political Foundation of Globalization 338

Positive Aspects of Globalization   339
    China and Globalization   340

The Negative Aspects of Globalization   342
    The Clash of Civilizations   342
    Unemployment and Economic Inequality   344
    Case Study: Wal-Mart and the Power of Global Corporations   344
    Loss of Cultural Identity   345
    Loss of Indigenous Economies   346
    Loss of Corporate Social Accountability   347
    The Weakening of Democracy   347

The Future: Collaboration and International Social Work   349
    International Social Work and the Importance of Social Work Values   349

Summary   353

PRACTICE TEST   354

MySocialWorkLab   354

16. Social Work, Policy, and Advocacy   355

Social Workers Engaged in Policy Practice   356
    Various Approaches to Problem Definition   356

The Social Worker as Advocate   358

Social and Economic Justice   360
    Diversity, Oppression, and Human Rights   360

Stakeholders, Collaboration, and Political Strategy   361
    Policy Research   361
    Major Stakeholders   362
    The Strengths Perspective and Policy Advocacy   363
    Policy Windows of Opportunity   364
    Collaboration and Political Strategy in Policy Advocacy   366
    Social Workers and Policy Debate   368
    Internet Advocacy   369

Social Workers and Advocacy Success   370

Summary   372

PRACTICE TEST   373

MySocialWorkLab   373

Notes   374

Text Credits   397

Photo Credits   399

Index   400

Preface

This text introduces students to social work as a profession in the context of the American social welfare system. Written with an emphasis on demonstrating student competency in relation to the CSWE 2008 Educational Policy and Accreditation Standards, the text utilizes "Demonstrating Knowledge, Values, and Skills," boxes that engage students in competency-based practice activities.

Additionally, student reflection regarding the value of applying social research to social work interventions is generated by "Research Informed Practice" boxes that employ recent studies with diverse sets of client populations.

The organization of this book begins with an overview of the profession, including important values and concepts in social work (Chapter 1) and continues with a discussion of the fundamental importance to social work of systems theory (Chapter 2), preparing students for an examination of the systemic context of social work—the U.S. social welfare system—in Chapter 3. Chapter 4 then explores how social workers actually practice at multiple system levels in their work by illustrating generalist practice methods as they relate to work with individuals, families, groups, organizations, and communities. Early in the text, the fundamental relationship of social work, diversity, inclusion, and social justice is discussed (Chapter 5). Similarly, to promote effective social work interventions and just social policy, professionals must have a historical knowledge of the influence of various policies on oppressed and disadvantaged populations, which is discussed in Chapter 6 on the history of social work and social welfare.

Once students have gained an understanding of the history behind how the U.S. social welfare system and professional social work developed, several chapters then present current social work services with specific client populations in specific settings. By presenting information about social work services in this way, the text will provide students with a better sense of career opportunities in social work, bringing the concept of the "social welfare system" to life for students. Knowledge of the current social welfare system is a prerequisite for a critical understanding of the social welfare system's strengths and weaknesses. It is our hope that students may then be ready to learn how to advocate for more inclusive and just social welfare policies. Consequently, we present a discussion of social work, policy, and advocacy as the final chapter of the book.

We want to make learning about social work fun and interesting for students; therefore, the text is "user-friendly," with boxed inserts throughout to draw students' attention to relevant and interesting information. For example, the book provides "Did You Know?" boxed inserts to provide students with interesting pieces of information. Other elements include "Social Work Stories" and "Case Studies" meant to generate personal reflection and class discussion regarding social justice, human rights, diversity, empowerment, self-determination, and other ethical issues.

Connecting Core Competencies Series

This new first edition is a part of Pearson Education's *Connecting Core Competencies* series, which consists of foundation-level texts that make it easier than ever to ensure students' success in learning the ten core competencies as stated in 2008 by the Council on Social Worker Education. This text contains:

- **Core Competency Icons** throughout the chapters, directly linking the CSWE core competencies to the content of the text. **Critical thinking questions** are also included to further students' mastery of the CSWE standards. For easy reference, page iv displays which icons are used in each chapter, in a chapter-by-chapter matrix.
- **An end-of-chapter Practice Test** with multiple-choice questions that test students' knowledge of the chapter content and mastery of the competencies.
- **Additional questions pertaining to the videos and case studies found on the new MySocialWorkLab** at the end of each chapter to encourage students to access the site and explore the wealth of available materials. If this text did not come with an access code for MySocialWorkLab, you can purchase access at www.mysocialworklab.com.

Acknowledgments

We would like to thank the many people involved in helping us through the development of this book. Jerry would especially like to thank Susan, Andy, and Becca for their love, support, and understanding. Anne gives personal thanks to her husband, Bob, for his support in all her writing endeavors. Fleur would like to thank Fiona Hopper, Sarah Andel, and Nathan Hall for four years of enormous patience and support, and Anne Funderburk, Layne Gregory, and Leah Otto for their invaluable insight and input. Dave thanks Karen Fuller for her love and support. And a thank you goes to Marianne McEnroe for her assistance during the research process.

We'd also like to thank the reviewers for their helpful feedback throughout this process: Patty Carlson, University of Nebraska at Omaha; Lynn Cooper, Sacramento State University; Donna Maria Daly, San Diego State University; Kathryn Dixon, Bergen Community College; Tammy Freelin, University of Missouri–Columbia; Makeba Green, Bowie State University; Tina Hancock, Campbell University; Sylvia Hawranick, Ohio University; Gayle Mallinger, University of Pittsburgh; John D. Matthews, Eastern Washington University; Kathryn McKinley, Buena Vista University; Murali Nair, Cleveland State University; Elizabeth Palley, Adelphi University; Humberto Reynoso, Boston University; Anita Sharma, University of Louisiana at Monroe; and Dianne Woods, California State University–East Bay.

1

Social Work as a Profession

CHAPTER OUTLINE

A Profession Defined 2
Would You Enjoy a Career in Social Work?
Social Work Defined
Social Work in Relation to Social Welfare

Possible Careers in Social Work 5
Social Work with Individuals
Social Work with Families
Social Work with Groups
Social Work with Communities
Social Workers in Administration
Social Workers in Policy Practice
Social Workers in Research
Social Work in Relation to
 Other Professions

Social Work: A Values-Based Profession 14
Values
Ethics
Competence in Relation to Diversity and
 Individual Dignity
Social Justice and Human Rights
Strengths and Empowerment

Baccalaureate Social Work Education 22

The Future of Social Work 25

Summary 26

Practice Test 27

 MySocialWorkLab 27

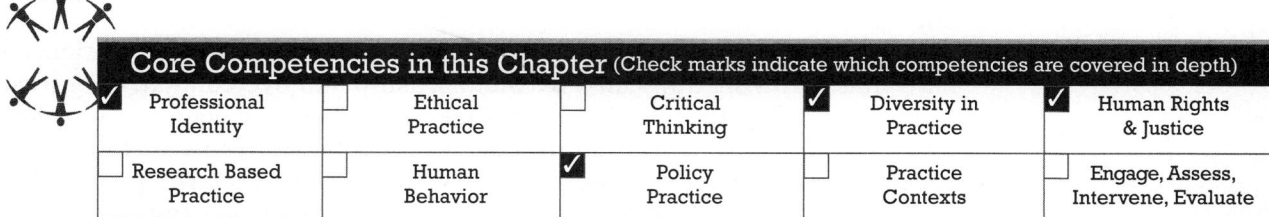

Core Competencies in this Chapter (Check marks indicate which competencies are covered in depth)									
✓	Professional Identity	☐	Ethical Practice	☐	Critical Thinking	✓	Diversity in Practice	✓	Human Rights & Justice
☐	Research Based Practice	☐	Human Behavior	✓	Policy Practice	☐	Practice Contexts	☐	Engage, Assess, Intervene, Evaluate

Chapter 1

A PROFESSION DEFINED

Would You Enjoy a Career in Social Work?

Would you enjoy a career in the profession of social work? In this chapter, we provide an overview of the purpose, values, methods, and educational requirements of social work. People enter social work for many reasons. Some people go into social work because they want their work to lead to a meaningful life—for themselves and others. Listen to Michael Pesce, a social worker in foster care and adoption services.

> I went to graduate school and had a field placement where I worked with the State Department of Social Services in the area of foster care. I've been in foster care and adoption ever since. . . . I need to do something that matters—that matters to somebody else and that matters to me, something that has value. That is a demonstration of caring. . . . I think back to that time when I went out and took these kids out of a foster home where there had been some abuse, and this little kid looked at me and said, "Thank you." And you go, "Wow! This is what this is all about." That is not a big gigantic success story, but it was a moment that I have never forgotten.[1]

Hannah Freese went into social work for similar reasons:

> For a long time, I heard the calling to social work, and I said, "I am going to ignore it." It was like I could hear the phone ringing and did not pick it up. It all started when I was in high school. They had a thing called "interim week," where you do something outside of your curriculum for a week or two. I did an internship at a day care center. I worked with under-privileged kids and it snowballed from there. Every project I did every year involved some type of social service with children. When I graduated from high school, I was waiting tables and thinking, "What am I going to do with my life?" So I moved to L.A. because I wanted to act. I didn't want to do social work. I ended up with a job at a homeless shelter for runaway kids, because I needed more money, and it was something I knew how to do. I realized when I got that job, though, that it wasn't just to pay the rent; I felt fulfilled.[2]

Social Work Defined

Okay, so you may be interested in a social work career, but you need to know more about it. American social work as a profession is about a century old now. It is a helping profession. It is for people who want to make a difference with their life. It is for people who want to leave the world a better place than they found it. Social work is for people who care about others, who are sensitive to the needs of others. It is for people who like to work and collaborate with others.

The profession of social work also attracts people who have experienced hard times growing up, who have met hardship and overcome it, or at least learned to cope with it. Social work is for people who respect and appreciate people who are different from themselves; people who know that diversity keeps the world from being boring. Social work is for those who believe that people ought to be able to live their own lives, free of coercion and oppression.

It is for those who value independence and want to help others become independent. It is for those who believe in social and economic justice.

But exactly what is "social work"? The National Association of Social Workers (NASW) states in its "Code of Ethics" that:

> The primary mission of the social work profession is to enhance human well-being and help meet the basic human needs of all people, with particular attention to the needs and empowerment of people who are vulnerable, oppressed, and living in poverty. A historical and defining feature of social work is the profession's focus on individual well-being in a social context and the well-being of society. Fundamental to social work is attention to the environmental forces that create, contribute to, and address problems in living.[3]

. . . being poor in a rich country may be more difficult . . . than being poor in a poor country.
—David Shipler, 2005, 9.

Similarly, the International Federation of Social Workers (IFSW) adopted this definition of social work:

> The social work profession promotes social change, problem solving in human relationships and the empowerment and liberation of people to enhance well-being. Utilizing theories of human behavior and social systems, social work intervenes at the points where people interact with their environments. Principles of human rights and social justice are fundamental to social work.[4]

Further, the *2008 Educational Policy and Accreditation Standards*, published by the Council on Social Work Education, states:

> The purpose of the social work profession is to promote human and community well-being. Guided by a person and environment construct, a global perspective, respect for human diversity, and knowledge based on scientific inquiry, social work's purpose is actualized through its quest for social and economic justice, the prevention of conditions that limit human rights, the elimination of poverty, and the enhancement of the quality of life for all persons.[5]

Critical Thinking Question
Social workers promote human rights and justice concerning people who are oppressed or vulnerable. As you observe the world around you, which groups do you think need assistance?

As a profession, social work consists of five essential elements:

Purpose: the object for which something exists

Values: a principle, standard, or quality considered desirable

Sanction: authoritative permission or approval that makes a course of action legitimate or legal

Knowledge: familiarity, awareness, or understanding gained through experience or study

Skills: proficiency with a set of techniques, particularly in relation to a regular or systematic way of accomplishing anything

In essence then, social workers use "knowledge," "values," and "skills"—with the "sanction" of society—for the "purpose" of promoting positive change for client systems.[6]

In pursuing their professional mission, social workers generally perform several roles, including enabler, teacher, broker, mediator, advocate, and activist. Social workers perform the "enabler" role by enhancing the coping and problem-solving capabilities of clients. They play the "teacher" role by providing clients with new information and, at times, role modeling new behaviors. Social workers serve as "brokers" when they link people with services, resources, and opportunities. They perform the role of "mediator" when they help resolve disputes between the client and other people or organizations. Further, social workers act as "advocates" when they represent, defend, and champion the rights of their clients. And they play the "activist" role when they plan and participate in organized demonstrations to support or protest a government policy.[7]

In fact, social workers practice at three levels:

1. **The micro level:** working on a one-to-one basis with an individual
2. **The mezzo level:** working with families and other small groups
3. **The macro level:** working in communities, administration, or policy practice[8]

Many students may wonder how "social work" relates to the term "social welfare." Social workers employed at the macro level certainly seem to concern themselves with social welfare.

Social Work in Relation to Social Welfare

The profession of social work has developed within the context of the United States' social welfare system. Pioneering social workers could be found in 19th-century institutions such as settlement houses and charity organization societies. Today, the **social welfare system**, by definition, refers to our nation's system of programs, benefits, and services that help people meet those social, economic, educational, and health needs that are fundamental to the maintenance of society. These programs and services, primarily located in the public and private nonprofit sectors of U.S. society, include Social Security, unemployment insurance, workers' compensation, Temporary Assistance to Needy Families, food stamps, public housing, Medicare, and Medicaid. Our social welfare system also includes Alcoholics Anonymous (AA) support groups, Mothers Against Drunk Driving, the YMCA, the Girl Scouts of America, Habitat for Humanity, the American Red Cross, the Salvation Army, United Way, local faith-based services, and other voluntary associations in the private nonprofit sector.

Social Work Stories: Homelessness

A shelter worker speaks about the housing problems in Annapolis, Maryland:

Housing here in Annapolis is so expensive that it's often unaffordable for the working poor. You can't even touch a small one-bedroom apartment here for less than seven hundred a month. Don't get me wrong, I'm not saying homelessness is always just a cost-of-housing problem. Some of our guests, even those who work full-time, have more complex problems. Some have experienced abuse as kids or they are unbalanced or have drug issues, and others are just kids themselves without the skills to manage. But there is a belief in our culture that if you work you will not be poor or hungry, and the truth is that many of the people who work, even the people who work full-time, are very poor and often very hungry.[9]

A more detailed discussion of social welfare in relation to social work will be provided in Chapter 3. But for now, the reader should remember that social welfare is a broader concept than social work. Most social workers are employed in the U.S. social welfare system. Social work is a profession; social welfare is a "system" that employs many professions. That is, professionals from many other fields also practice within the social welfare system, including people from fields such as public administration, law, nursing, sociology, psychology, and medicine. Social workers frequently collaborate with these other professionals when assisting clients. In any case, students interested in social work have a wide variety of jobs from which to choose!

POSSIBLE CAREERS IN SOCIAL WORK

Social workers practice their profession in many different types of settings. Many work in the public sector. Many also work in the private nonprofit sector, while other social workers work in the private for-profit sector. Public sector jobs include those in federal, state, county, and local government agencies. Typical jobs in government settings include child protection, adoption, adult protection, veterans' services, public schools, and the correctional system. Private nonprofit jobs include those in health and human services such as the Boys and Girls Clubs, Meals on Wheels, the YMCA, the YWCA, the Red Cross, Big Brothers/Big Sisters, substance abuse prevention services, family counseling agencies, parent education and support services, and various advocacy organizations.

The private for-profit sector is better known as the "business sector." Social workers find jobs in businesses in employee assistance programs, community relations, public affairs, corporate charitable contribution programs, and volunteer management programs. Social workers also work independently in private practice. In this case, social workers set up a proprietary practice that may involve consultation, research, educational workshops, and other non-clinical services. Many other social workers in private practice set up clinically oriented practices, usually providing mental health services. In any case, social workers in private practice need to be licensed, certified, or registered in accordance with state laws.

Social Work with Individuals

Depending upon the setting, many social workers provide services primarily to individual people. Social workers focused on work with individuals might provide case management, psychotherapy, and/or advocacy—usually all three. Social work with individuals has historically been referred to as "casework" or "social casework."

Casework, by definition, involves the use of social work knowledge, values, and skills in face-to-face relationships to resolve or reduce difficulties "arising out of disequilibrium between people and their environment."[10] This process involves helping people adjust to their environment, as well as intervening to change factors in the individual's environment. Casework with individuals includes helping people with concrete practical problems, with environmental deficits and pressures, and with interpersonal and intrapersonal difficulties.

Social workers involved in casework with individuals work in a wide variety of practice settings, including social service agencies, hospitals, outpatient clinics, state and local child protective services, and private practices. Social workers practicing casework with individuals include clinicians in an inpatient psychiatric facility, case managers in a residential shelter for homeless youth, social workers working with dialysis patients in a hospital, and adult protective service workers.

Case management is similar to casework. **Case management** is defined as a service done by "an individual or team of professionals who organize, coordinate, and sustain a network of formal and informal supports in order to optimize the functioning and well-being of people with multiple needs."[11] Because of their multiple needs, these people typically need several types of supports. It is the job of the case manager or member of an interdisciplinary case management team to link their client with all needed services and supports to which the client is entitled.

In other words, case managers plan, seek, and monitor needed services from one or more agencies on behalf of a client. In so doing, the case manager may play several roles, including that of a broker, mediator, or advocate. Case management makes it easier for an individual client to locate services in a social service system that is often complex and fragmented. Consequently, case managers require a detailed knowledge of the full range of services at the community level as well as a working knowledge of state and national services.

Be that as it may, some social work students may be primarily interested in working with families in the future. For these students, the profession of social work holds many opportunities!

Social Work with Families

Social work with families became a distinct field in social work practice beginning in the 1960s. Social workers who work with families help family members improve their patterns of interaction to better meet the needs of all family members.[13] In other words, social workers aim to help families with behavioral, emotional, and interactional problems. The process is usually viewed as one of problem solving within a system's context—the system in this case being the family. At times, families develop dysfunctional coalitions and alliances within the family system. Social workers, sometimes employed in agencies as "family therapists," help families to change problematic family structures, leading not only to positive transformation of the family, but positive change in each of the family members as well.

Social workers who work with families draw from a number of different theories about how families work and how families change. In doing so, social

Research Informed Practice with Latino Families

In 2007, a team of researchers led by Vincent Guilamo-Ramos did a study of Latino parenting practices in the Bronx borough of New York City. A total of 63 mother–adolescent pairs took part in the study. Results showed most of the teens understood that parental exercise of authority and close monitoring were reflections of parental love and a desire to keep them safe in the city. The researchers also found that the majority of adolescents in the study wanted "to communicate with their parents frequently, spontaneously, and openly, without fear of parental anger."[12]

As a social worker, how might you use these research results to work effectively with Latino families?

workers may use a number of techniques and play a number of roles. Some may focus on specific relationships, such as that between a between a parent and child, or may extend their work to include a range of extended family. Sometimes they videotape family members interacting during the therapeutic session. Sometimes one-way mirrors are used so that family interactional patterns can be observed by other family members. In addition, role-playing may be used where family members are asked to reenact prior conflicts. Sometimes a therapist acts as a model of more functional behavior when dealing with conflict. This may include ways to communicate more effectively. At other times, social workers doing family therapy perform the educator role in an effort to better inform family members regarding strategies for improved family relationships.

Furthermore, social workers working with families frequently attempt to link these families to community resources in an effort to provide additional or long-term support to the family. This may entail referring families to parenting programs, support groups, 12-step groups such as AA and Al-Anon, affordable housing, transportation services, or anger management classes. Such referrals may result from the social worker collaborating with other professionals—psychologists, nurses, and so on—in an interdisciplinary team.[14]

While some social work students may want to work with families, other students may be interested in working with a wider variety of groups. They see themselves in some aspect of "group work."

. . . the social rule that mothers should stay at home . . . has seldom been applied to poor women.
—Gail Collins, 2009, 337.

Social Work with Groups

Although group work as an intervention method in social work can be traced back to the settlement houses and mutual aid societies of the late 1800s in America, it became recognized as a distinct professional intervention method within social work in the 1930s. **Group work** or social group work as a social work intervention method is defined as an intervention that utilizes group process, based in large part on social systems theory, to promote positive change among group members. This process is typically goal-directed around common interests of group members. These interests may include common emotional problems, educational needs, skill development, or recreational opportunities.[15]

Consider the following examples. When working with individuals, social workers use groups to provide support to people who are coping with a common issue, such as the loss of a loved one or the diagnosis of a disease. At times, groups are used to educate clients around such issues as parenting or substance abuse prevention. Sometimes the groups are therapy groups that help group members with rehabilitation of a serious personal problem such as depression or violent anger. Many groups run by social workers incorporate both educational and behavior change components, such as groups designed to help individuals with diabetes improve their diet, teenagers avoid pregnancy and STDs, or college students reduce their stress level. These groups are often referred to as "psychoeducational" groups. Sometimes groups are used to address functional deficits, as with adolescents needing social and problem-solving skills. At other times, social workers use groups in a purely developmental sense, such as recreation groups, arts and crafts groups, reading groups, consciousness-raising groups, team-building groups, staff development groups, or other types of empowerment groups.

> **Demonstrating Knowledge, Values, and Skills**
>
> Take out a piece of paper and write down three groups that you have joined. What was the purpose or goal of each group? How often did each group meet? Were group members like you or very different? How do you feel you benefited from each group? Did you receive emotional support? Did you learn new skills? Did you get an opportunity for fun and recreation?

While many social workers like to work directly with individuals or groups, some prefer a more macro area of social work. If you feel this way, working to improve communities may be of interest to you!

Social Work with Communities

Social workers who work with communities are often called "community organizers." In this instance, the client is the community and the intervention process is called "community organization." **Community organization** is defined by its use of planned collective action to address the needs of people from the same geographic area or with some other common interests. The intervention typically involves community needs assessment and the development of community leaders, action strategies, and required resources to address unmet needs. To illustrate, the community need may be less crime, better schools, cleaner streets, or improved recreational facilities. Sometimes the need is greater economic opportunity, in which case social workers may get involved in planning for economic development within the community. In any case, social workers working as community organizers facilitate collective action in an effort to promote positive community change.

Social workers working to better community well-being perform a variety of tasks. They could help to establish a neighborhood organization. They may organize a meeting to discuss problems with neighborhood youth. They might help community residents establish a buyers club to purchase low-cost heating oil. Further, social workers may assist communities in planning and conducting neighborhood fairs and festivals that celebrate national holidays or the ethnic heritage of community members. Social workers in the community organization role might also help residents raise funds from local businesses to build better playgrounds for neighborhood children. Some may organize peaceful

> **Case Study: Community Organization**
>
> A young social worker is employed by a neighborhood organization in a city in Minnesota. The specific neighborhood in which he works consists primarily of poor and working poor families. The neighborhood organization works to improve community conditions. Its activities have included the development of a neighborhood crime watch, the establishment of a community newspaper, and the organizing of community tree planting. During his year as a community organizer, the social worker witnessed a neighborhood meeting in which the leaders of the neighborhood organization presented only three options to community residents for the spending of city community development funds. The leaders wanted to spend the money on a low-income housing project, and therefore presented this option in the most favorable way. They purposely made the other two options seem very unappealing. They hoped that no one would question why only three options were considered. Why not consider a fourth option? Why not a fifth option? The neighborhood leaders called for a quick vote and their housing project received the most votes and the subsequent funding from city government.
>
> 1. Was it right of the leaders to conduct a neighborhood vote in is so misleading of a way? Was this not a perversion of local democracy?
> 2. The young social worker observed the planning of the strategy, but did not question the ethics of the process. Should he have challenged the process during the planning stage? Should he have alerted neighborhood residents to the scheme?

demonstrations for improved city services to the neighborhood. Whatever the case, the goal of community organization is greater well-being for the residents of the community.

Working to better meet the needs of communities is great for some, but other social workers enjoy running organizations. Consequently, they seek administrative positions!

Social Workers in Administration

Many career paths lead social workers into administration. Frequently, these are social workers who concentrated on the more macro aspects of the profession while in school. Often administrative social workers find employment in private nonprofit agencies as Chief Executive Officers (CEOs), executive directors, or program directors. Many also find work in government agencies as heads of various government divisions, program directors, or even commissioners of entire departments. Social workers at the top levels of management are responsible for many administrative tasks. For example, they ensure their agency conducts regular strategic planning, which often involves community needs assessment. They oversee program development, which includes program design, fundraising, and program evaluation. Social administrators are responsible for staff development, including hiring, evaluation, and termination. Social administrators are also involved in policy advocacy and community education as well as interagency collaboration.

Administrators of private nonprofit agencies assist with board development for their organizations. This typically includes working with existing board members to recruit and train new board members. Social workers in nonprofit management, given the importance of volunteers in nonprofit organizations, must also take responsibility for recruiting, developing, and managing volunteers.

In addition, nonprofit administrators spend a great deal of their time in fund-raising. Funds are raised in many ways. Vehicles for fund-raising include grant writing, grass-roots events such as walkathons and road races, annual campaigns to solicit individual donations, planned giving involving bequests, and capital campaigns to raise money for the development of new facilities.

Social workers who go into administrative practice often enjoy developing and administering new programs to meet emerging community needs. Given their macro perspective, they like working with larger systems. And they enjoy collaboration, coordination, and leadership. But if you have a macro perspective, yet don't want administrative responsibilities, maybe social welfare policy development would be a better match for you.

Social Workers in Policy Practice

Social welfare policy defines the context in which social services are developed and delivered. Many social workers, particularly those who concentrated in macro practice as students, find employment in policy practice.[17] **Policy practice** in social work, by definition, involves the formulation, enactment, implementation, and assessment of social welfare policies. While some social workers in policy practice hold elected offices, social workers more often find jobs as policy planners or policy analysts. Some work for elected officials or in government agencies at the national, state, or local levels, while many others work in private nonprofit agencies, especially large nonprofit agencies at the national and state levels, agencies such as the Children's Defense fund, the Child Welfare League of America, or United Way of America. Social workers' firsthand knowledge of the needs of various client populations is highly valued by policymakers in national, state, and local government.

Social workers engaged in policy work carry out a variety of specific tasks. They help to define social problems, analyze the values underlying such problem definitions, set policy goals and objectives in relation to the problems, outline policy options for achieving these goals and objectives, consider various criteria for evaluating policy options, and ultimately, decide on final policy proposals to advocate and implement. Social workers involved with policy development sometimes are only involved in the research and analysis that goes into developing proposals, while at other times they make direct recommendations as to which policy options they consider best. This is because social workers' knowledge of how health and human services are produced, distributed, and consumed is critical to the policy development process.[18]

For this and other reasons, social workers in policy practice enjoy the opportunity to develop and influence policies that affect many people. If policy practice as well as case work, group work, and community organization are not for you, social work offers employment in still another area: research.

Did You Know?

According to the National Association of Social Workers in 2010, there are over 170 social workers elected to local, state, and national offices. These include two U.S. senators and seven U.S. representatives.[16]

Social Workers in Research

Social workers engage in research for several reasons. They identify research-based interventions to achieve client goals. They also use research to evaluate program outcomes and practice effectiveness. For example, social welfare policies typically result in social welfare programs and services that then need to be evaluated as one step in determining the success or failure of the original legislation. Social workers in administration are typically responsible for seeing that program evaluations are done, and social workers frequently conduct these evaluations of programs and services. What is more, some social workers earn a Ph.D. and gain employment at universities in teaching and research. These social work educators utilize their practice experience to inform their research—and ultimately, their students!

Okay, so we have established that social workers do many things. But what, you may wonder, makes social work different from psychology and sociology and other fields? We address this question in the following section.

Critical Thinking Question
Social workers in policy practice define social problems and advocate new policy options. If you had a chance to speak to your state's governor, what social problem would you say should be the highest priority?

Social Work in Relation to Other Professions

Social work is a profession within the social welfare system. As such, social workers apply scientific knowledge and technical skills to assist their clients. More specifically, social work is a professional activity focused on helping individuals, groups, organizations, and communities enhance or restore their capacity for social functioning. Social workers also strive to create societal conditions conducive to these goals. In so doing, social work requires knowledge of human development and behavior, societal institutions, and the interaction between individuals and larger institutional systems. In other words, social work focuses on three things: the person, the system, and the relationship between the person and the system.[20] Often when individuals have problems, these are the result of dysfunctional transactions between the person and his or her environment. Social workers are trained to focus on these transactions.

In carrying out their interventions, social workers apply various theories. Foremost among them are systems theory and ecological theory (to be discussed in more detail in Chapter 2). Systems theory suggests that no problem can be fully understood by breaking it down into component parts. The relationship among the various parts of the whole system is as important as each part individually. Most systems seek a balance in an effort to maintain and preserve the system, whether that system is a family, a group, or a community. Problems arise when systems experience an imbalance due to any number of factors. Similarly, the ecological perspective, or "ecosystems perspective," stresses that human beings develop and adapt to transactions with all elements in their environmental systems. Based in part on these theories, social work intervention emphasizes a focus on the person in his or her environment.[21]

Because social workers work in the social welfare system, they collaborate with professionals from other disciplines. These professional disciplines tend to have slightly different

Did You Know?

According to the Substance Abuse and Mental Health Services Administration (SAMHSA), social workers are the largest group of mental health services providers in the U.S. There are more clinically trained social workers (over 190,000 in 1998) than psychiatric nurses, psychologists, and psychiatrists combined. Social work is recognized by federal law and the National Institutes of Health as one of five core mental health professions.[19]

perspectives regarding people and their environments.[22] These related disciplines include sociology, psychology, and psychiatry. **Sociology** is the study of the origins, organizations, institutions, and development of human society. When going about their work, sociologists, who typically have five to seven years of graduate study, attempt to explain the ways in which human societies influence individual functioning within those societies. In addition, sociologists attempt to understand the differences among various human societies. Therefore, sociologists seek to understand, for example, the effect of living in a market economy on individual behavior, the effect of democratic institutions on individual behavior, the influence of racist institutions on individual functioning, and the effect of urbanization on human development.

A psychologist, in contrast, studies human behavior and mental processes in an effort to understand human behavior for individual functioning. That is, **psychology** is the study of mental processes and behavior. Because psychologists study mind and behavior, professionals in this discipline are interested in the function of the brain, child development, and, in general, "what makes people tick." Psychologists often specialize in certain areas, including clinical psychology, counseling, developmental psychology, or social psychology. Each of these specializations examines a different aspect of human behavior. Psychologists who specialize in clinical psychology often work in hospitals, clinics, and private practice. They often use interviewing techniques, diagnostic tests, and psychotherapy in their practice. Psychologists with a master's degree are able to administer and interpret tests, counsel patients, and conduct research. A Ph.D. in psychology typically requires five to seven years of graduate study and two years of professional experience for certification or licensure. Licensure requirements vary from state to state.

Psychiatry is the study of the diagnosis, treatment, and prevention of mental illness. In other words, psychiatrists specialize in the problem of mental illness. In so doing, psychiatrists work in private practice, in courtrooms, and in specialized medical settings such as coronary and intensive care units. In addition, they often serve as consultants to other agencies. Psychiatrists are medical doctors, requiring five to seven additional years of psychiatric training and experience. As a result, they are qualified to use the full range of medical techniques related to mental illness. Such techniques include medication, shock, and surgery, as well as counseling and behavior modification. Psychiatrists generally use a medical model, which views the individual's problem as a disease or sickness that needs to be cured. Utilizing the medical model, psychiatrists typically examine symptoms in an effort to make a diagnosis. Once the diagnosis is made, psychiatrists prescribe the treatment with the highest likelihood of curing the disease or sickness. In contrast to the social worker's dual perspective of the "person-in-environment," in psychiatry, the individual's problem is considered to be inside the individual. In other words, in contrast to examining the person's environment for factors contributing to the problem, psychiatrists tend to focus on other possible contributing factors, including genetic endowment, metabolic disorders, unconscious defense mechanisms, childhood traumatic experiences, or infectious disease. Psychiatrists believe that the individual's mind has been negatively affected by one or more of these factors. Psychiatrists, being medical doctors, view people seeking their services as patients and provide "treatment" of the patient's problem.

Often students get confused between the services of the aforementioned professions and those of "counselors." Counseling can be done by psychiatrists, psychologists, and social workers, as well as guidance counselors and clergy. Counseling is a broader category than the previously discussed disciplines. Many people get jobs as counselors, yet the required education, experience, and licensing varies considerably among these positions. Some require no licensing and only minimal education. And, as discussed, psychiatrists, psychologists, and social workers providing counseling services require many years of education and experience. Some counselors deal with mental health, while other counselors help people with their educational and career concerns. For example, mental health counselors help individuals with problems such as suicide, stress, and drug and alcohol addictions. Rehabilitation counselors, in contrast, help individuals with vocational needs affected by disabilities. These disabilities may be physical, mental, or social. Counselors work not only with individuals but often with the families of those individuals. In any case, counseling positions normally require one to two years of graduate study, a master's degree in a specific discipline, and supervised counseling experience. As previously discussed, requirements for licensing and certification vary depending upon specialty and state.

A major requirement in many social work jobs, therefore, is collaboration with a number of professionals from various disciplines, perspectives, and educational experiences. This collaboration, often in the form of partnerships, coalitions, or interdisciplinary teams, is becoming more and more important. Recent conservative social welfare policy, as well as the demands of managed care, has resulted in fewer resources for agencies in the social welfare system. This often results in limited services, more short-term interventions, and more narrow eligibility requirements for services. In an effort to provide comprehensive care, health and human service agencies are forced to collaborate in helping to solve individual and social problems. This collaboration can result in increased resources and expertise, thereby helping social workers and other professionals better address the multidimensional problems of individuals, families, and communities. Collaboration also requires better integrated services, which avoids service duplication and service gaps. Consequently, many funders of health and human services today require community agencies to collaborate to receive grants for service provision.

Social Work Stories: Professional Collaboration

Social worker Lorrie M. works for the city of Portland, Maine, in its Health and Human Service Department. When asked what she likes most about her job, she states:

I like the collaboration with a team of professionals. In my job, I work in an interdisciplinary team. The team consists of a physician, psychiatrist, nurse, nurse practitioner, and a dentist. Together, we decide the needs and service priorities of poverty-stricken people in our city. I see a wide variety of individuals, including many who are dually diagnosed with substance abuse and mental health problems. In addition to providing short-term counseling, I work with other agencies to obtain needed resources and services for each case I see.[23]

Social Work Stories: Why Did You Go into Social Work?

Emily S. is a graduate social work student at the University of New Hampshire. Emily has chosen social work after experimenting with other professions such as teaching. She chose social work because she has come to believe that the profession offers the widest range of opportunities to create change, both within the U.S. and internationally. Emily would like to work for social justice by collaborating with others to create solutions to social problems such as violence against women, gender inequality, and poverty.

Because social problems can be so all-encompassing, she feels that it is easy for social workers to become overwhelmed by the magnitude of the needed change. She believes that the complexity of social welfare systems within the U.S. and other systemic obstacles increase workers' frustration in their efforts to promote positive social change. Emily tries to face this frustration by celebrating small successes, honoring the strength of those who work to make the world better, and nurturing her spirituality and relationships with others.

Emily can see the powerful role of social workers by reflecting upon her experiences in her student internships. During her first-year internship at a high school, Emily established a strong relationship with a teenage girl who faced many difficulties within her family and social group. The relationship that developed between Emily and this student became a tool for helping the student to learn valuable coping skills. Emily feels that their relationship led to tremendous growth for both of them. In her second year internship at Sexual Assault Support Services, Emily provided programs to elementary school students to help prevent sexual abuse and teach the children personal body safety skills. Emily can see how these programs create change in children's lives, since after participating in the program, some of these children were able to find the courage to report abuse against them.[24]

SOCIAL WORK: A VALUES-BASED PROFESSION

Values

Now that you have a better idea of what social workers do in their field, let's take a closer look at the profession's ideological foundation. The profession of social work is based upon a set of core values. These values are service, social justice, the dignity and worth of the person, the importance of human relationships, integrity, and competence.[26] In terms of service, the primary goal of social work is to help people in need and to address social problems. This is the reason that many people choose to become social workers. Social workers believe

Social Work Stories: Homeless Shelters

A worker at the St. Vincent de Paul Village food and homeless shelter in San Diego, California, tells about their work:

The lunch line at St. Vincent's begins forming at nine A.M. each morning and stretches around the block by ten. We feed five hundred to six hundred people an hour, every day, seven days a week. Families always come first, and then the disabled, but the mass of people waiting for food includes the homeless and the working poor and military families. Some come only occasionally but we can usually pick out a hundred or a hundred fifty regulars, people who come everyday. We ask no questions because we don't want to make them feel uncomfortable about being here. We know that many of them are not homeless, at least not yet. So I always tell them, "save your money to pay your rent and your other bills and come here to eat with us. That way you won't become homeless."[25]

that service to others is more important than self-interest, the dominant value of the market economy. A second core value is social justice. Much of what social workers do involves social and economic justice. Social workers promote social change with and on behalf of vulnerable populations—groups such as women, racial and ethnic minorities, children, and people with disabilities. To accomplish this, social workers strive to develop more just policies, programs, and services for these groups in need. (*Note:* By "racial and ethnic minorities," we mean groups that, based on their race or ethnicity, are rendered subordinate to society's more dominant groups. More information on this topic will be provided in Chapter 5.)

They also emphasize "human rights" such as freedom, privacy, safety, education, health care, and decent standards of living. The aforementioned groups often suffer from social problems, including poverty, discrimination, unemployment, and oppression. Often these are groups that are either too young or too old to participate in the market or, because of race or gender, have been discriminated against in their efforts to participate in the market economy. Social workers, therefore, work to promote more just and humane policies as well as programs to address these issues.

Another core value in social work is the dignity and worth of each person. All social workers must respect the inherent dignity and worth of every individual. This is a prerequisite for developing effective helping relationships with individuals, families, and groups. In the process, social workers need to understand the unique cultures and backgrounds of the people with whom they work. This requires an openness and sensitivity to the unique experiences of every individual. It also involves the promotion of self determination for each individual.

A fourth core value of social work is the importance of human relationships. One reason for this is that social workers use human relationships to promote change in individuals, families, groups, and communities. Social workers also understand that helping people to develop healthy human relationships is a means to a high-quality life and happiness for all people. Healthy human relationships are a prerequisite for meeting the needs of love and belonging and for developing healthy families.

Integrity is a fifth basic value in social work. Professional social workers must act with integrity at all times. In so doing, social workers develop the trust of clients and coworkers. Social workers also work to promote ethical policies and practices in the organizations in which they are employed. Furthermore, integrity is an important factor for social workers if they are to have the credibility needed to promote social justice.

A final core value of the social work profession is competence. Social workers must practice within the areas of their competence and must continually work to develop and enhance their professional expertise. What is more, social workers should look for opportunities to contribute to the profession's knowledge base through education, scientific inquiry, and evaluation of programs and their individual practice.

Ethics

Values relate to what people consider desirable, while "ethics" relates more directly to what people consider right or wrong.[27] That is, ethics pertain to values in action. When considering the profession of social work, ethics are important because they relate to expectations associated with professional

Critical Thinking Question

Social work is based on values including service, social justice, individual dignity, importance of human relationships, integrity, and competence. Which of these values has been most important in your life so far?

conduct. Ethics are so important in social work that the profession has a "code of ethics." This code of ethics spells out social workers' ethical responsibilities to clients, to colleagues, to the social work profession, and to society at large, among other things. They are, in essence, guidelines for professional conduct. Ethics become a challenge for social workers when the professional social worker has a choice between two options, both seemingly ethical, but only one can be chosen. In such a case, which course of action is more ethical and how does one determine this? In other cases, a social worker may have ethical responsibilities to two different parties, say a parent and child, but can only meet his or her responsibility to one party at a time.[28]

Social workers also confront ethical dilemmas involving confidentiality. They are not supposed to share certain personal information conveyed to them by clients; however, some circumstances may require social workers to do just that in order to protect other people from harm or to protect clients from harming themselves. Examples include suicidal clients and violent spouses.

Other ethical dilemmas faced by social workers involve paternalism. Social workers believe in self-determination for clients; however, there are certain circumstances in which social workers may ethically have to direct client behavior in order to keep a client safe. An example would be a mentally ill homeless person who desires to sleep outside during a New England winter instead of using a nearby community shelter. Another illustration would be a social worker who works with children and youth, a population that is not fully mature and therefore does not always exercise mature judgment involving decisions on issues such as sexual relations, alcohol use, and other risk-taking behavior.

Social workers in policy and administrative jobs deal with ethical dilemmas that concern the allocation of scarce resources. How do social workers make ethical choices to fund one program instead of another program? In an environment of scarce resources, social administrators and policymakers must make these decisions frequently. Again, the question is, what is the most ethical option when choosing among several good options?

Furthermore, social workers must make ethical decisions involving their professional colleagues. When should a social worker report a colleague who divulges personal client information to others? At what point should a professional social worker report a colleague who makes a sexual comment? When should a social worker report a colleague suspected of drug abuse?

Social workers face these and other ethical dilemmas all too frequently. It is the task of professional social work education to assist students in acquiring specific knowledge about social work values and ethics and applying these values and ethics in the field. This includes an awareness of the student's personal values and how they may conflict with the values of the social work profession. It also requires teachers to stimulate awareness of ethical issues on the part of students and help them develop analytical skills to deal with these issues. What is more, by the time students graduate with a social work degree, they should have a sense of moral obligation and personal responsibility concerning the values and ethics of the profession.[29]

As previously stated, the **NASW Code of Ethics** provides social work students and professionals with values, principles, and standards to guide their professional conduct. Specifically, the NASW Code of Ethics serves six purposes. First, it identifies the core values of the profession. Second, the code summarizes the broad ethical principles related to social work values and provides ethical standards to guide social work practice. Third, the code offers social workers a set of considerations for use in ethical dilemmas. Fourth, it provides ethical standards by which the general public can hold the profession of social work accountable. A fifth purpose, particularly important for students, is that the code helps to socialize practitioners who are new to the field in terms of the profession's mission, values, ethical principles, and ethical standards. And finally, the code of ethics provides the profession with criteria for judging whether or not practicing social workers have been unethical in their conduct.[30]

More specifically, the aforementioned values and associated ethical principles provided by the NASW Code of Ethics to guide social work practice are quoted as follows:[31]

Value: *Service*
Ethical Principle: *Social workers primary goal is to help people in need and to address social problems.*

Social workers elevate service to others above self-interest. Social workers draw on their knowledge, values, and skills to help people in need and to address social problems. Social workers are encouraged to volunteer some portion of their professional skills with no expectation of significant financial return (pro bono service).

Value: *Social Justice*
Ethical Principle: *Social workers challenge social injustice.*

Social workers pursue social change, particularly with and on behalf of vulnerable and oppressed individuals and groups of people. Social workers' social change efforts are focused primarily on issues of poverty, unemployment, discrimination, and other forms of social injustice. These activities seek to promote sensitivity to and knowledge about oppression and cultural and ethnic diversity. Social workers strive to ensure access to needed information, services, and resources; equality of opportunity; and meaningful participation in decision making for all people.

Value: *Dignity and Worth of the Person*
Ethical Principle: *Social workers respect the inherent dignity and worth of the person.*

Social workers treat each person in a caring and respectful fashion, mindful of individual differences and cultural and ethnic diversity. Social workers promote clients' socially responsible self-determination. Social workers seek to enhance clients' capacity and opportunity to change and to address their own needs. Social workers are cognizant of their dual responsibility to clients and to the broader society. They seek to resolve conflicts between clients' interests and the broader society's interests in a socially responsible manner consistent with the values, ethical principles, and ethical standards of the profession.

Value: *Importance of Human Relationships*
Ethical Principle: *Social workers recognize the central importance of human relationships.*

Social workers understand that relationships between and among people are an important vehicle for change. Social workers engage people as partners in the helping process. Social workers seek to strengthen relationships among people in a purposeful effort to promote, restore,

We can realistically envision a world without extreme poverty by the year 2025 . . .
—Jeffrey D. Sachs, 2005, 347.

maintain, and enhance the well-being of individuals, families, social groups, organizations, and communities.

Value: *Integrity*
Ethical Principle: *Social workers behave in a trustworthy manner.*

Social workers are continually aware of the profession's mission, values, ethical principles, and ethical standards and practice in a manner consistent with them. Social workers act honestly and responsibly and promote ethical practices on the part of the organizations with which they are affiliated.

Value: *Competence*
Ethical Principle: *Social workers practice within their areas of competence and develop and enhance their professional expertise.*

Social workers continually strive to increase their professional knowledge and skills and to apply them in practice. Social workers should aspire to contribute to the knowledge base of the profession.

Given these values and ethics, social workers feel that it is important to consistently improve their competence in working with people from various backgrounds and experiences. This involves a special competence in relation to diversity and individual dignity.

Competence in Relation to Diversity and Individual Dignity

Social work programs must be culturally relevant to be effective in assisting all individuals and groups. That is, social work must recognize the interrelationship between culture and personal identity. Cultural diversity in social work often involves people of color, yet this concept also relates to gender, class, physical ability, and sexual orientation. Using a "strengths perspective" (to be discussed in Chapter 2 in more detail), social workers strive to recognize and utilize the strengths inherent in each group to facilitate positive

Social Work Stories: Immigration and Poverty

 tenant farmer in California reminisces about his life:

According to Mom, I was born on a cotton sack out in the fields, 'cause she had no money to go to the hospital. When I was a child, we used to migrate from California to Arizona and back and forth. The things I saw shaped my life. I remember when we used to go out and pick carrots and onions, the whole family. We tried to scratch a livin' out of the ground. I saw my parents cry out in despair, even though we had the whole family working. At the time, they were paying sixty-two and a half cents an hour. The average income must have been fifteen hundred dollars, maybe two thousand. . . . The bad thing was they used to laugh at us, the Anglo kids. They would laugh because we'd bring tortillas and frijoles to lunch. They would have their nice little compact lunch boxes with cold milk in their thermos and they'd laugh at us because all we had was dried tortillas. Not only would they laugh at us, but the kids would pick fights. My older brother used to do most of the fighting for us and he'd come home with black eyes all the time.

What really hurt is when we had to go on welfare. Nobody knows the erosion of man's dignity. They used to have a label of canned goods that said, "U.S. Commodities. Not to be sold or exchanged." Nobody knows how proud it is to feel when you bought canned goods with your own money.[32]

change. That said, social workers need to be careful not to stereotype individuals based upon membership in a specific group, but instead, recognize that diversity exists within diversity. Each individual is unique; each is worthy of dignity.[33]

"Culturally competent practice" focuses on the intersection between the diverse worldview of the individual or group and the dominant views of a given society; it requires social workers to understand how oppression and discrimination contribute to a set of values, roles, adaptations, and coping behaviors on the part of diverse individuals. This is because individuals from diverse groups often attain a set of values that include survival, combat, and street values that are quite different from the values that ordinarily would characterize a diverse social group free of oppression and discrimination. In short, social workers must develop a comprehensive understanding of clients, an understanding that includes their diverse background and associated characteristics—in contrast to using preconceived notions based upon demographic categories.[34]

Cultural diversity, by definition, includes social, racial, and ethnic diversity. "Social diversity" refers to differences based on age, class, or sexual orientation for example. The concept of "race" relates more to physiological differences. Because racial differences such as skin color are relatively noticeable, discrimination against individuals based on racial group membership is common and historically persistent. In contrast to race, "ethnicity" refers to distinct population groups that share common traits and customs. These customs are distinct in terms of their underlying values and the way these values are conveyed in language, traditions, child rearing, male–female relations, art, music, and so on.[35]

The concept of "cultural pluralism" seeks to respect and maintain ethnic differences. Cultural pluralism allows diverse groups to express themselves without suffering discrimination or oppression—even when they're a minority in a dominant culture. Respect for cultural pluralism demands that social workers avoid imposing their own culture on people they are trying to assist.[36] Social workers who understand cultural pluralism understand that every individual is like no other human being. That is, individuals are unique. Yet every individual is like some other individuals in that they belong to subgroups, whether male or female, or any other differentiator. And every individual is like all other individuals in terms of their basic human needs. We all need food, water, shelter, and relationships. Social workers must be knowledgeable about all three levels of diversity. Why? Because a knowledge of cultural diversity is the first step in respecting the dignity of every individual and a key to building trust in a helping relationship.

To respect cultural pluralism, social workers must develop cultural competency in their practice. **Cultural competency** may be understood through a five-dimensional framework.[37] This framework consists of informational, intellectual, interpersonal, intrapersonal, and interventional competencies. With regard to "informational competence," social workers must become aware of traditional and nontraditional knowledge in relation to oppressed and stigmatized populations. This knowledge would include information about theory, treatment, rehabilitation, empowerment, and community services. "Intellectual competence" requires social workers to adapt information in a way that best assists clients. This often requires or involves creative ways of thinking, particularly for social workers involved in difficult individual and social problems.

Critical Thinking Question

Social work involves an ability to feel comfortable with differences. Can you recall a time when you felt uncomfortable around a person very different from you, but later became more comfortable around them?

"Intrapersonal competence" involves empathy. That is, intrapersonal competence requires social workers to not only understand their own perspective, but also to understand another person's view of the world. In doing so, social workers need to understand, anticipate, and effectively deal with their own emotional and behavioral reactions to individual problems in relation to a distinctly different culture. This often requires that social workers monitor their own culturally learned behaviors in order to effectively help persons from other cultures.

"Interpersonal competence" includes the ability to work with people distinctly different from oneself. It involves communicating with and effectively engaging clients from different backgrounds. It involves empathy, warmth, and respect for clients even if one finds the client unappealing or frightening. "Interventional competency" refers to the synthesis and culmination by social workers of the first four competencies. To the extent that the social worker is competent in obtaining information about the client, applying information to strategies for helping the client, being able to understand and control his or her own cultural beliefs and behaviors in relation to a different culture, and work effectively on a personal basis with another person, then one can say that a social worker has achieved interventional competence.[38]

In developing interventional competence, social workers expect to find strengths and capabilities in clients even while helping a client to address a specific problem. In short, social workers must understand the influence of culture as a factor in problem definition and resolution. This involves the social worker's ability to view a client and their problems through the cultural lens of the client as well as that of a social worker. It involves an ability to feel comfortable with differences. It involves an ability to keep an open mind and examine presuppositions when viewing people of different cultures. It may also involve the ability to change one's own perspective in the face of new information about human differences. Overall, it requires an ability to be flexible in thinking and behavior.[39]

Social workers believe that cultural competence enables them to better promote social justice and human rights in their work. Because social justice is discussed at length later in this text, we briefly describe its importance to social work next.

Social Justice and Human Rights

Social work education programs examine the many factors that contribute to oppression and discrimination against certain populations, including racial and ethnic minorities, children, older adults, and women. People in these groups

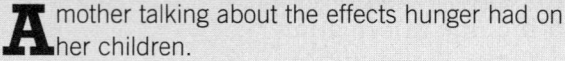

Social Work Stories: Hunger

A mother talking about the effects hunger had on her children.

Going to school without a decent breakfast was real hard on the kids. Their grades dropped, they became depressed, they also felt different and ashamed. Little things like not being able to afford a hamburger at a fast-food place and having to eat those damn beans really got to them. Let me tell you, this wasn't like eating soul food for fun. I tried to vary our diet. Once I got a neck bone and they scraped the fat off it and ate pure fat. That's how hungry they were.[40]

are more likely to suffer from poverty and related problems such as substance abuse and mental illness. Social work education examines strategies for producing laws, institutions, and services that better meet the needs of these populations, and therefore are more socially and economically just. In so doing, the concepts of distributive justice, human rights, civil rights, and global oppression are typically examined.[41]

Social work educators, students, and practitioners believe that these topics are important. They also believe that finding people's strengths and empowering them through those strengths are also important in their work as social workers.

Strengths and Empowerment

Social workers, as previously stated, believe in empowering their clients, whether those clients are individuals, families, groups, organizations, or communities. Each client has strengths that can be used in the helping process. The social worker's job is to collaborate with clients to discover those strengths and to use them for positive change and empowerment.[43]

Empowerment is defined as a multidimensional construct that applies to individuals, families, groups, organizations, and neighborhoods. It involves a psychological sense of self-control as well as actual influence and power in the greater society. In this sense, empowerment involves the study of "people in context," a primary distinction of the social work profession.[44] Empowerment refers not only to a state of mind, but also to a reallocation of power that results from altering social institutions.

Social workers who seek to empower clients see their clients as functional and healthy when given access to resources and opportunities. For individuals and families, informal social networks, such as friends and relatives, are important sources of support in the empowering process. In any case, if empowerment is to take place, client goals, means, and outcomes must be defined by the clients themselves in collaboration with a social worker. Social workers help to provide information to create client self-awareness in setting goals for positive change; they also help clients to access available resources and use them effectively.[45]

In short, social workers empower clients when they increase the clients' ability to control their destinies. This involves an ability to recognize client strengths and to find, increase, and/or redistribute opportunities and resources throughout society. For many clients, this is achieved by linking personal and political power.[46]

Social Work Stories: Poverty

Author Loretta Schwartz-Nobel tells of her struggle with poverty:

It wasn't until after the end of my marriage that I came to understand firsthand what it meant to be a suddenly single mother with two small children, promises of child support that didn't arrive, no regular income, and no health insurance.

I will never forget how alone I felt the morning my landlord called to say that my children and I would be evicted if the $425 I owed in back rent wasn't paid immediately. I had $200 in the bank, a stack of unpaid bills on the kitchen table and no food in the house. I tiptoed into the bedroom and looked at my children still asleep in their beds. For a while, I just stood there helplessly, wondering how I could possibly rescue them.[42]

Social Work Stories: Jobs for Unskilled Workers

Author Barbara Ehrenreich talking about the jobs that are available to unskilled workers:

The main thing I learn from the job-hunting process is that, despite all the help-wanted ads and job fairs, Portland is just another $6–$7-an-hour town. This should be as startling to economists as a burst of exotic radiation is to astronomers. If the supply (of labor) is low relative to demand, the price should rise, right? That is the "law." At one of the maid services I apply at—Merry Maids—my potential boss keeps me for an hour and fifteen minutes, most of which is spent listening to her complain about the difficulty of finding reliable help. It's easy enough to think of a solution, because she's offering "$200 to $250" a week for an average of forty hours' work. "Don't try to put that into dollars per hour," she warns, seeing my brow furrow as I tackle the not-very-long division. "We don't calculate it that way." I do, however, and $5 to $6 an hour for what this lady freely admits is heavy labor with a high risk of repetitive-stress injuries seems guaranteed to repel all mathematically able job seekers. But I am realizing that, just as in Key West, one job will never be enough. In the new version of the law of supply and demand, jobs are so cheap—as measured by the pay—that a worker is encouraged to take on as many of them as she possibly can.[47]

BACCALAUREATE SOCIAL WORK EDUCATION

Now that you have a sense of the profession, you may wonder what you have to do to earn a degree in social work. As an undergraduate student, you are primarily interested in a baccalaureate degree. A baccalaureate in social work (BSW) prepares graduates for a career in a generalist practice social work setting. As a graduate with a generalist social work degree, students are prepared to work in a variety of job settings and have the skills to uphold the ethics and values of the social work profession.

More specifically, the primary objective of the undergraduate social work education is to prepare students to function as generalist practitioners in a variety of agency settings with a variety of client situations. Students learn the necessary values, knowledge, and skills to enhance social functioning and improve the quality of life for clients and client systems. They also learn the importance of policy and political change as components of practice. The BSW curriculum emphasizes the interaction between client systems and their environments based on ecological and social systems theories. Students are provided varied but interrelated and integrated opportunities to mature intellectually, emotionally, and professionally as they acquire a generalist practice framework. Upper-level courses are designed to integrate, reinforce, and extend the learning that takes place in lower-level liberal arts and social work courses.[49]

Did You Know?

According to the Council on Social Work Education (CSWE), in 2007, 30,554 junior and senior students were enrolled in baccalaureate social work. There were also 23,299 full-time and over 13,000 part-time students enrolled in graduate social work programs. In the same year, 16,794 students graduated with their MSW degrees, while 12,018 earned their BSW degrees.[48]

"General education" courses are designed to encourage students to develop the value of independent, critical thinking and to stress the cultural and historical contexts of knowledge. By the students' third year, a more advanced and in-depth knowledge of social sciences and biopsychosocial theories is expected. Students progress from an introductory familiarity with theories to learning skills that enable them to understand and use social science and social work concepts to conduct purposeful intervention with client systems of all sizes.

Typically, introductory courses in social work focus on the previously discussed topics of Values and Ethics, Diversity, and Social and Economic Justice. Intermediate-level classes focus on Human Behavior and the Social Environment (HBSE) and Social Welfare Policy and Services. Advanced courses in social work focus on Practice, Research, and Field Education.

Human Behavior and the Social Environment

When students move into intermediate courses, they have a general knowledge of factors affecting individuals and intervention strategies. The (HBSE) curriculum explores the person-in-environment model in depth. Specifically, HBSE introduces the theoretical frameworks and models for the study of human development and behavior. It integrates and consolidates theories from the prerequisite social, behavioral, and biological science courses and provides the theoretical foundation for assessment and intervention in multiple systems. Consequently, these courses emphasize the systems approach and the person as a member of various systems (i.e., person-in-environment). Concepts of the family, primary groups, formal organizations, neighborhoods, and communities are presented as examples of significant social systems. Cultural factors, socialization, and the implications of racism, sexism, and other forms of oppression are usually discussed at each systems level. As part of these courses, students are expected to demonstrate knowledge of the interplay of biological, emotional, sociocultural, and cognitive factors in individual and family functioning and development.

Social Welfare Policy and Services

Students taking social welfare policy courses are typically provided with an overview of the origins and development of U.S. social welfare policy, the political processes in our federal and state systems, and the values and ethics that shape our present social welfare system. In addition, these courses introduce students to basic methods of policy analysis as well as to the effects various policies have on oppressed and disadvantaged populations, such as rural and urban poor, women, gays and lesbians, and people of color. Furthermore, social welfare policy courses educate students in the various ways they can influence policy formulation while advocating for social and economic justice.

Social Work Practice

Social work practice courses build on the knowledge gained in general education/liberal arts courses, introductory social work courses, and human behavior/social environment courses that students have completed during their first undergraduate years. Practice courses enable students to practice interviewing skills, problem assessment and contracting, intervention, and evaluation—all necessary for generalist practice in an entry-level social work position. Course content encourages the student to examine client strengths as well as cultural heritage as part of the assessment and intervention framework and to explore the value of collaborating with, rather than administering to, the client. Students are encouraged to assess clients from a systems perspective, viewing the client system in interaction with larger and smaller systems within the environment. For this reason, social work practice with families is a significant aspect of generalist practice.

In addition, students taking practice courses gain an understanding of diversity issues in service delivery, including how institutionalized forms of oppression may affect relationships with clients. A prominent theme throughout practice courses is ethnic-sensitive practice. Students apply their knowledge, skills, and values to role-playing situations and simulations.

Research

Social workers use research frequently in practice. Courses in research methods are designed to introduce students to the most common and important research methods in the social sciences, with emphasis on research in social work. The goal of these courses is for students to develop competence in all phases of planning social research. Often students demonstrate their competence by designing and conducting their own research proposals during the semester. Class sessions are typically used to discuss the basic precepts guiding social scientific research, the various types of research designs, as well as ongoing student projects. Necessary aspects of the research process include gathering, analyzing, and evaluating empirical studies in the professional literature; developing a research hypothesis and an appropriate research design; consideration of human subjects and ethical considerations; and demonstrating the writing skills required to report research findings. Exercises and assignments geared toward each of these skills normally are incorporated into the research courses.

Field Practicum

In an accredited baccalaureate of social work program, there is a minimum requirement of 400 hours of field work. This field practicum enhances student learning by providing opportunities to integrate and apply theories, research, values, and methods of generalist social work acquired in lower-level courses. Agency field instructors provide guidance and direction based on their experience and expertise in the field. Typically, students take a concurrent field seminar to better integrate course knowledge with their practice experience. Learning to recognize and respect the dignity and worth of client systems regardless of gender, race, religion, national origin, sexual orientation, or other aspect of difference is important in both the practicum and the concomitant seminar.

In summary, it is clear that undergraduate social work education prepares students for all areas of social work and a variety of careers. Combining a liberal arts education and social work courses, students are given the well-rounded, diverse education they will need to work with all types of clients in the field. When attending a school accredited by the Council on Social Work Education, students can be confident that they will receive an education that promotes the values of the profession and provides the tools for a successful career in social work.

Using the skills that a BSW student acquires in a social work education, students have the ability to meet their career goals as well as the goals of the profession. Students graduate with the ability to understand and change policy, work with diverse individuals, and use limited resources for change. Graduates are assured that they will enter the field ready to promote social justice and advocate for those in need. Social work graduates learn the skills to serve clients in the best way possible, and in turn help the people who need it most. Organizations hiring BSW students from an accredited school are assured that they are hiring an individual with the basic skills to fulfill a social work role, skills that will serve as the basis for more specialized roles in the future.

> **Did You Know?**
>
> According to the U.S. Department of Labor's Bureau of Labor Statistics (BLS), social work is one of the fastest growing careers in the United States. In 2008, 642,000 people were employed in social work, and social work employment is projected to grow by 16% between 2008 and 2018.[50]

THE FUTURE OF SOCIAL WORK

Future careers in social work look very promising for today's students.[51] The Internet, for example, presents new opportunities for casework, community organizing, social administration, and policy practice. In addition, social workers will find more and more employment opportunities in the business sector as global corporations strive to relate to diverse cultures and vulnerable populations in the U.S. and abroad. Social work in private nonprofit organizations will become more international in scope, paralleling the growth of international economic and political institutions. Specialization within the profession of social work will also increase. In fact, mental health appears to be the fastest growing area of social work.[52] That said, while specialization may become more prevalent in social work, the generalist skills, versatility, and broad perspective of the profession will continue to allow social workers to find work in a multitude of settings. If you take a close look, you will find social workers employed in hospitals, schools, prisons, senior centers, corporations, mental health centers, the military, elected public offices, United Way, and many other settings. According to NASW, social workers frequently obtain jobs in the following service areas: veterans' services, hospice and palliative care, adoption and foster care, family planning, disaster relief, homeless family assistance, employee assistance, domestic violence, parent education and support, HIV/AIDS services, school alternative programs, gerontology services, housing assistance, employment services, policy analysis, addiction treatment, crisis intervention, eating disorders, and neighborhood development.[53]

Social work is a challenging career! Social workers help people in the most difficult moments in life; social workers are there when people confront addiction, mental illness, disability, domestic violence, discrimination, and unemployment. Yet the social work profession has been assisting people, organizations, and communities in need for over 100 years—a wonderful history of social change and social justice. Would you enjoy a career in social work?

> **Research Informed Practice**
>
> How do social work, sociology, psychology, and other helping profession course curricula differ? Each of these disciplines is unique in its requirements for a degree. Research what courses are offered at your university for each profession. How do they vary? What are the similarities? Are the main courses similar? What do the required and elective courses in each major tell you about that profession? Use this information to determine your department's stance on what it believes is unique about its particular major.

SUMMARY

Social work is a helping profession. It focuses on individual well-being in a social context. The social work profession has developed within the U.S. social welfare system. Most social workers directly assist individuals, families, groups, and communities, while some work in administration, policy, or research. In all cases, social workers are guided by a Code of Ethics in their practice; issues related to individual dignity, respect for diversity, social justice, human rights, and empowerment are central to social work practice.

1 CHAPTER REVIEW

Succeed with mysocialworklab

Log onto **MySocialWorkLab** to access a wealth of case studies, videos, and assessment. (*If you did not receive an access code to* **MySocialWorkLab** *with this text and wish to purchase access online, please visit* www.mysocialworklab.com.)

PRACTICE TEST
The following questions will test your knowledge of the content found within this chapter. For additional assessment, including licensing-exam type questions on applying chapter content to practice, visit **MySocialWorkLab**.

1. A defining feature of the social work profession is:
   a. Its focus on human well-being
   b. Its focus on community well-being
   c. Its focus on individual well-being in a social context
   d. Its focus on the social context

2. The essential elements of the social work profession include:
   a. Knowledge, Information, and Power
   b. Knowledge, Values, and Skills
   c. Knowledge, Experience, and Credentials
   d. Knowledge, Power, and Members

3. Social workers practice at three levels:
   a. Low, Intermediate, and High
   b. Beginner, Advanced, and Professional
   c. Micro, Mezzo, and Macro
   d. Apprentice, Journeyman, and Master

4. Case managers require knowledge of services at the:
   a. Individual level
   b. Family level
   c. Agency level
   d. Community, state, and national level

5. Social workers who work with families typically view their work as one of problem-solving within a system's context, the system in this case being the:
   a. Individual
   b. Family
   c. Group
   d. Community

6. Social workers working as community organizers facilitate collective action in an effort to:
   a. Campaign for their favorite political candidate
   b. Become a community leader
   c. Provide community leaders with the solution to community problems
   d. Promote positive community change.

7. The profession of social work is based upon a set of core values which include:
   a. Service
   b. Trust
   c. Competition
   d. Personal gain

8. Social workers understand that relationships between and among people are:
   a. Different
   b. Oblivious to change
   c. A vehicle for change
   d. Parallel change

Diversity in Practice

9. Cultural diversity in social work relates to:
   a. Race, class, physical ability, and sexual orientation
   b. Exclusively race and ethnicity
   c. Ethnicity only
   d. Race only

Professional Identity

10. The values of the social work profession include:
    a. Freedom
    b. Social equality
    c. Liberty
    d. Competence

Log onto **MySocialWorkLab** once you have completed the Practice Test above to access additional study tools and assessment.

Answers

Key: 1) C 2) B 3) C 4) D 5) B 6) D 7) A 8) C 9) A 10) D

Theoretical and Conceptual Models of Social Work

CHAPTER OUTLINE

The Complexity of Social Work Theory and Practice 29

Human Behavior and the Social Environment 30
Multidimensional View: The Biopsychosocial Model of HBSE
Biological Domain
Psychological Domain
Social Domain
Expanding Our Perspective: The Spiritual and Physical Domains

Systems Theory and Social Work Practice 42
The Ecosystems Perspective
The Strengths Perspective in Social Work Practice

Summary 46

Practice Tests 48

 MySocialWorkLab 48

	Core Competencies in this Chapter (Check marks indicate which competencies are covered in depth)								
☐	Professional Identity	☐	Ethical Practice	☐	Critical Thinking	✓	Diversity in Practice	✓	Human Rights & Justice
☐	Research Based Practice	✓	Human Behavior	☐	Policy Practice	✓	Practice Contexts	☐	Engage, Assess, Intervene, Evaluate

THE COMPLEXITY OF SOCIAL WORK THEORY AND PRACTICE

Always remember that you are absolutely unique. Just like everyone else.
—Margaret Mead

After reading Chapter 1, you are aware that social workers occupy a wide variety of professional roles, from case manager to social activist. You may be wondering about the connection between social work's values and purpose and the practice of social work in a professional context. In this chapter we will examine this very question. We will explore the conceptual basis of social work and the models, perspectives, and approaches that unite the practice of social work and make social work practice unique.

Because this chapter will explore various levels of social work theory and practice—conceptual bases, models, perspectives, and approaches—it is useful to differentiate these levels from one another, although, in truth, their differences are not always clear-cut. A "conceptual base" is the idea, or collection of ideas, upon which a discipline, such as social work, is founded. The idea that human beings and their environments (e.g., social, physical) exist in a transactional relationship is a conceptual base of social work. **Models** are systems of data, suggestions, and inferences presented as a description or an analogy and are used to help us visualize something that cannot actually be seen, such as a conceptual base or a theory. When we speak of the **Biopsychosocial model**, for example, we are referring to a model of *how* the biological, psychological, and social components of human functioning exist in relation to one another. Social work "perspectives" are the viewpoints or lenses through which social work practice is conceptualized. For example, what is commonly referred to as the **strengths perspective** is an orientation toward social work practice that emphasizes the strengths, rather than the deficits, of human beings and their environments. Finally, social work "practice approaches" refer to the methods that social workers employ in their work. Practice approaches are derived from or informed by particular theories of human behavior such as cognitive theory, behavior theory, or psychodynamic theory.

Case Study: Louis B.

Louis B. is a three-and-a-half year old European American boy living in Jersey City, New Jersey. He recently began preschool at a local Head Start program. Workers there have observed that Louis appears be experiencing delays in his social, motor, emotional, and cognitive functioning. He rarely speaks and seems to have more trouble than his classmates following verbal directions. He occasionally acts aggressively towards his peers and has difficulty with tasks that require fine motor control.

Louis is the youngest of three children. His older sister Julia (6) and his older brother Joey (8) were removed from the care of his parents, Annemarie (24) and Jake (26), by his state's Office of Child Protective Services two years ago due to allegations of severe child neglect. The state is currently investigating allegations of neglect of Louis made against the couple several weeks ago.

Four years ago Annemarie and Jake left their home in another state after being evicted from their apartment due to nonpayment of rent. The couple lived on their own with their three children until Julia and Joey were removed. At that time, Annemarie experienced a severe episode of major depression and left Louis and Jake to live with an aunt in a nearby town for several months. She moved back into the couple's apartment three months ago. Annemarie attended high school though 10th grade

(Continued)

> **Case Study: Louis B.** (*Continued*)
>
> and then dropped out after becoming pregnant with Joey. While in school she received special education support for cognitive limitations that were never fully diagnosed. She is currently staying at home to care for Louis and is not employed in a paid position. Jake graduated from high school and has worked in road construction intermittently since then. He is currently working part time for the city's department of transportation and making above minimum wage. He is also looking for additional work. His current job does not include any benefits. Both parents have a history of substance use, including alcohol, marijuana, and nicotine. Annemarie reports she drank alcohol through the fifth month of her pregnancy with Louis.
>
> Annemarie and Jake are taking part in an intensive parenting education and support program in an effort to maintain custody of Louis. The program includes parenting education classes, case management for all family members, and individual and family therapy for all family members. As part of this program, a social worker visited the family in their home and reviewed the overall safety of the apartment with them. Given the age and poor condition of the apartment building, the social worker suspected there might be lead paint in the apartment and suggested the couple have Louis's blood lead levels tested. The results indicated levels significantly above the federal guidelines.
>
> Imagine you are a social worker working with Louis. How would you begin to assess and conceptualize what is "going on" with Louis? What information included here could help you understand his situation? What additional information would you like to know?

HUMAN BEHAVIOR AND THE SOCIAL ENVIRONMENT

The study of human behavior and the social environment (HBSE) is a core component of undergraduate social work education. The Council on Social Work Education outlines the areas of focus for HBSE courses:

> Content includes empirically based theories and knowledge that focus on the interactions between and among individuals, groups, societies, and economic systems. It includes theories and knowledge of biological, sociological, cultural, psychological, and spiritual development across the lifespan; the range of social systems in which people live (individual, family, group, organizational, and community); and the ways social systems promote or deter people in maintaining or achieving health and well-being.[1]

Clearly, HBSE is a broad area of study. Let's take a closer look at the two concepts joined under the HBSE banner: human behavior and the social environment. Human behavior refers to any action displayed by a human being in response to its internal physiology, its psychology, and/or its external environment. The social environment refers to all the external conditions and influences that surround and affect human beings, including all the individuals, communities, groups, organizations, and institutions an individual encounters, whether directly or indirectly. This would include an individual's physical setting—home, neighborhood, workplace, and broader geographical area, as

Theoretical and Conceptual Models of Social Work

> **Demonstrating Knowledge, Values, and Skills**
>
> **HBSE vs. SEHB**
>
> It is no coincidence that the phrase "human behavior and the social environment" starts with the micro and works outward. Critics of contemporary social work practice often cite the emphasis on individual psychological intervention, as opposed to social activism and the promotion of social change, as a problematic trend in the profession. Although the first U.S. social workers focused on community development and progressive political and economic reform, the emergence of the field of psychology changed the direction and emphasis of social work from the society to the individual. Social casework became the order of the day.
>
> How might social work education change if students were taught "the social environment and human behavior" rather than "human behavior and the social environment"? What might be gained or lost in this change?

well as his or her economic, political, and social circumstances, including class, race, gender, religious affiliation, sexual orientation, the political climate of his or her society, personal wealth, as well as the wealth of his/her locality, nation, and so forth.

The notion that all human beings exist in a reciprocal relationship with their environment is the core foundational concept in social work. This holistic, multidimensional view of human existence differentiates social work from traditional models of psychology and medicine, which focus primarily on the individual, and sociology or public policy, which focus on society's broader structures and institutions. The study of human behavior and the social environment requires attention to all the layers of human existence, from the functioning of neurotransmitters in the brain, to the functioning of the global economic system. This is a tall order, certainly, yet effective social work practice depends on a thorough understanding of the multilayered, transactional nature of human existence.

Social advance depends as much upon the process through which it is secured as upon the result itself.
—Jane Addams

Multidimensional View: The Biopsychosocial Model of HBSE

The study of human behavior and the social environment examines this reciprocal relationship between individuals and their environments across the human lifespan from a multidimensional point of view. This multidimensional point of view is referred to as the biopsychosocial model. The biopsychosocial model:

> allows the social worker to view the person holistically, as both an individual with inner biological drives and as a social and cultural being. . . . Each component in the system—whether biological, psychological, social, or spiritual—is intertwined with every other component. . . . It reminds social workers that even in individual micro-level intervention, a holistic, environmental approach will enhance understanding.[2]

The biopsychosocial model of HBSE views each of the domains of human existence—biological, psychological, social, spiritual, and physical—as wholly interconnected with each other. For the purposes of discussion, however, we will look at each of these individual domains in more depth.

Biological Domain

The biological domain is made up of everything intrinsic to the human body. Genetic inheritance, brain chemistry, organ function, nutrition, disease, physical injury, height, weight—all these physiological components affect how a person and his or her environment interact. Our understanding of how biology affects all the other domains, and vice versa, is constantly changing as discoveries in the biological sciences expand our knowledge. The fields of medicine, psychology, education, substance abuse treatment, and, of course, social work, are all affected by developments in the study of human biology. New information about the genetic and biochemical components of individual problems, such as depression and substance abuse, as well as discoveries regarding the workings of the brain, have provided an awareness of the link between the human mind and human behavior.[3] The genes we inherit from our parents not only determine what we look like, but are also implicated in our temperament, talents, and mental and physical health. Genes are implicated in predispositions to certain mental and physical health problems such as alcoholism, asthma, breast cancer, hypertension, and schizophrenia.[4] Brain scanning technology, such as functional magnetic resonance imaging (fMRI), have enabled scientists to examine the connection between activity in particular areas of the brain and everything from "emotional intelligence" to schizophrenia, thus creating new insights into the role of the brain in our physical, emotional, and cognitive well-being.

Research on brain development over the lifespan has given us new clues regarding how children grow and where troubles may begin. Early psychological models of human functioning paid little heed to the neurochemical workings of the brain, as so little was known about brain neurochemistry. Instead, the psychological models developed in 19th and early 20th centuries emphasized the role of the parental relationship and an individual's psyche in determining behavior. More recently, the field of genetics brought about a great shift in our understanding of the influence of biology and biochemistry on behavior. Neuroscience research, however, has recently shown that even genetics alone cannot illuminate the full picture of human development. Indeed, rather than a mysterious organ somehow related to our development and behavior, or a mass of predetermined chemical interactions over which neither we nor our environment have any control, the brain is, in fact, dynamic and ever-changing. According to Robin Karr-Morse and Meredith S. Wiley, authors of an influential book on child development and violence, *Ghosts from the Nursery,* genetics can "set broad parameters . . . [but] the actual matter of the brain is built."[5]

The transactional nature of human brain development is illustrated in the process of language acquisition—the ability to understand and produce human speech. Studies of language acquisition have demonstrated that children who are deprived of hearing human speech during the first years of life are unable to develop their own speech or to understand spoken language later in life.[6] The neural connections required for language acquisition only occur if they are needed—in other words, only in the presence of speech. Once the critical window for making these connections has passed, these neurons are "pruned," absorbed, or used elsewhere in the brain.[7] Not all developmental milestones follow this use-it-or-lose-it pattern, however. Important skills such as math, logic, and music are acquired most effectively during middle to late childhood, but our ability to learn them later in life is not lost entirely; it simply becomes more difficult.[8]

The role of neurochemistry in mental illness and human behavior also continues to be clarified. As noted above, the human brain adapts to its environment and needs a rich environment to develop to its full potential. Many mental disorders appear to be linked to neurochemical imbalances in the brain, but the neurochemistry of the brain itself is linked to one's environment throughout the lifespan. For example, brain research has begun to illuminate the importance of two neurochemicals in human behavior: serotonin and noradrenaline. The right balance of these two chemicals is essential for modulating our anxiety and arousal levels. Too much noradrenaline and too little serotonin lead to impulsivity and possibly to acting out in violent ways. Too little noradrenaline and too little serotonin lead to a state of chronic underarousal, leading to a high tolerance for risk and thus potentially dangerous behavior. Too much serotonin is related to rigidity and low tolerance for risk, and has been indicated in anxiety disorders, such as obsessive-compulsive disorder.[9]

Although the biological sciences have given us new insights into the complexities of the "nature" side of the nature–nurture debate, the crucial roles of the psychological and social domains remain unclear. For example, one child with low serotonin levels may grow up with a passion for extreme sports, whereas another might grow up to be a violent criminal.[10] A child's psychological, social, physical, and spiritual environments, and the interaction of these environments with each other and with the child's unique biological makeup, make all the difference.

Psychological Domain

The focus of the psychological domain of human development is the individual and his or her unique psyche. The concepts of consciousness and personality are key elements of human behavior and human development viewed through a psychological lens, as are mental processes such as emotion, cognition, communication, memory, and so on. Psychological theories regarding human development abound, and most are predicated on the concept of human growth or drive toward a developmental goal. Social work draws from a number of developmental theories to understand the nature of human behavior and human development over time. Psychoanalytic theorists, such as Sigmund Freud and Erik Erikson, focus on emotional and personality development. Erik Erikson's (1950) conception of development is compatible in many ways with social work's biopsychosocial model.[11] Erikson's theory of development focuses on the ways in which individuals' personalities evolve throughout the lifespan as a result of the interface between their physical maturation and societal demands. Erikson envisioned that humans develop in stages, and proposed that a psychological "crisis" occurs at each stage of development and must be resolved in order for development to continue successfully. Although the biological and societal demands propel individuals into and through successive stages, unresolved crises from the past, such as issues from early childhood, hamper psychological development and can come back to trouble people later in life. Erikson proposed eight stages of human psychological development. The stages are:

1. Basic trust vs. mistrust—birth to 18 months
2. Autonomy vs. shame and doubt—18 months to 3 years
3. Initiative vs. guilt—3 to 6 years
4. Industry vs. inferiority—6 to 12 years
5. Identity vs. role confusion—adolescence
6. Intimacy vs. isolation—young adulthood
7. Generativity vs. stagnation—maturity
8. Ego integrity vs. despair—old age[12]

Successful resolution of these crises leads to a balance between the tasks presented at each stage. For example, young toddlers, having successfully resolved the conflict between trust and mistrust, emerge from this first stage of development with a balanced internalized sense of safety and skepticism. This balanced sense of trust and mistrust allows the child to both avoid danger and embrace care from safe sources, and helps him or her to both survive and thrive.

Critics of Erikson's work have noted the assumption of "universality" in his theory of human development. Erikson's eight stages suggest that all humans follow the same developmental course and experience the same crises at the same ages, regardless of historical, social, or individual differences. For example, Erikson's life stage theory assumes that heterosexuality is the norm, which suggests that the successful resolution of the intimacy versus isolation phase will be heterosexual marriage in young adulthood. In contemporary society, many people find intimacy in nonmarital or non-heterosexual relationships. Feminist scholars have also noted limitations to Erikson's theory regarding the importance of human relationships to development throughout the lifespan. Although only the intimacy versus isolation stage clearly denotes the importance of relationships to human well-being, we know that social relatedness is crucial to wellness at every stage of life.

Although Erikson's work focuses on emotional and personality development, the psychological domain also encompasses other aspects of our inner experience, such as learning and cognition. In the first half of the 20th century, psychologist Jean Piaget proposed a stage-based theory of cognitive development focused on the way human thinking and intelligence develops and changes throughout the lifespan.[13] Piaget sought to explain the human tendency for greater cognitive organization and abstraction over time. Piaget disputed the commonly held notion that the variations between children's cognitions and adults' were simply a matter of children's lesser knowledge or experience.[14] He proposed, instead, that childhood cognitive structures were different from those of adults.

Piaget theorized that human cognitive development evolves throughout childhood, moving through four distinct periods. At the earliest period, babies' cognitive development focuses on organizing their physical action for efficient interfacing with the immediate environment in order to meet basic needs. At the most advanced period of development, adolescents develop the capacity for abstract thought. Piaget outlined the following four periods of cognitive development:

Period I: Sensori-Motor intelligence (birth–2 years)
Period II: Preoperational thought (2–7 years)
Period III: Concrete operations (7–11 years)
Period IV: Formal operations (11 years–adulthood)[15]

Although Piaget believed that these periods were an "invariant sequence" (i.e., they must be moved through in the same order), he also understood children to move through the periods at different rates.[16] The ages attached to these periods, therefore, are offered as general guidelines only.

Piaget's theories of cognitive development have been criticized by many for their lack of attention to the importance of culture and environment on children's development. Russian psychologist Leo Vygotsky (1896–1934) was also interested in understanding children's cognitive development, but unlike Piaget, Vygotsky looked to social interactions and culture to explain the nature of the developmental process. Vygotsky believed that cognitive development progresses due to the interaction of two intertwined developmental paths: elementary processes that are basically biological and psychological processes, which are primarily sociocultural.[17] Vygotsky believed that elementary processes are transformed into higher-order psychological functioning as a child develops through interactions with the boarder environment. Vygotsky was particularly interested in how children develop speech, and his theories on this process are illustrative of his overall theory of cognitive development. Vygotsky believed that a progression in a child's development occurs twice—once extrapshycologically and once intrapsychologically.[18] In the case of speech, Vygotsky theorized that the egocentric speech of toddler-aged children—the monologue that young children maintain while they play, even when they are alone—is transformed through development into the inner speech that older children and adults use to guide their behavior—that is, into an adult thinking process. He called this process internalization.[19]

Vygotsky was also very interested in how children learn. He argued that within a certain social environment, there are tasks that children can complete on their own with no assistance, and those that they can complete with guidance and assistance from others, including more capable peers or adults.[20] The space between these two he termed the "zone of proximal development," and it is in this space that learning occurs. Vygotsky believed that the process of scaffolding supports learning and is an important function of adults and peers as children develop. Scaffolding is the process of helping to move children from initial difficulties with a task to the point where they can gradually perform the task independently.[21] Parents and teachers use scaffolding all the time in their interactions with children. Consider the parent who assists her young child to learn to tie his own shoes. First she might tie one shoe herself, narrating the process as she does. Next she might ask the child to tie the other shoe, continuing to narrate as the child does so, and helping the child when he gets stuck. Over time the parent will stop tying either shoe, and eventually will stop narrating the process, stepping in only when the child gets stuck. Additionally, while this process is taking place, the child is also internalizing the process himself, transforming this interaction into internal thought.

Both Piaget's and Vygotsky's theories of cognitive development have significant implications for social work practice at nearly every level and in nearly every setting. Let's use Piaget's theory of development to imagine working with a traumatized young child. According to Piaget, young children think in the preoperational stage. They tend to focus on one dimension of a situation or

Critical Thinking Question

Theories of human behavior and recent brain research suggest that children and adults think and learn differently. How might this impact the ways that social workers work with children and adolescents?

problem and have great difficulty mentally holding multiple dimensions of a situation at once. Children at this stage cannot conceptualize the notion of cause and effect. A social worker helping a child cope with a traumatic event must keep this fact in mind when attempting to design an effective intervention, realizing that too much discussion or explanation about the complexities of a traumatic situation may just further overwhelm or confuse a child. Let's use Vygotsky's theory to imagine working with a child with disruptive behavior in the classroom. In this situation, a social worker's role may be to help a child manage his angry feelings and prevent violent outbursts. Using the idea of the zone of proximal development, a social worker would want to understand which feelings, and at what level of intensity, the child can successfully manage on his own, and then use interventions to scaffold more advanced affect management. Social workers working in the mezzo and macros levels also need to understand children's cognitive development. For example, social workers involved in designing a drug prevention program for adolescents would need to ensure the developmental appropriateness of the program's various components for its target audience.

Erikson's and Piaget's works have provided essential knowledge for social workers about the process of human development in both the emotional and cognitive arenas. Meanwhile, psychologist Abraham Maslow sought to understand the underpinnings necessary for optimal human development overall. Maslow's more holistic, humanistic approach to human development has made his work particularly relevant and useful to social work theory and practice. In attempting to explain the conditions needed for human beings to reach their fullest potential (in other words, for human "self-actualization"), Maslow developed a paradigm of human needs that he called the "hierarchy of needs". In Maslow's conception, each need must be fulfilled successively before the next level of higher needs can be realized.[22] Basic survival needs (e.g., food, water, sleep) must be met before higher-level needs can be achieved. As Figure 2.1

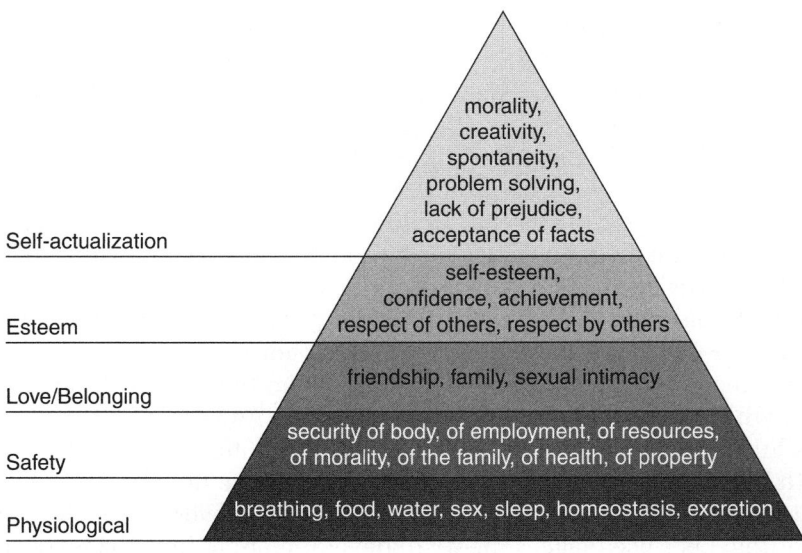

Figure 2.1

Maslow's Hierarchy of Needs

illustrates, Maslow considered safety, belongingness and love, esteem, and, finally, self-actualization as higher-order human needs (note, however, that even the highest-order needs are conceptualized as *universal human needs*, not privileges reserved for the lucky few).

Maslow's theory rests on the notion that each person attempts to satisfy these needs in order. Self-esteem and creativity, for example, are unlikely to occur without adequate nutrition and basic safety. Unlike Piaget's conception of human cognitive development, Maslow's hierarchy is not an invariant sequence. Circumstances in an individual's life may change, affecting the area of focus in the hierarchy. With the loss of a job or a loved one, community violence, or political conflict, the elements of self-actualization are affected, and an individual must focus on the lower rungs: safety or even basic survival. Although Maslow's theory is rooted in the psychological domain, it is also attentive to the transactional nature of individual psychology and the social environment, making it of particular interest and utility to social workers. Maslow's hierarchy, for example, offers "a paradigm for viewing a society's level of success in meeting its people's needs, or the needs of any group, in society."[23]

A family may have its basic needs met; however, if domestic violence exists, the safety needs of the children and the victimized adult are clearly not being met. The family members' higher-order needs of love, esteem, and self-actualization are thus imperiled, and could continue to be so without appropriate intervention. Maslow's needs hierarchy is therefore particularly useful in modeling the impact of setbacks caused by deficits in the social environment (e.g., violence, poverty, racism, food insecurity, poor health care) on individuals.

> *Poverty should be defined psychologically.*
> —Michael Harrington

Social Domain

In social work's transactional, multidimensional model of human development and behavior, the impact of the social environment is understood to be equally as important as the biological or psychological domains. The social domain encompasses everything that makes up our social worlds: our families, neighborhoods, schools, communities, places of work, and the major institutions of our nation—to name just a few—are all part of the social domain of human existence. Attention to the social domain is crucial for social workers, because individual biology and psychology do not exist in a vacuum, but within the context of broader social structures. These various social systems interact with each other as well as with an individual's biological and psychological makeup.

In the 20th century, the development of systems theory had a tremendous effect on the way scientists and researchers in the biological and social sciences understood the way environments—from the natural ecosystems to the human family—function. Systems theory, not surprisingly, has had a profound impact on contemporary social work practice and on the way social work professionals conceptualize the social domain and the interactions among all of the domains of human life. A system is a set of elements that affect, influence, and/or interact with one another. Systems theory and one of its outgrowths, ecosystems theory, will be discussed in greater detail a little later in the chapter. First, however, we will explore the theories of Urie Bronfenbrenner, a psychologist whose work draws heavily on systems theory, to expand our understanding of the social domain.

Bronfenbrenner identified four levels of social systems that make up the social context of human development. In Bronfenbrenner's scheme, the microsystem is comprised of a person's relationships in his or her immediate settings.[24] Individuals belong to multiple microsystems. Bronfenbrenner's mesosystem refers to interrelationships between or among microsystems. The exosystem refers to larger social systems that the individual does not participate in directly, but that influence his or her life. Finally, the macrosystem refers to the broader cultural contexts in which all the other systems are located.

Figure 2.2 offers a visual representation of Bronfrenbrenner's ecological model. This figure uses the life of a school-aged child to draw examples of elements of each system level. At the center are the child's most immediate relationships—those with caregivers, siblings, and grandparents. Links between or among microsystems comprise Bronfenbrenner's mesosystem layer. For example, if a child's microsystems include immediate family, school, and church, the link between the immediate family and the school represents one mesosystem. The link between family and church represents another mesosystem, and the link between school and church represents a third. If family values correspond to school values, the school–family mesosystem will be strong, whereas if family values are very different from school values or family and school have little communication, the child's family–school mesosystem will be weak, and so forth. We can imagine the many ways the school–family mesosystem might affect a child. Does a family member help the child with his

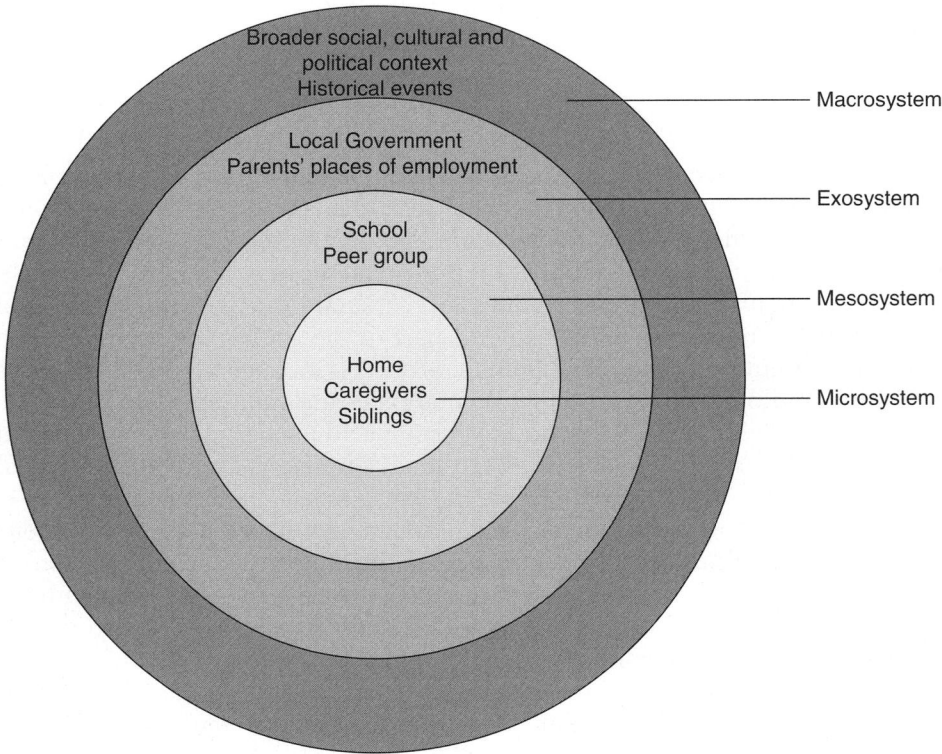

Figure 2.2
Bronfenbrenner's ecological model
Source: Based on Bronfenbrenner's ecological model.

or her homework? Does the child see members of his or her family microsystem reading books? Are behavioral norms at home similar to behavioral norms in the school setting? At the exosystem level are the systems that affect the child but which he or she is unlikely to interact with directly, including the school board, local government, or a caregiver's workplace. Again, it is not hard to imagine the range of ways these elements might affect a child. Are his or her caregivers paid a living wage? Was a caregiver laid off from his or her job recently? Does the local justice system enforce child abuse and neglect laws? Finally, at the macrosystem level are the child's broader cultural contexts—the social structures that surround him or her, the cultural values, norms, and laws. These systems are often more abstract, but have a profound impact on an individual's life. How is the society stratified? Is the child's gender, race, ethnicity, or religious group oppressed? Is the child's country experiencing civil unrest or war? The answers to these questions help a social worker more fully understand the topography of a given child's social domain, enabling the social worker to conceptualize the child's behavior, development, and overall functioning in a holistic, multidimensional way, and allowing the social worker to create a helping intervention that will be maximally useful and positive for the child.

Looking at Bronfenbrenner's scheme, it is clear that subsystems, including the family and social groups of various kinds, are a key part of the social domain. Social workers, therefore, must be aware of the groups that form the context of human life. In the most traditional sense of the word, the "family" is understood to be a group of people with genetic relationships to one another; however, families need not be defined so rigidly. Families are groups of individuals who decide (implicitly or explicitly) to act as a family. Families function as systems, just as other groups of living beings do, and also exist in the context of other, broader systems. Individuals within a family interact and affect one another, and these interactions also affect the family as a whole. Broader systems of which both individuals and the family as a whole are a part also affect the family. Families will be discussed in greater detail in upcoming chapters. For now, however, note that social workers who work with both individuals and with families must be aware of the countless influences on families and individuals it they are to design and initiate effective helping interventions.

Critical Thinking Question

It is important for social workers to understand that "family" is a broad concept. Identify as many family structures as can you think of. How do you feel about these different families?

Social groups, like the family, are a key component of an individual's social domain. Groups can be intentionally formed (e.g., a psychotherapy group) or naturally occurring (e.g., a group of professional colleagues). Social groups are generally categorized by function, such as recreational groups, self-help groups, civic organizations, charitable groups, psychotherapy groups, or neighborhood associations. Social workers often work with each of these types of groups in different ways and at all levels of practice. A social worker working in clinical practice might facilitate a psychotherapy group as part of an outpatient treatment program for individuals with mood disorders, whereas a social worker working in youth case management might refer his or her young client to Al-Anon, a mutual-aid group for family members and loved ones of individuals with alcohol and/or drug dependency. A social worker in macro practice might help a low-income neighborhood association navigate city politics in order to improve social services or public safety in the neighborhood. Social work with groups provides a key means by which to positively intervene in the social environment of a client, whether the client is a single person or an entire city.

Expanding Our Perspective: The Spiritual and Physical Domains

As the theory and practice of social work continues to grow in this new century, social workers are increasingly expanding their focus beyond the biopsychosocial conception of human development and behavior to include the additional domains of spirituality and the physical environment. Our spiritual lives and the physical world we inhabit affect our mental and physical health and well-being in profound ways. To be truly multidimensional in our understanding of human existence, social workers must also attend to clients' spiritual lives and their physical environments.

For centuries, spirituality has been practiced and taught primarily within organized religious groups. Historically, social work has had a significant connection to spiritual practice—Christianity in particular. The earliest American social workers, for example, were heavily influenced by the Protestant Social Gospel movement of the late 19th and early 20th centuries, which emphasized society's moral responsibility to attend to the welfare of its neediest citizens. In addition, many of the social sciences, from psychology to sociology, are historically rooted in Judeo-Christian notions of humanity, morality, and ethics. These roots aside, social work has always been a humanistic discipline—one focused on the daily life of real people in their present state of existence. In addition, social work ethics emphasize respect for difference and diversity, including religious and spiritual diversity. Social work practice, therefore, has not typically included much attention to the spiritual domain. Respect for difference has, unfortunately, often been understood to mean only that the social worker ought not impose his or her spiritual or religious practices or belief system on his or her client, and has not included the next essential steps: seeking to understand the role of spirituality in a client's life and harnessing this knowledge to create effective interventions. Increasingly, however, the role of spirituality, especially its role in individual and social empowerment and actualization, is being recognized.

Spirituality can play a key role in personal and community empowerment. According to Van Wormer:

> Disempowered people often need a purpose that transcends their mere existence. [In addition,] involvement in organized religions can provide much needed social and material support—witness the historic role of the African American church, which was the midwife of the civil rights movement.[25]

Practice Contexts

Critical Thinking Question

It can be helpful for a social worker to be well informed about the various spiritual resources in their community. What might be the benefits and pitfalls of building relationships with spiritual and/or religious organizations, leaders, or communities?

Spirituality can be a key component of the ways human beings make meaning out of existence—the way in which they understand and answer life's existential questions. Furthermore, spirituality can have an enormous impact on the way that an individual, community, or whole society conceptualizes the various challenges in which social work assistance is typically sought. Is mental illness understood to be indicative of a medical disease, an imbalance in an individual's life force energy, or possession by supernatural forces? Spiritual traditions and practices of the client may dictate the answers to questions about how an individual understands his or her difficulty and also give a social worker important guidance in designing culturally competent and effective interventions. For social workers practicing in communities where spirituality is deeply integrated into community life, awareness, sensitivity, and understanding of spiritual practices is essential. Building alliances with

spiritual leaders and healers can be enormously helpful and, in many cases, absolutely necessary.

The role of spirituality in physical and mental healing is increasingly emerging clearly and affecting social work practice. Many social workers in clinical practice are integrating mind–body based spiritual practices, such as meditation or prayer, in interventions with clients experiencing everything from eating disorders to anxiety to grief.

The relationship of the physical environment to other domains of human experience has always been a concern for social work. Thanks to the work of the environmental movement, however, we now have a far greater awareness than ever before of the degradation and depletion of the Earth's resources, and the impact of environmental hazards on human development and day-to-day existence. Global warming, climate change, air and water pollution, and dwindling nonrenewable resources affect all of us directly and indirectly. Many communities and individuals experience the direct effects of environmental destruction. For example, dwindling fish stocks due to overfishing and other environmental changes, such as water and air pollution, have affected fishing communities throughout the United States. Restrictions on days at sea, initiated to protect and revive fish stocks, have, in many cases, resulted in a variety of stressors on individuals and communities, including reduced income and occupational displacement. Using the biopsychosocial model, we can also imagine that these stressors in the social domain might interact with biological and physical domains, resulting in decreased mental health and social functioning in affected individuals, families, and communities.

Although we all experience the impact of changes in the physical world, certain populations tend to experience these more directly than others. The environmental justice movement has highlighted the connection among poverty, race, and exposure to the most damaging environmental hazards. Social work's historical and ongoing attention to poverty and social justice issues make this relationship one of particular interest and importance. In

Critical Thinking Question

Exposure to environmental toxins and other hazards disproportionately affects socially marginalized communities. How might a social worker work with a group or community to reduce their exposure to environmental hazards?

addition, examining connections among poverty, race, and exposure to environmental hazards also illustrates the interconnectedness of the domains of human existence. Poor people of color in the United States experience exposure to environmental toxins at a disproportionate rate.[26] There are a number of explanations for this disparity, including the greater likelihood that poor people of color will be living in substandard housing and the greater likelihood that such housing is located in neighborhoods in close proximity to major environmental toxin sources, including power plants and factories. Exposure to environmental toxins is related to a number of problematic health conditions, such as asthma and lead poisoning. High lead levels, furthermore, are well known to affect children's cognitive development.[27] Given the significant interactions that environmental hazards have on all the other domains, the physical domain is an essential addition to social work's multidimensional model of human development and existence.

SYSTEMS THEORY AND SOCIAL WORK PRACTICE

Systems theory, a framework to analyze and/or describe a group of entities (e.g., objects or beings) that work in concert and produce some result, was originated by biologist Ludwig von Bertalanffy (see *General Systems Theory*, George Braziller, 1968) and other scientists in the mid-20th century. Although developed in the context of the natural sciences, the systems theory concepts were quickly absorbed by other disciplines, including social work. The development of systems theory provided social work with the theoretical underpinnings necessary for conceptualizing and using the biopsychosocial (spiritual–physical) model. Systems theory postulates that all beings are systems and all beings reside within multiple systems. General systems theory foundational concepts include wholeness, feedback, homeostasis, and equilibrium.

Wholeness refers to the idea that the elements within a system, as well as a given system, are both whole and part.[28] Furthermore, a system is made of parts but is an entity greater than the sum of those parts. Thus, no system can be fully understood simply by examining its individual parts. For example, just as the biopsychosocial model suggests, a person cannot be fully understood by examining only a particular domain. Feedback refers to the structure of a system. Parts exist in relationship to each other, and information is exchanged within that relationship. Systems that are working well are in balance. Parts are in balance with each other, and the system is in balance with the other systems of which *it* is part. This is equilibrium. Systems must be adaptable to change to remain in equilibrium. Homeostasis refers to this state of flexible balance.

Systems theory provided social workers with a way of understanding that individuals are both systems themselves and parts of systems (e.g., families, groups) that are, in turn, parts of even greater systems (e.g., societies or nations). Although systems theory provides an excellent foundation for understanding the complexities of human existence, many have found that in its original form, it could not wholly capture the intricate dynamics that occur in social systems. The ecosystems perspective of social work draws from systems theory as well as other theories, models, and perspectives, to provide a framework for understanding the complex relationships between and within humans and their environments.

The Ecosystems Perspective

Drawing from concepts originating in systems theory, the ecosystems perspective holds that individuals can only be fully understood when viewed in the context of their environment. The ecosystems perspective was widely adopted into the practice of social work in the 1970s and has since become a, if not *the*, dominant framework for conceptualizing social practice. "Ecology," a subfield of biology that studies the complex relationship between a living organism and its environment, provides a useful metaphor for conceptualizing this simultaneous focus on the person, his or her environment, and the reciprocal relationship between them.[29] This multidimensional way of conceptualizing individuals and environments as an interrelated whole is referred to in social work practice as person-in-environment (PIE). The ecosystems perspective highlights not only the need to view people in their environment, but also the need to view the PIE system in the context of history and culture, as all these elements of the PIE systems continuously interact with each other.[30]

Goodness of fit is central to the ecosystems perspective and is closely related to homeostasis and equilibrium, but captures more of the complexity that arises in the PIE system. Goodness of fit refers to the fit between a person and his/her environment. The fit is said to be good when the environment is meeting the needs of the individual in a satisfactory way (think back to Maslow's hierarchy of human needs). When the fit is not good and the environment is not meeting an individual's needs, problems arise.[31] An individual's health, development, or social functioning may be compromised. A primary task for social workers is to assess the level of fit between their client(s) and client environments. This assessment not only helps social workers to understand the source(s) of difficulty, but also can point the way to a potential path toward resolution.

One way that social workers can begin to assess the level of fit between a person and his or her environment is by creating a visual representation of a person (or family, community, etc.) in his or her environment; this is known as an ecomap. Looking at an ecomap can help a social worker, in partnership with a client, locate areas where there are person–environment mismatches. Figure 2.3 depicts an ecomap of the case example discussed earlier in the chapter. Where do you think Louis's needs are and are not being met?

The concept of adaptation, defined as when people and environments both react to and act upon each other, is also central to the ecosystems perspective.[32] The relationships in PIE systems are dynamic. Change in one necessitates adaptation by the other to maintain fit. When adaptation does not occur, fit is compromised and, again, problems can occur.

If we take the fishing communities example discussed in the section on the spiritual and physical domains of human functioning, we can see this process in action. Dwindling fish stocks, caused by past overfishing, water pollution, and climate changes cause state and federal regulatory bodies to restrict the days that fishermen can go out to sea. This change, of course, affects the individual and families who depend on the income provided by fishing, and necessitates adaptation. Individuals with other personal and environmental resources, such as other job skills and interests, higher education, or other sources of income (e.g., an employed spouse) may find it fairly easy to adapt to this change. Individuals without extra resources may find it more difficult to adapt. The change in days-at-sea will have rendered their environment deficient in meeting their needs. For a good fit to be restored, personal and environmental adaptations are necessary. Perhaps the days-at-sea restrictions can be influenced by community activism; perhaps an occupational retraining

Poverty . . . represents the failure of an economic system.
—Brooks Atkinson

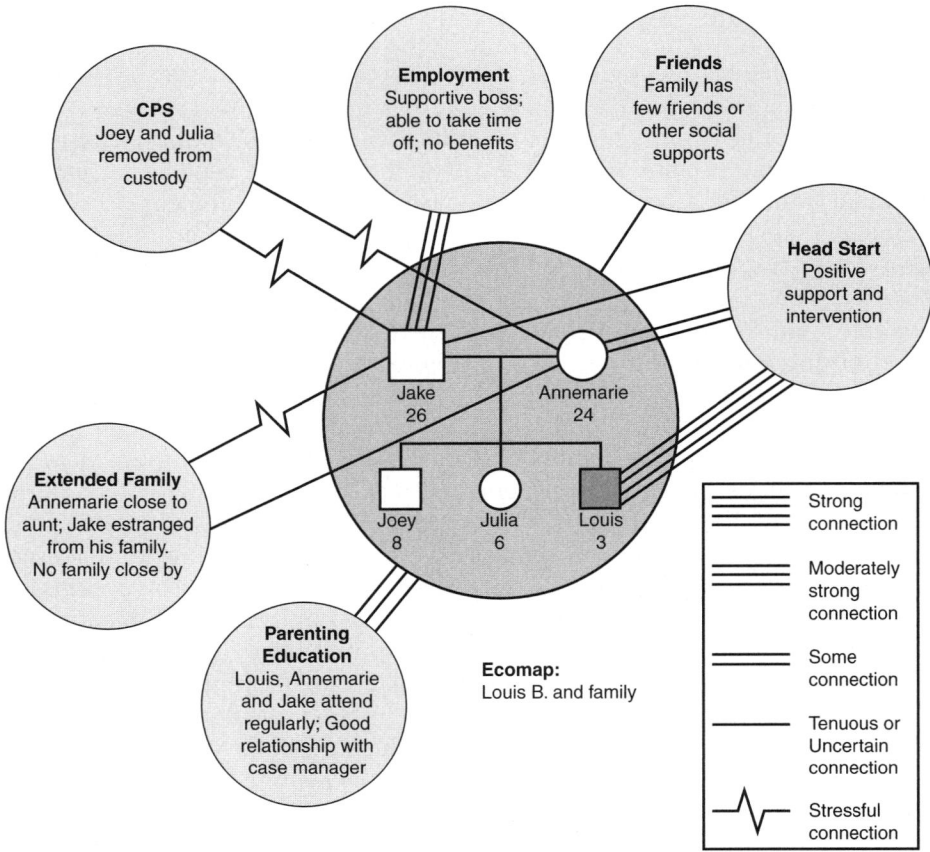

Figure 2.3
Ecomap

program can be started in the community; perhaps an individual may discover unrealized interests and talents that can point the way to new occupational and personal opportunities. Social workers could be called upon to initiate and assist with any of these interventions.

Demonstrating Knowledge, Values, and Skills

Ecomaps can be extremely useful tools for social workers and their clients as they work together to come to a mutual understanding of the client in his/her/their social environment. There are many variations in ecomap design, keys, etc. Use Figure 2.3 as a guide, or do your own web or library research on how to create an ecomap.

Activity 1

Role-play with a partner a scenario in which one student is the social worker and one student is the client. Work together to construct an ecomap of the client's life at this moment in time. The student playing the social worker should inquire about various aspects of the social environment, including work, school, family relationships, spiritual life, friends, community, neighborhood, etc. Ecomaps are highly flexible tools and can map a person's relationship with the social environment from the micro- to the macrosystem level.

Activity 2

Ecomap construction need not be limited to the social worker–client relationship. Developing an ecomap of one's own social environment can provide students and social workers alike with a valuable snapshot of their own lives, and foster greater self-awareness. Try creating an ecomap of your own life at this point in time and see what surprises emerge.

Several other ecosystems concepts are related to adaptation. In this example, the change in days-at-sea is a life stressor for the negatively affected individuals, families, and communities. A life stressor is an event or issue that is perceived by the individual to place excessive demands on his or her internal and environmental resources.[33] Perception is a key word in the definition of life stressor. As our previous example indicates, what one person experiences as a stressor may be a positive opportunity for another person.

Another important concept is coping, a multidimensional concept that refers to one's perceived and actual ability to manage a stressor.[34] "Relatedness," the extent of positive attachments and sense of belonging one has; "competence," one's sense of one's own capacity for effective action in the environment; "self-esteem," one's global positive sense of oneself; and "self-direction," one's sense of one's own power and agency, are all connected with coping. Individuals, families and communities that experience higher levels of relatedness, competence, self-esteem, and self-direction are more likely to cope with stress and to make the necessary adaptations in a successful way. Each of these four concepts is internalized (i.e., the individual does them without even thinking about them) in an individual, or not, through the continuous interaction between the individual and the environment. A child who is constantly criticized by her adult caretakers, for example, is unlikely to develop a strong sense of competence or self-esteem.

Also central to the ecosystems perspective are the habitat and niche concepts. Both are ecological terms that refer to the setting in which an organism exists. In social work practice, habitat refers to all the settings that make up a person's environment, such as homes, schools, workplaces, neighborhoods, cities, etc.[35] The settings, of course, affect the person (and via versa). Turning back to our case example, it's easy to see the impact Louis's habitat had on his functioning. The niche concept refers to the "status occupied by an individual in the social structure of a community."[36] Niche is a particularly important area of attention for social workers. Oppressed groups—such as individuals in poverty, people of color, GLBTQ people, children, and the elderly, to name just a few—occupy marginalized niches in our society. The habitat and niche concepts are related, of course. Turning again to our case example, we see how poverty affected the kind of habitat Louis experienced. Niche also points to another important concept in the ecosystems perspective: power. The extent to which groups and individuals experience personal and social power, or have power withheld and/or used against them, has an enormous impact on the PIE system.[37]

The holistic, transactional view offered by the ecological perspective is thoroughly in keeping with social work values, and provides a model for practice that is consistent with the biopsychosocial (spiritual–physical) model of human development, behavior, and functioning used by social work. The ecosystems perspective informs a number of specific approaches to social work practice with specific clients and client groups that are discussed in upcoming chapters such as case management, family therapy, and social and political activism.

The Strengths Perspective in Social Work Practice

The "strengths-based approach" to social work practice focuses on identifying, respecting, and enhancing what is "right" with individuals, groups, and communities. It emphasizes client–worker collaboration and client empowerment and is closely related to the ecological perspective discussed above. Proponents of the strengths-based approach to social work practice note that the helping professions, including social work, have traditionally been based on the notion that there is something wrong or abnormal about social work clients, and that a social worker's role is to identify and fix the problem.[38] This takes place at both an individual and a cultural level. On an individual level, this means that social workers focus on a client's problems (e.g., they are depressed, unemployed, or HIV positive) and often ignore the many things that are "right" with them (e.g., they take good care of their children, they are great basketball players, they love animals). On a cultural level, the deficit-based model can have dire consequences, especially for marginalized social groups.

The strengths-based approach to social work practice is predicated on several key ideas, including:

- Uncovering and recognizing client strengths
- Respecting client strengths
- Fostering client strengths
- Viewing the social worker as collaborator (rather than an expert)
- The importance of community to the helping process[39]

The goal of the strengths-based approach is to empower clients (individuals, groups, communities) to help them gain understanding, voice, and influence over decisions that affect their lives and to discover the power within themselves to make positive change happen. In this approach, social workers view the client as knowing something; they see the client as having learned something from experience. The social worker respects the fact that the client has ideas and energy, and can do some things very well.[40] The concept of "community" (i.e., a sense of belonging and membership) is central to the strengths-based approach because individuals do not gain a sense of power and strength in isolation from one another. When people feel isolated, it is hard for them to see and access inner and outer resources, or even to feel that such resources exist. Community, however, goes a long way in fostering a sense of hope and possibility. To these ends, the "help" provided by a social worker who uses the strengths-based approach emphasizes:

- Uncovering and supporting inner and outer resources/strengths/contingencies;
- Developing a caring helper–client relationship;
- Fostering positive expectations and hope; and
- Technical operations to promote change.[41]

By focusing on client strengths, social workers can provide temporary assistance that will have a lasting and empowering impact.

SUMMARY

The major values of the social work profession are service, social and economic justice, dignity and worth of the individual, importance of human relationships, and integrity and competence in practice. These core values form the foundation of social work theory and practice. In this chapter we explored the theoretical underpinnings of social work as a profession. We reviewed the major conceptual basis of social work, and the models, perspectives, and approaches that unite the social work practice.

The notion that all human beings exist in a reciprocal relationship with their environments is the core foundational concept in social work. This concept is captured in the term "human behavior and the social environment," or HBSE. HBSE is an essential area of study in social work education. To understand the relationships between human beings and their environments, social workers look to the biopsychosocial model of human development and functioning. The biological domain of human functioning encompasses everything that is physically intrinsic to a human being, including genetic inheritance, brain chemistry, organ function, nutrition, disease, physical injury, height, and weight. The psychological domain includes consciousness, personality, emotions, cognition, communication, and memory. The social domain encompasses everything that makes up a person's social environment, including families, neighborhoods, schools, communities, workplaces, and local, state, and federal government. Each of these domains, as with the spiritual and physical environment domains, interacts in unique and complex ways throughout a person's life course.

Systems theory has strongly influenced the contemporary practice of social work. Systems theory provides a framework for understanding that all beings are systems and all beings reside within multiple systems. The social work ecosystems perspective draws from systems theory, as well as other theories, models, and perspectives, to provide a framework for understanding the complex relationships between and within humans and their environments. The term person-in-environment (PIE) is used to refer to this system of relationships. Social workers take an ecosystems perspective when they approach a client, whether that client is a person, family, or community. They try to understand the relationships that exist in the PIE system, as well as the strengths and challenges that exist within that system. The strengths-based approach to the practice of social work is closely tied to the ecosystems perspective in social work practice, and focuses on identifying, respecting, and enhancing the PIE system strengths, and utilizing these strengths to address current problems and challenges.

2 CHAPTER REVIEW

Succeed with **PEARSON mysocialworklab**

Log onto **MySocialWorkLab** to access a wealth of case studies, videos, and assessment. (*If you did not receive an access code to* **MySocialWorkLab** *with this text and wish to purchase access online, please visit www.mysocialworklab.com.*)

PRACTICE TEST The following questions will test your knowledge of the content found within this chapter. For additional assessment, including licensing-exam type questions on applying chapter content to practice, visit **MySocialWorkLab**.

1. In social work, the "social environment" includes:
   a. A person's personality when with others
   b. A person's behavior when in social settings
   c. The way a person perceives group situations
   d. A person's extended family, faith community, and social status

2. According to the chapter, children who do not encounter human speech in the first years of life are:
   a. More likely to develop hearing loss
   b. Have higher rates of crime as adults
   c. Lose the capacity for speech themselves
   d. Suffer from a serious degenerative neurological disease

3. According to the chapter, noradrenalin and serotonin are:
   a. Two neurochemicals implicated in impulsivity and risk tolerance
   b. Two neurochemicals implicated in hearing impairment and language acquisition
   c. Two neurochemicals that decrease with age
   d. Two neurochemicals that cause violent behavior

4. According to Erikson, the major developmental task of a child's first 18 months is:
   a. Developing verbal communication skills
   b. Establishing a sense of competence and industry
   c. Developing gross motor skills such as sitting up and walking
   d. Establishing a sense of basic trust

5. In Vygotsky's theory of child development, scaffolding refers to:
   a. The process of assisting a child move from concrete operations to formal operations
   b. The process of assisting children to move from initial difficulty with a task to the point where, with help, they can perform the task independently
   c. The idea that culture and society influence the way a young child develops his/her superego
   d. The idea that children need a highly structured learning environment

6. Maslow's hierarchy of needs follows the following sequence:
   a. Love and belongingness needs, esteem needs, self-actualization needs, safety needs, physiological needs
   b. Physiological needs, safety needs, love and belongingness needs, esteem needs, self-actualization needs
   c. Safety needs, esteem needs, self-actualization needs, love and belongingness needs, physiological needs
   d. Physiological needs, safety needs, esteem needs, self-actualization needs, love and belongingness needs

7. In Bronfrenbrenner's model, the term mesosystem refers to:
   a. A person's immediate relationships and life settings
   b. The broader social and cultural context of a person's life
   c. The spiritual domain of an individual's life
   d. The interrelationships between or among the microsystems that make up a person's life

8. The ecosystems theory holds that:
   a. An individual's physical environment has the greatest impact on their well-being
   b. Systems must stay in homeostasis at all times
   c. An individual can only be fully understood when viewed in the context of his/her social environment
   d. The spiritual domain of social functioning is the most important

9. A visual representation of an individual in his/her environment is called a(n):
   a. Ecomap
   b. Genogram
   c. Family tree
   d. Venn diagram

10. One key premise of the strengths perspective of social work practice is:
    a. The idea that an individual is only as resilient as her family system
    b. The conceptualization of the relationship between social worker and client as one of collaboration
    c. The belief that an individual must be physically well before he/she can resolve psychological difficulties
    d. The belief that social workers should not be involved in advocacy or any work that involves taking a political position

Log onto **MySocialWorkLab** once you have completed the Practice Test above to access additional study tools and assessment.

Answers

Key: 1) d 2) c 3) a 4) d 5) b 6) b 7) d 8) c 9) a 10) b

Basic Concepts in Social Welfare

CHAPTER OUTLINE

Social Welfare: A Conceptualization 50
Ideological Input
Economic Institutions
Political Institutions
Social Institutions
Outcome: Societal Well-Being

Summary 60

Practice Test 61

 MySocialWorkLab 61

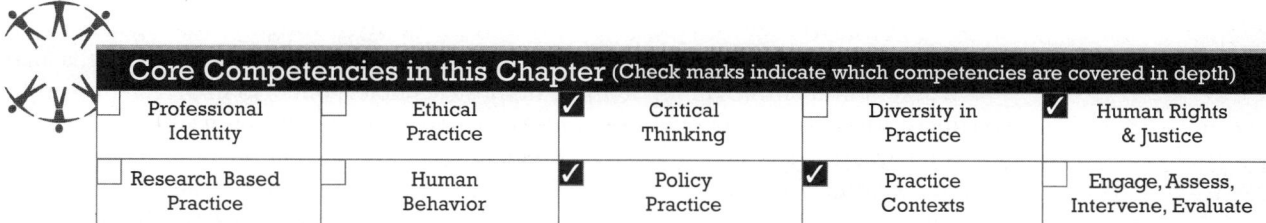

SOCIAL WELFARE: A CONCEPTUALIZATION

At this point, we should discuss further the institutional context in which social work takes place. Therefore, this chapter looks at the ideologies and institutions that comprise the U.S. social welfare system. The term **social welfare**, by definition, refers to a system of privately and publicly funded institutions, programs, benefits, and services that help people meet those basic social, economic, health, and educational needs deemed necessary for the maintenance of society. The term social welfare also refers to a state of societal well-being.[1]

The first part of the definition, a "system of institutions, programs, benefits, and services," refers to the means to some end, while the second part of the definition refers to the end itself, "societal well-being." As such, defining "social welfare" can be tricky, but understanding the concept of social welfare is key to understanding the profession of social work.

All societies develop and organize their major institutions to maximize the overall well-being of their citizens. In the United States, people buy and sell goods in a market economy to meet their individual needs. But there are some services that are considered necessary for societal well-being regardless of any one individual's ability to pay or the market's ability to produce them at a profit. Examples include housing for the homeless, soup kitchens for the hungry, and health care for older and poor Americans. These services are considered so important to the maintenance of overall societal well-being that society, through funding mechanisms such as taxation and philanthropy, pays for part or all of the cost of the service to the individual. By helping the individual, societal well-being is maintained as well. This array of programs and services is America's "social welfare system." Social work as a profession focuses on the promotion, planning, and delivery of many of these services. Van Wormer agrees, "the profession most closely related to the provision of social welfare services is social work." Social work as a profession helps individuals, groups, and communities enhance or restore their capacity for social functioning, while creating societal conditions favorable to this goal.[2] Other writers have also offered definitions of social welfare that emphasize a system of programs and services that promote individual well-being and, at the same time, societal well-being. For example, authors Romanyshyn and Romanyshyn claimed that social welfare refers to:

> [A]ll those forms of social intervention that have a primary and direct concern with promoting both the well-being of the individual and of the society as a whole. Social welfare includes those provisions and processes directly concerned with the treatment and prevention of social problems, the development of human resources, and the improvement in the quality of life. It involves social services to individuals and families as well as efforts to strengthen or modify social institutions.[3]

Social welfare services are delivered primarily through public agencies and private nonprofit agencies. However, in delivering social welfare services, social workers find employment, not just in these agencies, but also in private for-profit institutions (e.g., the business sector). Social workers can be found throughout the United States in state child welfare departments, adult protective units, state correctional facilities, and in mental health services. They can also be found in administrative and direct service positions in the private nonprofit sector—in

Critical Thinking Question

By helping the individual, the U.S. social welfare system enhances societal well-being as well. Can you think of an instance when you helped another person yet benefited yourself at the same time?

organizations such as United Way, the American Red Cross, the Boys and Girls Clubs, and Big Brothers/Big Sisters.

Yet social workers are also employed in corporate employee assistance programs, corporate foundations and charitable giving programs, child care centers, hospitals, and nursing homes. Social workers educated in subjects such as diversity, race, culture, oppression, and group process are expected to become more valuable to corporations competing in a global economy. The fact that social work skills, perspectives, and ethics are valued and in demand across all three sets of institutions in our country is a tribute to social work education.

A theme throughout this text is that well-being is an outcome of the efforts of three sets of institutions: economic, political, and social.[4] That is, a high standard of living requires collaboration among these three institutions. All three types will be discussed in more detail in the remainder of this chapter. But for now, it must be stressed that throughout American history, these three sets of institutions have collaborated to promote a high quality of life for American citizens. For example, our economic institutions, dominated today by large corporations, produce goods and services for a profit. Yet American political institutions have historically supported, and at times regulated, our business institutions to better promote societal well-being. And U.S. social institutions, often supported by progressive leaders in business and government, have done what business could not do at a profit and what government did not have the will to do alone.

At other times, social groups and agencies have needed to pressure business and government to "do the right thing," thereby creating a rich history of American activism. Thus, all three sets of institutions contribute to national well-being. At times, these institutions compete with one another, but ultimately, they must collaborate in "the national interest." Sometimes their collaboration takes the form of a "public–private partnership," a "coalition," a "league," a "federation," a "contracted service," or simply a "volunteer effort." National, state, or local organizations from one, two, or all three major institutional sectors may be involved. In any case, institutional cooperation and collaboration ultimately are needed to maximize individual and societal well-being. Social work is a profession that works with many other professions in all three sectors of the United States to promote societal well-being.

Ideological Input

To understand the social welfare system in the United States or any country, the dominant beliefs, values, and ideas—or **ideology**—of the nation must be made explicit. In other words, nations like the United States, in an effort to maximize individual and societal well-being, build and organize institutions based on a set of values. A **value** is a principle or quality that is considered desirable. Values serve as criteria for making choices, including choices involved in social welfare. Since the mid-1800s, the groups considered most influential in terms of American values have been conservatives, liberals, and the radical left.

In terms of promoting individual and societal well-being, "conservatives" support a free market economy and limited government. To this group, the market is the most fair and efficient institutional mechanism for distributing societal resources. Like an "invisible hand," the marketplace guides investment and consumption decisions in maximizing societal well-being.[5] In general, conservatives believe that individual profit is the great motivator, that leaving individuals free to pursue their own self-interest in a capitalist system works for the betterment of all. To this end, the role of government should be limited to defending private property rights and maintaining social order. A more expanded role for government, according to conservatives, only drains resources that could be invested in business. Government resources are resources that cannot be used for creating wealth and employment in a capitalist economy.

In cases where for-profit entities do not meet the needs of certain groups of people, conservatives prefer the use of local private nonprofit groups to deliver social welfare services. That is, for people who cannot participate in the workplace—some people with disabilities, older Americans, and children, for example—conservatives typically choose to rely on support provided by the family, churches, and other private nonprofit organizations, such as local United Way member agencies (e.g., Meals on Wheels, the Girl Scouts). In addition, conservatives prefer that these voluntary efforts to support needy people be funded, when necessary, from private charitable giving. Conservatives, therefore, tend to be big promoters of philanthropy on the part of individuals, corporations, and foundations. In short, conservatives tend to value private delivery of social welfare services.

In contrast to conservatives, "liberals" advocate for a more regulated market and an activist government. Liberals typically agree with conservatives that the market economy is the best promoter of a high standard of living; however, based in part on the U.S. experience in the Great Depression, traditional liberals believe that the market economy has certain negative tendencies that should be monitored and regulated by government to maximize societal well-being. These tendencies include erratic business cycles, racism, sexism, and environmental pollution. Thus, liberals support an expanded role for government in areas such as unemployment insurance, health care, affordable housing, civil rights, affirmative action, and environmental protection. This group tends to be associated with the New Deal under Franklin Roosevelt and the Great Society under Lyndon Johnson.

In summary, liberals tend to support more of a "mixed economy" in the manner of European welfare states than do conservatives.[6] Therefore, liberals believe that all three sets of institutions—political, economic, and social—need to play significant roles in promoting social well-being.

The "radical left" in the United States has consisted historically of socialists and communists. While it is even harder to generalize about the beliefs of this group, the radical left typically supports a major reorganization of the three sets of U.S. institutions, one that would result in a greatly reduced role for capitalists in the economic and political sectors. This might include a government-planned economy. It might also include increased workplace democracy, where workers would have a much greater role in business decision making. This group tends to see the source of social problems such as poverty and racism as inherent in the capitalist economy. In other words, social problems are the result of structural defects in the capitalist economy; therefore, only fundamental reform of our current institutional structure will maximize societal well-being.

Another important part of the societal ideological input, especially for social workers, is the predominant belief regarding the cause of poverty at any given point in history. For example, during the Middle Ages, poverty was much more likely to be seen as a matter of fate. Droughts, military invasions, plagues, and the feudal class hierarchy were thought to be relatively uncontrollable determinants of poverty. At other times, the individual was considered to be the major cause of poverty. For most of the 1700s and 1800s, for example, the immorality of the individual was blamed for poverty. If only the person could be reformed to live a more moral life, that person would be more prosperous. In this case, "moral" generally meant more hard-working, sober, and pious. Conservatives tend to stress this view of poverty. During other points in history, the U.S. system of institutions was considered to be the primary cause of poverty. For example, while America struggled with mass unemployment during the Great Depression, the U.S. institutional structure, especially business, was criticized. As a result, institutional reforms such as the Securities and Exchange Commission and the Federal Deposit Insurance Corporation were passed. Liberals, and to a greater degree leftist radicals, are more apt to emphasize this perspective on poverty.

In any case, a society's value set—its ideology—will strongly influence the way that society organizes its major institutions. In the next sections of this chapter, the current major political, economic, and social institutions operating in the United States are discussed.

Economic Institutions

Capitalism is an economic system that "emphasizes private business initiative in the pursuit of profits through the use of private property."[7] Under capitalism, the basic economic unit is the individual. That is, capitalist ideology stresses individual initiative in the market economy. Three essentials of a capitalist economic system follow from this definition: First, property is primarily privately owned. Second, this private property is used for the accumulation of private gain or profits. And third, these private property owners and profit-seekers are primarily responsible for the level and direction of the national economy.

In addition, a central characteristic of capitalism is that it is a **market system** in which the **factors of production** are commodities for sale.[8] These factors of production are land, labor, and capital. In contrast to economies run by tradition (as in the feudal society of the Middle Ages) or command (as in the 20th-century Soviet Union), in a capitalist economy, individual men and women operating freely in the marketplace decide what to do with these factors of production.[9]

Further, a basic philosophy espoused by these individual capitalists is **laissez-faire**. This French term refers to "leaving things alone."[10] It underlies the basic argument that government should not interfere with the operations of the marketplace. Through the market dynamic of "supply and demand," many argue that a market economy is self-regulating and the fairest and most efficient mechanism for allocating and distributing society's resources.

This "free-market" philosophy, with its emphasis on free trade and competition, characterizes the capitalist economy found today in the United States. It is an economy increasingly dominated by large corporations, as opposed to small businesses. And it is an economic system that is now being spread with increasing speed throughout the world through the process of **globalization**.[12] Globalization is defined as ". . . the inexorable integration of markets,

Did You Know?

Did you know that it is said that a group of merchants called on the French finance minister, Colbert, who served between 1661 and 1683. Colbert thanked the merchants for their contributions to the French economy and asked them what he could do for them. The merchants replied, "Laissez-nous faire"—leave us alone.[11]

Globalization, as a general business principle, can bring more benefits to the poor than any alternative.

—Muhammad Yunus

Critical Thinking Question

If a global economy allows corporations to move all or part of their business operations to nations throughout the world, how might this impact the work of social workers?

nation-states, and technologies to a degree never witnessed before."[13] What makes this trend unique are the technologies that make it possible, including computerization, digitization, satellite communications, fiber optics, and the Internet. Such technologies are allowing corporations to create a global market for their goods and services, a market that increasingly reaches across national borders, defense systems, and cultures. The fall of the Berlin Wall and the Soviet Union are dramatic illustrations of globalization. Further, globalization means that corporations are freer to move all or part of their business operations to countries all over the world. It means that investors can move their funds in and out of countries with lightening speed. And while globalization is creating or exacerbating certain social problems,[14] the optimists swear that all of this means a rising standard of living for all participants, including developing countries.

As the 21st century began, the United States was the leading national economy in the global economic system. Beginning in the 1990s, the U.S. economy experienced its longest continued expansion in modern history. The "extraordinarily robust technical progress in the computer and communication industries" was a central factor in this economic success.[15] Households in the United States benefited from improved employment opportunities, real income gains, and a substantial increase in their net worth.[16] Overall unemployment rates were the lowest in 30 years, including record low rates for minorities. As of early 2010, the United States is still the largest economy in the world, ahead of both China and Japan.[17]

At the same time, some experts fear that globalization is creating a two-tiered employment system:[18] a full-time, highly paid group and a lower-paid, part-time or temporary group. The first tier of employees being hired by corporations includes core personnel with relatively high salaries, full benefits, and comfortable working conditions. These employees typically are engaged in finance, marketing, or technology. While providing high-paid jobs for a small number of employees, corporations are increasingly manufacturing their products with a second tier of people. This second tier of employment is part-time or temporary, pays low wages, and includes few benefits. Thus, while the U.S. economy is a world leader in many ways, social workers will inevitably face the challenge of addressing the problematic aspects of globalization as vulnerable populations, such as children, minorities, and single mothers, deal with the vast technical and economic changes ahead. The banking crisis and worldwide economic recession of 2008–2009 is the most immediate example of this instability.

Political Institutions

Americans live under a democratic system of government. The three major branches of government in the U.S. are the **Executive Branch**, which is responsible for enforcing the laws of the land; the **Judicial Branch**, which is responsible for interpreting and assuring the constitutional validity of laws; and the **Legislative Branch**, which is responsible for making laws. This chapter covers the federal level of these political institutions, meaning the presidency, the Supreme Court, and Congress. The influence of the various U.S. presidential administrations and the Supreme Court on American social policy and social welfare will be addressed in the history section of this book. Congress will be discussed in greater detail here, because Congress is the source of much legislation that leads to the creation of social welfare services.

The U.S. Congress is a **bicameral** legislature. That is, Congress is composed of two legislative bodies: the House of Representatives and the Senate. The **House of Representatives** contains 435 voting members.[19] Also, there are five nonvoting delegates representing the District of Columbia and U.S. territories and possessions. United States representatives serve two-year terms. Each representative must be at least 25 years old, a U.S. citizen for seven or more years at the time he or she begins service, and a resident of the state from which he or she is elected.

The **Senate** contains 100 members, two from each state. Senators serve six-year terms. Each senator must be at least 30 years of age, a U.S. citizen for nine or more years, and a resident of the state from which elected.[20] Each Congress lasts two years and is numbered. For example, in 2008, the U.S. Congress was the 110th.

Social work advocates, and advocates from other fields, must regularly make contact with the staff of members of Congress.[21] House members typically have about 20 people on their personal staff, and staff size is roughly the same for all House members. In contrast, a senator's staff size is based on his or her state population size. The larger the state population, the larger the senator's staff. Senators from large states may have 60 or more staff members.[22] Personal staff members are usually divided between offices in Washington, D.C., and the home state.

Each member of a congressional representative's personal staff performs many tasks. In addition to routine clerical duties, staff members write speeches and assist with policy development. They also meet with constituents and lobbyists. For these reasons, congressional staff members are key contacts for social work advocates. Similarly, social workers involved with policy development will want to know the staff members of pertinent congressional committees. The committee staff provides support to congressional members on individual committees. The most common approach is for the committee chair to hire a staff to work with the committee members from the majority party in Congress. Likewise, the ranking minority party member hires a staff for the minority party members.[23]

Since the early decades of the 1800s, the "party system" and the "committee system" have been the primary means of organizing congressional work. First, let's look at the political parties in the House of Representatives. The majority party has the primary responsibility for organizing the legislative agenda. The majority party controls the selection of the **Speaker of the House** (i.e., the presiding officer), and its members constitute a majority on each committee. The Speaker, along with the **majority leader**, the leader of the party holding the majority of seats in the house (along with other party leaders called **whips**, who act as assistants to, and proxies for, the leaders), determine the issues that will be given top priority during the session. In addition, the minority party elects a **minority leader** and a minority whip to work with (or against) the majority party on legislation.[24]

Members of political parties also elect their leaders in the Senate. The majority party elects a majority leader and an assistant majority leader (whip). In similar fashion, the minority party elects a minority leader and an assistant minority leader (whip). (The Vice President serves as President of the Senate, the presiding officer.) The majority leader, with the help of colleagues, performs numerous duties. These include organizing the Senate's work, scheduling policy issue debates, and helping to gather enough votes to pass specific pieces of legislation.[25]

Critical Thinking Question

Social workers promote social welfare policies that advance social and economic well-being. What policies would you like to see changed in order to improve the well-being of your family?

As stated, the committee system is the second major arena for congressional work. In fact, most congressional work is done in committees. This work consists of various duties. Congressional committees initiate and prioritize specific policy proposals. They hold public hearings on various policy issues and conduct investigations. Committees initiate studies and publish reports. And congressional committees perform administrative oversight, such as reviewing budget requests and passing judgment on presidential appointees. These congressional committees generally have the most expertise in Congress on a given policy subject. Senior members of committees have often dealt with certain issues for a number of years. Also, the staffs that support these committees are often specialists in the policy issue.[26]

Through the party system and congressional committees, and with the help of congressional office staff, Congress performs three major functions.[27] The first is legislation or *lawmaking* (see Figure 3.1). Lawmaking involves

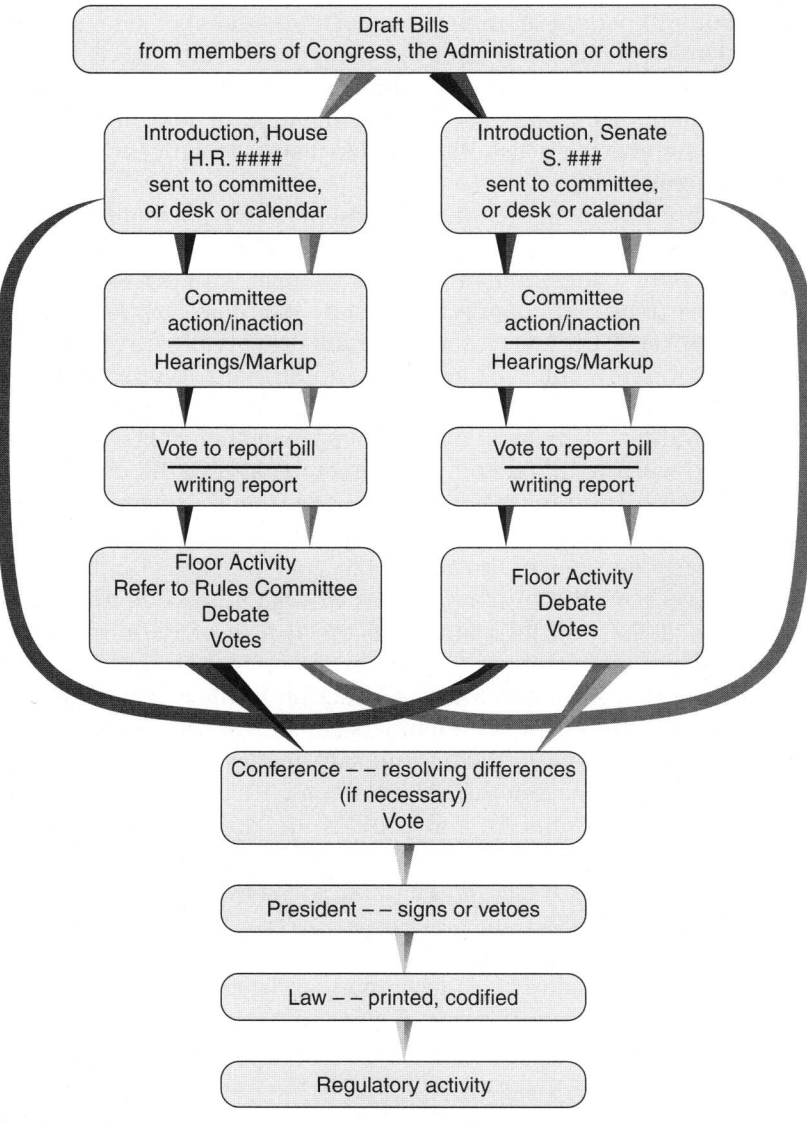

Figure 3.1

How a bill becomes law

Source: Retrieved from the World Wide Web on Feb. 24, 2010 from http://www.lexisnexis.com/help/CU/The_Legislative_Process/How_a_bill_Becomes_Law.htm

> **Demonstrating Knowledge, Values, and Skills**
>
> **Case Study Ethical Considerations in Policymaking**
>
> When the former Soviet Union fragmented into several smaller nations, many in the United States breathed a sigh of relief. The "Cold War" was over; the communist threat to the U.S. had dissolved. Consequently, policymakers decided to cut defense spending, which would mean closing many naval yards and air force bases around the nation. While many in Congress thought it in the national interest to do so, few, if any, lawmakers wanted a military installation closed in their district or state. These military installations employ many workers, who, if they lost their jobs, would blame the local congressional delegation. Further, local businesses and governments would be opposed to such closings because they benefit from a large workforce living in their communities.
>
> When in conflict, should a member of Congress vote in accordance with the prevailing opinion of their district/state or in the interests of the nation as a whole? Should congressional representatives vote the prevailing opinion of their district/state or their personal convictions on the policy issue?

information-gathering, discussion, negotiation, and compromise. About 90% of bills introduced in a typical Congress never become law. In addition, lawmaking is influenced at every stage of the process by special interest groups. These special interest groups, which include the National Association of Social Workers, help draft legislation, testify at hearings, lobby members of Congress in committee and during floor debate, and pressure the president to sign or veto legislation.

The lawmaking process is governed by a set of rules and precedents. Legislation is considered at a number of points in the process. Each is a veto point. Therefore, the rules favor the status quo rather than social change. Proponents of change must be successful at each point in the process. Furthermore, the rules work to slow the pace of lawmaking, which also favors the status quo. An example would be a "filibuster," where a member of the Senate does not relinquish the floor during debate. In any case, social work advocates must be well prepared in order to work successfully in such an environment.

A second major function of Congress is *representation*. Each member of Congress represents two groups of citizens: his or her own congressional district or state and the nation as a whole. Sometimes these interests conflict. What is more, the individual may have strong personal feelings on any given policy issue. No wonder politicians appear to try "to be all things to all people."

Finally, the third major function of Congress is *administrative oversight*. This function is partly the result of the American public's feeling that citizens should not only be served by government, but protected from it as well. Often, bureaucratic agencies make expert or administrative decisions; Congress then reviews those decisions. Techniques for oversight include special investigations by congressional committees, budget hearings, Senate confirmation of presidential appointments, and impeachment.

In a democracry, every citizen, regardless of his interests in politics, "holds office."

—John F. Kennedy

Social Institutions

Social institutions are referred to in various ways: the private nonprofit sector, the voluntary sector, the charitable sector, even the independent sector and the third sector. For the most part, these social institutions will be referred to in this text as either the private nonprofit sector, or the nonprofit sector.

This sector of American society is large, and provides much of the nation's social welfare services. It includes churches, health and human service agencies, civic and community groups, elementary and secondary schools, arts and cultural organizations, and mutual benefit societies. In fact, there are over one million charitable, or nonprofit, organizations in the United States, and these organizations employ over 10 million people.[28]

More specifically, the definition of a **private nonprofit organization** is an organization "that is not part of government and does not exist to make a profit."[29] Nonprofit organizations are often characterized as philanthropic, charitable, or public benefit organizations. They usually exist to provide a service or promote a cause. For the most part, they are private organizations serving a public purpose. Philanthropic nonprofit organizations include those with the **501(c)(3)** classification. These organizations are exempt from federal income tax under section 501(c)(3) of the federal tax code. Charitable donations to 501(c)(3) nonprofit organizations are tax deductible.[30]

A small percentage of nonprofits focus on aid to their members, in contrast to a "public good." These nonprofits are called **mutual benefit organizations**. Examples of these organizations include labor unions, veterans' organizations, credit unions, and fraternal organizations. Donations to mutual benefit organizations are not tax deductible.[31]

In any case, 501(c)(3) organizations represent the vast majority of agencies in the nonprofit sector, and their number is growing fast. The total number of charitable 501(c)(3) organizations registered with the U.S. Internal Revenue Service nearly doubled from 1996 to 2006.[32] There were 654,186 of these nonprofit agencies in 1996, a figure that increased to 1,064,191 by 2006.[33] In 2006, the Giving USA Foundation reported total charitable giving to these agencies of close to $300 billion. Health and human service organizations received about $50 billion, or approximately 17% of the total.[34]

The nonprofit sector, as you can see, plays an important role in the United States. In fact, it plays six roles. First, and perhaps most important for social work, this sector provides a context for advancing social change. In fact, most, if not all, major social movements in U.S. history started in the nonprofit sector, including women's suffrage, civil rights, consumer protection, and environmentalism.[35] Second, the nonprofit sector preserves American heritage through nonprofit historical societies, museums, and theaters. Third, this sector offers recreation to the public through organizations such as the YMCA, Girl Scouts, and Little Leagues. Fourth, the private nonprofit sector provides support to American business through its nonprofit educational and research institutions, institutions like Harvard University. Fifth, services that cannot be delivered at a profit by the business sector are often provided in the private nonprofit sector. An example would be Habitat for Humanity's effort to build decent and affordable housing for low-income Americans. And finally, this sector of society promotes the general welfare through its many health and human service agencies throughout the country. In fact, as the reader will learn in the subsequent history chapter, the private nonprofit sector is the birthplace of the profession of social work.

Demonstrating Knowledge, Values, and Skills

Make a list of the ways private nonprofit organizations in your community have served you, your friends, or family. Next, break into small groups, and if comfortable, share your stories with other students in the group. Are there needs in your community that local nonprofit agencies currently do not address? How could these agencies collaborate to better serve your community?

Basic Concepts in Social Welfare

A fundamental point to remember at this juncture is that the private nonprofit sector has historically worked closely with government to deliver social welfare services. Indeed, all three sets of institutions—political, economic, and social—collaborate to deliver social welfare services and benefits. Researcher Lester Salamon comments on this concerted effort:

Did You Know?

The Massachusetts colony passed a tax to help support Harvard College; it also paid part of the Harvard president's salary until 1791. Today, Harvard University has an endowment of several billion dollars.[37] How's that for a collaboration!

> In short, by the latter 1970s, the U.S. had developed a complex system of social welfare protections providing significant levels of assistance not just to the poor but to the middle class as well and involving an extensive partnership between government and both nonprofit and for-profit providers.[36]

Outcome: Societal Well-Being

When people refer to societal well-being, they frequently use terms such as "standard of living," "quality of life," or simply "the nation's health." Whatever term is used, societal well-being is typically measured by one or more indicators. Socioeconomic indicators commonly used in the United States include the Gross Domestic Product, and unemployment and inflation rates.[38] Gross Domestic Product (GDP) measures the dollar value of total output of all goods and services produced within the U.S. by both domestic and foreign entities. Given that a high GDP is generally associated with high employment rates, the GDP is a much-utilized indicator of national well-being.[39]

Unemployment and inflation rates are also frequently reported. A person in the U.S. is counted as "unemployed" if he or she does not have a job, but has searched for work in the past four weeks, and is currently available to work. The

Government's job is not to shield workers from . . . reality, but to empower them to deal with it.

—Thomas L. Friedman

> **Research Informed Practice**
>
> Social welfare programs and services can help shape and support a community. What types of social welfare agencies, programs, and services are located in your community or near your university? What types of programs are most prevalent? Which programs are well known? Are there programs in other communities that your community does not have? What do the results of this research activity tell you about your community or university? Describe what your experience was like finding social welfare programs and organizations in your area.

Critical Thinking Question

Social workers measure societal well-being using indicators such as poverty rates, teen pregnancy percentages, child abuse statistics, infant mortality rates, and school graduation rates. Which indicators do you feel are most important and why?

"unemployment rate" is the percentage of the labor force that is unemployed. The U.S. unemployment rate was 5.7% in January of 2005, but by January of 2010, during an economic recession, the rate had risen to 10.6%. From a consumer's perspective, "inflation" refers to a general increase in the prices of the goods and services they purchase. If prices rise quickly, this means consumers cannot buy as many goods and services with their relatively fixed paycheck. Put simply, during periods of high inflation, the buying power of the consumer's paycheck decreases. From 2005 to 2008, U.S. inflation rates were low, ranging between 2.8% and 3.8%. In December of 2009, U.S. inflation stood at 2.7%.[40]

Although indicators such as the GDP, unemployment, and inflation rates are widely used, like most "indicators," they do not capture all aspects of society's welfare. Consequently, social workers use several other social indicators as well. To illustrate, social workers in the health and human services tend to deal more with indicators such as poverty rates, adult and juvenile crime rates, teen pregnancy percentages, child abuse and neglect statistics, and infant mortality rates. Social workers employed in the field of education are more familiar with indicators such as graduation and school dropout rates, literacy statistics, and school violence incidence. Similarly, social workers involved in political advocacy organizations are particularly concerned with voter registration levels and voter turnout.

What is more, when considering the overall welfare of the nation, the profession of social work emphasizes social justice, respect for diversity, self-determination, and empowerment of vulnerable populations. These principles are part of the ethics of the profession, and therefore must be included by social workers when evaluating societal outcomes. Many of these measures of well-being will be discussed as part of the history chapter that follows.

SUMMARY

All societies organize their major institutions—economic, political, and social—to maximize the overall well-being of their citizens. In the United States, people buy and sell goods in a market economic system to meet their individual needs. In addition, there are some services that are provided for societal well-being regardless of any one individual's ability to buy or sell them, services such as health care for poor children, housing for the homeless, soup kitchens for the hungry, health care for older Americans, and fuel assistance for the needy during the winter. These services are considered so important to the maintenance of overall societal well-being that the government pays for part or all of the cost of the service to the individual. Both the individual and society benefit at the same time. This system of programs and services is what we mean by America's "social welfare" system.

3 CHAPTER REVIEW

Succeed with MySocialWorkLab

Log onto **MySocialWorkLab** to access a wealth of case studies, videos, and assessment. (*If you did not receive an access code to* **MySocialWorkLab** *with this text and wish to purchase access online, please visit www.mysocialworklab.com.*)

PRACTICE TEST The following questions will test your knowledge of the content found within this chapter. For additional assessment, including licensing-exam type questions on applying chapter content to practice, visit **MySocialWorkLab**.

1. Societal well-being is an outcome of the efforts of three sets of institutions: economic, political, and:
   a. Executive
   b. Judicial
   c. Social
   d. Senate

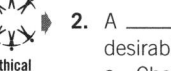
Ethical Practice

2. A _____ is a principle or quality that is considered desirable.
   a. Choice
   b. Value
   c. Measured outcome
   d. Policy

3. Capitalism is an economic system that emphasizes private business initiative to make profit using:
   a. Private property
   b. Government
   c. Taxpayers
   d. Land

4. A fundamental characteristic of capitalism is that it is a market system in which the factors of production are:
   a. Executive, judicial, and legislative
   b. Social, economic, and political
   c. Private, public, and nonprofit
   d. Land, labor, and capital

Practice Contexts

5. New technologies are allowing corporations to create a global market for their goods and services, a market that increasingly reaches across national borders, defense systems, and cultures. This process is called:
   a. Internationalization
   b. Capitalization
   c. Globalization
   d. Digitization

6. The three major branches of government in the U.S. are:
   a. The executive, judicial, and legislative
   b. The social, political, and economic
   c. Senate, House of Representatives, and Congress
   d. Legislative, financial, and defense

7. The definition of a "private nonprofit organization" is an organization that:
   a. Is a social business that does not make a profit
   b. Works with government for a public cause
   c. Is not part of government and does not exist to make a profit
   d. Is licensed as a mutual aid entity

8. Nonprofit organizations are often characterized as:
   a. Socialistic
   b. Capitalistic
   c. Philanthropic
   d. Globalistic

Research Based Practice

9. Social workers are concerned with social indicators such as:
   a. Child abuse statistics
   b. Profit margins
   c. Inflation rates
   d. Family socialization

Policy Practice

10. Services considered so important to the maintenance of overall societal well-being that the government pays for part or all of the cost of the service to the individual are referred to as:
    a. Charity
    b. Philanthropy
    c. Social welfare
    d. Corporate welfare

Log onto **MySocialWorkLab** once you have completed the Practice Test above to access additional study tools and assessment.

Answers

Key: 1) c 2) b 3) a 4) d 5) c 6) a 7) c 8) c 9) a 10) c

4

Generalist Social Work Practice

CHAPTER OUTLINE

Roles and Functions of Social Work 63

The Nature of Helping Relationships 64

Diversity and Cultural Competency 65

Engagement 66

Data Collection and Assessment 68
Family Assessments
Group Assessments
Organization and Community Assessment

Planning and Contracting 72

Intervention in Generalist Social Work 73
Generalist Social Work with Individuals
Generalist Social Work with Families

Generalist Social Work with Groups
Generalist Social Work with Organizations and Communities

Evaluation 78

Termination 80

Summary 83

Practice Test 85

 **MySocialWorkLab 85**

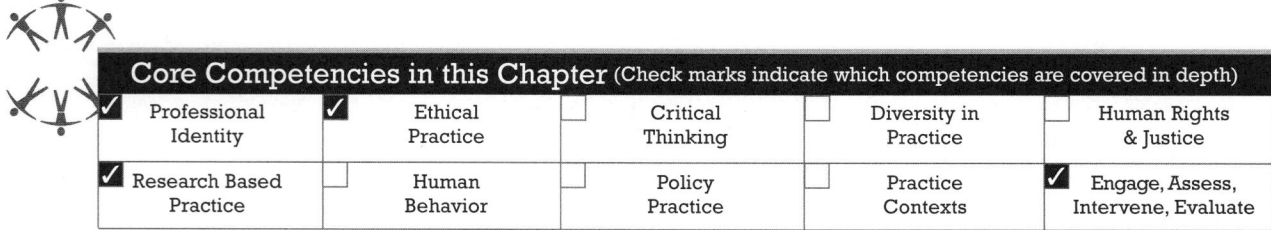

Core Competencies in this Chapter (Check marks indicate which competencies are covered in depth)									
✓	Professional Identity	✓	Ethical Practice	☐	Critical Thinking	☐	Diversity in Practice	☐	Human Rights & Justice
✓	Research Based Practice	☐	Human Behavior	☐	Policy Practice	☐	Practice Contexts	✓	Engage, Assess, Intervene, Evaluate

ROLES AND FUNCTIONS OF SOCIAL WORK

Now that you have a beginning understanding of social work as a profession, including its theoretical framework and institutional context, in this chapter we want to discuss more specifically the relationships, values, theories, and methods involved in "generalist social work." This is because the purpose of a BSW education is to prepare students for generalist practice through the mastery of several core competencies. These competencies (i.e., demonstrated practice behaviors) ensure that entry-level social workers have the knowledge, values, and skills needed to practice with individuals, families, groups, organizations, and communities. Such an education involves a knowledge of the biological, psychological, and social factors that affect human behavior, providing a social worker with the versatility to promote positive change among client systems of various sizes.[1] The goal of social work is to reconcile the well-being of individuals with the welfare of society. In doing so, social workers are concerned with aiding individuals in need of service as well as changing societal conditions that cause social problems. In short, this requires a generalist education and is referred to as **generalist social work practice**.

Generalist practice provides a perspective—the ecosystems perspective—from which to do social work. This perspective, as discussed in earlier chapters, is based in part on systems theory. That is, social workers focus on the interaction between the person and the systems that comprise the person's environment, including family, ethnic group, neighborhood, workplace, and religious institution. The social worker then takes a practice approach based upon the unique situation of the client. This is in contrast to applying a strict methodology to every intervention regardless of client characteristics. Social workers are not educated in the use of one tool that is used to fix every problem; rather, social workers have an entire toolbox from which to select specific tools given the uniqueness of each job they encounter. This makes for a great carpenter or mechanic and it also makes for a great social worker!

This focus on the person-in-environment (PIE) means that social workers must understand the culture in which they practice and the cultural background of the individuals, families, and groups they serve. They must also be familiar with the array of services available in any community. Understanding the culture in which they work enables social workers to better understand the social problems that impact that culture. In short, social workers use a broad range of knowledge and skills to address many different social problems. Hence, much of social work can be characterized as "generalist practice."[2]

Some authors see generalist social work practice as characterized by three collaborative roles: (1) consulting with clients regarding their problems, (2) managing the resources of systems in which clients function, and (3) offering clients information regarding both.[3] The consulting role pertains to the activities through which social workers and their clients promote change by clarifying problems, outlining options, and deciding on action plans.[4] The resource management role refers to the social work practice of advocating for new policies and programs that result in new resources to meet client needs. They also manage resources by coordinating the delivery of services, helping clients access the services, and evaluating programs and services. Such resources might include a soup kitchen for the homeless, a support group for young mothers, or a crisis hotline for a community. Finally, social workers play an educator role by helping clients to better understand themselves, their problems, and the systems in which they function.

Critical Thinking Question

Social workers must develop a helping relationship with clients. In order to form this relationship, they must trust each other. How does the social worker's professionalism and proper use of authority reinforce a trusting relationship?

THE NATURE OF HELPING RELATIONSHIPS

A mechanism through which social workers and their clients promote positive changes in client functioning is known as the "helping relationship." A helping relationship both structures change efforts and supports change efforts to the extent that the change is a collaboration between the client and social worker. Therefore, the ability of social workers to form helping relationships is fundamental. Through this collaborative helping relationship, the social worker assists the client in better defining problems, exploring alternative courses of action, and deciding which change strategies to pursue. Such collaboration empowers clients to be more aware, to make better decisions, and to take responsibility for their decisions and their future. This process also promotes self-determination and self-efficacy for the client.[6]

Forming a helping relationship does not precede the social work intervention; rather, it is an integral part of the intervention. Forming a helping relationship begins at the very start of the helping process. Whether the client is a person or group of persons, the helping relationship evolves through simultaneous attention to the client's problem and his or her emotional well-being.[7]

The kind of helping relationships that social workers form with their clients is different from casual friendships or other types of relationships. Clients normally don't ask social workers for assistance in order to develop a helping relationship; they ask for assistance with specific problems and issues with which they are trying to cope. Again, the helping relationship is a means to a goal, but it isn't the goal itself. Promoting a mutually beneficial interaction between clients and their environments is a fundamental goal of social work. And promoting positive change for individuals, families, groups, organizations, and communities is the immediate objective of any intervention effort. The helping relationship facilitates this positive change.[8]

Sometimes helping relationships are voluntary—as when a depressed person calls a therapist in private practice or an individual accepts the outreach efforts of a social worker to enroll in a program. At other times, the relationship is involuntary—as when an individual, such as a habitual drunk driver, is mandated by a court to see the social worker. Whether the interaction is voluntary or involuntary determines, to some extent, how difficult it will be to form

---

Social Work Stories: Domestic Violence

A social worker named Wanda remembers her work with victims of domestic violence:

I was a BSW student when I first came to volunteer, and then to work as an employee, in a small shelter for battered women and children who were escaping life-threatening situations in a small, north Texas college town. . . . I received a call from a woman who had found the shelter's number in the phone book. She had run away from her abuser and was homeless now, but had a job working at the local truckstop. She was sleeping under a bridge in a nearby park. . . . I told her I would come pick her up and take her to the shelter, which I did. . . . She was wearing dirty white tennis shoes. On the way to the shelter, she told me that her boss was going to fire her if she didn't get a pair of brown shoes to wear. She told me "Goodnight" with tears in her eyes. . . . I went to the garage . . . and began . . . to rummage through the black garbage bags. . . . I was about to quit when my fingers touched what felt like a pair of shoes. . . . They were in really good shape too. . . . I cleaned the shoes the best I could. . . . Then I went upstairs to her door and placed the shoes outside. . . . I heard from the other social worker that the woman believed that the shoes had come from an angel. . . .[5]

a helping relationship with a client. But in any case, forming a helping relationship with the client is an integral part of the helping process for social workers.

Helping relationships depend upon good communication skills on the part of the social worker. Effective communication, consequently, is a critically important tool for the social worker. To be a social worker, you must have the ability to listen to clients' stories and to show that you hear and understand their problems and that you respect their ability to address problems. Social workers develop a "third ear" that listens for the deeper meaning behind what clients are saying. This requires the social worker to interpret what the client is saying and to develop hypotheses that can be tested by the social worker and either accepted or rejected depending upon the course the helping relationship takes.

Generalist social work practice—and more specifically, the helping relationship—is based, therefore, on a set of interpersonal skills and a predisposition toward people. Social workers believe that all people have dignity along with the right to self-determination and social justice. They have a sense of kinship toward their fellow human beings and realize the commonalities of humanity (e.g., "If not for the grace of God, there go I").

Effective social workers also seek to understand the diversity inherent in the human condition and try to become more sensitive to the diverse perspectives of other cultures. They show **Empathy**, which is an emotional understanding of what the client is going through. Effective social workers exhibit genuineness and warmth toward other people. They show genuineness to their clients by being unpretentious, authentic or "real," and spontaneous throughout the helping relationship.[9]

From all of these traits and skills comes acceptance on the part of the social worker for the client and the client's story. Acceptance suggests understanding, but not necessarily approval. In other words, acceptance refers to an understanding of what it's like to be a human being faced with problems. Ultimately, trust develops—trust that the social worker understands and accepts the client and trust that the social worker has the knowledge and skills to help the client. This trust in the helping relationship is reinforced by the social worker's professionalism. "Professionalism" includes the proper use of authority by the social worker in the helping relationship. At its best, the helping relationship becomes a medium of human interchange, one that can ultimately lead to a rewarding job and career for the social worker. Therefore, if you have some of these skills, if you enjoy interacting with people, if you have a natural curiosity about people who are different from you, and if you believe in the positive possibilities of all people, a social work career may be for you![10]

DIVERSITY AND CULTURAL COMPETENCY

Differences in individual characteristics, such as sex, age, ethnicity, and social class, can be barriers to establishing effective helping relationships. Therefore, social workers expect that their clients will be unique individuals with unique values and perspectives that may differ greatly from their own. This is especially true when the client comes from a different cultural background. Individuals are more likely to trust people who have values, beliefs, cultures, and histories common to their own; they tend to distrust those who are different in any or all of these respects. Social workers who assist minority clients remain aware of these challenges. In fact, they acknowledge

We live in a culture that discourages empathy . . . that too often tells us our principal goal in life is to be rich, thin, young, famous, safe, and entertained.

—Barack Obama

Critical Thinking Question

Social workers must develop a helping relationship with clients. In order to form this relationship, they must trust each other. How does the social worker's professionalism and proper use of authority reinforce a trusting relationship?

> **Focus on Professionalism and Ethics**
>
> **Value:** "*Dignity and Worth of the Person*
> **Ethical Principle:** *Social workers respect the inherent dignity and worth of the person.*
>
> Social workers treat each person in a caring and respectful fashion, mindful of individual differences and cultural and ethnic diversity. Social workers promote clients' socially responsible self-determination. Social workers seek to enhance clients' capacity and opportunity to change and to address their own needs. Social workers are cognizant of their dual responsibility to clients and to the broader society. They seek to resolve conflicts between clients' interests and the broader society's interests in a socially responsible manner consistent with the values, ethical principles, and ethical standards of the profession."[11]

Critical Thinking Question

Treating individuals with respect is important to the helping relationship. Which social work values apply to understanding the differences between client interests and broader societal interests in order to resolve conflicts between the two?

Diversity makes for a rich tapestry. We must understand that all the threads of the tapestry are equal in value, no matter their color.
—Maya Angelou

differences directly early in the helping relationship. At the same time, they demonstrate respect and appreciation for client differences by showing curiosity and asking questions based upon a genuine desire to better understand the client's perspective. This is good social work practice.[12] Groups that have historically faced discrimination and oppression often exhibit an intensified need for respect. Also, they may have greater needs for support and empowerment. Acknowledging differences while showing a genuine desire to know and understand diverse clients is the best approach for effective interventions.[13]

Lum defines "minority social work practice" as "the art and science of developing a helping relationship with an individual, family, group, and/or community whose distinctive physical, cultural characteristics, and discriminatory experiences require approaches that are sensitive to ethnic and cultural environments."[14] Lum emphasizes that when working with minority groups, two concepts are important for social workers to remember. The first concept is **cultural commonality**, which refers to the fact that major minority groups share certain experiences in their history, including discrimination and oppression. The second concept, **cultural specificity**, emphasizes that, although they have commonalities, major minority groups have unique cultural histories, unique social problems, and unique strengths. Therefore, social workers must be aware that different minority groups, as well as different individuals within minority groups, require different intervention approaches.[15]

ENGAGEMENT

Engaging the client is part of establishing a helping relationship with the client. **Engagement** means "to draw into; to involve; to attract." It also means "to agree or commit to some aim."[17] The first part of the engagement process in generalist social work establishes the purpose for being together. Remember that a client may seek out a social worker voluntarily or may be there involuntarily as a result of some mandate, which may affect engagement.

During the early phase of the engagement process, the social worker and client discuss and establish the basic parameters of the helping relationship. This includes agreeing upon a time and place to meet, the frequency of meetings, relationship duration (i.e., whether the meetings will continue on an open-ended basis or whether there will be an established termination date for service). If the client is expected to pay for services, they will work out

> **Focus on Professionalism and Ethics**
>
> **Value:** "*Importance of Human Relationships*
> **Ethical Principle:** *Social workers recognize the central importance of human relationships.*
>
> Social workers understand that relationships between and among people are an important vehicle for change. Social workers engage people as partners in the helping process. Social workers seek to strengthen relationships among people in a purposeful effort to promote, restore, maintain, and enhance the well-being of individuals, families, social groups, organizations, and communities."[16]

payment details. If the relationship between social worker and client is expected to be confidential, social worker and client discuss and agree upon the details of how confidentiality will be maintained. In this early phase of engagement, if a contract is expected or desired, the social worker and client discuss the contract development process. Thus, the beginning phase of the engagement process establishes a context and structure for the helping relationship. It establishes norms for behavior on the part of the social worker as well as the client.

As part of this process, the social worker typically explains his or her position and expected role in the helping relationship. At times, the social worker may find it helpful to briefly inform the client of his or her professional credentials and qualifications for working with the client. The social worker and client also discuss the client's rights and responsibilities during their sessions. This is especially important if the client is mandated to attend the sessions and does not come voluntarily. If the client is seeing the social worker involuntarily, the early stage of the engagement process is used to minimize client resistance to attending sessions. The key to minimizing this resistance is to establish some level of client confidence, trust, and hope that working with a social worker will help the client to live a happier and healthier life.[18]

As the social worker and client start to meet on a regular basis, the social worker in generalist practice typically collaborates with the client to identify and define problem areas in the client's life and to establish goals for addressing the problem(s). Skilled social workers know that during this phase of the engagement process, it is effective to help clients identify their own goals for the helping process. In other words, it is not as important for social workers to tell clients what social workers think clients should do as it is for clients to identify and communicate what they believe they need to do and accomplish in their lives. This builds client motivation to continue working with the social worker. As they work together, the social worker and the client can explore alternative courses of action to achieve client goals. In this way, the social worker attempts to help the client establish realistic goals and strategies to better his or her life. Otherwise, unrealistic goals and strategies can frustrate the client's motivation and the change efforts.[19]

As the social worker and client establish goals and plans for achieving these goals, the social worker also takes care to be realistic about what he or she can do to help the client. Thus, the social worker attempts to establish hope for success on the part of the client, but must also be open and honest regarding his or her professional limitations. This is all part of engaging clients in a realistic attempt to help them. The engagement process typically ends when the social worker and client terminate the helping relationship.[20]

DATA COLLECTION AND ASSESSMENT

Critical Thinking Question

During assessment, social workers collect and analyze information related to the client's problems and issues. Consulting the research literature is often the next step. In what ways can social workers use research to inform practice?

The intervention **Assessment** phase is when the social worker does an in-depth collection and analysis of information related to the problems and issues presented by the client.[21] The specific information collected and analyzed during the assessment phase varies depending on the mission of the agency in which the social worker works, the types of clients served by the agency, and the clinical orientation of agency staff.[22] Most individual client assessments collect demographic information, including gender, age, race, marital status, and religious affiliation. In addition, assessments normally include the client's health history, as well as a history of any health problems experienced by other family members.

At times, social workers also ask clients for information regarding dramatic childhood experiences, such as parental divorce, abuse and neglect, and major accidents or illness. Other psychosocial data typically gathered in the assessment phase includes information regarding peer, family, and friend relationships; academic performance; cultural, spiritual, or religious affiliations; group and organizational memberships; and other sources of support.

Social workers employed in mental health care and psychiatric settings gather detailed information regarding a client's past mental health treatment, medications, and hospitalizations. Also, social workers in this type of setting usually administer mental status exams. These exams collect information on the client's appearance, behavior, mood, affect, speech patterns, thought patterns, attention, and concentration ability.[23]

Social workers employed in agencies that feature a psychodynamic orientation tend to emphasize information related to a client's early development, parental history of separation and divorce, childhood abandonment, peer relations, physical and psychological traumas, significant issues regarding physical and sexual development, and issues concerning sexual orientation.

Social workers in agencies that employ behavioral assessments will gather information related to observable, measurable client behaviors, while social workers who emphasize the "strengths perspective" will make sure to identify apparent client strengths, including assets and resources contained in the family and community systems in which the client lives. Similarly, social workers doing cognitive assessments emphasize detailed information about the client's cognitive abilities.[24]

In any case, the assessment process includes all significant and relevant data related to the client's biopsychosocial history. In short, the assessment phase of the intervention is the phase where detailed information regarding client problems is collected and analyzed using the social work profession's PIE perspective. Good social workers know that a balanced assessment requires a look at both the individual and the environment in which he or she functions. There may be problematic issues in both the individual and the environment. There will also be resources in both the individual and in the individual's environment. Consequently, social workers gather information in all of these areas. This ecosystems perspective, emphasizing the PIE context, allows the social worker to gather a broad array of detailed information with which to develop an intervention plan.

Using the ecosystems perspective, social workers doing assessments stay alert to imbalances related to individual needs and environmental resources, individual wants and environmental opportunities, and individual strengths

Generalist Social Work Practice

> **Research Informed Practice**
>
> Using the Internet, find the home page of your city government. Take note of the various city services listed, whether they are recreational, educational, health, or human services. In addition, find the home page of your local United Way agency and make a list of the different member agencies, programs, and services supported by your United Way. These are potential resources that social workers use to assist people in your community. They are community assets that represent an opportunity and resource for residents. They represent a potential source of strength for people in need of help.

and environmental demands. Thus, the PIE context helps the social worker to develop and maintain a balance in these client–environment interactions.[25]

In doing their assessments, social workers try to maintain mutuality in the process by closely listening to the client's story and probing for more details related to that story. This collaboration with the client illustrates that assessment is both a process and a product. It requires both analytical and interactional skills from the social worker. It requires the social worker to use rational analysis and subjective experience with the client. It includes both dispassionate data collection and compassionate understanding from the social worker. The final assessment product results in an integrated objective and subjective appraisal of the client's situation.[26]

Family Assessments

In addition to assessments with individual clients, social workers do assessments with other types of clients. As with individuals, family assessments start with the perception of the problem as presented by family members. And, as with individuals, the social worker listens to each person's story as a beginning step in assessment.[27]

Social workers attempt to help family members understand that they comprise a system in which all members' behaviors influence the behaviors of other family members. Seldom is the problem as simple as first presented by family members, and seldom is the problem located solely in the family member identified as the problem. In doing family assessments, therefore, social workers gather and examine information on the family's structure, communication patterns, boundaries, life-cycle stage, ethnicity, culture, and emotional state.

"Family structure" refers to the way the family organizes itself. Is there a stepparent in the family? Is the family headed by a single parent, male and female, or a same-sex partnership? Family structure also includes currently accepted patterns of family behavior. Is dad the "head of the household," is it the mother, or do adults in the family share authority equally? Is mom the authority in the kitchen or is this authority shared more equally among family members?

Boundaries refer to the degree of accessibility or approachability within the family, and between its subsystems and external systems. "Open family systems" are characterized by a great deal of interaction with people outside the immediate family, while "closed family systems" are characterized by little or no interaction with people outside the family. "Random family systems" are characterized by a lack of family structure and defined boundaries.

Like individuals, families also pass through life-cycle stages with each addition or loss of family members. For instance, families often move from being childless couples to couples with children living at home to couples with grown children living independently. Each of these transitions requires adjustments among family members.

A family's ethnicity and culture will affect its values, beliefs, and perspectives on family roles and its view of the very meaning of life. Family communication patterns will influence not only the development of family problems but also the solutions to, and prevention of, these problems. Families are often unaware of their communication patterns, and therefore may benefit from education by the social worker.

Finally, the social worker doing family assessments takes note of the emotional status of the family and its members, as well as family strengths and resources. For example, certain family members may have a great sense of humor, or a strong sense of family loyalty may be apparent. The family may show unusual resilience in the face of a natural disaster such as Hurricane Katrina. These resources and strengths are often not clearly understood by family members. Social workers can help to identify and use family strengths to promote better family functioning in the future.[28]

Group Assessments

Social workers also do group assessments. Sometimes the assessment is of a treatment group; other times, the assessment is of a group focused on completing a task. Treatment groups are used to enhance members' awareness and coping abilities around some shared problem, while task-related groups are organized to accomplish a specific responsibility or carry out a mandate. In doing group assessments, social workers gather and analyze information regarding group purpose, structure, culture, and life-cycle stage. In addition, social workers gather and analyze information regarding alliances among group members, and the specific task the group wants to achieve.

With groups, "structure" refers to group size and composition, diversity, and receptivity of the group to new members. "Group culture" refers to traditions, values, beliefs, and norms established by group members, while "group alliances" pertain to group characteristics such as leadership, power, and shared opinions. As with individuals and families, social workers also note the group life cycle—has the group formed only recently or has it been in existence for a long period of time? Also of interest is whether the group has clear traditions, beliefs, and norms or whether these are still developing. Does the group have a large and active membership or is its membership declining and inactive? This is all useful information. Further, the social worker assesses the group's ability to carry out identified tasks. Often, the inability of the group to define, organize, and complete tasks is the main problem. In any case, the social worker starts with the group's perception of its presenting problem and group member strengths and resources to address group problem(s).[29]

Organization and Community Assessment

Social workers also perform assessments with organizations and communities. Organizational assessments are done, in part, because organizational functioning influences the ability of social workers to serve their clients. Social workers doing organizational assessments focus on such areas as organizational policies, resources, and culture. Policies provide the framework in which social workers deliver their services, while organizational resources support social workers in their duties. Abundant resources increase the probability that interventions will be successful, while resource shortages increase the probability that services will be of lesser quality. Similarly, organizational culture affects organizational services and effectiveness—either positively or negatively. A culture in which social work practitioners feel supported, valued, and respected promotes effective interventions. In contrast, an organizational culture filled with sexism, racism, and cynicism frequently leads to less effective interventions.[30]

Finally, some social workers do assessments of entire communities. Social workers employed in administrative, community organization, or policy analysis positions are the most likely to be involved in community assessments. In doing these assessments, social workers gather and analyze data related to community demographic profiles, community conditions, and community resources. Demographic data includes information such as average age, percentage of women and men, ethnic and racial percentages, and the percentage of children.

In terms of community conditions, social workers look at such things as housing conditions, school quality, traffic congestion, pollution levels, crime rates, and resident mobility. Community resources include the availability of child care, health and human services, recreational services, religious organizations, job opportunities, and public transportation. Social workers believe community factors like these have a significant influence on individual, family, and group functioning.[31]

Moreover, social workers doing community assessments look for significant community strengths, assets, and resources. In this way, social workers seek to gain the knowledge to develop and empower communities, knowing that strong and healthy communities affect the strength and health of the individuals and families that reside there. This empowerment process depends on the ability of community members to make choices, and on the availability of choices for them to make.

In summary, social workers not only help individuals, families, and groups to make choices regarding problems; they also help organizations and

Case Study: Ethics and Community Work

A social worker, Gary L., was hired by a neighborhood organization to do an assessment of community conditions as expressed by the neighborhood residents. The neighborhood, located in Albuquerque, New Mexico, was populated primarily by low- and middle-income households. To Gary, the neighborhood looked and felt neglected. Houses were in various stages of repair. Litter was all too prevalent. Dogs roamed about unsupervised. To collect further information from residents, Gary conducted door-to-door interviews with people who happened to be home at the time. One day, at roughly 10:30 a.m., a woman invited him into her home to conduct an interview. The woman was an attractive woman in her early 30s and appeared to be alone in the house. As the social worker started the interview in the living room, he became concerned that the woman might be wearing a nightgown. It was not obvious, however. Since he had already started the interview, he was not sure what to do.

Should he have ended the interview suddenly? Should he have asked the woman if she wanted time to throw on a robe? He didn't want to insult her—especially if it wasn't sleep attire—but he also wanted to conduct himself professionally. What should he have done? Should he have been in the house alone with the woman in the first place? What practice should he follow in the future to prevent predicaments like this one?

> **Research Informed Practice with Abused Children from Diverse Neighborhoods**
>
> Social work researchers Bridget Friesthler, Emily Bruce, and Barbara Needell published a study in 2007 that examined the association between child maltreatment and various neighborhood characteristics.[33] These characteristics included neighborhood population density, impoverishment, instability (percentage of people moving), child care burden (ratio of children to adults), racial/ethnic composition, and alcohol outlet density (number of bars, restaurants, and stores in relation to population). In this study, black children were three times more likely than Hispanic children, and five times more likely than white children, to have experienced substantiated maltreatment. For the black children, neighborhood rates of child abuse and neglect were positively associated with the percentage of neighborhood residents living in poverty, and the number of "off-premise alcohol outlets" (e.g., stores that sell alcohol) per 1,000 population. For Hispanic children, maltreatment rates were positively associated with the neighborhood's percentages of female-headed households, poverty, and unemployment.
>
> What does this study tell you about social work's ecosystems perspective? How could a study such as this better inform you as you work with children?

communities to identify and make choices in an effort to promote healthy functioning.[32] Once the assessment is finished, social workers are then ready to develop more precise and focused plans for client intervention.

PLANNING AND CONTRACTING

The assessment process often leads social workers to collaborate with clients to develop a written intervention plan or **client contract** that includes arrangements for payment for services, specifying what services will be offered and at what cost.[35] Additionally, contracting involves a written intervention plan similar to a legally binding agreement that delineates the problem to be worked on by the social worker and client, specific tasks required by the client and the social worker, and expected intervention outcomes. Contracts typically include specified dates of service and, at times, specified dates for achieving identified goals and tasks.[36]

Social workers use contracts for several reasons. First, they encourage or require the social worker and client to collaborate to clearly define the immediate problem to be addressed. Second, because the contract suggests a binding agreement between worker and client, it helps motivate the social worker and client to seriously attempt to alleviate the problem without giving up. In a sense, it is a commitment by both the social worker and the client to make a good-faith effort to follow through on agreed-upon goals. Third, a contract encourages both the social worker and the client to be precise and concrete in

> **Focus on Professionalism and Ethics**
>
> **Value:** "*Integrity*
> **Ethical Principle:** *Social workers behave in a trustworthy manner.*
>
> Social workers are continually aware of the profession's mission, values, ethical principles, and ethical standards and practice in a manner consistent with them. Social workers act honestly and responsibly and promote ethical practices on the part of the organizations with which they are affiliated."[34]

delineating agreed-upon courses of action—including specific tasks for each party. Because goals and action plans are specific and written, there is less chance for later disagreement between the social worker and the client regarding the initial purpose of the helping relationship. Contract specificity also helps prevent the social worker and client from drifting from one problem to another during the helping process, and from drifting from one strategy to another while addressing the problem.[37]

Social workers also use contracts because as they work together with clients to draw up contracts, they can help clients prioritize the most important problems on which to work, the most important goals to achieve, and the most immediate tasks to begin. This process is especially helpful for clients who tend to feel overwhelmed and disoriented by the myriad issues facing them. Thus, a contract can instill hope on the part of the client that something can be done and that they know where to begin.[38]

Furthermore, developing a written agreement in contract form encourages collaboration, mutuality, and a balance of power in the relationship. The process shows respect for the client and promotes independence and self-determination on the client's part. Similarly, written contracts promote both client and social worker accountability. In short, contracts empower clients.[39]

In the process of developing written intervention plans and contracts, the social worker may make suggestions regarding alternative courses of action and educate the client regarding community resources, but it is the client who must ultimately take responsibility for the quality of his or her life. The social worker does not attempt to solve the problem for the client, but rather, *with* the client.[40]

INTERVENTION IN GENERALIST SOCIAL WORK

Generalist social work practice uses a **generalist intervention model** that is based upon four characteristics. First, it is based on the knowledge, skills, and values of the social work profession. At the core of this professional education model is an ecosystems perspective that maintains that social workers must work with individuals as they interact in the various systems they encounter on a daily basis, systems such as families, ethnic groups, work groups, and communities.[42] Second, the generalist intervention model involves micro, mezzo, and macro systems as targets of change. Third, generalist interventions stress that individual and social problems should be addressed through multiple theories and perspectives. And finally, the generalist model employs a problem-solving methodology that includes assessment, planning or contracting, intervention, evaluation, termination, and follow-up.[43]

Within the ecosystems perspective, the generalist social worker can choose from a wide range of theories and intervention methods depending on the type of client system and the nature of the presenting problem.[44] Among the theories

Focus on Professionalism and Ethics

Value: "*Service*
Ethical Principle: *Social workers' primary goal is to help people in need and to address social problems.*

Social workers elevate service to others above self-interest. Social workers draw on their knowledge, values, and skills to help people in need and to address social problems. Social workers are encouraged to volunteer some portion of their professional skills with no expectation of significant financial return (i.e., pro bono service)."[41]

used by social workers are psychoanalytic theory, learning theory, cognitive theory, and biological theory.[45]

Historically, social workers have used **psychoanalytic theory** based upon the work of Sigmund Freud and others. Traditional psychodynamic interventions use techniques such as free association and dream interpretation to help individuals work through repressed psychological material. Psychodynamic treatments typically require relatively lengthy treatment plans. During this type of treatment, the social worker encourages "transference," a process by which the client relates to the therapist as if the therapist were a significant person in the client's life (e.g., a father or mother). Psychodynamic interventions are used less often today for several reasons, including managed care requirements that limit the length of time a service can be offered to the client, research showing that brief treatments can be just as effective as longer-term interventions, and the demands of contemporary fast-paced lifestyles.

Today, social workers use a range of theoretical perspectives in their interventions. For example, social workers use learning theory when they enter into behavioral interventions with clients. That is, social workers use **learning theory** to, among other things, weaken maladaptive responses to stress and other external stimuli, and to reinforce more adaptive client behaviors. Social workers in schools use behavior modification techniques from learning theory when they employ rewards and punishments with individual students or student groups.

Cognitive theory is another theory often used in social work interventions. Cognitive theorists maintain that dysfunctional behavior begins with faulty understandings or "cognitions" on the client's part that can lead to dysfunctional feelings and behaviors. Social workers apply cognitive theory in their work when they challenge clients to rethink faulty beliefs, attitudes, and behaviors, and subsequently to consider other, more realistic explanations and behaviors.

Another theory social workers use is **biological theory**, which attributes dysfunctional client behavior to biological origins and calls for biological treatments, including medications. Social workers do not dispense medications directly, but make referrals to physicians who are trained and licensed to prescribe medications to clients suffering from biological problems (e.g., brain dysfunctions). These clients, who often experience severe mental health problems, see a physician to receive medications and a specialized clinical worker (e.g., clinical social worker or psychiatrist) for more traditional insight therapy and support services.[46]

Generalist Social Work with Individuals

Depending on the setting, many social workers provide services primarily to individuals. Social workers focused on individual work might offer emotional support, facilitate problem solving, provide case management, or conduct advocacy—perhaps all four. As previously described, social work with individuals is usually referred to as **casework**, although casework is not necessarily limited to work with individuals (for example, a social worker in an agency serving families would provide casework to a family). Casework involves resolving or reducing difficulties "arising out of disequilibrium between people and their environment."[47] This process involves helping individuals adjust to the environment, as well as intervening to change factors in the individual's environment. Casework with individuals includes helping people with concrete practical problems, with environmental deficits and pressures, and with interpersonal and intrapersonal difficulties. Social workers involved in casework with individuals work in a wide variety of practice settings, including social service agencies, hospitals, outpatient clinics, state and local child protective services, and in private practice.

Case management is defined as a collaborative form of intervention in which the individual social worker, perhaps working in an interdisciplinary team, links clients with needed services by playing the roles of facilitator, broker, mediator, and advocate. It may be a part of casework. Case management requires knowledge of the full range of agencies, benefits, and services available to the client.[48] Social workers doing case management at times monitor individuals' progress as they access community services and intervene on an as-needed basis when the client requires additional support or service referrals. Social workers typically use their planning skills to coordinate needed financial, educational, health, and human services. That is, social workers doing case management coordinate a mix of needed services for the client in a way that is nonduplicative, synergistic, and cost-effective.

Generalist Social Work with Families

Generalist social workers also work with families. Sometimes, they help families with behavioral, emotional, and interactional problems. The process is usually viewed as one of problem solving within a systems context, the system in this case being the family. They utilize a variety of techniques in family work. They try to reframe and relabel family perceptions and interactions in a way that promotes new insights and improves family functioning. Social workers depathologize family problems so that family members do not see themselves as weird or deviant, which can facilitate more frequent and open communication regarding their issues. Also, they examine family interactional patterns between and among adult partners, parents, and children and siblings. Again, the purpose of such examination is to promote family insight about patterns that lead to dysfunctional behavior and unhappiness.

To develop more constructive and correctional patterns, a social worker may try to restructure family interactions, sometimes by assigning homework in the form of "directives" to family members. Directives might call upon family

Social Work Stories: Working with Families

Social worker, Heidi, talks about her work with families:

I was in my last six months of college, broke, ready to quit school, and only a few months away from graduation. I wanted to enter the field of social work and stop working these "mall jobs" where respect is rare. I went to my professor at Hawaii Pacific University and informed her of my frustrations . . . she pulled up an e-mail she had received that day. A family was looking for a companion to work with their 18-year old son who had Down Syndrome. "Could you possibly be interested in this?" I jumped at the opportunity . . . something about the job appealed to me. . . . Over the next six months, I worked with "Steve," teaching him to live independently by riding the city bus, budgeting, and preparing . . . meals (even though we burned the spaghetti!). Steve and his parents introduced me to a new population, a group that goes unrecognized by the rest of society all too often—those with developmental disabilities/mental retardation, and their families. I was "hooked."[49]

members to practice certain interaction patterns until the next time they see the social worker. Part of this work includes attention to alliances between or among family members that have been dysfunctional and that need to be changed. In all of this work, the social worker maintains a systems perspective on family functioning, pointing out that a happier family life requires give-and-take, compromise, and negotiation, as well as gains and losses on the part of individual family members.[50]

Frequently, the generalist social worker uses a problem-solving approach to assist a family with resources such as housing, transportation, child care, or schools. The social worker subsequently encourages discussion among family members regarding strategies and options to better address key issues. In the process, the social worker may lead a discussion on various community services and resources available to individual family members and to the family as a whole and may refer families to support groups, local housing authorities, transportation services, or evening classes. By referring family members to community resources, the social worker begins to help family members develop a wider support system outside of the immediate family system, one that may enhance and extend the support given by the social worker to the family.

Generalist Social Work with Groups

Generalist social work practice also involves working with groups other than the family. As stated earlier, generalist social workers may get involved in many types of groups, including educational groups, support groups, psycho-educational groups, recreation groups, reading groups, youth groups, staff development groups, and team-building groups. When facilitating therapeutic groups, the social worker tries to promote several processes—processes that typically characterize effective therapeutic group work. For example, the social worker uses the group experience to instill hope in its members that they can deal with personal problems more successfully. Participation in a group can be particularly effective at instilling hope because group members see other individuals in the group becoming successful in dealing with the shared problem. Members start to believe that "if they can do it, I can do it." In addition, groups promote imitation from group members. That is, individuals tend to imitate the successful behaviors of other group members when dealing with their own problems and issues. Group members are able to imitate other group members because they learn from the interactions that take place at each group session. Group members exchange stories, observations, insights, and advice with one another from session to session.

The social worker guides the group so that discussion among group members is open, honest, and focused on self-growth. Making the session safe in this way promotes greater self-disclosure from participants. It also promotes reality testing by participants. Individuals share stories and see if other group members have had similar experiences. In this way, individual members do not feel they are alone or deviant in their experiences. This environment helps group members learn to accept one another and themselves. A sense of empowerment develops as group members help one another while, at the same time, helping themselves. Social workers look for opportunities to promote insights among group members as they interact, often in the same ways they behave with family members or coworkers. This process leads to self-understanding.[51]

The generalist social worker keeps the group focused on shared problems while facilitating discussions among group members about alternative behaviors that have worked in the past. Also, he or she assists the group to explore various community services and resources available to group members. Thus, the problem-solving model inherent in generalist social work can be applied to groups.

Generalist Social Work with Organizations and Communities

At the macro level, generalist social workers perform a wide array of duties with organizations and communities. Their roles and responsibilities include education and training, program planning, and community development.[53] Often, generalist social workers are asked to assist in improving service delivery or in developing new services. Similarly, generalist practitioners doing community organization, sometimes called community organizers, help to develop new community resources, educate community residents regarding emerging community issues, organize community residents to work on neighborhood projects, and in general, help to improve community conditions.

Generalist social workers do education and training within their organizations by assisting with staff development and continuing education activities. At the community level, social workers get involved with education and training by organizing community forums, workshops, and presentations. At times, they may participate as facilitators or educators in these community meetings.

Generalist social workers also perform many tasks related to program planning at the organizational and community levels. They may work with organizational task forces and agency program committees to improve existing services and develop new services to meet emerging community needs. They might assist in coordinating interagency service networks. Additionally, social workers in generalist practice use their research skills to conduct community needs assessments and program evaluations. They sometimes engage in resource development by identifying possible program funding sources and coordinating various fund-raising activities such as community festivals, road races, auctions, or garden tours. And finally, they may write grants to fund new programs and services.

Community organization refers to specific intervention methods in which generalist social workers participate using planned collective actions. Community organization may involve development activities (i.e., "community development") that bring together leaders from various socioeconomic groups in an effort to find consensus in creating or revitalizing local institutions. At

---

Focus on Professionalism and Ethics

Value: *"Social Justice*
Ethical Principle: *Social workers challenge social injustice.*

Social workers pursue social change, particularly with, and on behalf of, vulnerable and oppressed individuals and groups of people. Social workers' social change efforts are focused primarily on issues of poverty, unemployment, discrimination, and other forms of social injustice. These activities seek to promote sensitivity to, and knowledge about, oppression and cultural and ethnic diversity. Social workers strive to ensure access to needed information, services, and resources; equality of opportunity; and meaningful participation in decision making for all people."[52]

It is never too late to give up our prejudices.
—Henry David Thoreau

other times, community organizers seek to improve community conditions by empowering community residents. Thus, community organization contains a social action component that requires the social worker to perform a variety of advocacy roles. This involves everything from organizing meetings and starting task groups to building powerful coalitions and conducting class advocacy.

Coalition building refers to collaborating with, and at times challenging, public and private institutions that control needed community resources. This requires generalist social workers to use their skills in organizing, public speaking, mediation, and negotiation. **Class advocacy** is defined as social work activities that involve whole groups of people whose rights have been violated in some way. Generalist social workers may help to educate these groups regarding their civil rights. In so doing, the social worker mobilizes such groups to take action and confront public policymakers regarding an identified problem.[54]

In summary, generalist social workers take part in interventions at multiple systems levels. The system may be an individual, a family, a group, an organization, or a community. Using systems theory and the generalist intervention model, the generalist social worker chooses among various systems in assisting clients to identify problems, consider alternative courses of action, explore resources, and take action.

EVALUATION

Government, managed care companies, United Way, and other funding sources are increasingly requiring social workers to document service effectiveness. This means that social workers need to use interventions that research has shown to be effective (i.e., "evidence-based practice"). They also need to monitor intervention processes and outcomes on a regular basis, a process called **evaluation**. The purpose of evaluation is to improve and document the effectiveness of social work interventions. Social workers have many ways to evaluate their interventions, some very basic and simple, others more complex and scientific. Most practitioners do this on a regular basis by simply taking time to reflect on the effectiveness of their intervention efforts. This may be done after each interaction with the client as well as after the case is terminated. Social workers who want to improve or document their effectiveness typically use good supervision and case consultation on a regular basis.[55]

In doing evaluation, generalist social workers ask themselves several questions: Are the social worker and client following the plan as originally written and agreed upon? Is the plan working? Which actions have been most effective? Which have been least effective? Which parts of the intervention plan have produced the most positive results using the fewest resources? Conversely, which strategies have required the most resources with the least positive results? Is the intervention a true collaboration—meaning, are the social worker and client actively performing their parts? Is the client becoming more independent and empowered? Have client goals and strategies originally agreed upon changed in any way?

The evaluation of an intervention with a single client is called a **client outcome assessment**; it allows the social worker to evaluate whether or not the intervention plan has been successful. If successful, the assessment determines whether the intervention or other factors led to the positive results. The assessment allows the social worker and client to decide whether to stay with the current course of action or to modify their strategy to produce better results for the client.[56]

Social workers give attention to several tasks when doing evaluations. They make sure to define client problems and related goals clearly. They establish measurable objectives in relation to each goal. Since measures aren't perfect, they use multiple measures to assess client progress. That is, most measures do not capture all aspects of a problem. Using multiple measures, social workers aim to collect the most relevant information regarding client goals and objectives. Similarly, they try to use the most accurate measures in terms of reliability and validity. **Reliability** refers to the degree to which a measurement instrument produces consistent results, while **validity** is the degree to which an instrument measures what it is intended to measure (and not something else). Furthermore, social workers collect information at the beginning phases of the intervention in order to establish a baseline by which to judge future client progress.[57]

Social workers use a number of measurement tools in their evaluations. One such tool is a "client journal," sometimes called a client log, where the social worker may ask the client, or each person in a family, or group, to keep a journal to document their thoughts, emotions, activities, and overall progress on a daily basis.

Social workers also use a variety of scales to rate client progress. Scales are used to measure client goal attainment, behaviors, thoughts, or emotions. Most scales use a point system ranging from high to low (or low to high). A client typically collaborates with the social worker to describe or define his or her low points and high points; these descriptions then become the endpoints of the scale.

In addition to scales that the social worker and client develop together, social workers at times use "standardized scales," which refer to scales that have already been developed, used, and evaluated. They have a known reliability level. Standardized measures tend to be relatively easy to use and therefore do not require extensive training. Such measures are available to measure a variety of client emotions, thoughts, and behaviors, including self-esteem, depression, anxiety, and marital satisfaction.[58]

In doing their evaluations, social workers choose a specific evaluation design in which to conduct their measurements. One of the most frequently used designs is the **single system design**, also known as single subject or single case design. Single system designs evaluate interventions with a single client system, whether that is a single individual, a single family or other small group, a single organization, or a single community. Whatever the "client," the process is the same. It always involves taking multiple measurements of a target problem.

In the single system design, a series of measurements of the problem are taken before the social work intervention begins; then a series of measurements are taken during the intervention to assess progress on the target problem. These designs can be made more or less complex by the social worker, but they all build on the basic baseline-intervention design (called the Basic AB Design). In this case, single system designs can be used to evaluate individual client outcomes or to evaluate entire programs or policies.

In the case of program evaluation, a social work intervention with an entire program can be considered. With program evaluation, the target problem usually involves many clients rather than just one or two individuals or one small group. Furthermore, social workers involved in policy analysis can evaluate the effectiveness of policies in the same way. Again, in this case, the policy is the intervention, and the target problem relates to larger populations rather than a single individual or single small group. In summary, the generalist intervention model can be readily evaluated by social workers in many different settings and with many types of clients.[59]

TERMINATION

For the generalist social worker, the last stage in the helping process with a client is referred to as **termination**. Terminations can be planned or unplanned. Unplanned terminations occur when an individual or family drops out (i.e., stops attending sessions) or when the client is transferred to another social worker. Clients may be transferred to a different social worker for several reasons. Sometimes a client requires more advanced treatment than the generalist social worker can provide, and therefore the social worker refers the client to a more experienced, advanced, or specialized social worker. Other times a client may be transferred to a new worker because the original worker has been promoted to another position within the same agency, transferred to another

---

Focus on Professionalism and Ethics

Value: "*Competence*
Ethical Principle: *Social workers practice within their areas of competence and develop and enhance their professional expertise.*

Social workers continually strive to increase their professional knowledge and skills and to apply them in practice. Social workers should aspire to contribute to the knowledge base of the profession."[60]

agency office, taken a job with another agency, or been fired from his or her current position.

There are also several reasons for planned, agreed-upon terminations between the social worker and client. The social worker and client may have left the service contract open-ended with no fixed time limits, but have reached a point in the intervention where the client has achieved her or his goals and does not feel a need to continue with the service. Conversely, the social worker and client may agree to end the service due to a lack of progress in the intervention process. Termination with a social worker may also occur because the client requires a different type of helping professional, such as a psychologist or psychiatrist, for example. Another typical reason for planned termination is managed care specification.[61]

Termination is often a time of heightened emotions between the social worker and client. If the intervention has been highly successful, termination may be a time of achievement and happiness. If the intervention termination has been mandated by managed care, a social worker and client may become more anxious, feeling that time is running out. Termination can also bring up feelings of loss and abandonment for the client—frequently the very reasons the client began to see the social worker in the first place. That is, clients often seek counseling and support after experiencing a loss of a relationship with a spouse, partner, parent, or child. Therefore, terminations can bring back feelings of disappointment, resentment, rejection, and anger. Most often, clients experience mixed emotions about terminating a relationship with the social worker.[62]

The social worker, too, must deal with personal emotions regarding ending the helping relationship. On one hand, the worker may have really enjoyed working with a particular individual. Perhaps the client made the social worker feel very competent and needed. At times like these, social workers may regret having to end the relationship. On the other hand, the social worker may feel disappointed or a little guilty about not having been more successful with the client. Perhaps the worker would prefer to continue to try to achieve intervention goals with the client, but cannot due to managed care limits or because the client wishes to end the service. In any case, the social worker must be aware of his or her feelings, and verbalize them to the client during the termination process.

In addition, because of their negative or mixed feelings, clients may experience behavior regression during termination. That is, they may revert to exhibiting earlier dysfunctional behaviors or they may show deterioration in newly learned coping skills. The social worker makes sure to identify and discuss these issues with the client as part of termination.[63]

In any case, social workers terminating services with clients attempt to do three things: (1) review the progress and outcomes of the intervention; (2) review the helping relationship itself; and (3) plan for the client's future. First, because the social worker and client review the progress they have made during the intervention, the termination stage of intervention has an evaluative feature to it. A final comprehensive review of client progress may serve to support or cancel the decision to terminate. For instance, in the case where the client has either met her or his goals or clearly failed to meet these goals, the social worker and client may decide to terminate the service. However, a review needs to take place in order to determine the amount of progress that has been made. A review of client progress and outcomes gives the social worker and client a chance to summarize client progress in terms of

Social Work Stories: Social Work Student

Stephanie K. is an undergraduate student in the social work department at a California university. As a high school student, Stephanie had the opportunity to see the work of the social workers in a nursing home. At this time, she realized how much she enjoyed working with people and how important it was to offer help to other people. Stephanie believes that she can offer help to people by connecting them with resources that are unknown to them. Stephanie feels that we can help people by empowering them to achieve even small changes in their lives. She feels that a small change can be a big success for people who go through many challenges in life. Stephanie is surprised that social work can be applied in a variety of settings and with a variety of populations.

As a social work student, Stephanie mostly enjoys her internship because she has the opportunity to apply theories, practices, and knowledge that she has learned in her classes. Stephanie finds the practical work very interesting because she is able to work with individuals and groups in the real world. During her internship she has done several home visits and she has learned a great deal by observing her coworkers interacting with the families in a variety of situations.

Stephanie feels that "Practice I" was the best course because it helped her to get an idea of the role of social workers. She believes that in "Practice I" she learned how to put together skills, techniques, and "use of herself" professionally. Stephanie found the role-plays the most powerful part of this course. Although she recognizes how difficult it was for her to be a client or a therapist in each of the scenarios, she values the benefits of the experience in her understanding of practicing social work. The feedback that she was getting from the group leader and the fact that she was videotaped helped her to use verbal and body language effectively. Through this process she also learned her strengths, her limitations, and ways to improve her skills. Stephanie also recognizes the positive contribution of all the classes (research, HBSE, social policy), which gave her a better understanding of social work as a profession.

In the future, Stephanie would like to do family therapy or couples therapy. After studying social work, Stephanie finds herself listening and interacting with friends and family members in a different way than she did before. She has become less judgmental about the people around her and more understanding of the situations that they are in. She has been able to listen better to her family and friends too. She feels that learning about different racial/ethnic and socioeconomic backgrounds has really made her realize the differences between people and the issues with which they struggle. Stephanie believes that social work really does open up a whole new world to the way we think as human beings. She feels that people in this society care too much about themselves and not enough about helping others around them. Stephanie believes that as social workers, we need to change the way people think about certain issues such as mental illness, homelessness, disabilities, socioeconomic status, and racial backgrounds. She hopes to do this in her future career.

---

newly learned coping mechanisms, insights, and strengths. This review also serves as a prerequisite for future planning. The information and conclusions developed during the termination process can be used to assess the client's future service needs.

The second step during the termination process is to review the helping relationship itself. During this time, the social worker and client openly and honestly discuss their feelings about working together. This is the point at which the client can be encouraged to share any positive feelings of accomplishment and negative feelings around the loss of the relationship or lack of progress. As noted, clients typically have mixed emotions about relationship termination. The social worker explores these feelings with the client so that the client and social worker can feel some sense of closure to the helping process. An open and honest discussion about what the client liked and disliked about working together also serves to provide evaluative feedback to the social worker on his or her intervention skills. Further, such a discussion, as in the review of progress, provides information on the client's future service

> **Demonstrating Knowledge, Values, and Skills**
>
> **Generalist Social Work Practice Activity**
>
> Students should organize themselves into groups. Identify one classmate as the client and one as the social worker. The others will be observers. The student playing the client is coming to the social worker for assistance on a problem. The social worker sits with the client and discusses what has brought the client in today. Given this is a short session, the social worker and client must define and solve the problem to the best of their abilities. The observers should pay attention to client–social worker interactions, and how the social worker frames the session with the client. Each session should last 15–20 minutes. After a session is over, come together as a group and discuss the observations that were made.
>
> How did the client feel during the session? How did the social worker feel? How was the client assisted? Is there a plan for future meetings? Trade places so that other students have a turn being client, social worker, and observer.

needs. Conversely, this discussion may confirm that the client no longer needs services.

Finally, the client progress review and the worker–client relationship review lead to the final step in termination: planning for the client's future. During this step, the social worker and client develop a plan for maintaining the emotional and behavioral gains the client made during the intervention. This may include practicing strategies that have worked during sessions with the social worker, but practicing them in new and different settings that await the client. It may involve helping the client to forecast expected difficulties and leading a discussion of alternative strategies and community resources. In this way, the social worker helps ease the client's transition out of the intervention by making the client's future more concrete as opposed to vague and, possibly, threatening. As before, the generalist social worker uses a problem-solving approach within the profession's ecosystems framework.[64]

When the client is a system larger than individuals and families, termination involves a ritual such as a farewell get-together. A party or dinner allows the social worker and client to review group, organizational, or community achievements. It also allows individuals to say goodbye and to thank other members of the group, organization, or community.[65]

SUMMARY

Social workers are concerned with aiding individuals in need of service as well as changing societal conditions that cause social problems. This requires a generalist education and is referred to as generalist social work practice. Generalist social work practice requires a broad knowledge base. It also requires a range of skills on the part of the social worker. In order to help clients, social workers must first be able to develop good relationships with clients. They must be able to engage clients by both establishing the purpose of their work together and mutually setting goals for addressing client problems.

The social worker must be able to do an assessment in which detailed information regarding client problems is collected and analyzed according to the social work profession's PIE perspective. Good social workers know that a balanced assessment requires a look at both the individual and the environment (e.g., home, community) in which the individual functions.

The assessment process often leads to a written plan and/or contract between the social worker and the client. The plan typically delineates the problem to be worked on by the social worker and client, specific tasks required by the client and the social worker, and expected intervention outcomes.

In carrying out the contract, the generalist social worker selects from a wide range of theories and intervention methods depending on the type of client system and the nature of the presenting problem. This intervention may involve the client's family, other significant groups, significant organizations, and the community.

Finally, social workers must be able to evaluate the effectiveness of their interventions and terminate with clients in a professional manner.

4 CHAPTER REVIEW

Succeed with PEARSON mysocialworklab

Log onto **MySocialWorkLab** to access a wealth of case studies, videos, and assessment. (*If you did not receive an access code to MySocialWorkLab with this text and wish to purchase access online, please visit www.mysocialworklab.com.*)

PRACTICE TEST
The following questions will test your knowledge of the content found within this chapter. For additional assessment, including licensing-exam type questions on applying chapter content to practice, visit **MySocialWorkLab**.

Professional Identity

1. Meredith has just graduated with her master's in social work and will be starting her first job soon. As a generalist social worker, her overall practice goal will be:
   a. To promote child welfare
   b. To reconcile the well-being of individuals with the welfare of society
   c. To help individuals and groups assimilate to U.S. society
   d. To ensure that state-level social policies are enforced

Professional Identity

2. Meredith's practice approach as a generalist social worker will be based upon:
   a. The unique situation of each client
   b. Applying a strict methodology to every intervention regardless of client characteristics
   c. Applying a strict methodology to interventions with children while focusing on the unique situation of adult clients
   d. Facilitating support groups for children and adults

3. Generalist social work practice is characterized by three collaborative roles:
   a. Consulting with clients regarding their problems; referring clients to physicians to determine whether medications might help them; and working collaborative with physicians on the plan of action to be undertaken
   b. Consulting with clients regarding their problems; making contact with all systems with which clients interact; and participating as activists to reduce social problems at the federal level
   c. Consulting with clients regarding their problems; managing the resources of systems in which clients function; and offering clients information regarding both
   d. Consulting with clients regarding their problems; coordinating services by collaborating closely with other professionals regarding mental health diagnosis and need for medications; and prescribing medications to help alleviate client problems

4. The "helping relationship" refers to:
   a. The manner in which social workers assess their clients
   b. The relationship that forms between a social worker and a client when the social worker–client relationship has been mandated by a court
   c. State and local child protective services relationships with families
   d. A mechanism through which social workers and their clients promote positive changes in client functioning

5. The formation of a helping relationship depends upon:
   a. Social class similarity between the social worker and the client
   b. Good communication skills by the social worker
   c. An authoritarian approach on the part of the social worker
   d. An advocacy role on the part of the social worker

Ethical Practice

6. Ms. Barrios, a social worker, always listens deeply to her clients in order to gain an emotional understanding of what each client is going through and to interpret what each client is saying. According to the text, Ms. Barrios is showing _____ when she does this:
   a. Social justice
   b. Empathy
   c. That she has the upper hand in the helping relationship
   d. Advocacy

Diversity in Practice

7. The concept that refers to the fact that major minority groups share certain experiences in their history, including discrimination and oppression, is referred to as:
   a. The helping relationship
   b. Cultural specificity
   c. Engagement
   d. Cultural commonality

8. The beginning phase of the engagement process:
   a. Changes significantly with each client
   b. Establishes a context and structure for the helping relationship
   c. Is always characterized by the administration of mental status exams
   d. Is defined by advice the social worker gives to the client

9. The degree of accessibility or approachability within a family and between its subsystems and external systems is also known as:
   a. Boundaries
   b. Cultural commonality
   c. Cultural specificity
   d. Engagement

Log onto **MySocialWorkLab** once you have completed the Practice Test above to access additional study tools and assessment.

Answers

Key: 1) b 2) a 3) c 4) d 5) b 6) b 7) d 8) b 9) a

5

Social Work and Social Justice: Diversity, Difference, and Oppression

CHAPTER OUTLINE

Human Difference and Diversity 87

Diverse Peoples of the United States 90
Major Social Groups in the United States

Organizing Principles of Diversity and Difference in Society 98
Social Groups
Inequality: Discrimination and Prejudice
Inequality: Domination and Subordination
Identity
Oppression, Power, and Privilege

The Lived Experience of Oppression: "The Isms" 104
Racism
Ethnocentrism

Xenophobia
Classism
Sexism
Homophobia and Heterosexism
Ableism

Social Work and Social Justice 109
Empowering Practices: Social Justice in Action
Practice Focus: Strengths-Based Practice

Summary 111

Practice Test 113

 MySocialWorkLab 113

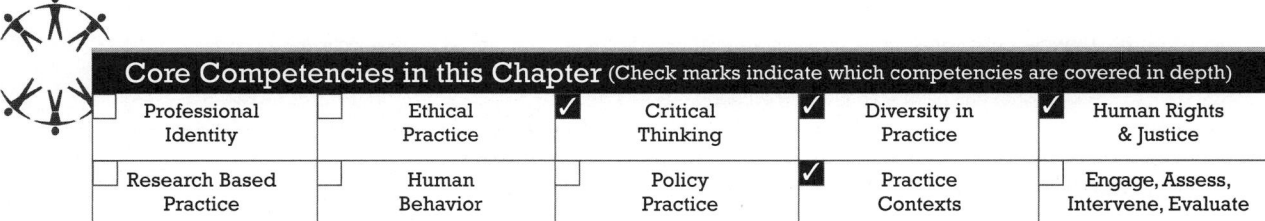

	Core Competencies in this Chapter (Check marks indicate which competencies are covered in depth)				
☐ Professional Identity	☐ Ethical Practice	✓ Critical Thinking	✓ Diversity in Practice	✓ Human Rights & Justice	
☐ Research Based Practice	☐ Human Behavior	☐ Policy Practice	✓ Practice Contexts	☐ Engage, Assess, Intervene, Evaluate	

HUMAN DIFFERENCE AND DIVERSITY

It is crucial for social workers to be aware of the diversity that exists among the human population. **Human diversity** refers to the range of differences among human beings, including "age, class, color, culture, disability, ethnicity, family structure, gender, marital status, national origin, race, religion, sex, and sexual orientation."[1] This chapter examines various categories of human difference and the many groups facing social injustice through discrimination and oppression. As professionals dedicated to social justice and empowerment, social workers must be alert to discrimination and oppression and their effects on the individuals, groups, and communities we serve. Moreover, being aware of, alert to, and curious about clients' values, beliefs, cultural practices, concerns, and experiences allows social workers to collaborate with clients with sensitivity and effectiveness and to recognize, support, and build upon their many strengths.

If we are to achieve a richer culture, rich in contrasting values, we must recognize the whole gamut of human potentialities.

—Margaret Mead

Although the value placed on human diversity in U.S. society has been increasing significantly since the civil rights movement and other social liberation movements of the mid-20th century, the differences among human beings continue to be used to justify the oppression of some and privileging of others. It is therefore important to understand exactly—or as exactly as possible—what the many categories of human diversity represent. To fully understand and appreciate the topics discussed throughout this chapter, we offer the following working definitions of some major categories of human difference:

Race has historically referred to categorizing people based on phenotypical differences, such as skin color. This definition, however, is inaccurate. Contemporary scientists reject race as a biological category[2] because phenotypical difference do not correlate with genotypical differences, or differences in personality, intelligence, and so on.[3] Although differences in physical appearance do exist, Smedley (1993) explains that race is a social concept:

> Historical evidence shows that race . . . was not a mere objective sorting of human physical diversity into convenient categories, nor was it a scientific term invented and defined by scholars . . . race was a social mechanism for concretizing and rigidifying a universal ranking system . . . [of European] dominance. . . .[4]

This doesn't diminish its historical importance. In the words of scholar and cultural critic Cornell West (1994), race matters.[5] In our contemporary nomenclature, the concept of race tends to reference shared culture, traditions, values, beliefs, and history, along with any real or perceived differences in physical appearance.

Ethnicity refers to "traditions, customs, activities, beliefs, and practices that pertain to a particular group of people who see themselves and are seen by others as having distinct cultural features, a separate history, and a specific socio-cultural identity,"[6] while "ethnic group" refers to a group of people who share the aforementioned characteristics. Ethnicity can be a confusing concept, as it involves several other interrelated categories of difference. For example, a person might be white (race), American (nationality), of Slavic (i.e., Eastern European) origin (ethnicity), speak English (language), and practice Islam (religion).

Culture refers to the various customs, traditions, arts, sciences, political ideologies, and religious beliefs of a group of people in a particular time period. Every individual is born into a "cultural matrix" of values, beliefs, norms, rules, and behaviors.[7] The way we live our lives, from the food we eat to the jokes we laugh at to the art we think is beautiful to our beliefs about major social phenomena like work, gender equality, and environment, are enormously influenced by our culture. The term "dominant culture" refers to the culture whose values, language, and ways of behaving are imposed on subordinate cultures through economic, political, and/or social power.[8] American culture has historically been dominated by values, beliefs, and social practices of its Western European settlers, and although aspects of many other cultures have been incorporated into the dominant U.S. culture over time, "Western" (reflecting the culture of Western Europe) culture and values continue to be privileged.

Social class refers to individuals' rank in their society. In the United States, we typically speak of five classes or five levels of SES: *lower class*, *working class*, *middle class*, *upper middle class*, and *upper class*. These correlate roughly to the income distribution quartiles used by the U.S. Census Bureau, but class involves more than a person's income. It incorporates both achieved status (earned income plus educational and occupational attainment) and inherited or ascribed status (wealth, privilege, power, and access derived from a person's family and cultural background).[9] Langston defines class as "composed of ideas, behavior, attitudes, value and language; class is how you think, feel, act, look, dress, talk, move, walk; class is where you shop, restaurants you eat in, the schools you attend and the education you attain; class is the very jobs you will work throughout your adult life."[10]

Gender refers to a person's identity as a woman or a man. Gender and sex are not the same, and it is important for social workers to be aware of the

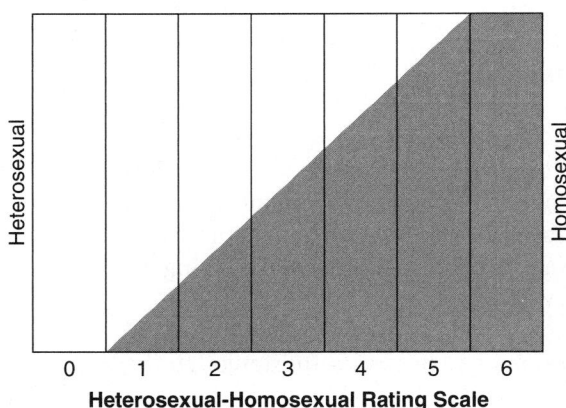

0–Exclusively heterosexual with no homosexual
1–Predominantly heterosexual, only incidentally homosexual
2–Predominantly heterosexual, but more than incidentally homosexual
3–Equally heterosexual and homosexual
4–Predominantly homosexual, but more than incidentally heterosexual
5–Predominantly homosexual, only incidentally heterosexual
6–Exclusively homosexual

Figure 5.1
The Kinsey Scale of Sexual Orientation
Source: See Alfred Kinsey et al. Sexual Behavior and the Human Male. (Bloomington, IN: Indiana University Press, 1948).

distinction between the two. Sex refers to biological division between females and males, while gender is a socially constructed concept that incorporates expectations associated with femininity and masculinity. Although men and women are biologically different, the ways of being we have come to associate with those differences, and the value we place on those ways of being, are created by our society. **Gender identity** refers to a person's view of him- or herself as one or another gender. The pioneering work of gender identity activists and scholars has pointed out that an individual's gender identity is not necessarily parallel to that individual's biological sex. This is not pathological, but is another source of human diversity.

Sexual orientation refers to affection, love, and/or attraction for another person, ranging along a continuum with same-sex attraction (i.e., homosexual) at one end and "opposite" sex attraction (i.e., heterosexual) at the other end. The scientist Alfred Kinsey noted that sexual attraction, behavior, and identity do not always fit neatly into categories and that most people exist somewhere on this continuum from entirely heterosexual to entirely homosexual (see Figure 5.1).[11]

A **disability** is a physical or mental impairment that leads to a loss of functioning that can be permanent. The U.S. Social Security Administration, the federal agency that controls the administration of federal benefits to individuals with disabilities, considers a person disabled if he or she cannot do work that he or she did prior to becoming disabled, cannot adjust to other work because of the disabling condition(s), and expects the disabling condition to last for at least one year or to result in death.[12] This way of understanding disability is typically referred to as the medical model of disability, and locates the "problem" of disability within the individual (i.e., she or he has an impairment). There are alternative ways of understanding the concept of disability. The social model of disability conceptualizes disability by locating the problem of disability within society, rather than within the individual. In the social model, disability is understood to result from society's poor response to individuals with impairments, rather from the "impairments" themselves (or the people who possess them).[13] Thus, if society provided adequate facilities, services, and other resources, physical and mental impairments would not necessarily result in a loss of functioning, and thus would not create a disability.

Critical Thinking Question

What might be the costs or benefits of adapting the medical or social model of disability to individuals with disabilities and to society at large? Why do you suppose many in the disabled community reject the medical model of disability?

Prejudice is the child of ignorance.

—William Hazlitt

Focus on Professionalism and Ethics

NASW Ethical Standard 1.05: Cultural Competence and Social Diversity

The National Association of Social Workers identifies the importance of understanding and valuing diversity in our clients within the Code of Ethics:

a. Social workers should understand culture and its function in human behavior and society, recognizing the strengths that exist in all cultures.

b. Social workers should have a knowledge base of their clients' cultures and be able to demonstrate competence in the provision of services that are sensitive to clients' cultures and to differences among people and cultural groups.

c. Social workers should obtain education about and seek to understand the nature of social diversity and oppression with respect to race, ethnicity, national origin, color, sex, sexual orientation, age, marital status, political belief, religion, and mental or physical disability.[14]

DIVERSE PEOPLES OF THE UNITED STATES

The U.S. is diverse in many respects. According to the U.S. Census Bureau, in 2005, over 25% of the U.S. population were people of color, 12.1% were over 65 year of age, 12.4% were born in a country other than the U.S., 19.4% spoke a language other than English at home, 13.3% were poor, and 14.9% met the federal definition of disability.[15] The U.S. population has also grown increasingly diverse over the past several decades. The percentage of people over 65 in the United States tripled in the 20th century.[16] From 1980 to 2000, the U.S. minority population increased by 88%.[17] In the same time period, the Latino population nearly doubled, growing from 6.4% of the total U.S. population in 1980 to 12.5% in 2000.[18] Recent years have brought continued shifts in the racial and ethnic makeup of the U.S. The Census Bureau reports that between 2000 and 2004, the population of the United States grew by 4.3%; however, the number of Asian Americans grew by 16.2% and the number of Latinos grew by 17%.[19]

There are several explanations for the increasing diversity of the U.S. population. Immigration, differing birthrates, globalization, and increased visibility of some groups are all factors. Immigration from all over the world more than doubled between 1950 and 2000 and rose by 50% from 1980 to 2004.[20] Although the immigration rate is far smaller now than at the turn of the last century, immigration appears to be on the increase, and it continues to play a leading role in the ongoing U.S. diversification. Changes in the fertility rate are another source of increasing diversity. For example, African American women have the lowest fertility rate among all ethnic and racial groups in the United States, while Asian American and Latina women have significantly higher fertility rates than either African American or European American women.[21] Additionally, foreign-born female residents of the U.S. have a significantly higher birthrate than native-born residents.[22] Another source of increasing diversity is access to the cultural heritage, practices, and products of the world within and outside our borders, made possible by globalization. Finally, increased visibility of cultural and other social groups, such as GLBTQ (i.e., Gay, Lesbian, Bisexual, Transgender, and Queer/Questioning) persons due to hard-won civil rights advances contributes to growing visible diversity in the United States.

Major Social Groups in the United States

We have established that the United States is a diverse nation and is becoming more so every day. In this section, we'll take a closer took at some of the many racial, ethnic, social, and cultural groups in the U.S., focusing on groups most often marginalized within our society. The information provided here is intended only as a very basic and broad overview. We strongly caution you to avoid making broad generalizations based on the material presented here, and encourage you to do your own exploration through reading, research, and conversation to deepen your understanding of any cultural group (including your own!).

Indigenous Peoples of the United States

There are hundreds of indigenous nations within North America, and there are as many languages, belief systems, and traditions among indigenous peoples. Awareness and sensitivity to diversity among indigenous peoples prevents broad generalizations about this group; however, this section will briefly review some basic shared history and some themes common among the various nations.

The history of the relationship between the Euro-American government of the U.S. and the indigenous peoples is characterized by "internal colonization" practices, whereby native populations were and are treated as if they were foreigners in their own homeland.[23] Historically, the U.S. government pursued a policy of obliteration of indigenous peoples, initially through death and later through forced assimilation into Euro-American culture. **Assimilation** is the practice of coercively absorbing a minority group into the dominant group and causing the group to lose important elements of its identity.

Beginning in the late 1700s and early 1800s, the U.S. coerced or physically forced large numbers of indigenous peoples off their ancestral lands and onto reservations. The U.S. attempted to undermine virtually all traditional cultural practices from spiritual rituals to sophisticated systems of tribal governance to ancient languages under the guise of "civilizing" American Indians. Mismanagement and deception have also been hallmarks of U.S. dealings with American Indians. The Bureau of Indian Affairs (BIA), founded in 1824 and charged with managing the 55.7 million acres of land reserved in treaties and held in trust by the U.S. government and providing education for Native American youth through tribal schools, has been a source of much contention and controversy to this day.

During its first two centuries, the U.S. government's policy regarding the education of Indians was intended to "educate" the Indian out of them.[24] Indian boarding schools were founded to assimilate Indian children into Euro-American society. Children were removed from their families, denied access to their heritage and culture, forbidden to speak their own languages, and intentionally humiliated for their "Indianness." This policy was officially

---

Empowerment in Action

White Bison and the Wellbriety Movement

Over the past several decades, substance abuse has been an issue of major concern among Native American communities. According to the U.S. Substance Abuse and Mental Health Services Administration, Native American and Alaskan Natives had among the highest rates of alcohol and drug use and the highest rate of tobacco use in 2008.[27] Native peoples also suffer a much higher alcoholism mortality rate than the U.S. general population.[28] Concern about the tremendous toll of substance abuse on Native American communities, particularly among youth, and the lack of culturally competent substance abuse treatment and prevention programs has inspired native communities to organize unique recovery and prevention initiatives. Among them is White Bison, and nonprofit organization located in Colorado Springs, Colorado, and the Wellbriety Movement it started in the 1990s. Founded in 1988 by Don Coyhis, a member of the Mohican Nation, White Bison's mission is to "bring 100 Native American communities into healing by 2010" through addiction prevention, recovery support, and education.[29] According to White Bison, "wellbriety" means "to be both sober and well. It means to have come through recovery from chemical dependency and to be a recovered person who is going beyond survival to thriving in his or her life and in the life of the community. The Well part of Wellbriety means to live the healthy parts of the principles, laws and values of traditional culture. It means to heal from dysfunctional behaviors other than chemical dependency, as well as chemical dependency itself. This includes codependency, ACOA behavior, domestic or family violence, gambling, and other shortcomings of character."[30] The Wellbriety Movement emphasizes the importance of returning to traditional indigenous cultural values in the recovery process, and has created an adapted version the 12-step model of Alcoholics Anonymous for native communities called the Medicine Wheel 12-Steps.[31] In 2009, Coyhis was awarded a Purpose Prize by the California think tank Civic Ventures for his successful and innovative efforts.[32]

ended in 1975 with the Indian Self-Determination and Educational Assistance Act.

Alcoholism and substance abuse, youth suicide, domestic violence, and child abuse are experienced at disproportionately high rates among American Indian peoples.[25] There is a direct connection between these problem areas and the cycle of "colonially induced despair" caused by oppressive U.S. policies.[26] There has been progress toward reversing oppressive U.S. policy since the mid-1970s. For example, the Indian Child Welfare Act of 1978 officially ended the practice of removing indigenous children from their families and placing them in boarding schools as well as the practice of placing Indian children in non-Indian homes due to both legitimate and illegitimate child welfare concerns. The law now grants tribal courts the ability to claim jurisdiction over the child welfare proceedings of their members and requires that children be placed with extended family, other tribal members, or other American Indian families.

African Americans

Over the approximately 300 years of the active slave trade, approximately 650,000 African men, women, and children were brought by force to the U.S. as slaves. The institution of slavery had, at its core, the total dehumanization of its victims. Africans who were enslaved brought their own rich cultural traditions, spiritual beliefs, and family patterns with them to the U.S. African slaves were officially forbidden to practice these traditions; however, many continued to do so in secret while also integrating European and Euro-American cultural practices by necessity. African slaves were denied all human and civil rights: They couldn't marry, didn't have custody over their own children, were forced to labor without limits on time or difficulty, and couldn't be taught to read or write. Physical and sexual abuse by slave owners was commonplace—and indeed a primary tool for maintaining submission. The practice of slavery was officially ended with the conclusion of the Civil War in 1865. The legacy of slavery, however, remains profoundly powerful in shaping race relations and the lives of African Americans to this day. Following the Civil War, "Jim Crow" laws were established in Southern and border states. These laws maintained the system of white supremacy and oppression from 1865 until the civil rights movement of the 1960s. Jim Crow laws mandated "separate but equal"—that is, segregated—treatment for African Americans in all arenas of life, and "equal" nearly always translated into inferior. In the Jim Crow South, nearly every element of African Americans' personal and public lives was circumscribed: schools, universities, churches, public transportation, even public restrooms, were segregated. In the north, de facto segregation occurred due to racial discrimination in housing, education, and employment, and had much the same impact, though it was not enforced by law.

A major turning point for civil rights for African Americans was the 1954 U.S. Supreme Court decision in *Brown v. Board of Education*, which ruled racial segregation in public schools unconstitutional. The civil rights movement of the late 1950s and 1960s brought an end to Jim Crow and pressed for civil rights protections in housing, voting, employment, public transportation, and other areas. Dr. Martin Luther King, Jr. is, of course, the best-known civil rights leader and had a profound impact on the success of the movement, forever changing the course of race relations and social justice in the U.S. Thousands of African American activists, however, sacrificed their safety and even their lives to the movement for civil rights.

Social Work and Social Justice: Diversity, Difference, and Oppression

According to the U.S. Census, about 12.2 % of the U.S. population identifies as black or African American.[33] Despite the many gains in equality made possible by the civil rights movement, major inequities continue to exist. African Americans have higher levels of unemployment, poverty, and incarceration than Euro-Americans. They also experience higher rates of AIDS and chronic diseases such as diabetes and heart disease. African American youth are more likely to die by homicide than white youth.[34] And African Americans' lifespan is 5–7 years shorter than that of Euro-Americans.[35] There has long been a significant gap in education between African Americans and Euro-Americans. While this gap has decreased over the past several decades, it remains large. Racism and oppression are key factors in the creation and maintenance of these disparities in health, education, employment, and incarceration.

Significant diversity exists within the African American community. Although the majority of those identified as "black" in the U.S. Census are descendants of African slaves, recent increases in Caribbean and African immigration have added to the diversity of the population.

Latino/as

Latinos (i.e., individuals of Mexican, Central American, South American, Spanish-speaking Caribbean, or Spanish descent) are currently the largest minority group In the U.S., accounting for 12.5% of the population.[36] The number of Latinos in the U.S. has grown rapidly over the past decade. In several states, including California, New Mexico, and Texas, Latinos account for over a third of the population (see Figure 5.2). The Latino population in the U.S. is diverse.

Critical Thinking Question
Psychologist David Wing Sue notes that class differences can result in an added level of "bicultural stress" for middle- and upper-class African Americans. What do you think "bicultural stress" could involve?

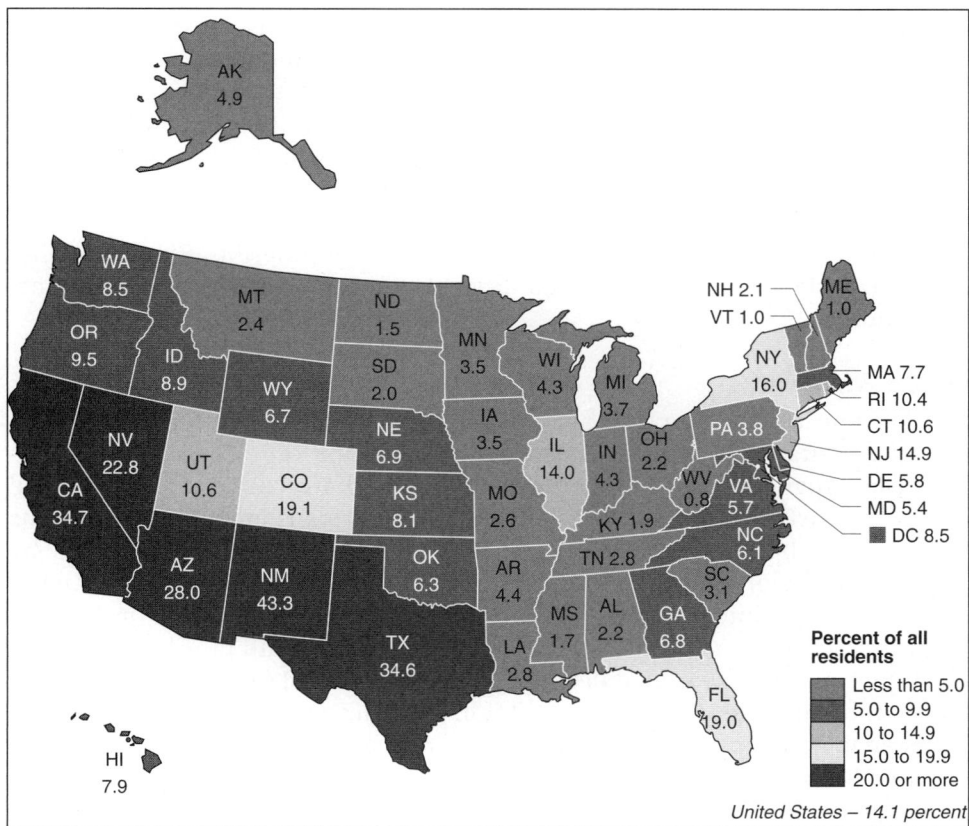

Figure 5.2
Percent Latino in the U.S. Population, 2004
Source: U.S. Census Bueau, Population Estimates Program, July 1, 2004

It includes families that have lived within the current U.S. borders for centuries, and those that have just arrived. It includes those with little education or employment opportunity and those who have obtained the highest levels of educational and professional prestige. It also represents a wide range of nationalities; the majority of the U.S. Latino population is of Mexican origin (59.3%), followed by Puerto Rican (9.7%), Central American (5.1%), and South American (4.0%).[37] Although linguistically similar (about 75% of U.S. Latinos speak Spanish at home[38]), many Latinos trace their roots to European and indigenous ancestors. Moreover, due to the active slave trade in the Spanish-speaking Caribbean (including Cuba, Puerto Rico, and the Dominican Republic) and parts of South America until the late 1880s, many Latinos of Caribbean and South American origin are of mixed European, indigenous, and African descent.

Immigration is a major cause of stress for Latinos, even those who have lived in the U.S. for many years. As with any immigrating group, the resources that a family or group has had access to in their country of origin—education, income, professional experience—has a significant impact on their economic and professional success in the U.S., and acculturation pressures and racism face many Latinos regardless of origin. Recent immigrants, especially undocumented immigrants, face frequent hostility and exploitation in their new country. Racism and anti-immigrant sentiment have led to increased depression and suicide rates among Latinos.[39] Moreover, undocumented immigrants, because of their "illegal" status, are particularly vulnerable to violence and exploitation, and have added barriers to accessing any form of publicly funded assistance—from legal services to physical and mental health care to domestic violence protection.

Given the reality of discrimination and oppression, it is not surprising that, as a group, Latinos experience higher rates of poverty and unemployment, and lower household incomes and educational attainment, than the overall population.[40] Moreover, Latinos tend to be overrepresented in lower-paying economic sectors, including service, construction, transportation, and sales. Latinas, especially, are overrepresented in the service industry.[41] Latinos also suffer from higher rates of disease (including tuberculosis, obesity, and AIDS), and are less likely to have health insurance than the general population. Finally, Latino youth experience higher rates of adolescent pregnancy, adolescent parenting, and suicide.

Asian Americans

Asian Americans in the U.S. are a highly heterogeneous group, with over a dozen cultural, national, and/or linguistic groups represented, including Chinese, Japanese, Korean, Vietnamese, Cambodian, Laotian, Filipino, and Thai. The distribution of Asians and Asian Americans among these various groups has changed significantly throughout U.S. history, influenced by national and global political and economic forces. The first major wave of Asian immigration occurred in the mid-1800s, when Chinese men were recruited, often by coercion and without their wives and children, to build the transcontinental railroad between the East and West Coasts. U.S. immigration policy towards Asia remained highly restrictive until 1965, when Congress enacted changes to the Immigration and Nationality Act that repealed prior restrictions and began to emphasize family reunification and U.S. skilled labor needs. Discrimination in housing, employment, and education, as well as the need and desire to maintain cultural ties to their country of origin, spurred the formation of Asian enclaves in large U.S. cities. The United

States's xenophobic policy toward Asians and Asian Americans reached its pinnacle during World War II, while the U.S. and Japan were at war. Beginning in 1941, Japanese Americans were forced to leave their homes and businesses and move into internment camps. In many cases, Euro-American families took over these families' now deserted farms and other prosperous agricultural businesses.[42] The U.S. did not formally apologize to Japanese Americans affected by its internment policy for over 40 years. In 1988, President Reagan issued a formal apology and offered up to $20,000—a fraction of what was typically lost—to camp survivors.[43]

After 1965, U.S. policy regarding Asian immigration loosened considerably, and that change, combined with a number of serious regional conflicts, including the Vietnam War in the 1960s and early 1970s, spurred a significant rise in Asian immigration, especially from Southeast Asia. Over 1.5 million Southeast Asian refugees have entered the U.S. since 1975.[44] Currently, a majority of Asian-descended people residing in the U.S. were born in Asia.

Asian Americans are sometimes described as "the model minority" due to the generally high rates of education, employment, and entrepreneurship, and low rates of crime, teen pregnancy, and poverty among Asian American communities. Although many Asian Americans and Asian immigrants to the U.S. experience success on a number of fronts, this so-called "positive" stereotype is problematic in many ways. It is frequently used in divisive attempts to compare Asian Americans with other U.S. minority groups and, as such, it clearly seeks to pit different ethnic and racial groups against one another, blame certain groups for their struggles, and undermine the value of diversity in our society. Furthermore, it erases diversity within the Asian American population. For example, poverty rates are much higher among Southeast Asian refugee communities than among many other Asian American groups due to a number of sociopolitical factors. Refugees from areas such as Cambodia and Laos fled brutal dictatorial regimes, often with few resources. In many cases, their U.S. experience has been quite different from those who have come to the U.S. by choice and with education, financial resources, and career skills. As social workers, it is crucial that we look past such stereotypes and not dismiss the suffering, or strength, of any segment of the population.

Gay, Lesbian, Bisexual, and Transgendered Persons

GLBTQ is an acronym for Gay, Lesbian, Bisexual, Transgender, and Queer/Questioning, commonly used to refer to individuals who consider themselves as having a homosexual or bisexual orientation, transgender gender identity, or an undefined sexual orientation and gender identity. The U.S. Census does not collect data on sexual orientation, so it is impossible to know the number of GLBTQ people living in the U.S. Estimates suggest that anywhere from about 4% to about 20% of the total population are GLBTQ, depending on how homosexuality is defined (i.e., by behavior only, by attraction only, or both).[45] For much of the past two centuries, homosexuality and "gender nonconformity" were regarded by the health and mental health professions as diseases or mental disorders that could be cured. This stance changed dramatically in the 1970s. The American Psychiatric Association voted to remove homosexuality from the *Diagnostic and Statistical Manual of Mental Disorders* (DSM) in 1973. In 1975, the American Psychological Association decided that homosexuality was not a mental disorder, followed by the National Association of Social Workers (NASW) in 1977. Homosexuality is now accepted by all major medical, educational, and psychological professional organizations as a normal expression of sexual orientation. Our contemporary understanding of homosexuality is recent; the concept of sexual identity, in general, has not been around long. Before the late 1880s, sexual orientation was not even conceived of as homosexual, bisexual, or heterosexual. In fact, the 1901 edition of the *Oxford English Dictionary* did not even include an entry for the word "homosexual."[46]

Changes in U.S. social policy toward GLBTQ people have been brought about by the work of GLBTQ individuals and allies active in the gay rights movement since the late 1960s. The Stonewall Riot of June 28, 1969, in New York City is generally recognized as the official start of the Gay Liberation movement. The riots at the Stonewall Inn, a popular gay and transgender club in Greenwich Village, were sparked by a violent police raid on the club that took place early in the morning on June 28. The protests lasted for several days, and the energy and connections generated by these events led to the creation of a number of gay rights organizations pivotal to the gay rights movement. Previously, GLBTQ people were not protected in any way from discrimination in housing, employment, education, or service access. They were not protected from anti-gay violence or hate crimes. Most kept their sexual identity and same-sex relationships secret from friends, family, and coworkers. Both the legal and cultural climate for GLBTQ people have shifted substantially over the past 30 years. Currently, 25 states have some form of antidiscrimination laws to protect at least some GLBTQ people from discrimination in employment, housing, and/or public accommodations, although there are wide variations among these laws regarding the extent of the protections and who exactly is protected (i.e., gay and lesbian vs. all GLBTQ people).[47] Thirty-one states have laws that address hate or bias crimes based on sexual orientation; ten of those states also have laws that address hate or bias crimes based on gender identity.[48]

Relationship recognition and parenting are among the areas in which GLBTQ individuals and families continue to face substantial discrimination. In the 1990s, significant positive changes in the GLBTQ rights on the state and federal levels concerned many conservative lawmakers. In 1996, the U.S. Congress enacted, and President Bill Clinton signed, the so-called Defense of Marriage Act (DOMA), restricting the federal definition of marriage to a union between one man and one woman. While the statistics are changing rapidly, at the time of this writing, 37 states had passed their own DOMAs and two additional states had strong language defining marriage as a man–woman union. Thirty states have amended their state constitutions to reflect this limitation.[49] Also at the time of this writing, only five states—Connecticut, Iowa, Massachusetts, New Hampshire, and Vermont—have passed laws to recognize same-sex marriage. One state, New Jersey, recognizes "civil unions" between same-sex couples; these grant the same benefits as marriage but are not defined legally as marriage.[50]

GLBTQ people still face significant discrimination, especially outside of major metropolitan areas. As the above statistics illustrate, discrimination at the state and federal levels in regard to the right to marry and receive the benefits associated with marriage has increased, rather than decreased, over the past decade. The NASW has advocated for the right of GLBTQ people to marry legally. In 2004, the NASW issued a position statement on the issue, noting:

> The NASW encourages the adoption of laws that recognize inheritance, insurance, same-sex marriage, child custody, property, and other rights in lesbian, gay, bisexual, and transgender relationships. The Association firmly believes that all federal protections and responsibilities available to legally married people in the United States should be available to

people who enter same sex unions (including domestic partnerships, civil unions, and same sex marriages). NASW encourages the adoption of laws that recognize inheritance, insurance, same-sex marriage, child custody, property, and other rights in lesbian, gay, bisexual, and transgender relationships.[51]

Furthermore, acts of discrimination, from the brutal hate-motivated murder of Wyoming college student Matthew Shepard to limiting sexuality education in hundreds of public schools to heterosexuality-exclusive curricula, take place across the country every day.

Because so little data is collected nationally on GLBTQ people, statistics regarding education, employment, and income are scarce. Data regarding the health and mental health of GLBTQ people is more available, although notably only 1% of all health research funding goes to study their health.[52] Given the negative social messages regarding GLBTQ individuals and relationships, and given that nearly all GLBTQ people grow up as minorities, not only in their larger communities, but even within their own families, we might expect GLBTQ people to suffer from higher rates of mental health and physical health issues. Although this is in some ways accurate, it is not true across the board. GLBTQ adults and adolescents have higher rates of substance abuse than the general population.[53] Lesbians, however, are reported by some studies to suffer from lower rates of both depression and eating disorders than heterosexual women.[54] Men who engage in homosexual behavior, regardless of how they identify their sexual orientation, are at higher risk for suicide, especially during their late adolescent and young adult years.[55] Overall, GLBTQ people have relatively high utilization rates for mental health services; however, lack of access to health and mental health care of all kinds remains a significant issue in GLBTQ communities.

Critical Thinking Question

Despite much progress in attitudes towards GLBTQ people, anti-GLBTQ bias continues to be commonplace across social settings. What role, if any, do social workers have in fighting and preventing this bias?

Individuals with Disabilities

Over 72 million U.S. families (nearly 30%) have at least one member with a disability, and in 18% of households the head of household is living with a disability.[56] An individual is considered to have a disability, according to the Americans with Disabilities Act, if he or she has "a physical or mental impairment which limits major life activities."[57] Life activities include "caring for oneself, performing manual tasks, walking, seeing, hearing, speaking, breathing, learning, and working."[58] The two major types of disabilities are physical disabilities and mental disabilities. Physical disabilities "affect the body's participation with its environment," and include chronic diseases, physiological disorders, sensory disabilities (for example, blindness and deafness), and limb losses.[59] Mental disabilities "affect psychological, emotional, or developmental experiences" and include mental illness, cognitive limitations, learning disabilities, and developmental disorders such as autism.[60]

Individuals living with disabilities are more likely to be poor than individuals without disabilities. About 12.8% of U.S. families with at least one disabled member live in poverty, compared with

Did You Know?

A Note on "Queer"

The word "queer" has long been used as a pejorative for GLBTQ folks. However, activists and scholars involved in the "queer" movement have sought to reclaim this word from its pejorative use and turn it into an empowering and inclusive way to reference the GLBTQ community and others who consider themselves as outside of strict heterosexual social norms. There continues to be controversy about the use of the word, given the pain associated with its pejorative use, but GLBTQ youth are increasingly finding it a useful way to claim their "non-heterosexual" identity without limiting their sexual orientation to strictly homosexual or bisexual. It is important for social workers to be aware the new use of "queer," as it allows us to understand how our clients define their own identity; however, it is also important to be alert to the context of its use, given its continued popularity as a pejorative, hateful putdown.

9.2% of all families.[61] Families with at least one disabled member have lower median incomes than those without a member with a disability. As expected, families where the primary worker—the head of household—has a disability are the most likely to be impoverished.[62] Families raising children with a disability also tend to have lower incomes,[63] and families of color with children with disabilities experience among the highest poverty rates. For example, 42% of African American families headed by a single female parent with at least one child with a disability live below the poverty line.[64]

Historically, individuals with disabilities have been treated as "deserving poor" by the public sector and were offered "indoor relief" as early as the Elizabethan Poor Laws of 1601. This does not mean, however, that individuals with disabilities have experienced a history of respect from public institutions or from society at large. In the U.S., individuals with disabilities were typically cared for by their families, as they are today; however, if a family was unable to provide care, individuals with disabilities were often "cared for" in public institutions, where they were housed with everyone from criminals to the elderly. Such institutionalization continued until the 1960s. Institutionalization went through major reforms beginning in the early 1800s, however. In the mid-1800s the pioneering reformer Dorothea Dix crusaded against the horrific conditions of what were then called "asylums," which housed individuals with mental illness, and helped create hospitals specifically for the care and treatment of individuals with mental disabilities. Specialized educational institutions also began to appear starting in the 19th century. Gallaudet, the first school for deaf students, was founded in 1817. The first residential school for children with cognitive limitations was founded in 1948 in Massachusetts. The Social Security Act of 1935, enacted as part of Franklin Roosevelt's New Deal, set aside public funds for rehabilitation and assistance to individuals with disabilities. The Americans with Disabilities Act of 1990 (ADA) granted "class" status to individuals with disabilities—that is, it recognized "the disabled" as a unique group—and added them to the existing classes (racial minorities, women, etc.) protected from discrimination in housing, employment, and public access. The disability rights movement, which became active as a grassroots movement in the early 1970s, has pointed out that the U.S. has a history of progressive improvement in its policies regarding individuals with disabilities but does not have a strong history of including individuals with disabilities in the process of creating policies.[65]

ORGANIZING PRINCIPLES OF DIVERSITY AND DIFFERENCE IN SOCIETY

We now know some of the basics related to human diversity in the U.S., but the phenomenon is complicated and multifaceted. To gain a better sense of how difference and diversity operate in society and in our individual lives, let's turn to some of the organizing principles of social diversity and difference.

Social Groups

In the preceding sections we discussed the major social groups in the U.S. It was likely no surprise that the groups we included were described as "social groups," but just what are social groups, really? Young defines a social group as "a collective of persons differentiated from at least one other group by cultural forms, practices, or way of life."⁶⁶ Group members tend to associate more with each other than with members of other groups because of their shared history and experiences. Social groups only understand themselves as such when they are faced with other groups that differ from them in some way. According to Young, "group identification arises . . . in the encounter and interaction between social collectivities that experience some difference in their way of life and forms of association, even if the also regard themselves as belonging to the same society."⁶⁷

It is important to understand how social groups come to identify themselves, and be identified by others, because the existence of different social groups is the foundation of a diverse society. Social groups are also the way in which we experience difference and, often, prejudice, discrimination, and oppression. In other words, our identification as part of a group—either a group that is privileged or dominant, or a group that is marginalized or subordinate—determines if, when, and how we experience oppression.

Inequality: Discrimination and Prejudice

Prejudice and discrimination are two interrelated systems by which inequality and power differences are maintained between individuals and groups. **Prejudice** is the prejudgment (usually negative) of an individual or group without sufficient information to support the judgment. Usually prejudice is related to a belief that another individual or group is inherently inferior to oneself or one's social group. Individuals, and even societies, are frequently unconscious of their prejudices, yet even unconscious prejudices profoundly affect behavior. **Discrimination**, usually derived from prejudice, is the practice of treating individuals and groups differently. There are countless examples of individual discrimination in everyday life: A white woman gets up from her seat on the subway when an Arab man sits next to her; a doctor talks to the sign language interpreter rather than to his deaf patient. When major social institutions—schools, churches, and courts—reinforce prejudice and discrimination, this is called "institutional discrimination." The current federal law that limits marriage to a man and a woman is an example of institutional discrimination. Often policies like these are not consciously intended to be discriminatory, and yet they have a discriminatory effect when put in to practice.

Inequality: Domination and Subordination

Jean Baker Miller, a pioneering feminist psychologist, wrote that "in most instances of difference there is also a factor of inequality."⁶⁸ Miller suggested that this inequality exists at many levels, but "fundamentally [in] status and power."⁶⁹ How does inequality play out in individual and social relationships? Miller posited that two interconnected phenomena affect the relationships among different parties: domination and subordination. Miller described some key characteristics of dominant groups, including how they interact with subordinate groups:

- A dominant group usually "impede[s] the development of subordinates and block[s] their freedom of expression and action." This process may occur overtly or covertly.
- A dominant group has the "greatest influence in determining a culture's overall outlook," including everything from art to science to popular culture.

- Through this power and control over culture, the dominant group's values, traditions, ways of behaving, and so on become the norm for a given society.
- Because of its influence in all aspects of life, the existence of inequality between the dominant and subordinates groups is obscured.[70]

Dominant groups have an unequal share of power, status, access, and other societal resources. Power allows the dominant group to obscure the existence of this inequality: It's "normal" or "just the way things are." We need only to look at the majority of individuals in positions of power in the major sectors of our society, including government, business, and media/entertainment, to see who constitutes the dominant group in American society: white, heterosexual, Christian, able-bodied males. While this has shifted significantly over the past 30 years—and continues to do so due in large part to the hard work of social movements and the recognition by many that the current state of inequality is unacceptable—the vast majority of power in our society remains in the hands of this social group.

Miller (1986) also examined the experience of subordinates. She noticed that subordinates are required by necessity to know much more about the dominants than the dominants know about them, and often even more than they know about themselves.[71]

Clearly, inequality does significant damage to groups and individuals in the subordinate position, but what about those in the dominant position? Are they immune from suffering because of their power? Many experts argue that dominants and subordinates both suffer from isolation, although for different reasons. Dominants are denied the richer understanding of themselves and of the broader human experience because their position of power isolates them from connecting with and learning from subordinate groups.

Power tends to corrupt and absolute power corrupts absolutely.
—Lord Acton

Identity

Identity is a fundamental part of our collective and individual "humanness." It is the answer to the basic question, "Who am I?" **Identity** refers an individual's and/or a group's unique sense of self and similarity and/or difference in comparison to others. Identity exists on three basic levels: universal, group, and individual.[72] The "universal level" includes the things all humans share as members of the same species, such as our basic biological and physical make-up, general self-awareness or consciousness, and the ability to use symbols. The "group level" includes our identification with various social groups, including gender, age, ethnicity, religion, and culture. Many elements at this level can and

---

Demonstrating Knowledge, Values, and Skills

Noted psychologist, author, professor, and president of Spellman College in Atlanta, Georgia, Beverly Daniel Tatum, developed the following exercise called "Who Am I?" for use with university undergraduate students learning about racial identity:

Complete the following sentence: "I am _____." Write down as many descriptors as you can think of in one minute. What do you notice about what you wrote down and what you didn't write down? Looking at Figure 5.3, how many descriptors fit into the "individual" level of identity? How many in the "group" level? The "universal" level?

Adapted from Beverly Daniel Tatum, *"Why Are All the Black Kids Sitting Together in the Cafeteria?" and Other Conversations about Race* (New York: Basic Books, 1997).

do change over time and circumstance. For example, your identity as a child has changed as you have aged. Finally, the "individual level" includes elements that are unique to an individual, such as particular genetic makeup and unique life experiences. Figure 5.3 illustrates this three-part concept of human identity.

If you completed the preceding practice exercise, you probably came up with several individual-level answers. You might have described yourself as "smart," "outgoing," "tall," or "afraid of snakes." You may have noticed that many, or few, of your answers to the question "Who am I?" were group-level characteristics. Tatum describes her experience using this exercise with students in her classes:

> . . . over the years I have noticed something . . . students of color usually mention their racial or ethnic group: for instance I am Black, Puerto Rican, and Korean American. White students who have grown up in strong ethnic enclaves occasionally mention being Irish or Italian. But in general, White students rarely mention being White. . . . I notice a similar pattern in terms of gender, religion and sexuality. Women usually mention being female, whereas men don't usually mention their maleness. Jewish students often say they are Jews, while mainline Protestants rarely mention their religious identification. A student who is comfortable revealing it publicly may mention being gay, lesbian, or bisexual. Though I know most of my students are heterosexual, it is very unusual for anyone to include their heterosexuality on their list.[73]

Tatum's experience makes it clear that membership in a dominant social group (e.g., men, whites, heterosexuals) makes this part of our identity invisible to us and to those around us who are also part of this group. This makes sense when we remember the idea that identity as a social group starts with the recognition of difference. As Tatum notes, "the parts of our identity that do capture our attention are those that other people notice, and reflect back to us. The aspect of identity that is the target of others' attention, and subsequently of our own, often is that which sets us apart as exceptional or 'other' in their eyes."[74] At a social group level, this phenomenon means that socially dominant groups

Critical Thinking Question

Our cultural and social group identities can give us valuable perspective in some areas but may cause blind spots in others. How can we better recognize and work with our own cultural and social blind spots?

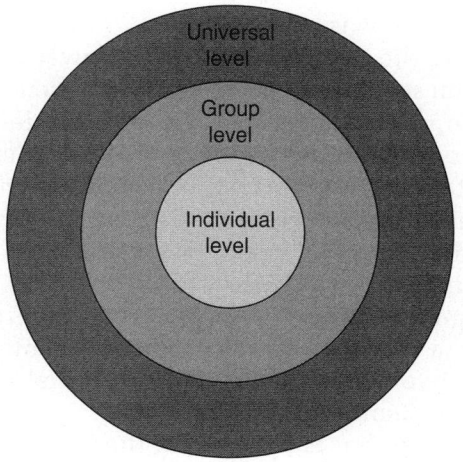

Figure 5.3
Levels of identity
Source: David Wing Sue, Multicultural Social Work Practice (Hoboken, NJ: John Wiley & Sons, 2006) p.17

are rarely forced to recognize their difference because the greater culture, of which members of their group are in control, reflects themselves back to them, and thus makes them unremarkable.

Every level of identity is relevant to the human experience, and every level is relevant to social work practic. The group level of identity, however, is particularly salient to a discussion of human diversity, oppression, and social justice. It is at this level where we may develop blind spots—incorrect assumptions about the ways individuals and groups different from ourselves experience the world. As social workers, these blind spots impede our ability to effectively and empathetically assist and empower our clients.

Oppression, Power, and Privilege

This section describes some of the ways in which difference is lived in our society. The role of social groups, domination and subordination, and identity are all important ways that we understand ourselves and others in context. As noted earlier, one of the ways difference is lived in our society is through inequality mediated by domination and subordination. Oppression is the system by which domination and subordination (i.e., differences in power) are maintained and reinforced and by which nondominant groups are denied access to power (e.g., economic, educational, legal, etc.).

It is impossible to discuss oppression without also examining the concept of **power**. The two are instrumental to one another's existence. At its core, to be oppressed is to be without the power to effect change. Power is what enables individuals to advance themselves and to control or exploit others.[75] In her 1984 work, *Feminist Theory: From Margin to Center*, bell hooks argued that in the U.S., power is most accessible to the dominant social groups. hooks imagined social power like a bull's eye, with those with the most social power in the center and those with less power located further away. She argued that nondominant groups are marginalized; that is, they are outside the circle of power. Moreover, hooks argued that marginality builds upon itself: The greater the number of memberships in marginalized groups, the further away from the center of power one is.

Appreciating the dynamics of social power is critically important for social workers on several levels. As has been discussed, socially subordinate, marginal, and oppressed status—location outside the power sphere in our society—renders individuals and groups more vulnerable to social problems, from violence to illness to poverty. It is also important for social workers to understand that there is more than one type of power. Although dominating power (i.e., "power over") is oppressive and exploitative of others, power itself is not inherently so. Miller refers to power as "the power to implement."[76] This understanding of power is closely linked to the concept self-determination, a core social work value. Part of our professional role as social workers involves empowering clients—helping them to access power to create positive change.

For every group that is oppressed, there is a corresponding privileged group. **Privilege** is the set of unearned advantages that are associated with being in a powerful or dominant social group, or, put another way, the advantages that come with being socially recognized as "normal." Privilege is the subtle, usually unrecognized ways that certain groups get certain social benefits (e.g., a sense of personal safety, seeing people who look like them in popular media, knowing that the clothes they can afford to buy will not be considered "unprofessional" and keep them from getting a job). As discussed in the preceding section on identity, when we belong to a dominant social group, we often are unaware of how doing so affects our lives. For example, if you are heterosexual, how often do you think about the fact that you are heterosexual? Do you think about it before you hold your significant other's hand when walking across campus? Do you think about it when you take your significant other to a large family function? Do you think about it when you are watching a romantic comedy in which all the characters are heterosexual? The answer to these questions is probably "no." If you are gay, lesbian, bisexual, or transgender, however, your answers to at least some of these questions will more likely be "yes." GLBTQ individuals in the U.S. are often in the position of needing to do some extra "work" that heterosexuals need not do. This extra work might involve assessing a public place and the people in it for safety, steeling oneself for disapproving looks or comments from family members, or spending a half an hour looking for a DVD with a positive GLBTQ relationship as the focus of the plot. Not needing to do this extra work is part of heterosexual privilege. Heterosexuals didn't do anything to "earn" their privilege; they are just being who they are.

Most people are privileged in one way or another. If you can walk up the stairs to your classroom without looking for a ramp or an elevator, you are experiencing the privilege of being "able-bodied." But we rarely recognize the privilege we experience. We are much more likely to recognize the privilege we do not experience—in other words, the ways we may be discriminated against or oppressed. When we don't recognize our privilege, we are less likely to feel motivated to do anything about the injustices it might produce. If you are not somebody who needs to use a wheelchair to get around, ask yourself when was the last time you thought about how hard or easy your classroom was to access for individuals in a wheelchair, let alone felt compelled to start a campus-wide campaign to improve wheelchair access? As social workers, part of our professional mission is to promote justice in our society. To do this in an effective and meaningful way, we must become aware of the ways we unconsciously experience social privilege in our lives, and the ways that our clients may or may not share in our privilege. Without awareness of our own privilege, we are almost certain to remain blind to the more subtle (yet equally damaging) ways that oppression affects our clients socially and psychologically, to miss opportunities to reduce the presence of injustice, and even to unconsciously perpetrate injustice against our clients. Furthermore, social workers experience a level of privilege associated with their professional role that many of our clients do not share. This power both enables us and obliges us to be agents of positive social change.

THE LIVED EXPERIENCE OF OPPRESSION: "THE ISMS"

Many of the concepts discussed so far may seem too abstract, complex, and challenging to relate to our own lives. However, if you've ever experienced it, oppression is anything but an abstract concept. The psychological and social costs of oppression are enormous for those who experience it. Statistics collected about all areas of daily life, from health to employment to education to political participation, demonstrate that this is true. Individuals from oppressed social groups are more likely to experience everything from mental and physical illness to homelessness to natural disasters. But we don't need statistics to illuminate this reality. All we have to do is take a walk to our local soup kitchen, community health clinic, or domestic violence shelter. In these settings and all the other settings in which social workers practice, the realities and costs of oppression are inescapable.

Racism

The traditional definition of **racism** is prejudice and discrimination based on race. We usually think of individuals who hold racist views as people who consciously believe that others of a different race are inferior (in intelligence, moral character, etc.) to them. We usually think of racist acts as blatant acts of discrimination, such as not promoting an Asian American to a better position because of her race, or refusing to rent an apartment to an African American family because of their race. Certainly, these are accurately understood as racial discrimination, but they provide an incomplete definition of racism. Just as oppression encompasses the concepts not only of conscious discrimination, but also of conscious and unconscious domination, subordination, and privilege, racism is a complex and pervasive social phenomenon. Tatum defines racism as "a system of advantage based on race" that privileges one race, whites, above other races.[77] Her definition is particularly powerful, and challenging, because it draws attention to prejudice and discrimination against people of color, clearly key factors in racism, and also to the systematic benefits racism bestows on the dominant racial group. Are there really benefits of racism? No form of oppression comes without benefits to the dominant group. During the period of U.S. history when slavery was legal, one benefit among many was the availability of free labor to drive the U.S. economy. Now we might think of the benefits of racism as more seats available for whites in the U.S. Congress, or more roles for white actors in mainstream movies. Of course, we rarely think of racism in terms of its benefits, because if we are white, we rarely see "business as usual" as either an effect of racism or as any personal benefit to us, and yet one significant result of racism is the overrepresentation of white people (and thus Euro-American culture, values, etc.) in the powerful institutions of our society.

Ethnocentrism

Ethnocentrism is the belief that one's ethnic group is inherently superior to other groups. Among the most extreme and brutal examples of the costs of an ethnocentric worldview is the Nazis' systematic extermination of Jews in

Eastern Europe during 1930s and early 1940s. Central to the Nazi worldview was the belief in the inherent, "natural" superiority of the Aryan "race" to all others. This belief was the underlying justification for the internment and murder of millions of Jews during the Holocaust. Subtler, and less violent, forms of ethnocentrism operate within American culture in ways most of us are oblivious to, especially if we are part of the dominant social group. One example of subtle, yet pervasive, ethnocentrism is using the Christian calendar as the standard calendar in all major international institutions. The fact that we operate on a Western European, Christian calendar (i.e., we count the year from Jesus's birth) is ethnocentric, given that a significant portion of the U.S. population practices a religion other than Christianity, most with their own ways of documenting and counting the passage of time. Few would argue for a change in our calendar system, and most would argue that the benefits of a universal calendar far outweigh the costs. Is the Western European Christian calendar an inherently superior way of keeping time? Doubtful, yet it is accepted as being so, and the topic of change is hardly up for discussion.

> **Did You Know?**
>
> **Racism Is Hazardous to Health!**
>
> In 2002, the National Institute of Medicine released a major study that found serious disparities between the health and health care of people of color and whites in the U.S. Although the source of disparities involved a number of individual and institutional factors such as lack of access to medical care, a fragmented healthcare delivery system, higher treatment refusal rates, and health insurance coverage differences, the study found that even when participants had the same health insurance coverage, whites were more likely than African Americans to receive the tests and other follow-up care required to treat their conditions appropriately. This proved true across a range of clinical settings (e.g., private versus public hospitals) and, unsurprisingly, was related to higher mortality rates among African Americans. The study attributed at least some of this difference to provider bias, stereotyping, and prejudice.
>
> *Source:* Biran D. Smedley, Adrienne Y. Stith, and Alan R. Nelson (Eds), *Unequal Treatment: Confronting Racial and Ethnic Disparities in Health Care* (Washington, DC: National Academies Press, 2003).

Xenophobia

Xenophobia is a fear of all things foreign, including people who originate from foreign countries. Xenophobia is an underpinning of the anti-immigrant movement, which opposes immigration into the U.S. from other countries, on the basis that immigrants take jobs away from native-born workers, flood publicly funded social services, and pose possible national security threats. The first two of these objections, of course, are based on the incorrect assumption that all immigrants are poor and that all poor people overuse publicly funded programs (see the classism section below). The third objection has gained more currency as an argument against immigration since the events of September 11, 2001, although many also regard this as a dubious argument for restricting immigration as well.

The experience of oppressed people . . . is the experience of being caged in: all avenues . . . are blocked or booby trapped.

—Marilyn Frye

Classism

Classism is usually defined as prejudice and discrimination based on social class. We rarely talk about class or classism in the U.S., largely due the myth that we are a classless society and that the same opportunities are available for everyone. It can be hard to image what class looks like, let alone what classism looks like. When we believe there is no U.S. class system and that everyone has an equal shot at a "middle-class" lifestyle, it leads us to several erroneous assumptions. The first, of course, is that those who do not have a middle-class lifestyle have not worked as hard as those who do. Obviously, this assumption fuels prejudice and contempt for poor and working-class people and high regard for the wealthy. This line of thinking underlies all kinds of social policies regarding poor and working-class people, especially those that limit public support due to concerns that this will only reinforce the deficiencies that lead to their lack of wealth in the first place.

Another way of understanding classism is parallel to Tatum's definition of racism: a system of advantage based on class. Again, this definition draws attention not only to the discriminatory elements of classism, but also to the benefits that middle and upper classes derive from classism. For example, low-paid workers in the service and agricultural industries keep the price of food low, allowing us to spend less on food and more on other things. If agricultural workers, grocery clerks, cashiers, and stockroom workers made, say, $12.00 an hour rather than $6.00, we would all pay a lot more for food. Our diets would probably change; we'd have less money to spend on a gym membership, rent, or college tuition. Therefore, the existence of lower classes enables the existence of upper classes, and class privilege allows the middle and upper classes to remain ignorant of this fact if they choose. Langston remembers an interaction with a college professor when she was attending college in addition to being a mother of two children, including an infant, and working two jobs to keep the family afloat: "I had to work to support my family. The only choice I had was between school or sleep. Sleep had become a privilege. A white middle class feminist instructor told me, quite sympathetically, that I ought to hire someone to clean my house and watch the baby. Her suggestion was totally out of my reality both economically and socially. I'd worked for years cleaning *other* people's houses."[78] This professor, well-intended though she was, made a suggestion that completely ignored the reality of class—both her own and her student's.

Sexism

Sexism is the system of power and privilege based on gender. Hackman writes that:

> . . . these systems of power and control take place at institutional, cultural, and individual levels. Examples of sexism range from degrading jokes, to objectifying females in the media, to job discrimination, to acts of violence against women. Sexism can be directed at a girl or woman individually or, on a larger scale, can encompass cultural views, social attitudes, or institutional practices. . . .[79]

Sexism is also predicated on the idea that women and men innately act, think, feel, and behave in different (even opposite) ways; that things masculine are superior to things feminine; and that females are feminine and males are masculine. This translates into cultural beliefs about who and what are valuable in society. A social system that systematically values masculine over feminine, one in which the positions of power, from major institutions to individual families, are occupied by men, is referred to as "patriarchal." Frey understands sexist oppression like a bird cage.[80] Instances, even at an institutional level, of sexual harassment, domestic violence, or rape; of exploitative media images; of not voting for a female lawmaker because she's "too emotional" (or not emotional enough); or of having low performance expectations or girls in math or science, are the wires of the cage. Viewed individually, it is hard to

> **Demonstrating Knowledge, Values, and Skills**
>
> It's not so unusual today to hear the word "feminism" thrown around like it's something you couldn't say in a G-rated movie, but just what is feminism, anyway? The well-known Christian evangelical preacher Pat Robertson made the famous statement that "feminists encourage women to leave their husbands, kill their children, practice witchcraft, become lesbians, and destroy capitalism." Most people see that definition for the hyperbole it is, yet many people these days are uncomfortable referring to themselves as feminists. For some, the word feminist conjures up images of women criticizing men in broad, sweeping generalizations. For others, it brings forth images of white, middle-class women who have successful careers and rely on lower-class women of color to care for their homes and children. These unfortunate stereotypes of feminists are readily available in popular media and contribute to resistance to the concept of feminism by many young women and men. Feminism, however, is not about "male-bashing" or the advancement of some women on the backs of others. It is not about hating men, trying to be like men, or trying to remove all men's power. Feminism is, according to bell hooks: "a movement to end sexism, sexist exploitation, and oppression. . . ." If you believe that women deserve equal pay for equal work, if you believe that no woman or man should ever be sexually assaulted, if you believe that child care should be more affordable for parents, if you believe that no woman or man should have her or his life choices restricted due to social stereotypes about gender roles . . . guess what? You're probably a feminist.

see how these instances trap women and limit their life possibilities and potential. Can't they just fly around it? Yet, taken together, the ways in which systematic sexism undermines women's power, safety, and freedom become clear.

Homophobia and Heterosexism

Homophobia is the fear and/or hatred of gay, lesbian, and bisexual people. It underlies the belief system that enables and justifies sexual orientation–based discrimination. Like the other "isms," homophobia can (and does) exist on all three levels—individual, institutional, and structural. Hate crimes against GLBTQ people are violent examples of individual homophobia. Institutional homophobia is rarely as violent as individual acts of homophobia can be, yet the impact is devastating. One example of deliberate institutional homophobia is state laws that bar GLBTQ individuals from marrying. In many states, this means that GLBTQ people cannot visit a sick partner in the hospital, make important medical decisions on their partner's behalf, or retain custody of shared children if the biological parent dies, all benefits that heterosexual people are automatically entitled to when they marry. "Internalized homophobia" refers to homophobic beliefs that many GLBTQ people, by virtue of their socialization into a homophobic culture, hold within themselves.

Heterosexism is a closely related concept that refers to the "system by which heterosexuality is assumed to be the only acceptable and viable life option."[81] Examples of institutional heterosexism include neglecting homosexuality as a topic in sexuality education in schools or including "spouse" or "husband/wife" rather than "partner" on client forms in social service agencies. Whether intentionally designed to or not, these heterosexist acts systematically send the message to GLBTQ people that their sexual identity and their romantic relationships do not exist.

> **Demonstrating Knowledge, Values, and Skills**
>
> **Social Justice Starts with You**
>
> Later in this chapter, you will read more about cultural competence in social work practice, but you can begin creating a more just world right now, even if you are not working as a social worker. The Teaching Tolerance program at the Southern Poverty Law Center, a nonprofit organization that works to end racism and promote social justice, suggests these six steps for combating intolerance wherever you encounter it:
>
> *Whatever situation you're in, remember these six steps to help you speak up against everyday bigotry. In any situation, however, assess your safety, both physical and emotional. You must acknowledge your risk as you make your own choice to Speak Up!*
>
> **Be Ready:** You know another moment like this will happen, so prepare yourself for it. Think of yourself as the one who will speak up. Promise yourself not to remain silent.
>
> **Identify the Behavior:** Sometimes, pointing out the behavior candidly helps people hear what they're really saying: "Janice, what I hear you saying is that all Mexicans are lazy" (or whatever the slur happens to be). Or, "Janice, you're classifying an entire ethnic group in a derogatory way. Is that what I hear you saying?"
>
> When identifying behavior, however, avoid labeling, name-calling, or using loaded terms. Describe the behavior; don't label the person.
>
> **Appeal to Principles:** If the speaker is someone you have a relationship with—a sister, friend or co-worker, for example—call on their higher principles: "Bob, I've always thought of you as a fair-minded person, so it shocks me when I hear you say something that sounds so bigoted."
>
> **Set Limits:** You cannot control another person, but you can say, "Don't tell racist jokes in my presence anymore. If you do, I will leave." Or, "My workspace is not a place I allow bigoted remarks to be made. I can't control what you say outside of this space, but here I ask that you respect my wishes." Then follow through.
>
> **Find an Ally/be an Ally:** When frustrated in your own campaign against everyday bigotry, seek out like-minded people and ask them to support you in whatever ways they can.
>
> And don't forget to return the favor: If you aren't the first voice to speak up against everyday bigotry, be the second voice.
>
> **Be Vigilant:** Remember: Change happens slowly. People make small steps, typically, rather than large ones. Stay prepared and keep speaking up. Don't risk silence.
>
> ---
>
> *Adapted from* Teaching Tolerance Project, *Speak Up! A Response to Everyday Bigotry* (Montgomery, AL: Southern Poverty Law Center, 2006), pp. 77–79.

Ableism

Ableism is defined as pervasive and systemic discrimination towards people with disabilities.[82] Like all other forms of descrimination, it can be blatant or subtle, individual, institutional, or structural. Often, having a disability necessitates more assistance from family, friends, medical professionals, the federal government, and other institutions than is considered "ideal" in the dominant American value system. Americans value independence, which fuels prejudice against individuals with disabilities. We prize the individual's ability to take care of him- or herself financially, physically, and emotionally, without recognizing that few—regardless of disability status—truly achieve anything completely alone. An ableism-informed worldview sees individuals with disabilities as people with problems that need to be "fixed" in order to function in society, rather than seeing society as needing to shift in order to accommodate their needs. The 1990 Americans with Disabilities Act was passed in order to address some of most the pervasive forms of institutional discrimination that individuals with

> **Focus on Professionalism and Ethics**
>
> **Value:** *Social Justice*
> **Ethical Principle:** *Social workers challenge social injustice.*
>
> Social workers pursue social change, particularly with and on behalf of vulnerable and oppressed individuals and groups of people. Social workers' social change efforts are focused primarily on issues of poverty, unemployment, discrimination, and other forms of social injustice. These activities seek to promote sensitivity to and knowledge about oppression and cultural and ethnic diversity. Social workers strive to ensure access to needed information, services, and resources; equality of opportunity; and meaningful participation in decision making for all people.[83]

disabilities face in housing, education, and access. Despite improvements that have resulted from the ADA, those without disabilities (both as individuals and as a social group) are rarely aware of their able-bodied privilege.

SOCIAL WORK AND SOCIAL JUSTICE

Promoting social justice and eliminating social injustice are among social work's core values and goals. What is social justice? The concept of **social justice** speaks to the commonly held notion that an ideal society is a just one. However, justice looks different to different individuals, cultures, and societies, based on their political and philosophical ideals. Later in this book, we'll examine the major philosophies of social justice that influence contemporary social work ethics, policy, and practice in greater detail. In general, from the social work perspective, a just society is one in which all individuals have rights and opportunities as well as obligations and responsibilities—a society in which oppression does not exist. As social workers, a core part of our work is to ensure that society moves closer to this state of justice. This is no easy task, so where do we begin? Since its founding in the Settlement House movement of the 19th and early 20th centuries, social work has been a source of creative thinking and practice regarding social justice. The next section offers a beginning look into some promising practices.

Empowering Practices: Social Justice in Action

How do social workers pursue social change? They might advocate for new legislation regarding domestic violence. They might help a low-income neighborhood plan economic development projects. They might help a female client see the connection between media images of women and her personal struggle with an eating disorder. Across nearly every practice setting, social workers are answering the call to practice in a way that promotes social justice.

Practice Focus: Strengths-Based Practice

The strengths-based model is predicated on collaboration with the power that exists within the individual (or community) towards a life that the client defines as better.[84] Proponents of the strengths-based model note that the helping professions, including social work, have traditionally been based on the notion that there is something wrong or abnormal about clients, and our

Social Work Stories: Learning to Work Across Difference

Alexandra, a white female MSW student, writes about her experiences in clinical practice in Boise, Idaho, with Melinda A., a female American Indian university student:

One of the most important lessons I will take away from working with Melinda is the challenge of being a truly culturally competent clinical practitioner. Being culturally aware and engaged is a strong part of my personal values; however, this case challenged me to put my values into practice—to step outside my comfort zone, and to step away from de-contextualized psychodynamic theory. I learned through the course of my work with Melinda that my reliance on traditional theories of psychology and psychotherapy allowed me ignore, or even to pathologize, many of her tremendous strengths. Amazingly, Melinda has continued to seek empowerment in our relationship even when I was too clueless to attend to it.

One assumption I made in working with Melinda was that calling attention to difference in a relationship will promote disconnection rather than connection. When we began therapy, I felt that to call attention to the fact that we were different and that I am unfamiliar with many aspects of her worldview, values and spiritual beliefs would make her feel uncomfortable or not well understood. I also think that my own guilt over my association with the colonial enterprise—my very existence as a white American—caused me to shrink from attending to aspects of difference in our relationship. Connected to this is my assumption that admitting I don't know or understand about a certain aspect or her culture, life experience, etc. communicates that I don't care.

As the year has gone on and I have become more aware and more willing to engage with our differences, rather than try to hide from them, our work has shifted in a positive direction. Early this semester, Melinda attended a conference hosted by a student of color leadership organization about class issues. She brought her questions and struggles and impressions to session the following week. We talked about her experience as a both a student of color and a student from a lower class background on campus. After half an hour, even despite all my trepidation, I couldn't help but ask "given all this, what is it like for you to sit here every week and talk to me—a white person from a different class background—about your life?" What followed were the beginnings of an honest discussion about the challenges of talking to someone "like me": could I really understand what her life has been like? Could I really understand her? We both had to acknowledge that there are times when I couldn't, even despite my best efforts. Since then, Melinda seems to trust me more and she has shared more about her life and struggles in therapy. I have learned that a willingness to engage difference, rather than turn away from it, can be a connecting experience. It can build trust, and I hope, also help foster a sense of empowerment. As I look back on my work with Melinda, I am so thankful for the experience, and feel I have grown in personal and professional confidence and competence from it."

role is to find that thing and fix it.[85] This takes place at both an individual and a cultural level. On an individual level, it means that professionals focus on a client's problems (e.g., they're depressed, unemployed, HIV positive) and ignore the many things that are "right" with them (e.g., they take good care of their children, they love animals, they have survived many obstacles). On the cultural level, this deficit-based model can have dire consequences, especially for nondominant groups. With social privilege comes that acceptance of the dominant groups' characteristics as "normal." Thus in contemporary U.S. culture, the behaviors, thoughts, and values associated being Euro-American, heterosexual, able-bodied, middle class, and male are considered normal. Thus, it is easy to see how in the traditional deficiency-based model, being different from the dominant definition of "normal" becomes the problem that needs to be fixed.

Proponents of the strengths-based approach also note that in a deficit model, "the relationship between the helper and the client is almost always going to be marked by distance, power inequality, control, and manipulation"[86] because the helper is seen as the one who knows what is wrong and how to fix it. Note the connection here between the description of the helper–client relationship and that of the dominant–subordinate relationship in our earlier discussion of inequality. The strengths-based approach incorporates the idea that a client–social worker relationship based on models of domination and subordination is not only unhelpful to the client, it is oppressive and ineffective in fostering client empowerment.

The strengths-based approach is founded on several key tenets:

- uncovering and recognizing client strengths;
- respecting strengths;
- fostering strengths;
- viewing the social worker as collaborator (rather than an expert);
- the concept of "membership"; and
- the importance of community.[87]

The goal of the strengths-based approach is to empower clients (e.g., individuals, groups, communities) to help them gain understanding, voice, and influence over decisions that affect their lives and to discover the power within themselves to make positive change happen. This means the "client is best known as someone who knows something, who has learned something from experience, who has ideas, who has energies of all kinds, and who can do some things quite well."[88] The concept of community is seen as central to the strengths-based approach because individuals do not gain a sense of power and strength in isolation from one another. When people feel isolated, it is hard to see and access inner and outer resources, or even to feel that such a thing is possible. A sense of belonging and membership, however, goes a long way in fostering a sense of hope and possibility. To these ends, the "help" provided by a social worker using the strengths-based approach emphasizes:

- uncovering and supporting inner and outer resources/strengths/contingencies;
- developing a caring helper–client relationship;
- fostering positive expectations and hope; and
- technical operations to promote change.[89]

The strengths-based approach has gained currency among many social workers and social work agencies. Its emphasis on empowerment through building critical consciousness, community relationships, and a sense of strength and hope can guide social workers in their efforts to put the value of social justice into practice.

SUMMARY

Understanding and valuing difference and diversity is a core social work value. In this chapter, we reviewed basic terms that describe social location, including race, class, gender, ethnicity, sexual orientation, and disability status. The U.S. population is quite diverse and has been growing in ethnic, religious, and cultural diversity throughout its history. Social groups that are minorities in the U.S. population, including women, people of color, poor people, people with disabilities, immigrants, religious minorities, and GLBT people, are often marginalized. Each of these groups has a unique history and current strengths and challenges that social workers must understand. Concepts such as social groups, inequality, identity, power, and privilege are among the organizing principles of diversity and difference in our society. Each functions independently and also interacts with the others. Understanding these concepts is a crucial first step in understanding the structure and function of discrimination and oppression. Discrimination and oppression take many forms based on various social locations, including race, religion, gender, sexual orientation, national origin, and disability status. Promoting social justice—that is, reducing and preventing oppression and discrimination, and advancing empowerment and equality in society—are among social workers' core responsibilities. The emergence of the strengths-based approach in social work practice emphasizes consciousness raising, clients' unique strengths and gifts, client empowerment, community relationships, and hope and illustrates the professions ongoing commitment to social justice.

5 CHAPTER REVIEW

Log onto **MySocialWorkLab** to access a wealth of case studies, videos, and assessment. (*If you did not receive an access code to **MySocialWorkLab** with this text and wish to purchase access online, please visit www.mysocialworklab.com.*)

PRACTICE TEST

The following questions will test your knowledge of the content found within this chapter. For additional assessment, including licensing-exam type questions on applying chapter content to practice, visit **MySocialWorkLab**.

1. Achieved status and ascribed status are elements of:
   a. Racism
   b. Social class
   c. Environmental damage
   d. Social work licensing

2. Gender refers to:
   a. A person's sexual orientation
   b. Maleness- or femaleness-based biological differences
   c. A person's identity as a male or woman
   d. Discrimination based on sex

Diversity in Practice

3. According to this chapter, each of the following contribute to increasing diversity in the U.S. *except*:
   a. Immigration
   b. Increased social visibility of some group
   c. Changes in birthrates for different groups
   d. Religious conversion

4. In the U.S., the majority of individuals identifying themselves as Latino or Hispanic trace their national origins to:
   a. Mexico
   b. Puerto Rico
   c. Argentina
   d. El Salvador

Practice Contexts

5. Assimilation refers to:
   a. The practice of requiring new immigrants to speak only English in schools
   b. The practice of enforcing racial segregation
   c. The practice of coercively absorbing a minority group into the dominant group
   d. The practice of collaborating with clients to enhance their unique strengths

6. As of 2010, marriage between two individuals of the same sex is illegal in:
   a. Twenty states
   b. Thirty-six states
   c. Every state except Alaska and Hawaii
   d. Forty-five states

7. Institutional discrimination refers to:
   a. Overt and covert discriminatory practices embedded in major social institutions
   b. Discrimination against institutions in the awarding of government grants
   c. Racist laws in effect during the time of slavery
   d. Corporate policies that limit time off for family obligations

8. As discussed in this chapter, social privilege refers to:
   a. The fact that some states have better public education systems than others
   b. A social system that favors males and/or masculine qualities over females and/or feminine qualities
   c. The ability of an entity to ensure other entities do as it wishes
   d. An unearned advantage based on some aspect of one's social identity

9. Two models for understanding disability presented in this chapter are:
   a. The social model and the inequality model
   b. The medical model and the social model
   c. The ableism model and the medical model
   d. The ableism model and the psychosocial model

10. Heterosexism refers to:
    a. Discrimination based on sex and/or gender
    b. The fear or hatred of individuals who identify as transsexual or transgender
    c. The (often unconscious) assumption that heterosexuality is the only acceptable and viable life option
    d. Long-term sexual dysfunction

Log onto **MySocialWorkLab** once you have completed the Practice Test above to access additional study tools and assessment.

Answers

Key: 1) b 2) c 3) d 4) a 5) c 6) d 7) a 8) d 9) b 10) c

6

History of Social Work and Social Welfare

CHAPTER OUTLINE

The Beginnings of a U.S. Social Welfare System 115
Caring for the Poor: Poverty and the Workhouse
The Central Role of Organized Religion and the First Amendment
The Influence of American Philanthropy

Industrialization of America 117
The Poor Laborer
The Antipauper Movement
The Growth of Private Nonprofit Agencies for the Poor
The Development of Charity Organization Societies
The Progressive Era
The Social Advocacy of Women and the Settlement Houses
Business Charitable Contributions: The Growth of Community Chests and Service Clubs

The Great Depression and Creation of a National Social Welfare System 124
The Great Depression
The New Deal

The Role of Social Work in the New Deal
Successes and Failures of the New Deal

Lyndon B. Johnson and the Great Society 129
The Great Society

Nixon and the Federal Social Welfare Partnership 131

The Women's Movement 132
Impact of the Civil Rights and Women's Movements on Professional Social Work

Reagan and New Federalism 134
The First President Bush: George H. W. Bush
Bill Clinton and Welfare Reform
Developments in Social Work
Social Welfare Developments: George W. Bush–Barak H. Obama

Summary 137

Practice Test 138

 MySocialWorkLab 138

Core Competencies in this Chapter (Check marks indicate which competencies are covered in depth)									
✓	Professional Identity	✓	Ethical Practice		Critical Thinking		Diversity in Practice	✓	Human Rights & Justice
	Research Based Practice	✓	Human Behavior	✓	Policy Practice	✓	Practice Contexts		Engage, Assess, Intervene, Evaluate

THE BEGINNINGS OF A U.S. SOCIAL WELFARE SYSTEM

Caring for the Poor: Poverty and the Workhouse

Subsequent chapters address the policies, programs, benefits, and services of the current U.S. social welfare system. However, before presenting this information, we want to discuss in this chapter how this system developed. Such a historical overview helps the reader to understand the complexity of the current system and the complex personalities who created it.

Social welfare institutions and practices in the American colonies were modeled after the British Elizabethan Poor Law Act of 1601. Despite the opportunity and prosperity of the American colonies, there were still a considerable number of people in need. In any society, vulnerable children are born, sturdy adults get old and frail, some people are born with disabilities, disease is spread, and accidents happen. Many people lost jobs due to seasonal and other periodic unemployment. Immigrants, a critical source of labor, needed help acclimating to a new environment. War veterans and widows were vulnerable to poverty.

The populations of colonial cities, such as Boston, New York, Philadelphia, and Charleston, increased by 100% or more during the 1700s.[1] Colonial government was ultimately responsible for assisting poor people, a practice called "poor relief." Yet, in practice, government and private groups collaborated to deliver it.[2] Thus, the distinction between "public" and "private" responsibilities often was blurred in colonial America and throughout American history.

Jonathan Katz, in his study of American welfare, concludes the colonies dealt with poor relief in one or more of four ways.[3] Churches provided relief to "deserving" people in their homes: the young, the old, and the sick. Children from poor families were apprenticed to private individuals, such as artisans or farmers. Some, especially poor people, who appeared able to work—the "less deserving poor"—were given "indoor relief"—assistance provided in public institutions, variously referred to as poorhouses, workhouses, or almshouses. They were made to work in these institutions in exchange for assistance. Lacking other options, some public authorities auctioned off poor people to the highest bidder, a private individual who agreed to undertake their care.

Unlike England, land in America was plentiful, but labor was scarce. Early colonists, who depended on one another's labor for survival, demanded that able-bodied colonists work. This economic demand for labor was reinforced by colonial religious doctrine, most notably **Calvinism**.[4] According to John Calvin, the French Protestant reformer, work was sacred and represented God's calling on earth. If you were able-bodied, yet poverty-stricken, you were considered immoral, wicked, undeserving, and not destined for salvation. Beginning in the late 1600s, able-bodied vagabonds were put to work in "workhouses," which combined work projects with religious instruction. The work projects, weaving cloth and making shoes, helped meet the cost of poor relief.[5] Workhouses were considered economically beneficial to the colony and morally therapeutic to the poor.

Residency requirements for public assistance (meaning one had to be a local resident to receive aid) were established, but enforcement was often loose.[6] High taxes and high public assistance costs were a concern even during the colonial era. Needy frontier settlers would seek assistance in wealthy towns such as Boston and New York. These towns eventually started to request funds from colonial governments to help meet the needs of these nonresident poor, an early form of state public assistance.

For the poor that remained in rural areas, the workhouse was often not an option, as local residents couldn't afford to build and maintain one.[7] In these cases, the poor often were auctioned to the highest bidder; the town typically provided clothing and medical care in addition to some financial support to the winning bidder.

Black colonists were not served in the workhouse because they were judged subhuman by most whites.[8] Furthermore, local government officials didn't assist black colonists, fearing slave owners would turn slaves over to localities when they were no longer able to work.

The Central Role of Organized Religion and the First Amendment

Much of the U.S. private nonprofit sector can be considered a direct result of organized religion.[9] The Puritans, a group of religious nonconformists who first landed in present-day Massachusetts in 1620, brought their version of the English poor relief system to America.[10] When able, families were expected to care for their needy members. The church was seen as an extended family. Church officials aided poor families in providing basic health and human services to their needy members. Overseerers of the poor were elected to collect taxes to fund relief of poor parish members.

Over time, religion became more diverse, with Quakers, Anglicans, Baptists, and Catholics becoming influential. These groups gradually developed an increasingly sophisticated network of education and health and human services for their individual denominations.[11] Additionally, ethnic, trade, and other social groups organized to assist their members as well as the community at large. These self-help networks became a large part of the current private nonprofit sector in the U.S.

By the colonial period, the growth of this sector was already evident.[12] The Scots Charitable Society, the Friends Almshouse of Philadelphia, the Ursuline Sisters' New Orleans Orphanage, and the Charitable Irish Society of Boston are examples of private nonprofit charitable organizations that helped the needy. Groups of this sort became an integral part of the poor relief system, complementing public officials' efforts to help the poor and the ill.

The First Amendment to the Constitution provides the legal foundation for the private nonprofit sector of American society.[13] It provides for freedom of religion, assembly, speech, and the right to petition government over grievances. It established the principle at the federal level that government is inherently different from religion. Thomas Jefferson and the rest of the Founding Fathers believed government should not be used to prevent citizens from congregating and exercising their distinctive faith or from speaking out on more secular issues.[14] This had great significance for the ongoing development of voluntary associations, including voluntary health and welfare organizations. Not surprisingly, the profession of social work originated in this sector of society.

The Influence of American Philanthropy

American charitable giving fueled the growth of the private nonprofit sector. The Puritans, believing in predestination, viewed wealth as a sign that the individual was destined for salvation.[15] The harder individuals worked, the more prosperous they would become. The more prosperous they became, the more moral they must be. And the Puritans viewed charitable works as an obligation of all people.[16]

By the mid-1700s, there was a growing belief that living a charitable life could increase a person's chances of salvation. Charitable giving to needy community members, including black and other minority colonists, became an investment in one's own salvation, a good deed that was good for the donor *and* the donee.

By the 1700s, numerous colonists were beginning to amass fortunes, enabling them to become philanthropists.[17] Their increased charitable giving helped fund the growth of charitable agencies in the nonprofit sector, allowing them to recruit health and human service volunteers and employees, pioneers in the profession of social work.

INDUSTRIALIZATION OF AMERICA

The Poor Laborer

During the 1800s, the U.S. developed into a leading world industrial power. Millions of immigrants arrived in search of jobs, land, and opportunity. America offered higher wages and hope for social advancement.[18] In fact, many poor immigrants did improve their lives. A few, like Andrew Carnegie, became rich. However, some immigrants remained or became needy, victims of a young industrial power with little regulation and few safeguards. Dramatic industrial growth was followed by periods of recession. In 1837, 50,000 people in New York City were unemployed.[19] Nationwide, an estimated 200,000 were left unemployed by the economic crash in 1857.[20] About 40,000 of these unemployed people lived in New York City. Around the end of the Civil War, about 12,000 women in New York City worked as prostitutes—out of desperation![21]

Eastern industrial cities lacked adequate food, water, and sanitation due to rapid growth. Streets often were filled with garbage; outbreaks of disease could be disastrous. During the first week of July in 1877, 139 infants died in Baltimore. Poor populations were crowded, suffering the worst during hot summers and freezing winters.[22]

Immigrants lucky and healthy enough to work in factories suffered oppressive heat, polluted air, dangerous machinery, and long hours.[23] Some worked from sunrise to sunset. Long hours and dangerous machinery led to many disabling accidents, rendering the victims unable to work—resulting in poverty and dependency.

The Antipauper Movement

The 19th century was an era of epic events: westward expansion, the Civil War, immigration, and industrialization. It was also an era of great national movements: the Abolition Movement, the Women's Rights Movement, the Temperance Movement, and the Antipauper Movement. The Antipauper Movement is of special interest to social workers because much of the social work profession found its origins in this movement.

The Anti-Pauper Movement produced an increase in the number of poorhouses.[24] (Note that a "pauper" is one who is extremely poor, especially one dependent on public assistance or charity.) According to historian Michael Katz, author of *In the Shadow of the Poorhouse*, the American poorhouse had several goals, including to: prevent starvation; deter pauperism; minimize public relief costs; rehabilitate the poor person; prevent pauper children from becoming pauper adults.[25]

Poorhouse supporters believed that all of these goals, with the possible exception of preventing starvation, could be achieved better in a public institution like the poorhouse than outside of such institutions in private homes (called "outdoor relief").[26] To achieve these goals, the poorhouses combined religious instruction with work projects.[27]

Although not without critics,[28] belief in the merits of "indoor relief" led to an increase in the number and specialization of public institutions during the 1800s.[29] The old poorhouse system contained many different people: unemployed, "able-bodied" people, those with mental illness and other disabilities, those too old to work, and children. Social advocates began to lobby government policymakers for separate institutions for people with mental illness, for criminals, for delinquent and neglected youth, and for the "deaf, dumb, and blind."[30]

The Growth of Private Nonprofit Agencies for the Poor

The 1800s also witnessed the growth of private nonprofit agencies to assist the needy. These voluntary efforts were an extension of the churches' colonial role in providing for the poor. During the early 1800s, business and professional leaders in New York, Philadelphia, Baltimore, and Boston established a Society for the Prevention of Pauperism in their respective cities.[31] They also encouraged using "district visitors" to visit and advise poor families in each district. After 1840, "provident associations" and "associations to improve the condition of the poor" employed similar strategies to help the poor.[32] All were direct forerunners of later social work institutions. Other organizations founded during the late 19th century, beyond denomination services (e.g., Catholic Charities), included the YMCA, YWCA, Salvation Army, and American Red Cross.[33]

Professional Identity

The Development of Charity Organization Societies

Critical Thinking Question

U.S. society increasingly wanted services based upon technical expertise, empirical information, and rational planning. Can you think of ways that social workers fulfill these expectations?

Business and professional groups increasingly called for more professionalism in health and human services. They wanted services based on technical expertise, empirical information, and rational planning instead of people receiving jobs or services based on their political support at election time.[34] As advocated by Dorothea Dix and state mental health hospitals, other health and human services needed to be predicated on the latest scientific information. Thus, philanthropy became more scientific, and health and humans services began to reflect this new concept of **scientific philanthropy**.[35]

Charity organization societies began to emerge to better coordinate and deliver services based on scientific philanthropy. Buffalo, New York, gets credit for the first official American charity organization society, started there in 1877 by the Reverend S. Humphrey Gurteen. Although the concept was imported from Europe, charity organization societies in America were the result of collaboration among business and professional leaders in urban communities.[36] Aiming to be more scientific, professional, and businesslike, the charity organization societies emphasized individual needs assessment, case histories, case conferences, service referrals, and interviewing skills, as well as community service coordination.[37] This point about service coordination needs to be emphasized. In the beginning, these organizations did not deliver services directly.[38] Instead, they provided a community organization function for the many direct service agencies in the community. To accomplish this role, charity organization societies kept a registry of relief applicants, a history of services provided to various individuals and families, and a list of the many health and human services. Referrals to appropriate agencies were made after information about the relief applicant was collected.

"Friendly visitors," primarily female volunteers from the business and professional classes, did home visits to investigate and document family needs.[39] The goal of this more rational philanthropy was to "restore the recipient of charity to the dignity of as much self-sufficiency and personal responsibility as he could manage."[40]

During home visits, friendly visitors aimed to establish a personal relationship with the family. It was also hoped that a personal connection between the rich and poor would improve class relations.[41] Furthermore, home visits allowed volunteer to collect information on the individual needs of the family. A case conference was set up with other civic-minded leaders from the community to better determine what services were needed by the individual or family.[42] At the same time, the conferences enabled business and professional leaders to identify and fund services needed in the community.

Home-based service also allowed the friendly visitor to role model appropriate behavior—some related to health and safety, some related to morality.[43] However, the charity organization societies at that time aimed to separate health and human services from religion.[44] Being simply moralistic, yet not requiring a religious conversion to receive aid, was another step toward professionalization.[45]

Charity organization societies were an improvement over the old poorhouse system. As stated, they helped to professionalize American health and human services. The origin of social work as a profession can be traced to them as they pioneered the development of "casework" and "community organization." Ironically, their emphasis on research, documentation, and technical skills led to the conclusion that part-time volunteers were not adequate. As a result, charity organization societies later helped to establish professional social work education programs at such schools as Indiana University, Ohio State, Bryn Mawr, the University of Minnesota, and Columbia University.[46]

The Progressive Era

The period in American history from about 1900 to 1920 is known as the **Progressive Era**.[47] It was a time of major reforms in the economic, political, and social institutions of the nation. A capitalist economy based on small business competition increasingly was overshadowed by large-scale industry. The enormous industrial growth following the Civil War featured unregulated competition among individual entrepreneurs—survival of the fittest, in a sense.[48] Consequently, at the end of the 19th century, many liberal reformers believed that American institutions needed better coordination, collaboration—even regulation. These reformers, firsthand witnesses to the Industrial Revolution, understood both the positive and negative social welfare aspects of an industrial economy.[49] They believed that new, more civic-minded organizations needed to be created. Social cooperation needed to supplement individual initiative and competition. In the end, progressive reformers were remarkably successful in achieving these objectives.

Social reformers documented many problems in America; poverty existed not just among laborers in industrialized regions of the country. Historian James Patterson, in his study of American poverty, states that the highest incidence of poverty was found in the agricultural economy of the southern states.[50] Yet much of the Progressive Era reforms targeted the poverty-related problems of industrial centers, such as decent housing for poor industrial laborers—a major social problem during the Progressive Era. At the time, the poorer neighborhoods of the largest industrial cities, places like New York's Lower East Side, had the most crowded conditions in the world.[51] To illustrate, the Lower East Side contained 330,000 people per square mile, compared to 175,000 people per square mile in London at its worst. According to the famous social worker and eyewitness, **Jane Addams**, industrial cities such as Chicago had grown so fast that much of the housing when built was considered temporary, and therefore of poor quality.[52] But poor families lived for years in these dwellings. Sometimes several families crowded into housing meant for single families.

Addams, in her book *Twenty Years at Hull-House*, tells of the unhealthy tenement activities of immigrants families, many of them from rural European regions and unused to city living.[53] Some slaughtered sheep in their basements; others sorted rags retrieved from city dumps; still others baked bread beneath the pavement of filthy city streets.

In addition to unhealthy living conditions, new problems associated with mass food production were discovered. In his influential 1905 book about the Chicago stockyards entitled *The Jungle*, **Upton Sinclair** vividly alerted the public to the problem of food impurities due to the use of diseased cattle, illegal animals, and other foreign matter in the mass production of meat products.

The harsh and dangerous working conditions in the slaughterhouses, other factories, and various mines continued to be a social problem at the end of the 1800s. It was common to see a worker repeat the same simple task for 12 hours, six days per week. These long hours doing repetitive work with dangerous machinery contributed to many industrial accidents. To illustrate, 35,000 workers were killed and 700,000 injured in industrial accidents in 1914 alone, many of them left permanently disabled.[54]

The use of child labor in dangerous factory settings also became a public issue during the Progressive Era. Some children worked as many as 80 hours per week in U.S. factories.[55] Most were only between the ages of 10 and 15. Many children worked in factories for years, turning over most, if not all, of their wages to their parents.

Harsh as factory conditions were, the alternative for most immigrant families was unemployment and poverty, while their children slipped into juvenile delinquency as members of turn-of-the-century street gangs. Note, though, that it was increasingly difficult to blame many of these social problems on the individual. Issues such as impure food, unsafe housing, and dangerous factories were increasingly viewed during the Progressive Era as institutional failures, as problems in the individual's environment.[56]

The Progressive Era social reformers addressed these social problems primarily through government regulation.[57] In so doing, progressive reformers did not advocate for many federally funded social services. They feared federal relief programs would be used by national political parties as patronage prizes.[58] Middle- and upper-class Progressive Era reformers believed federal social program costs would escalate also, due to the corruption of patronage-oriented political parties and the lack of professionally trained public administrators in Washington, D.C.

Progressive Era activists, therefore, used government regulations to pursue social change. One set of reforms involved safety regulation.[59] Fire codes were passed to address unsafe housing in urban neighborhoods. Upton Sinclair's influential writing led to the passage in 1906 of the Meat Inspection Act and the Pure Food and Drug Act.[60] And increasingly, work conditions at factories were regulated.

Social work was also impacted by the Progressive agenda. Reformers of the era called for increased licensing and accreditation of professions such as medicine, law, and nursing.[61] In accordance with the times, the New York Charity Organization Society started a summer training course in 1898, an initiative that led to the development of the New York School of Philanthropy, which later became the Columbia University Graduate School of Social Work.

The progressive reformers, although primarily focused on regulation, did institute a limited number of government social programs. Workmen's compensation, for instance, was adopted in most states by 1920.[62] Between 1911 and 1919, most states also enacted "mothers' pensions," providing money to poor, widowed, single mothers to help them care for their children.[63] Reformers argued the alternative to mothers' pensions was foster care, orphanages, or unsupervised children roaming the streets.

The Children's Bureau, established in 1912, addressed child labor, infant mortality, birth rates, child diseases, and juvenile courts. In addition to these government services, Progressive Era activists created many of the most well-known, voluntary, nonprofit agencies in the U.S. today: Goodwill Industries, Big Brothers, Boys Clubs of America, YWCA, Big Sisters, Boy Scouts, Camp Fire Girls, and Girl Scouts.[64]

Critical Thinking Question
Advocates during the Progressive Era saw the environment as a major contributor to individual problems such as poor health. To what problems does the current social environment contribute?

The Social Advocacy of Women and the Settlement Houses

The grassroots political advocacy of women was the driving force behind much reform during the Progressive Era.[65] Of most interest to social workers was the community organizing and social advocacy of the various **settlement houses**. The first settlement house, Toynbee Hall in London, England, was a residence in a poor section of the city for Oxford University men. This "settlement in the slums" was an outpost from which to teach students social responsibility in accordance with Christian social ideals.[66]

Using Toynbee Hall as a model, American settlement houses were private nonprofit organizations, established in poor inner-city neighborhoods to promote the social welfare of community residents. In cities such as New York and Chicago, the vast majority of residents were poor immigrants. Women—including several famous social workers—became the dominant force in American settlements, eventually comprising 70% of settlement residents.[67] Jane Addams, Edith Abbott, and Grace Abbott were all settlement house residents who became identified as social workers. Often inspired by religious conviction, settlement leaders moved beyond their city mission predecessors to further emphasize scientific methods.

The most famous early settlements were Chicago's **Hull House**, founded by Jane Addams and Ellen Starr in 1889, and New York City's Henry Street Settlement, established by Lillian Wald in 1895.[68] By 1900, there were 100 settlement houses in existence; ten years later, about 400 settlements were operating in the U.S.[69]

These settlement houses were significant influences on the community organization and group work methods in the emerging social work profession. Like charity organization societies of the time, settlement houses were founded on the principle of scientific philanthropy. Observation, information gathering (or in today's terms, "data collection"), and documentation were believed to be prerequisites to social advocacy and change. In fact, Residence, Research, and Reform were the "three Rs" of settlement house work.[70] For the most part, settlement leaders targeted their reform efforts on the social environment of immigrant neighborhoods in the large industrial cities. In so doing, their goal was to prevent poverty and class conflict while promoting the health and welfare of industrial communities.

The settlement houses aimed to promote social integration, facilitating the functioning of immigrant groups as they adapted to industrial life. Most settlement leaders encouraged cooperation among classes in promoting social welfare.[71] In short, the settlement mission was to make the existing system better, not to replace it.

You might be surprised at the range of activities organized at some settlements. Hull House first started a kindergarten, which helped to establish a positive relationship with immigrant parents and children in the neighborhood.[72] This was followed by a public kitchen, called a "coffee house," and then a gymnasium, adapted from a former saloon.[73] Hull House became the neighborhood's social center.

In providing space to the neighborhood, the settlement house workers were able to see and hear the needs of the various immigrant groups. It made the settlements attractive sites for young professionals, especially young women, interested in social research and advocacy. Given the significant amount of social legislation passed during the Progressive Era, the community organization and social advocacy efforts of settlement house leaders must be considered a success.[74] Yet settlement leaders were aware of their limitations as voluntary charitable organizations.[75] Leaders such as Jane Addams recognized the importance of coordinated efforts among various community stakeholders, both public and private, in promoting social welfare.

To illustrate, in 1899, long before Ralph Nader's consumer movement, settlement leaders such as Florence Kelley worked with other reformers to create the National Consumers League, an organization that used consumer pressure to advocate for child labor laws, minimum wages, and shorter work days for women, as well as safer consumer products.[76] Settlement house leaders working with other reform groups established the National Women's Trade Union League in 1903. Settlement reformers helped racial minorities by supporting the founding of the National Association for the Advancement of Colored People (NAACP) in 1909. In helping to organize the NAACP, Lillian Wald hosted the National Negro Conference at the Henry Street Settlement in 1909.[77]

Did You Know?

Florence Kelley became a resident of Hull House while fleeing a violent domestic situation. In late December of 1891, after being hit and spit on by her husband, Florence packed up her three children and belongings and moved to Chicago, becoming a resident of Hull House within a week of her arrival.

> **Social Work Stories: Jane Addams and International Social Work**
>
> Jane Addams was voted in public opinion polls the most "exemplary" American?[79] Can you imagine a social worker receiving that honor today? Her father had been a prosperous businessman in Illinois, and perhaps the biggest ethical influence on her life. In addition to establishing her Chicago settlement, Hull House, Addams helped found the American Civil Liberties Union in 1920 and was a leader in national and international peace efforts. For this latter work, she received the Nobel Peace Prize in 1931.

Their focus on collaboration eventually led settlement house leaders to join forces with charity organization societies, further contributing to the emergence of the social work profession.[78] A significant event in this evolution of the profession was the 1905 merger of the settlement house journal, *The Commons*, with the New York Charity Organization Society's journal, *Charities*. And in 1909, Jane Addams became the first settlement house leader to be elected president of the National Conference of Charities and Corrections, the most prominent national conference at the time for social workers.

Business Charitable Contributions: The Growth of Community Chests and Service Clubs

Progressive Era charity organization societies also were concerned about community organization and collaboration. One result was the "community chest," now called United Way. Considered to be the first federated fund-raising organization in American history, this Denver charity organization society centrally organized fund-raising for several community charities. Denver's religious leaders took the lead in establishing the organization; community business people also supported the effort. Later, the community chest model became very popular among business leaders around the country for several reasons.[80] Businesses saw private philanthropy as a preferred option to the higher taxes and political patronage associated with public agencies. Some business leaders recognized the public relations benefits of their philanthropy. Others participated for religious reasons or for social status. Still others may have provided support in the hope that business charitable contributions would defuse the social criticism of radicals and the press at the time.

Importantly, community chests provided a vehicle by which to assess community needs and services on a macro basis—again reflecting the scientific philanthropy concept.[81] Local health and human service agencies' requests for support could be investigated and evaluated similar to charity organization societies' investigation of individual need. This allowed business and professional leaders to identify duplication of effort and opportunities for partnerships among various health and human services. Thus, community chests were an instrument for coordinating charitable efforts.

Furthermore, the federated fund-raising drive proved to be an efficient, well-organized method of raising support for needed health and human services—including services used by the local businesses' employees.[82] Instead of requesting multiple donations throughout the year, the federated campaign solicited funds from local businesses in a single community-wide drive.[83]

Business and professional groups also made charitable donations to community projects through an expanding array of local "service clubs."[84] In 1910, Rotary International was started as a federation of 16 local clubs. The Rotary was followed by the Kiwanis in 1916 and the Lions in 1917. These groups typically targeted their donations to a selected group in need: needy children (especially boys and crippled children) and blind people. Mutual aid societies and fraternal organizations, such as the Masons, Odd Fellows, Eagles, and Loyal Order of Moose, joined these service clubs in providing social workers with grassroots resources by which to help the needy.

THE GREAT DEPRESSION AND CREATION OF A NATIONAL SOCIAL WELFARE SYSTEM

The Great Depression

America in the 1920s was a prosperous nation. Savings during the decade quadrupled.[85] A housing boom enabled millions of Americans to own their own homes. By 1924, about 11 million families were homeowners. Automobiles, electricity, radio, and mass advertising became increasingly influential in the lives of average Americans. Additionally, corporations increasingly offered workers fringe benefits and stock-sharing opportunities.[86]

The overall prosperity of the 1920s U.S. overshadowed the chronic poverty of certain vulnerable populations. These were the same populations that had always been at risk in American history: children, older Americans, racial and ethnic minorities, female-headed families, people with disabilities, and workers with unstable or low-paying jobs. According to James T. Patterson, author of *America's Struggle Against Poverty: 1900–1994*, about one-fourth of the population in Southern rural areas consisted of poor sharecroppers and tenant farmers.[87] African Americans made up over a third of these small farmers.

This is what Patterson refers to as the "old poverty."[88] The "new poverty" began with the famous stock market crash of 1929 and the onset of the Great Depression. This was when many middle- and upper-income families first experienced poverty in America. The sudden and severe downturn of the American economy left many in shock and denial. Some became suicidal.

Between 1929 and 1933, U.S. unemployment jumped from 3.2% to 24.9%, almost a quarter of the official labor force.[89] This represented 12.8 million workers.[90] Unemployment in some cities was as high as 80%—8 out of 10 workers.[91] During this period, consumer spending declined 18%, manufacturing output dropped 54%, and construction spending plummeted 78%. Eighty percent of production capacity in the automobile industry came to a halt.

By 1932, many politicians, businessmen, and journalists started to contemplate the possibility of massive revolution in the U.S.[92] Thousands of the most desperate unemployed workers began raiding food stores; this looting became widespread by 1932. Demonstrations by the poor demanding increased relief often resulted in fights with the police. In places like Harlem, the "sit-down strike" became part of the strategy during these relief demonstrations.

The so-called New Deal was, of course, nothing more than an effort to preserve our economic system.

—Eleanor Roosevelt

Five thousand war veterans demonstrated in Washington in the spring of 1932, with Army infantry and tanks, tear gas, and bayonets required to quell the demonstration.[93]

The New Deal

When Franklin Roosevelt was elected in 1932, the traditional ideologies and institutions of the United States were in a state of upheaval.[94] Americans had grown up promoting the ideology of the deserving and undeserving poor, both of whom were now standing in line for relief. Private nonprofit organizations were overwhelmed with requests, unable to meet the needs of their communities. State and local governments, ultimately responsible for their poor throughout U.S. history, now looked for financial assistance.

America needed an expanded institutional partnership between the federal government and other societal sectors to promote social welfare. Earlier Americans believed the federal government should not be involved in providing poor relief.[95] But now the size of the national crisis required a national solution. Progressive leaders and average Americans increasingly demanded the federal government take greater responsibility in relieving and preventing poverty.

To address nationwide social unrest, FDR took immediate action to create job opportunities and provide insurance and relief programs. This first set of reforms was an emergency stopgap measure. The Federal Emergency Relief Administration (FERA) was given primary responsibility for distributing to individual states federal relief funds used to sustain unemployed families during the immediate crisis. The Civilian Works Administration (CWA) created jobs in public works, including road repair, digging drainage ditches, and maintenance of local parks. The Public Works Administration (PWA), created in 1933, focused on more complex public works such as dams and airports. The Civilian Conservation Corps (CCC), supervised by the U.S. Army, provided jobs for youth in various parks.

Federal reforms during the Roosevelt Administration also included reforms to stabilize the economic sector.[96] In 1933, the Federal Deposit Insurance Corporation (FDIC) was established to restore public confidence in the banking system. A year later the National Housing Act established the Federal Home Administration (FHA) to insure home mortgages and home improvement loans and to refinance needy families' loans at lower interest rates.

Many people felt rampant stock market speculation played a significant role in causing the stock market crash and subsequent depression. Consequently, the Securities and Exchange Commission (SEC) was established in 1934 to regulate speculation abuses by investors and stockbrokers.

From November of 1934 to November of 1936, the Roosevelt Administration implemented a second set of reforms meant to define the ongoing social welfare responsibility of the federal government. The **Social Security Act of 1935 (SSA)** was the major piece of legislation passed during this period. The SSA was a package of social programs consisting of both insurance and poor relief (which eventually became known as "public assistance" or "Welfare"). The act contained both unemployment insurance and old age pensions (commonly known as "Social Security"). Unemployment insurance was very unpopular with business leaders. Yet FDR was able to

pass the legislation by packaging unemployment insurance with more popular programs (e.g., old age pensions).

The Social Security Act also contained several federal poor relief programs including Old Age Assistance, Aid to the Blind, and Aid to Dependent Children (ADC).[99] These were meant to be a continuing federal responsibility. ADC targeted relief to poor children in single-parent families. It was not until 1950 that the parent became officially eligible for assistance.

Note that prior to the New Deal, relief was a tool used by social workers to rehabilitate.[100] To get relief, a person had to accept rehabilitation services from a social worker. With the New Deal, poor relief became a right of American citizens meeting certain eligibility standards, such as financial need. In other words, poor relief became, not a means to rehabilitation, but rather an end in itself.

Demonstrating Knowledge, Values, and Skills

Presidents and Disabilities

Franklin D. Roosevelt is generally considered to be one of the three greatest presidents in American history, along with Lincoln and Washington. FDR also happened to have a disability, coping with "infantile paralysis" or polio throughout much of his adult life. Because the disease left his legs paralyzed, he could not walk without assistance.[97] Yet, during his campaign for president, FDR traveled 13,000 miles by train and made 16 major speeches.[98] Throughout his presidency, people were amazed at his energy and optimism. He held office longer than any president in our history, leading the U.S. through two of its biggest 20th-century crises, the Great Depression and World War II.

Could Roosevelt be elected president today? How would the press cover his disability? How would the voters react to a candidate who could not walk without assistance?

The Roosevelt Administration, however, continued to confront massive unemployment and labor unrest. Numerous strikes took place throughout the country. The Wagner Act was passed in 1936, establishing the National Labor Relations Board, which was empowered to enforce workers' right to start their own unions.[101]

The Roosevelt Administration also implemented a number of major federal initiatives during this "second New Deal" that were later terminated.[102] One was the Works Progress Administration (WPA), which replaced the Federal Emergency Relief Administration created at the start of the New Deal. Program eligibility was limited to one member of each family, typically a male. Some considered this program to be discriminatory. The WPA employed two million people a month to build libraries, schools, hospitals, parks, and sidewalks.[103]

FDR's legislative momentum slowed after 1936, but he did manage to get the Wagner-Steagall Housing Act passed in 1937, establishing the U.S. Housing Authority, which provided low-interest loans to local government to develop public housing.[104] The 1938 Fair Labor Standards Act was another late New Deal success. It established minimum wages and maximum work hours similar to the Progressive Era policy agenda.

The Role of Social Work in the New Deal

By the beginning of the Great Depression, U.S. social work had grown and matured as a professional discipline. Responding to the criticism that social work was made up of kind-hearted people doing activities that almost anyone could do, **Mary Richmond**'s 1917 publication *Social Diagnosis* provided a body of knowledge for professionalization.[105]

As the decade of the 1920s progressed, the social work profession increasingly reflected the conservative trend across the nation.[106] Times were good; jobs were plentiful. Once again, social problems such as poverty and unemployment were traced to the individual. Psychiatric social work, led in part by Smith College, became the rage within the profession. In this process, Sigmund Freud's psychoanalytic work viewed individual dysfunction as a sign of emotional disorder, not so much of immorality.

The social work profession fit the social, economic, and political needs of the conservative and prosperous 1920s. By 1929, there were 25 graduate schools of social work.[107] Several professional organizations had been established, including the American Association of Social Workers in 1921. Also, to further research-based knowledge, several professional journals appeared, including *The Compass*, renamed *Social Work*.

When Franklin Roosevelt took office, he made several social workers prominent figures in his administration, and social workers played major roles in policy development. FDR's wife, **Eleanor Roosevelt**, was probably the most influential person in the White House. Although she did not hold a social work degree, Eleanor received on-the-job training working in New York settlement houses.[108] As First Lady, she reflected the settlement philosophy of "research and reform." She traveled around the nation and the world collecting information for her husband. He counted on her to bring back detailed information concerning public sentiment and social need—"research" on which the social policy of the New Deal was based.

Harry Hopkins, a social worker with settlement house experience, was the next most influential person close to the president. After managing Roosevelt's relief program in New York, Hopkins was selected to head the Federal Emergency Relief Administration (FERA) and later its successor, the Works Progress Administration (WPA). As indicated earlier, these entities were at the core of Roosevelt's efforts to provide for the massive numbers of unemployed Americans, making Hopkins FDR's top official in the rescue effort.[109] In fact, this social worker was so respected by President Roosevelt that, before Hopkins' health started to deteriorate, some believed that Roosevelt was grooming Hopkins to be the next president of the United States. Hopkins lived in the White House with Franklin and Eleanor, and during World War II, Roosevelt sent Hopkins to be his special representative in talks with both Winston Churchill and Joseph Stalin.

A third prominent member with social work training and settlement house experience was Frances Perkins. She was the first woman appointed in U.S. history to a president's cabinet, serving as secretary of the Department of Labor.[110] She had worked at two Chicago settlement houses, Hull House and Chicago Commons.[111] In 1909, she had attended the New York School of Philanthropy (which became the Columbia University Graduate School of Social Work) to learn survey research methods, receiving her master's degree in political science from Columbia University. Earlier, she had advocated for safer factory and labor standards as Roosevelt's head of the New York State Safety Board.[112]

In addition to these prominent policy development roles, the New Deal created thousands of new social work rank-and-file jobs. In fact, the Federal Emergency Relief Act required that every local public relief administrator hire at least one experienced social worker on staff.[113] This requirement introduced social work ethics and methods into every county and township in America. During the 1930s, the number of employed social workers doubled, from about 30,000 to over 60,000 positions. This job growth created a major shift in social work practice, from primarily private agency settings and clinical roles to public agencies and social advocacy. The New Deal also expanded the scope of social work from a primarily urban profession to a nationwide profession practicing in rural areas as well.

Successes and Failures of the New Deal

The New Deal had many shortcomings.[114] For example, it didn't establish any major national health programs. Furthermore, to appease Southern politicians and get some reform legislation passed, FDR did relatively little to help African Americans.[115] Many worked as domestic servants, migrant workers, or farm laborers—occupations not covered by New Deal legislation (e.g., old age pensions, minimum wages, or unemployment insurance). Moreover, from an ethical standpoint, the New Deal involved no anti-lynching legislation—even though beating and lynching of black citizens was still common in some parts of the nation. If America as a nation suffered during the Great Depression, African Americans and other racial and ethnic minorities suffered worst of all.[116]

Critical Thinking Question

Should social workers primarily practice in terms of what *should* be done *ethically*? In what situations should they think in terms of what *can* be done *politically*?

Eleanor Roosevelt was probably the most powerful political ally of African Americans during this Administration. As historian Doris Kearns Goodwin has noted, Franklin Roosevelt thought in terms of what *could* be done politically, while Eleanor thought in terms of what *should* be done ethically.[117] While inspecting conditions in Southern states for her husband, Eleanor discovered discrimination against African Americans in several New Deal programs.

A 1935 executive order from the president barred discrimination in WPA programs. Actions such as these showed African Americans that Franklin and Eleanor Roosevelt did care about them. More importantly, this advocacy gave young African Americans a glimpse of the potential power of the federal government regarding civil rights.

Whatever its shortcomings, the New Deal prevented many Americans, black and white, from starving to death during the Great Depression. It also reformed national institutional structures to meet the massive needs of millions of Americans in poverty. It created a major federal health and human service system, adding to the services of local public and private agencies. The Social Security Board, set up to administer the Social Security Act, later became the U.S. Department of Health, Education, and Welfare.[118] And the Social Security Act became, and still is, the foundation of the American health and human service system.

LYNDON B. JOHNSON AND THE GREAT SOCIETY

The Great Society

President Lyndon Johnson significantly expanded the federal partnership with private and other public institutions to promote social welfare via his legislative agenda called the **Great Society**.

The Great Society consisted of numerous pieces of legislation. The first, and perhaps most important, was the Civil Rights Act of 1964. When Johnson took office, the civil rights movement was already well under way through court action and the voluntary efforts of various groups in the nonprofit sector. In 1954, the Supreme Court had ruled that school segregation was unconstitutional.[119] In 1955, Rosa Parks, an African American, refused to give up her seat to a white rider on a Montgomery, Alabama, bus, leading to a public bus boycott in that city by African Americans. The Reverend Martin Luther King, Jr. organized the successful boycott, in which African Americans refused to spend their money on bus transportation until the buses were desegregated. In 1961, 11 youth calling themselves Freedom Riders began a protest of segregated bus stations and other discriminatory interstate travel laws. In 1963, the Southern Christian Leadership Conference, headed by King, and the Alabama Christian Movement for Human Rights led a campaign to protest segregation in Birmingham, Alabama, the largest industrial city in the South. King's coalition used a nonviolent strategy, employing peaceful mass marches, sit-ins, and business boycotts. His advocacy attracted media attention nationwide, indeed worldwide, forcing the federal government to cooperate in enforcing African Americans' civil rights.

King believed public pressure generated from the Birmingham demonstrations contributed greatly to the Johnson Administration's passage of the **Civil Rights Act of 1964**.[120] The act promoted black voting rights, called for desegregation of public facilities, and prohibited employment discrimination in organizations receiving federal money.

The **Civil Rights Act of 1965** was also passed, giving the federal government the right to presume discrimination in any state (or its subdivisions) where less than 50% of racial minorities voted in the latest federal election and in any area using screening methods such as literacy tests.[121] In these cases, federal authorities could directly administer elections. Within one week of the bill signing, the federal Justice Department had filed suits to have poll taxes voided in Texas, Virginia, Mississippi, and Alabama.[122] In addition, voter screening tests were suspended in several states.

To help older Americans with health care, the Johnson Administration passed Medicare in 1965.[123] To assist the poor with health care, the administration passed Medicaid that same year.[124] This legislation was funded through matching grants with states. The weaknesses of Medicaid were similar to those of Medicare. Neither promoted outreach and preventive services, and there were few cost controls in the legislation.

A fifth major piece of legislation passed as part of Johnson's Great Society was the Older Americans Act of 1965, authorizing the creation of a national network of Area Agencies on Aging. Today, these agencies coordinate and subsidize services (e.g., home care and nutrition programs for older Americans).

The Johnson Administration also passed the Elementary and Secondary Education Act in 1965, providing federal assistance to low-income public school districts[125] Other Great Society programs included the Work Incentive Program, which funded training programs and child care for women on welfare[126] and the Food Stamp Program, which assisted the poor in purchasing food.

The centerpiece of Johnson's Great Society legislative agenda, however, was the **War on Poverty**. This antipoverty legislation, officially entitled the Economic Opportunity Act of 1965, consisted of several programs including Job Corps and the Neighborhood Youth Corps.[127] Job Corps provided urban school dropouts with alternative educational and training programs, while the Neighborhood Youth Corps provided part-time jobs to youth in local agencies.

Volunteers in Service to America program, better known as VISTA, was a domestic version of the popular Peace Corps program. Instead of sending Americans to work in foreign countries for a stipend, VISTA sent them to do community organizing in poor U.S. neighborhoods. Furthermore, the "War" included legal aid to the poor and the creation of medical clinics in poor neighborhoods.

The most controversial part of the War on Poverty were the Community Action Programs, referred to as "CAP" agencies.[128] Housed in the Office of Economic Opportunity, these CAP agencies were given several objectives: to plan and coordinate local services for the needy, to fund and deliver certain services (e.g., the preschool program, Head Start), and to advocate for the poor. Not only were CAP agencies supposed to advocate for the poor, they were instructed to encourage "maximum feasible participation" of the poor in their programs. Maximum feasible participation of the poor was viewed as a way to bridge social reform and individual change. More specifically, proponents reasoned that empowerment through participation in social change activities would lead to better mental health for the individual. To promote empowerment and maximum feasible participation of the poor, many CAP agencies employed paraprofessionals from their neighborhoods and client populations.

The Great Society programs have been criticized.[129] Some feel that Johnson's administration did not pay enough attention to adequate funding and proper implementation.[130] However, those close to Johnson maintain that his commitment to the poor and civil rights was genuine.[131] He accomplished in civil rights and national health care what Franklin Roosevelt and the New Deal did not. As a result, millions of needy Americans have benefited from the right

> *For practically every family . . . the ingredients of poverty are part financial and part psychological.*
> —David Shipler

to vote, Medicare, Medicaid, legal aid, Head Start, student financial aid, and other Great Society programs.

NIXON AND THE FEDERAL SOCIAL WELFARE PARTNERSHIP

Richard M. Nixon succeeded Lyndon Johnson as president in 1968. Although Nixon was a Republican who was highly critical of Johnson's Great Society, he continued to expand the federal partnership in social welfare.[132] Nixon's policy views on the Great Society reflected the anger and resentment of the middle class and many local community leaders toward the concept of maximum feasible participation of the poor in local services. In short, the practical realities of empowering the poor to take more control of local community institutions and services threatened local community politicians and administrators, leaving a resentment that Nixon capitalized on politically.

At the same time, however, Nixon sought to build voter support for his presidency and the Republican Party by enacting more and better social legislation than the Democratic Party.[134] He did so by promoting legislation that helped the working poor and what America has historically viewed as the deserving poor—older Americans, people with disabilities, and children. Nixon added expansive amendments to Democratic policy proposals designed to assist the working and/or deserving poor. This resulted in a considerable amount of health and human service legislation during Nixon's presidency and a substantial addition to the federal government's responsibility for social welfare.

Legislation enacted by the Nixon Administration included the Supplemental Security Income program in 1972, bringing Old Age Assistance, Aid to the Blind, and Aid to the Disabled under the sole administration of the Social Security Administration of the federal government.[135] Most of the cost for the program was assumed by the federal government. Supplemental Security Income, better known as SSI, provided assistance to people with mental and physical disabilities, including deinstitutionalized mental health patients. Nixon, the Great Society critic, greatly expanded the number of people receiving assistance in the various categorical services that comprise SSI.

Nixon also expanded the federal government's role in the Food Stamp Program, making the federal government responsible for program funding and administrative oversight.[136] While doing this, Nixon established national eligibility standards for food stamps, including the working poor, and made participation in the Food Stamp Program mandatory for all states.

During his first term, Nixon also approved a 20% increase in Social Security benefits and indexed Social Security to inflation.[137] This meant that as the cost of living went up, benefits would also rise. Unfortunately, the legislation did not include a corresponding increase in the payroll tax to fund the benefit increase. This, along with double-digit inflation and an increase in the number of retired people per worker, contributed to an eventual funding crisis in the Social Security Program.

Nixon also pioneered in the use of revenue sharing and block grants.[138] **General revenue sharing** provided federal funds to local governments for general operating expenses, while **special revenue sharing** (including block grants)

Did You Know?

President Richard Nixon detested social workers! He felt that they coddled the undeserving poor. He also felt that many Great Society services were ineffective programs that served bureaucrats and social workers more than the country.[133]

contributed federal funds to local governments for broad categories of services. For example, Title XX of the Social Security Act, passed during the Nixon Administration, was designed as a block grant. This legislation contributed federal funds to states for a broad array of social services—including critically needed services such as child care and domestic violence shelters.

Nixon was also the first president to sign legislation that used the tax system to give resources to the poor. This was the Earned Income Tax Credit.[139] The credit was a payment to the working poor with dependent children of up to $400, based on a percentage of their earned income for the year.

Other legislation passed during the Nixon Administration included the Rehabilitation Act (1973), the Education for All Handicapped Act (1975), the Health Maintenance Act (1973), the Family Planning Services and Population Act (1974), the Juvenile Justice and Delinquency Act (1974), and the Child Abuse Prevention Act (1974).[140] The Rehabilitation Act led to major efforts to make buildings, public transportation, and jobs accessible to people with disabilities, while the Education for All Handicapped Act "mainstreamed" students with disabilities in public schools. A bill that would lead to significant changes in the U.S. healthcare system, the Health Maintenance Act, provided funding to develop health maintenance organizations. Another Nixon health bill, the Family Planning Services and Population Act, helped low-income women obtain family planning services.

The final two pieces of legislation dealt with child welfare–related issues. In the early 1970s, Americans were becoming more concerned about child abuse. One concern was the physical abuse of children found guilty of minor delinquencies but institutionalized in adult facilities. Consequently, amendments to the Juvenile Justice and Delinquency Act in 1974 offered support to local juvenile diversion services for runaway and truant youth, while the Child Abuse Prevention Act provided funding to universities and demonstration projects for research on child abuse and neglect.

Nixon also took some positive steps on the issue of civil rights, following through on desegregation of southern schools.[141] In addition, his "Philadelphia Plan" promoted affirmative action in the employment of women and racial minorities. Yet Nixon's agenda in his second term became more conservative with respect to federal spending on programs that might benefit these groups. Public opinion polls showed that many white, ethnic, blue-collar, and middle-class groups resented the militant tactics of activist groups and opposed further social spending. Thus, during his second term, Nixon attempted to focus more on the concerns of this "silent majority"—issues such as inflation, government spending, and, ironically, crime. Nixon was forced to resign the presidency in 1974,[142] facing impeachment because of his involvement in the burglary cover-up at the Democratic National Headquarters in Washington, D.C.

THE WOMEN'S MOVEMENT

Throughout the 1960s and 1970s, a growing sense of agency among women resulted in a rekindled women's movement.[143] Women of this era drew on the past victories of American women in such causes as the abolition movement, the temperance movement, the antipauper movement, and, most recently, the civil rights movement. In addition to this history, numerous recent events and issues galvanized women.[144] Among these were the publication of best-selling books (e.g., *The Feminine Mystique*), prevention of violence against women,

> **Social Work Stories: African American Women as Policy Advocates**
>
> Two of the most high-profile female activists of the 1960s and '70s were Fannie Lou Hamer and Shirley Chisholm. Born in 1917 in Montgomery County, Mississippi, Hamer dropped out of school at age 6 to help support her family by picking cotton.[145] Yet during her civil rights career, she would receive honorary degrees from two colleges, including the prestigious Howard University. In August 1962, Hamer tried to register to vote but was rejected when she failed to interpret a section of the Constitution correctly.[146] She finally passed the screening test in December 1962. However, when she tried to vote in August 1963, she was rejected again, because she had not paid a poll tax for two years. This occurred after she had been arrested in June 1963 in Winona, Mississippi, while trying to integrate a segregated bus terminal with a busload of other African Americans. While in jail, two inmates beat her severely on orders from police officers.
>
> Showing incredible courage, Hamer continued her community organizing around voter registration and other social issues throughout her life. In September 1965, she was asked to testify at a closed hearing of the House Elections Committee. During her testimony, Hamer stated that if "Negroes were allowed to vote freely, I could be sitting up here with you right now as a Congresswoman."[147]
>
> A second prominent female activist, as stated, was Shirley Chisholm. Born in 1924 in Brooklyn, New York, to immigrants from Barbados and British Guiana, Chisholm went on to earn a master's degree in education from Columbia University.[148] She was elected to Congress in 1969, emphasizing such social issues as job training, equal education, adequate housing, enforcement of antidiscrimination laws, child care, and an end to the Vietnam War. In 1971, Chisholm ran for president of the United States, becoming the first viable female candidate of color. She ended up receiving 151 delegate votes for the presidential nomination. After the campaign, Chisholm stated, "What I hope most, is that now there will be others who will feel themselves as capable of running for high political office as any wealthy, good-looking white male."[149]

discrimination in the workplace, the 1973 *Roe v. Wade* Supreme Court decision legalizing abortion, and the Great Society's failure to address women's issues (such as child care) adequately. These types of issues came up repeatedly in the growing number of women's groups and women's studies courses. The result was a major campaign to pass an Equal Rights Amendment to the Constitution. In the end, the amendment passed Congress but was never ratified by enough states. Yet, the campaign helped women to see that they could have power through advocacy, leading to successful efforts in the future. These eventual victories included an increase in rights and services involving sexual harassment, domestic violence, sexual assault, child care, family leave, and educational and athletic opportunities.

Impact of the Civil Rights and Women's Movements on Professional Social Work

By the 1960s, social workers were no longer leaders in developing social policy on a national level. As discussed previously, social work was more concerned with casework and professionalization in the 1950s. Therefore, social work, as a profession, was not at the forefront of policymaking during the Great Society, as it had been in the New Deal. According to John Ehrenreich, there were very few articles on civil rights in *Social Work* before 1963.[150] Ironically, those most influential in 1960s social policy, such as Michael Harrington and the Reverend Martin Luther King, were not social workers.

In fact, the social work profession came under attack.[151] The **National Welfare Rights Organization**, established in 1967, advocated for public welfare

Critical Thinking Question

Social work practice responded to the sociopolitical context of the 1960s and '70s. Can you cite three societal trends today that social work should address?

clients' rights. The advocacy target was often social workers in administrative positions in the public welfare bureaucracy. Also during the 1960s, social work students protested against schools of social work, claiming social work curricula were irrelevant to key social issues such as civil rights and welfare rights. As a result, schools of social work started adding courses in community organization, social planning, and race, culture, and oppression. Furthermore, newer social work courses included more information on systems theory, prevention, and the causes of social problems. During the 1960s, casework itself was attacked for not doing enough to help the poor.[152]

Later, the women's movement also had an impact on professional social work. The theoretical base of casework, with its heavy Freudian emphasis, was criticized for being sexist.[153] Consequently, during the 1960s and early '70s, social work once again began to reflect the sociopolitical environment at the time, emphasizing systemic causes of social problems and social action to remedy these problems.

REAGAN AND NEW FEDERALISM

The Reagan Administration accelerated a conservative trend in social policy that began in Richard Nixon's second term and continued through the presidencies of Gerald Ford and Jimmy Carter. Nixon began proposing cuts in federal spending on numerous programs in his second term, while Ford and Carter passed very little health and human services legislation (although the Carter Administration did enact legislation supporting adoption and foster care in 1980).[154] During the 1970s, the general public became increasingly concerned with a stagnant economy, high inflation rates in consumer prices, rising taxes, and the increasing deficit in the federal government budget. In addition, government regulation of the business sector had increased enormously during the 1960s and 1970s, reflecting public concern at the time for worker safety, product safety, and environmental quality.[155] By the early 1980s, business leaders, in particular, were concerned with overregulation.

Republican Ronald Reagan defeated incumbent Democratic President Jimmy Carter in 1980. Reagan's political priorities consisted of balancing the federal budget through cuts in wasteful government spending, cutting individual and corporate taxes, reducing government regulations (particularly on businesses), and increasing military spending.[156] To achieve this, Reagan sought to decrease the federal government's role in the American partnership for social welfare, preferring to rely more on private for-profit and nonprofit institutions. In Reagan's view, poverty-related programs, such as AFDC and food stamps, once again should become primarily the responsibility of state and local governments. Although Reagan referred to this agenda as "New Federalism," it was really a return to the old role of the federal government in advancing social welfare.[157]

The essence of Reagan's economic recovery plan, known as **supply-side economics**, was that tax cuts for the wealthy would be reinvested in business expansion, which would create more jobs and consumer goods. More jobs would create the income needed to buy those consumer goods. In short, increased production would create increased demand for the goods produced.[158]

Reagan believed that he had a mandate from the people for his political agenda due to his large victory over Jimmy Carter. His administration moved fast during its first term to enact several pieces of legislation to meet this conservative mandate. Part of Reagan's strategy was to take numerous categorical programs and combine them into relatively few block grants, while at the same time cutting total federal funding for the programs. Thus, the Omnibus Budget Reconciliation Acts of 1981 and 1982 reduced or eliminated many "means-tested" programs (i.e., programs in which eligibility is based upon a certain income level).[159] AFDC, food stamps, SSI, unemployment insurance, and low-income housing were cut. Funding for Title XX social services, which became the Social Services Block Grant, was capped. In addition, incentive payments in the Aid to Families with Dependent Children program were eliminated. The legislation confirmed the belief by liberals that much of what Reagan called "government waste" was, in fact, federal-level health and human services.

The Reagan Administration also passed the Job Training and Partnership Act during its first term.[160] Its distinctive feature was the establishment of "Private Industry Councils." These councils awarded contracts to job placement agencies, which received a fee for every person placed in private-sector jobs. This emphasis on private, rather than public sector, employment reflected the more conservative nature of Reagan's approach to social welfare.

Furthermore, Reagan supported reform in Social Security and Medicare programs.[161] To address growing concern about the solvency of Social Security, Reagan taxed some Social Security benefits of wealthy Americans and returned the money to the Social Security Fund. This reform also included a phased-in delay in Social Security benefits until eligible citizens reached the age of 67. To reform Medicare, the Reagan Administration established national levels for payment in 467 specific diagnostic categories to help control rising healthcare costs.

The First President Bush: George H.W. Bush

Reagan's vice president, George H. W. Bush, defeated the Democratic governor of Massachusetts, Michael Dukakis, for president in 1988. During his campaign, Bush repeatedly told voters to "stay the course" of the previous eight years under Reagan. And when he became president, that is essentially what Bush did, proposing very little new health and human service legislation. In his single term in office, Bush did enact legislation resulting in the "Child Care and Development Block Grant," signing the legislation in 1990.[162] This federal grant provided funding to local child care providers for administration, staff training, and direct care. Also in 1990, the Bush Administration passed a major civil rights act called the **Americans with Disabilities Act**. This legislation forbade discrimination against people with disabilities in several areas, including employment, education, housing, and public accommodations. The act required employers to make "reasonable accommodations" for people with disabilities, including building modifications and the provision of interpreters.

Bill Clinton and Welfare Reform

In the presidential election of 1992, Arkansas Governor Bill Clinton defeated the incumbent, George H. W. Bush. Clinton's subsequent legislative successes reflected the more conservative mood of voters around the country. In fact, although Clinton was known as "The Great Empathizer," his policies were much more conservative than his rhetoric.

Clinton signed the 1993 Omnibus Reconciliation Bill, which began cutting the federal deficit through a combination of spending cuts and tax increases, including increases on wealthy Americans.[163] By 1999, Clinton succeeded in erasing the federal budget deficit. In cutting the huge federal deficit, he supported the business sector in the global economy by attracting more international investors.

The Clinton Administration's major social reform was the **Personal Responsibility and Work Opportunities Act (PRWOA)**, passed late in Clinton's first term.[164] Meant to satisfy anti-welfare sentiment and further reduce federal social welfare spending, the legislation had been a campaign promise of Clinton to "end welfare as we know it." In so doing, the act ended Aid to Families with Dependent Children as an entitlement and replaced the program with a block grant called **Temporary Assistance to Needy Families (TANF)**. Under this new legislation, no individual or family is "entitled" to welfare. Although the law gives states some flexibility in administering federal funds, as a general rule, individuals must participate in work activity within two years of receiving assistance, and families are limited to a total of five years assistance in a lifetime.

Other important legislation passed during the Clinton Administration included the 1993 Family and Medical Leave Act and the 1994 Crime Bill. The Family and Medical Leave Act requires public and private employers with 50 or more employees to offer family or medical leave for up to 12 weeks.[165] Legitimate reasons for leave under the act include the illness of an employee or family member or maternity-related reasons. Although employers are not required to provide paid leave, the employer is mandated to continue health benefits and to offer the same or a comparable job when the employee returns to work. The Crime Bill provided funding to increase the size of police forces, build new prisons, and deliver certain crime-related services (including domestic violence services).[166] Although Clinton failed in his attempt to enact new national health insurance legislation, it should be noted that he achieved a more incremental victory when he increased federal funding to states in 1997 for children's health insurance. Moreover, legislation was passed in 1996 that prevented private insurance companies from discriminating against mental health coverage.[167]

Developments in Social Work

Reflective of the conservative trend in American society during the late 1970s through the 1990s, the social work profession returned to a casework emphasis—specifically, clinical social work (i.e., casework with a strong psychotherapy orientation).[168] Accordingly, the National Federation of Societies for Clinical Social Work was established in 1971. This period in social work history also witnessed a trend toward private practice. This was, in part, the result of the profession's successful lobbying for private insurance reimbursement as well as Medicare reimbursement. Schools of social work experienced healthy enrollments of students wanting casework concentrations, while the number of students focusing on macro-level practice, including administration and community organization, decreased. With the growth of managed health care in the 1990s, this broadness and flexibility within the social work profession allowed it to redefine its role in an increasingly cost-controlled healthcare system.[169]

Social Welfare Developments: George W. Bush–Barak H. Obama

George W. Bush defeated Democratic candidate Al Gore in a close and highly contested presidential election in 2000. President George W. Bush turned out to be more overtly religious than his father in the role of president. His faith was reflected in his conservative views on gay marriage, abortion, and embryonic stem cell research. His strong religious views also influenced his policy on the church's role in health and human services. More specifically, the Clinton Administration's 1996 welfare reform contained a "charitable choice" clause, a provision that encourages states to increase religious organizations' involvement in federal programs like Temporary Assistance to Needy Families. George W. Bush's administration intensified and extended this policy shift with a major effort to funnel federal social service funding to religious institutions as part of his "faith-based" policy initiative.[171] With respect to other significant legislation, Bush reformed Medicare to include prescription drug benefits, "Part D," for American senior citizens.

Barack H. Obama became the first black man to become United States president when he took office in 2009. Obama inherited a failing economy similar to that awaiting Franklin Roosevelt when he was elected in 1932. Consequently, in February 2009, his administration passed a $787 billion economic stimulus package, which consisted of a combination of federal spending and tax cuts. One of the largest pieces of economic legislation in U.S. history, the bill aimed to provide assistance to banking and other industries, while saving millions of jobs. In addition, in 2010, Obama signed major healthcare reform legislation. The 10-year, $940 billion bill brought coverage to 32 million uninsured Americans, expanded Medicaid, and prevented insurance companies from denying coverage based on preexisting health conditions.[172]

> **Did You Know?**
>
> Bill Clinton was the first American president to reveal he had undergone psychotherapy. He participated in family counseling with his mother and brother. Also, did you know that First Lady Hillary Rodham Clinton was the first First Lady to hold a professional degree?[170]

The danger of too much government is matched by the perils of too little.
—Barack Obama

SUMMARY

Social welfare institutions and practices in the American colonies were modeled after the British Elizabethan Poor Law Act of 1601. During the late 1800s and early 1900s, charity organization societies and settlement houses based on scientific philanthropy began to emerge to better coordinate and deliver services to the needy. By the 1930s, social work had emerged as an important profession in the American social welfare system.

The social welfare policies, programs, and services created by Franklin Roosevelt's New Deal during the Great Depression established a truly national social welfare system. President Lyndon Johnson's Great Society expanded this social welfare system. The New Federalism of President Ronald Reagan returned more responsibility for social welfare services to the states, and President Bill Clinton's welfare reform, through the Personal Responsibility and Work Opportunity Act, attempted to return more responsibility for well-being to individuals.

6 CHAPTER REVIEW

Log onto **MySocialWorkLab** to access a wealth of case studies, videos, and assessment. (*If you did not receive an access code to **MySocialWorkLab** with this text and wish to purchase access online, please visit www.mysocialworklab.com.*)

PRACTICE TEST
The following questions will test your knowledge of the content found within this chapter. For additional assessment, including licensing-exam type questions on applying chapter content to practice, visit **MySocialWorkLab**.

1. Social welfare institutions and practices in the American colonies were modeled after the:
   a. Quaker religious beliefs
   b. Those of Jamestown, Virginia
   c. Native American concepts of community
   d. British Elizabethan Poor Law Act of 1601

2. "Indoor relief" in colonial social welfare referred to:
   a. Assistance provided in public institutions
   b. Assistance provided in one's own home
   c. Assistance provided in a wealthy family's home
   d. Assistance provided in a shelter

3. The American poorhouse was:
   a. A place to rehabilitate poor people
   b. A poorly constructed house
   c. A place normally dedicated to one poor family
   d. A shelter built by the poor themselves

4. The first official American charity organization society was started in 1877 in:
   a. Boston, Massachusetts
   b. New York City, New York
   c. Buffalo, New York
   d. Philadelphia, Pennsylvania

5. Charity organization societies were based primarily on what concept:
   a. Calvinism
   b. Scientific philanthropy
   c. Self-help
   d. Mutual aid

6. The "Progressive Era" in U.S. history refers to:
   a. A time of great increases in social services
   b. A time of great increases in social work jobs
   c. A time of increased sociopolitical advocacy
   d. A time of great increases in civil rights for U.S. minorities

Policy Practice

7. The vast majority of residents in U.S. settlement houses were:
   a. Poor Native Americans
   b. Poor African Americans
   c. Poor American colonists
   d. Poor immigrants

Human Rights & Justice

8. The Social Security Act was a package of social programs consisting of:
   a. Insurance
   b. Poor relief
   c. Both insurance and poor relief
   d. Old age pensions only

9. The "Great Society" referred to:
   a. President Lyndon Johnson's legislative agenda
   b. The progress made by Progressive Era advocates
   c. President John Kennedy's legislative agenda
   d. The progress made by 1960s social advocates

10. President Ronald Reagan's "New Federalism" maintained that assistance to the poor should be:
    a. Primarily a responsibility of the federal government
    b. Primarily a responsibility of state and local government
    c. Primarily a responsibility of poorhouses
    d. Primarily a responsibility of philanthropy

Log onto **MySocialWorkLab** once you have completed the Practice Test above to access additional study tools and assessment.

Answers

Key: 1) d 2) a 3) a 4) c 5) b 6) c 7) d 8) c 9) a 10) b

7

Poverty and Social Welfare

CHAPTER OUTLINE

Introduction to Poverty 140

Definition and Causes of Poverty 140
Defining and Measuring Poverty
Federal Poverty Thresholds and Guidelines
Current Federal Poverty Thresholds: Problems and Alternatives
Who Are the Poor?
Demographic Trends in Poverty

Causes of Poverty 145
Economic System Factors: Work, Income, and the Labor Market
Education and "Human Capital"
Oppression and Discrimination
The Impact of Changing Family Structures
The "Culture of Poverty"

Publicly Funded Services to the Poor 154

Social Insurance Programs 155

Public Assistance Programs 156
Current Issues in Public Assistance: A Critical Analysis of Welfare Reform

Food and Shelter Programs 158
Food Stamps
The Special Supplemental Food Program for Women, Infants, and Children
Public Housing and Section 8 Housing Assistance
Contributions of Business and the Private Nonprofit Sector to Housing
Current Shelter Issues: The Homeless
Other Publicly Funded Programs in American Social Welfare

Summary 163

Practice Test 164

 MySocialWorkLab 164

	Core Competencies in this Chapter (Check marks indicate which competencies are covered in depth)								
☐	Professional Identity	☐	Ethical Practice	✓	Critical Thinking	☐	Diversity in Practice	✓	Human Rights & Justice
☐	Research Based Practice	☐	Human Behavior	✓	Policy Practice	✓	Practice Contexts	☐	Engage, Assess, Intervene, Evaluate

139

> *The other America, the America of poverty, is hidden. . . . Its millions are socially invisible to the rest of us.*
>
> —Michael Harrington

INTRODUCTION TO POVERTY

When we begin to examine contemporary social problems, we have to start with poverty. Poverty is one of the most pressing problems in the U.S. and around the globe. More than 37 million people in the U.S. were poor in 2007.[1] Poor Americans get sicker, stay sicker, and die younger than nonpoor Americans. They are more susceptible to crime and victimization, food insecurity, and homelessness. The plight of children in poverty, who make up 35.7% of all poor Americans, is especially discouraging.[2] Children born into poor families experience significantly higher infant mortality rates than those born into middle-class or wealthy families.[3] Children who live in poverty grow up to experience lower educational outcomes, lower lifetime earnings, more adolescent pregnancy, and poorer physical and mental health than those who do not.[4]

Despite the painful reality of poverty, defining it is a complicated business, one that is often driven more by political processes than rational policymaking. The same can be said for the programs and services in place to reduce U.S. poverty and to help individuals and families move out of poverty.

In 1962, Michael Harrington argued in his book, *The Other America*, that the majority of Americans were blind to the realities of poverty. Harrington noted that the poor were hidden in inner-city ghettos and isolated rural areas far from the eyes of the middle class, whose economic privilege allowed them to avoid encountering the poor except by choice. We might say the same is true today, although the information-technology revolution, the expansion of suburban sprawl further into once rural areas, and the renewed movement back into cities over the past few decades may have made poverty more visible. In either case, few social workers fail to encounter poverty and its effects on individuals, families, and society in their work. A mental health case manager, a child welfare worker, a policy analyst, a social activist, a school social worker—all encounter the effects of poverty at the micro, mezzo or macro level. Indeed, many in the field, including the Council on Social Work Education, regard eliminating poverty and ameliorating its effects on individuals and families as one of the profession's core tasks.[5] It is crucial, then, that social work students understand a few things about poverty: What it is? What causes it? Who experiences it? What policies, programs, and services are in place to assist with it? How well do those policies and programs actually work? In this chapter, we will examine these questions and pay special attention to how social workers collaborate with people from other professional and academic disciplines to help individuals and families in poverty and to reduce poverty overall.

DEFINITION AND CAUSES OF POVERTY

Defining and Measuring Poverty

Defining poverty is anything but clear-cut, but it is an important first step in understanding its impact on individuals and society. In the United States, the federal government plays a primary role in defining what we understand as the meaning of poverty. The federal definition of poverty rests on the concept of **Deprivation**.[6] A family is considered poor if they do not have enough income to maintain a minimum standard of living, including housing, food, and medical care. This is known as **Absolute Poverty**. Individuals and families that fall at or below a certain income threshold deemed the minimum needed to meet basic needs is considered poor, and everyone above this threshold is not poor. The threshold changes each year based on price changes that occur in the economy.

Absolute poverty measures are not the only measures of poverty. If we define poverty as deprivation plus inequality—inequality in the distribution of income—a relative measure of poverty might appear more appropriate. **Relative poverty** measures the extent to which an individual's or family's income falls below the average income threshold for the economy. According to this definition, a family is poor if they have considerably less access to income and wealth than other people living in their society—for instance, those in the bottom fifth or tenth of the U.S. income distribution. Under this definition, a family of four that makes one dollar over the absolute poverty threshold (i.e., poverty line) would be defined as poor, whereas, using the absolute poverty measure, the family would likely not be eligible to participate in poverty-related programs.

Federal Poverty Thresholds and Guidelines

As you can see, the type of measure a country uses—relative or absolute—changes the way we understand poverty. Each year the U.S. Census Bureau issues **federal poverty thresholds**—the absolute measures that identify the amount of before-tax cash income, based on family size and members' ages, that a family needs to be considered able to meet family members' basic needs. How does the government decide on the income level needed to maintain this basic standard of living? In 1963, Mollie Orshansky, an economist employed at the Social Security Administration, developed the formula used to calculate the federal poverty thresholds. She constructed the formula using the U.S. Department of Agriculture (DOA) food budgets for families in economic stress and then multiplied the cost of this budget by three. While the DOA had four such food plans at the time, Orshansky used the least expensive plan, the economy food plan which was designed for temporary use in tough times, for her calculations. She multiplied her original number by three based on information from the 1955 Household Food Consumption Survey, which found that an average U.S. household spent about one-third of its budget on food. In 1969, Orshansky's formula was adopted as the official U.S. poverty definition, and it has been used since that time. The thresholds are updated annually to reflect inflation using data from the Consumer Price Index for all Urban Consumers (CPI-U).[7]

The Department of Health and Human Services and many state and local government agencies use a simplified version of the poverty thresholds, called **poverty guidelines** or poverty levels, to determine eligibility for a number of means-tested programs and services, including most of the programs that we address later in this chapter. Take a look at the 2009 poverty guidelines in Table 7.1. The 2009 poverty level for a family of four is an annual income of $22,050. When you take into account the wide variety of basic expenses for a family with children—health care, child care, food, housing, utilities, transportation, clothing, school supplies—this is very low indeed! In fact, the Economic Policy Institute estimates that the average yearly cost of meeting the basic needs of a family of four (two parents and two children), was $48,778 in 2008, more than double the 2009 threshold for a family that size![8]

Table 7.1	2009 HHS Poverty Guidelines
Persons in family	Poverty guideline
1	$10,830
2	$14,570
3	$18,310
4	$22,050
5	$25,790
6	$29,530
7	$33,270
8	$37,010

Source: *Federal Register*, Vol. 74, No. 14, January 23, 2009, pp. 4199–4201

Current Federal Poverty Thresholds: Problems and Alternatives

Defining and measuring poverty is a complicated business, and the formula employed by the federal government is imperfect at best. Although suggestions for reform vary widely across the political spectrum, most experts agree that the current measurement provides an inaccurate picture of U.S. poverty. It was even criticized by Orshansky herself in 1995. She noted that the formula she developed was intended for use specifically with elderly households, rather than across the board.[9]

Many argue that an absolute measure does nothing to identify and equalize the highly skewed U.S. income distribution. Even among proponents of an absolute measure, there are concerns about the current formula's ability to calculate whether a family is poor or not. One common criticism is that food occupies a smaller portion of the average U.S. household budget than it did in the 1960s. Current estimates suggest that the average household food expenditure has dropped to one-seventh of total household expenditures; thus, multiplying an average low-cost food budget by three underestimates the income needed to meet basic needs, and thus underestimates the number of poor individuals and families in the U.S.[10] A second criticism is that the thresholds do not take into consideration expenses such as child care, transportation, or other work-related expenditures. A third criticism rests on the lack of cost-of-living adjustments for geographic differences (e.g., housing), especially between urban and rural areas.[11] Of course, some critics are also concerned that the thresholds are based on cash income and do not reflect in-kind benefits or the Earned Income Tax Credit, thus underestimating a family's gross income and possibly overestimating the number of families who are poor.[12]

Suggestions as to how to amend the poverty thresholds or to develop a new way of measuring poverty altogether are abundant, and they come from individuals and organizations with diverse political affiliations and interests.

Among the measures that have received the most attention are those proposed by the National Academy of Sciences. In 1995, the National Academy attempted to address some of the criticism directed at the current measure and developed several alternative formulas for calculating poverty thresholds.[13] Their recommendations included using data from the Consumer Expenditure Survey, which calculates what families actually spend on food, clothing, and shelter, rather than the CPI-U, to update the thresholds each year. They also recommended adjusting the poverty rate to allow for geographic differences in the cost of necessities. Another recommendation they put forth was to update the definition of family income to include the value of some in-kind benefits (e.g., food stamps, housing subsidies, free and reduced school lunches, and heating assistance) and to exclude income and payroll taxes, some medical costs, child care, and work-related expenses.[14] To date, however, none of their recommendations have been adopted.

Critical Thinking Question

Current federal poverty thresholds impact the ability of U.S. families in need to qualify for assistance. The current formula for determining these thresholds has many problems. What role, if any, do social workers have in reforming the current formula?

WHO ARE THE POOR?

Now that we have a rough idea about how poverty is defined and measured, the next questions have to do with what U.S. poverty looks like: Who are "the poor"? How many people are poor?

Every year the U.S. Census Bureau attempts to answer these questions, and many others, through a nationwide survey called the Current Population Survey. Remember that the Census Bureau uses the federal poverty thresholds to identify who qualifies as "poor." Figure 7.1 details the poverty rate trends over the past 45 years. According to the Census Bureau in 2007, 12.5%, or over 37 million people in the United States, are officially poor. This is up from 11.3% of the population and 31.6 million in 2000. Theories abound to explain why this is trend is occurring, and as you might have guessed, much of the debate is politically charged. Certainly, as is clear from Figure 7.1, the most recent upswing in the poverty rate began during the 2001 recession. We'll look at some theories about the causes of poverty in the next subsection.

I see one-third of a nation ill-housed, ill-clad, ill-nourished.

—Franklin D. Roosevelt

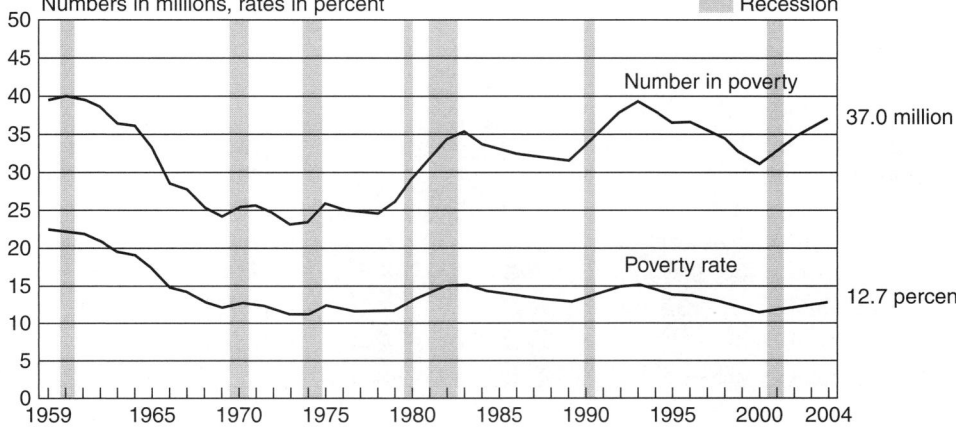

Figure 7.1
Number in Poverty and Poverty Rate, 1959–2004
Source: U.S. Census Bureau, Current Population Survey, 1960 to 2005, Annual Social and Economic Supplements.

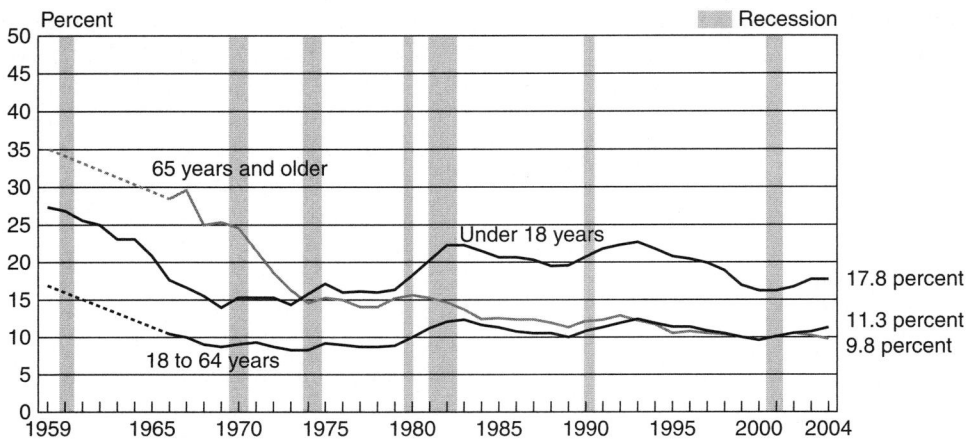

Figure 7.2
Poverty Rates by Age, 1959–2004
Source: U.S. Census Bureau, Current Population Survey, 1960 to 2005. Annual Social and Economic Supplements.

Demographic Trends in Poverty

In addition to collecting information on how many people are poor, the Census Bureau also collects information on who is poor, broken down by age, gender, race, and labor force status. We will examine some of this data next.

One major positive trend that has occurred in the U.S. since the 1950s has been a downward trend in poverty among individuals over 65. As Figure 7.2 illustrates, individuals over age 65 experience the lowest poverty rate in the U.S. The elderly poverty rate, 10.2% in 2003, dropped to 9.7% by 2007. Unfortunately, the same is not true for the youngest Americans. Children have the highest poverty rate of all age groups. Since 1959, the child poverty rate has increased significantly except for a dip during the 1990s. By 2007, more than 13 million children aged 18 years or younger were living in poverty. Although children under 18 make up about a quarter of the U.S. population (24.8%), they make up more than a third (35.7%) of those living in poverty.[15]

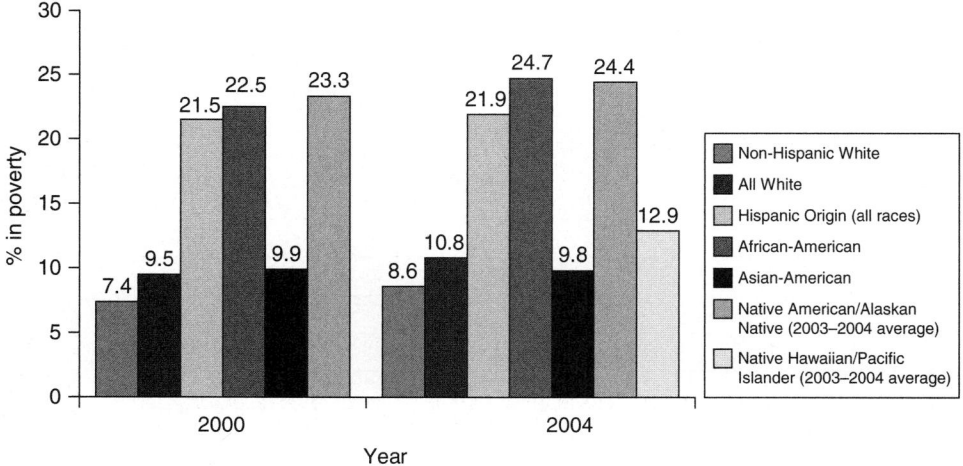

Figure 7.3
Poverty Rates by Race and Latino/a Origin, 2000–2004
Source: U.S. Census Bureau, Current Population Survey, Annual Social and Economic Supplements, 2004.

Poverty and Social Welfare

> **Demonstrating Knowledge, Values, and Skills**
>
> **Differences in Poverty Rates by Group Membership**
>
> This brief overview of differences in poverty by age, gender, and marital status shows how poverty disproportionately affects those who are oppressed in U.S. society: children, women, and people of color. As the poverty data show us, those who are located in multiple oppressed groups (e.g., black *and* a child) suffer most of all. Just looking at the numbers tells only a small fraction of the story of U.S. poverty, however. The data cannot tell us why those in poverty are poor, how they came to be poor, or why some groups experience higher poverty than others.
>
> Take a minute to jot down your guesses about the answers to these questions. In the next section, we will examine some of the causes of poverty, both long and short term. See how your guesses match up.

When child poverty is compared to adult poverty, we find that 18% of children lived in poverty in 2007, significantly higher than either adults (10.9%) or seniors (9.7%).

In 2004, the poverty rate among men of all races was 11.5%, whereas among women it was 13.9%. Two related pieces of data can give us some more information about the levels of poverty among women as compared to men. The first statistic reflects women's median income relative to men's. In 2004, the median earnings of individual women working full time in the U.S. were $31,223; for men it was $40,798. This translates to an earnings ratio for women to men of 77:100 (the source of the often cited statistic that a woman makes $0.77 to a man's $1.00).[16] The second statistic examines poverty households broken down by the gender of the "householder." The difference is stark: close to 30% of female-headed households (households where there is no husband present) are poor, compared to 5.5% of married-couple households and 13.5% of single-male–headed households.[17]

Data also show significant differences in poverty among whites and people of color (see Figure 7.3). In 2007, nearly a quarter (24.5%) of African-Americans lived in poverty compared to 21.5% of Latinos and 8.2% of whites. For other groups, data from 2004 shows that about 10% of Asian Americans, over a quarter (25.3%) of Native American/Alaskan Native peoples, and nearly 13% of Native Hawaiian/Pacific Islanders lived in poverty.[18]

Children of color also disproportionately experience poverty. In 2007, over one-third (34.5%) of all black children, and close to one-third (28.6%) of Latino children, were living at or below the poverty line, compared to about 15% of white children.[19]

Individuals born outside the United States also experienced a higher poverty rate in 2007 that native-born individuals. The poverty rate among non–U.S. born residents was nearly 17%, compared to 11.9% for native-born residents. The poverty rate was particularly high (20%) among individuals who had not become U.S. citizens.[20]

CAUSES OF POVERTY

Why are people poor? What causes poverty? Why are some people more likely to be poor than others? These are important questions for social workers and society, but like other poverty-related questions, they are much more complex than they sound. In the social sciences, questions of cause and effect are the most challenging to answer with certainty. We do know many of the variables that are associated with poverty: changes in the economic climate (e.g., recessions), unemployment, low educational attainment, lack of skills/training, discrimination and oppression, loss of primary wage-earner, one-parent family structure, illness, disability, and government spending on social-welfare programs. Both structural and individual variables interact to create poverty, but just how they do so is often highly complex and dynamic. Let's look at some of these factors in greater detail.

Economic System Factors: Work, Income, and the Labor Market

One theory about poverty is that it stems from a lack of work, and, indeed, loss of employment is the single event most likely to trigger entrance into poverty.[21] Although there are many reasons a person might lose a job, one major source of job loss is low demand in the economy. Unemployment and the macroeconomic forces that cause unemployment have a significant impact on the U.S. poverty rate. The poverty rate tends to rise during times of high unemployment and to fall during periods of lower unemployment.[22] Moreover, the poverty level also correlates with macroeconomic changes, such as recessions (see Figure 7.1) and periods of real wage declines or increases. Recessions trigger generally low demand for workers in the market, but certain sectors of the economy are often disproportionately affected. In addition, larger changes in the national and global economy can trigger low demand for workers in a particular sector even when the economy is growing. For example, since the 1970s the U.S. has seen a significant loss of jobs in the manufacturing sector due to globalization. The loss of these jobs, which typically provided workers without postsecondary education benefits and livable wage, has moved many of the previously nonpoor into the ranks of the working poor.

Although lack of employment—and thus lack of income—is a major source of poverty, to say that poverty always is a result of a lack of employment is incorrect. Using the official federal definition of poverty, more than a third of the poor worked at some point during 2007.[23] Almost 12% of the poor worked full-time and year-round.[24] Yet working families with incomes below the poverty line earn, on average, only 76% of the poverty threshold.[25] Working families actually made up the majority (52%) of families with incomes at or below 200% of the federal poverty level ($44,100 for a family of three) in 2009.[26] These families have attracted increased attention in recent years, especially as welfare reform pushed millions of recipients of Temporary Assistance to Needy Family (TANF) off welfare and into low-paying jobs. The **working poor** challenge our assumptions about the relationship between work and poverty. Here are a few details about the working poor (those working at least 1,000 hours per year and with incomes at or below 200% of the FPL):

- A majority of these families have children (80%) and two or more adults present (65.3%);[27]
- They are more likely to have jobs in lower-paying industries such as services or transportation;[28]
- These jobs are typically less stable and provide fewer benefits such as health insurance and retirement plans;[29]
- These jobs are less likely to have daytime hours, adding the burden of child-care expenses to one-parent or dual-income families even after their children reach school age;[30]

Table 7.2 Federal and State Minimum Wages

>Federal MW	Equals Federal MW of $7.25	< Federal MW	No MW Required
AK - 7.75	AZ	AR - 6.25	AL
CA - 8.00	DE	CO - 7.24	LA
CT - 8.25	FL	GA - 5.15	MS
DC - 8.25	HI	MN - 6.15	SC
IL - 8.00	IA	WY - 5.15	TN
MA - 8.00	ID		
ME - 7.50	IN		
MI - 7.40	KS	5 States	5 States
NV - 7.55	KY		
NM - 7.50	MD		
OH - 7.30	MO		
OR - 8.40	MT		
RI - 7.40	NE		
VT - 8.06	NH		
WA - 8.55	NJ		
	NY		
	NC		
14 States + DC	ND		
	OK		
	PA		
	SD		
	TX		
	UT		
	VA		
	WV		
	WI		
	26 states		

Source: US Department of Labor, Wage and Hour Division, 2010

- Their median wages are far below the nonpoor: $7.55 per hour versus $16.67 per hour; For working-poor families headed by one adult, the difference is even greater—they earn a median wage of only $6.73;[31]
- The poor in the United States work more hours per capita than in any other wealthy nation.[32]

Clearly, many of the poor work, and working is not always an effective antidote to poverty. In fact, according to one study that simulated the effects of stringent work requirements, even if all able-bodied adults worked at least 2,000 hours per year, only about 20% of the working poor would move to above 200% of the FPL, whereas one-third of nonworking poor would become working poor and only one-sixth of the nonworking poor would move to above 200% of the FPL.[33]

One of the reasons that even people who are participating in the labor force remain poor is low wages. In 2007, Congress enacted the Fair Minimum Wage Act, triggering the first minimum wage increase in over a decade. In July 2007, the minimum wage increased from $5.15 to $5.85; in July 2008 the minimum wage increased from $5.85 to $6.55, and as of July 2009, the federal minimum wage in the United States was $7.25 per hour. This means that a person working full-time and year-round at a minimum-wage job will earn about $15,000 before taxes (assuming that this person has paid sick days and holidays or does not take any days off). This figure is barely above the 2009 FPL for a family of one of two, and about $3,000 below the 2009 FPL for a family of three. States are able to set their own minimum wage laws, and many set them higher than the federal minimum wage (see Table 7.2). As of 2010, no state has mandated a minimum wage high enough for an individual in a minimum-wage job to earn enough to meet the 2009 FPL for a family of three (about $8.80/hour).

Many tout raising the minimum wage by a substantial amount as a simple way to reduce U.S. poverty; however, what effect such changes actually have on the U.S. economy is the subject of contentious debate. Concerns include whether employers can afford to pay workers a higher minimum wage without laying people off, whether higher minimum wages encourage large corporations to send jobs outside the U.S., and the potential impact on the inflation rate in the U.S.

Wage Inequality

is another economic phenomenon connected to poverty,[34] one that is tied, at least in part, to the low end of the U.S. wage spectrum. As the difference between the median incomes of the top 20% of the country and the bottom 20% of the country has grown, poverty levels have, in general, increased.[35] As Table 7.3 shows, the after-tax incomes of the lowest 20% of wage earners rose only 8.7% during the two decades between 1979 and 2000, whereas the incomes of the highest fifth increased by 68.3%. This makes sense when we consider that the minimum wage has been raised only $4.35 since 1979, whereas there is no upper limit on what Americans can earn.

Why is wage inequality connected to poverty? One argument is that as the wealthy become more distant from those in the lower quartiles of the earning bracket, they find it easier to opt out of, or not lend their political support to, publicly financed programs that help "redistribute" some of the wealth, especially to those who are most in need.[36] The wealthy are not likely to gain anything (financially) from programs like food stamps or TANF, so they may be less supportive of funding such programs. They can send their children to better public schools (because they can afford to move to wealthier school districts) or to private schools, so they are likely to be less invested in the quality of poorer schools;

Table 7.3   Average After-Tax Income by Income Group (in 200 dollars), 1979–2000.

Income Category	1979	1989	2000	Percent Change 1979–2000	Dollar Change 1979–2000
Lowest Fifth	12600	12100	13700	8.7	1100
Second Fifth	25600	25100	29000	13.3	3400
Middle Fifth	36400	37500	41900	15.1	5500
Fourth Fith	47700	51800	59200	24.1	11500
Fifth Fith	87000	10800	141400	68.3	57400
81st–95th percentile	65300	75800	88700	35.9	23400
96th–99th percentile	103600	129100	158600	53.1	55000
Top 1percent	286300	506500	862700	201.3	576400

Source: Timothy Smeeding, "Public Policy, Economic Inequality and Poverty: The United States in Comparative Perspective" *Social Science Quarterly*, 86: 977 (2005).

and they can afford good health insurance, and so are less likely to consider the quality and accessibility of Medicaid. Thus higher economic inequality produces lower levels of investment in programs that help redistribute both actual money (through programs like TANF) and resources (like public schools or Medicaid).

Education and "Human Capital"

It should come as no surprise that education and poverty are intimately connected. Low educational attainment is a key predictor of poverty, a fact highlighted in Table 7.4. Across all races and both genders, Americans with less than a high school education experience the highest poverty rates. Over one-fifth of those without a high school education have incomes at or below 100% of the FPL, and this figure goes up to 51.2% for those with incomes at or below 200% of the FPL. For all races and both genders, there is a significant drop in poverty rates for those who have completed a high school education. Those who have completed a college education experience the lowest rates across groups. One of the reasons for the connection between educational level and poverty is obvious: Most jobs, even many minimum wage jobs, require at least a high school education. In addition, an increasing number of jobs, even at the paraprofessional level, require at least some college or postsecondary training.

Human capital refers to the range of qualities a worker brings to employment, including education, training, skills, and past work experience. Education is typically the foundation on which these other qualities are built. It's hard to get the work experience needed for a higher-paying position without enough education. Individuals with low human capital are typically less appealing to employers.

Although human capital offers a more complete picture of the individual qualities needed for employment and economic upward mobility, lack of human capital is hardly the only factor that keeps people from finding employment that offers advancement opportunities and thus a way out of poverty.

When someone works for less pay than she can live on . . . then she has made a great sacrifice for you.

—Barbara Ehrenreich

Table 7.4 **Percent (%) of U.S. Population in Poverty by Education Level and Race and Gender, 2004**

	Less than High School	High School	Some College/ Post-Secondary Training	College (4yrs)
All	21.9%	11.9%	8.5%	4.3%
All Male	18.3%	10.9%	7.1%	3.8%
All Female	25.3%	13.5%	9.7%	4.8%
White (non-Latino/a)	15.8%	9.4%	7.0%	3.7%
African-American	34.8%	22.0%	14.9%	7.1%
Latino/a	26.7%	15.4%	10.6%	7.5%
Asian-American	15.8%	11.3%	11.5%	6.1%

Source: U.S. Census Bureau

Structural forces in our society (e.g., oppression and discrimination) can both keep individuals and/or groups from acquiring human capital and prevent them from advancing despite their possessing human capital. We can see this phenomenon in evidence if we look again at Table 7.4. Notice that poverty rates, even among college graduates, are higher among women and people of color. Even when in possession of a college education, so often touted as the "ticket out of poverty," poverty is harder to avoid for women and people of color.

Oppression and Discrimination

In the previous section on the demography of poverty, we saw that poverty disproportionately affects women, children, and people of color. Much of this is due to the effects of institutional oppression and discrimination on these groups. Institutional oppression and discrimination refers to practices that are deeply embedded in our social, educational, legal, and political institutions. Often institutional forms of oppression and discrimination are covert and "just the way things are," rather than clear, overt acts of individual discrimination. Indeed, although the U.S. has many federal and state laws designed to prevent overt discrimination on the basis of race, sex, religion, national origin, and disability, institutional oppression and discrimination continues to impede the ability of minorities, women, immigrants, and the disabled to obtain employment, safe housing, financial resources (e.g., mortgages or car loans), health care, quality education, and equal representation in the legal systems. It is not hard to find examples of this phenomenon in action. Years of legal discrimination against African Americans in housing and employment (before the 1964 Civil Rights Act) contributed to the development of poor urban ghettos in most U.S. cities. Because of the way U.S. public schools are funded (i.e., primarily through local tax revenue), the schools in these neighborhoods suffer the consequences: less-qualified teachers, larger classes, crumbling buildings, few enrichment activities, and harsher discipline. Many students drop out. Without even a high school education, their employment opportunities are limited to jobs that pay a minimum wage, which, as we know, does not even provide enough income for a single person to live above the FPL. The cycle continues, despite federal and state antidiscrimination laws.

Human Rights & Justice

Critical Thinking Question

Some individuals and groups argue that access to free high-quality education is a basic human right. Do you agree? What role might a social worker play in advancing this right nationally or globally?

> ### Did You Know?
>
> **Being Poor Isn't Cheap . . .**
>
> If you think that poor individuals could simply remedy their circumstances by spending less money, you might want to rethink your position. A recent study by the Brookings Institution illustrates just how expensive being poor can be. The researcher, Matt Fellowes, found that lower-income families in 12 U.S. cities pay higher than average prices for a wide range of basic necessities than do higher income families. Some of these are:
>
> - **Financial Services:** Lower-income families often have to rely on check-cashing businesses because they don't have enough income to maintain a bank account. These businesses charge up to a 10% fee per check.
> - **Tax Refund Services:** Lower-income consumers are more likely to pay high fees to get their tax returns more quickly. Many tax preparation services may charge over 1,800% interest on refund anticipation loans, and may target these loans directly to their lowest-income customers.
> - **Car Insurance:** Drivers living in lower-income neighborhoods can pay between $50 and $1,000 per year in higher car insurance premiums than those living in higher-income neighborhoods.
> - **Home Loans:** 4.2 million lower-income homeowners pay an average of 4.2% more in mortgage interest than higher-income households.
> - **Furniture:** Lower-income consumers are more likely to shop at rent-to-own business for pricier home wares such as furniture, computers, and washing machines, which they cannot afford to pay up front for. The interest on these items can end up costing the customer over three times the products' value.
> - **Groceries:** Grocery stores in lower-income neighborhoods are often smaller and more expensive than those in higher-income neighborhoods, and there are fewer large stores accessible to lower income neighborhoods. Both factors mean less opportunity for comparison shopping and efficient use of a grocery budget.
>
> *Source*: Matthew Fellowes, From Poverty, Opportunity: Putting the Market to Work for Lower Income Families (Washington, DC: Brookings Institution, 2006).

Finally, the poor, regardless of their race, gender, ethnicity, or disability status, often face covert and overt discrimination and exploitation on the basis of their poverty status. It is no coincidence that predatory retail and financial outlets set up shop in poor neighborhoods. Many large companies, such as grocery store and retail chains, choose not to open stores in poor areas, leaving the poor no choice but to shop at higher-priced markets. Blatant cases of individual discrimination occur as well, like the fast-food worker who was fired because of her unkempt appearance, which was due to the worker's inability to afford to pay the $4.00 fee to use the washing machine at the local laundromat. Institutional and individual oppression and discrimination keep many, many Americans locked in a poverty trap.

The Impact of Changing Family Structures

During the early to mid-1990s, the years in which welfare reform was the topic of many a national headline, there was lots of talk about single motherhood and poverty. Some blamed single, unwed mothers, citing their poor choices and lack of self-control, for perpetuating a cycle of poverty and driving up the number of Americans receiving welfare. Others decried the forces of institutional oppression that keep women dependent on undependable male partners and/or earning $0.77 to a man's $1.00. One fact became unavoidable: Families headed by a single woman were, and are, the most likely to be poor. This phenomenon has been termed the **feminization of poverty**.[37]

Why this the case? Some of the many reason for high rates of poverty among women with children include:

- Sex/gender discrimination
- Insufficient child support from child(ren)'s fathers
- Concentration of women in low-paying jobs

- Economic changes leading to decline in mid-level jobs and increase in lower-paying service industry jobs
- Increase in divorce, separation, and "singleness"
- High cost of childcare
- Early child-bearing
- Low educational attainment[38]

Having children is expensive in both time and money. Raising children can easily be unaffordable on one income. Furthermore, a single mother is not only the only potential wage earner; she is also the only source of child care. For single women with very young children—the groups that are the most likely to be poor—the choice is impossible: they cannot leave their children alone to go to work, but they cannot feed their children without working. The high cost of child care can make it an untenable option for low- and even some moderate-income single mothers. Add to all of these barriers the fact that women, especially those without advanced education and training, are generally herded into low-paying "pink collar" jobs (e.g., food service, domestic work, etc.), and it is no wonder that so many female-headed households are living below the poverty line.

Although women have increasingly made up the majority of the poor, the vast increase in the number of women in the labor force over the past several decades has reduced poverty among married-couple families. Families where both husband and wife are employed have the lowest rates of poverty among all family types. It is interesting to note that among one-income married-couple families, families where only the wife works have lower rates of poverty than families where only the husband works.[39]

Critical Thinking Question
What do you suppose accounts for the fact that married households with one income provided by the female wage earner have lower rates of poverty than those with one income provided by a male wage earner?

The "Culture of Poverty"

For some, the experience of poverty is temporary. A laid-off employee gets a new job, a single parent remarries, a temporarily disabling condition improves. For others, however, poverty seems a permanent state, passed down from generation to generation in an endless cycle. This phenomenon, and the explanation for it, has been termed the **culture of poverty**. The concept originated in the early 1960s, when middle-class America was just waking up to the reality of poverty in the U.S. Oscar Lewis, an anthropologist, argued that the culture of poverty was an adaptation by the poor to their social and economic marginalization and alienation as lower class members in a capitalist society experiencing a period of economic stress, high unemployment, and high inequality.[40] Lewis defined "culture of poverty" characteristics as apathy, hostility, social disorganization, lack of participation in civic life, early sexual activity and childbearing, poor impulse control, and a present-time orientation.[41] He argued that these characteristics helped the poor cope with the feelings of hopelessness, helplessness, and despair that arise from their experience of marginalization, and he believed these characteristics could be passed down to succeeding generations, causing them to become embedded in communities even when the economic and social factors precipitating them had improved, leading to even further marginalization and social isolation.[42] According to Lewis, the antidote to the culture of poverty lay in the poor becoming a viable social movement that could advocate for their rights and agitate for changes in oppressive institutions.[43]

Other authors of the time used similar terminology to describe and explain intergenerational poverty, although most did not share Lewis's belief

Figure 7.4
Variables Associated with Poverty

in a radical, empowerment-focused remedy. Many of Lewis's contemporaries appropriated his theory for more conservative ends, describing the culture of poverty in a way that closely echoed the older idea of the "undeserving poor." Writing in the 1970s, Edward Banfield described the culture among the poor as one that is so present-oriented that it "attaches no value to work, sacrifice, self-improvement, or service to family, friends or community."[44] Unlike Lewis, Banfield's solution was not empowerment among the poor through organization or redistribution of resources. An advocate of a laissez-faire approach, Banfield instead argued that because the solutions he identified, such as removing children from poor parents and placing them with middle-class parents, were not legal, the government had better just stay out of the whole business.[45]

Indeed, the distressing similarities between the conservative view of the "culture of poverty" concept and the old notions of the "undeserving poor" have resulted in significant controversy surrounding the phrase in general. The concept has become almost entirely identified with an emphasis on the individual characteristics of the poor, rather than on the structural forces that cause poverty. Focusing only on individual issues can easily lead to stigmatizing the poor and blaming them for their own circumstances. This attitude, in turn, easily leads to political and social apathy, and even hostility, to the need for policies that promote structural change as a means to reduce U.S. poverty.

We have explored some of the major theories about what causes poverty (see Figure 7.4). There are also many life events, circumstances, social forces, and

> **Social Work Stories: The Intersection of Poverty and Mental Health**
>
> Rebecca O., a case manager for chronically mentally ill adults at a religiously affiliated social service agency in Kentucky, reflects on the challenges that arise when mental illness and poverty intersect:
>
> > One of the most challenging aspects of poverty for my clients is that it is so limiting to their lives. Poverty impacts all of their basic needs. If you don't have food, a roof over your head, or heat in the winter those issues become priority number one in my work with them. Even though there may be other pressing issue—mental and physical health issues, for instance—that need attention as well, there's only so much we can do at once. Poverty also seems to create a cycle of crisis throughout people's lives. Let's say an individual gets a monthly pay or public assistance check at the beginning of the month that just isn't enough to cover everything it's supposed to, his or her food stamp allowance can't quite cover their food needs, and it's just not possible for that person to go to work to make some extra income. Towards the end of the month everything gets really emotionally elevated—that person is under very intense stress and a mental health crisis becomes much more likely. . . .
> >
> > Sometimes I find I can get overwhelmed working with people who are struggling with the combined affects of poverty and serious mental illness. The challenges they face can feel so monumental. I try to remember to maintain a focused balance: to do my best to deal with the things I have the power to help with, but also remain focused on building and sustaining the relationship I have with my client. The relationship is what helps bridge the gap between my own life experience [as someone who has not lived in poverty] and my client's. I also try to view my work with clients through the lens of empowerment: getting to know a client as a unique individual with strengths and challenges, accepting that their goals and capacities are unique to them and may be different than mine, and using the strength of our relationship to promote a sense of stability and groundedness.

Poverty is a reflection also on those who are not poor.
—Brooks Atkinson

other phenomena that are potential causes of poverty. Chief among these is the effect of poor physical and mental health. Poor physical health, injury, and/or disability can push people out of the labor force and into poverty. If any of these problems occur in a family's primary wage earner, they can cause the family to fall below the poverty line. Mental illness, emotional disturbances, trauma, and drug and/or alcohol dependence can also prevent individuals from working at all, or working enough to support themselves and their families. These issues can affect anyone; however, certain types of chronic physical and mental illness are associated with poverty and oppression—they operate in a loop, like many of the other variables discussed in this section, where they are both the cause and the effect of poverty. For social workers, this loop is especially deserving of attention. We will return to these important topics in later chapters.

PUBLICLY FUNDED SERVICES TO THE POOR

You are now familiar with the definitions and some of the many complex causes of poverty in the United States. Social workers encounter the real and often devastating effects of poverty regardless of their field of practice. Social workers have often been at the forefront of attempts to address and remedy the challenge of poverty through work creating and managing public and privately funded antipoverty programs, advocating with poor communities, and providing direct service to individual and families in need. In this section we will survey some of the key public and private sector antipoverty programs active in the U.S.

SOCIAL INSURANCE PROGRAMS

Social Security

U.S. social welfare is comprised of two major categories of cash support programs: social insurances and public assistance.[46] Social insurances are based on the prior earnings and payroll contributions of an individual, whereas public assistance, typically referred to as welfare, is based on the financial need of an individual. The primary social insurance programs today are Old Age, Survivors, and Disability Insurance; unemployment insurance; and workers' compensation.

Old Age, Survivors, and Disability Insurance (OASDI), commonly known as Social Security, is an example of a universal program, because U.S. citizens are entitled to participate in the program as a social right.[47] Program participation is not based on financial need. In 2007, close to $577 billion in Social Security benefits was paid.[48] In that year, about 49.4 million Americans received benefits. Funding for Social Security comes from a payroll tax shared in an equal proportion by the employer and employee. Social Security benefits are adjusted when the cost of living increases, a practice that began during the Nixon Administration.[49]

To receive Social Security, a person must contribute payroll taxes during his or her working years, earning "credits" toward future Social Security benefits.[50] Those individuals contributing payroll taxes for a minimum of 10 years (or 40 quarters in Social Security eligibility terms) are covered permanently under the program. The level of covered earnings and age determines individual benefit levels at retirement. People born before 1938 can receive full Social Security retirement benefits at age 65, whereas this age gradually increases for others. For example, for those born in 1960 or later, the full retirement age is 67.

The disability insurance part of Social Security assists people of any age who meet certain eligibility criteria. Specifically, people can qualify if they have sufficient Social Security credits and show medical proof of a disability that will prevent them from substantial employment for a year or more. A person with a condition expected to result in death may also qualify.[51] When the individual turns 65 years of age, disability benefits automatically become old-age benefits. Finally, survivors insurance covers various categories of dependent children, parents, widowers, and widows. These categories of recipients receive benefits when a worker insured through Social Security dies.

As we saw in the previous section on contemporary poverty demographics, the poverty rate among those 65 and older has declined over the years and continues to decline, evidence that Social Security is an effective antipoverty program. That is, most recipients are raised above the poverty line by Social Security.[52]

Unemployment Insurance

Unemployment insurance is a second major social insurance program. Like Social Security, unemployment insurance can be an effective poverty prevention program, although it is a temporary aid,[53] since unemployment benefits normally last a maximum of 26 weeks. In fiscal year 2006, close to $30 billion was spent in the U.S. on unemployment insurance benefits, with a little over 7 million people benefiting from the program. Although governed by federal standards, individual states determine eligibility for unemployment benefits, the amount and duration of the benefits, and the amount that employers must contribute. Except for three states, which require a minimal employee contribution, funding for unemployment insurance is derived solely from an employer payroll tax.

About 85% of the total U.S. labor force is covered by unemployment insurance. Farmers, domestic workers, and self-employed workers are not eligible for unemployment benefits. In addition, few of the poor receive unemployment insurance. The poor can be excluded from benefits for several reasons. A poor individual may not qualify if that person worked less than two of four quarters in the qualifying year or if the person earned less than a minimum income. Also, if the individual was terminated from a job for misconduct or quit voluntarily, he or she may be excluded. Furthermore, in most states, time spent in job training can prevent an individual from qualifying for unemployment benefits, because the individual is not immediately available and looking for work.

Workers' Compensation

The third major social insurance program in the United States is **workers' compensation**. It is the oldest major social insurance program in the nation, dating back to the Progressive Era.[54] Spending by employers nationally on direct written premiums for workers' compensation totaled $31.7 billion in 2001.[55] There are no federal standards, so each state oversees its own workers' compensation program. The program provides victims of work-related injuries with cash, medical care, and, to a limited extent, rehabilitation services. It also compensates survivors if an injury is fatal. Like unemployment insurance, workers' compensation does not cover all workers. Farm and domestic workers are not covered in many states. For those wage and salary workers in the U.S. that are covered, state laws generally specify a payment rate of two-thirds of the injured worker's previous pay.

In contrast to injuries, coverage for occupational illnesses is a weak part of workers' compensation. Most states only pay benefits for illnesses that appear within "several" years after the worker leaves a company. In other words, workers have a relatively short period of time to prove their case.

PUBLIC ASSISTANCE PROGRAMS

The second major category of U.S. cash support programs is public assistance. Public assistance programs are "selective" programs in that benefits are based on individual need. Need is determined by a **means test** (i.e., an income test).[56] The three primary sources of U.S. public assistance are Temporary Assistance to Needy Families, Supplemental Security Income, and general assistance.

Temporary Assistance to Needy Families (TANF)

The 1996 welfare reform enacted by the Clinton Administration ended "Aid to Families with Dependent Children" (AFDC) as an entitlement and replaced the program with a block grant, called Temporary Assistance to Needy Families (TANF), discussed in Chapter 6.[57] In 2007, the federal government appropriated close to $16.5 billion for TANF. To receive federal funds in the AFDC program, states had to provide matching funds. Under the 1996 legislation, states do not provide matching funds, but they do need to

Poverty and Social Welfare

meet a "maintenance of effort" requirement. That is, states must maintain spending equal to at least 75% of their Fiscal Year 1994 spending on AFDC and related services (80% if work participation rates are not met by the state). TANF gives states some flexibility in administering federal funds. For example, states can transfer up to 30% of their TANF block grant funding to either their Child Care Development Block Grant or 4.25% to their Social Services Block Grant.

The fundamental difference between the new TANF and former AFDC programs is that, under TANF, no individual or family is "entitled" to welfare.[58] As a general rule, individuals must participate in work activity within two years of receiving assistance and families are limited to a total of five years assistance in a lifetime. If a program participant refuses work requirements, states have the option to reduce or eliminate assistance to the family. This could include the loss of Medicaid. The exception to this provision is when the participant refuses work because they cannot find or afford child care for a child under 6 years old. Although the 1996 legislation did not guarantee that this needed child care would be provided to the participant, states are mandated to spend 70% or more of Child Care Entitlement funding, which is part of the Child Care and Development Fund, on families receiving TANF, transitioning from TANF, or at risk of becoming TANF eligible.

Another important feature of TANF, as originally designed, concerns minor parents.[59] Minors who are parents cannot receive TANF assistance unless they are living at home with their parents or in another adult-supervised setting. In addition, these minors must attend high school or an alternative educational or training program when the child is 12 weeks old.

Critical Thinking Question

Imagine you are a social worker working with a low-income adolescent girl about to give birth to her first child. What financial, social, emotional, educational, and housing challenges could you assist her with?

Supplemental Security Income

The **Supplemental Security Income (SSI)** program was established in 1974 during the Nixon Administration.[60] It was essentially a restructuring of the Social Security Act's public assistance programs for blind and older Americans. Aiming to assure a minimum monthly income, the program supplements the income of poor people who are aged 65 or older, blind, or disabled.[61] SSI recipients have grown from 4 million in 1974 to 7.8 million in 2006. The federal government spent more than $38 billion in SSI benefits in 2005. Contrary to the misconception that SSI is funded by Social Security trust funds, the program is funded out of general tax revenues.

People with disabilities are the largest group of SSI clients, representing 72% of total recipients in 2005. "Disability" is defined under SSI guidelines as a "physical or mental impairment that prevents substantial employment activity and has lasted or probably will last for at least a year or may result in death."[62]

General Assistance

The third major public assistance program in the United States is **General Assistance**.[63] It is a program for the needy that do not qualify for previously described federal assistance. Forty-one states and the District of Columbia offer general assistance, although in some states, only certain counties provide assistance. As the name suggests, the program provides general "safety net" help to the poor. Benefits include cash and/or in-kind payments. Similar to TANF, 21 states require "employable" adults to work or enter job training in order to maintain eligibility for general assistance benefits. Some states also impose

> **Did You Know?**
>
> Welfare reform got its major push from city and state governments.[65] These levels of the public sector began experiencing severe budget crises during the 1970s and 1980s. A primary example was New York City, which experienced a fiscal crisis in 1975. Public assistance, among other things, was blamed for the city's fiscal problems, precipitating a movement to reform city welfare. During the 1980s, other cities followed New York City's example. At the same time, state governments around the country began asking for federal regulation "waivers" concerning public assistance. As a result, many features of TANF, including time limits and teen parent restrictions, had already been implemented at the state level when the 1996 federal legislation was enacted.

time limits on all or certain categories of their general assistance caseload. These requirements reflect the increased tightening by many states of general assistance eligibility for adults considered employable during the 1990s.

Current Issues in Public Assistance: A Critical Analysis of Welfare Reform

There are many issues of concern to the social work profession regarding the TANF program.[64] PRWORA, the 1996 Personal Responsibility and Work Opportunity Act that established TANF, contained no explicit requirement that poor families get cash assistance. Under this welfare reform legislation, states can opt to limit aid to vouchers or services. These features of the new approach to public assistance present a threat to the social work principle of self-determination, because they provide less flexibility to caseworkers and clients in the use of welfare assistance. The provisions of the law allowing states to reduce spending on welfare to 75% of Fiscal Year 1994 state spending and to transfer TANF funds to child care or social services block grants gives states some flexibility. However, there are potential negative ramifications to this aspect of the law as well. TANF funds spent on other services could result in less basic subsistence support to poor families. Another issue concerning TANF involves the right of clients to appeal TANF decisions. The former federal law regarding public assistance was specific in guaranteeing clients the right to appeal decisions against them. The 1996 legislation, however, is more general on this issue. States must submit their own plans, which may vary considerably in the protection of client rights.

FOOD AND SHELTER PROGRAMS

Food Stamps

The federal government provides food to poor Americans through a variety of programs. Public, private nonprofit, and private for-profit organizations all cooperate in the provision of these programs. For example, child nutrition programs, including the school lunch program, reach out to poor children in schools, child-care centers, and summer camps. The largest federal food program, representing about two out of every three federal dollars in the food and nutrition category, is the **Food Stamp Program**.[66] In 2007, 2.6 million people received food stamps, and total benefits equaled about $30 billion. The average benefit per person was $95.46.[67] These benefits are adjusted yearly in accordance with changes in food prices generally. Food stamp households, however, are expected to contribute about 30% of their resources to food costs. Although states administer their food stamp programs, the federal government pays for the direct costs of food stamps and a portion of state administrative expenses.

Participants in the food stamp program receive a monthly allotment of "stamps" through an electronic benefit transfer system. Using a plastic debit card, food stamp recipients can purchase food at most retail stores. Participants may not purchase alcohol, tobacco products, or hot ready-to-eat foods with "stamps." In recent years, consistent with the push for welfare reform in general, work requirements have been attached to food stamps. PRWORA limits able-bodied recipients between the ages of 18 and 50 (without children) to three months of food stamps in a three-year period unless the person is working or engaged in a workfare program for 20 or more hours per week.[68]

The Special Supplemental Food Program for Women, Infants, and Children (WIC)

"WIC" is a specialized preventive nutrition program that provides nutritious foods, nutrition education, and access to health care to low-income pregnant women, new mothers, infants, and children at nutritional risk. WIC has been proven to increase the number of women receiving prenatal care, reduce the incidence of low birth weight and fetal mortality, reduce anemia, and enhance the nutritional quality of participants' diets. Like the Food Stamp Program, WIC is administered at the federal level through USDA's Food and Nutrition Service. The program is available in all 50 States. Also like food stamps, WIC has income eligibility restrictions. To be eligible for the WIC program, an applicant must be a pregnant, postpartum, or breastfeeding woman, an infant, or a child under the age of five. Applicants must live in the state in which they apply, must be certified by a health professional to be at nutritional risk (for medical or dietary reasons), and must have a household income below 185 percent of the federal poverty line. In addition, a person who participates or has family members who participate in certain other benefit programs, such as the Food Stamp Program, Medicaid, or TANF, automatically meets the income eligibility requirement.[69] According to the USDA, about 8 million individuals relieved WIC benefits in 2007.[70]

Public Housing and Section 8 Housing Assistance

The federal government assists many middle- and upper-income families with housing through its tax policies and loan programs. The federal government also collaborates with local public and private entities to provide housing assistance to low-income individuals and families. Most of this support is provided through the Department of Housing and Urban Development (HUD) in two major programs: the **Public Housing Program** and the **Section 8 Program**. In fiscal year 2007, HUD's budget was $33.6 billion.[71]

The **Public Housing Program**, dating back to the New Deal, provides federal subsidies for construction costs on housing units built by local public housing authorities.[72] These local housing authorities subsequently own and operate the units. As part of the program, the federal government offers rent subsidies to cover the difference between the operating cost of individual housing units and 30% of the tenant's adjusted household income.

During the Reagan, G. H. W. Bush, Clinton, and G. W. Bush administrations, federal funding for public housing was cut drastically. One reason for this diminishing support was the tendency of public housing projects to concentrate families facing multiple challenges into low-income neighborhoods. Increasingly, this approach has witnessed a high incidence of crime and vandalism, resulting in relatively high operating costs for local public housing authorities and high social costs for victimized families. These problems, along with rising construction costs, compelled policymakers to look for alternative low-income housing proposals.

The **Section 8 program** (referring to Section 8 of the Housing and Community Development Act) emerged in the 1980s as the major alternative to public housing.[73] Subsequently, it became the largest federal housing assistance program for the poor. To illustrate, in 1996, the U.S. government spent $15.8 billion on Section 8 assistance, whereas the public housing program received $4.5 billion. Section 8, now called the **Housing Choice Voucher Program**, is essentially a rent supplement program. Tenants typically pay 30% of their adjusted income on rent; the federal government pays the difference between the tenant's contribution and the market rate for the apartment. In contrast to public housing, tenants have a "choice" of using their subsidy in publicly or privately owned housing where available in their community. The 1990 Housing Act, passed by the George H. W. Bush Administration, sought to increase the supply of low-income rental housing through block grants to state and local governments.

To address the ongoing challenge of funding affordable housing, some states and cities are now establishing housing trust funds to assist in creating more affordable housing units. State or local governments usually establish local housing trust funds. The funds receive ongoing public revenues that can only be spent on affordable housing initiatives, including new construction, preservation of existing housing, emergency repairs, homeless shelters, housing-related services, and multifamily building for nonprofit organizations. At least 257 housing trust funds operate in the U.S., spending over $500 million on housing opportunities each year.[74] There is also legislation (pending at time of press) to create a national housing trust fund. In December 2007, Congress passed the National Affordable Housing Trust Fund Act. If signed into law by President Bush, the bill will establish a dedicated funding source for the production, preservation, and rehabilitation of 1.5 million affordable homes over 10 years. At least 75% of the funds will be for housing for households that are extremely low income, earning less than 30% of an area's median income.[75]

Contributions of Business and the Private Nonprofit Sector to Housing

The federal government encourages business investment in low-income housing through the low-income rental housing tax credit.[76] The tax credit was established as part of the Reagan Administration's Tax Reform Act of 1986. Between 1990 and 1994, this tax incentive added about a quarter million low-income housing units to the housing supply. Developers qualify for the tax credit if they set aside specified percentages of their rental units for low-income tenants.

Habitat for Humanity International is probably the most well-known voluntary housing development program. Between 1976 and 2000, this nonprofit, nondenominational Christian organization, using donated material

and voluntary labor, produced about 30,000 affordable houses in the United States.[77] The program refers to recipients of the houses as "partners" because the partner family helps build their house. Upon completion, Habitat for Humanity sells the home to the partner at no profit, while ensuring the partner a no-interest mortgage. The average sale price for a Habitat home built in the United States in 2008 was about $60,000.[78] Although Habitat for Humanity, by itself, is not capable of solving the shelter problem in the United States, it is a valuable part of the collaborative effort to address the problem.

Current Shelter Issues: The Homeless

Despite various public and private efforts to provide decent low-income housing and temporary shelter, including the 1987 Stewart B. McKinney Homeless Assistance Act, the National Coalition for the Homeless believes the number of homeless people in the U.S. continues to grow.[79] Estimates of homelessness vary, in part, because the definition of what constitutes "homelessness" varies. The National Coalition for the Homeless uses a broad definition, claiming that people who live in unstable housing arrangements and lack a permanent place to stay are experiencing homelessness. Although the National Law Center on Homelessness and Poverty estimates that as many as 2 million people experience homelessness during a given year, the National Coalition for the Homeless, because of the difficulty in counting the homeless, chooses to cite the shortage of available services for the homeless. In 2006, 29% of requests for emergency shelter went unmet due to a lack of resources.[80] Moreover, another study showed that in 50 cities around the U.S., the individual city's official estimated number of homeless typically exceeded that city's available number of shelter and transitional housing spaces.

Case Study: Inter-Professional Collaboration—Integrating Antipoverty and Domestic Violence Advocacy in Iowa

Poverty is among the most pervasive challenges facing individuals most likely to seek out social work services. For victims of domestic violence, poverty creates and maintains real danger. Almost half of the women receiving welfare have experienced physical abuse at some point in their lives, and over half of homeless and housed low-income mothers report physical abuse by an intimate male partner.[84] In 1997, the Iowa Coalition Against Domestic Violence (ICADV) and the Building Comprehensive Solutions to Domestic Violence Initiative (a project of the National Resource Center on Domestic Violence, in collaboration with Greater Hartford Legal Aid, Inc. and the University of Iowa School of Social Work) joined together to attempt to address the challenges of poverty and housing stress for victims of domestic violence in a more comprehensive, effective way. Correia and VonDeLinde write about the issues that initiated the creation of the coalition:

> In Iowa—as in many parts of the country—the general domestic violence advocacy strategy to meet the economic needs of battered women was primarily to provide them with information and referrals. For example, when a battered woman sought safety at a shelter, an advocate might refer her to the welfare agency and subsidized housing programs (if she specifically requested that information). . . . Recent policy changes, however, have dramatically limited the amount and duration of welfare benefits and reduced housing resources, as well. Such sweeping changes to social support programs also increase the advocacy needs of battered women. As a result, domestic violence advocates in Iowa began to ask themselves new questions about their work. For example, how often are battered women forced to return to an abusive partner because they are unable to secure permanent housing? What happens to women who lose their welfare benefits because of time limits or because their abusive partner sabotages their efforts to comply with program rules? What role should domestic violence advocates play in helping battered women meet their families' basic human needs?[85]

ICADV worked to help build the capacity of its members to address the economic and housing needs of its clients by taking the following steps:

1. Identifying and recognizing battered women's economic needs
2. Developing leadership and staff commitment to economic issues
3. Building the capacity of advocates to provide economic advocacy and collaborate with new partners
4. Providing economic advocacy and collaborating with new partners at several pilot sites
5. Securing necessary funding and technical support
6. Institutionalizing economic advocacy[86]

Economic advocacy was identified as a crucial element in reducing poverty and improving safety for victims of domestic violence. Domestic violence support workers (referred to as advocates) and victims of domestic violence both needed skills in economic advocacy. A significant focus of the ICADV included providing education and training for its domestic violence advocates in economic advocacy. While DV advocates typically provide referrals to public assistance and/or housing assistance agencies for clients in need, most do not have the skills or knowledge to provide these services themselves. Advocates learned how to teach financial planning skills to enable women to be their own economic advocates, as well as learning how to integrate policy analysis into their everyday work with women. Additionally, advocates were training in skills needed for successful community collaboration to better prepare them for advocacy in a collaborative context. The skills learned included how to create and maintain a collaborative mindset, negotiation techniques, strategic thinking, and meeting facilitation.[87]

As the ICADV example shows, social workers, whether they are working as domestic violence advocates, clinical case managers, or school social workers (to name only a few), must be aware of the economic issues facing their clients and be willing to enter into collaborative partnerships for training, support, skills building, and coalition-based advocacy if they are to effectively address their economic needs.

Rural areas generally have even fewer resources for the homeless. Thus, in a nation that has never adequately housed all of its people, homelessness continues to be a serious policy issue. The home foreclosure crisis of 2008 threatens to worsen the problem.

Other Publicly Funded Programs in American Social Welfare

A wide range of other publicly funded programs contributes to U.S. social welfare. Many services are funded by government—through vehicles such as the Social Services Block Grant—but delivered by private organizations. Hence, they are part of an interdependent network of public and private efforts to further social welfare. These services include child welfare programs such as child abuse and neglect prevention, foster care, adoption, shelter, and outreach services.[81] Other programs benefiting children include publicly funded health insurance (State Children's Health Insurance Program or S-CHIP), child care, education, and family planning services.[82] Head Start (the preschool program) and student loan programs are part of the education category. In addition, the U.S. government supports employment and training programs for those seeking employment.[83]

SUMMARY

Poverty is among the most pressing U.S. social problems. Poverty renders children, adults, families, and communities vulnerable to a host of additional social ills, from poor health to crime and violence. Poverty is of particular concern to social workers, as its impacts are felt by so many social work clients, from individuals to entire communities. The Council on Social Work Education regards eliminating poverty and ameliorating its effects on individuals and families as one of the core tasks of the field of social work.[88]

Defining exactly what poverty is, who suffers from it, and what causes it is a complicated task. In this chapter, we examined two ways of measuring poverty: absolute and relative. In the U.S., poverty disproportionately affects groups with lower social power: children, women, people of color, and immigrants. Determining the causes of poverty is a challenging and potentially controversial undertaking. Major factors that contribute to poverty include changes in the economic climate (for example, recessions or downsizing in a certain economic sector), under- or unemployment, low educational attainment, lack of skills/training, discrimination and oppression, loss of primary wage-earner, one-parent family structure, illness, disability, and government approaches to poverty (e.g. cuts or gains in antipoverty spending, etc.). Many of the factors that contribute to poverty are systemic factors (economic decline, oppression) that interact both with each other and with individual factors (poor health, lack of education).

Publicly funded antipoverty programs exist on the federal, state, and local levels, and encompass a wide range of services targeted at particular issues that either contribute to or are a result of poverty. In this chapter, we surveyed social insurance programs, public assistance programs, and food and shelter programs. Social insurance is based on the prior earnings and payroll contributions of an individual; public assistance, typically referred to as welfare, is based on the financial need of an individual or family. Old Age, Survivors, and Disability Insurance; unemployment insurance; and workers' compensation are social insurance programs. Temporary Assistance for Needy Families (TANF) and general assistance are among the public assistance programs currently operational in the U.S. Food and shelter programs include food stamps, Section 8 rental assistance, and public housing. In addition to publicly funded programs, many antipoverty programs are provided by the nonprofit sector.

7 CHAPTER REVIEW

Log onto **MySocialWorkLab** to access a wealth of case studies, videos, and assessment. (*If you did not receive an access code to **MySocialWorkLab** with this text and wish to purchase access online, please visit www.mysocialworklab.com.*)

PRACTICE TEST The following questions will test your knowledge of the content found within this chapter. For additional assessment, including licensing-exam type questions on applying chapter content to practice, visit **MySocialWorkLab**.

1. The federal poverty guidelines refer to:
   a. The number of U.S. residents living in poverty in a given year
   b. The way the U.S. Census Bureau counts the number of poor children
   c. The wage a worker must make to support him/herself and one dependent child
   d. Income guidelines used by to determine eligibility for federal, state, and/or local publicly funded antipoverty programs

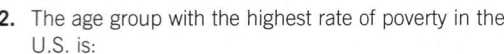
Human Rights & Justice

2. The age group with the highest rate of poverty in the U.S. is:
   a. 18–24 year olds
   b. Children under 18
   c. Individuals over 65
   d. 25–40 year olds

3. As of July 2009, the federal minimum wage is:
   a. $8.50/hour
   b. $7.25/hour
   c. $6.55/hour
   d. $5.15/hour

Diversity in Practice

4. The following racial group experienced the highest rate of poverty in 2004:
   a. African Americans
   b. Latino/as
   c. Whites
   d. Native Americans/Alaskan Natives

5. The formula created by Orshansky and used to calculate the federal poverty threshold:
   a. Was based on controversial poverty regulations from the Progressive Era
   b. Is no longer in use
   c. Remains accurate and appropriate because the cost of food and other household items have not changed
   d. Was originally intended for use only with elderly households

6. The following is NOT among the causes of the high rate of poverty among female-headed households:
   a. Higher numbers of women in the workforce overall
   b. The high cost of child care
   c. Sex and gender discrimination in employment
   d. Early child-bearing

7. The cost of food, clothing, and other essential goods and services available in poor neighborhoods tends to be:
   a. More than in middle-class neighborhoods.
   b. Less than in middle-class neighborhoods.
   c. About the same as in middle-class neighborhoods
   d. Less than in middle-class neighborhoods, but also of poorer quality

8. This federal program provides income assistance to poor parents and children for a limited time period:
   a. Medicaid
   b. AFDC
   c. The Section 8 voucher program
   d. TANF

9. SSI provides a monthly minimum income to:
   a. Individuals with disabilities
   b. The elderly
   c. Children under 3
   d. Veterans

10. The largest federal food support program for low-income families and individuals is:
    a. WIC
    b. Food stamps
    c. Food pantries
    d. The Healthy Families Partnership

Log onto **MySocialWorkLab** once you have completed the Practice Test above to access additional study tools and assessment.

Answers

Key: 1) d 2) b 3) b 4) d 5) d 6) a 7) a 8) b 9) a 10) b

8

Health, Health Care, and Medical Social Work

CHAPTER OUTLINE

Social Workers in the Healthcare Profession 166

Major Health Problems 166

Heart Disease 166
Cancer
Obesity
Asthma
AIDS

Socioeconomic Aspects of Illness 171

Health Services 171
Medicare and Medicaid
Private Insurance and Managed Care
Problems in the Healthcare System
Problems with Managed Care
Uninsured and Underinsured
Why Don't People Have Health Insurance?

The Un-Covered Middle Class
Prescription Drugs
Innovations and Proposed Solutions
Policy Proposal: National Healthcare System

Social Work in a Medical Setting 180
Hospital Social Work
Community Health Clinics
Hospice
Health Promotion and Prevention

Interprofessional Collaboration: Social Work and Healthcare Professionals 185

Summary 186

Practice Test 187

 MySocialWorkLab 187

Core Competencies in this Chapter (Check marks indicate which competencies are covered in depth)									
☐	Professional Identity	☐	Ethical Practice	☐	Critical Thinking	☐	Diversity in Practice	✓	Human Rights & Justice
☐	Research Based Practice	✓	Human Behavior	✓	Policy Practice	☐	Practice Contexts	✓	Engage, Assess, Intervene, Evaluate

165

SOCIAL WORKERS IN THE HEALTHCARE PROFESSION

The U.S. healthcare system is a comprehensive and interdisciplinary service network that encompasses the full range of medical care, from diagnosis and treatment to wellness and health maintenance activities, for people from all walks of life. Social workers in the healthcare system specialize in providing biopsychosocial supports to individuals and families on a variety of issues related to their health and wellness, illness and disability. Hospitals set the stage for health care and medical social work starting in 1905 when a physician named Richard Cabot created a social work position in the Internal Medicine Clinic at Massachusetts General Hospital. A few years later, services were extended to the Neurology Clinic there, and some say these few positions heralded the beginning of hospital social work, one of the oldest specializations in the social work profession. In this chapter, you will learn about the American healthcare system along with social workers' roles in hospitals and other healthcare settings. Some of the major health problems that face Americans are described, along with typical micro- and macro-level roles for social workers in dealing with these illnesses. Also, since social workers who work in these areas collaborate with other healthcare professionals on a daily basis, we have included a section on interprofessional collaboration.

Although hospitals still employ the majority of social workers in health care and medical social work, horizons have expanded to include many other settings, such as community health clinics, family planning clinics, health maintenance organizations and other managed care settings, hospice and home health care, industry settings, labor unions, public and state health agencies, substance abuse programs, residential care and rehabilitation facilities, and the Veterans Administration. All of these types of organizations and more employ healthcare and medical social workers in both direct practice with individuals, families, groups, and in macro-level positions (e.g., administration, planning, and policy and program development). The Bureau of Labor Statistics (BLS) estimates that social workers hold approximately 642,000 U.S. jobs, and about 21% of these jobs (138,700 jobs) are in medical and public health areas.[1] Moreover, the BLS estimates that the demand for social workers to fill medical and public health positions will grow by 22% to 169,800 by 2018, much faster than the average projected growth for other occupations![2] As managed care continues to limit the length of hospital stays, more social workers will find jobs in home health care. And as the elderly population continues to grow (by 75% over the next 20 years), more social workers will find jobs in nursing homes, assisted living, long-term care facilities, and hospice care.[3]

MAJOR HEALTH PROBLEMS

Although it would be impossible to provide details for all major health problems that people confront daily, the following section highlights a handful of serious illnesses that healthcare social workers address at the micro and macro levels.

Heart Disease

Heart disease, also called **cardiovascular disease** or CVD, comprises a number of abnormal conditions that affect the heart. It is the leading cause of death in the U.S. for both women and men. Nearly 700,000 people die from heart disease every year.⁴ In fact, each year heart disease kills more people than cancer, respiratory diseases, accidents, diabetes, and flu or pneumonia—the next five leading causes of death after heart disease—combined. It is also a major cause of disability. More than 6 million Americans are living with active heart disease.⁵ The biggest risk factors for heart disease (and stroke) include high blood pressure, high cholesterol, diabetes, tobacco smoking, physical inactivity, and obesity. Poor, uninsured, and medically underserved people suffer disproportionately from heart disease, and it is more common among older adults.⁶

Many social workers are employed in hospital cardiac care, working with patients and their families. In this age of brief care, some heart attack victims are released from the hospital less than a week after a heart attack occurs, so cardiac care social work tends to be short and focused on how the patients will behave at home.⁷ In a few short meetings with the patient and his or her family, the cardiac care social worker must develop rapport, provide support and guidance, and address the stress associated with heart attacks. Generally, patients must make large lifestyle modifications, including dietary changes, smoking cessation, exercising, and reducing stress and anxiety, among other things. Often, social workers meet with heart attack victims several times after they have left the hospital, during their rehabilitation period. Social workers who work with cardiac patients outside hospital settings tend to provide education, individual, family, and group counseling, and to lead support groups and self-help groups. Social workers in macro practice might perform community outreach for cardiac disease prevention and education or legislative advocacy around health access and patient care issues.

Cancer

In general, **cancer** refers to the uncontrolled division, growth, and spread of abnormal cells in the body. Whether or not a person develops cancer depends on multiple factors, including heredity, immune system health, diet, age (older cells are more likely to make "mistakes" during division), tobacco inhalation, excessive sun exposure, exposure to chemicals and other substances, ionizing radiation exposure, and viruses. Different combinations of factors tend to lead to different types of cancers. As with heart disease, cancer incidence, prevalence, death, and illness burden vary by minority group status, with poor, uninsured, and medically underserved populations suffering disproportionately more than the general U.S. population.⁸

Social workers who work in the cancer field are called **oncology social workers**; they practice in hospitals, outpatient clinics, hospice and home care agencies, community wellness programs, patient advocacy organizations, and many other settings, where they perform counseling, educational programs, support groups, community referrals, and consultations.⁹ Through their work, oncology social workers help patients and their families: (1) learn to talk with doctors and other members of the treatment team; (2) talk with children, family, friends, and coworkers about diagnosis, treatment, and aftercare; (3) cope with emotions, such as anger, fear, sadness, and worry; (4) reduce stress and learn to use relaxation techniques; (5) understand how cancer might affect fertility and sexual intimacy; (6) understand and link to complementary and alternative medicines; (7) understand and find appropriate clinical trials; (8) learn to live with cancer and negotiate life as a cancer survivor; (9) access resources (e.g., affordable medical care, medical equipment, transportation, temporary housing, home health care and hospice care); and (10) plan for continued care using advance directives (e.g., documents written and signed in advance that explain a person's medical wishes).[10] Oncology social workers who practice in macro settings, like those in cardiac care, often perform community outreach or education activities or work as legislative advocates.

Obesity

The incidence of overweight and **obesity** among adults and children in the U.S. has increased over the past 30 years, such that it now afflicts more than 55% of the adult population, 17.4% of children aged 12–19 years, 18.8% of the child population aged 6–11 years, and nearly 14% of children between ages 2 and 5. These numbers represent growth that is double and triple 1980 proportions.[11] In response to this growing problem, in June 1998, the U.S. established the first federal guidelines to address overweight and obesity identification, evaluation and treatment,[12] and made lowering obesity among adults to less than 15% of the population by the year 2010 a priority. However, obesity appears to be growing rather than shrinking.

Why the big hoopla over obesity and overweight? One reason for concern is that overweight individuals are at higher risk for illness from certain cancers, high cholesterol, coronary heart disease and stroke, and a number of other diseases. Another reason for concern is that obesity carries psychosocial implications because of stigma, discrimination (particularly in hiring and promotion), social anxiety and depression related to self-image, self-blame, and fear of rejection. Seipel writes:

> . . . stigma against overweight people is still considered a socially acceptable form of prejudice because many believe that overweight people have control over their weight. Overweight people are often viewed as gluttonous, lazy, of weak character or even immoral. Because of stigmatic stereotypes for overweight people, many experience difficulty obtaining jobs. Others experience forms of ostracism, discouragement and violence from preschool to college. Some even encounter hostile attitudes from healthcare providers instead of compassionate care.[14]

Physicians and medical students have been found to use adjectives such as bad, difficult to manage, lacking self-control, sad, and ugly to describe obese patients.[15]

As you might guess, social workers play multiple roles in relation to overweight and obesity through micro-level direct practice and macro-level advocacy to raise local and national awareness about obesity-related health and social problems and to change policies that target vulnerable populations.[16]

Is there an alternative explanation for the hoopla over obesity and overweight? Yes, indeed, and it has implications for social workers. In recent years, an obesity controversy has developed in the scientific community. One side, as described previously, focuses on health consequences associated with excess weight. The other side argues, among other things, that obesity is socially constructed according to middle-class Western ideals of beauty and has "as much to do with a social and cultural response to particular kinds of bodies as it has to do with health."[18] In a book entitled *The Obesity Epidemic, Science, Morality and Ideology*,

w?

nouth Medical School study, researchers
n aged 9–12 who have televisions in
gnificantly more likely to be obese.
despite socioeconomic status,
and amount of physical activity,
ports teams.[13]

> **Demonstrating Knowledge, Values, and Skills**
>
> **Increasing Activity among Overweight Children**
>
> Current research suggests that one way to increase activity among overweight children is to encourage *active* video game play. For example, Mayo Clinic researchers reported that 8- to 12-year-olds who played video games while walking on a treadmill expended 40% more energy, those who played activity-promoting video games expended 40% more energy, and children who danced to gain points in a popular dancing video game used close to 70% more energy than children who played video games while seated. Participants reportedly enjoyed the games and played them repeatedly.[17]
>
> Social workers in macro practice settings often inform, educate, and help to organize communities to address issues like how to grow healthy children.
>
> For this activity, students should organize into groups of four and brainstorm ways to engage children in healthful activities in each of the following settings: (a) in school; (b) after school; and (c) at home. Remember that some children may enjoy organized sports, while others may not. Think about how to engage children who claim not to like sports-like activities. After the brainstorming session is finished, the whole class can discuss their ideas for each setting.

Gard and Wright argue that the way medical and public health professionals and health educators have characterized obesity-related health problems pathologizes overweight people, creates anxiety for all, and sets the stage for the medical community to seek a "cure" that would surely include new pharmaceutical products aimed at both children and adults.

Asthma

Asthma is a chronic respiratory disease that affects the lungs. It affects about 34 million Americans; about 9 million are children under age 18 and close to 3,500 people (mostly adults) die each year due to asthma complications.[19] Although asthma prevalence has been increasing among all age, racial, and gender groups, like many other illnesses, asthma incidence and prevalence, along with asthma deaths, remain higher among vulnerable populations.

Social workers play multiple roles in asthma education, prevention, and management. For example, Parker-Oliver suggests that social work interventions with asthmatic adults and children ideally include: (1) educating individuals and families about asthma management; (2) teaching individuals and families about stress reduction, relaxation techniques, and nonmedical interventions; (3) mediating support groups for individuals and families dealing with asthma; (4) referring families to community resources; (5) providing links to financial resources; and (6) advocating within the medical system.[20] Macro-level social work practice would include advocating to change policy that affects poor and minority populations, who are more likely to live in substandard environments that contain environmental triggers known to cause asthma.

> **Research Informed Practice: The Obesity Controversy**
>
> This activity will give you the opportunity to learn more about the obesity controversy, to take a stand on an issue, and to support your position. Using your library's research databases, perform a search using keywords such as "obesity controversy," "social construction of obesity," and "obesity myth." Write a two-page paper that describes the controversy briefly and explains your position regarding obesity. Use some of the sources you located to support your points.

AIDS

Researchers believe that **Human Immunodeficiency Virus** (HIV) began to develop into an epidemic as early as World War II. Although the first cases were not identified until 1981, recent blood sample analysis dates the first confirmed HIV death to 1959. This deadly virus attacks T-helper cells associated with the immune system, cells that are required to fight disease. Over time, an immune system compromised by HIV leaves the body vulnerable to malignancies and infections that eventually lead to death. The end stage of HIV is known as AIDS. Of course, HIV/AIDS is not a problem just in the United States; experts identify it as the leading global health concern today. Approximately 25 million people worldwide have died from HIV/AIDS since the beginning of the epidemic. The Centers for Disease Control and Prevention (CDC) report that over 1 million people in the U.S. are living with HIV/AIDS currently, and about a quarter of those people are yet to be diagnosed.[21] An additional 40,000 children, adolescents, and adults, many under age 25, become infected each year.

HIV/AIDS sufferers face many health-related issues, ranging from symptom recognition and diagnosis to healthcare access and treatment to everyday disease management. In addition to all the health issues, researchers have identified a number of psychosocial stressors, such as lack of acceptance (even by family and friends) and stigmatization, lack of intimacy and social isolation, feelings of disempowerment and diminished self-esteem.[22]

Social workers who work with this population often provide direct practice support to patients and their families to help them learn to accept and manage the illness. They might also provide information and conduct group therapy and support groups with HIV/AIDS sufferers. Studies have shown that group therapies are a very important treatment technique with this disease and with other chronic illnesses, because contact with others suffering from the illness can promote social bonds and a sense that victims are not alone.[23] Group therapies have also been found to reduce stigma, foster social acceptance, and encourage reciprocal support from other sufferers.[24] At the macro level, social workers advocate to reduce stigma against HIV/AIDS-infected individuals. **Stigma**, which differs by race and gender, remains strong and includes: (1) misconceptions about how the disease is transmitted; (2) blaming the victim; and (3) social rejection.[25] Stigma can deter individuals from seeking treatment or following treatment guidelines. Indeed, many HIV/AIDS sufferers have recounted stigmatization and insensitivity from administrative personnel in healthcare settings and from healthcare and social service professionals.[26] Social work training and experience are especially helpful in reducing the stigma and discrimination surrounding HIV/AIDS because "the social work profession, by virtue of its holistic perspective is capable of responding to the needs of vulnerable populations, helping people gain more control over their lives—in partnership with them—and addressing major political, social and economic issues."[27]

SOCIOECONOMIC ASPECTS OF ILLNESS

The populations more likely to suffer from the diseases discussed in this section and many other diseases include blacks, Hispanics, American Indians, Asian Americans, and poor whites. These minority groups are at a disadvantage because they tend to hold lower socioeconomic status in society. Remember that

---

Self-esteem isn't everything: it's just that there's nothing without it.

—Gloria Steinem

> **Focus on Professionalism and Ethics**
>
> **Value:** *Social Justice*
> **Ethical Principle:** *Social workers challenge social injustice.*
>
> Social workers pursue social change, particularly with and on behalf of vulnerable and oppressed individuals and groups of people. Social workers' social change efforts are focused primarily on issues of poverty, unemployment, discrimination, and others forms of social injustice. These activities seek to promote sensitivity to and knowledge about oppression and cultural and ethnic diversity. Social workers strive to ensure access to needed information, services, and resources; equality of opportunity; and meaningful participation in decision making for all people.[30]

socioeconomic status (SES) is defined as a combination of education, occupation, and income. SES is the most important predictor of living standards that indicate the likelihood of an individual's or a group's access to adequate living conditions (e.g., safe from environmental toxins), education, certain occupations, and health insurance. For example, blacks experience the highest cancer death rates, with a rate about 25% higher than whites for the most common cancer types. And in recent years, Puerto Ricans were almost 125% more likely to have been diagnosed with asthma than whites, whereas blacks and American Indians were 25% more likely to have been diagnosed with asthma than whites.[28] Moreover, the asthma death rate for Puerto Ricans was 350% higher than for whites, and blacks had an asthma death rate 200% higher than whites.[29]

Other populations more likely than the general population to hold lower socioeconomic statuses and to be at higher risk for serious health problems include women, the elderly, people with disabilities, and those that live in rural areas or in highly populated urban areas.

It is easy to understand health and healthcare inequities from a social justice perspective. Social justice, as previously discussed, means that all people are entitled to equal participation in the social, educational, and economic spheres of society. To achieve social justice, collective goods, institutional resources, and opportunities must be distributed equitably. Social justice also implies that all members of society are empowered. In reality, as economic inequality increases, health declines. Therefore, social position determines health in the current social order.

You . . . need to be a flea against injustice. Enough committed fleas biting strategically can make even the biggest dog uncomfortable and transform even the biggest nation.

—Marian Wright Edelman

HEALTH SERVICES

During the mid-1800s, urban areas were crowded, dirty, and teeming with disease. The first steps toward public health addressed sanitation. Fifty years later, advocates tackled contagious diseases. By the early 1920s, the demand for hospital care was so great that a group of teachers in Dallas, Texas, contracted with Baylor University Hospital to provide three weeks of hospitalization for a fixed payment of $6.00.[31] Prepaid plans like this one multiplied throughout the 1920s, enabling individuals to pay their hospital bills and providing guaranteed income for hospitals, benefiting both groups. After the Depression, when more patients had difficulty paying medical bills, physicians and hospitals organized to develop the first health insurance companies; Blue Shield, developed in 1933, was among the first such companies. At first, **Health Insurance** was a controversial topic—so controversial that it was not included in early Social Security system proposals. But 20 years later, employers were providing health insurance as a benefit, and in the 1960s, coverage was expanded with the development of Medicaid and Medicare.[32]

Medicare and Medicaid

In 1965, healthcare coverage in the U.S. expanded for the first time in 30 years. Medicare and Medicaid, two new social insurance programs, were part of the new package. Medicare was added to the Old Age, Survivors, and Disability Insurance program (OASDI) to cover citizens over age 65 who met eligibility requirements for Social Security benefits. Medicare also covers specific medical needs categories for people under age 65. The special needs categories include some people with disabilities and all individuals with end-stage renal disease, which means they have permanent kidney failure that can only be treated with regular dialysis or with a kidney transplant. There are three main parts to **Medicare** coverage: Part A, Part B, and a prescription drug program. Part A of Medicare provides hospital insurance to people who meet certain conditions (in addition to those listed above) and is funded by payroll taxes and employee contributions. Since most people who work (or their spouses) have had payroll taxes deducted from their paychecks during their working life, this means that most people do not pay premiums to get coverage. Part A helps to cover costs for hospital services, post-hospital skilled nursing facility services, hospice care, and some home health services. Part B of Medicare is a voluntary program that covers physician services, outpatient care, some medical supplies, and some diagnostic tests. Although the federal government subsidizes Part B, most people who choose to participate must pay monthly premiums plus an annual deductible and service copayments. The Medicare Prescription Drug Improvement and Modernization Act of 2003 started a voluntary prescription medication coverage program. In January 2006, coverage began for anyone eligible for Medicare. People who want to participate in this program must pay a monthly premium. More than 14% of Americans (more than 44 million people) were covered by Medicare in 2008.[33]

The **Medicaid** program, another social insurance program enacted in 1965 under the Social Security Act, provides healthcare coverage to certain low-income individuals and families whose income falls below a certain amount. This federal program is administered by individual states, which set their own eligibility and service guidelines, so services and group coverage can be highly variable across states. Eligible individuals receive services from physicians, hospitals, and other healthcare providers that agree to participate in the program. Basic Medicaid covers physician services, diagnostic tests, home health services, and long-term care. States may elect to offer additional services, such as prescription drug coverage and dental care. Medicaid covered just over 55 million individuals—about 13% of the population—in 2007, and for the majority this is the only form of health insurance they can access.[34] Figure 8.1 depicts Medicaid coverage by selected populations.[35]

The federal government hoped that the combination of employer health benefits, Medicare, and Medicaid would provide sufficient healthcare coverage for everyone in the U.S.; however, within about 10 years it became evident that many individuals and families still did not have access to any type of healthcare coverage. Statistics indicated that the number of uninsured was on the rise.[36] At the same time, healthcare costs have skyrocketed.[37] The federal response to increasing healthcare costs, coupled with increasing numbers of uninsured individuals and families, was to enact the Health Maintenance Organization Act of 1973, which began the managed care movement, which is described in the next section.

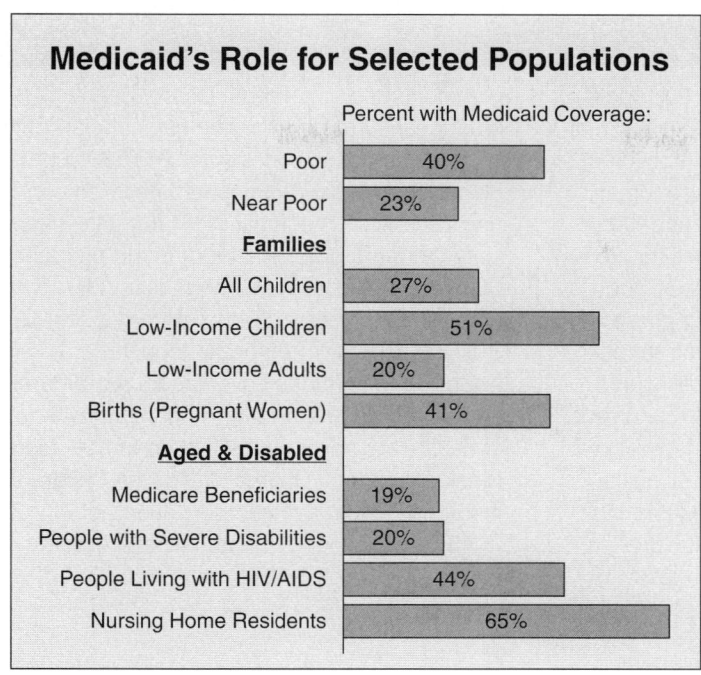

Figure 8.1
Medicaid's Role for Selected Populations
Source: KMCU, KFF, and Urgan Institute estimates; Birth data: NGA, MCH Update

Private Insurance and Managed Care

Although the number of people who obtain health insurance through an employer-based voluntary health insurance system has decreased recently, work-related health insurance still covers the majority of people in the U.S.[39] Fewer than 10% of Americans purchase their own insurance directly from insurance companies, either because they do not work or because they do not want the health insurance offered by their employers.

For those who are insured, health insurance plans typically fall into two categories, called fee-for-service and managed care. People insured under **fee-for-service** plans choose a doctor, clinic, or hospital, and the insurance pays for part or all of the cost according a predetermined fee schedule; the insured person pays the remainder of the bill, which may include a deductible amount (per year) and a copay (per visit). Managed health care has replaced fee-for-service plans because it provides insurers more control over healthcare expenditures they must make on behalf of their clients.

Managed care began in the 1930s and 1940s when Henry Kaiser attempted to control healthcare costs in his businesses by hiring salaried physicians to provide health care to his employees. This was the first time patients had to get permission—referrals—from primary care physicians in order to see specialists.[40] In 1973, President Nixon favored legislation aimed at developing more managed care plans and enacted the Health Maintenance Organization Act of 1973. Health maintenance organizations evolved, and managed care was credited with slowing the rise of healthcare costs during the 1990s.

The managed healthcare system controls both financing and service delivery to insured individuals. In general, managed healthcare plans have

Did You Know?

The **Children's Health Insurance Program** (CHIP, formerly known as S-CHIP) represents the first real attempt to provide health care to children not covered by any other health insurance programs. It was created by the federal government in 1998 through Title XXI of the Social Security Act to provide low-cost healthcare coverage for children in families that were poor, but not poor enough to be covered by Medicaid. The government provided broad guidelines and matching funds to states, which then designed their own programs. Individual states determined how much to spend (and thus how much the state would receive from the federal government in matching funds). States also set eligibility requirements and outlined benefits packages and pay scales. Although all 50 states developed CHIP programs, states that chose to pay less received less money in matching funds. Consequently, CHIP varies a great deal across states. The original plan provided matching funds to states from 1998 through 2007. Since the number of uninsured children continued to rise throughout the initial CHIP funding years, some states ran into problems funding the program. As the CHIP expiration date neared in late 2007, two proposals to revise CHIP passed Congress. President George W. Bush vetoed both proposals, though he did sign a CHIP extension to continue coverage through March 2009. In the meantime, the number of children without any form of healthcare coverage continued to rise. More recently, President Barack Obama signed the Children's Health Insurance Program Reauthorization Act of 2009 (CHIPRA, or PL 111-3) into law on February 4, 2009. CHIPRA finances CHIP through FY 2013.[38]

several goals that aim to deliver quality services while at the same time controlling costs. People insured by managed healthcare organizations are required to use physicians, clinics, and hospitals that are members of an approved provider network. Patients can elect to see doctors outside the plan, but out-of-network services may be only partially covered or not covered at all. Often, providers are constrained by managed healthcare plans to recommend certain types of care or to prescribe generic rather than brand-name medications. There are several types of managed healthcare structures, including health maintenance organizations (HMO), preferred provider organizations (PPO), and point-of-service plans (POS). HMOs and PPOs are similar in structure, whereas POS plans fall somewhere in between managed care and fee-for-service plans.

Problems in the Healthcare System

Critics point to a number of inadequacies in the U.S. healthcare system.[41] First, it is fragmented, complex, highly individualized, and localized. Second, there is so much money to be made. Healthcare costs continue to increase at twice the rate of workers' wages and faster than government tax revenues. Third, the number of uninsured individuals and families is high and continues to rise each year. Fourth, workers with preexisting health problems often cannot obtain insurance; in fact, sometimes they cannot get jobs because employers consider them to be poor risks. Many of these problems are not new; government officials and politicians, healthcare professionals, employers, and workers have been struggling with them for decades, and good alternatives have not been forthcoming. While healthcare experts hope problems related to fragmentation, high costs, large numbers of uninsured individuals and lack of coverage for individuals with preexisting conditions will be lessened or even eliminated by the Patient Protection and Affordable Care Act signed into law in March 2010, it is likely that some of these problems will linger for some time. Let's look at how these problems have effected Americans.

Problems with Managed Care

Healthcare fragmentation presents a real problem for consumers. Providers tend to work in separate, unrelated practices and are paid for services in a piecemeal fashion. In recent years, it has been profitable for some specialists to join forces in single-specialty groups, where they can pool resources to establish their own labs, purchase equipment and compete with nearby hospitals.[42] Terry describes the process this way:

> Patients see a primary-care physician and are referred to a specialist, handed off to another consultant, admitted to a hospital, discharged to a nursing home or rehab facility and then sent back to the hospital. Along the way, they may have tests at different labs and may pick up prescriptions at multiple pharmacies. And every time they move from one care setting to another, information about their previous care is lost.[43]

The high costs are partially due to the pool of highly trained medical professionals, who are becoming increasingly specialized. Specialists are receiving more referrals than they did a decade ago, and most trips to specialists require one or more new laboratory tests. State-of-the-art hospitals and medical technology are expensive to develop, purchase, and maintain, but the investment is worth the cost because they increase hospital profits manyfold.[44] Insurance companies enjoy the big profits too, and pharmaceutical companies are among "the most profitable businesses in the nation."[45]

Uninsured and Underinsured

Individuals and families that are **uninsured** do not have access to any health insurance coverage at all, whereas **underinsured** individuals and families have insurance coverage but are at high risk for incurring medical debt. The number of uninsured individuals and families is skyrocketing. It is not enough to have a job, as many of the uninsured work full time for employers that to do not offer healthcare benefits. Moreover, as insurance premiums grow, they consume more of the workers' income; and as health coverage becomes too costly for employers to purchase, more people will become uninsured or will incur medical debt on top of paying insurance premiums. Close to 29 million people have recently accrued medical debt, and 70% of those with debt were insured when they incurred their debt.[46] At the same time, preexisting health problems disqualify individuals from healthcare plans in many states.

Why Don't People Have Health Insurance?

According to a 2007 report from the U.S. Census Bureau, the percentage of Americans without health insurance increased from 15.3% (44.8 million people) in 2005 to 15.8% (47 million people) in 2006.[47] At the same time, health insurance premiums have increased rapidly. They jumped by more than two-thirds from 2001 to 2006, about twice as fast as workers' wages have increased. Moreover, the higher the proportion of low-income workers, the less likely a firm is to offer employee health benefits. From 2005 to 2006, both the percentage and the number of people without health insurance increased, and it is likely that the number of uninsured will continue to rise. Children and racial minorities are disproportionately represented among the uninsured. About 12% of children are uninsured. In 2006, less than 11% of whites, 20.5% of blacks, and more than 34% of Hispanics did not have health insurance.[48]

The Un-Covered Middle Class

As you probably know from listening to candidates during the 2008 presidential campaign, health insurance coverage is not just a problem for the poorest poor. In fact, this problem has found its way into the middle class. Individuals and families that are underinsured can be poor *or* middle class. They may be covered with minimal health insurance, but still not be adequately protected, meaning that they are at high risk of incurring medical debt. Oswald, Bodurtha, Willis, and Moore noted that:

> there is no universally accepted definition, [but] the term "underinsurance" is generally used to refer to healthcare insurance that requires excessive out-of-pocket expenditures, that has significant limits with respect to what healthcare services are covered or that fails to cover healthcare expenses that are perceived by the insured person to be essential for his or her health.[49]

Estimates of the number of underinsured vary depending on the definition used. At least 58 million adults in the U.S. are at high risk of incurring medical bills that they will not be able to pay.[50] About 40 million of these adults were uninsured for all or part of the previous year. Another 76 million adults with private insurance report problems paying medical bills.[51]

Prescription Drugs

No matter what the symptom, today there is a prescription drug being marketed to make it go away. At the same time, most drugs on the market have long lists of potential side effects; the advertisements always run through the side effect list in double-time, then tell potential customers to decide with their physicians if a particular drug is "right" for them. Mentioning brand-name drugs to physicians will often prompt them to write prescriptions for the drugs, and that is exactly what the pharmaceutical companies hope for.

Critical Thinking Question
Current U.S. health policy has allowed pharmaceutical companies to medicalize common conditions and promote drugs heavily, which increases profits. How might social workers intervene to advance social and economic well-being for affected groups?

The most marketed medications are supposed to: (1) treat widespread chronic conditions; (2) be the only drug "proven" to reduce symptoms, even though most "new" drugs are basically the same as myriad other drugs already on the market; and (3) be taken for a long period of time (maybe forever). Medications to treat erectile dysfunction, high cholesterol, and depression are among the most widely advertised.[52] In fact, pharmaceutical companies are known for developing drugs for common conditions that people have learned to live with and that were not treated historically (e.g., insomnia, mild allergies).

It behooves pharmaceutical companies to medicalize common conditions and promote drugs heavily because this increases their profits manyfold. Aggressive advertising to consumers and physicians increased prescription drugs from an $81 billion dollar business to a $252 billion dollar business in just eight years (1997 to 2005).[53] In addition to creating consumer demand, doctors and health plans have bought into the advertising and popularity of many drugs.

Pharmaceutical companies claim that prescription drug costs are high solely because research and development (R&D) costs are prohibitive. However, it is important to note that research and development costs are not as high as the drug industry claims they are. Although R&D estimates for a single new drug have ranged from $230 million to over $800 million, in fact, the majority of "new" drugs are not significantly different from drugs already on the market. And when a new drug is patented and hits the market, "the company has the ability to set its own price; without competition, there is no downward pressure on the price from other drug suppliers."[54] In contrast, the Canadian Patent Medicines Prices Review Board sets the prices of drugs marketed in Canada and compares the price of a given drug to be marketed in Canada to U. S. and European prices. Their competitive pricing strategy results in drug prices that are one-third lower in Canada than they are in the U.S.[55]

As drug prices in the U.S. continue to rise, fewer American can afford to buy the medications they need. Prescription drug costs to consumers rose threefold from 1990 to 2001, and they didn't stop there. Between 2004 and 2007, the costs for the 122 drugs most commonly prescribed jumped by nearly 14%; a common sleep aid increased in cost by nearly 28% during 2007 alone; and "by 2012, spending is projected to increase to $445 billion or more."[56]

Innovations and Proposed Solutions

Increased healthcare and prescription drug costs, decreased healthcare coverage, and inequitable coverage and services across groups (e.g., racial, class) has left Americans disenchanted and looking a government-based solution. A majority of Americans (64%) believe that the federal government should guarantee healthcare coverage for all; and nearly two-thirds (65%) believe that providing healthcare coverage to all Americans is more important than keeping healthcare costs down.[57] Even more (84%) believe that government programs should be expanded to provide healthcare coverage for all uninsured children.[58]

Healthcare reform is certainly needed. What are the alternatives? Victor Fuchs, an economist who specializes in healthcare reform believes reform must be comprehensive to make a difference. He comments that comprehensive reform is a tall order because:

> it must reduce the huge inefficiencies in the way the country funds healthcare by eliminating employment-based insurance and income-tested subsidies. It must improve efficiency in medical practice by providing physicians with the information, infrastructure and incentives they need to deliver cost-effective care. Reform must also eliminate gross lapses in quality and must tame but not destroy the development and diffusion of expensive new medical technologies.[59]

Another leading healthcare economist, Jonathan Gruber, believes that a move toward universal healthcare coverage must address three issues: (1) pooling; (2) affordability; and (3) mandate issues. Pooling means that national health care must include large groups or pools of participants spanning the range of health statuses from healthy to unhealthy.[60] Otherwise, insurers will charge higher rates to make up for the possibility that a large percentage of individuals to be insured have serious and costly health problems. Affordable health insurance is a must if the U.S. wants to reduce the number of uninsured and underinsured individuals and families. Yet, no matter how it is defined, providing health insurance is a costly enterprise and many individuals and families would need large government subsidies in order to purchase health insurance.

Critical Thinking Question
Individuals, regardless of societal position, have basic human rights, including freedom, safety, adequate standard of living, and health care. Yet certain groups lack access to the health care they need. Why does this problem persist?

> **Research Informed Practice**
>
> **Purchasing Insurance and Supporting a Family of Four in California**
>
> Bill and Susan W. have been married six years and live in a working-class San Francisco suburb, where Bill works in the security department of a large firm that offers family health insurance coverage. Susan works part time on an hourly basis and doesn't receive benefits. The total cost of family health insurance for Bill's family totals $12,243, a sum that would be even higher if he worked for a smaller company. Since Bill's salary is $40,000, which weighs in at 200% of the poverty line, it takes 30% of his annual income to purchase healthcare coverage for himself, Susan, and their two small children.[61] This leaves about $28,000 from Bill's salary plus the $6,000 Susan earns at her part-time job to cover all other expenses (e.g., housing, food, clothing, maintenance for their 1983 car, child care).
>
> Search the Internet to determine the average costs of housing, food, clothing, and other items and services necessary to support a family of four. Are Bill and Susan W. able to cover their costs if they shell out the money for health insurance, or are they better off foregoing insurance and hoping they and their children remain healthy this year?

To be sure, there are uninsured and underinsured individuals and families who choose to forego health insurance, despite moderately priced employer packages and despite government subsidies. Therefore, many believe that mandates are necessary.[62] To mandate that individuals and families purchase some kind of health insurance "would be similar to auto insurance . . . where individuals are required to have insurance if they want to drive a car."[63] In April 2007, Massachusetts became the first state to mandate health insurance coverage for all residents.

Another approach that has been supported by conservative politicians is the **Health Savings Account** (HSA), an alternative to more traditional health insurance plans introduced under the Medical Modernization Act of 2003. Although HSAs are an interesting alternative to consider, they are not without problems. For example, individuals cannot predict health crises that might occur in a given year and might not set aside enough money in an HSA to cover cancer treatments, organ transplants, or serious accidents.[64] Neither are consumers as knowledgeable as physicians regarding clinical decisions, yet HSA accounts would require consumers to make such decisions. Finally, some fear that HSAs might prompt some employers to do away with employee health insurance plans, which could increase rather than reduce the numbers of uninsured and underinsured Americans.

Policy Proposal: Health Care Reform in the United States

During his campaign, President Barack Obama proposed to overhaul the U.S. healthcare system with a national healthcare plan that would provide affordable coverage to all Americans. Since his election in November 2008, President Obama has continued to pursue accessible and affordable healthcare coverage. For example, on February 4, 2009, the President signed the Children's Health Insurance Reauthorization Act (CHIP), which provides health care to approximately 11 million children. At least 4 million of these children did not have coverage prior to this 2009 reauthorization. Also in February, on the 13th, the President signed the American Recovery and Reinvestment Act of 2009 into law. This act has among its goals to: (1) protect healthcare coverage for Americans losing their jobs; (2) improve computerized medical records, which would

> ### Case Study: Dirigo—Maine State Healthcare Program
>
> Maine has struggled with rising healthcare costs and a rising number of uninsured individuals and families for years. For example, from 1996 to 2002, the cost of a family health insurance policy increased by 77%, at a time when the median family income in Maine increased by only 6%.[65] In response to the rising numbers of uninsured, Governor John Baldacci signed the Dirigo Health Reform Act into law in 2003. The reform aims to provide quality health care that is safe, effective, patient-centered, timely, efficient, and equitable. Dirigo, which takes its name from the state motto, meaning "I lead," is a set of healthcare reforms encompassing three complementary components aimed at reducing healthcare costs while increasing healthcare access and coverage to all Maine residents. Dirigo components include: (1) a new healthcare plan called DirigoChoice, designed to provide universal coverage to Maine residents; (2) a newly designed cost control system; and (3) multiple initiatives to ensure the availability of high-quality healthcare throughout the state. DirigoChoice is a partly subsidized program for small businesses (50 or fewer employees) and people without employer-sponsored insurance plans. A number of state agencies participate in Dirigo Health.
>
> The governor's Office of Health Policy and Finance oversees the reform and serves as the government liaison to the DHA, an independent agency with its own board of directors that is responsible for administering the health plan and establishing a clearinghouse of best practices and information called the Maine Quality Forum. By February 2009, DirigoChoice was covering some 29,251 Maine residents and had changed their America's Health Ranking from 19th in 2003 to 5th in 2008.[66]
>
> Maine hopes that Dirigo Health will be able to put a lid on rising healthcare costs by: (1) reducing bad debt and charity care (through increased healthcare access); (2) creating an annual budget (called the Capital Investment Fund) to pay for new construction and technology acquisition that is deemed necessary and in the best interest of Maine residents; and (3) requiring hospitals and physicians to maintain a price list for the 15 inpatient and 20 outpatient services they perform most often and to provide this "Transparent Price List" to healthcare consumers upon request.

contribute to reduced healthcare costs and greater patient privacy; (3) allot federal monies to prevention and wellness program in order to improve health nationally and to help reduce healthcare costs; (4) fund research on treatments with an eye to providing patients with objective information about the comparative benefits of various treatments; and (5) increase funding to train nurses and doctors for the future.[67]

As this book goes to press, the U.S. is another step closer to implementing quality, affordable health care for all Americans. On March 21, 2010, Congress approved a bill that will extend coverage to 32 million Americans over the next decade. On the same day, Congress approved a separate reconciliation bill that makes changes to the companion healthcare legislation passed by the Senate in December 2009. This wide-reaching healthcare bill, called the Patient Protection and Affordable Care Act, was signed into law on March 23, 2010. Provisions in this act include: (1) prohibiting private health insurance exclusions for preexisting conditions and making other immediate changes in the way health insurance companies conduct business; (2) changing the role of public programs and improving the quality and efficiency of care, such as expanding Medicaid coverage, protecting and strengthening Medicare for the elderly, continuing to fund CHIP through 2015, and ensuring that minimum covered benefits include services and products that enable people with disabilities to maintain and improve function; and (3) improving access to innovative medical therapies.[68] This legislation also extends dependent coverage up to age 26, promotes preventive health care in a variety of ways, and provides funding for community health centers in underserved communities.[69]

For all those whose cares have been our concern, the work goes on, the cause endures, the hope still lives, and the dream shall never die.

—Edward Kennedy

While health care remains contentious and will continue to be argued for years to come, many social historians describe this healthcare bill as the most important piece of social welfare legislation in the more than 40 years since President Lyndon Johnson launched government health care for the elderly. According to award winning historian Doris Kearns Goodwin:

> The domestic bills that we consider historic have had one thing in common: They have extended social or economic justice to the American people. Each of the 20th-century bills we remember did precisely that: Social Security, the civil-rights bill ending segregation, voting rights, fair housing, Medicare. . . . By extending health care to almost all Americans as a right and not a privilege, this bill is indeed historic.[70]

SOCIAL WORK IN A MEDICAL SETTING

Medical social work is practice that takes place in hospitals and other healthcare settings.[71] Although social workers in medical settings do work with physically ill clients and their families, they also facilitate health and wellness. In addition to hospitals, social workers find jobs in an array of healthcare settings, including community health clinics, family service agencies, health maintenance organizations, prepaid medical plans, private fee-for-service medical practices, and university health clinics, where they perform clinical duties, such as crisis intervention, clinical assessments, and individual, family, and group counseling. In some settings, they take part in prevention activities, such as community education, health screenings, and self-help groups.[72]

Hospital Social Work

Whatever the setting, social workers take a biopsychosocial, holistic approach to working with clients, always paying attention to the interface between the client and his or her environment (the PIE approach). The hospital setting differs from other settings in two ways. First, managed care pressure to contain costs has led to fewer, shorter hospital stays; second, hospital social workers work alongside professionals from many disciplines. Hospital social workers perform some or all of the following jobs: (1) make referrals and facilitate links with community resources; (2) plan preadmission and discharge; (3) screen patients at social risk for difficulties related to medical conditions; (4) provide patient and family counseling; (5) perform psychosocial evaluations; (6) provide health education within the community; (7) conduct research; (8) plan activities; and (9) collaborate with other hospital staff.[73]

Hospital social workers collaborate with an interdisciplinary team that might include physicians, psychiatrists, nurses, physical therapists, nutritionists, and others. Team composition may differ based on the type of hospital and the section of the hospital to which the social worker is assigned. Teams might work together to complete patient assessments, team-teach other hospital staff, develop intervention plans, collaborate to make ethical decisions, and evaluate outcomes. Social work services, although tailored to particular medical needs and patient characteristics, are holistic and almost always include acting as a liaison between the hospital and the family, providing patient and family education and referral information, making families and patients aware

> **Social Work Stories: Practicing Social Work in a Hospital Setting**
>
> Anne Marie O. knew social work was the right place for her when she found herself agreeing with the social work ethical code and philosophy. In her hospital position, Anne Marie provides psychosocial support to patients and families, links patients and their families to community resources, and leads therapeutic support groups. She explains that "hospital patients often feel like they have little control over what is happening to them so social work staff work with them around their feelings of helplessness." Anne Marie also develops discharge plans for patients leaving the hospital, works with the hospital legal department, runs community education clinics on patient-related topics, and is part of a social work team that leads other hospital staff through "critical incident debriefing," which means they help hospital staff process highly emotional or serious incidents. Anne Marie notes that of all the things she had to learn when she joined the hospital staff, hospital terminology and illness diagnoses were the most difficult. "There was a huge learning curve for me. It is important to be able to relay information to families in layman's terms. The doctors and nurses tell patient and their families what is going on, but they don't always understand the information, so we have to be able to explain it to them."

of typical stressors related to particular illnesses or disorders, providing individual and family support, and the like. Large hospitals employ multiple social workers who work in different units of the hospital. For example, hospital emergency rooms (ERs) often have social workers on staff, along with ER physicians and nurses. Emergency room services are fast-paced and crisis oriented. Social workers in the ER may see many clients in one day, addressing issues that range from simple concerns to complex crises to death. Assessments, services, and discharge may need to take place quickly. In an organ transplant unit, social workers use biopsychosocial techniques to help patients and families through referral, assessment, the waiting period, hospital admission and discharge, post-transplant follow-up, and rehabilitation services. Social workers in pediatric oncology units typically provide both concrete services and support services. Concrete services might include community referrals, transportation help, and financial aid, whereas support services might include patient and family counseling through diagnosis, treatment, and possibly death.[74]

Community Health Clinics

Although the community health center (CHC) model dates back to the 1800s on the global level, it did not spread to the U.S. until 1965 as a possible means of addressing healthcare inequality.[75] The original CHC was part of a pilot program sponsored by the Office of Equal Opportunity as part of President Johnson's War on Poverty. The federally funded CHC program set out to provide family-focused primary and preventive healthcare services to rural and urban residents living in medically underserved communities, regardless of their ability to pay. The first CHC, called the Tufts-Delta Health Center, aimed at serving a black population of around 14,000 in the Mississippi Delta region and grew into a network of over 900 "federally qualified health centers" nationwide.[76] The Tufts-Delta Center program included healthcare outreach and personal medical services, health education, an empowerment program, and a variety of public health interventions that addressed housing, water supplies, and sanitation. Health centers overcome economic, geographic, and cultural barriers to primary health care and they tailor services to the needs of the community.[77]

As the community health clinic movement has grown over the past 40 years, the federal government has focused on providing care while balancing cost, access, and quality.[78] Healthcare access has remained a problem since the early days of the movement, and access problems have increased as the number of uninsured and underinsured individuals and families has skyrocketed. Decreases in Medicaid coverage have also created problems for community health centers. Increased need makes it difficult for centers to provide consistently high-quality services. To ensure high quality, high access, and cost-efficiency as we move into the future, the federal government must pay attention to two structural features: (1) community health centers should be owned and operated by the local community; and (2) federal management and guidance should be consistent across all health centers throughout the U.S.[79]

Social workers in community health and other public health settings usually collaborate with colleagues from a number of disciplines to provide a full range of services, from educational and outreach services related to health and wellness, to health planning and assessment and direct individual and family therapy, to home healthcare services. In general, the primary focus of community and public health social work is prevention.

Hospice

The word "hospice" comes from the Latin word "hospitium," which means guesthouse. The first medically related hospice was developed in the 1960s and was located near London, England. **Hospice care** spread to the U.S. in 1974, "when it became clear that the traditional medical model did not meet the complex needs of people at the end of life; in this void hospice workers built a system of interdisciplinary care designed to meet the physical, psychological, social and spiritual needs of terminally ill people and their families."[80]

Hospice care is designed to give supportive attention to people of all ages who are in the final phase of terminal illness. It focuses on quality of life rather than cure, and the goal is to facilitate comfort and relieve pain. Social workers in hospice care are an important part of a multidisciplinary team that typically includes doctors, nurses, home health aids, and clergy. Many hospice care facilities incorporate trained volunteers to offer **respite care**, which offers family members relief from caring for their terminally ill family member for brief periods of time. Social workers in hospice settings provide both inpatient and in-home care to patients as well as family members or other caretakers. The most important role hospice social workers play is helping clients adjust to and make plans for the illness and death of a loved one. Hospice social workers participate in all stages of care, beginning with the intake interview and continuing through regular and crisis intervention for home care and inpatient care.[81] Social workers often facilitate regularly scheduled family conferences to inform family members about the patient's condition and what to expect. They also provide services to the family through support groups, home visits, and calls that are sometimes continued for months after the patient's death.

Critical Thinking Question

Social workers are in a position to promote physical activity and health care tailored to individual and age-group needs across the lifecycle. Brainstorm strategies for promoting healthy living in (a) childhood; (b) adolescence; and (c) old age.

Health Promotion and Prevention

Since the settlement house days, social workers have been active in health promotion, prevention, and public health activities designed to help individuals and

Case Study: National AIDS Prevention

U.S. HIV/AIDS prevention efforts are administered through the Centers for Disease Control and Prevention (CDC). The CDC prevention strategy over the past 20 years has focused on helping individuals at high risk for HIV/AIDS change and maintain healthful behaviors in order to remain uninfected.[84] The CDC has taken steps to reduce barriers to early HIV diagnosis and to increase access to high-quality medical care, treatment, and ongoing prevention services. The CDC initiative uses best practices in public health to reduce the incidence and spread of HIV/AIDS and to stay on top of new test technologies and interventions, with a focus on four strategies: (1) making HIV testing a routine part of medical care; (2) implementing new models for diagnosing HIV infections outside medical settings; (3) preventing new infections by working with persons diagnosed with HIV and their partners and with individuals at high risk for infection; and (4) decreasing mother-to-child HIV transmission.

CDC prevention and intervention programs are focused on changing risky behaviors. Interventions include encouraging early HIV diagnosis; providing counseling, testing, and referral services; providing educational programs and materials; and training peers to be role models. CDC funds and works with governmental and nongovernmental programs that are delivered in multiple locations and formats, including storefronts, gay bars, health centers, housing communities, faith-based organizations, and schools. The CDC also uses street outreach techniques, like mobile testing vans, offering incentives for participation or referral and recruiting peers to help.

families maximize their chances of living long, healthy, and productive lives. Recent areas of health-related activity have included diseases such as HIV/AIDS and Alzheimer's disease as well as social issues such as teenage pregnancy.[82] Social workers have actively educated individuals and families about healthful lifestyles, proper diet and exercise, smoking termination, and other activities that promote lifelong health. They have led many efforts to change attitudes and behaviors, because doing so is compatible with the person-in-environment and holistic perspectives embraced by the profession. One area in which social workers have been less active until recently is promoting healthful lifestyles for elderly individuals. Marshall and Altpeter suggest eight strategies to promote physical activity and health across the life cycle, including: (1) developing activity-friendly communities; (2) advocating for transportation-friendly communities and adequate community infrastructures that enhance mobility (e.g., speed limits, pedestrian safety); (3) developing healthy work environments; (4) fostering coordination and collaboration across jurisdictions, government levels, and agencies; (5) creating opportunities to promote health among the aging through clinical services; (6) enhancing community competence; (7) supporting economic development for health; and (8) promoting professional community research and information partnerships.[83]

> **Case Study: Statewide Prevention of Tobacco Use**
>
> Tobacco is the greatest preventable cause of illness and premature death in the U.S. Each year, nearly 440,000 deaths are attributed to tobacco use—more deaths than alcohol and drug use, automobile accidents, suicides and murders, and HIV/AIDS combined.[85] Smoking has been linked to cardiovascular disease and stroke. In fact, smokers' risk of developing heart problems is two to four higher than the risk for nonsmokers, and smokers are at twice the risk for strokes.[86] Furthermore, smoking is expensive to smokers, the healthcare system, and to employers. Most states have programs aimed at reducing tobacco use, and in some circles tobacco use is now called "tobacco dependence disease."
>
> In 1993, Hawaii received a grant from the Centers for Disease Control and Prevention to develop a tobacco prevention and control program. Called the Hawaii Tobacco Prevention and Education Project, this program has involved the community, professional business, grassroots organizations, volunteers, and youth groups to participate in tobacco prevention and control efforts throughout Hawaii. The Hawaii project has as its goals to: (1) reduce youth access to tobacco products; (2) reduce smoking rates among adults; (3) reduce exposure to environmental tobacco smoke(rs); (4) build coalitions/community support; (5) improve data/surveillance; (6) increase media and awareness; and (7) increase treatment and cessation options.[87]
>
> Each aim involves multiple programs and activities designed to educate, encourage, and support Hawaiian children and adults in their efforts to avoid using tobacco. For example, to achieve the first aim, the project has developed the Youth Initiation Prevention and Cessation program, which encourages youth to avoid tobacco use through school- and community-based activities, services for teachers, and a tobacco-free policy promotion at the college level. There are multiple school-based activities that target children in K–12 and post-secondary education. For example, a K–12 curricular program includes take-home coloring books for younger children and factsheets for older children. Also, there is media literacy project that educates students about media portrayals of smoking and then provides free movie passes in exchange for written movie reviews; there is also a teen video awards program that buys air time, then works with middle and high school students to write and perform public service announcements. The community-based program complements and coordinates with school programs by celebrating national and international events each year, such as the Great American Smoke-Out, Kick Butts Day, and World No Tobacco Day. Other community celebration activities include a student rally at the state capital, street marketing (sign-waving by youth), school presentations, tobacco-free dance events, and a rally in memory of victims of tobacco exposure. There is also a youth summit to provide information and teach leadership and advocacy skills. Teachers are targeted through free tobacco training, a statewide conference for health and physical education teachers, and workshops to provide teachers with the most up-to-date tobacco education information.
>
> In November 2006, Hawaii strengthened its resolve against tobacco use by enacting the Hawaii Smokefree Law, a comprehensive statewide law that prohibits smoking in all enclosed or partially enclosed places of employment, including bars and restaurants. More than 85% of all Hawaii voters were in favor of the law.[88]

INTERPROFESSIONAL COLLABORATION: SOCIAL WORK AND HEALTHCARE PROFESSIONALS

Interprofessional collaboration, which is both dynamic and complex, is essential in most healthcare settings. This refers to the process that occurs in healthcare settings "when two or more healthcare providers cooperate and assist one another in the service of a patient or family members."[96] It is important to

> ### Case Study: Local Prevention—Diabetes
>
> Diabetes mellitus is a group of diseases distinguished by high blood glucose levels due to defects in insulin production and/or insulin action. More than 18 million Americans have diabetes, though more than 5 million remain undiagnosed currently. Diabetes is a very serious disease that can lead to kidney failure, limb amputation, and blindness in adults. Moreover, people with diabetes are 2 to 4 percent more likely to develop heart disease than non-diabetics.[89] One type of diabetes—Type 2 diabetes—can be prevented if a person makes lifestyle changes during the "pre-diabetic" period. Individuals at risk of developing Type 2 diabetes include overweight adults age 45 years and older and obese individuals under age 45 who have one or more of the following characteristics: (1) family history of diabetes; (2) low HDL cholesterol and high triglycerides; (3) high blood pressure; (4) giving birth to a baby weighing over 9 pounds or a history of gestational diabetes; (5) belong to a minority group, including blacks, Hispanics, American Indians, Asian Americans, and Pacific Islanders.[90]
>
> Local communities can play a part in encouraging lifestyle changes that lower their risk of developing Type 2 diabetes. For example, in Keene, New Hampshire, several organizations joined together to promote regular physical activity and healthy eating habits in an effort to prevent Type 2 diabetes. The Advocates for Healthy Youth (AFHY) program sponsored the project, called "Take 10," with grant money from the New Hampshire Department of Health and Human Services.[91] The Take 10 project is part of a larger AFHY effort to improve overall health among elementary school-aged children and their parents.
>
> AFHY joined with a local elementary school in Keene and the Keene Parks and Recreation Department to offer in-school and after-school physical activity and nutrition programs for children.[92] Teachers take part in school-day activities. One Keene teacher described Take 10 as "a curriculum-based program that encourages kids to take 10 minutes in the school day to be physically active. Teachers lead the sessions, which are matched to lessons in history, math, English, art, etc."[93] She and other teachers at school also "mapped out a walking route around the school for children to get some extra exercise during recess."[94] After school, Keene Parks and Recreation takes over with programs that teach the children about fitness, activities they can do at home, and how to make healthy snacks for themselves.
>
> The adult portion of the program encourages teachers and parents to increase their physical activity by gradually working their way up to walking 10,000 steps per day, the equivalent of about five miles. One parent commented, "What folks should keep in mind is that every step counts. Steps to your co-worker's desk, steps from your car to the store, steps up the stairs . . . all the little efforts through the day can make the difference."[95]

well-rounded patient care because diverse healthcare professionals assigned to one case bring with them different kinds and levels of knowledge and diverse skills, which can be combined to deliver better services. Team members might include physicians, psychiatrists, social workers, psychologists, nurses, physical therapists, nutritionists, and others.[97] Team members might differ depending on the level of care the patient needs and the diagnosis, the type of hospital,

> ### Research Informed Practice with Chinese Immigrants
>
> In 2007, Daniel W. L. Lai and Shirley B. Chau completed a survey study on the influence of service barriers on the health status of 2,214 older Chinese immigrants in Canada. "Circumstantial" barriers included "lack of transportation" and "lack of knowledge about existing health services." In fact, "lack of knowledge about existing health services" was the third most frequently cited service barrier among survey participants. Circumstantial barriers such as these were significant predictors of poor physical health in this study population.
>
> How could this research inform a social worker's efforts to help older Chinese immigrants in the Canadian health care system? Could the findings be relevant to older Chinese immigrants in the United States?[101]

Critical Thinking Question

Social workers collaborate with other human services and medical professionals during engagement, assessment, intervention, and evaluation. There are many benefits to collaboration. Are there situations when collaboration might create problems for social workers and clients?

and other factors. Typical functions of interprofessional teams include: (1) shared assessment of patient problems and needs; (2) relevant information exchange; (3) team teaching of staff; (4) intervention plan development; (5) ethical decision making; (6) task and responsibility delegation; and (7) outcome evaluation.[98] Interprofessional collaboration is not without problems, especially since different professions operate according to different professional values, attitudes, and service orientations, but the outcomes of such deliberations are so valuable that most medical settings value such teamwork.[99]

SUMMARY

Healthcare and its associated cost is one of the most urgent issues Americans face today. This chapter discusses the many roles social workers play in the healthcare profession. In all healthcare settings, social workers specialize in providing biopsychosocial supports to individuals and families on a variety of issues related to their health and wellness, illness, and disability. The settings in which they provide services are highly variable, and as the American healthcare scene evolves, the roles for social workers are likely to continue to grow. Several sections of this chapter emphasize that a large proportion of Americans do not have access to health insurance and cannot afford health care. The populations least likely to have health care access—including members of minority groups, the elderly, and persons with disabilities—also have higher risk for serious health problems. A history of the U.S. health services system details problems that have developed within the system over time. While most Americans agree that the U.S. healthcare system is in need of reform, there is a great deal of disagreement about the direction reform should take. In early 2010, the U.S. healthcare debate reached a fever pitch and resulted in a new law called the Patient Protection and Affordable Care Act. This new law, which will be put into effect over a period of several years, has been designed to address many problems in the U.S. healthcare system.

8 CHAPTER REVIEW

Log onto MySocialWorkLab to access a wealth of case studies, videos, and assessment. (*If you did not receive an access code to* **MySocialWorkLab** *with this text and wish to purchase access online, please visit www.mysocialworklab.com.*)

PRACTICE TEST
The following questions will test your knowledge of the content found within this chapter. For additional assessment, including licensing-exam type questions on applying chapter content to practice, visit MySocialWorkLab.

Research Based Practice

1. Lily is an 11-year-old girl with a television in her bedroom. According to a recent study at Dartmouth Medical School, Lily is significantly more likely to:
   a. Develop cancer than other children her age
   b. Suffer from obesity despite her level of physical activity
   c. Develop asthma
   d. Experience a higher risk of obesity the lower her family's socioeconomic status

2. Charley is an oncology social worker in a cancer center. As an oncology social worker, which of the following duties is she likely to perform?
   a. Learn to talk with doctors and other members of the treatment team
   b. Refer patients that are experiencing stress to medical professionals outside the cancer center
   c. Discourage patients from pursuing complementary and alternative medicines outside the cancer center
   d. Pay home visits to the homes of children with cancer to better understand family dynamics

3. As a medical social worker who works in an asthma clinic, Ben plays multiple roles in asthma education, prevention, and management. He is likely to engage in all of the following except:
   a. Mediating support groups for individuals and families dealing with asthma
   b. Providing links to financial resources for individuals and families dealing with asthma
   c. Advocating to change policy that affects poor and minority populations, who are more likely to live in substandard environments that contain environmental triggers known to cause asthma
   d. Working with environmental firms to remove environmental triggers from the homes of his clients

4. Medicaid is a social insurance program enacted in 1965 under the Social Security Act that provides:
   a. Healthcare coverage to individuals age 65 and over whose income falls below a certain amount
   b. Healthcare coverage to certain low-income individuals and families whose incomes fall below a certain amount
   c. Healthcare coverage to individuals under age 10 and over age 65 provided their family income falls below a certain amount
   d. A mechanism through which social workers and their clients promote positive changes in client functioning

5. Critics of managed care contend that managed care:
   a. Is fragmented
   b. Provides better care for children than S-CHIP provides
   c. Is not fragmented enough
   d. Has improved health care for all Americans

Diversity in Practice

6. Suzanne is a medical social worker. As such, she is likely to:
   a. Work with physically ill clients and their families
   b. Tend to work only with clients who are eligible for health insurance
   c. Work with the parents of children with cancer, but not directly with the children
   d. Work in a hospital setting, as medical social workers rarely find jobs outside of hospitals

7. Socioeconomic status (SES), which is a combination of education, occupation, and income:
   a. Is the most important predictor of living standards that indicate the likelihood of an individual's or a group's access to adequate living conditions (e.g., safe from environmental toxins), education, certain occupations, and health insurance
   b. Is the least important predictor of living standards that indicate the likelihood of an individual's or a group's access to adequate living conditions (e.g., safe from environmental toxins), education, certain occupations, and health insurance
   c. Has not been found to be related to asthma deaths in the U.S. population
   d. Determines which clients social workers

8. Larry is a medical social worker whose work focuses on quality of life rather than cure, and the goal is to facilitate comfort and relieve pain. Which of the following represents the kind of care Larry provides?
   a. Respite care
   b. Hospice Care
   c. Community health care
   d. Medicare

Log onto **MySocialWorkLab** once you have completed the Practice Test above to access additional study tools and assessment.

Answers

Key: 1) b 2) a 3) d 4) b 5) a 6) a 7) a 8) b

Emotional and Behavioral Problems and Social Work Treatment

CHAPTER OUTLINE

Mental Health in the United States 189

Mental Health and "Illness": Conceptualizations of Mental Disorder 189
The Medical Model
Developmental Models
Sociological Theories and the "Myth of Mental Illness"
The Diagnostic and Statistical Manual of Mental Disorders (DSM)

Mental Disorders 195
Disorders Usually First Diagnosed in Infancy, Childhood, or Adolescence
Delirium, Dementia, Amnesic, and Other Cognitive Disorders
Schizophrenia and Other Psychotic Disorders
Mood Disorders
Anxiety Disorders
Sexual and Gender Identity Disorders
Eating Disorders
Personality Disorders
Culture-Bound Syndromes

Social Work and Mental Health Services 200
Micro Practice: Services to Individuals
Mezzo Practice: Practice with Groups and Families
Macro Practice: Policy, Administration, and Advocacy
Practice Settings

Challenges and Trends in Mental Health and Social Work Practice 208
Racial Disparities in Mental Health Care
Managed Care
Evidence-Based Treatment

Interprofessional Collaboration in Assertive Community Treatment (ACT) 210

Summary 212

Practice Test 213

 MySocialWorkLab 213

Core Competencies in this Chapter	(Check marks indicate which competencies are covered in depth)			
Professional Identity	✓ Ethical Practice	✓ Critical Thinking	✓ Diversity in Practice	Human Rights & Justice
Research Based Practice	Human Behavior	Policy Practice	✓ Practice Contexts	Engage, Assess, Intervene, Evaluate

Emotional and Behavioral Problems and Social Work Treatment

MENTAL HEALTH IN THE UNITED STATES

Mental health disorders affect millions of Americans every year. According to the National Institute of Mental Health (NIMH), a federally funded institution that is the largest scientific organization in the world dedicated to mental health research, more than 26% of Americans over age 18 suffer from at least one mental disorder every year.[1] In 2004, 57.7 million Americans were struggling with a diagnosed mental disorder.[2] About 6% of the U.S. population suffers from a serious mental disorder such as schizophrenia.[3] The impact is significant. Mental disorders are the leading cause of disability among 15- to 44-year-olds.[4] In 2003, care and treatment of mental disorders accounted for 7.5% of all health care spending, totaling $121 billion.[5] Of course, even these numbers say little about the real impact of mental disorders on the individuals who suffer from them or on U.S. society at large.

Mental health problems do not affect three or four out of every five persons but one out of one.

—William Menninger

Social workers play a major role in providing mental health services, providing the vast majority (60%) of mental health care in the U.S.[6] In addition, mental health is the most common social work specialty, with 37% of social workers specializing in mental health.[7] Mental health social workers work in a variety of settings. For example, they might provide psychotherapy services at a community mental health center, run educational groups for family members of individuals with schizophrenia at a partial hospital program, or provide school-based mental health case management services to children. In addition to providing direct care, social workers also participate in developing mental health policy at national, state, and local levels, advocate on behalf of persons with mental disorders, and administer and oversee public, private, and nonprofit mental health organizations. Social workers have a unique perspective on mental health and wellness issues. Social workers strive to understand a client (e.g., individual, family, group) in his or her life context—the social environment. In order to work in the mental health field, social work students must receive special education and training in mental health, mental disorders, psychotherapy, and mental health treatment. They are typically referred to as **clinical social workers** and must hold at least an MSW to provide most clinical services, including psychotherapy. Social workers with a BSW degree may be qualified to provide case management and crisis services in some agencies. Even social workers who do not specialize in clinical work need to understand the basics of mental health and social work treatment, however. Macro-level work in this field requires training in mental disorders and treatment, as well as in administration, planning, and policy. In this chapter we will explore the concepts of mental health and mental "illness," survey mental health services provided by social workers, and examine the fundamentals of social work treatment for mental health disorders.

MENTAL HEALTH AND "ILLNESS": CONCEPTUALIZATIONS OF MENTAL DISORDER

Any exploration of social work and mental health must begin with the concept of mental health itself. What is a mental disorder, and what does it mean to experience a mental disorder? What makes one person depressed, whereas another is just having a difficult life transition? These are simple questions with complex answers. Just what constitutes a mental disorder, or whether mental disorders even exist, is a topic of some controversy. There is no one unifying or standard perspective on mental disorders or their causes. The various views and conceptualizations of mental disorders can be divided into three general categories: the medical or biological model, developmental models, and sociological models.[8]

The Medical Model

Early conceptions of mental disorders ranged from demonic possession to personal eccentricity. During the first 150 years of the existence of the United States, the prevailing notion was that metal illness was derived from faulty morals and poor personal character. Interventions derived from such conceptualizations ranged from simply ineffectual to shockingly dangerous and inhumane. Clifford Beers, a Connecticut businessman who suffered from what we would now characterize as bipolar disorder, described the daily violence and neglect in an early 20th-century asylum in his 1909 autobiography, *A Mind That Found Itself*:

> My observations convinced me of an anomaly; namely, that the only patients in a hospital for the insane who are not likely to be subjected to abuse are the very ones least in need of care and treatment. The violent, noisy, and troublesome patient is abused because he is violent, noisy, and troublesome. The patient too weak physically or mentally to attend to his own wants is frequently abused because of that very helplessness which makes it necessary for the attendants to wait upon him. And so of the forty men in the violent ward during my fourteen weeks of confinement there, at least twenty were at one time or another viciously beaten by some one of the three attendants, frequently by two at once.[9]

In the early 19th century, the concept of mental disorder as a physical disorder of the brain began to emerge in the U.S. in tandem with a new medical specialty called psychiatry.[10] This understanding of mental illness as a brain disorder very gradually began to supplant old notions of mental illness as failures of character and morals, though as Beers's experiences illustrate, the process was very slow indeed. Modern concepts of mental disorders as comparable to physical illnesses have reduced some of the stigma and blame associated with prior conceptualizations and helped advocates argue for more humane and scientifically informed treatment.

Often referred to as the **medical model** of mental disorders, the concept of mental disorder as equivalent to physical illness remains the dominant theory in the field of mental health today. The medical model emphasizes the role of human biology, especially the brain, as the source—and solution—to mental disorders. The dominance of the medical model is reflected in the mission of many of the United States' major mental health treatment and research institutions.[11] For example, the first point in the National Institute of Mental Health's mission statement reads: "[to] support the integrative science of brain and behavior providing the foundation for understanding mental disorders."[12]

Proponents of the medical model believe that mental disorders have an *organic* cause—that is, a physical, biological cause—including genetic anomaly, the effects of a pathogen (such as a virus or bacteria), or environmental exposure.[13] Indeed, evidence for this view of mental disorders is growing rapidly as researchers develop more sophisticated methods for understanding that most complex of human organs, the brain. Brain dysfunction appears to be indicated in many disorders, including post-traumatic stress disorder (PTSD), bipolar disorder, and schizophrenia. The medical model, with its emphasis on scientific inquiry, also eschews any particular psychological or sociological theory of what causes mental disorders. This, some argue, renders it less vulnerable to subjective personal opinion and professional dogma.[14] In addition, the concept of mental disorder as bodily illness takes the blame away from the individual and his or her family. We do not blame individuals or their parents for having a stroke or cancer, after all. Advocates for people with mental disorders emphasize this aspect in particular. The National Alliance for the Mentally Ill (NAMI), a prominent national advocacy group, states on their Web site that "mental illnesses are biologically based brain disorders . . . they cannot be overcome through 'will power' and are not related to a person's 'character' or intelligence."[15]

Developing medicines that can correct brain dysfunction has been a major focus of mental health research for the past half century. If mental disorders are illnesses of the brain, then medicine that acts on the brain should help reduce or even eradicate mental illness. Positive research results from the use of **psychotropic medication** (medication that affects mood, behavior, and/or mental processes) in managing and reducing symptoms of many serious disorders, including depression, bipolar disorder, and schizophrenia, seem to support this conception of mental disorder. The extent of positive impact current antidepressant medications have on depression remains a subject of debate, however. A 2008 study published in the *New England Journal of Medicine* notes that many trials of antidepressant medication that show poor results (in other words, show the medication to be no more effective than a placebo) are not published in the medical, academic, or general media, skewing public perceptions of the effectiveness of such medication.[16] Indeed, the study found that when the results of these unpublished trials were included, trials of antidepressant medication from 1987 until 2004 show antidepressant medication as having only a modest positive effect on adult depression.[17] Of course, even if current antidepressant medications are not as effective as is widely believed, that fact alone doesn't necessarily call into question the overall concept of mental disorder as akin to physical illness. It does, however, point to the limitations in our current understanding of the nature of major mental disorders.[18]

Although predominant, the medical model of mental illness is not the only way to think about mental illness. Indeed, although thinking about mental disorders as equivalent to physical illness has helped reduce the stigma and suspicion that have long surrounded mental disorders and the individuals who experience them, the medical model has been criticized for ignoring society's role in determining what is and is not considered normal or disordered, and the societal role in causing mental disorders. Other models of mental illness focus on psychosocial rather than biological explanations.

Developmental Models

Developmental models of mental disorder are informed by the same principles that guide developmental models of general human functioning. In fact, a hallmark of the developmental perspective is the belief that the same principles govern both normal and "abnormal" human functioning. Normal and abnormal are viewed not as discreet, separate categories, but as lying on a continuum.[19] Developmental models emphasize the role individuals' past experiences in shaping their present functioning, including the development of mental disorders.[20] All of the various psychological models of human functioning, including psychodynamic, cognitive, and humanistic models, fall under the developmental model umbrella.

Psychodynamic is a term used to describe the family of theories and approaches to human psychology that have their origins in the work of Sigmund Freud. Freud theorized that human beings are fundamentally motivated by innate drives.[21] He believed that these drives were primarily sexual and aggressive and that they create psychic energy, which has different focuses at different stages of development. When these drives are not gratified appropriately at the appropriate stage of development, "fixation" occurs and leads to inner conflict.[22] Freud also described the **unconscious**. He believed that important psychological processes that drive thinking, emotions, and behavior occur outside of our conscious awareness.[23] One of the roles of the unconscious is to hold back threatening or disturbing information (such as urges or wishes that originate from sexual or aggressive drives), from our conscious minds—that is, to defend us from ourselves. This conflict between the conscious and the unconscious leads to too much psychic energy being spent on defending ourselves. Although some defense is necessary for day-to-day functioning, overusing our energy on defense and the types of **defense mechanisms** we use, can lead to problems in functioning.[24] The most problematic defenses are those that significantly distort reality, such as denial (a defense in which a person denies the existence of a distressing reality) or projection (a defense in which an individual attributes his or her uncomfortable feeling or wish to another person). Conversely, when no defenses are in place—when drives continue unchecked—problems can also occur. Mental disorders occur when reality-distorting defenses become fixed and rigid or when an individual lacks adequate defenses. Many later psychodynamic theories do not include or emphasize sexual and aggressive drives, but all focus on the belief that intrapsychic conflict, and the way the mind copes with it, are at the core of mental disorders.[25] Furthermore, all such theories emphasize the role of early life experiences, particularly in key relationships (e.g., with parents or caregivers), in creating the unresolved inner conflict that leads to mental disorders.

The **cognitive-behavioral** perspective on mental disorder shares with psychodynamic theories the idea that humans are shaped by past and current events and interactions with their environments, as well as the belief that human beings are innately motivated by inner forces. The cognitive-behavioral concept of inner forces, however, is different from Freud's "drives." Rather, the cognitive-behavioral perspective on human motivation views human beings as ultimately seeking to increase their feelings of pleasure and reduce their feelings of pain.[26] The cognitive-behavioral perspective emphasizes the role of learning, which is acquired through rewards and punishments accrued in our environments, and of cognition, which we use to understand and interpret interactions and events. Human beings themselves are viewed as "information processing systems," constantly interacting with the environment and interpreting these interactions.[27] According to the cognitive-behavioral perspective, behavior influences the way we think, and thinking influences the way we behave. All individuals are believed to operate in keeping with these principles, mental disorder or no. Mental disorders occur due to problematic environments or events and/or unusual or inaccurate ways of thinking.[28] For example, a woman with a history of parental emotional neglect may come to interpret the neglect as resulting from her unlikeability. This belief may lead her to stay away from others, assuming that she will be neglected and disliked by everyone. This behavior prompts feelings of loneliness and poor self-esteem, which can lead to depression. In this case, the combination of thinking patterns derived from negative events and reinforced by behaviors results in mental disorder.

Finally, the "humanistic" perspective offers another view of mental health and mental disorder. The concept of "mental illness" as distinct from mental wellness does not figure into the humanistic perspective. Rather, it views human beings as unique, distinct, and innately driven to self-actualize—that is, to live to their fullest potential.[29] This process can be thwarted by negative life events and unsupportive social environments (see Maslow's hierarchy of needs, discussed in Chapter 2). Difficulties—what others refer to as "mental disorders"—are thus understood to arise from differences or conflicts between a person's inner experience of him- or herself and the way he or she is treated by other people and the world at large.[30] Along with both psychodynamic and cognitive-behavioral perspective, the humanistic perspective has been a major influence on the field of clinical social work.

Sociological Theories and the "Myth of Mental Illness"

Sociological theories emphasize society's role in defining what is and is not mental illness, and in determining who has a mental disorder. Sociological theories generally take a social constructionist perspective, holding that mental disorders are what a society constructs them to be. Some sociological theories conceptualize mental disorder as a means of social control—a way to keep individuals in line with approved social norms by stigmatizing behavior that is not in keeping with those norms (norms, it should be noted, that are defined by those in power). For example, according to **labeling theory**, mental disorders originate from the way society views certain behaviors.[31] Societies have rules for normal behavior that govern all aspects of life, such as when it is appropriate to be loud or quiet or to wear clothes or be naked. Most individuals break social rules at some time or another, but if the rule-breaking is infrequent and minor, the behavior tends to be ignored or rationalized. When rule-breaking behavior is frequent or severe and/or when the rule breakers have little social power (e.g., members of a marginalized social group), society labels the behavior as deviant or abnormal.[32] A "mentally ill" label is applied to the behavior and to the persons who exhibit it.[33] Over time, individuals come to identify with their labels, and the labeling becomes a self-fulfilling prophecy.[34]

Social labeling theory suggests that mental illness exists more subjectively than objectively, a conception at odds with the medical model, which suggests that mental disorders are an objective, biological reality. Psychiatrist and academic Thomas Szasz represents, perhaps, an extreme position on the continuum of challenges to the medical model of mental disorders. Szasz suggests that the entire concept of mental illness is a myth.[35] According to Szasz, mental disorders are not illnesses or diseases, and the term "mental illness" is a metaphor for describing deviant behavior and human suffering, rather than physical reality.[36] He argues that although all illnesses, physical or mental, are deviations from norms, physical illnesses are deviations from anatomical or biological norms, whereas behaviors and mental states commonly interpreted as indicative of mental illnesses are, in fact, deviations or violations of social,

> *To live in poverty is to live with constant uncertainty.*
> —Barbara Ehrenreich

ethical, and/or legal norms.[37] Thus, from his perspective, although many people struggle with emotional pain and suffering, their reality is due to "problems in living" rather than a brain disease.[38]

The Diagnostic and Statistical Manual of Mental Disorders (DSM)

Conceiving of mental disorders as illnesses suggests that mental disorders, like physical ailments, have a cure. In medicine, a diagnosis is a critical first step in treatment. Physical illnesses can be identified by careful medical observation, laboratory testing, or after death, by autopsy. Mental disorders, however, are much more difficult to identify. For example, there are no tests to measure the neurochemical imbalances thought to contribute to depression. Historically, diagnosis of mental disorder has very been subjective. There has been an increasing emphasis on identifying, classifying, and developing a more objective system for diagnosing mental disorders since the mid-20th century, however. The first edition of the *Diagnostic and Statistical Manual of Mental Disorders* (DSM) was published in 1952 by the American Psychiatric Association (APA). The DSM, now in its fifth revision, is a diagnostic handbook for mental health professionals that lists different categories of mental disorders along with diagnostic criteria. The first two editions were based on a psychoanalytically informed biopsychosocial framework for understanding human psychology and psychopathology, and in time were critiqued for a lack of any clearly delineated way to distinguish between normal and abnormal.[39] The third edition, published in 1980 (the DSM-III), used a medically informed model with diagnostic criteria identified for each disorder.[40] In addition to helping mental health service providers distinguish a mental disorder from "normal" life challenges, the APA hoped this edition would make diagnosis more consistent and reliable.[41] Reliability, in this context, means that two mental health professionals assessing the same individual would come to the same conclusion about what, if any, mental disorder the individual is experiencing. The current DSM-IV-TR, released in 2000, is modeled on the same principles as the DSM-III. A new revision of the DSM, DSM-V, is scheduled for release in 2013.[42]

Critiques of the DSM, including its specific use in social work practice, are wide ranging. Criticisms of DSM include questions about how it is created and revised, about its reliability, about its use and utility in contemporary clinical

---

Demonstrating Knowledge, Values, and Skills

The Pharmaceutical Industry and the DSM

Among the critiques of the DSM as the primary diagnostic tool for mental health research and practice are concerns about the potential influence of pharmaceutical companies on the DSM revision process.[43] A 2006 study of the financial connections of the DSM-IV and DSM-IV-TR task force members—the mental health professionals who help develop and revise the DSM—found that 56% had at least one connection with the pharmaceutical industry. The study also found that 100% of the members of the subcommittees studying mood disorders and schizophrenia—two classes of mental disorders in which treatment with psychotropic medication is commonly utilized—had financial ties to drug companies.[44]

What impact do you suppose this might have on how the DSM is developed? What could the potential benefits and costs of task force members' connections to the pharmaceutical industry be to the DSM? For mental health professionals? For clients?

practice and in the education of mental health professionals, and about its lack of attention to cultural difference and other social factors.

Herb Kutchins and Stuart Kirk, prominent critics of the DSM and its usefulness in social work practice, note that "the DSM does not provide social workers with a useful language to talk about social deprivation, individual abilities and strengths, oppression, accumulated disadvantage, racism, sexism, accessing community resources, client advocacy, family and group dynamics, interpersonal struggles and conflict, networking or clarifying what the client really wants."[45] Some family therapy practitioners also criticize the DSM for its emphasis on problems as originating in an individual rather than in the family system. Feminist critics point to gender bias in a variety of DSM diagnoses, especially those categorized as personality disorders.

Homosexuality is often cited as evidence of both the fact that mental disorders are based in culture rather than science *and* the lack of acknowledgment of this fact by the DSM and the medical model in general. Homosexuality was included as a mental disorder in the DSM-I and II, but was eliminated from the DSM-III. Including homosexuality as a mental disorder in the original DSM was influenced by the norms and values (including religious values) of the dominant culture at that time, which viewed homosexual behavior as aberrant. Furthermore, categorizing homosexuality as a mental disorder perpetuated discrimination, disrespect, and stigmatization of GLBT people. Advocacy efforts by the GLBTQ community, allies, and mental health practitioners heavily influenced the APA's decision to remove it from the DSM-III. This change has had a very significant and positive impact on reducing the stigma associated with homosexuality and also reflected evolving social attitudes about sexual orientation. The change, however, does raise an interesting question: If mental disorders are truly medical disorders—that is, if they are truly organic in nature—how can changing social norms influence what is and is not considered a disorder? It is hard to imagine the medical community changing its understanding of cancer or diabetes as diseases for similar reasons.

Critical Thinking Question
Some professionals suggest that while there are personality disorders associated with stereotypical feminine characteristics, the same is not true for stereotypically masculine characteristics. Looking at the various personality disorders described here, do you agree?

The nature of mental health is deeply complex, and professionals in the field of mental health are far from a definitive understanding of exactly what constitutes mental wellness and disorder, how mental disorders come to exist, why individuals suffer from them, and how to help individuals end that suffering. There are many theories, but far less proof. Amidst all of these competing theories, social work emphasizes a multidimensional model. Chapter 2 detailed the biopsychosocial (spiritual–ecological) model of human existence. Social work practice in mental health uses the same model to conceptualize mental disorders. Social workers in clinical practice, especially those who practice psychotherapy, draw on particular theories of mental disorder and human psychology to inform their interventions; however, the biopsychosocial approach reminds us of the overarching, unifying principles of social work practice.

MENTAL DISORDERS

Despite important criticism of the DSM, the diagnostic process, and the medical model of mental disorders, all are real and prominent features of the contemporary mental health field. The DSM remains the dominant framework for defining what is and is not a mental disorder, and it is widely, if sometimes uncomfortably, used by social workers practicing in the mental health field.

The DSM-IV-TR identifies 16 categories of mental illness, and includes a glossary of "culture bound syndromes." The 16 categories of mental disorders include Disorders Usually First Diagnosed in Infancy, Childhood, or Adolescence; Delirium, Dementia, Amnesic, and Other Cognitive Disorders; Schizophrenia and Other Psychotic Disorders; Mood Disorders; Anxiety Disorders; Sexual and Gender Identity Disorders; Eating Disorders; and Personality Disorders.[46]

Disorders Usually First Diagnosed in Infancy, Childhood, or Adolescence

Many disorders in this category are found in both children and adults; however, they usually are diagnosed in childhood. These disorders include mental retardation, learning disorders, pervasive developmental disorders (also referred to as *Autism Spectrum Disorders* [ASDs]), *Attention Deficit Disorder* (ADD), and *Attention Deficit Hyperactivity Disorder* (ADHD), which involve symptoms of inattention and, in the case of ADHD, hyperactivity. ASDs are usually diagnosed by the time a child is preschool aged, and are about four times more common in boys than girls.[47] ADD and ADHD are among the most commonly diagnosed childhood disorders; however, ADHD also affects an estimated 4% of adults in a given year.[48]

Delirium, Dementia, Amnesic, and Other Cognitive Disorders

These disorders are characterized by memory and/or cognition losses that represent a significant change from previous functioning. *Alzheimer's disease* is in this category. Alzheimer's is the most common cause of dementia,[49] a state in which a person experiences memory loss and cognitive deficits, including difficulty identifying objects despite adequate sensory functioning, speech difficulties, and/or difficulties with physical movement, despite intact motor functioning.[50] Symptoms of Alzheimer's disease typically emerge after age 65. About 10% of adults over 65 suffer from Alzheimer's disease, and about half of adults over age 85 experience the disorder.[51]

Schizophrenia and Other Psychotic Disorders

The mental disorders in this category are severe and are characterized by psychotic symptoms—thinking and behavior marked by a significant disconnection from reality. Schizophrenia, a serious and debilitating mental disorder, is in this category. Individuals suffering from schizophrenia typically experience delusions and/or hallucinations, confused or incoherent speech, unusual or bizarre behavior, restricted emotional responses, significant impairment in functioning in work/school and interpersonal relationships, and ability to care for themselves, depending on the subtype of the disorder they experience.[52] Schizophrenia typically first appears in men in their late teens to early twenties, and in women in their twenties and early thirties.[53] It affects about 1% of U.S. adults in a given year.[54]

Mood Disorders

Disorders in this category include major depressive disorder and bipolar disorder. Mood disorders are characterized by significant disturbances in mood—that is, a person's emotional state and attitude—that affect a person's ability to function in day-to-day life. A person suffering major depression experiences a consistently low mood and several of the following symptoms for two or more weeks: lack of interest in activities he or she usually enjoys, loss of energy/fatigue, feeling hopeless and pessimistic, insomnia or oversleeping, significant weight change (unintentional weight loss or gain), difficulty concentrating, loss of motivation, and preoccupation with death (including suicidal thoughts).[55] Bipolar disorder is characterized by extreme mood shifts: depressive episodes on the one end and manic episodes on the other. Manic episodes are characterized by vastly increased energy, elevated or irritable mood, inflated sense of self-esteem, racing thoughts, excessive involvement in pleasurable activities with potentially painful or dangerous consequences (for example, risky sexual behavior or spending sprees).[56] Approximately 9.5% of U.S. adults experience a mood disorder in a given year.[57] Major depression is the most common of the mood disorders, affecting about 6.7% of the U.S. adult population, and is more prevalent among women than men.[58] In the past decade, there has been a large increase in the numbers of children diagnosed with bipolar disorder, and it remains unclear whether this is a reflection of long-overdue diagnosis for children struggling with this serious mood disorder, or if it has become a "catch-all" diagnosis for kids who experience moodiness, irritability, and/or "hard to control" behavior (a similar conundrum exists for ADHD).[59]

Anxiety Disorders

Anxiety disorders are the most common mental disorders in the U.S. About 40 million people, or about 18% of the adult U.S. population, experience an anxiety disorder in a given year. Anxiety disorders are characterized by excessive fear, worry, apprehension, and even dread, as well as avoidance of situations associated with these feelings. Disorders in this category include Generalized Anxiety Disorder (GAD), Obsessive-Compulsive Disorder (OCD), Post-Traumatic Stress Disorder (PTSD), panic disorder, and a range of phobias. Of the anxiety disorders, GAD and PTSD are the most common, affecting between 3% and 3.5% of the adult U.S. population in a given year, respectively.[60] Individuals suffering from GAD experience persistent excessive worry about a number of events or activities, as well as several of the following symptoms: restlessness, irritability, sleep problems, muscle tension, fatigue, and difficulty concentrating.[61] As the name suggests, PTSD is a disorder that occurs in reaction to a traumatic event in which a person experienced a perceived or actual threat to his or her own life or bodily integrity, or that of others, and felt intense fear, helplessness, or horror. Examples of such trauma include combat, sexual assault, domestic violence, and natural disasters. Individuals suffering from PTSD re-experience the trauma through intrusive memories, flashbacks, and/or nightmares, avoid stimuli associated with the trauma (including actually avoiding places or people associated with it, or repressing associated memories, thoughts, and/or feelings), and increased physical and emotional arousal, such as trouble sleeping, difficulty concentrating, and/or exaggerated startle response (i.e., excessive "jumpiness").[62]

> **Did You Know?**
>
> **The Controversy over GID**
>
> There is significant controversy regarding the GID diagnosis. Many believe that it is no more a disorder than homosexuality, and that its inclusion in the DSM reflects cultural and social norms, values, and bias about gender and sexuality rather than a genuine mental disorder. Moreover, many believe that its inclusion reinforces and even promotes stigma and misunderstanding of transgender people. Its existence, however, also serves an important function for transgender people who are interested in sex reassignment surgery. Currently an individual cannot receive such surgery without a GID diagnosis, creating an unfortunate and unjust double bind for transgender people.

Sexual and Gender Identity Disorders

Disorders in this category involve sexual dysfunction or identification with the other gender. The diagnoses in this category are particularly controversial. Sexual dysfunction disorders include *male erectile disorder*, characterized by difficulty in achieving or maintaining an erection long enough to allow for engagement in or completion of sexual intercourse.[63] In recent years, this disorder has received increased attention, especially from pharmaceutical companies, several of which have launched aggressive print and television advertisements for drugs such as Cialis. *Gender Identity Disorder* (GID) diagnosis is characterized by two major features: a significant and persistent identification with the other gender, which in adults may be manifested in stated desire to be the other sex, passing as the other sex (including altering physical appearance and dress to correspond with other sex,); and persistent discomfort with one's own sex (including the feeling of being born into the wrong body).[64]

Eating Disorders

Disorders in this category are characterized by significant disturbances in eating behavior and a preoccupation with body weight and shape. The two disorders in this category are anorexia nervosa and bulimia nervosa. Both affect women in greatly disproportionate numbers as compared to men, especially anorexia. Less that 15% of individuals with anorexia are male, and just over a third of individuals with bulimia are male.[65] Between 0.5% and 4.2% of women will experience an eating disorder in their lifetime.[66] Individuals who suffer from anorexia are unable to maintain a body weight at or above a minimally normal weight for their height and age; have an intense fear of gaining weight, despite being underweight; experience a disturbance in their own sense of their bodies (in other words, experience themselves generally, or in particular areas, to be fat when they are not); and, in women, experience a disruption in the menstrual cycle due to being underweight. People with anorexia might attempt to lose weight by restricting their food intake severely, purging (e.g., vomiting, abusing laxatives), exercising excessively, or a combination of all three.[67] Bulimia is characterized by binging (consuming a large amount of food) accompanied by a feeling of being "out of control," using one or more of a variety of methods to prevent weight gain and get rid of food (e.g., vomiting, fasting, excessive exercise, abusing laxatives), and a preoccupation with body weight and shape.[68] Eating disorders can have significant negative effects on overall physical health, and can even be fatal. Binge-eating disorder—characterized by binging accompanied by a sense of loss of control and shame, guilt, and/or physical discomfort, but not accompanied by purging, is not included as a diagnosis in the current DSM, though it may be in future editions.[69] Approximately 2–5% of U.S. adults experience binge-eating disorder.[70]

Emotional and Behavioral Problems and Social Work Treatment

Personality Disorders

Personality disorders are characterized by long-term rigid patterns of behavior, thinking, emotions, attitudes, and worldviews that deviate strikingly from societal expectations, cause significant stress and distress to self and/or others, interfere with day-to-day functioning, and result in problematic social and interpersonal interactions. These patterns begin in adolescence or early adulthood and tend to remain in place over a significant amount of time. There are ten personality disorders listed in the DSM, clustered into three subcategories based on prominent features.

Cluster A personality disorders include:

- **Paranoid:** characterized by a pattern of mistrust and suspiciousness of the motives of others.
- **Schizoid:** characterized by a pattern of detachment from social relationships and a limited range of emotional expression.
- **Schizotypal:** characterized by a pattern of acute discomfort in social relationships, cognitive/perceptual distortions, and odd or eccentric behavior.

Cluster B personality disorders include:

- **Antisocial:** characterized by a pattern of overt disregard for and violation of the rights of others.
- **Borderline:** characterized by a pattern of impulsivity and instability in emotions, self-image, and relationships.
- **Histrionic:** characterized by a pattern of excessive emotionality and attention seeking.
- **Narcissistic:** characterized by a pattern of grandiosity, need for admiration, and lack of empathy.

Cluster C personality disorders include:

- **Avoidant:** characterized by a pattern of social discomfort and inhibition, feelings of insufficiency, and hypersensitivity to negative feedback.
- **Dependent:** characterized by a pattern of submissive behavior "related to an excessive need to be taken care of."
- **Obsessive-compulsive:** characterized by a pattern of preoccupation with control, order, and perfection.[71]

Most personality disorders describe characteristics that are not uncommon or unfamiliar to most people. Almost everyone knows someone who seems to never stop talking about themselves, is "overly dramatic," is very shy, is a "neatnik," or is just plain odd or eccentric. These characteristics, in and of themselves, do not signify the presence of a personality disorder. The human personality is complex and each individual's personality is distinct and unique—made up of many traits and characteristics, some more pleasant and socially accepted than others. What makes personality disorders different from personality quirks is the persistence and rigidity of problematic characteristics and the level of distress or impairment they cause to the person, others around him or her, and society in general. Individual personality disorders are relatively rare in the adult U.S. population. Some studies suggest that no more than 2% of people experience an individual personality disorder;[72] however, they are more common in certain subpopulations. For example, antisocial personality disorder is disproportionately common among incarcerated individuals.[73]

Culture-Bound Syndromes

In an attempt to improve the inclusiveness and cultural competency of the DSM, the DSM-IV-TR included, for the first time, a glossary of 25 identified culture-bound syndromes. Culture-bound syndromes are disorders unique to a cultural group or society and do not easily fit into current DSM diagnostic categories. A few culture-bound syndromes are described below:

- **Amok:** This disorder was first reported in Southeast Asia, but is also found in Pacific Rim societies, Puerto Rico, and among the Navajo. Amok is a dissociative episode characterized by a period of brooding, followed by an outburst of violent, aggressive, or homicidal behavior. It is experienced almost exclusively by males and can include delusions, amnesia, and exhaustion followed by a return to pre-episode functioning.
- **Ghost sickness:** A disorder observed among many Native American communities, ghost sickness is characterized by a preoccupation with death and the deceased. Symptoms include bad dreams, physical weakness, feelings of danger, loss of appetite, fainting, dizziness, and anxiety. Ghost sickness is sometimes associated with witchcraft.
- **Mal de ojo:** Found primarily in Mediterranean cultures, mal de ojo is a Spanish term meaning "evil eye." Children are especially at risk, and symptoms include fitful sleep, crying for no apparent reason, vomiting, and fever.
- **Nervios:** The term *nervios* is an idiom of general distress common among Latino/as both in the United States and in Latin America. Associated symptoms include difficulty functioning, headaches, sleep difficulties, nervousness, tearfulness, dizziness, and other somatic disturbances.
- **Zar:** A syndrome occurring in the Middle East and Northern Africa, *zar* is a term used to describe spirit possession and is characterized by dissociative episodes, shouting, laughing, and weeping.[74]

For social workers in mental health practice to be effective in working with culturally diverse client populations, they must be knowledgeable about their clients' cultural backgrounds and the specific disorders that occur within their cultural and social contexts. Without such knowledge, social workers are in danger of over-pathologizing clients and assigning what are actually culture-specific disorders an inappropriate DSM diagnosis, such as schizophrenia.[75]

SOCIAL WORK AND MENTAL HEALTH SERVICES

Social workers working in the mental health field practice at the micro, mezzo, and macro levels. They also work in a variety of settings.

Micro Practice: Services to Individuals

Micro-level social work practice in mental health, as noted earlier in this chapter, is usually referred to as psychosocial casework or **clinical social work**. Psychosocial casework (see Chapters 1 and 4) is a method of working with clients that dates back to the beginnings of the social work profession.[76] Although the practice has evolved over the years to incorporate new theories,

Critical Thinking Question

The "Westernization," of mental health and illness (such as major depression and eating disorders) across the globe appears to be growing. What potential problems—or benefits—might arise from the Westernization of mental illness?

Isolation is the primary source of suffering for people.

—Judith Jordan

biomedical and scientific developments, and the principles of social justice movements, the core features of social work practice with individuals remain:

- Human functioning encompasses biological, psychological, and social elements.
- Problems arise from a disruption in fit between individuals and their environment.
- Treatment is a collaborative endeavor between the social worker and the client.
- The goals of treatment are to mobilize strengths and coping skills, locate resources (internal and external), and find "optimal fits" between clients and their various social and physical environments.[77]

Social workers in micro practice in mental health may provide different types of services or use different psychological theories or approaches to guide their interventions with clients, but the basic tenets of psychosocial casework provide a solid foundation for practice.

Social workers practicing at a micro level in mental health typically provide case management, counseling/psychotherapy, and/or other individual support services to clients with mental disorders. Social workers who provide mental health **case management** coordinate multiple, ongoing services for individual clients with mental disorders. For example, a social worker working with an adolescent male who has been diagnosed with bipolar disorder and a learning disorder might coordinate individual psychotherapy services, family therapy services, psychiatric services (including medication management), recreational programming, and school-based support services. Depending on his circumstances, a case manager might also coordinate transportation to and from all these services, assist him or his family in accessing public or private health insurance to pay for these services, help him access special services or programs in his community (e.g., find information, help fill out applications), and/or provide other support as needed. Case managers help plan treatment strategies, including identifying appropriate services and assisting clients to identify needs and goals; monitor the effectiveness of various services; and advocate for improved or new services as needed. Case managers may also provide "psychoeducation" and/or help clients find information about their particular disorders. Depending on the setting and client population, BSW social workers may provide case management services. Some types of specialized case management, such as case management for individuals with chronic serious mental disorders, require the additional skills, training, and expertise of an MSW degree.

Psychotherapy (also referred to as therapy or counseling) is another way that social workers work with individuals. Social workers who provide psychotherapy may work with clients who are struggling with a mental disorder as well as with clients who are not experiencing a mental disorder but are facing particularly challenging life events and/or transitions. Freud originated the "talking cure" we know as psychotherapy as a specialized way to help individuals resolve inner conflicts and improve their psychological health. Human beings have always used verbal communication to work through difficult situations, however. For example, spiritual consultation and support provided by religious leaders is common in most religious traditions.

There are numerous approaches to psychotherapy that social workers may use in their work with clients. Three major therapeutic approaches—psychodynamic, cognitive-behavioral, and humanistic—are derived from the

> **Social Work Stories: Working with Clients in Private Psychotherapy**
>
> Anne F, a social worker in Lafayette, Louisiana, for over 20 years, discusses the types of mental health issues she encounters in her private psychotherapy practice, and how she works with clients on these issues:
>
> > From a DSM-IV point of view, I'd say the problem I encounter most frequently is depression. From a trauma-response, cognitive behavioral point of view, which is my primary theoretical orientation, I'd say the most frequent struggles I see are the inaccurate beliefs, the negative beliefs of "I'm not OK," "I'm unworthy," which, I think, create a filter that creates depression and are often based in trauma. I don't see people with chronic mental illness or psychosis in my practice because I think they need a higher level of treatment than I can provide, including a psychopharmacological treatment and case management. The core of what I do, though, is listen and witness. Fundamentally, listening, witnessing, and holding the belief that this person is OK and loveable the way they are is the core of what I do. I believe there are logical reasons that clients are thinking and behaving in ways that aren't working for them and it's not something to be ashamed of, just something to understand and make choices about. Sometimes, really, I think that's all I do. There are times, of course, when we're problem solving, coming up with resources, or scripting and rehearsing how to talk to someone, but fundamentally, we're creating a place where the client can just be who they are.

models of human development and psychological functioning described earlier in this chapter and in Chapter 2. There are dozens of sub-approaches derived from these approaches, some focused on particular populations or particular disorders. Some psychotherapeutic approaches are designed to be used over a short period of time (often referred to as "brief treatment" approaches); other approaches are more effective given a longer course. Despite this diversity, however, all psychotherapies have some basic components in common. Almost all therapies follow the same general path:

- **Assessment:** Before an intervention can begin, the client and worker must come to a joint understanding of what is going on for the client. In assessment, the social worker gathers pertinent biological, psychological, and social data about the client. The social worker gathers data about both the client's present circumstances and past experiences. They may also use specialized assessment tools to determine the presence of a particular symptoms of mental health disorders. Assessment typically, and logically, begins with the social worker inquiring about what prompted the client to seek psychotherapy. Although assessment is an essential first step, it is also an ongoing process, as clients' lives and circumstances change over time.
- **Establishing the client–worker relationship:** Therapy is hard work for clients (and for therapists!), requiring a substantial level of commitment, trust, and courage on the part of the client. As discussed in earlier chapters, establishing a positive client–therapist relationship is an essential component of effective therapy. Goldie and Alfred Kadushin call this positive relationship (also referred to as a "working alliance") an "anesthetic to sharing painful material."[78] In fact, the presence of a good working relationship has been shown in numerous studies to be the ingredient common to all successful therapy, regardless of the specific therapeutic approach used.[79] Developing a positive relationship begins at the first interaction between a worker and client. Developing a positive working alliance relies on several key elements in the worker's approach toward the client, including acceptance and a nonjudgmental

attitude, empathy, genuineness and authenticity, warmth, interest, and trust, respect for client's right to self-determination, respect for the client's individuality, and respect for the principle of confidentiality.[80] Self-awareness, including awareness of one's strengths and challenges and personal and sociocultural values, is another key component in developing an effective therapeutic relationship.

- **Intervention:** Change begins to occur during the intervention phase of psychotherapy. The social worker makes choices about how to proceed in the intervention phase based on information gleaned from the assessment and the strength and status of the relationship, as well as on her or his own theoretical framework. For example, social workers specializing in cognitive-behavioral therapy are likely to engage clients about their cognitive processes and beliefs. Informed by the principles of behaviorism, they might assign homework to clients to try out new behaviors. Although we often refer an intervention "phase," interventions happen in all phases of psychotherapy treatment. Kadushin and Kadushin note that the development of a good client–therapist relationship can be an intervention in and of itself, especially for clients who experience challenges with trust and interpersonal interactions.[81]
- **Evaluation:** In the evaluation phase (see Chapter 4 also), the social worker and client evaluate the effectiveness of the treatment. They assess progress toward the client's goals to date, perhaps make changes in focus or direction, add new goals, or modify initial goals. Sometimes social workers use standardized evaluation instruments to determine progress, especially regarding a particular mental disorder. Evaluation—especially evaluation with standardized tools—has become particularly important in recent years, as an increasing number of health insurance providers are requiring that social workers justify continuing treatment with hard evidence of the impact of the treatment thus far. Beyond that, evaluating your own practice is just good social work practice.
- **Termination:** Termination is, of course, the final treatment phase. As indicated in Chapter 4, there are many reasons termination can occur. Termination can be a difficult process for clients, especially if they have experienced unresolved prior losses, have inadequate social supports, are facing challenging life circumstances, have found the treatment to be unsatisfactory, and/or if the termination is forced rather than mutually agreed upon.[82]

Mezzo Practice: Practice with Groups and Families

Frequently, social workers practicing in the field of mental health work at the mezzo level with families or other groups. Social workers practicing with groups may facilitate a variety of groups of clients with mental illness, including therapy groups, support groups, psychoeducational groups, and/or socialization groups.[83] "Therapy groups" can be formed of individuals diagnosed with the same mental disorder, such as depression or borderline personality disorder, or of individuals with different disorders. Therapy groups may be process-oriented and focus on interactions among the clients and between the clients and the social worker, or skills-based groups, which focus on teaching and supporting specific skills for coping with a particular disorder or general

Critical Thinking Question

Groups can provide a unique and highly effective context for individuals to resolve mental health issues, due to "curative factors" present in group therapy. What do you imagine might be the benefits or drawbacks of group therapy?

distress. A group in which residents of an inpatient mental health treatment facility meet and discuss their experiences is an example of a process-oriented group. A group for individuals with anxiety disorders to learn and practice relaxation techniques is an example of a skills-based group. Skills-based groups often have a cognitive-behavioral approach. **Support groups** include groups where the members offer ongoing support to each other. Support groups may begin by being facilitated by a social worker, but once established can often continue without the social worker's participation. "Psychoeducational groups" in the mental health field might include groups to inform individuals with mental illness about the medications they are taking or about new community resources that are available. Finally, social workers in mental health practice with groups might facilitate "socialization groups," which focus on assisting clients in building social support networks and developing social and interpersonal skills. These groups can be particularly beneficial for those who are socially isolated and/or dealing with mental disorders that affect their comfort and/or ability to engage socially with others, such as those suffering from social anxiety disorder or depression.

Social work practice with families in the mental health field often takes the form of **family therapy**. The family therapy perspective on mental illness holds that the forces that both contribute to and ameliorate mental illness exist in the context of family functioning, and see difficulties, at least in part, as arising from problematic relationships within family systems.[84] Family therapy deemphasizes the role of the "problem" person (often identified as the person with a mental disorder) and instead is directed at changing family structure, which in turn changes family members' lives.[85] Family therapy is a diverse field and, like individual

---

Social Work and Social Justice: The Stigma Associated with Mental Disorders

Along with abusive and inhumane "treatment" like that described by Beers in his 1909 autobiography and call to action, *A Mind That Found Itself*, individuals with mental illness have historically and currently suffer from individual and institutional prejudice and discrimination. While much progress has been made in reducing the stigma around certain types of mental illness, including depression and anxiety, the social stigma surrounding disorders such as schizophrenia remains significant and can affect every area of life, from facing treatment to finding employment. In his 2006 book *Shunned*, British psychiatrist Graham Thornicroft details the discrimination and prejudice faced by individuals with mental illness across the globe, in areas such as housing, employment, medical and mental health care, civic life, and interpersonal relationships. For example, Thronicroft notes that as of 1999, 19 U.S. states limited the participation of individuals with mental illness in voting, serving on juries, and holding public office.[86] Among the most widely held misconceptions about individuals with mental illness is that they are more prone to violence and are therefore dangerous.[87] This is, in fact, not the case. Individuals with mental illness are far more often the victims of violence than the perpetrators.[88] Individuals with mental illness also experience discrimination in insurance coverage. Indeed, despite gains made by mental health parity legislation, most major insurance carriers cover only a select group of "major" mental disorders. Additionally, mental health disorders are often considered preexisting conditions that can result in exclusion from health coverage.

Social work ethics obliges social workers to fight against prejudice and discrimination and for social justice. Several organizations dedicated to serving individuals with mental illness, including NAMI and Mental Health America, have stigma-reducing campaigns. Check out the Web sites of these and other organizations and consider the following questions:

What small changes can you make in your day-to-day life that can reduce stigma associated with mental illness? What major policy changes are being proposed to reduce discrimination and prejudice against individuals with mental illness? Are these enough? What changes would you propose?

psychotherapy, includes a wide range of theoretical orientations and approaches. The essential goal of family therapy is similar across these varying perspectives, however—to help families learn to function more effectively and thus meet the emotional and developmental needs of all family members. Frequently, family therapy is a component in multidimensional treatment for individuals, especially children and adolescents, with major mental disorders.

Macro Practice: Policy, Administration, and Advocacy

Social workers in macro practice in the mental health field typically take on at least one of several roles: advocate, administrator, and/or policy planner/developer. As in all other aspects of social work, macro social work mental health practice is focused on promoting a social justice agenda that includes reducing all forms of social inequality and discrimination. Social workers in mental health advocacy might lobby their state legislature to cover mental health disorders as extensively as medical disorders under state health insurance (referred to as **mental health parity**). Or they may lobby their city council to improve access to mental health services for marginalized populations, including recent immigrants or the homeless. Social workers in mental health administration often work in higher-level and/or supervisory positions in public or nonprofit mental health agencies, outpatient clinics, hospital psychiatric departments, and even health insurance companies. Social workers in these roles direct and oversee service provision, develop and implement agency policies and procedures, manage an agency's finances and raise money (in the case of nonprofit agencies) from public and/or private sources, and oversee and supervise employees. For social workers in administration, this includes developing a culturally competent staff.[89]

Along those lines, social workers in administration have a major role in creating the climate of the agencies and institutions in which they work, including the extent of their cultural proficiency. According to David Wing Sue, an expert in multicultural mental health practice, "culturally proficient" organizations operate with a very high degree of multicultural adeptness. In addition to having a diverse and multiculturally aware staff at all organizational levels, culturally proficient organizations: (1) add to the existing knowledge base of culturally competent mental health practices through original research and demonstration projects; (2) actively pursue a social justice agenda and advocate for diversity; (3) hire staff with specialized training and supervisory skills in cultural competent practices; (4) regularly evaluate their multicultural policies, practices, and overall environment; and (5) use culture-specific programs as a resource.[90]

Social workers in mental health policy may focus their work in a wide range of areas. Their many activities in mental health policy include developing policies regarding mental health delivery systems, including increasing access to services for individuals with mental disorders—especially those who are socially marginalized and/or reside in marginalized communities. Also, they may evaluate existing services and programs or conduct research into important issues mental health, such as prevalence rates and diagnostic disparities.

Practice Settings

Social workers in mental health work in a wide range of practice settings. Typically, the area of focus (in other words, micro, mezzo, or macro) helps to determine the setting in which they work. Social workers in micro and mezzo

Research Informed Practice with African American Boys

In 2006, Michael Lindsey et al. published the results of a study of depression among urban African American boys. Extensive interviews were done with 18 boys aged 14–18 who had been recruited from community-based mental health centers and after-school programs. The majority of boys who were receiving mental health treatment reported that the problems they experienced related to issues in the school environment. These issues included behavioral and academic achievement problems. Although family and school officials eventually helped to access support and mental health services, these boys reported that initially they tried to solve their mental health problems on their own.

How could these research findings inform your efforts as a social worker to assist boys in this situation? What do the results tell you about the "person-in-environment" perspective?[91]

Critical Thinking Question

Social workers promote client self-determination unless clients pose a serious risk to themselves or others. How might a social worker determine that a client's self-determination should be limited?

practice work in four major setting categories: inpatient, outpatient, residential, or private practice. Social workers in macro mental health practice may work in these same settings as administrators, policy planners, or researchers. They might also work in local, state, or the federal government, in policy organizations designing or researching mental health policy, or in advocacy groups, such as NAMI, advocating for the needs of individuals with mental disorders.

One of the key principles guiding the setting in which individuals receive mental health services is the concept of a **least restrictive setting**. The least restrictive setting for a client is that setting which allows a client the highest level of self-determination, a core value of social work, while providing the proper treatment intensity needed for services to be effective.[92] The U.S. Supreme Court decision in *Olmstead v. L.C.* (1999) provides additional legal support for this principle, requiring that states place individuals with mental disorders in community settings when assessed as appropriate by mental health professionals and not opposed by the affected individual, taking into account the community resources available.[93]

Inpatient settings include both general and mental health hospitals. Until the 1960s, most inpatient hospitals specializing in mental health care were run by individual states and funded with state and federal funds. Many people diagnosed with major mental disorders spent years in these facilities, often under conditions that were overly restrictive, coercive, or even abusive. Some patients' mental health improved, but even more languished in state hospitals with minimal improvement. A movement towards **deinstitutionalization** began in the early 1960s under the Kennedy Administration, resulting in the release of thousands of long-term state mental health hospital residents into local communities and the development of community mental health centers to provide care and treatment on an outpatient basis. The advent of managed care has also added to the reduction of inpatient services, as inpatient services are far more expensive than outpatient services. The number of individuals in public mental health hospitals in the U.S. dropped significantly in the second half of the 20th century, from over 560,000 resident patients in 1955 to 60,000 in 2000.[94]

Today, most mental health hospitals are run by private companies, some for profit and others as nonprofits. Typical stays in these facilities tend to be much shorter than they once were; the average inpatient stay has fallen to fewer than ten days and continues to decrease.[95] Specialized mental health hospitals and mental health units in general hospitals typically focus on short-term crisis intervention and stabilization, and then work to connect a patient with community resources to meet long-term mental health needs. Social workers in working in inpatient settings might provide psychological assessment, short-term psychotherapy, and/or discharge planning (in other words, helping patients connect to mental health and other support services in their local communities).

The decrease in inpatient services is a subject of some controversy. Although most agree that clients are "immeasurably better off in the deinstitutionalized care system than they ever could be in mental hospitals,"[96] many experts in mental health care policy are concerned that continued reductions of inpatient services may be negatively affecting clients who truly need the intensive level of care offered by such services, and can pose a safety risk to both the client and society at large.[97]

Social workers in mental health may also work in **residential treatment programs**. Clients receiving residential treatment reside in same place where they receive mental health and/or substance abuse treatment and other support services. Sometimes a mental disorder is so chronic or severe that it interferes with a person's ability to be safe or to properly care for him- or herself. In such circumstances, residential treatment can be an important and helpful option. Residential treatment programs exist for a number of specific disorders, including eating disorders, substance abuse, and schizophrenia, and for specific populations, including children with severe emotional and/or behavioral problems or homeless men who have chronic mental illness. Residential treatment is generally more holistic (i.e., focuses on a wider range of psychosocial needs) and of a longer duration than inpatient hospital treatment. Social workers with MSWs employed in residential settings often provide services similar to what they might in an outpatient setting: case management, individual and group therapy, and psychoeducation. BSW social workers working in residential care often handle the majority of contact with clients, and provide assistance and support with daily living skills, medication management, transportation, and monitoring residents' progress on behavioral goals.

Most individuals with mental health disorders receive treatment in outpatient programs. Diverse settings provide a range of outpatient mental health services, including the outpatient units of general or specialized mental health hospitals, social service agencies, or community mental health centers. In rural areas, mental health services are often provided through multi-service sites that include medical and even dental services. Educational institutions,

Research Informed Practice: Mental Health Agency Profile

Mental health services are provided in a wide rage of settings. Among these are hundreds of mental health agencies across the U.S. Becoming knowledgeable about community resources is an important part of a mental health social worker's professional responsibilities. To learn more about mental health agencies and the services they provide, choose a mental health service agency in your geographical area and complete an agency profile. Questions to answer in your profile include:

- Where is the agency located?
- What services do they provide?
- What client populations does the agency serve?
- How many employees work in the agency? What are their professional qualifications?
- How is the agency funded?
- What is the agency's annual budget?
- Describe the agency's environment? Is it welcoming and friendly? Cold and formal? To what extent is the agency culturally competent or proficient?
- What are the agency's future plans for service expansion or new programs?

including some public and private K–12 schools, colleges, and universities, offer individual and/or group outpatient mental health services for their students. Many large employers (e.g., corporations, public and private institutions) offer **employee assistance programs** (EAPs). These employers may have in-house clinicians to provide short-term counseling and substance abuse treatment to employees, or they may contract with local clinicians to provide these services. Outpatient services include case management, psychotherapy, family therapy, group therapy, psychoeducation programs, and short-term crisis services.

Social workers interested in mental health can also work in private practice. Private practice social workers are self-employed in their own psychotherapy practices or are a part of privately run group practice. Social workers practicing psychotherapy privately must have at least a master's degree in social work and be licensed by their state at the highest level of clinical social work licensure. According to the NASW, 37% of social workers in the mental health field are employed in private practice settings,[98] and the number continues to grow.[99] Social workers in private mental health practice are both therapists and small business owners, and must be knowledgeable in both psychotherapy and business management, including how to receive proper reimbursement from health insurance providers.

CHALLENGES AND TRENDS IN MENTAL HEALTH AND SOCIAL WORK PRACTICE

Racial Disparities in Mental Health Care

I'm a pessimist about probabilities; I'm an optimist about possibilities.
—Lewis Mumford

One of the most pressing and enduring problems in mental health is the alarming disparities in access to and receipt of mental health care between people of color and whites. According to the U.S. Surgeon General, racial and ethnic minorities have less access to mental health services, are less likely to receive needed mental health care, receive poorer quality care, and are underrepresented in mental health research, all despite experiencing mental disorders at the same rates as Euro-Americans.[100] Barriers to mental health care for people of color include: (1) fear and mistrust of treatment, which exist due to a number of factors, from negative past experiences to differing cultural attitudes and beliefs regarding mental health and treatment; (2) racism and discrimination, which can occur at the individual or institutional level (e.g., where services are located, how culturally competent and inclusive they are); and (3) language and communication factors, including lack of multilingual services or qualified interpreters.[101]

African Americans, for example, experience challenges in accessing mental health services due to a number of factors, including lack of health insurance, unemployment, and/or employment in jobs without health insurance benefits (about 25% of African Americans are uninsured); minimal availability of African American treatment providers; and location of service providers in hard-to-access areas.[102] Furthermore, African Americans are more likely to be misdiagnosed than Euro-Americans.[103] There are many interconnected reasons for the bias, including individual clinician bias and lack of cultural competence as well as bias within DSM diagnostic criteria. Because racial and ethnic minorities are less likely to receive care, and receive a poorer quality of care when they do, they bear a disproportionate burden of the impacts of mental illness.[104]

Managed Care

Over the past 20 years, managed care has emerged as the primary mode of health care delivery in the United States. Managed care refers to any kind of health care services (including mental health care services) that are paid for by a third party (in other words, not the person receiving or providing the services) and for which any part of clinical decision making rests with any entity other than the client or the health care provider.[105] Two principal and interconnected issues exist regarding managed care for mental disorders: parity and cost control. Underlying the concept of mental health parity is the idea that the same range of insurance benefits should exist for mental illness as for physical illness.[106] Because of its ongoing nature and the frequent need for specialized care, however, mental health care is expensive, particularly for more severe and chronic disorders like schizophrenia. Many managed care plans do not include mental health care coverage, or if they do, require that only "medically necessary" treatments be covered.[107] Although such restrictions put mental health coverage on a par with medical health coverage, determining what is medically necessary in the treatment of a mental disorder is more complicated than for many physical health problems. For example, a psychoeducational group focusing on living skills can be beneficial for a person with a chronic and severe mental disorder, but is it necessary?

Both because the standards for mental health care are less clear than for other medical care, and because all health care costs continue to grow, many managed care organizations—often private, for-profit businesses—have instituted more rigorous management policies for mental health care to reduce costs.[108] One of the ways managed care organizations attempt to contain their costs is by using gatekeeping procedures, whereby individuals can only receive coverage for services approved by a company gatekeeper, whose role is to determine what services a consumer does or does not need. Many managed care companies also mandate that approved services be provided in the least restrictive setting possible, and limit who a client may obtain services from and for how long.[109] These procedures, often referred to as utilization management, introduce a third party into the mental health care decision-making process.[110] Although this is not necessarily a problem in and of itself—many people consult third parties (e.g., relatives, friends, and professionals) when making health care decisions—utilization management is often criticized for leaving control of important mental health care decisions in the hands of insurance company employees who do not know the patient and are not practicing mental health professionals. At the same time, many employees in utilization management positions are trained as mental health professionals, including as social workers.

> **Research Informed Practice: Mental Health and the Wars in Iraq and Afghanistan**
>
> In recent years, the challenges faced by returning Iraq and Afghanistan war veterans have received substantial media attention. Among the issues that veterans face are challenges related to mental health. Social workers often work with veterans and their families in veterans' hospitals, outpatient programs, on military bases, and in veterans' home communities. In doing your research, review both popular media sources (e.g., newspapers and reputable news-oriented Web sites) and academic sources (e.g., scholarly journal articles). As you review these sources, pay attention to the following questions: What are the major mental health issues that veterans struggle with upon returning home? What are the causes of these issues? What impact do these issues have on veterans' families and communities? How accessible and effective are treatments for veterans? How is treatment funded? To expand your knowledge about social workers' professional work with veterans, check out the National Association of Social Workers Web site on this issue: http://www.helpstartshere.org/kids-and-families/veterans-affairs.

Evidence-Based Treatment

As health insurance companies exercise more control over mental health care services, there has been a shift in emphasis toward treatment modalities that have been proven effective to reduce or resolve mental disorders. The emphasis on these treatments, referred to as **evidence-based treatments**, in contemporary mental health practice and policy has many benefits for managed care, service providers, and clients. Treatments that are supported by evidence of their effectiveness have the potential to save health care insurers, including private companies and state and federal government, a significant amount of money as they reduce the funds "wasted" on treatments that do not work for clients. Evidence-based treatments can benefit mental health service providers, as they supply providers with tools for effectively assisting clients—any mental health treatment provider's ultimate goal—and prevent providers from becoming overly reliant on particular treatment approaches just because they are familiar or fit with their particular theoretical orientation. Mental health service agencies, as well as individual providers, who use evidence-based treatments in their practice are also more likely to be approved as service providers by managed care entities and to receive appropriate compensation for their work. Clients also benefit from receiving treatments that are proven to work. Clients save money, given that even clients *with* health insurance must pay for at least part of any treatment they receive through copayments and deductibles. Clients can avoid the frustration and discouragement that often accompanies ineffective treatment. Most beneficial of all, of course, is that clients' lives improve as their mental disorder remits. All of this said, many mental disorders and treatment approaches remain unstudied, representing a future challenge for social workers.[111]

INTERPROFESSIONAL COLLABORATION IN ASSERTIVE COMMUNITY TREATMENT (ACT)

Social work in mental health is, by necessity, a collaborative undertaking. Clients with mental health disorders often need multiple services from multiple providers. Many mental health service settings are multidisciplinary, meaning that they include professionals from a number of disciplines, including social work, psychology, psychiatry, and psychiatric nursing. Clients with severe mental health disorders require comprehensive—and thus multidisciplinary—services. *Assertive community treatment* (ACT) is a collaborative, multidisciplinary mental health service model for individuals with serious and persistent mental illness in which social workers play an important role. ACT teams are made up of professionals whose backgrounds and training include social work, rehabilitation, counseling, nursing, and psychiatry. ACT teams provide comprehensive services, including case management, initial and ongoing assessments, psychiatric services, employment and housing assistance, family support and education, substance abuse services, and other services, and supports critical to an individual's ability to live successfully in the community. One of the most critical and effective elements of ACT teams is their around-the-clock nature: services are available 24 hours per day, 365 days per year. Several research students have shown the ACT model to be effective. For example, clients receiving ACT services are more likely to find and remain in stable housing and to spend less time in psychiatric inpatient hospitalization.[112]

Social workers in ACT often function as intensive case managers. Their responsibilities can include home visiting, skill development, resource brokering and problem solving. In this capacity, they help clients with housing, financial security, medications, job skills and training, recreation, daily living skills, physical health management, and, when applicable, navigating the criminal justice system. The assistance they provide can be very concrete, such as accompanying a client to a doctor's appointment, helping with grocery shopping, or even assisting with basic home repairs. ACT emphasizes creating and maintaining trusting, solid relationships between client and provider. Providing reliable, concrete assistance helps foster and maintain this relationship, and the relationship in turn allows the client to trust the team to provide more in-depth assistance, such as medical and psychological treatment and support.[113]

Collaboration among professionals is a key component of ACT. Professionals work together to form a network of support around a client, and this network is part of what makes ACT an effective treatment. According to the ACT Association, ACT team principles include:

- Team members communicate their professional assessment of people's needs and suggest treatment strategies based on their professional knowledge.
- Team members teach their teammates as much as possible about their area of expertise.
- Team members ask other team members questions and learn as much as possible about their areas of expertise.
- Team members pitch in and help when needed, even if it means doing something that draws on their life experience rather than professional expertise (for example, helping someone move furniture into a new apartment).[114]

ACT teams are only one among a wide range of settings that call on social workers to collaborate with other mental health professionals. Given the social work emphasis on the multidimensional model of human functioning and mental health, social workers are uniquely qualified to collaborate with professionals in all areas of mental health.

SUMMARY

Mental health is a major health issue in the U.S. Over a quarter of Americans over age 18 suffer from at least one mental disorder every year.[115] The mental health field is an exciting, fascinating, and ever-changing area of social work practice. Currently, mental health is the most popular specialty among social workers, and this trend is likely to continue. There are several models and theories regarding the origins of mental disorders and how best to treat them. These models and theories fall under three headings: the medical model, developmental theories, and sociological theories. Regardless of their theoretical perspective, social workers maintain a multidimensional view of mental health and wellness.

The mental health field is constantly changing, as debates continue about the nature of mental illness and wellness, disorder and "normality." Social workers have a unique perspective to bring to these debates!

9 CHAPTER REVIEW

Succeed with mysocialworklab

Log onto **MySocialWorkLab** to access a wealth of case studies, videos, and assessment. (*If you did not receive an access code to **MySocialWorkLab** with this text and wish to purchase access online, please visit www.mysocialworklab.com.*)

PRACTICE TEST

The following questions will test your knowledge of the content found within this chapter. For additional assessment, including licensing-exam type questions on applying chapter content to practice, visit **MySocialWorkLab**.

1. According to the chapter, mental disorder is:
   a. The leading cause of disability among 18–44-year-olds in the U.S.
   b. A dangerous social problem
   c. The largest source of health care spending in the U.S.
   d. A less significant social issue in the 21st century than it was in the 20th century

2. According to the chapter, one potential benefit of the medical model of mental illness is:
   a. Society now realizes that mental health issues are easily resolved with medication
   b. Treatment for mental health issues now takes place primarily in hospitals and other inpatient settings, reducing the need for outpatient care
   c. There is less stigma associated with mental illness, whereas historically it was viewed as resulting from an individual's faulty moral character
   d. Less attention is paid to the impact of culture on our conceptions of health and disorder

3. The cognitive behavioral perspective emphasizes the role of _____ in mental health and illness:
   a. Innate drives, including sexual and aggressive drives
   b. Learning and cognition
   c. Self-actualization
   d. Substance abuse

4. According to social labeling theory, mental disorders originate from:
   a. Society's perception of and response to certain behaviors
   b. Early parent–child relationships
   c. Racial and gender discrimination
   d. Too few social supports, such as extended family and social networks

5. The next edition of the *Diagnostic Manual of Mental Disorders* is due for release in:
   a. 2010
   b. 2020
   c. 2017
   d. 2013

6. In the DSM-IV, attention deficit disorder, autism, and mental retardation are all examples of:
   a. Other cognitive disorders
   b. Disorders usually first diagnosed in infancy, childhood, or adolescence
   c. Mood disorders
   d. Personality disorders

 Diversity in Practice

7. According to the DSM-IV, mal de ojo is a culture-bound syndrome characterized by:
   a. A preoccupation with death and the deceased, sometimes associated with hallucinations
   b. Poor sleep, tearfulness, fever, and gastrointestinal upset
   c. Dissociative episodes and incongruent affect
   d. Heightened anxiety, headaches, dizziness, and other somatic complaints

8. Deinstitutionalization:
   a. Began under the Kennedy Administration, and resulted in the release of thousands of long-term hospital patients and the development of community mental health centers
   b. Began in the early 19th century, initiated by the efforts of pioneers such as Dorothea Dix
   c. Resulted in an increase in crimes committed by individuals with mental illness and is now considered a failure
   d. Is at odds with the social work ethic of self-determination

 Diversity in Practice

9. Barriers faced by minority groups in accessing mental health treatment *do not* include:
   a. Mistrust of treatment due to cultural attitudes and beliefs regarding mental health and treatment
   b. The growing number of teaching hospitals in poor, urban areas
   c. Racism and discrimination, which can occur on at the individual or institutional level
   d. The lack of multilingual services or qualified interpreters

10. According to the chapter, current challenges in managed care include:
    a. Governmental mismanagement
    b. Low rates of participation
    c. The role of third parties in determining what services are "medically necessary"
    d. Poor compensation for health insurance industry employees

Log onto **MySocialWorkLab** once you have completed the Practice Test above to access additional study tools and assessment.

Answers

Key: 1) a 2) c 3) b 4) a 5) d 6) b 7) d 8) a 9) b 10) c

10

Children, Youth, Family Problems, and Services

CHAPTER OUTLINE

Families in the United States: Decades of Change 215
Demographic Changes in the Family
Changes in Functions of the Family
Diverse Family Forms
Monica McGoldrick and the Family Life Cycle

Major Challenges Facing Children, Youth, and Families 219
Divorce
Single-Parent Families
Blended Families
Family Violence
Partner Abuse
Sexual Violence
Child Abuse and Neglect
Types of Abuse
Child Sexual Abuse and Incest

The Family-(Un)friendly Workplace 227

Major Services to Children, Youth, and Families 228
Child Welfare and Child Protection
Family Intervention

Out-of-Home Placements and Foster Care
The Removal vs. Reunification Debate
Adoption Services
Parenting Support Services and Education
Self-Help: Parents Anonymous
Adolescent Pregnancy and Parenting
Family Planning Services
Family Violence Services
Services to Survivors
Services to Batterers
Services to Families in an Educational Setting
Head Start and Early Head Start
School Social Work
Alternative Education Programs
Child, Couple, and Family Therapy
Therapeutic Work with Children: Play Therapy
Couples Counseling, Marital Therapy, and Family Therapy
Child Abuse and Family Violence Prevention
Adolescent Pregnancy Prevention

Summary 240

Practice Test 241

 MySocialWorkLab 241

	Core Competencies in this Chapter (Check marks indicate which competencies are covered in depth)								
☐	Professional Identity	☐	Ethical Practice	☐	Critical Thinking	☑	Diversity in Practice	☑	Human Rights & Justice
☑	Research Based Practice	☑	Human Behavior	☐	Policy Practice	☐	Practice Contexts	☐	Engage, Assess, Intervene, Evaluate

FAMILIES IN THE UNITED STATES: DECADES OF CHANGE

In recent decades, the U.S. has witnessed rapidly changing patterns of marriage, divorce, remarriage, and cohabitation. Throughout most of history, Americans have thought of themselves as the marrying kind. Indeed, marriage was highly valued prior to the 1800s, when the economy relied on agriculture. At that time, families tended to live on small farms near their relatives, which created an **Extended Family Structure**. Men and women were expected to marry early and stay married permanently. Women who delayed marriage or never married were called "spinsters" or "old maids" and were stigmatized by family, friends, and community. Because marriages were expected to last a lifetime, divorces were difficult, even impossible, to obtain and evoked extreme disapproval, so families tended to stay together whether they wanted to or not. During this time, large families were valued because children contributed to the many tasks that had to be performed to keep farms running smoothly; children were an economic asset.

However, during the Industrial Revolution, large families became unnecessary. In fact, because child labor was no longer needed to keep the farms running, their need to be sheltered, clothed, and fed made children an economic liability. Family sizes began to shrink. Changing times also led to increased mobility and relocation for employment. Smaller families were less expensive to move from place to place. Over time, expectations about early, permanent marriage and large families relaxed and trends began to change. Today there are many alternative family forms that may have existed but were not recognized as viable until very recently. The next section defines some of these family forms and their prevalence in U.S. society. Later in this chapter you will learn about the major problems families are grappling with today. Finally, we will address policies and services that are in place for U.S. families.

Demographic Changes in the Family

Recent decades have witnessed a stabilizing divorce rate, a dramatic decrease in the number of married-couple families, and an equally dramatic increase in single-parent families. These changes, along with an unprecedented increase in the number of cohabiting couples, means that "more children are seeing their households reconfigured several times," such that 40% of children are likely to live in a cohabiting household by age 16.[1]

As alternative household configurations have become more common, the U.S. government has had a difficult time keeping track of changing family structure. This has happened partly because the Census Bureau defines family households as those that include two or more individuals related by marriage, birth, or adoption. All other groups that live together in one place are called "households," and individuals who share a household with unrelated individuals are said to live in "nonfamily households." According to this definition, cohabiting couples and gay or lesbian family groupings are not defined as families unless the household includes children. Currently, the Census Bureau is investigating new definitions.

> **Research Informed Practice: Children Raised in Nontraditional Families**
>
> This activity will help you learn more about outcomes for children raised in nontraditional families. Form a group of three, select a topic (blended families, cohabiting families, gay or lesbian families); then, using library research databases, find three articles that address your topic. Make a 2 × 2 table that lists positive and negative outcomes (findings) for children raised in your chosen family type by age group (children and adolescents). Compare your findings to your group members and/or share them in class.

Changes in Functions of the Family

Living in a market-driven economy (as opposed to a farm-based economy in which families were self-sufficient) has required that major institutions in society, such as healthcare, educational, and economic institutions, assume greater responsibility for certain aspects of health maintenance, education, and the distribution of goods and services. New institutions have developed, including child care and elder care, and we have moved into an age where information can be obtained and exchanged almost instantly.

To us, family means putting our arms around each other and being there.
—Barbara Bush

The family system has also undergone extensive changes. It has expanded beyond the "traditional nuclear family" unit to include families in which both parents work outside the home for pay, single-parent families, lesbian and gay families, multigenerational families, and cohabiting families—all viable family forms. Despite these broad changes, the four basic functions of the family have remained relatively constant for over two centuries. The first, reproduction, ensures the population is maintained. The second function, "socialization" of the young, is very important because it is through socialization that members of society learn about societal expectations and what is highly valued at the macro level. Families provide the cultural context for early development, teaching language and basic methods of communication. An important socialization component is the hidden social identity agenda that children begin to internalize at birth. For example, children learn what it means to be a member of a particular racial or ethnic group, and they develop gender and religious identities within the family setting before moving into other institutions, such as education, that advance the hidden agenda. Third, families provide economic support in the form of shelter, protection, and nourishment. The fourth function of the family is emotional support and social interaction. The family system buffers the relationship between its members and society, providing a safe retreat from outside pressures.

Diverse Family Forms

As divorces became easier to obtain, tolerance for divorce increased, and reasons for granting divorces multiplied, a steady increase in the number of divorces ensued from approximately 1860 to 1960. From 1950 through 1995, the U.S. witnessed higher probability for all races that first marriages would break up, slightly lower likelihood that divorced individuals would remarry, and higher likelihood that second marriages would end in separation or divorce. In 2005, married couples became a minority for the first time in U.S. history.

Why did this happen? In addition to high divorce rates, age at first marriage has been creeping up since 1950, when it was approximately age 20 for women and 23 for men. Today the median age at first marriage is nearly 26 years for women and 27 for men. Many couples are choosing to live together—**Cohabit**—rather than marry. Experts suggest that since the 1990s, as many as 50% of couples may be choosing to live together *in order* to bear children and as a first step toward marriages that may or may not ever take place. Indeed, in recent years, unmarried births have accounted for over half of all births to women ages 20 to 24 years. Nearly three of every ten births to women ages 25 to 29 occur outside of marriage. By the end of 2006, even though the divorce rate had dropped to it lowest point since 1970, a lower marriage rate and a higher cohabitation rate meant that fewer people were married at any given time.

Social workers often work with families that are going through divorce. For example, many social workers perform couples therapy as part of their family practice, while social workers in educational settings conduct groups for children experiencing divorce.

In recent years, same-sex marriages have received a great deal of media attention. As you learned in Chapter 5, three states recognize same-sex marriages currently, and by 2010, three more states that have voted to recognize same-sex marriage will have added their laws to the books. At the same time, legislation to prohibit same-sex marriages has been proposed in several states. Other states prohibit marriage, but recognize **Civil Unions**. States that recognize civil unions provide same-sex couples various benefits enjoyed by legally married couples. Legally recognized or not, a growing proportion of American families are composed of same-sex partners with and without children. According to the Census Bureau, which counted same-sex, unmarried partners in the 2000 census, about a quarter of same-sex couples are raising children (a third of lesbian couples and just under a quarter of gay couples). Although same-sex couples were undercounted, these numbers give an idea of how many same-sex couples are raising children. In comparison, 45.6% of married, heterosexual couples and 43.1% of unmarried couples had children in the household.[2]

Critical Thinking Question

Social workers face extreme diversity and difference in practice. Think about the diverse family forms that currently exist in the U.S. Can you identify examples of strengths associated with each?

Did You Know?

Unlike past decades when marital status gave a fairly clear idea of the number of adults in a household, it is less telling today. Unmarried mothers often live with the fathers of their children, and well over half of women aged 25 to 39 have cohabited at least once. Moreover, many unmarried parents experience multiple relationships—sometimes called repartnering—within a couple of years of the birth of a child.[3]

The steady increase in cohabitation, delayed age at marriage, and the decision not to marry at all, along with high divorce rates, have changed the life course of the American family. Today, most new marriages and remarriages begin with cohabitation, divorce rates remain high, and the number of single-parent families has reached an all-time high.

Monica McGoldrick and the Family Life Cycle

Monica McGoldrick, a social worker and director of the Multicultural Family Institute in Highland Park, New Jersey, obtained her B.A. degree from Brown University, her M.A. in Russian Studies from Yale University,

FAMILY LIFE CYCLE STAGE	EMOTIONAL PROCESS OF TRANSITION: KEY PRINCIPLES	SECOND-ORDER CHANGES IN FAMILY STATUS REQUIRED TO PROCEED DEVELOPMENTALLY
Leaving Home: single young adults	Accepting emotional and financial responsibility for self	a. Differentiation of self in relation to family of origin b. Development of intimate peer relationships c. Establishment of self in respect to work and financial independence
The joining of Families through marriage: The new couple	Commitment to new system	a. Formation of marital systems b. Realignment of relationships with extended families and friends include spouse
Families with young children	Accepting new members into the system	a. Adjustment of marital system to make space for children b. Joining in child rearing, financial and household tasks c. Realignment of relationships with extended family to include parenting and grandparenting roles
Families with adolescents	Increasing flexibility of family boundaries to permit children's independence and grandparents' frailties	a. Shift of parent/child relationships to permit adolescent to move into and out of system b. Refocus on midlife marital and career issues c. Beginning shift toward caring for older generation
Launching children and moving on	Accepting a multitude of exits from and entries into the family system	a. Renegotiation of marital system as a dyad b. Development of adult-to-adult relationships between grown children and their parents c. Realignment of relationships to include in-laws and grandchildren d. Dealing with disabilities and death of parents (grandparents)
Families in later life	Accepting the shifting generational roles	a. Maintaining own and/or couple functioning and interests in face of physiological decline: exploration of new familial and social role options b. Support for more central role of middle generations c. Making room in the system for the wisdom and experience of the elderly, supporting the older generation without overfunctioning for them d. Dealing with loss of spouse, siblings, and other peers and preparation for death

Figure 10.1
Six Family Life Cycle Stages and Tasks Associated with Each Stage
Source: B. Carter & M. McGoldrick, *The Expanded Family Life Cycle: Individual, Family, and Social Perspectives*, 3rd ed. (Boston: Allyn & Bacon, 2005), p. 2

and her MSW and honorary doctorate from the Smith College School for Social Work. Professor McGoldrick is fourth-generation Irish American and is married to a Greek immigrant. She reports that she learned little about her cultural heritage during childhood, but her family therapy work has shown her the importance of connections to family and cultural history. Dr. McGoldrick has written volumes on many topics, including the family life cycle, class, culture, gender, family patterns, sibling relationships, and remarried families.

McGoldrick, together with Betty Carter, another social worker, developed a framework that depicts the family as a system that moves through time. It emphasizes the intergenerational connectedness of families and the multiple transitions that families make as they move through the life cycle. Carter and McGoldrick believe "family stress is often greatest at transition points from one stage to another of the family developmental process and symptoms are likely to appear when there is an interruption or dislocation in the unfolding family life cycle."[4] One goal of therapeutic interventions with families is to help those facing stress to reorganize so they can move forward. Figure 10.1 depicts Carter and McGoldrick's six family life cycle stages and the tasks associated with each stage. Their framework, which recognizes multiple family forms, enables social workers to understand what families might look like as they move through the life cycle. Diverse families proceed through life cycle stages within their own cultural context, and social workers take this into account when using the **Family Life Cycle** paradigm.

Critical Thinking Question

Based on the section "Monica McGoldrick and the Family Life Cycle," what are potential needs and sources of strength for families as they move through the family life cycle?

MAJOR CHALLENGES FACING CHILDREN, YOUTH, AND FAMILIES

Divorce

Divorce can lead to a host of difficulties for parents that fall roughly into five areas, each with a unique set of consequences: (1) legal; (2) financial; (3) psychological/emotional; (4) parent relationship; and (5) interparent relationship.[5] The legal process with the greatest consequences, financial and otherwise, for divorcing parents is child custody. **Child custody** is a multidimensional concept that includes legal and residential custody, visitation, child support, and other financial issues. Another part of the legal process in some states is spousal support. Financial consequences are greater for women, given their lower earning capacity, the high cost of child care, and poorly enforced child support laws. Also, personal property division contributes to the financial consequences of divorce. Psychological and emotional consequences are high because divorce has repeatedly been ranked as the top life stressor. Parents may feel like they have failed at both marriage and parenthood. They may experience self-doubt, loneliness, and worry about whether they will be able to survive on their own. Although the stigma attached to divorce has lessened, they may still worry about stigma and the disappointment of family members and friends. Divorced parents are at heightened risk of physical and mental illness, suicide and homicide, accidents, substance abuse, depression, and anxiety. At the same time,

There are two marriages in every marital union, his and hers, and his is better than hers.

—Jesse Bernard

divorce often decreases positive parenting strategies, while increasing negative parenting strategies, at least in the short term. Finally, the interparental consequences of divorce refer to conflicts between parents during the first three years after the divorce occurs.

It is not entirely clear how divorce affects children. Most scientific studies have focused on negative consequences for children, with little to no discussion about positive adjustment after divorce. Although divorce certainly has negative consequences for children, pre-divorce marital conflict may be far more damaging. And other issues that arise as a result of the divorce—many stemming from poverty and associated financial pressures—complicate the effects of divorce. For example, problems children experience after a divorce may stem from leaving the family home for substandard housing in a dangerous neighborhood rather than from the divorce itself.

Single-Parent Families

Single-parent families, those with one adult and one or more children, grew sixfold from 1970 to 2006. Today, nearly 13 million children live in single-parent families, and experts predict that more than half of all American children under age 18 will spend part of their childhoods living with a single parent. Although many people imagine teenage mothers juggling three or four children when they think about single-parent households, the "average" single parent is a divorced mother in her early thirties with one or two children. About half of these households result from divorce, whereas less than a third of the mothers have never been married. Not surprisingly, single-mother households tend to be poorer than two-parent households. In 2006, more than eight in ten single-parent families were mother-headed, and close to a third of those families lived below the poverty line. The poverty rate in black and Hispanic single-mother families was even higher.

Single motherhood has multiple consequences for both the mothers and their children. A 1995 quote accurately sums up the financial consequences for the mothers: ". . . single mothers in poverty may increasingly find themselves in a 'catch 22' situation: They may earn just enough from employment to move them beyond the income threshold necessary to qualify for means-tested public assistance, but not enough to provide for an adequate level of subsistence or to free them from the grasp of poverty."[6]

Indeed, single mothers face unemployment, low wages coupled with increased cost-of-living, food insecurity, high child care costs, discrimination, and the poor health of their children. They are more likely to live in unsafe neighborhoods, where they and their children face violence, heightened environmental health risks from pollution, and substandard housing. Moreover, single mothers are more likely than the general population to have experienced childhood adversity and family violence. The chronic nature of their day-to-day stressors affects their physical and mental health, leading to physical illnesses, including diabetes, psoriasis, and mental disorders (e.g., clinical depression, anxiety, substance abuse, and post-traumatic stress disorder).

Today, studies are examining a type of single-parent family that has been increasing: **Custodial grandparent families**. In recent years, more grandparents have assumed responsibility for raising their grandchildren and, more often than not, these grandparents are single. In 2000, nearly

Critical Thinking Question

Single-mother families suffer inequities in many areas of their lives. Can you describe anyone in your community who has suffered disadvantages related to rearing children alone?

> **Research Informed Practice**
>
> This activity will help you learn more about the legal situations that grandparents raising grandchildren must face. Using your library's research databases, perform a search using keywords such as "grandparents raising grandchildren," "legal issues," and "courts." Write a two-page paper outlining the problems and policy changes you believe would be necessary to resolve the issues that grandparents performing kinship care must face on a daily basis.

6 million grandparents were living with their grandchildren under age 18 and close to half were responsible for child care. Although grandparents raising grandchildren have more health, mental health, and financial problems, they also experience a number of positive consequences, including the pleasure of being close to their grandchildren and feeling needed and productive.[7]

Blended Families

Shifting patterns of marriage, divorce, remarriage, cohabitation, and repartnering have a big impact on family life when multiple families join to form new families. First marriages join two families; second marriages can combine three or more families. **Blended families**—also called remarried, reconstituted, or stepfamilies—can include biological parents and offspring and partners who bring their children to the new family unit. Many blended families add new children. The extended family often includes stepsiblings who do not live in the blended family unit, grandparents and stepgrandparents, plus multiple uncles, aunts, and family members from former marriages. Multiple remarriages can add myriad relatives to the mix.

Professional social workers who work with families play multiple roles in the lives of parents and children. In addition to working directly with families on solutions to various problems they may be facing, some social workers advocate for families in local or national settings as community organizers, lobbyists, or lawmakers, for example.

Adolescent Pregnancy and Parenting

Decades of research have revealed that multiple factors contribute to the high adolescent pregnancy rate, including age at puberty, age at first sexual intercourse, poor parenting skills, less educationally enriched home environments, poor educational and career opportunities, family poverty, and growing up in a single-parent household.[8] There is also an **intergenerational effect**, which means that the children of young mothers are more likely to become pregnant during adolescence than the children of mothers who wait until their twenties to have their first children.

> **Did You Know?**
>
> The U.S. adolescent birthrate reached an all-time high in 1991 at 61.8 births per 1,000 females aged 15–19 and then went through a steady decline to 40.4 births per 1,000 in 2005. While the birthrate for all groups declined significantly, the biggest drop was among black teens (declined by nearly two-thirds). Despite substantial declines, nearly a million girls become pregnant each year, and the U.S. teen pregnancy rate tops all other industrialized countries.

Pregnant adolescents are less likely than older mothers to get adequate prenatal care or to be properly nourished. They are more likely to experience premature or prolonged labor. All teen mothers, but especially those under age 15, are at higher risk for birth complications, such as abnormal bleeding, anemia, premature rupture of the uterine membrane, hypertension, toxemia, and death. After the birth, young mothers are more susceptible to depression and feelings of helplessness, low self-esteem, and stress. Moreover, they attempt and complete suicide more often than older mothers.

Many younger teen parents continue to live at home, but older teens tend to be forced into adulthood earlier than their classmates. If they cannot continue to live at home, they often drop out of high school in order to pay for housing, food, child care, and other necessities.

Historically, social scientists have argued that the economic consequences for young parents, especially teen mothers, are devastating and affect them for the rest of their lives. Stuck in lower-paying, less-skilled jobs, their lifetime earnings are reduced, leading to poverty, unemployment, and public assistance. On the brighter side, recent studies suggest that the lifelong outlook for single teen mothers may, in fact, be better than the outlook for other poor teens. Although teen mothers are less likely to receive a high school diploma, they are more likely to obtain a GED and to work longer hours than their peers who drop out of school. This behavior could lead to higher lifetime earnings than equally poor teens who delay childbearing beyond adolescence. Such findings are encouraging because they suggest that in the long run, adolescent mothers who complete high school may be less likely to be poor or to have to rely on public assistance. Also, they confirm that the primary problem is poverty and not adolescent pregnancy.

Children born to adolescent mothers are different from children born to mothers in their early twenties in two key areas. First, home environments provided by teen mothers tend to be less cognitively stimulating and less nurturing that those provided by mothers aged 20–21 years at the time of birth. Second, teen mothers' children score lower on cognitive achievement tests.

Family Violence

Critical Thinking Question

Social workers work with families experiencing violence within the larger societal context. Why is it important to engage in practice activities that include individual and family treatment and practice activities aimed at social reform simultaneously?

Although researchers and the general public use the term **family violence** to refer to many different types of violence, particularly adult-to-adult married couple violence, family violence is officially defined as all types of violent crime committed by an offender who is related to the victim, either biologically or legally, through marriage or adoption. A crime is considered family violence if the victim is the offender's current or former partner, parent, or adoptive parent, stepparent, legal guardian, biological or adoptive child, stepchild, sibling, stepsibling, grandchild, stepgrandchild or adoptive grandchild, grandparent, stepgrandparent or adoptive grandparent, blood relative (e.g., aunt or uncle), or relative by marriage.[9]

Family violence services are another area where social work skills can be used. Many social workers are employed by domestic violence shelters, where they may perform various jobs, from working with children who have been abused or have witnessed domestic violence, to working with adult victims, performing individual or group therapy, connecting people to services (medical, financial, or housing, for example), or advocating for victims' rights and social reform. Social workers are also employed by hospitals, where violence victims often go for treatment, by prisons that house batterers, and by other community

> **Case Study: Family Violence**
>
> In 2008, Erica and her children left suburban Denver home quickly. Erica had been living with what she called "minor abuse," which included broken arms and blackened eyes, since her wedding day. Cliff was romantic and solicitous throughout their courtship and Erica kept hoping he would "return to his old self." Over time, she resolved to take the abuse to keep a roof over the children's heads, but at a birthday celebration for 7-year-old Timmy, Cliff blew up and threw a chair at the boy. This was the first time Cliff had threatened to harm one of the children. The chair missed Timmy, but at that moment Erica made the difficult decision to leave her seven-year marriage. When Cliff stormed out after the attack, Erica locked the doors and blocked them with furniture. She considered calling the police, but the last time she did Cliff was home within hours. Later that evening, Cliff returned and apologized through the door, then made verbal threats and kicked the doors for hours while Erica, her mother, and the children huddled in the bedroom. Erica was pretty sure Cliff would not break in since her mother was visiting. Indeed, Cliff gave up and left after three hours. The next morning Erica took Timmy and his two younger siblings to a nearby emergency shelter. The family was whisked away from the shelter to a safe house in an undisclosed location, where they remained for three months. During that time, Erica and the children saw a shelter social worker regularly for individual and group therapy. Now, feeling safe again, they are living in transitional housing waiting for permanent housing to become available.

agencies that work with batterers. Also, social workers can serve as expert witnesses in family violence court cases.

Partner Abuse

Adult family violence falls into four categories, including physical abuse, psychological abuse, financial abuse, and neglect. **Physical abuse** refers to physical pain and injury that includes, but is not limited to, punching, bruising, restraining, or abusing sexually. **Psychological abuse** occurs when abusers cause mental anguish, such as humiliation, intimidation, or threats of harm. **Financial abuse** refers to illegal or improper exploitation of a victim's property or financial assets, whereas **neglect** is defined as the deliberate failure or refusal to fulfill caregiving obligations, such as providing food and health care. Often, family violence results in hospitalization or death.

Most Americans recognize that family violence is widespread and extremely dangerous, but this was not always the case. Family violence and trauma research only began in the 1970s, and people were surprised to learn that adult-to-adult intimate violence occurred not only among heterosexual, married couples, but also among dating couples, cohabiting couples, and among lesbian and gay couples. Many people were surprised to learn that all forms of violence perpetrated against adult family members cut across social classes, educational levels, and racial groups and that violence can occur at any stage of the family life cycle, including old age.

Today, social workers and other health care professionals are aware of family violence and are on the lookout for signs of violence. There are laws that prohibit partner and family violence. Nevertheless, family violence statistics remain high and vary widely because many cases are never reported to authorities and because various states and organizations compile their data differently. For example, a 2000 Department of Justice report that calculated adult-to-adult violence statistics concluded that two to four million adult women are abused every year.[10] An additional 1 to 2 million elderly adults are abused or neglected each year. A different report from the FBI's Uniform Crime Reporting (UCR) program found that 1.5 million family violence incidents were reported from 1996 to 2001 for all adults, including adult women and the elderly.[11] Nearly a third of the UCI cases involved girlfriend/boyfriend violence, followed by married partner violence, at nearly 25%. Over 1 million of the victims were aged 18 to 65 years. A third report that included individuals aged 12 and older, conducted by the Department of Justice,[12] found that three-quarters of family violence victims were white. In fact, whites and blacks were considerably more likely to be victimized than were Hispanics or individuals from other racial and ethnic groups. This report noted that nearly two-thirds of victims were between the ages of 25 and 54. By any measure, family violence statistics are high and violence exposure, whether direct or indirect, has devastating effects on victims.

Like their victims, abuse perpetrators come from all social classes, educational levels, and racial groups. From 1996 to 2001, 79% of abusers were white and 62% were at least 30 years old.[13] Abusers can be clergy, college professors or K–12 teachers, doctors, farmers, police officers, and social workers. They may be charming and helpful to others much of the time. Bragg[14] compiled research on perpetrators of violence against both adults and children and developed a list of characteristics and the behavioral tactics they commonly use to gain control over victims. He found that they: (1) behave differently in public than in private; (2) abuse power and control; (3) tend to blame the victim(s) for their violent behavior (i.e., "project blame"); (4) frequently claim that they lost control *temporarily*; and (5) minimize or deny the abuse.

Did You Know?

Family violence perpetrators tend to be men and about 95% of victims are women. While female-to-male violence does occur, usually women perpetrate violence in retaliation for abuse or in attempts to escape their abusers. Given the greater strength of most men compared to most women, violence against women has been shown to cause more injury and to be more repetitive than violence perpetrated by women against their male partners.

The consequences of abuse are severe and long lasting. Many studies have documented the extent to which emotional abuse, physical abuse, and sexual violence contribute to mental and physical health problems in women. Women who have been abused by their partners suffer from long-term gynecological (e.g., STDs, infections, and urinary tract infections), neurological (e.g., fainting, seizures, back pain, and headaches), and chronic stress-related problems (e.g., gastrointestinal disorders, cardiac problems, and appetite loss) at a rate about 50% to 70% greater than women who have not been abused by their partners.[15]

Sexual Violence

Sexual Violence refers to sexual activity that is forced or that takes place without the victim's consent. It can include physical contact (e.g., unwanted touching and rape) and other behaviors, such as intimidation, peeping, sexual harassment, and threats. Although anyone can be a victim of sexual violence, most victims are women and most perpetrators are men. More often than not, victims know the offenders. Although sexual violence statistics are grossly underreported, the Centers for Disease Control and Prevention surveyed a national sample of high school students and found that 11% of females and 4% of males reported that they had been forced to have sexual intercourse.[16] Among college students, the numbers are higher, with almost a quarter of women reporting attempted or completed rapes. Sexual violence underreporting occurs for multiple reasons, including: (1) fear of making a report; (2) fear that others will not believe them or that the police will not help them; and (3) fear of retaliation by the offender.

Child Abuse and Neglect

Child Abuse, like other forms of family violence, has only recently been defined as a social problem. In fact, English common law recognized that fathers had the right to issue arbitrary and severe discipline against their children. Today, the federal Child Abuse Prevention and Treatment Act (CAPTA), as amended by the Keeping Children and Families Safe Act of 2003, provides a minimal federal definition of child abuse and neglect that applies to children under age 18 and their parents or other caregivers. It reads:

- Any recent act or failure to act on the part of a parent or caretaker which results in death, serious physical or emotional harm, sexual abuse or exploitation; or
- An act or failure to act that presents an imminent risk of serious harm.[17]

Each state goes beyond these minimum federal guidelines to provide a three-part (typically) definition of child maltreatment within its own criminal and civil code, including: (1) mandatory child maltreatment reporting statutes; (2) criminal statutes; and (3) juvenile court jurisdiction statutes.[18] Although laws vary from state to state, all states require social workers and other professionals to report suspected abuse or neglect to proper authorities.

Types of Abuse

In general, child abuse can be broken down into the following categories:

- **Physical abuse** refers to non-accidental physical injuries inflicted on children by parents or guardians and includes beating, biting, burning, kicking, punching, shaking, and death.
- **Child neglect** is a broad category that refers to failure by a parent or guardian to provide for basic physical, emotional, educational, or medical needs. An example of physical neglect is leaving a child alone for an excessively long period of time. Examples of emotional neglect include encouraging a child to steal or engage in other illegal activities. Failure to enroll a child in school exemplifies educational neglect, whereas medical neglect means failure or refusal to obtain medical, dental, or mental health care.
- **Emotional abuse**, perhaps the most difficult to recognize, refers to verbal abuse, lack of affection or attention from a parent or guardian, isolation or rejection, terrorism, and unreasonable expectations.
- **Sexual abuse** includes sexual exploitation, sexual fondling, mutual masturbation and other hand–genital or oral–genital contact, and sexual intercourse. Online sexual assault represents a relatively new and increasingly prevalent area of sexual abuse.

Research Informed Practice

Child maltreatment definitions for all 50 states and the District of Columbia are available at http://www.childwelfare.gov/systemwide/laws_policies/state/. Choose the state where you live as well as a couple of states in other parts of the country and compare child abuse reporting laws across states.

How does your state stack up against the others?

> **Focus on Professionalism and Ethics**
>
> **Social Workers' Ethical Responsibility to Clients Regarding Child Abuse and Neglect**
>
> **Ethical Responsibility:** *Privacy and Confidentiality*
>
> Social workers should protect the confidentiality of all information obtained in the course of professional service, except for compelling professional reasons. The general expectation that social workers will keep information confidential does not apply when disclosure is necessary to prevent serious, foreseeable, and imminent harm to a client or other identifiable person. In all instances, social workers should disclose the least amount of confidential information necessary to achieve the desired purpose; only information that is directly relevant to the purpose for which the disclosure is made should be reviewed.[21]

Just as with adult-to-adult family violence, most child abuse and neglect cases go unreported. This is especially true of emotional and sexual abuse. Children's Bureau statistics estimated that in 2005, 3.3 million referrals involving the alleged maltreatment of about 6 million children were made to child protective services agencies.[19] The abuse was substantiated—found to show evidence of abuse or neglect—for nearly 900,000 children. Almost two-thirds of the cases involved neglect. More than half of the children were under 8 years of age, and the group with the highest victimization rate was birth to 3 years. Of these child victims, more than half were girls. About half the victimized children were white, a quarter black, and less than a fifth were Hispanic.[20]

The effects of abuse are pervasive and can be exhibited in a number of ways, including eye contact avoidance, difficulty regulating and communicating emotions or intimacy, hyperactivity, sexually provocative behaviors, low school achievement, and low self-esteem.

Social workers, other health care professionals, and social researchers consider how multiple individual and larger systems factors interact when trying to understand the causes for child abuse. Various factors immediate to the individual, such as feelings of isolation, poor self-esteem, low frustration tolerance, and high stress, are important to consider. Also, interpersonal relationship quality and social support networks are essential resources for parents. Lack of resources contributes to feelings of isolation and stress. Moreover, work-related and financial problems combine with other characteristics and situations to increase stress and negative feelings. Lack of information about child development (and thus expectations that exceed the developmental level of the child), along with authoritarian personality characteristics, also plays a large part. Finally, larger social problems (macro-level), such as poverty, substance abuse, societal expectations for males and females, and the significance of societal values like independence and family privacy, are also very important to consider.

Child Sexual Abuse and Incest

As noted earlier, child sexual abuse includes sexual exploitation and/or fondling, sexual intercourse, mutual masturbation, and other hand–genital or oral–genital contact. Perpetrators of sexual abuse against children include strangers and individuals known or related to the children (incest). Sexual abuse by nonfamily members is also known as "sexual assault" and "extrafamilial abuse." David Finkelhor, director of the Crimes Against Children Research Center at the University of New Hampshire, identified several risk factors associated with child sexual abuse, but noted that the relationship between the abuse and the identified characteristics remains tenuous.[22] Risk factors include: (1) absence of natural parents; (2) disability, illness, or employment of the mother; (3) female gender; (4) parental conflict or violence; (5) poor parent and child-victim relationship; (6) preadolescent age; and (7) presence of stepfather.

Sexually abused children exhibit both short- and long-term effects from abuse. Short-term effects include feelings of guilt, fear, shame, hostility, and anger. Victims are often anxious and experience problems in school, and some children report feeling betrayed and powerless. The list of long-term effects is lengthy and includes repeated bouts of depression, anxiety, suicidal ideation (and completed suicides), self-destructive behaviors, difficulty in interpersonal relationships, lack of trust, and continued low self-esteem. Adults who were victimized as children may be more likely to be victimized in their adult relationships and more likely to abuse substances.

It is important to note that there was a 40% drop in substantiated child sexual abuse cases from 1992 to 2000. Researchers question whether the decline resulted from prevention, treatment, and law enforcement or from decreased identification and child sexual abuse reporting. Although experts believe sexual abuse is a substantially underreported crime, in recent years nearly 10% of reported cases of child abuse involved sexual abuse of some kind.

THE FAMILY-(UN)FRIENDLY WORKPLACE

Despite continued rhetoric about the importance of families, the American labor market has historically failed to support families both on and off the job. Social welfare policy scholar Mimi Abramovitz writes, "Despite a '24/7' work environment and the mounting rhetoric about 'family values,' few companies offer the flexibility or the supports needed by working women and men to care for their families, to pursue their careers or just to hold on to their jobs."[23] Although parents who work for smaller companies suffer the most, many families from companies of all sizes give up or shorten their family leave (e.g., childbirth, child care, elder care, health-related) because they cannot afford to forego their paychecks or lose their jobs. Since the late 1990s, there have been jumps in food prices (23%), housing (29%), medical care (43%), and child care (52%).[24] Gasoline had increased by a whopping third in the first half of 2008 alone. Most of these increases occurred during a long period when the minimum wage remained constant at $5.15 per hour. In May 2007, the U.S. Congress voted to increase minimum wage to $7.25 over a three-year period, a welcome increase but not enough to alleviate the problems.

Family leave policies aren't the only problem. Over the past 30 years, as more women have entered the labor market, work supports have became less rather than more available. For example, workplace discrimination against pregnant women has increased, and the number of pregnancy discrimination cases filed with the Equal Employment Opportunity Commission (EEOC) has jumped nearly 40% since 1992.[25]

Finding reliable, high-quality, yet affordable child care during working hours may well be the biggest problem facing low- and middle-income working families, and single parents are hardest hit. Almost three-quarters of single mothers and single fathers with children under age 18 work, and child care

> **Social Work Stories: Choosing a Practice Area**
>
> Bill M., who has his MSW from the Smith College School of Social Work, is a family therapist. Bill started his undergraduate education in psychology and then completed a master's degree in education before spending ten years trying to decide what to do with his life. After several jobs and three years volunteering in Africa, he settled on social work. "I realized that social work talked the same language as I did in terms of the macro and micro work involved. I also liked the fact that I would be able to go into clinical work right away." Bill's first MSW field placement involved family therapy with couples and families. For his second placement, he was part of an outpatient team of social workers and other professionals. Today Bill counsels children, adults, and families in his office and in a school. What Bill loves most about being a social worker is that each new client system brings different characteristics to the helping relationship, which means the work never gets old. His advice to students who might want to pursue a career in child and family social work is to *volunteer* to get an idea what social workers do on a daily basis.

can take upwards of 40% of their income. In fact, the lower the family income, the higher the proportion that goes to child care. Also, many parents work long, irregular hours when child care centers are closed. These problems lead many parents to seek informal care from relatives or neighbors, a low-cost but unreliable and often poor-quality alternative. To compound matters, because the cost of living has increased faster than wages, both one- and two-parent families have increased their working hours to make up for low wages, resulting in less time with the children; parent–child time has decreased by over 20 hours per week since 1969.

Employment and child care problems are heightened for single mothers moving from TANF to work. Until 1996, AFDC provided cash assistance to parents who met particular financial criteria. However, in 1996, with the passage of the PRWORA, the number of families receiving cash assistance fell by half. Current TANF guidelines require states to move women from welfare to work quickly *and* to keep families from receiving welfare whenever possible. Yet there are not enough jobs available, especially in rural areas, and families leaving TANF cannot find work, which increases their likelihood of experiencing food insecurity, health problems, and housing problems, among other difficulties. When they do find work, the prohibitive cost of child care threatens their ability to keep their jobs.

Caring for elderly relatives presents similar problems. Well over 20 million families provide care for elderly relatives currently.

MAJOR SERVICES TO CHILDREN, YOUTH, AND FAMILIES

Child Welfare and Child Protection

The child welfare system is a complex service network that promotes child and family well-being. Multiple public, private, and community organizations that vary by state and even by local community make up the network. Many of these organizations, which span a wide range of disciplines, employ social workers. These organizations coordinate and collaborate with one another to some extent to provide a variety of family services, including adoption, family preservation, financial or housing assistance, foster care, mental health care, parenting skills classes, permanency planning, residential treatment, and substance abuse treatment.

Family Intervention

The complexity of the U.S. child welfare systems is heightened because specific procedures vary so widely by state. In general, though, state systems:

- Receive and investigate reports of possible child maltreatment and then work with state juvenile justice systems to make decisions about removing abused children from their homes.
- Arrange foster care for children who are not safe at home and provide permanency planning services to promote permanent living situations for children in the foster care system.
- Provide services to families who need assistance protecting and caring for their children, including family preservation services designed to keep families together whenever possible.
- Arrange permanent adoptive homes or independent living services for children leaving foster care who cannot return to their homes.

Federal legislation provides general guidelines within which each state carries out these tasks.

Out-of-Home Placements and Foster Care

Foster care is an important part of the child welfare network. Placing a child in foster care refers to making alternative residential arrangements for that child outside his or her own home. Often, it is social workers who remove children from their homes and coordinate alternative living situations. Pecora and his colleagues defines foster care as "the provision of planned, time-limited, substitute family care for children who cannot be adequately maintained at home and the simultaneous provision of social services to these children and their families to help resolve the problems that led to the need for placement."[26]

The primary goal of placement is to resolve family problems and reunify families (**reunification**); however, when families cannot be reunited safely, alternate permanent arrangements must be made (called **permanency planning**). Unfortunately, many children remain in foster care for long periods of time, moving from one substitute care arrangement to another in private foster homes, other residential arrangements, or group homes. These children remain on social worker caseloads throughout their involvement in the system. Many children remain in foster care until their 18th birthday, when they "age out" of the system. Approximately 20,000 children become too old for child welfare services each year. Sadly, many of these children lack skills and resources that would enable them to support themselves, and many of them end up homeless. Currently, a number of studies are attempting to follow samples of these children to learn more about how they fare in adulthood. After leaving foster care, some seek help at other agencies where social work professionals manage their cases. Marly's experience is typical of children who age out of the foster care system.

Although child abuse and neglect occur across all social classes and educational levels and within all racial and ethnic groups, "a combination of

> **Case Study: Marly's Foster Care Story**
>
> Marly knows a great deal about the system, having first entered foster care as an infant. Marly and her mother were both addicted to drugs when Marly was born, and Marly went directly from the hospital into foster care. She lived with her mother on and off until she turned 4, then went from placement to placement, living in more alternative placements than she could count. When Marly aged out of foster care at 18, she went to a homeless shelter, then bounced from shelter to shelter for a year. She landed a job in an after-school program, but it did not provide enough money for her to live on her own and buy groceries. Now, at 19, she has found shelter in a building that provides semipermanent housing for homeless young adults. In exchange for her apartment, Marly works in a secondhand clothing store located in the building.

socioeconomic factors and various state and federal policies as well as disparate reporting and service delivery increase the likelihood that poor and minority children will enter the foster care system."[27] The families of poor and minority children are more likely to lack the resources needed to pay for the child care they need in order to meet TANF work requirements, placing single-parent families at even greater risk for findings of child maltreatment and contributing to their disproportionate representation in the foster care system. In fact, in some states, over half the children in foster care come from single-mother households. The U.S. foster care system serves approximately 800,000 children per year, and children of color comprise about over half the total population.

The Removal vs. Reunification Debate

The original intention of the U.S. foster care system was to provide a temporary living situation for children who were not safe in their own homes. Although the children were away from home, supportive family services would set the stage for reunification whenever possible and permanent placement with relatives or adoptive families when reunification could not guarantee the safety of the children.

We are willing to spend the least . . . money to keep a kid at home, more to put him in a foster home and the most to institutionalize him.
—Marian Wright Edelman

Although reunification remains the goal in permanency planning, foster care (impermanent homes) has become a much more permanent arrangement than originally planned—so permanent that many children remain in foster care until they age out at age 18. In fact, throughout the 1990s, more children entered foster care than were leaving foster care in most large states. In 2002, children remained in out-of-home care for an average of nearly three years; about 20% of children who left care that year had been there over three years

> **Demonstrating Knowledge, Values, and Skills: Best Interests of the Child**
>
> A controversy has developed around whether to remove children from their homes permanently (moving them out of foster care into adoptive homes as quickly as possible) or to make repeated attempts to reunify children with their families.
>
> To think about: Based on your reading, which course of action do you believe serves the best interest of children in the foster care system?

and children waiting to be adopted had been in the system at least three years.[28] Juxtaposed against the large numbers of children remaining in foster care for long periods are children (between 8% and 13%) who have been reunited with their families only to reenter the foster care system within 6 to 12 months of reunification due to re-abuse.[29] At the same time, supportive family services to prepare families for reunification have been substandard or even nonexistent.

Adoption Services

The Adoption and Safe Families Act of 1997 (ASFA) addresses the adoption needs of the growing population of children in the child welfare system. AFSA promotes: (1) permanency (moving children from foster care to permanent placements); (2) adoption (by rewarding states that increase their adoption rates, especially for children with special needs); and (3) safe and stable families (family preservation and family reunification or keeping families together whenever possible). Children are eligible for adoption when their parents voluntarily relinquish parental rights or when court action terminates rights. As many as half a million families in the U.S. are seeking to adopt at any given time, more than enough families to adopt all the children in need of placement. Yet half a million children in the U.S. foster care system remain unadopted.

It isn't that people have stopped adopting children. Indeed, the number of domestic adoptions—adoptions within the U.S.—rose fairly dramatically over time, from 72,000 in 1951 to an all-time high of 175,000 in 1970. After 1970, the domestic adoption rate dropped before it began to increase again, this time more gradually. In 2002, 151,332 children were placed—130,269 domestic adoptions and 21,063 between countries (called "intercountry adoptions") Relatives adopted more than 54,000 of these children and 76,013 were placed in unrelated homes (adoptions in which neither adopting parent was related to the child).[30]

The problem for all those unadopted children is that not all adoptive parents seek to adopt through the public child welfare system. In 2001, 50,000 of the 176,000 children available for adoption through the public child welfare system were adopted.[31] Often, prospective adoptive parents are apprehensive about adopting children who have been placed in foster care. Demick attributes their ambivalence about adopting foster children to: (1) misconceptions about the psychological outcomes for children separated from their biological parents under traumatic circumstances; and (2) strongly held cultural biases about the importance of "biological kinship and the traditional nuclear family."[32] He asserts that these misconceptions are based on myths that are not supported by scientific research on attachment or adoption outcomes.

In addition, most adoptive families would prefer to adopt infants, so older children who have been in foster care are less likely to be adopted. Neither do many families prefer to adopt "special needs" children, those who need special health care and related services due to chronic behavioral, developmental, emotional, or physical conditions. Risk factors are defined as biological (e.g., low birth weight) or environmental (e.g., child abuse or neglect) and the services referred to include regular physical or mental health care, early intervention services, special education services, family support services, or therapeutic services, such as speech therapy. Under this broad definition, an

> **Focus on Professionalism and Ethics**
>
> **Value:** *Social Justice*
> **Ethical Principle:** *Social workers challenge social injustice.*
>
> Social workers pursue social change, particularly with and on behalf of vulnerable and oppressed individuals and groups of people. Social workers' social change efforts are focused primarily on issues of poverty, unemployment, discrimination, and other forms of social injustice. These activities seek to promote sensitivity to and knowledge about oppression and cultural and ethnic diversity. Social workers strive to ensure access to needed information, services, and resources; equality of opportunity; and meaningful participation in decision making for all people.

estimated 13% of children in the general population and more than 80% children in foster care have special healthcare needs.

Who arranges U.S. adoptions? Because for-profit adoption is illegal in all U.S. jurisdictions, not-for-profit intermediary adoption agencies arrange all legitimate adoptions. Lawful adoption agencies handle approximately three-quarters of all non-relative adoptions and provide the best services and safeguards for all parties involved: children, biological parents, and adoptive parents. Despite the illegality, for-profit adoption remains a thriving business in the U.S. and throughout the world. There is a great deal of variability in how these independent adoptions, often called "black-market" or "gray-market" adoptions, take place. Sometimes children, especially infants, are sold for large sums (black market), whereas lawyers and other individuals outside of state-regulated agencies place other children (gray market). What all independent adoptions have in common is that neither the mothers (often young and unmarried) nor the adoptive parents receive the much-needed pre- and post-adoption services to which they are entitled. Adoptive parents who seek to adopt through independent means do so for various personal reasons. For example, some families do not qualify to adopt through licensed agencies; others may choose to adopt independently to avoid long waiting periods or to exercise more control over child selection.

Parenting Support Services and Education

Parent support services vary by locale but typically include a combination of classes and support groups. In some areas, families might be encouraged to participate, while in others participation is court mandated. Parents lead some groups (parent-to-parent support), whereas social workers and other experts lead others. Typical formal class topics include active parenting, positive discipline techniques, relationship enhancement, and nurturing children. Although the bases for support groups vary considerably, typical reasons for developing or joining such groups address special needs (e.g., autism, ADHD, dyslexia, cerebral palsy) or parenting issues (e.g., grandparents raising grandchildren, single parenting, gay and lesbian parenting, father involvement). The most successful programs include well-articulated goals and procedures; multiple components, such as take-away materials; sections that focus on children in addition to parents; and multiple delivery modes (e.g., individual, group and, perhaps, home visits).

Self-Help: Parents Anonymous

A frustrated single mother founded Parents Anonymous (PA) in 1969. Today there are more than 250 accredited affiliates in the U.S. and Canada, administered by volunteers who work together to (1) build strong communities and strengthen families and (2) achieve meaningful parent leadership.[33] The ultimate goal of PA is to strengthen families in order to prevent child abuse and neglect.

Did You Know?

Jolly K., the single parent who established PA, struggled with the urge to use severe discipline with her daughter from the time she was born. When her daughter was 4 years old, Jolly K. sought help from a local clinic. During therapy, she had the idea to develop an Alcoholics Anonymous–like organization to help parents struggling with abuse issues, and Mothers Anonymous was born. Later the name was changed to Parents Anonymous to welcome fathers.

Adolescent Pregnancy and Parenting

Adolescents need family planning services that are multidisciplinary, preventive, and extend over longer time periods. They should go beyond regular family planning services provided at clinics to include a variety of community- and school-based services. Important components of comprehensive adolescent services and care include sexuality education, family planning information and

assistance (including pregnancy and new parent education programs and adoption information), mental health and counseling services, job training and help finding jobs, tutoring and extracurricular activities that build self-esteem, provide alternatives to childbearing, and motivate teens to complete high school. All of these services should target both adolescent mothers *and* fathers. In reality, however, although individual services are good, overall they tend to be piecemeal and incomplete, and few programs target adolescent fathers.

Many health clinics subsidized by the U.S. Department of Health and Human Services specialize in maternal and child health issues important for pregnant and parenting adolescents. Other government-subsidized programs include TANF, Medicaid, food stamps, and other food supplement programs including Women, Infants, and Children (WIC).

Model adolescent parenting education programs provide a comprehensive array of informational, mentorship (e.g., role modeling and home visits), and practical services that promote: (1) high school completion; (2) building self-worth; (3) strengthening job skills; (4) delaying subsequent pregnancy; (5) stabilizing the current family situation and preventing child maltreatment; and (6) achieving optimal health and development for the child(ren) and the mother. Quality child care is a key component of successful programs.

Family Planning Services

Nearly two-thirds of women of childbearing age (about ages 15–44) seek family planning services from a medical provider in any given year. Many seek services from private physicians, but family planning services supported by public funds are among the most critical and most widely used services available to women. Publicly funded clinics provide extensive reproductive healthcare information and contraceptives to millions of women each year. Often, public clinics are the healthcare gateway for young women and low-income women. Family planning clinics' services are in high demand, and they must remain available and even expand services throughout the country. In fact, nearly half of all U.S. pregnancies are unintended, defined as such because they occurred among women who were using contraceptives at the time of conception.

Family Violence Services

In recent years, increased public and professional knowledge about family violence issues has resulted in more services. Yet services differ by state and local community, making them uneven across the U.S. Available services tend to fall into four categories: (1) transitional services; (2) shelters; (3) mental health services; and (4) child-centered services.

Services to Survivors

Transitional services are often the entry point into the service delivery system. They include crisis lines; information and referral services; professional services provided by family doctors, clergy, and attorneys; hospital emergency room services; and police departments. Shelters, frequently the second service level for women and children running from family violence, provide refuge from continued abuse along with a multitude of services including emergency housing, emergency financial assistance, counseling, legal advice, child care, and access to other community services, including health care, employment services, and the like.

Professionals agree that mental health services are an essential component of recovery for victims of family violence, rape, and sexual assault; these are provided by mental health professionals from several disciplines including social work, psychology, and medicine. Child-centered services are provided through the child welfare system.

Services to Batterers

The first batterer intervention programs began over 25 years ago and have since improved services and outcomes. In most states, men arrested for partner violence are required to participate in interventions. The majority of interventions are composed of abuser groups treated weekly with a combination of rehabilitation and punishment techniques over a period that lasts anywhere from three months to a year. Unfortunately, intervention programs appear to be inconsistent and program effects remain small. In fact, men who are arrested and undergo treatment have only slightly lower recidivism (relapse) rates than men who are arrested but do not undergo treatment or who drop out of treatment. Research suggests that batterer intervention treatment decreases sexual violence by just over 5%, and victims report that treatment provides no benefits at all. This implies that sexual violence perpetrated against partners tends to continue unabated. Many professionals believe that batterer treatment programs could be improved with a multidimensional focus that addresses: (1) motivational rather than confrontational strategies; (2) tailored treatment (to meet the needs of those in treatment); (3) substance abuse treatment; and (4) couples therapy, currently prohibited in many states because of potential danger to victims.

Services to Families in an Educational Setting

Social workers who serve families in educational settings apply social work principles and methodologies in working with children in preschool through grade 12 environments and post-secondary environments, with the primary goal of removing barriers that prevent students from fulfilling their academic potential.

Head Start and Early Head Start

Head Start, a national program for preschool children aged 3 to 5, promotes school readiness by providing educational, health, nutritional, and social services to enrolled families and children. It was founded in 1964 as part of President Johnson's War on Poverty. The goal was to enhance cognitive and social development for poor children in order to "level the playing field" before they entered school and, ultimately, to enhance their ability to escape poverty as adults. The major focus of the school readiness programming has been on early mathematics and reading skills. Early Head Start was established in 1995 to serve younger children, from birth to 3 years. These combined programs, which have served more than 24 million children, have been the primary funder of local agencies, but in recent years, local programs have combined Head Start funds with other child care funding to provide extended day services to children whose parents work full time. In 2007, more than 908,000 children participated in Early Head Start and Head Start programming. Almost 40% of these

> **Did You Know?**
>
> Head Start programming encourages parent participation. In 2005, nearly 900,000 current and former Head Start parents volunteered with the program by assisting in classrooms, fundraising, serving on policy councils, and other activities. That year, more than 207,000 Early Head Start and Head Start fathers participated in regularly scheduled activities designed to involve fathers.

children were white, 34.7% were Hispanic, about 30% were black, 4% were American Indian, and less than 2% were Asian.[34] In 2005, three-quarters of the children served lived in households where more than one language was spoken and more than 10% had identified disabilities, including speech and language impairments and developmental delays.

Studies evaluating Head Start and Early Head Start programs have produced conflicting results. Recent studies affirm the importance of early intervention programs. For example, Gorey meta-analyzed long- and short-term benefits of preschool programs and found large positive effects on academic achievement and intelligence as measured by standardized tests.[35] In general, the improvements were evident for at least 5 to 10 years. Studies in Gorham's analysis also reported fewer social and personal problems over a 10- to 25-year period, including lower school dropout rates and lower rates of unemployment, poverty, and welfare dependence. Gorey did note that Head Start results were near the bottom of the performance continuum compared to all other preschool programs in the study.[36] Caputo confirmed that Head Start programming might need additional improvements to make it comparable to non–Head Start preschool programs.[37] His results showed that children whose mothers completed high school started school with an advantage over Head Start children whose mothers did not complete high school, leading him to conclude that Head Start programs should be modified to ensure that "Head Start graduates can achieve roughly comparable income-to-poverty ratios throughout their young adult lives."[38] Improvements may be in the works, as President Bush signed into law the Improving Head Start for School Readiness Act of 2007 in December 2007.

School Social Work

Generally, school social workers collaborate with administrators, teachers, and support staff to provide a range of services within the school setting. School social workers address issues related to: (1) stress that arises within the school (micro) context, such as bullying and other peer problems, truancy, low academic self-esteem, low motivation, or underachievement; (2) difficult family transitions, such as divorce or remarriage, the illness or death of a parent, or parental incarceration; (3) stress related to the societal (macro) context, including discrimination, gang-related activities, poverty, homelessness, and family violence; (4) mental health and behavioral problems, such as depression or substance abuse; and (5) special educational needs, including learning disabilities, attention disorders, developmental disabilities, and other special health needs.

They can be employed by individual schools or by single or multiple school districts, and may serve one or more schools in a community. School social work requirements vary by state. In some states, school social workers practice with a BSW, whereas in other states, they need their MSW to practice. Still other states require MSW graduates to take a credentialing exam in order to practice school social work. The School Social Workers Association of America provides links to state education Web sites (http://www.sswaa.org/).

As concern about the mental health needs and barriers to care for children, adolescents, and their families have heightened, some social workers have advocated for collaboration with professionals outside the school

> **Research Informed Practice with Children in the U.S. South**
>
> Fram, Miller-Cribbs, and Van Horn published a study in *Social Work* (2007, Volume 52) that examined the educational experiences of children in the Southern region of the U.S. The study included data on 3,501 children in 246 schools. "High-ethnic minority schools" were defined as schools "with more than 50% ethnic minority students." The researchers found that classrooms in these schools had teachers with lower certification levels and significantly fewer years of experience at the school than teachers at others schools. In addition, the high-ethnic classrooms were less adequately equipped and had higher percentages of students with low reading skills.
>
> How does this study relate to the "person-in-environment" practice approach of social work? How could the results of this study inform your efforts as a social worker working with children, families, and schools?

setting: ". . . [S]chools and systems of education around the country are joining forces with community mental health and health systems, families and community stakeholders to promote youth mental health and remove it as a barrier to learning."[39] Such collaboration is compatible with guidelines set forth by the No Child Left Behind Act of 2001 (P.L. 107-110), through partnerships authorized by the 21st Century Community Learning Centers (Title IV, Part B) initiative.

Alternative Education Programs

Alternative schools became popular in the late 1960s and early 1970s. The Department of Education defines an "alternative school" as "a public elementary/secondary school that addresses needs of students that typically cannot be met in a regular school, provides nontraditional education, serves as an adjunct to a regular school, or falls outside the categories of regular, special education or vocational education."[40] Unfortunately, not everyone with a stake in alternative education defines it this way, so count estimates vary according to the source. According to most estimates, there are more than 20,000 alternative schools in the U.S.

There are three general types of alternative schools: (1) schools of choice that emphasize innovative programs or strategies designed to attract students; (2) last-chance schools (often involuntary) that precede expulsion and that tend to use behavior modification or remediation techniques; and (3) remedial schools (often involuntary) that focus on social/emotional issues and/or academic issues. Some question whether this typology is accurate today, but given the lack of agreement about what constitutes an alternative school, no other typology exists currently. Alternative school programs generally have small enrollment and high teacher–student interaction, emphasize student decision making, provide opportunities and curricula that are relevant to student interests, exhibit structural flexibility, and have supportive environments; but it has been difficult to assess quality and success rates. As the number of facilities continues to increase to meet the needs of students who have not succeeded in traditional schools, it will be increasingly important to develop evaluation methods that accurately measure outcomes.

Child, Couple, and Family Therapy

A strong social work theme is addressing individuals in their environments (as stated earlier, the person-in-environment approach). Child, couple, and family therapy proceeds from this perspective and can be divided into two general types: couples therapy (premarital, marital, or other, such as cohabiter) and family system therapy. Constable and Lee provide a comprehensive definition of social work with families:

> . . . comprises interventions with persons in families, with couples and with family units. The social worker works in the midst of complex interaction between persons in families and with social institutions, when these institutions can assist families to carry out relational tasks. The fundamental tasks of the social worker in this process are to assist families to reconstruct their relationships when these are at risk and to work with the broader institutional context, so that the institutions are able to assist family members, particularly the most vulnerable, in carrying out their functions.[41]

Therapeutic Work with Children: Play Therapy

Play therapy, used with children up to about 12 years of age, employs play techniques to carry out counseling interventions. Play as a form of therapy is useful because children are often developmentally unable to express their feelings and thoughts in a straightforward manner. Social workers who specialize in this form of therapy use play-based techniques and concrete objects and methods, such as toys and art, to provide children with emotionally and developmentally appropriate means for expressing difficult or traumatic experiences. Social workers vary activities according to the child's age and responsiveness to play options available in the room. Ideally, play therapy rooms should offer a wide range of play materials, including art supplies, board games, clay, dolls and puppets, playing cards, sand, and running water.

Conducting therapy through play is not as easy as it sounds. Social workers must first establish rapport with the child and then adapt the therapy to the individual child in order to use play to interact with the child. A key component of the play therapy method is that children are alone with the social worker without parents, guardians, or other significant adults present in the room. This is important because it enables social workers to get to know their small clients in a different way than if the other adults were present during the therapeutic session. It also gives the social worker the opportunity to meet the child at his or her level. Working with children through play, as with any other type of therapy, includes working with significant adults in the child's life. This always includes the child's parent(s) or guardian, but may also include teachers and other professionals who have contact with the child and may have helpful information.

Couples Counseling, Marital Therapy, and Family Therapy

All couples and families experience problems off and on throughout the family life cycle. Usually, they work through crises and high-stress periods. Sometimes, however, problems persist or heighten in severity, and then families must turn to professionals for help in finding solutions to their problems. Couples counseling and marital therapy are comparatively new developments. For generations, couples and families with problems turned to relatives or religious leaders when their problems became too difficult to handle on their own. Of course, some couples and families still do this, especially if they feel reluctant about seeking outside help for personal problems. One thing that has changed over time is that when problems persist, many couples and families today go beyond their relatives and ministers and turn to professionals for help. Couple and family counseling is one of the many areas in which social workers can choose to specialize.

Sometimes engaged, cohabiting, or married couples consult professional therapists before their problems become severe, or even before problems surface. This type of therapy is sometimes called "prevention therapy"; it is focused on helping couples develop skills and resources that can help them avoid potential problems. Couples can work on expressing their expectations, something that may sound easy but usually isn't. We base our expectations on our experiences (e.g., childhood experiences, media, friends, and relatives) and may not even realize that we have them. Couples can also develop better communication skills and learn how to problem-solve in this kind of therapy.

For couples and families who turn to therapists after problems become evident, the main goal of therapy is to modify relationships among family members by working on communication and interaction patterns. The social work approach to therapy is "holistic," which means that social workers assess client functioning across multiple contexts (at the individual level, community level, and societal level, for example)

Child Abuse and Family Violence Prevention

Some social scientists believe that the only way to reduce family violence is to address violence and violent masculinity at the societal level. According to Jackson Katz, an educator, filmmaker, and author, the U.S. must institute widespread gender violence prevention education with boys and men, especially in sports and the military.[42] Katz believes that all forms of partner violence are rooted in American culture and must be addressed at the cultural level. Presumably, addressing violence at the cultural level would reduce child abuse as well. Barring a widespread social problem approach, the best way to prevent family violence is to improve systems responses at the local level and to develop interventions that decrease recidivism.

Macro Case Study: How One State Attempts to Get Juvenile Offenders Back on Track by Providing Programming and Enlisting Community Volunteers

The Children's Advocacy Council in South Portland, Maine, aims to promote child and family well-being by mobilizing the community against child abuse and neglect. The council educates and trains individuals and organizations that work with children and facilitates collaboration among organizations throughout a large Maine county in an attempt to provide the best educational and support opportunities available anywhere. Over the years, the council has launched a number of programs aimed at wrapping services around at-risk juveniles, juvenile offenders, and their families. For example, the council includes a family mediation program staffed by community volunteers; a juvenile jail diversion program; separate transitional, short-term group homes for boys and girls; an attendant care program that houses high-needs juvenile offenders waiting to appear in court; a bridge home for children entering state custody; substance abuse services; a parenting outreach program; and an organization that promotes job satisfaction and self-sufficiency for youth and adults.

Adolescent Pregnancy Prevention

A variety of approaches aimed at reducing adolescent pregnancy have been attempted in recent years. Approaches tend to focus on sexual behavior and/or future outcomes. Most existing programs have addressed: (1) sexuality education (increasing knowledge about decision making, abstinence, and/or contraceptive use); (2) youth development (employing strategies to improve self-esteem, goal orientation, and life skills); and (3) role-playing and/or parenting simulations (using computerized infant simulators or other methodologies to educate adolescents about the negative aspects of infant care). Most programs are integrated into existing biology and health classes, though sometimes brief add-on programs are inserted into empty class periods or added to the end of the school day. It is well documented that most programs increase student knowledge, but often this isn't enough to change risky sexual behaviors.

In an attempt to ascertain methods that adolescents themselves find useful, one group of researchers conducted focus groups with of American Indian adolescents.[43] The adolescents perceived that they had limited access to information and contraceptives and believed it was important to: (1) discuss teen pregnancy and its consequences; (2) enhance/develop more pregnancy prevention programs in schools and community-based organizations; (3) improve contraceptive access; and (4) use the media to reach youth. Recommendations varied by age and sex and were consistent with differences in cognitive and emotional development

> **Did You Know?**
>
> RealCare® Baby (RCB) is a lifelike doll (called a simulator) programmed to present realistic infant responses. It replaces the flour sack babies used for years in high school health classes. RCB simulators are equivalent in size and weight to newborns, can be male or female, and represent multiple racial and ethnic groups. Like newborns, they cry randomly and for varying lengths of time. A computer chip records information, including crying, rocking, diapering, neglect, and certain types of abuse (e.g., head support, rough handling, and shaking). Adolescents "care" for the infants by inserting a key attached to a wireless wristband into the simulator's back. Like human infants, the simulators do not always respond and may continue crying. During the assigned care time (several days to a week), the wristband cannot be removed. Although study results have been mixed, many studies show that students, especially girls, who have taken care of infant simulators have more realistic perceptions of parenting newborn infants.

SUMMARY

Social workers who work with children, youth, and families work in a variety of settings, including homes, private offices, hospitals, and schools. Because social workers must be able to complete assessments for their clients that use the person-in-environment perspective, they must understand human behavior and development across the life cycle. Working with children, youth, and families also requires social workers to be knowledgeable about macro-level issues, including laws that govern behavior in the state(s) in which they practice and societal practices and expectations that affect individuals and families as they move through life.

10 CHAPTER REVIEW

Log onto **MySocialWorkLab** to access a wealth of case studies, videos, and assessment. (*If you did not receive an access code to* **MySocialWorkLab** *with this text and wish to purchase access online, please visit www.mysocialworklab.com.*)

PRACTICE TEST The following questions will test your knowledge of the content found within this chapter. For additional assessment, including licensing-exam type questions on applying chapter content to practice, visit **MySocialWorkLab**.

1. During recent decades:
   a. The divorce rate has increased dramatically
   b. The proportion of single-parent families has increased steadily
   c. Cohabitation has decreased while the number of married-couple families has increased
   d. Family violence has decreased dramatically

2. Although the family system has undergone extensive changes, the functions of the family have remained relatively constant for over two centuries. They include:
   a. Reproduction, socialization, economic support, and emotional support/social interaction
   b. Reproduction, socialization, child support, and health care
   c. Reproduction, emotional support, and social interaction throughout childhood, elder care, and family protection
   d. Reproduction, child education, economic support, and socialization

3. Which of the following statements is correct?
   a. Nearly half of all births to women ages 25 to 29 and three-quarters of all births to women ages 20 to 24 occur outside of marriage
   b. Since the 1990s, as many as 50% of couples may be choosing to live together *in order* to bear children and as a first step toward marriages that may or may not ever take place
   c. Forty-eight states recognize civil unions and provide same-sex couples various benefits enjoyed by legally married couples
   d. Fewer than 3% of births occur outside of marriage

4. John and Susan have decided to get a divorce. According to research, parents experiencing divorce:
   a. Suffer psychologically and emotionally; divorce has been rated one of the top life stressors
   b. May feel like they have failed at marriage but not parenthood
   c. Are likely to be highly stigmatized in their communities
   d. Have a higher likelihood of interparental conflict during the first year after the divorce; however, the level of conflict reduces drastically by the beginning of the second year

5. Jenny is 65, widowed, and lives alone on a very small pension. Since her daughter, Marian, was convicted of using cocaine and put in prison, she has lived with and taken care of her two young grandchildren. The authors would call Jenny a:
   a. Residential grandparent
   b. Custodial grandparent
   c. Surrogate mother
   d. She is simply called a day care provider

6. Since the early 1990s, the greatest drop in the adolescent birthrate has been among:
   a. White teens
   b. African American teens
   c. Latino Teens
   d. American Indian teens

7. After being divorced for three years, Terry, who is 31, has been struggling to make ends meet. She holds two jobs to earn enough money to cover food costs and child care expenses for her 4-year-old son and 5-year-old daughter, but her employer does not provide health care benefits. As a single parent:
   a. Terry can be considered the "average" single parent
   b. Terry is much older than the "average" single parent, who is most likely to be between the ages of 20 and 24 with three small children
   c. The majority of single mothers have never been married
   d. More than half of the children born to single mothers spend one or more years in foster care

8. The authors use the term "intergenerational effect" in relation to:
   a. Family violence and partner abuse
   b. The children of older mothers, who are less likely to marry or have children
   c. The children of young mothers, who are more likely to become pregnant during adolescence than the children of mothers who wait until their 20s to have their first children
   d. Family violence that spans three or more generations

Log onto **MySocialWorkLab** once you have completed the Practice Test above to access additional study tools and assessment.

Answers

Key: 1) b 2) a 3) b 4) a 5) b 6) b 7) a 8) c

11

Physical and Developmental Disabilities

CHAPTER OUTLINE

Defining Disability 243
Physical Disabilities
Developmental Disabilities
Cognitive Disabilities
Disabling Illness: Stroke, ALS

Social Response to Individuals with Disabilities 252
Historical Perspective
Current Trends

Major Services to Individuals with Disabilities 256
Publicly Funded Services

Rehabilitation and Vocational Services
Residential Services
In-Home Services
Special Education

Interprofessional Collaboration: Social Workers and Occupational Therapists, Physical Therapists, Speech Therapists 265

Summary 266

Practice Test 267

 MySocialWorkLab 267

Core Competencies in this Chapter	(Check marks indicate which competencies are covered in depth)			
✓ Professional Identity	☐ Ethical Practice	☐ Critical Thinking	✓ Diversity in Practice	✓ Human Rights & Justice
☐ Research Based Practice	☐ Human Behavior	✓ Policy Practice	✓ Practice Contexts	☐ Engage, Assess, Intervene, Evaluate

Physical and Developmental Disabilities

DEFINING DISABILITY

Social workers often work with people with disabilities, helping to reduce prejudice and discrimination as well as providing direct services. In this chapter, we clarify the various forms of disability for the reader, examine society's response to this group, and provide an overview of the specific services delivered by social workers and their colleagues.

The way in which our society defines disability is reflected in social attitudes and, more recently, in legal definitions of disability. From a legislative standpoint, an individual is considered to have a **disability** if he or she has a physical or mental impairment that substantially limits one or more major life activities, has a record of this kind of impairment, and/or is regarded by others as having an impairment. Congress has added "contagious and non-contagious" diseases, including HIV and tuberculosis, as qualifying disabilities. At the same time, the Americans with Disabilities Act (ADA) excludes some conditions, such as gender identity disorders, sexual behavior disorders, and psychoactive substance use disorders.[1]

Defining disability in a practical sense is a complex issue. Disability, unlike most other individual characteristics, can be an ever-changing situation, with wide variations in impact. Many people who have disabilities were not born with them. And in some cases, medical or technological advances can lessen or even resolve a disability.[2]

The four commonly practiced disability perspectives include the medical, social, materialist, and postmodernist perspectives. The **medical perspective on disability** is the most prevalent model. It emphasizes that disability stems from a biological or physiological malfunction within the person that has led to impaired functioning in the activities of daily living. This perspective casts clients in the "sick role," as people who can be excused from social obligations or other responsibilities (e.g., school or work) due to their inability to function. For people with this perspective, the goal is to find medical cures to eliminate disability. "Sick" individuals must follow a professional's orders to become "well." If individuals resist professional/medical orders, they are labeled as "noncompliant," "maladjusted," or "failing to accept reality"—what social workers know as **blaming the victim**.

The **social perspective on disability** takes the view that disability derives from social arrangements that restrict the activities of people with impairments by placing social barriers in their way. According to this view, then, disability refers to how a physical or mental characteristic affects an individual's functioning in his or her environment and establishes expectations for future functioning. This model emphasizes changing the individual's social systems and pursuing social justice. The **materialist perspective on disability** asserts that economic factors lead to the oppression of people with disabilities. As a result, they are less valued as workers by employers, viewed as less competent by

There are two kinds of "disabled" persons: Those who dwell on what they have lost and those who concentrate on what they have left.

—Thomas Szasz

Research Informed Practice

Conduct a literature review of the "right to refuse treatment." Try to find out if there are laws in your state that address commitment to an institution and enforced or coerced treatment. Have any relevant court cases been decided in your state? Does your state chapter of NASW have a stance on this issue?

coworkers, and generally believed to experience greater difficulty learning new technologies, all of which further the attitudes that marginalize them in the first place—a vicious cycle. The **postmodernist perspective on disability** holds that disabilities are so varied and complex that no single theory can adequately explain them. Instead, professionals with this perspective support using multiple approaches based on each individual's circumstances.[3]

A fifth alternative to the medical model is the **disability paradigm**, which defines disability as a product of interactions between the individual's characteristics (e.g., condition and type of impairment, functional status, and other psychosocial factors) and environmental characteristics. According to this model, disability is a natural part of life rather than a tragedy that implies dependency or loss of value. People with disabilities are viewed as typical humans, capable and deserving of taking risks, making mistakes, and learning from failure.[4]

Unfortunately, despite advances in the past 30 years, individuals with disabilities and their families continue to face considerable prejudice and stigma, ranging from stereotyping and oppressive perceptions to indifference and outright hostility.[5] The social work profession, along with advocates and allies from other fields, continues to work to reduce prejudice and discrimination. Another common reaction to disability is discomfort, which occurs because people who do not have disabilities often feel uncertain as to how to act when encountering someone with a disability. Spending time around persons with disabilities can reduce these feelings of uncertainty.[6]

Critical Thinking Question
Social workers must be aware of social stigma that people with disabilities experience daily in order to empower their clients to cope effectively. How can social workers learn about the stigmatization their clients face?

Physical Disabilities

One in five people in the U.S. must cope with a physical disability. About half of these have disabilities classified as severe. Projections indicate that the prevalence of disability is likely to increase due to increases in life expectancy and the actual number of people over age 65. Data show a greater frequency of disability among older adults and people who have low levels of income and education, population groups that are likely to be served by social workers.[7]

People with disabilities often experience multiple challenges to completing common daily activities successfully (e.g., feeding, bathing, and toileting). Architectural and transportation barriers, communication disorders, or hearing and visual losses contribute to these challenges. According to the Disability Rights Movement, social workers should understand that "the physical and attitudinal barriers to employment, mobility and other life activities may create more problems than the actual impairments."[8] Persons with physical disabilities may experience disruptions in social relationships as a result of being ignored, rejected, or avoided by peers who do not have disabilities.

Social workers must be aware of the social difficulties and stigma that people with physical disabilities experience in order to empower their clients to deal with their feelings and work out effective methods of confronting and countering the effects of stigma.[9] Practitioner attitudes that devalue clients undermine empowerment. Limiting expectations for persons who have disabilities actually enhances negative self-identity and reduces their sense of personal control. Research focused on client perceptions of disabled individuals' relationships with their social workers identified several key negative components in client–social worker relationships, including prejudgment of clients based on their disabilities, disregard for each client's uniqueness, presumption of familiarity with clients' circumstances based on their records rather than on face-to-face interaction, failure to consider client capabilities and draw on clients' expertise regarding what works for them.[10] Collaborative, strengths-based approaches enhance client competence and social functioning and allow clients to determine their own needs, priorities, and hopes for the future, with a goal of maximizing the range of life choices and facilitate client decision making.[11]

Developmental Disabilities

Developmental disability is a non-diagnostic term that refers to the criteria that determine a person's eligibility for relevant federally funded programs. Developmental disabilities include mental retardation, cerebral palsy, epilepsy, autism, and other organic impairments. To qualify for federal programs, the developmental disability must be: (1) severe and chronic; (2) identified in individuals 5 years of age or older and manifested before age 22; (3) attributable to a mental or physical impairment or a combination of the two; (4) likely to continue indefinitely; (5) the cause of substantial functional limitations in three or more of the following areas of major life activity: self-care, receptive and expressive language, learning, mobility, self-direction, capacity for independent living, and economic - self-sufficiency; and (6) reflective of the person's need for a combination and sequence of special, interdisciplinary, or generic care, treatment, or other services that are lifelong or extended in duration and are individually planned and coordinated. It is applied to infants and young children from birth to age 5 who have substantial developmental delay or specific congenital or acquired conditions with a high probability of resulting in developmental disabilities if services are not provided.[12] Under this model, learning disabilities that interfere with activities such as writing, spelling, reading, and math calculations are considered to be different from retardation and emotional disturbances or vision, hearing, and motor disorders.[13]

Legislative mandates provide a comprehensive services framework for people who have developmental disabilities and underwrite many services, including: (1) institutional and residential programs, income maintenance (e.g., SSI, OASDI, Medicaid, food stamps, and Title XX) to support people living in their own homes, in adult foster care, and in group homes; (2) community-based support services, including day activity programs, case management, respite care, family support, planning, and advocacy; and (3) preventive programs such as screening for at-risk disorders and services for children with physical impairments.[14] Legislative provisions include counseling services for individuals, preparing functional assessments and evaluations, arranging alternative housing, supporting employment activities, accessing community resources, and advocating clients' rights in the policy milieu. Service objectives include promoting personal competence, establishing self-respect, acquiring life skills, and fostering independence. Social workers and clients mutually develop individualized, flexible plans of action (commonly know as ISPs—**Individual Service Plans**) that consider clients' growth potential and provide assistance appropriate to their competence level. Throughout the life course, there is a continuum of individualized support services, ranging from total assistance to independent living. These services touch on all aspects of living—housing, employment, education, health, family, and community.[15]

Large-scale institutions are no longer considered best-practice environments to house people with developmental disabilities. Empirical evidence overwhelmingly indicates that people with developmental disabilities living in community-based settings have significantly better outcomes across a range of psychosocial and behavioral domains than those who are institutionalized,

Critical Thinking Question

Many people have lower expectations for persons with disabilities, damaging their self-esteem and leaving them feeling powerless. Think of lowered expectations between a teacher and a child in a school classroom. What are the possible results?

and over the years large-scale deinstitutionalization has taken place.[16] **Deinstitutionalization** is the process of placing developmentally disabled and mentally ill individuals, formerly housed in large state-run institutions, into community-based programs and living situations. Social workers have benefited from deinstitutionalization because it has increased the likelihood that they will encounter people with developmental disabilities in settings outside the traditional settings that serve this population. Indeed, the National Association of Social Workers has openly supported independent living programs, accessible community resources and public services, education, employment opportunities, adequate income, and affordable and accessible healthcare services for persons with developmental disabilities. Further, ethical professional practice supports self-determination and social inclusion for people with disabilities.[17]

The lifelong support needs of people with developmental disabilities make it imperative that they and their caregivers plan for the future; in particular, they should arrange for services that take effect after parent caregivers are deceased, incapacitated, or otherwise unable to provide care. "Long-term care" includes a variety of treatment and legal considerations, including living arrangements, guardianship, financial advising, and employment. The need for care and related support systems far exceeds available services. Many factors contribute to this emerging crisis. One important contributor is that people with developmental disabilities are living longer today than in previous decades.[18]

Social Work Stories: Practicing with the Disability Field

As an undergraduate in Rhode Island, Dennis studied social science education and completed a special education placement that foretold what was to come. After college, while he was managing a gift shop in a bus terminal, an opportunity arose to work with disabled elders. Later he and his family moved to New Hampshire, where he found work at a center for autistic children. Although initially preferring community care to institutional work, Dennis soon learned to enjoy the setting and, ultimately, that led him to a job at the state training center for the developmentally delayed and a more than 30-year social work career in the State of New Hampshire developmental services system.

For Dennis, the most rewarding part of being a social worker is "to give to others less fortunate than we are." Social work always "seemed right"; it was an opportunity to "give back," "to affect social change for the better." Knowing he can make a difference, even if it's just for one person, is very powerful for Dennis. "Any time we can help an individual with a disability succeed at something, we help break down stereotypes and change public perceptions for the better." Dennis says his guiding principle comes from Norman Goroff, a professor at the University of Connecticut School of Social Work: "Never do anything that would denigrate another human being—our job is to lift them up."

Dennis notes that "you have to take care of yourself as well as the work, it's not being selfish! I learned to focus on what's important: Leave work at work, stay in the moment, do your best and be satisfied when you have done that. Remember, it's not about you." From Dennis's perspective, the biggest social work challenge is helping the people who work day-to-day with this population to develop a more positive set of expectations regarding their clients' ability to succeed. "It is hard to measure progress in this population at times, but it is critical that you see them as progressing." Another challenge in social work practice is to always bring social work values and ethics into the discussion, even when it may not be "popular" to do so.

For those beginning in the disabilities field, Dennis has a number of suggestions: (1) learn medical terminology; (2) develop a basic understanding of biology, how we learn and change; and (3) learn about psychiatric medications. Having mentors who encourage growth and development and networking are important parts of getting into the profession. One last comment from Dennis: "Social work in the disability area can seem scary at first—keep in mind that no one volunteers to be disabled. To be truly effective, you have to be able to go beyond the fear and negativity to see the promise in the future."

Social workers are in a position to advocate for the political changes that will be necessary to meet the future demands for services as more developmentally disabled individuals live into old age.

Two federal Medicaid programs, the Intermediate Care Facilities/Mentally Retarded (ICF/MR) and the Home and Community Based Services Waiver (HCBS) programs, provide support for the current developmental services system. The ICF/MR program provides funds for services that are essentially medical in nature and close in form to the institutional models that existed when this program was developed in the early 1970s. The HCBS Waiver provides federal reimbursement to states for community services including case management, homemaker assistance, home health aides, personal care, residential habilitation, day habilitation, respite care, transportation, supported employment, adapted equipment, home modification, and occupational, speech, physical, and behavioral therapy. Currently, states opt to fund a variable array of services, and no states finance all of these options. State and local family support services fill in some of the gaps by providing respite care, environmental adaptations, assistive devices, personal assistance, mental health care, crisis intervention, and behavior management. These supports allow families to care for their children with developmental disabilities at home rather than at expensive, and generally publicly financed, out-of-home institutions.[19]

Families bear the majority of responsibility for caring for family members with developmental disabilities. One study found that more than 60% of people with developmental disabilities lived with their families of origin; the remainder lived independently or in long-term care settings.[20] Women make up the majority of caregivers, many working outside the home as well as caring for their relatives with developmental disabilities. Families are smaller than in past generations, and increased mobility means extended families are less likely to live nearby, which has reduced the availability of unpaid and informal supports for the disabled.[21]

Individualized Service Plans (ISPs) offer a useful tool to structure housing, employment, leisure, health care, and advance directives for aging parents planning their transition out of caregiving roles. They offer the supports necessary to ensure that aging adults with developmental disabilities maintain functional skills and enjoy a higher quality of life. ISP implementation varies by location, but typically includes social workers who coordinate with a publicly or privately operated umbrella agency that provides residential services and support for daily living activities. Joining a state's long-term care waiting list is often the requisite first step to implementing ISP plans.[22]

The inadequacies of the present system and potential future deficits suggest three necessary aspects of social work practice with this population:

1. *Political advocacy:* Sustained political activism is required to achieve levels of funding and support that respectfully and responsibly meet the needs of people with developmental disabilities and their families. One particularly promising area for advocacy is coalition building, which offers great potential in energizing and sustaining efforts to assure future growth of the service system.
2. *Organizational development:* As the developmental disabilities service system continues to strain under the escalating demand for long-term care services, social workers in other settings will increasingly be called upon to work with people with developmental disabilities and their families in generic agencies. Social workers and other community

Critical Thinking Question

Social workers can play many roles in working in the disability field, including promoting cultural awareness and advocating for human rights. In what ways might you be involved as a social worker?

leaders should help community service organizations to appropriately structure services to address these needs.

3. *Inclusive, family-centered practices:* Community service systems need to address the needs of people with developmental disabilities and their families in inclusive ways. Given social work's focus on the "person-in-environment," social workers are well prepared to support people with developmental disabilities and their families as equal partners.[23]

Cognitive Disabilities

Mental retardation

Mental retardation is a specific diagnostic condition that is often part of developmental disabilities. Mental retardation has more than 23 associated syndromes that affect nearly 3% of the U.S. population.[24] Mental retardation "refers to significantly sub-average general intellectual functioning existing concurrently with adaptive behavior deficits and manifested during the developmental period."[25] As you probably know, intelligence refers to the general mental capability to reason, plan, solve problems, think abstractly, comprehend complex ideas, learn quickly, and to learn from experience. Adaptive behaviors include performing functional tasks, the ability to develop successful social interactions, and a sense of community orientation. Individual strengths often exist side-by-side with individual limitations. The causes of mental retardation often fall into broad categories: (1) genetic conditions (e.g., Down syndrome, fragile X); or (2) problems during pregnancy (e.g., fetal alcohol syndrome, problems related to the birth itself). Causes remain unknown for about one-third of the people affected.[26]

The social work mission to enhance social functioning meshes very well with the adaptive behaviors focus in mental retardation work. Also, social workers in other practice areas (e.g., child welfare, school social work) encounter this population regularly. Social workers may provide mental retardation services as therapist, advocate, ombudsman, service broker, or educational resource. The deinstitutionalization movement and the accompanying expansion of community-based services have created a complex service network. A key social work practice component with this population is to address the way diverse systems—health care, income maintenance, education, legal assistance, housing, self-help groups, mental heath, employment, and vocational training—interact with one another to meet the ever-changing needs of mentally retarded individuals and their families.[27] As in other areas of social work, mental retardation practitioners operate from a strengths perspective, focusing on abilities rather than limitations, understanding that people with disabilities, like all clients, have a right to control their own destinies.[28]

Worldwide, the Independent Living (IL) Movement has long encouraged the development of a long-term care system that maximizes the independence and self-sufficiency for this population. Specific goals in all settings include "normalization" and community integration as specific goals, along with service development tailored to the individual's needs and desires, which are provided as a right, not charity. NASW's (2000) policy statement on people with disabilities is clear about the importance of self-determination, encouraging a continuum of options "in which the client may be involved in decision making about the treatment plan up to a model in which the person with a disability defines the goals of such a plan."[29]

Brain injury

Traumatic brain injury (TBI) is an injury to the brain caused by impact (e.g., car accident, sports injury, or fall) or internal damage (e.g., gunshot wound, surgical intervention, or oxygen loss). Over the past three years, increasing concern has been expressed over the extent of TBI in soldiers returning from Iraq and Afghanistan.[30] Although TBI is similar to a stroke, a stroke is an *internal* event that disrupts the brain in specific ways as opposed to one caused by an *external* source. Traumatic brain injury can be focal (i.e., confined to one area of the brain) or diffuse (i.e., involving more than one area of the brain). TBI symptoms include seizures, headache, nausea, confusion, and emotional and behavioral problems. Depending on injury severity, the specific area of the brain affected, and injury type, the brain-injured person may not only face adjustment to a physical disability, but frequently must contend with cognitive deficits as well. The emotional stress of being brain injured may lead to psychological problems, such as depression, anxiety, lack of motivation, and low self-esteem resulting from a reduced ability to cope. Rehabilitation needs may range from acute in-hospital care to chronic care requiring social reintegration and adjustment.[31]

The family of a brain-injury survivor must also cope with overwhelming stress, an area that may be best suited to social work practice. Social workers

Continuum of Care	Roles and Functions
Trauma Unit (Acute care)	• Crisis intervention • Family support • Liaison with family & medical professionals

Rehabilitation Unit:	• Patient and family education
	• Social assessments
	• Individual, marital and family counseling
	• Group sessions
	   • Patient's peer support group
	   • Family/significant others support group
	• Discharge planning

Community re-entry	• Referrals to and liaisons with community resources • Advocate for community resources (e.g., financial services, housing, legal services, insurance companies, assistive devices, home care, vocational services, schools and employers, local head injury associations)
Follow-up & Auxiliary Services	• On-going out-patient groups for patient and family • Advocacy for head injury programs • Public awareness education • Head injury rehabilitation research

Figure 11.1
Social Work Roles and Function in Head Injury Rehabilitation from Early Trauma to Follow-Up Services[32]
Source: REHABILITATION FROM EARLY TRAUMA TO FOLLOW-UP SERVICES: footnote 32 from J. Beder, Hospital Social Work (New York, Routledge, 2006) pp. 113–116.

can help to facilitate a comprehensive rehabilitation program and provide multiple interventions, including crisis stabilization; individual, marital, and family counseling; group work; social support; and community networking.[32]

Because TBIs are sudden and tend to result from accidents, family members are often unprepared and uninformed about what to expect and how to proceed.[34] Social workers in this area offer crisis support, which includes answering questions about what may be expected in the course of acute treatment when the medical team is unavailable, client and family education about the long-term effects of brain injury, and acting as liaison between family members and other healthcare professionals. Given their knowledge of community services and resources, social workers are typically responsible for coordinating team discharge planning processes to determine appropriate follow-up care.[35]

Learning Disabilities

Learning disabilities describe neurological disorders that affect the brain's ability to receive, process, store, and respond to information; they often run in families. Although affected children are often average or above average in intelligence, they experience difficulty with basic reading and language skills—the most common learning disabilities. Learning disabilities can also affect a person's ability in other areas, including listening, speaking, reading, writing, or mathematics, leading to gaps between expected and actual achievement. They should not be confused with other disabilities such as mental retardation, autism, deafness, blindness, or behavioral disorders. Nor should they be confused with lack of educational opportunities resulting from frequent school changes or attendance problems. Attention disorders, such as attention Deficit/Hyperactivity Disorder (ADHD), and learning disabilities may occur at the same time, but are not the same.[36]

Do not worry about your problems with mathematics, I assure you mine are far greater.
—Albert Einstein

Experts are not certain what causes learning disabilities. Often there is no apparent cause. Factors that may contribute to the development of learning disabilities include heredity, problems during pregnancy and birth, and birth incidents. Head injuries, nutritional deprivation, and exposure to toxic substances (e.g., lead) can contribute to learning disabilities. Most experts do not believe that learning disabilities are caused by economic disadvantage, environmental factors, or cultural differences. Fifteen percent of the U.S. population is classified as having specific learning disabilities and approximately 5% of all school-aged children in public schools receive some kind of special education support.[37]

While there is no cure for learning disabilities, there are ways to help those with disabilities meet the challenges they present. Under the **Individuals with Disabilities Education Act** (IDEA) of 1997 and the ADA, people of all ages with learning disabilities are protected against discrimination and have a right to classroom and workplace assistance. The **Education for All Handicapped Children Act** of 1975 established the right of all children to education, mandated an integrated, mainstreamed program for children with special needs, and called for development of individualized educational plans.[38]

Legislation, research, and practice have increasingly called for educational programs and services based in evidence. As discussed previously, evidence-based practices are grounded in scientific research that demonstrates certain actions are likely to produce predictable and beneficial outcomes. Theory, research, professional experience and judgment, and child/family values and preferences all combine to inform evidence-based practice.[39]

Although many families and caregivers may first suspect problems early in a child's life and seek assistance, other families may initially deny that problems exist because they are fearful of or threatened by the possibilities and consequences. Social workers must be sensitive to differences in family responses, including cultural differences in viewing and addressing disabilities, and provide informed supports. When a child is determined to be at risk for learning disabilities, professionals should conduct periodic evaluations to determine whether the child's development is following expected patterns. An effective early identification program must take into account the myriad biological, environmental, and cultural factors that may influence the child's development. It is important to recognize that there is a wide range of individual differences in developmental progression, some of which may fall within the "normal" range of expected behaviors. The initial assessment process includes looking for risk indicators and protective factors, making systematic observation and conducting a comprehensive evaluation, if indicated. An interdisciplinary approach is especially valuable in interpreting evaluation information from a variety of sources. Social workers should include the child's family throughout the process.[40]

Professionals performing comprehensive learning disability evaluations use multiple standardized instruments and procedures, including valid, culturally appropriate tests, teacher/parent rating scales, and developmental checklists. Accurate understanding of the child's status and needs depends on an integrated assessment of the child's functioning in cognition, communication, literacy, sensory-motor functions, and social–emotional adjustment. If a learning problem or delay in development has been suggested, professionals should give priority to providing services that may include: (1) special education interventions that meet the child's developmental, behavioral, and pre-academic learning needs; (2) effective preschool programs; and (3) affirmative home environment. A variety of professionals may become involved to ensure that children, caregivers, and family members have access to a range of services and supports.[41]

It is commonly accepted wisdom that social workers and other professionals providing services to young children should be able to work with families to provide culturally and linguistically sensitive services, promote interagency coordination, engage in professional collaboration, and advocate for matching the needs of individual children to a continuum of available services and supports. In order to ensure competent practice, social workers should have knowledge and skills about typical and atypical child developmental patterns.[42]

It is never too late to get help for a learning disability. Finding out about a learning disability can be a great relief to an adult who could not explain the reason for their past struggles. Specialized testing is available for people of all ages, as is age-appropriate assistance. Many adults (some of whom are unaware of their disabilities) have developed effective ways to cope with their difficulties and have been able to achieve their life goals successfully.[43]

Disabling Illness: Stroke, ALS

A "stroke" is a sudden impairment in brain function that can cause brain damage. The two main categories of stroke are hemorrhage, caused by too much blood within the closed cranial area, and ischemia, caused by too little blood to supply an adequate amount of oxygen and nutrients to a part of the brain. Each year about 700,000 people in the U.S. experience a new or recurrent stroke, with men's rates 1.25 times greater than women's. Rates increase with age, history of heart disease or diabetes, cocaine use, and bleeding disorders. Heavy smokers and people with high blood pressure have an increased risk, whereas those who are physically active have a decreased risk.[44] The effects of a stroke may be short-lived, with patients recovering rapidly, sometimes within hours or days. More serious strokes can result in paralysis, speech impairment, or damage to parts of the brain involved in thought and muscle control, leaving the victim dealing with a loss of ability to function independently. Most stroke survivors are eventually able to resume their previous activities, but for those who have had a crippling stroke, a difficult and demanding rehabilitative challenge awaits.[45]

Strokes can necessitate modifying family functioning patterns to accommodate both temporary and permanent changes caused by the stroke. Between 40% and 60% of stroke victims have long-term effects that require assistance with daily living activities. Facing major disruption in their usual social, economic, personal, sexual, and emotional behaviors, many stroke victims and their caregivers become prone to depression. Creating a balance between providing care and assistance, while encouraging the stroke victim to function independently as much as possible, is a major challenge for caregivers and family.[46]

In contrast to stroke care is care provided for those suffering from amyotrophic lateral sclerosis (ALS). ALS, which commonly strikes people between ages 40 and 70, is a degenerative disease that usually attacks both upper and lower motor neurons and causes brain and spinal cord deterioration, affecting voluntary muscle control and movement. Described in 1869 by French neurologist Jean-Martin Charcot, it was first brought to national and international attention in 1939 when Lou Gehrig retired from baseball after an ALS diagnosis.[47] A common early symptom, present in more than half of all cases, is a painless weakness in a hand, foot, arm, or leg. Other early symptoms may include difficulties in speech, swallowing, or walking. Persons with late-stage ALS are totally paralyzed, yet in most cases their minds remain sharp and alert. The cause of ALS is not completely understood, and the average life expectancy of a person with ALS is about two to five years from time of diagnosis; however, recent advances in research and improved medical care have resulted in better clinical outcomes and increased hopes for the future.[48]

In both stroke and ALS cases, social workers play a major role in helping families and sufferers address the psychosocial effects of adjustment to chronic illness and developing plans for rehabilitation and/or respite. In particular, social workers may be of assistance in helping caregivers find balance and cope with the emotional realities.

SOCIAL RESPONSE TO INDIVIDUALS WITH DISABILITIES

Historical Perspective

At this point, let's review how society has treated individuals with disabilities. Throughout history, societies have considered individuals with disabilities as "outsiders" with little social value. Often they have been totally excluded by society. Disability responses have ranged from viewing disabled people as having supernatural powers or being possessed by demons to being useless or a source of amusement and derision.[49] Prior to the transition from feudalism to capitalism, many disabled individuals worked alongside their families. As you learned in Chapter 6, policies dating from the early English Poor Laws defined disabled people as one of a very few groups worthy of receiving so-called "outdoor relief," which did not require them to live in the dreaded almshouses or workhouses. For much of human history, however, the idea of providing legal rights to individuals with disabilities was never even considered. Individuals with disabilities were more often locked away against their will in prisons, asylums, and monasteries, where they were killed, exiled, neglected, and shunned.[50]

In the American colonial period, individuals with disabilities were primarily relegated to dependence on family members or placed in poorhouses. Various colonial laws related to disability included statutes that mandated deportation of persons with physical disabilities, classified all persons with disabilities as indigent, or required all persons with disabilities to wear distinguishing symbols on their garments that showed their classification.[51] In contrast, the U.S. government and many states and localities did attempt to meet the needs of disabled war veterans and their families by providing financial compensation for physical losses. Unfortunately, after every war, interest in veterans with disabilities has proved to be very short-lived.[52]

Social advances for individuals with disabilities first began to be made in the 1800s. The movement to create asylums to treat people with mental disabilities gained momentum in the mid-1840s, due in large part to the efforts of Dorothea Dix, who wrote and lectured about the pervasive mistreatment of person with mental disabilities. Inventor Alexander Graham Bell, who invented the telephone, also worked to popularize special education. Helen Keller gave disability a publicly identifiable face through her childhood accomplishments in the 1880s by learning to read, write, and speak despite being blind and deaf and not having the benefit of a trained special educator. After graduating from Radcliffe in 1904, Keller became an advocate for the rights of women, racial minorities, the poor, and persons with disabilities.[53]

In the mid-19th century, British scientist Francis Galton popularized a movement known as "eugenics," based on the principle that reproduction should be regulated based on an individual's characteristics and endowments, raising the standards of humankind by weeding out "unfit" elements, specifically persons with disabilities. Many areas of the U.S. established laws based on eugenics, laws that prohibited marriage, mandated "asexualizations," and/or institutionalized or banished individuals with any one of a number of physical, emotional, or mental disabilities. The U.S. Supreme Court upheld the legality of these practices so the U.S. wouldn't be "swamped with incompetence" and to "prevent those who are manifestly unfit from continuing their kind."[54]

Physical disability became a concern in the early 20th century with industrialization, which led to increasing numbers of industrial accidents and occupational hazards. At that time, the trade union movement and workers' rights groups began to push for workers' compensation for those who suffered disabling injuries on the job. World War I generated further attention to physical disability. Much of the effort focused on compensation for lost wages and working potential as opposed to reintegration into society through education and health services.[55] Vocational rehabilitation programs were first adopted for disabled veterans of World War I, and they were broadened in the 1920s to include unemployed disabled civilians. When the demand for labor in defense industries increased during World War II, due to the absence of young nondisabled, heterosexual, and predominantly white males serving in the military abroad, disabled workers, aging individuals, gays and lesbians, African Americans, Latino/as, and housewives were temporarily admitted to the work force until the return of nondisabled veterans after the war. [56]

As you know, the Social Security Act of 1935 included a social insurance program of retirement pensions for the elderly, but it stipulated that pensions could not be paid to persons residing in institutional care. In 1945, the Hill-Burton Act was passed by Congress to provide direct grants to public and other nonprofit organizations to construct nursing homes and other healthcare facilities.[57] Interestingly, after Medicare and Medicaid were enacted in the mid-1960s, many states transferred significant numbers of individuals residing in large state-supported institutions to nursing homes, largely in an effort to shift state costs to the federal government, giving the appearance that the structure of long-term care in the U.S. has been determined by reimbursement policy as opposed to identified "best practices."[58]

Current Trends

Social workers have become more active in the field of disabilities in various settings in recent decades, in large part due to increased demands for services brought about by medical/technological advances and the advent of community care. Social workers are trained in assessment, evaluation, and the provision of services that are developmentally appropriate across the lifespan of the person with developmental disabilities. Often, social workers are able to effectively lobby to obtain some individual or family services. Based on social work's emphasis on social justice, social workers attempt to ensure that people with disabilities have a right to the same opportunities to participate in community life and have access to services that are available to other citizens as well as access to any specialized services they may require. Disabled individuals and their families are most often served by state systems and other social welfare programs that must compete with one another each legislative session for limited and/or dwindling public resources. Social workers often practice political advocacy as a means of addressing these challenges.[59]

Disabled individuals are rightfully viewed as a population at risk, with an increased potential for abuse at all ages. In the U.S., in spite of the passage of laws to protect the rights of persons with disabilities, the average rate of unemployment for adults with disabilities is around 70%, compared to 5% unemployment rates for other adults. Overall, people with disabilities are much more likely to live in poverty and are less likely to have adequate access to education, health care, and housing than other members of society. Disabled people tend to be less likely than the nondisabled to participate in everyday activities such as shopping at supermarkets, eating at restaurants, attending concerts or seeing films, and visiting neighbors or friends. Much of this isolation and exclusion can be attributed to the continued existence of architectural and communications barriers.[60]

Research Informed Practice with Families of Children with Disabilities

Susan L. Parish and Jennifer M. Cloud published a study in 2006 (*Social Work*, Vol. 51, pp. 223–232) on the financial well-being of young children with disabilities. The authors concluded that "children with disabilities and their families are significantly more likely to live in poverty than typically developing children and their families." Factors contributing to this are the high costs of raising children with special needs, an insufficient income transfer system, and parental employment that is severely limited by available child care and family leave policies.

How could these findings inform your efforts as a social worker to help children with disabilities? Specifically, what could you do to promote a more inclusive life for these young children?

The goal of social work intervention is always to remove the obstacles society has placed in the way of self-fulfillment for people with disabilities. The **Americans with Disabilities Act** (ADA) established civil rights for people with disabilities, with the goal of assuring equal opportunity, full participation, independent living, and economic self-sufficiency and to protect qualified individuals from discrimination. To qualify under the ADA, people must meet the prerequisites of the program, job, or activity. They must be able to perform the essential functions with or without a **reasonable accommodation**, that is, a change in structure or approach that results in equal opportunity or access for a person with a disability. ADA requires reasonable accommodation in employment, public accommodations, and other areas of everyday life unless it imposes "undue hardship," although this concept is not well defined and is still being argued in the courts.[61] This was the first legal provision to impose an obligation upon dominant majority members to grant equal rights for a disadvantaged group.[62] In September 2008, Congress approved the ADA Amendments Act of 2008 (S. 3406), which overturned a number of employer-friendly U.S. Supreme Court decisions and expanded the definition of "disability." This legislation clarifies that the determination of whether an individual is "substantially limited" in a major life activity, and thus "disabled," must take into account any measures that a disabled person may be taking to correct for a physical or mental impairment. The new amendment requires "substantially limits" to be interpreted consistently with Congress's intent that courts define "disability" broadly and extends ADA protections to employees whose conditions are to some extent controlled, even when the employee is currently experiencing no symptoms.[63]

Perhaps the most popular recent social change strategy has revolved around the concept of empowerment. A fundamental empowerment goal, as discussed in earlier chapters, is to increase the political influence of relatively powerless sectors of society, allowing them to eventually rise to the same level of benefits traditionally enjoyed by their nondisabled counterparts. The process involves attempting to "level the playing field" as a beginning point by establishing the same rights and assumptions for disabled individuals as for nondisabled persons. Perhaps the most effective means of empowering disabled people would involve permanent systematic alterations in the decision-making process. An alternative possibility could be seeking sweeping changes in the economic system. If capitalism is considered to be a root cause of the oppression of disabled people, then diminishing this form of control would be a gain. Social work has demonstrated through community organization that empowerment is historically associated with intervention into a neighborhood or locality that is intended to have lasting and sustained effects. Whatever the structures that are finally adopted, empowering disabled peopled should be made permanent.[64]

Let me win, but if I cannot win, let me be brave in the attempt.
—Special Olympics Athlete's Oath

Disability Rights Movement

Inspired by the civil rights movement for racial equality of the 1950s and 1960s, persons with disabilities became active in battling for legal rights in the early 1970s. The disability rights movement was fueled by publicity around President Kennedy's disabled family member and a focus on returning Vietnam veterans with disabilities. In 1973, the federal government passed the first law to grant specific affirmative legal rights to individuals with disabilities. However, although most of the bills endorsed by the disability rights movement were passed without major opposition and enjoyed overwhelming legislative majorities, they often met with inaction regarding implementation and enforcement of the laws and pervasive noncompliance in many U.S. communities.[65]

Chapter 11

MAJOR SERVICES TO INDIVIDUALS WITH DISABILITIES

Publicly Funded Services

Although the reader was introduced to some of the following programs in earlier chapters, they are discussed in depth here as they relate to individuals with disabilities.

SSDI

Two major federal government programs provide benefits for qualified individuals with disability or blindness. One of these programs, Supplemental Security Income (SSI) is funded from general tax revenues and makes cash assistance payments to aged, blind, and disabled individuals, including children under age 18, who have limited income and resources. The other program is Social Security Disability Insurance (SSDI), which constitutes a significant and growing proportion of the Social Security program. SSDI assists insured disabled workers, spouses, and children by providing cash benefits, health insurance through Medicare after a two-year waiting period, and vocational rehabilitation services. To be eligible for this assistance, a worker must be totally disabled, meaning that he or she is unable to perform any substantial gainful activity because of physical or mental impairments that are expected to last for 12 months or result in death. Children under age 18 are defined as disabled if they do not engage in substantial gainful activity and their impairment or combination of impairments results in marked and severe functional limitations that are expected to result in death or have lasted or can be expected to last at least 12 months.[66]

While some programs give money to people with partial disability or short-term disability, Social Security does not. In general, to qualify for disability benefits, an individual must meet two different earnings tests: (1) a "recent work" test based on age at the time the disability occurred; and (2) a "duration of work" test to show that the individual worked long enough under social Security. Applicants must supply, in part, information about their medical diagnosis, how the condition limits their activities, a summary of treatments received, and how treatment may be expected to affect the person's ability to do work-related activities. Disability determination is based on whether or not the person is currently working, whether the medical condition is "severe" enough to significantly limit ability to do basic work activities (e.g., walking, sitting, lifting, and remembering) for at least one year, whether the medical condition is on the "List of Impairments" considered so severe that they automatically qualify as disabling by law, assessment of ability to do the work the person did previously, and ability to do some other type of work.[67] The dollar amount of the monthly benefit is based on an individual's average lifetime earnings. Certain family members of a disabled person may also qualify for benefits.[68]

Workers' Compensation

Although workers' compensation is the nation's oldest social insurance program, it is less well understood than others, partially because the laws and program administration vary from state to state. This occurs because there is virtually no federal role in the state workers' compensation programs. State programs include widely different coverage and disparate benefits, apply different rules, and have different administrative practices. Furthermore, there is little uniformity in terminology and in data collected and reported. When employees are injured on the job or suffer work-related illnesses or diseases that prevent them from working, they are eligible to receive benefits from their state workers' compensation program. Employees are also entitled to free medical care. Workers' compensation systems define disability purely in terms of a reduction in wage-earning capacity as a result of an injury, illness, or occupational disease that arose out of, or in the course of, employment. The Federal Employees' Compensation Act (FECA) provides workers' compensation for nonmilitary federal employees with provisions similar to most state laws [69]

Currently, there is a trend toward combining various programs, such as short-term disability, long-term disability workers' compensation, group health, and statutory programs required by the **Family and Medical Leave Act** (FMLA) of 1993 and the Americans with Disabilities Act (ADA).[70] FMLA is a federal law that entitles employees to up to 12 weeks of job-protected, unpaid leave during any 12-month period. Employees may use it to help deal with life situations such as the birth, adoption, or foster care of a child; to care for an immediate family member; or to deal with the employee's own serious health condition. FMLA applies to private as well as public sector employers. Generally, to be eligible, employees must meet certain criteria. During such leave, an eligible employee is entitled to continue group health plan coverage as if the employee had continued to work. Upon return from leave, the law dictates that employees be restored to the same or an equivalent position, with equivalent pay, benefits, and working conditions. State laws, which vary from state to state, may also apply.[71]

Many companies are making attempts to integrate their private programs related to disability and/or health care. Short-Term Disability (STD) Insurance Benefits can provide disability income for individuals absent from work because of non-occupational illness or injury. STD insurance can cover the period of disability up to 26 weeks following the disability. It usually has a liberal definition of "disability" and may require a short period deductible or period of elimination. This often means no benefits during the first 7 or 15 days. Many employers provide this coverage for short durations either through sick leave or self-insured plans. Long-Term Disability (LTD) Insurance Benefits are designed to protect an employee's income during extended absences from work that are caused by injuries, illnesses, and/or diseases that are not covered by sick leave or workers' compensation. Over the past 20 years, many companies have adopted **employee assistance programs** (EAPs). Sometimes the factors that lead to a decrease in an employee's productivity are not obvious. A comprehensive Employee Assistance Program provides confidential assessment and referral resources designed to help employees balance work and family life and cope with the mounting array of personal and family work pressures. The employer gains by keeping the employee fully productive, thereby avoiding replacement and retraining costs.

Many companies are also implementing "wellness programs" that help to reduce disability costs by encouraging workers to undertake preventive activities to better manage their healthcare needs. These programs educate and motivate employees and their families to adopt better health habits. Smoking, controlling weight, lowering cholesterol and blood pressure, wearing seat belts, improving nutritional food choices, and achieving a moderate level of fitness are frequently targeted behaviors in wellness programs. Most wellness programs also screen employees for disease because treatment is almost always more effective and less expensive in the early stages of a disease.

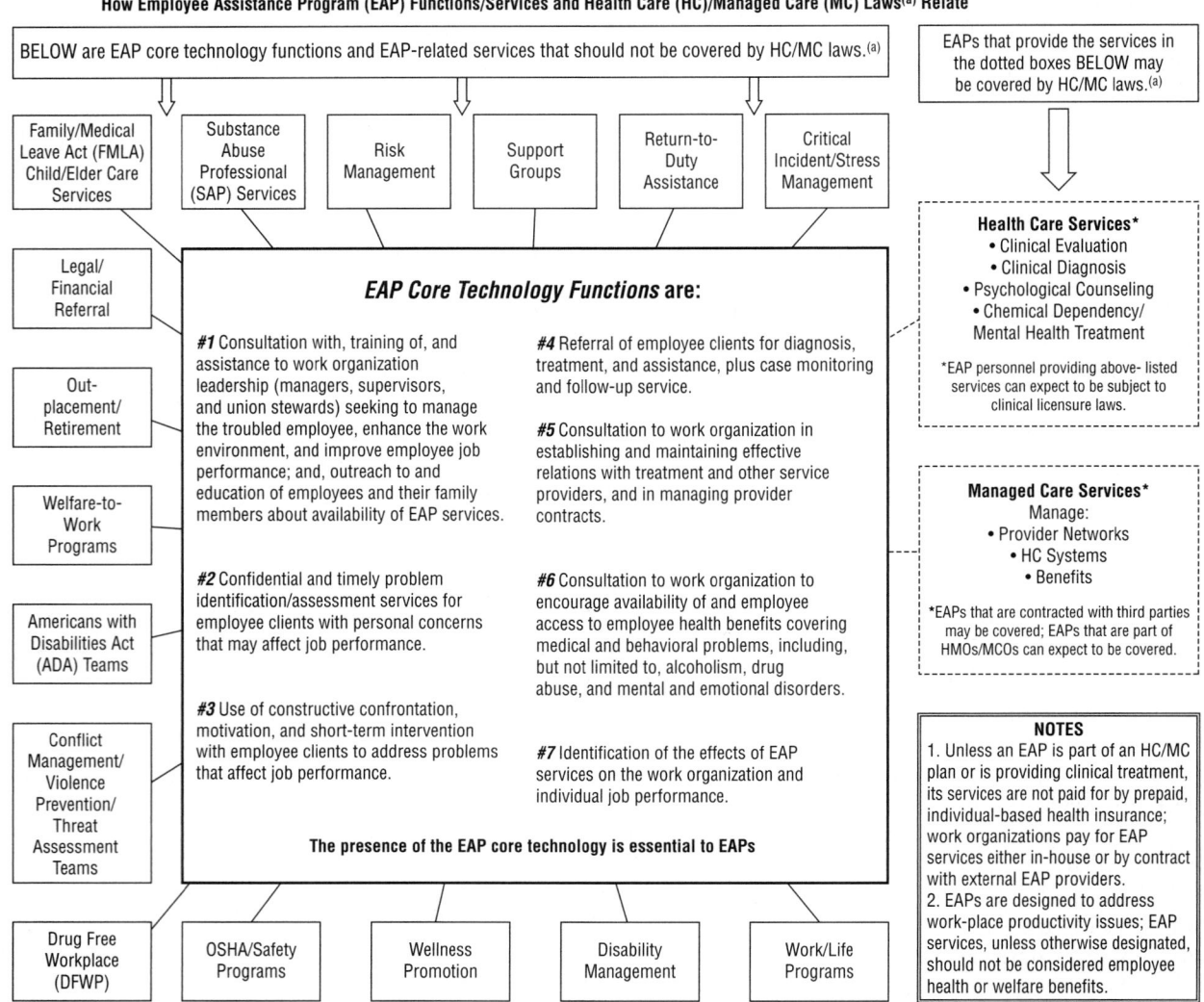

Figure 11.2
Employee Assistance Roles and Functions

Some workplaces have a safety prevention program to help reduce injuries and lower costs. Programs may include ergonomics, back injury prevention, worker fitness, wellness, and chemical safety. Effective safety programs are tailored to a company's individual needs, but have some common basic elements: management and employee commitment, hazard identification, hazard control, and training for workers. Return-to-work programs are designed to identify the causes of disability, manage the frequency and duration of disabilities, and encourage appropriate treatment and eventual return to the workplace. Integrated Disability Management Programs (IDM) combine disability management and insurance claims administration, seeking to manage the disability case and help employees to return to work as soon as they can reasonably do so.[72]

Rehabilitation and Vocational Services

Individuals who have been treated for a given medical condition such as stroke, spinal cord injury, or traumatic brain injury, but who are in need of additional rehabilitation before they can return home or to a long-term care facility, frequently use rehabilitation settings to help in restoring their former functional capacity.[73] **Rehabilitation** is the process whereby a person with a physical disability seeks to gain or regain independence and autonomy in different areas of functioning through participation in specialized medical programs, each with a unique multidisciplinary team. The social worker's goal in this setting is to help the client and family achieve their optimal level of psychosocial functioning and return to a fuller quality of life.[74]

Social work practice roles in this setting include assessment, counseling, education, and advocacy. Often, the social worker is the most accessible member of the healthcare team and is able to "translate" medical jargon into more usable and familiar language. While conducting a complete psychosocial review, social workers may use the assessment process to help orient the client and family as to what to expect from their team's treatment planning meetings and prepare families for family conferences, where holistic treatment and discharge planning is explained and problem solving occurs. The social worker's responsibility is to identify and present as many options as possible to clients and their families so that they are able to choose treatment options for themselves. Client and family goals should be realistic and mutually agreed upon.[75]

Counseling and problem solving are central aspects of the social work role in assuring the client's successful adaptation to a disability. Often, adaptation requires making major psychosocial readjustments, including dealing with grief over potential or actual functional losses, modifying the client's physical environment to accommodate new realities, learning new skills, and providing appropriate long-term emotional and financial resources. Social workers facilitate opportunities for clients and family members to voice and understand one another's concerns and develop effective plans. Social work intervention through the counseling process elevates actual, as well as perceived, levels of social support.[76]

Social workers may be active in the education of clients, their families, community members, and other health professionals about the disabilities; examining lifestyle implications; and teaching coping mechanisms for clients and their families, all of which may be done both individually and in groups. As you now know from reading earlier chapters, advocacy is a role every social worker performs. In this case, she or he acts as an information broker and liaison in obtaining housing, disability pensions, social assistance, wage loss insurance payments, and so on; facilitates provision of home support services or development of such services where the need exists; helps the client locate community coalitions to take political action to redress service gaps; and/or provides representation on various committees or decision-making bodies to represent the client, family, and community interests.[77]

Like work with other clients, social work with individuals with disabilities requires a collaborative approach, often in the context of family systems. The collaborative approach to working with those who are disabled and in need of long-term rehabilitation is based on the understanding that people with disabilities are people first and disabled second. They are neither their diagnoses nor their conditions. In many instances, the social work services a disabled person may need may not be disability-related at all. Generalist social work practice is, as you know, rooted in support for self-determination and empowerment. One important intervention strategy is helping clients retrieve past successful coping experiences that may have been overlooked or unidentified and use them to develop successful current coping strategies. A family systems perspective would suggest that the patient is not the only one who has sustained an injury, and the family should also be a focus of any intervention. Forming a therapeutic alliance with the family can be most helpful in addressing client needs.[78] Service decentralization may also indicate a special role for social workers trained in multidisciplinary approaches to rehabilitation. In recent years, a major trend in hospital and rehabilitation centers has been to extend services outside the institution into the community, delivering professional services to the local areas where the client lives. Social workers often act as liaisons between rehabilitation centers and community agencies, providing case consultation, referral, and education.[79]

In terms of vocational services, people with disabilities had few employment options prior to the mid-1980s. Social workers have come to understand that real employment provides an opportunity for long-term dignity, a chance at upward mobility, and the possibility for the disabled to break out of the perpetual cycle of unemployment or underemployment. Supported employment is one approach to this problem, involving paid competitive employment for people who have severe disabilities and a demonstrated inability to gain and maintain traditional employment. Supported employment can occur in a variety of normal, integrated business environments; it includes being paid minimum wage or better, getting support to obtain and maintain jobs, and having opportunities for career development. Studies have shown that the percentage of people dependent on public assistance/disability benefits as their primary source of income drops dramatically as a result of participation in supported employment. A state-by-state comparison indicates that costs for supported employment are from 40% to 80% of the costs of other day services, such as sheltered workshops or work activity centers.[80]

Residential Services

Long-term care services exist in a number of forms, including rehabilitation hospitals and clinics, nursing homes, intermediate care facilities, supervised boarding homes, home healthcare agencies, hospices, and hospital home care units. Elders use acute hospital services, physician services, and long-term care services more than any other age group, accounting for 30% of the nation's annual healthcare costs despite their making up only 12% of the total U.S. population. Growth within the elder population, especially among the "oldest" old (those over age 75), combined with remarkable improvements in medical care, has led to increased interest in promoting and understanding the factors that lead to longer and healthier lifespans.[81]

Skilled nursing facilities provide basic nursing care, helping residents with daily living activities (e.g., walking, bathing, dressing, and eating), ensuring necessary medical care, and providing a safe environment for residents.[82] Important health issues facing long-term care residents generally fall into two major categories: chronic physical impairment and mental health concerns. **Rehabilitative services** typically include physical therapy, occupational therapy, and speech therapy, but too often do not include any type of mental health services, despite the frequent presence of mental health concerns, such as life stresses, including widowhood and social and occupational losses, in addition to the adjustment to any physical health problems. Social workers are frequently the default resource for providing mental

> **Case Study: Living with Developmental Disability**
>
> "Joe was an imposing young man—tall, well-muscled—and extremely over-active when I first met him. Now in his 20s, he had been institutionalized with development services since age 2 when his family could no longer meet his needs. Essentially nonverbal, his behavior was occasionally aggressive and uncontrolled; and many of the organization's staff feared him—including the community staff where we intended to place him. However, we worked hard to address these concerns and Joe was eventually returned to his home community of Columbus, Ohio, to live in a shared residence. . . . I made a home visit to Joe three months following his placement to check on progress. The man who greeted me at the door when I rang the bell was almost unrecognizable. He was neatly dressed and groomed with a smile on his face. I noted the pride with which he showed me his room and the rest of his home. . . . I was particularly impressed when lunchtime arrived and he prepared the sandwiches for the group. . . ."

health-related services for mentally impaired residents in long-term care facilities, especially residents who were admitted as a result of deinstitutionalization. Medications are heavily emphasized as the primary method of treatment. Anecdotal evidence suggests the lack of mental health services in this setting is slowly being addressed, but it cannot be assumed that such services will be provided.[83]

"Respite" or long-term care programs provide a clinically appropriate, cost-effective alternative to hospital admissions and may decrease the length of hospital stays as well. In addition, these programs can benefit hospitals by reducing emergency rooms (ER) use, resulting in cost savings and improved medical care quality by providing better continuity and treatment follow-through. This is especially important because ERs are serving increasing numbers of homeless, poor, and underinsured or uninsured individuals despite their status as the most expensive service delivery point in the U.S. healthcare system.[84] Long-term care social workers encourage residents' independence and work to maximize personal dignity, justice, culture, respect, autonomy, and spiritual beliefs. A comprehensive psychosocial assessment, including cognitive patterns, mood and behavior patterns, and psychological status, is completed for each client upon admission and every three months thereafter unless a significant change in physical or mental status occurs. There is considerable evidence supporting the importance of family members' involvement in creating a general sense of well-being in the elderly individual. Responsible social work practice requires education for the family about the client's medical condition, including signs, symptoms, and how to deal with emergency situations. Families should be encouraged to communicate needs, problem solve, and participate in support groups.[85]

In-Home Services

Deinstitutionalization has resulted in greater numbers of people with disabilities living and working in community settings. Experts predict that by 2025 the world population will top 8.5 billion and the elderly population will exceed 1.1 billion. All countries will have to develop long-term service delivery systems focused on expanded community-based care options and related social services to support the needs of this population. A combination of factors will have significant ramifications for this developing system, including changing family demographics, increased life expectancy, resource competition, and the size of the direct service workforce.[86]

Medical social work services can improve the client's psychosocial situation while reducing overall treatment costs.[87] When appropriate, a social worker responsible for case management arranges, coordinates, monitors, evaluates, and advocates for a package of multiple services to meet the specific client's complex needs. In today's managed care environment, however, this traditional definition has been modified, and case managers (many of whom are not social workers) often serve as gatekeepers and are capable of initiating or disallowing service provision. Often the primary role of the managed care case manager is referring clients to the most cost-effective and efficacious service possible.

"Home care" refers to health care and social services that are provided to individuals and families in their homes or in communities offering a wide range of services, including nursing, rehabilitation, social work, home health aides, and other services. Home care agencies have been providing in-home services to Americans for more than a century and are viewed as a humane and compassionate way to deliver health and supportive services.[88] Today, Medicare is the largest single payer of home health care services.

A home care referral is generally triggered when patients and families have unmet discharge planning needs. A dramatic decrease in hospital lengths of stays over the past 20 years has been caused by technological advances in medical/surgical care and the advent of "Diagnosis Related Groups" (DRGs), which have led to patients being discharged "quicker and sicker" from hospitals; this decrease has increased the need for home care. Additional factors that have led to increased demand for home health care include: (1) a shift from acute infectious diseases to chronic diseases as major health problems; (2) advances in medical technology that allow people to be cared for at home in spite of the need for medical equipment such as IVs, portable oxygen machines, and infusion pumps; (3) reluctance to consider nursing home placement for aging family members; (4) the AIDS epidemic; and (5) increased survival rates for medically fragile children.[89] Formal caregivers include professionals and paraprofessionals who provide in-home care, including nursing and personal care. A multidisciplinary approach, including medical social workers, is crucial to developing client appropriate, high-quality, low-cost services. Healthcare social workers help patients and their families cope with chronic, acute, or terminal illnesses and handle problems such as adjustment to illness, grief and loss, concerns about dying, behavior management, and caregiver stress. As always, social workers document standardized biopsychosocial screening criteria for the client's care plan. Social workers are uniquely qualified to provide clinical services for home care and to provide support for the interpersonal and psychosocial aspects of clients' lives, while supporting other staff providing client care. By blending their knowledge of environmental and systems assessment and intervention with psychosocial expertise (i.e., person-in-environment), they can play a vital role in meeting client, caregiver, and family needs. Social work interventions with this population are best when they start from the strengths perspective and are both proactive and creative.[90] Because social worker home care visits are generally short term and time limited in nature, proper referrals and interdisciplinary collaboration are also key to successful interventions. Many social workers in home care have assumed supervisory responsibilities related to the interdisciplinary nature of the work and provide training and consultation, as well as ongoing provision of support to staff from various disciplines.[91]

Unfortunately, social workers represent only a small segment of home healthcare service workers. Despite recent advances, much of the home care industry is still driven by the medical model. In fact, the majority of home healthcare recipients are never even referred for social work services and may never receive additional supportive services, such as meals-on-wheels, mental health services, case management, transportation, financial services, Medicaid, day care, assistive devices, assistance in paying for prescriptions, companion services, support groups, legal services, and protective services.[92]

Special Education

The original Individuals with Disabilities Education Act (IDEA) legislation, which outlined the right to have a Free and Appropriate Public Education (FAPE) provided in the least restrictive environment and to receive needed special education and related services, was designed to ensure that children with disabilities were not excluded from public schools. IDEA covers children ages 3–21 in need of special education and related services because of a disabling condition. A child with a "disability" is defined as one with mental retardation, a hearing impairment (including deafness), a speech or language impairment, a visual impairment (including blindness), a serious emotional disturbance, or an orthopedic impairment; autism; traumatic brain injury; other health impairment, specific learning disability, deaf-blindness, or multiple disabilities. IDEA requires that, to the greatest extent possible, students with disabilities be educated with students who do not have disabilities. This is referred to as the **least restrictive environment** (LRE) and requires children only be removed from the regular classroom when education in regular classes cannot be achieved satisfactorily with the use of supplementary aids and services.[93]

Life is a succession of crises and moments when we have to rediscover who we are and what we really want.
—Jean Venier

Children with disabilities are now required to have an **Individualized Education Program** (IEP). IEPs are designed specifically for each child who receives special services. They are reviewed and rewritten yearly to reflect current functioning and progress toward educational goals. A transition planning process to prepare young adults with disabilities for adulthood is also required. Children with disabilities who also are homeless or whose primary language is not English have historically faced additional difficulties in obtaining appropriate special education services. Social workers routinely advocate for children to be tested in their native languages to protect them against erroneous disability diagnoses. Social workers who provide services to caregivers through healthcare, mental health, and child welfare settings should ensure that caregivers are aware of their rights and should be prepared to assist them in obtaining needed educational services for their children. Children with ADD or ADHD can now legally qualify for special education and related services under the category "other health impairment." Expanding the age range of children with developmental delays to include those between ages 6 and 9 allows more children to qualify for special education and related services without having to give them a potentially more severe label, such as "mental retardation," at too early an age. Social workers can advocate for families of children with ADD or ADHD and with developmental delays so these children receive appropriate services in a timely manner.[94]

Federal law recognizes that social work services in schools include a home–school–community approach. The term "social work services in schools" includes collaboration with parents and others on those problems in a child's living situation (home, school, and community) that affect the child's adjustment in school. This requires mobilizing school and community resources to enable the child to learn as effectively as possible in his or her educational program. It also involves preparing social or developmental histories and group and individual counseling with the child and family. This allows social workers in the schools the opportunity to foster relationships among diverse adults who work with the child both inside and outside the school setting. Strong advocacy skills, as stated throughout this book, are fundamental for social workers. Social workers can and should advocate for families to obtain meaningful educational opportunities for their children at school, at home, and in the community.[95] Social workers from outside the school system can advocate for their clients to receive social work services within the school system because these services support the child's educational functioning, and school social workers can refer students to outside agencies for more intensive, noneducational services. In so doing, all social workers who practice with children in whatever setting should remain aware of the developments in legal rights and protections for children and families.[96]

Social workers practice in many settings that offer prescreening for developmental problems including medical settings, well-baby clinics, and schools. In each setting, social workers work with parents as they deal with the results of the screening, linking parents with resources for special education, speech therapy, and support groups for parents, to name a few. Social workers offer information and education to parents to enhance parenting skills and enrich children's early learning environments.[97] In addition, social workers make sure that school districts solicit parent input. They also act as parent advocates, since they are often in a better position to ensure that parents' voices are heard during IEP sessions. In the process, social workers educate parents about their rights and mediate conflicts that might develop between parents and school personnel. Also, social workers can connect parents with parent organizations that focus on children with disabilities and special education (e.g., Parents Helping Parents, All Our Children), which can help strengthen the role of other families and family organizations supporting parents. Social workers,

Critical Thinking Question

Social workers provide services to clients with disabilities in a variety of settings. How might services be modified depending on the setting? Compare and contrast service delivery approaches in two settings you read about.

both inside the schools and in community child welfare and mental health agencies, have traditionally offered parenting education and skills training programs to help parents attain crucial knowledge and skills related to child development and parenting.[98]

INTERPROFESSIONAL COLLABORATION: SOCIAL WORKERS AND OCCUPATIONAL THERAPISTS, PHYSICAL THERAPISTS, SPEECH THERAPISTS

Social workers serve on interdisciplinary teams designed to assist individuals and family members in almost all settings. As you know from earlier chapters, interdisciplinary teams collaborate, using each discipline's knowledge base, skills, and process to help assess, formulate goals, and direct needed intervention, ensuring that clients receive the benefit of broad range of professional expertise to obtain optimal outcomes. Social workers typically identify psychosocial needs and often serve as team coordinators. Medical doctors, nurses, occupational therapists, physical therapists, and other professionals typically provide profession-specific services. Medical doctors and nurses attend to healthcare-related issues. Occupational therapists work with the ways people perform everyday activities, such as self-care and hygiene, as well as socializing, work, recreation, or education, and other activities of their community life. Psychologists provide neuropsychiatric testing and related services as well as share counseling duties with social workers, while physical therapists help clients with gross motor skill/coordination issues and services aimed at preventing or slowing the progress of problems resulting from injury, disease, and other causes. When needed, audiologists provide nonmedical hearing and balance management. Speech–language pathologists assess, diagnose, and intervene with speech, language, literacy, cognitive communication, social communication, and swallowing problems. The client's specific needs determine the mix of professionals on the team.[99]

Treatment approaches have become more client/family centered in recent years and actually include clients and their families in team processes more often than previously. Keeping the primary effort focused on clients and families is a necessary condition of effective collaboration, along with active participation and commitment to teamwork by team members and quality relationships among clients, caregivers, and service providers.[100]

Demonstrating Knowledge, Values, and Skills

Terminology is an important part of a social worker's role. Putting the person before the disability is a standard that social workers are expected to understand and adhere to. Discuss the importance of this in your class.

Does it matter if someone says "the disabled person" or "an individual with a developmental disability"? Why is this so important in the social work profession? How do social workers advocate for individuals with developmental disabilities and their families? What services are available? How does our government support individuals with disabilities?

SUMMARY

Throughout history, societies have considered individuals with disabilities as "outsiders," having little social value, often totally excluding them from society. Today, the way in which our society defines disability is reflected in social attitudes and in legal definitions of disability. An individual is considered to have a disability if he or she has a physical or mental impairment that substantially limits one or more major life activities.

There are four commonly practiced approaches to considering disabilities: the medical perspective, the social perspective, the material perspective, and the postmodernist perspective. The disability paradigm is a less common approach. Disabilities may be experienced in terms of physical disabilities, developmental disabilities, cognitive disabilities (mental retardation, brain injury, learning disabilities), or disabling illnesses. The responsibility for caring for people with disabilities is borne largely by families. Women make up the majority of caregivers, but this has grown more problematic as more women have joined the paid workforce.

Social workers have become more active in the disability field over the past few decades, in large part due to increased demand for services brought about by medical/technological advances and the advent of community care. Social workers are typically involved in every aspect of service delivery to individuals with disabilities, from government-run service, such as SSDI or worker's compensation, to coordinating rehabilitation and vocational services, residential services, in-home services, and school settings. Social workers serve on interdisciplinary teams designed to assist the individual and family members in almost all settings. Interdisciplinary teams use each discipline's knowledge base, skills, and process to help assess, formulate goals, and direct needed intervention, ensuring that clients receive the benefit of a broad range of professional expertise to obtain optimal outcomes. Rooted in social work's value of social justice, social workers attempt to ensure that people with disabilities have access to the same opportunities to participate in community life and services that are available to other citizens as well as to access any specialized services they may require. The goal of social work intervention is always to remove the obstacles society has placed in the way of self-fulfillment for people with disabilities.

The inadequacies of the present system and its potential future deficits and concerns suggest three necessary aspects of social work practice with this population: political advocacy, organizational development, and continued building of inclusive, family-centered practices.

11 CHAPTER REVIEW

Log onto **MySocialWorkLab** to access a wealth of case studies, videos, and assessment. (*If you did not receive an access code to MySocialWorkLab with this text and wish to purchase access online, please visit www.mysocialworklab.com.*)

PRACTICE TEST The following questions will test your knowledge of the content found within this chapter. For additional assessment, including licensing-exam type questions on applying chapter content to practice, visit **MySocialWorkLab**.

1. An individual is not considered to have a disability if they:
   a. Have a physical or mental impairment that substantially limits one or more life activity
   b. Have a record of impairment
   c. Are regarded by others as being impaired
   d. Believe they have a disability

2. Viewing a disabled personal as *personally* responsible for their own limited functioning is called _____ by social workers:
   a. Adopting a "sick role"
   b. "Individual accountability"
   c. "Blaming the victim"
   d. "Veritas theory"

3. Legislation that provides persons with disabilities legal safeguards and protection from discrimination is:
   a. ADA
   b. OBRA
   c. Social Security Act of 1935
   d. HIPAA

4. In modern social work practice, which of the following theoretical understandings of approaches to working with individuals with disabilities are most frequently supported by social workers?
   a. "Medical model" approaches
   b. "Disability paradigm" approaches
   c. Materialist approaches
   d. Social constructionist approaches

5. People with disabilities may seldom encounter:
   a. Easy handicap accessibility
   b. Effective communication from others
   c. Difficulties with transportation
   d. Understanding and accommodation

6. Adult individuals who have been identified as in need of services due to one or more disabilities *must* have:
   a. An ISP if over age 21
   b. Medicaid or SSI
   c. A battery of psychological tests
   d. A complete medical examination

7. Social workers often advocate for individuals with disabilities to be able to live:
   a. In group homes
   b. In their own homes
   c. In large institutions
   d. In specialized residences

8. Social workers have found _____ to be the most effective strategy to address current inadequacies in the social service delivery system for individuals with disabilities and potential future service gaps in the future:
   a. Become politically active
   b. Develop more appropriate service delivery systems in their agencies
   c. Practice in an inclusive, family-centered way
   d. Encourage families and clients to seek legal remedies

9. If current trends continue, social workers may expect to working with:
   a. Decreasing numbers of individuals with disabilities
   b. Increasing numbers of individuals with disabilities
   c. About the same numbers of individuals with disabilities
   d. Sharply increasing numbers of individuals with disabilities

10. Social workers are not providing _____ as part of their practice:
    a. Coordination of multidisciplinary teams
    b. Medical advice and information to clients
    c. Supportive counseling to families as well as clients
    d. Advocacy for appropriate service delivery

Log onto **MySocialWorkLab** once you have completed the Practice Test above to access additional study tools and assessment.

Answers

Key: 1) d 2) c 3) a 4) b 5) d 6) a 7) b 8) d 9) d 10) b

12

Substance Abuse and Social Work

CHAPTER OUTLINE

Substance Use and Abuse Defined 269
What Is Substance Abuse?

Current Issues in Substance Use and Abuse 271
Preventing Youth Smoking
Youth, Drugs, and Alcohol
The Debate over the Legalization of Marijuana
Crystal Methamphetamine Abuse: An Emerging National Epidemic?
Status of the Federal "War on Drugs"

Models of Addiction 278
The Biopsychosocial Model of Addiction
Sociocultural Models of Addiction
Psychological Models of Addiction
The Disease Model

Substance Abuse Intervention 280
Self-Help: Twelve-Step Support Groups
Professional Treatment Programs and Services
Treatment Facilities
Needle Exchange Programs
Drug Courts
Future Challenges in Drug Treatment: Dual Diagnosis
Substance Abuse Prevention

Summary 289

Practice Test 290

 MySocialWorkLab 290

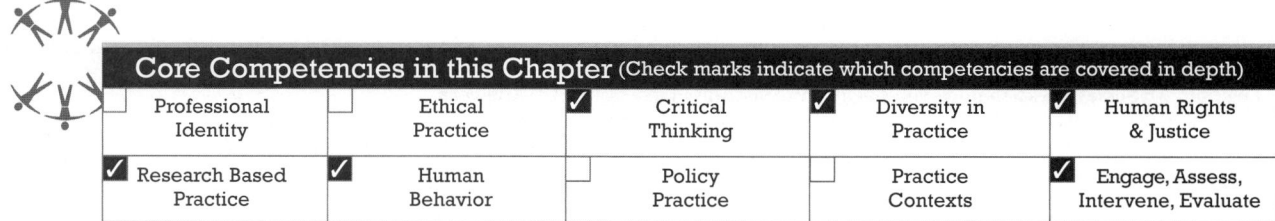

	Core Competencies in this Chapter (Check marks indicate which competencies are covered in depth)								
☐	Professional Identity	☐	Ethical Practice	✓	Critical Thinking	✓	Diversity in Practice	✓	Human Rights & Justice
✓	Research Based Practice	✓	Human Behavior	☐	Policy Practice	☐	Practice Contexts	✓	Engage, Assess, Intervene, Evaluate

SUBSTANCE USE AND ABUSE DEFINED

The lives of millions of Americans are adversely influenced by substance abuse. It could be a father who misses work because of alcoholism. It could be a baby born to a crack-addicted mother, or it could be a teen driver hurt driving while drunk. Given this fact, it is no surprise that the jobs of many social workers involve substance abuse treatment and prevention. In this chapter, we define some key terms and present current issues in the field of substance abuse treatment. We then provide an overview of the major treatment models and standard services with which social workers should be familiar. Finally, we examine the future challenges for social workers in this field and ways to prevent substance abuse.

If we're looking for the source of our troubles, we shouldn't test people for drugs, we should test them for stupidity, ignorance, greed and love of power.

—P. J. O'Rourke

What Is Substance Abuse?

To discuss the problem of substance abuse and related treatment programs, we first have to define carefully what is meant by some key terms in the field. **Intoxication** refers to the state of being under the influence of alcohol or other drugs such that the thinking, feeling, and behavior of the individual are affected. The state is sometimes referred to as "getting high" or "getting a buzz."[1] Many people get intoxicated occasionally without significant negative consequences. Alcohol, for example, is a regular part of sporting events, cookouts, and other social gatherings in the U.S. Yet frequent intoxication can lead to more serious health problems for the individual.

Substance abuse is "a maladaptive pattern of using certain drugs, alcohol, medications, and toxins despite their adverse consequences"[2] So, how does a social worker determine when an individual has crossed the line into substance abuse? Some of the symptoms include being preoccupied about the substance, taking greater amounts than intended, making persistent efforts to control its use, reducing occupational or social identities, and continually using the substance despite recognizing that it is causing recurrent physical, psychological, or social problems[3] (see Figure 12.1).

Drug addiction is defined here as a more severe stage of the problem. That is, **Drug addiction** is a compulsion to use chemical substances that results in a physiological dependence in which the body tissues require the substance to function comfortably. In the absence of the substance, the individual experiences withdrawal symptoms, which may include physical discomfort, emotional distress, impaired judgment, and belligerence.[4] Although there are many drugs to which people can become addicted, this discussion will focus on those most commonly abused in the U.S.

Tobacco is a drug frequently used and abused by Americans. In 2007, 43.4 million adults aged 18 and over in the U.S. were current smokers. This number comprised 19.8% of all adults—22.3% of men and 17.4% of women. American Indians/Alaska Natives represented the largest percentage of smokers (36.4%), followed by whites (21.4%) and African Americans (19.8%). More recent data, from January through June of 2008, indicates that close to 21% of the adult U.S. population currently smoked[5]. The active ingredient in tobacco is nicotine. **Nicotine** acts as a stimulant for the user. It causes the heart to beat faster, resulting in elevated blood pressure. Prolonged tobacco abuse can result in several negative respiratory and cardiovascular health consequences. For example, the tar in tobacco smoke causes cancer, shortness

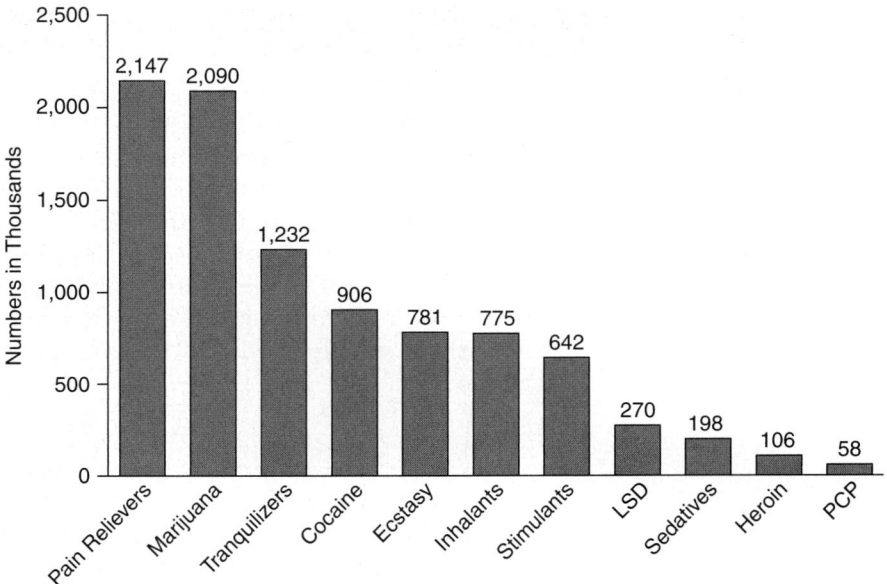

Figure 12.1
Entry Drugs of Abuse
Source: SAMSHA statistics for 2007/2008.

of breath, coughing, and other cardiovascular problems. Prolonged tobacco use can also cause heart failure, arteriosclerosis, emphysema, chronic bronchitis, heart disease, lung cancer, and other types of cancer. Smoking while pregnant can produce negative effects for newborn babies, including lower birth weights and a greater probability of stillbirth.[6]

Alcohol is a widely used drug in the U.S. and is generally socially accepted, particularly when used in small amounts. According to the Centers for Disease Control, 61% of the adult U.S. population drank alcohol on at least one occasion in 2006. Of these people, 20% had five or more drinks on at least one day during that year.[7]

It comes as no surprise, then, that millions of Americans abuse alcohol. It is one of the most common U.S. addictions. The term **alcoholism** refers to the compulsive drinking of beverages that contain the drug, alcohol. Some 17.6 million people abuse or are addicted to alcohol according to recent research.[8] Alcoholism can lead to liver damage (including cirrhosis or scarring of the liver). In 2006, for instance, there were 13,050 alcoholic liver disease deaths in the U.S. Alcoholism also contributes to heart disease (including congestive heart failure) and malnutrition, because alcohol may interfere with the digestion of food but has no nutritional value in itself. Alcoholics (i.e., those who abuse alcohol) may experience delirium tremens, usually called the DTs. These are alcohol (and barbiturate) withdrawal symptoms and may include disorientation, memory impairment, and hallucinations. Alcoholism can also lead to brain damage and may damage the fetus in pregnant women who abuse alcohol. In fact, excessive consumption during pregnancy can lead to a variety of neurological impairments, the most serious of which is **Fetal Alcohol Syndrome**, which is characterized by irreversible mental, physical, and/or behavioral problems.[9]

Did You Know?

Did you know that a "drink," by definition, is a 12-ounce bottle of beer, 5 ounces of wine, 1.5 ounces of 80 proof liquor, or 8 ounces of malt liquor? Moderate drinking is defined as up to one drink per day, on average, for females and up to two drinks a day, on average, for males.[10]

> **Social Work Stories: Drinking: A Love Story**
>
> Caroline Knapp talks about her alcoholism in *Drinking: A Love Story*:
>
> It happened this way. I fell in love and then, because the love was ruining everything I cared about, I had to fall out. This didn't happen easily, or simply, but if I had to pinpoint it, I'd say the relationship started to fall apart when I nearly killed my oldest friend's two daughters. I'd been visiting my friend Jennifer over Thanksgiving weekend a few years ago, and we'd all gone for a walk after dinner, she and her husband and the two daughters and me. The kids were five and nine years old, beautiful little blue-eyed girls with freckles and wide grins, and I'd been playing Rambunctious Friend of Mom's. I chased them around, and hoisted them into the air, and then, in a blur of supremely bad judgment, I dreamed up the Double Marsupial Hold. I put the older girl, Elizabeth, on my back, piggyback, and then I picked up the younger one, Julia, and held her facing me, so that her arms were around my neck and her legs around my waist. I was sandwiched between them, holding 130 pounds of kid. Then I started running across the street, shouting like a sportscaster: "It's the Double Marsupial Hold! They've accomplished the Double Marsupial Hold!" And then I lost my balance. I flew forward and came crashing down and I still believe it's a miracle that Julia's tiny, five-year-old skull wasn't the first thing to hit the pavement. Somehow, I kept her in my arms and allowed my right leg to take the fall, and I remember hitting the ground and feeling something like a minor explosion of my knee. The kids were okay, but I ended up in the emergency room with a gash on my knee so deep the nurses could see my kneecap. This is the truth: I was extremely drunk that night and I put those kids in serious jeopardy. Three months later I quit drinking, beginning the long, slow process of disentangling myself from a deeply passionate, profoundly complex, 20-year relationship with alcohol.[11]

So how can a social worker determine when a person moves from alcohol use to alcohol abuse to alcohol addiction? It can be difficult to assess. Sometimes the drinker comes to the realization that his or her alcohol use has become some kind of a personal "problem" after a scary experience. Consider the following story.

Marijuana—also called "pot," "grass," or "weed," is a third drug widely used in the U.S. In fact, it is the most commonly used illicit drug in the world. It is a natural drug that has been known for nearly 5,000 years. The psychoactive ingredient in marijuana that alters the user's mood is a chemical called THC. Flowers and leaves of the cannabis plant are dried and then smoked; the user's thinking and mood are affected. Marijuana's effects on the user vary according to dosage and conditions. These effects may be hallucinogenic, sedating, or stimulating. Marijuana's adverse effects include impaired short-term memory, slow learning, lung dysfunctions, decreased sperm count and sperm motility, interference with ovulation and prenatal development, impaired immune response, and, possibly, negative effects on the heart. Legalizing marijuana use in the U.S. is a hotly debated issue, especially given reports of positive medical benefits of marijuana use in reducing the negative effects of cancer treatment.[12]

CURRENT ISSUES IN SUBSTANCE USE AND ABUSE

In this section, we present several key issues currently being discussed by social workers involved in substance abuse–related policy and practice. These include preventing youth smoking, substance abuse on college campuses, binge drinking, the minimum drinking age, drinking and driving, marijuana legalization, the rise in "crystal meth" use, and the "War on Drugs."

Preventing Youth Smoking

About one in five U.S. adults smoke cigarettes (see Figure 12.2). This is despite the fact that an estimated 400,000 people a year die from smoking-related causes. Everyday almost 4,000 U.S. youth try their first cigarette.

Percentage of persons aged ≥18 years who were current smokers, * by sex and selected characteristics — National Health Interview Survey, United States, 2004

Characteristic	Men (n = 13,903) % (95% CI†)		Women (n = 17,423) % (95% CI)		Total (n = 31,326) % (95% CI)	
Race/Ethnicity§						
White, non-Hispanic	24.1	(±1.1)	20.4	(±0.9)	22.2	(±0.8)
Black, non-Hispanic	23.9	(±2.4)	17.2	(±2.1)	20.2	(±1.7)
Hispanic	18.9	(±1.9)	10.9	(±1.3)	15.0	(±1.2)
American Indian/ Alaska Native¶	37.3	(±12.1)	28.5	(±11.4)	33.4	(±8.3)
Asian**	17.8	(±4.4)	4.8	(±2.1)	11.3	(±2.4)
Education††						
0–12 yrs (no diploma)	31.5	(±2.4)	21.2	(±2.0)	26.2	(±1.6)
<8 yrs	23.5	(±3.2)	10.5	(±2.0)	16.7	(±2.0)
9–11 yrs	38.3	(±3.7)	29.8	(±3.1)	34.0	(±2.4)
12 yrs (no diploma)	29.9	(±6.5)	21.9	(±4.6)	25.5	(±3.8)
GED§§ diploma	42.1	(±5.9)	36.6	(±5.9)	39.6	(±4.4)
High school graduate	27.2	(±1.8)	21.1	(±1.4)	24.0	(±1.1)
Associate degree	24.6	(±3.1)	18.0	(±2.1)	20.9	(±1.9)
Some college	24.6	(±1.8)	20.3	(±1.3)	22.2	(±1.1)
Undergraduate degree	13.5	(±1.7)	10.1	(±1.4)	11.7	(±1.1)
Graduate degree	7.9	(±1.5)	8.1	(±1.5)	8.0	(±1.0)
Age group (yrs)						
18–24	25.6	(±2.9)	21.5	(±2.3)	23.6	(±2.0)
25–44	26.3	(±1.5)	21.4	(±1.2)	23.8	(±1.0)
45–64	25.0	(±1.6)	19.8	(±1.2)	22.4	(±1.0)
≥65	9.8	(±1.4)	8.1	(±1.0)	8.8	(±0.8)
Poverty status¶¶						
At or above	23.5	(±1.1)	17.7	(±0.9)	20.6	(±0.7)
Below	31.9	(±3.3)	27.1	(±2.2)	29.1	(±2.0)
Unknown	20.8	(±1.6)	17.4	(±1.4)	19.0	(±1.1)
Total	**23.4**	**(±0.9)**	**18.5**	**(±0.7)**	**20.9**	**(±0.6)**

* Persons who reported smoking ≥ 100 cigarettes during their lifetime and at the time of interview reported smoking every day or some days. Excludes 349 respondents whose smoking status was unknown.
† Confidence interval.
§ Excludes 332 respondents of unknown or multiple racial/ethnic category or whose racial/ethnic category was unknown.
¶ Wide variances in estimates reflect small sample sizes.
** Does not include native Hawaiians or other Pacific Islanders.
†† Among persons aged ≥ 25 years. Excludes 345 persons whose education level was unknown.
§§ General Educational Development.
¶¶ Based on family income reported by respondents and 2003 poverty thresholds published by the U.S. Census Bureau.

Figure 12.2
U.S. Adult Smokers
Source: NIH Health Interview Survey, US, 2004.

Of these youth, 1,000 will eventually become addicted—even though tobacco use is the single most significant avoidable cause of death in the nation. Cigarette smoking has been linked to several diseases, including lung cancer and emphysema.

Because of the danger of nicotine addiction, the U.S. has set a goal of reducing adult tobacco use to 12% of the adult population. To achieve this goal, the American Academy of Pediatrics (AAP) has recommended that the movie industry require an R rating for all new films that portray smoking to their audiences. An exception to this would be a film showing a real historical figure who smoked. The AAP also is advocating other measures to prevent smoking. For example, it has recommended that anti-smoking messages be shown before all films that portray smoking. Additionally, the AAP is asking the film industry to verify that no payments were made for tobacco product placements in U.S.-made movies and that the industry discontinue tobacco brand identifications in all films.

Hollywood has long been criticized for making cigarette smoking appear glamorous. Films from the 1930s, 1940s, and 1950s routinely showed leading men and women smoking cigarettes. Ironically, many of these glamorous Hollywood stars eventually died of smoking-related illnesses. Unfortunately, most of the viewing public never realized this fact. All they remember are the wonderful movies and glamorous stars and wanting to be like them. The resulting influence on American tobacco smoking habits was incalculable, particularly among American youth. With this in mind, the AAP's advocacy is considered a preventive measure in helping to reduce childhood smoking and eventual health complications in adulthood.[13]

> *Tobacco use remains the most serious substance problem in the United States, with 430,000 tobacco-related deaths annually. . . . It is the leading preventable cause of death and morbidity.*
> —C. Aaron McNeece and Diana M. DiNitto

Youth, Drugs, and Alcohol

Over 75,000 U.S. deaths per year are caused by excessive drinking. This makes excessive drinking the third leading preventable cause of death in the country, following smoking and the combination of poor diet and inactivity. Of these 75,000 deaths, 46% result from chronic conditions such as liver disease and 54% are caused by acute conditions such as motor vehicle accidents (see Figure 12.3). Of the 75,000 deaths, almost three-quarters (72%) are men. Another astounding statistic is that drunk drivers kill three times as many people on New Year's Eve as on other nights.[14]

Abuse of alcohol and other drugs continues to be a problem for young people in the U.S. College students (22.9%) exhibit higher rates of alcohol or drug addiction than does the general public (8.5%). Alcohol is the most widely abused substance on college campuses, although marijuana and prescription drug abuse has increased since the mid-1990s. For example, abuse of painkillers such as Vicodin, Percocet, and OxyContin rose between 1993 and 2005. During that same period, college students showed an increase in heavy marijuana use ("heavy" meaning smoking marijuana at least 20 days during the previous month). According to a 2005 study by the National Center on Addiction and Substance Abuse (CASA) at Columbia University, about two-thirds (68%) of college students reported drinking alcohol occasionally, while about 40% of students reported engaging in binge drinking during the previous two weeks. **Binge drinking** is defined as having five drinks (male students) or four drinks (female students) on one occasion. And, according to the 2005 study, 82% of college campus arrests involve alcohol. Furthermore, white students are more likely to use drugs and alcohol than minority students.[15]

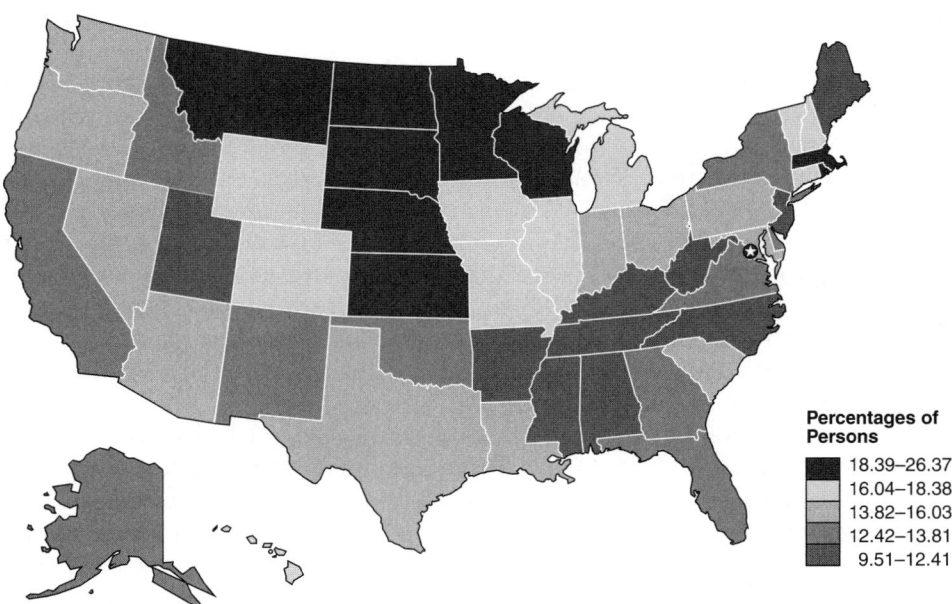

Figure 12.3
Young Driving under the Influence
Source: SAMHSA, 2004–2006 NSDUHs.

Critical Thinking Question

Social workers in policy practice define social problems and advocate for or against various policy options. What policy would you advocate regarding the minimum drinking age?

With respect to alcohol and young people, some policymakers believe that the minimum drinking age should be lowered nationwide from 21 to 18 years of age. Those who advocate for this proposal argue that 18-year-olds can serve in the military and are allowed to vote; therefore, they ought to be allowed to drink legally. In addition, having the minimum drinking age at 21 forces students to hide their drinking in dormitory rooms, fraternities, and sorority houses, where they are more likely to binge drink. Such drinking prevents students from learning to drink responsibly at home and in public. The argument for keeping the minimum drinking age at 21 relates to highway deaths. Many studies have shown that moving the drinking age from 18 to 21 years of age results in about a 16% drop in highway fatalities.[17]

Demonstrating Knowledge, Values, and Skills

Critical Thinking About Student Drinking

Some researchers recommend universities offer more required classes on Friday mornings to cut down on campus drinking. Why? The recommendation came about because there are about 1,700 drinking-related college student deaths each year. Experts believe a greater number of required classes on Friday mornings would reduce the amount of Thursday night drinking, thereby preventing college students from starting their weekend partying early. According to a 2007 study, the later in the morning that Friday classes started, the more some students drank the night before. Experts believe that less drinking on Thursday nights would result in less college drinking overall.

What do you think? Is this fair to students who do not abuse alcohol? Would such a policy really save student lives? If not . . . what do you think might help?[16]

The Debate over the Legalization of Marijuana

Marijuana legalization continues to be a controversial issue in the U.S. Legalization advocates have long claimed that marijuana use should be legalized for medicinal reasons. In 1996, California became the first state in the U.S. to legalize marijuana use in the treatment of seriously ill patients. Part of the reason for California's move is that marijuana helps in the treatment of glaucoma and generally alleviates nausea and pain related to treatment of certain illnesses, including cancer. Since 1996, many marijuana dispensaries have been established across California.

A growing public issue in California is that, while some of these dispensaries are selling marijuana for medicinal reasons and at no profit, many others are suspect. Critics claim that some dispensers are selling marijuana at a profit for a variety of reasons and not just for medicinal purposes. Purchasing marijuana at one of these sites only requires a doctor's note recommending its use for medicinal reasons, but not a prescription. Consequently, it is very easy to buy marijuana at these establishments. The Drug Enforcement Administration, as a result, has started to crack down on dispensers, calling them fronts for unregulated marijuana distribution; this is a problem because marijuana is a federally controlled substance. Furthermore, many of these questionable dispensaries place flyers near schools. Some give first-time buyers free grams of the substance; some give discounts to veterans. Others stay open until 2 a.m. Unfortunately, the federal Drug Enforcement Administration confuses the legitimate marijuana sellers (i.e., those who deal strictly in marijuana for medicinal reasons) with the more questionable sellers. Ultimately, severely sick people who could actually benefit from the marijuana use will be penalized.[18]

Crystal Methamphetamine Abuse: An Emerging National Epidemic?

Methamphetamine, better known as "crystal meth," has become a popular drug in the U.S. It is known by many names including ice, chalk, crack, glass, and G. Crystal meth use started on the West Coast and has spread throughout the country. The latest research indicates that percentages of persons 12 years and older illicitly using the drug were highest in Nevada (2.2 percent), followed by Montana (1.5%), Wyoming (1.5%), Arizona (1.3%), and New Mexico (1.3%). The drug appears to be popular with many groups, including American Indians stricken by poverty and street youth looking for a cheap high, as well as high-achieving college students trying to stay awake while studying for exams. It costs relatively little to purchase and offers a powerful high to those who use it. It can be snorted or injected, and it is often smoked. Methamphetamine is a highly seductive drug, but it is also one of the most damaging drugs. In particular, methamphetamine use injures the individual's brain cells. The damage makes the abuser more dependent on the drug, abusers finding it increasingly harder to get pleasure from anything else in life other than the drug. Over time, the drug user becomes dependent on larger and larger quantities of the drug to produce the dopamine high. Once addicted, the methamphetamine drug user may risk anything to obtain the high—including his or her life.

Social workers are educating themselves about crystal meth use for several reasons. As stated, it is very easy to obtain and it is inexpensive, which makes young people very susceptible to getting addicted to it. Also, because it is often injected, crystal meth use can contribute to the spread of HIV and AIDS. With Mexico becoming a new source of this very addictive and lethal drug, crystal meth will continue to be a concern in the foreseeable future for social workers and others in the substance abuse field.[19]

Status of the Federal "War on Drugs"

Given ongoing problems in the U.S. with marijuana and crystal meth, among other illicit drugs, the success of the 30-year "War on Drugs" is debatable. This war has focused on cutting off the supply of drugs to U.S. citizens from areas such as Latin America. It has also focused on detention, arrest, and incarceration. Emphasis on incarceration, in contrast to treatment, has created a problem in terms of U.S. prison overcrowding and a disproportionate incarceration of black males. As of June 2005, over 2.1 million Americans were serving time in U.S prisons and jails. About a quarter of these were black men between the ages of 20 and 39. Black males are seven times as likely to be incarcerated as are white males in the U.S. As a result of high rates of incarceration, due in part to drug arrests, prison crowding has overwhelmed the prison healthcare system. These incarcerated individuals suffer from afflictions such as mental illness, including schizophrenia, post-traumatic stress disorder, anxiety disorders, and depression. Chronic and infectious diseases, such as tuberculosis, hepatitis, and HIV, are also found among U.S. prison populations. Yet the health care these prisoners receive is suspect at best.

What is more, the War on Drugs is expensive. The cost of caring for one imprisoned individual is much greater than the typical cost of providing treatment. And when a person who has been incarcerated is finally released back into the community, a number of problems soon present themselves. The person must deal with unemployment, inadequate health care, limited housing, and the ongoing stigma of having a criminal record. Furthermore, while in prison, the family of the incarcerated individual suffers as well. Children go without consistent parenting, partners and spouses go without income, and the entire family lives with the stigma of having a family member in prison. Depending on the state in which the convict lives, upon release the individual may have difficulty accessing welfare benefits, public housing, or higher education loans. For these reasons, community reintegration is difficult and increases the probability of recidivism by the individual. As a result, the War on Drugs, with its emphasis on incarceration over treatment, has produced questionable outcomes.

Consequently, many social workers are advocating for a return to an emphasis on drug treatment rather than incarceration. Advocates are calling for more treatment services, more comprehensive case management, increased use of drug courts, better mental health care, traditional vocational training and literacy programs, and greater affordable housing access. A comprehensive treatment approach such as this might also include drug education and drug prevention efforts in the schools. And it should also emphasize evidence-based intervention strategies rather than a strategy based on moral or political concerns (see Figure 12.4).[20]

Issue	Substance Use and Abuse	Domestic Violence	Violence	Mental Health
Statistics	• **8.2%** of full-time workforce use an illegal drug • **9.4 million** illicit drug uses • **10.1 million** heavy alcohol uses	• **31%** of women are physically or sexually abused • More than **1 million** report violent assault	• Women are the victims in **80%** of workplace violence • **1.8 million** workdays are lost per year as a result of non-fatal acts of violence • **75%** of all workplace violence is committed by unarmed offenders • **80%** homicides are committed with firearms	• **1 in 5** adults will experience a diagnosable mental illness in any given year • **15%** of those also will experience a co-occurring substance use disorder • prevalence of mental illness and/or substance abuse in any given year approaches **25%**

Symptoms/ Signs	• Absenteeism
	• Reduced productivity
	• Reduced trustworthiness
	• Job instability
		• Job performance decreases
		• Absenteeism/lateness
		• Inability to focus
		• Poor self-esteem
		• Low productivity
		• Low morale
			• Risk factors include:
			  Mental illness
			  Substance abuse
				• Stress (**5.3%**)
				• Anxiety (**18.1%**)
				• Obsessive compulsive disorder (OCD)
				• Panic attacks
				• Posttraumatic stress disorder (PTSD)
				• Social phobia

Solutions	• Education about the signs of substance use	• Training and awareness programs • Taking measures to limit an abuser's contact with the employee and access to the workplace • Designate someone to keep in close contact with the abuse victim	• Develop and implement workplace violence policies • Report incidents and threats of workplace violence in accordance with policy	• Insurance programs that adequately cover mental health • Information and education about mental health issues available • Provide assessment and links to appropriate treatment resources

Figure 12.4
Substance Use Symptoms and Solutions
Source: SAMHSA

MODELS OF ADDICTION

There are several theoretical models that offer explanations for addiction and, therefore, help to guide social work interventions in the field.[21] Services for individuals with alcohol and other drug problems vary depending upon the model to which the service provider adheres. Therefore, the theoretical rationale social workers use to consider alcohol and drug addiction guides the mutual development of goals and strategies for client intervention.

The Biopsychosocial Model of Addiction

The theoretical model most consistent with the social work "person-in-environment" perspective is the **biopsychosocial model of addiction**. This model, by definition, explains alcohol and other drug addiction as a result of the interaction of multiple factors in the life of the individual addict. These include biological, psychological, and social factors. As such, this model incorporates many aspects of other addiction models, but it does so in a discretionary manner, depending upon the unique characteristics of each addict. Social workers who adhere to this model do a careful assessment before deciding what approach to take in treatment. No options are closed. No perspective is considered superior to others. Such an assessment might include several hypotheses to explain the addictive behavior. A variety of treatment methods and interventions might be used rather than just one approach. In this way, the full range of the social worker's knowledge and skills are used to help the individual suffering from alcohol or other drug addiction.[22]

As stated, the biopsychosocial model of addiction uses other models of addiction popular in the substance abuse treatment community. These include sociocultural models, psychological models, and the disease model. In order to apply the biopsychosocial model of addiction competently in practice, social workers must have a strong knowledge foundation in these other treatment models from which to develop intervention strategies.

Sociocultural Models of Addiction

Sociocultural models are theoretical models that explain individual addiction to alcohol and other drugs as caused by social and cultural factors. Social workers in the substance abuse field consider elements of this model in helping clients who abuse alcohol in particular. While doing so, social workers are careful not to stereotype all members of a specific group or culture.

Fisher and Harrison, in their 2009 book *Substance Abuse: Information for School Counselors, Social Workers, Therapists, and Counselors*, point to the low rates of alcoholism among certain groups, such as the Chinese and Jewish populations.[23] According to Fisher and Harrison, families in the Chinese and Jewish cultures allow the use of alcohol but strongly disapprove of excessive alcohol use because it can lead to inappropriate behavior. In these cultures, young people are allowed to use alcohol in ceremonial and other social situations, but are monitored for excessive use.

The sociocultural model of addiction does not focus just on ethnic groups. It also attributes alcoholism to other social groups such as the family.[24] In fact, research has shown that, in general, children of alcoholic parents are more likely to become alcoholics. Of course, this does not mean that because you have a

> **Research Informed Practice**
>
> We have noted the danger in stereotyping certain cultural groups regarding alcohol or other drug abuse. Go to the Internet site of the U.S. Department of Health and Human Services, Substance Abuse and Mental Health Services Administration, Office of Applied Studies. Review the various reports and information, looking for substance abuse differences among diverse racial/ethnic groups.
>
> Are there other socioeconomic variables that appear to be important considerations in any variation across racial/ethnic groups?

parent who suffers from alcoholism, you will necessarily become an alcoholic. One study found that 30% of children with alcoholic parents eventually developed alcoholism themselves. This is compared with 5% of children from parents who used alcohol moderately and 10% of children with parents who abstained altogether from using alcohol.[25]

Psychological Models of Addiction

Social workers also consider **psychological models of addiction** that offer explanations for alcohol and drug addiction. Professionals who adhere to this model believe people become addicted to alcohol or other drugs as a way to cope with the pain of a primary psychological problem. Perhaps the individual was molested as a child or suffers from depression currently. Maybe the person has been unemployed a long time and cannot find a decent job. Maybe the person is a domestic violence victim and sees no way out of an abusive marriage. Some people who have experienced such difficulties turn to alcohol or other drugs in an effort to relieve their pain (this is sometimes called "self-medication"). To illustrate, a 2007 national survey showed that the rate of illicit drug use among adults aged 18 and over was 18.3% for those who were unemployed and only 8.4% for those who were employed full-time.[26]

Other proponents of psychological explanations for alcohol and drug addiction maintain that there is an "addictive personality" at the root of the problem. Individuals addicted to one drug are more likely to become addicted to other drugs as well. As evidence, the aforementioned 2007 national survey found that, of those youth ages 12–17 who were heavy drinkers, nearly two-thirds (60.1%) were also currently using illicit drugs. In contrast, the rate of illicit drug use among nondrinkers in the study was just 5%. Also, the study showed that the frequency of illicit drug use was nine times higher for youth who also smoked. Furthermore, proponents of the addictive personality explanation point out that many people addicted to alcohol or other drugs also demonstrate other addictive behaviors. These addictive behaviors may involve gambling, sex, work, or food. Sometimes individuals believed to have an addictive personality will recover from their drug addiction only to evidence addictive behavior toward some combination of these other activities.[27]

"Social learning theory," which you read about in Chapter 4, is another psychological theory that has been used to explain alcohol and drug addiction. In this perspective, individuals addicted to alcohol or other drugs learned the addictive behavior from significant others, especially role models. These negative role models could be parents, but might also be friends, athletes, rock stars, or movie stars. The behavior is viewed as glamorous, macho, or sexy. In any case, the addiction is considered a bad habit that has been learned and can be unlearned. A good illustration of this theory is youth smoking. We have already described the AAP concern with Hollywood films that portray glamorous movie stars smoking in their various roles and the negative influence this may have on youth. Again, the addictive behavior is seen as a bad habit—one that was learned (in this case, by watching and emulating film stars) and can be unlearned.[28]

The Disease Model

One of the most commonly accepted explanations for alcohol and other drug addiction in America today is the disease model. This model is an integral component of the Alcoholics Anonymous and Narcotics Anonymous 12-step programs, which are part of many social workers' treatment plans for their clients and will be discussed in further detail in the following section. In contrast to other models, the **disease model** explains alcohol and drug addiction as a primary illness rather than the result of some other primary condition. Hence, the addictive behavior is not a symptom of some other personal problem, but a disease in itself. In fact, since 1956, the American Medical Association (AMA) has viewed alcoholism as a treatable illness.

Social workers guided by the disease model in their interventions with clients see the addiction progressing through several stages. In the early stage, the social worker sees the individual becoming increasingly tolerant to alcohol, perhaps having blackouts, starting to hide or gulp drinks, and often feeling guilty about his or her behavior. The middle stage of the disease is characterized by the individual losing control over her/his behavior. This phase also may include personality changes, a preoccupation with having a supply of alcohol on hand, and the loss of employment and friends. In the final stage, the individual starts to violate societal ethical standards, or to have tremors and hallucinations. According to the disease model, these stages are not reversible; the addiction is considered chronic and incurable, and must be coped with on a daily basis.[29] Just how social workers in the substance abuse field help clients to cope with alcoholism and other drug addictions is explained in further detail in the following section.

SUBSTANCE ABUSE INTERVENTION

Specific treatment approaches depend on the model of addiction underlying the treatment program. As stated in previous sections, social workers generally prefer the biopyschosocial model of addiction, because it considers several biopyschosocial theories to guide the choice of treatment interventions. This philosophy is reflected in treatment programs today, which are increasingly eclectic in their approaches rather than adhering strictly to one treatment approach. One component of many treatment programs is self-help groups such as the popular Alcoholics Anonymous and Narcotics Anonymous groups.

Self-Help: Twelve-Step Support Groups

Twelve-step support groups have become popular in the substance abuse field. This is, in fact, unique. No other mental health area uses support groups established and run by nonprofessionals as much as the substance abuse field. Alcoholics Anonymous (AA) is the most common version of the 12-step group and the oldest, dating back to 1935. Other popular 12-step groups include

Critical Thinking Question

Social workers utilize various theoretical models. If you were a social worker in the substance abuse field, where might you employ sociocultural, psychological, and disease models to help a family dealing with substance abuse?

For most normal folks, drinking means conviviality, companionship and colorful imagination. But not so with us in those last days of heavy drinking.

—Alcoholics Anonymous

Narcotics Anonymous (NA) for drug users and Al-Anon and Alateen for family members of substance abusers, CODA meetings for codependent people, and ACOA meetings for adult children of alcoholics. Twelve-step groups in other areas have followed on the success of AA and NA. Some of the more common ones include Overeaters Anonymous, Emotions Anonymous, Gamblers Anonymous, Spenders Anonymous, and Sex Addicts Anonymous. As discussed earlier, AA and NA support groups are often required or strongly encouraged as part of a formal treatment plan for an individual.

Did You Know?

Did you know that June 10, 1935, is considered the birthday of Alcoholics Anonymous? This is the date that Bob Smith, a surgeon, and Bob Wilson, a stockbroker, first talked to one another about their respective alcoholism problems. Both eventually achieved sobriety with the mutual support of one another. Many of the basic principles and traditions of AA groups are based on a book that Bill Wilson read—a book by William James called *The Variety of Religious Experiences*.[30]

Alcoholics Anonymous groups, as stated, are not treatment programs run by professionals. They are support groups run by nonprofessionals. A desire to stop drinking is the only requirement for participating in these groups. They are a fellowship of men and women who want to achieve sobriety and to remain sober. Because there is a strong spiritual component to the meetings, the gathering is considered a fellowship of people who want to share their common experiences and strengths regarding alcoholism. There are no fees to become a member. However, all groups are self-supporting through participant contributions. AA groups do not align themselves with any institutions or organizations, including any specific religious denominations or sects.

There are two types of AA meetings: closed meetings and open meetings. Closed meetings focus on one of the 12 steps, whereas open meetings are meetings in which speakers voluntarily share their stories about drinking and recovery. Also, there may be discussion meetings based on selected topics related to drinking and recovery.

The 12 steps of AA meetings are a set of principles by which participants achieve sobriety. In the first step, a person admits his or her powerlessness over alcohol. The remaining 12 steps are all spiritual in nature and are focused on self-improvement. They include a mention of a "Higher Power" as understood by the individual as well as the themes of surrender, forgiveness, humility, personal limitations, and service to others. In so doing, the 12 steps offer participants an alternative way of life. AA participants use a book called *Alcoholics Anonymous* that includes the 12 steps as well as helpful slogans and a set of traditions for running meetings . Some of the more well-known slogans include "one day at a time" and "live and let live."

AA meetings do not allow participants to comment on what other participants in the group have stated. This is the "no crosstalk" rule. This prevents people from judging others in the group. It also prevents nonprofessionals from playing the therapist role within the group. Meetings typically open with participants admitting their problem with alcoholism and reciting the Serenity Prayer.[31]

> "God grant me the serenity to accept the things I cannot change, the courage to change the things I can, and the wisdom to know the difference."[32]

Meetings often end by passing around a basket meant for contributions, similar to Christian church ceremonies. The meeting chair may document attendance for those who are court-ordered to attend the meeting. Sobriety milestones—whether they are 30 days, 90 days, nine months, or nine years—are often recognized. And the Lord's Prayer is often recited as part of the meeting closing. Although AA does not adhere to any specific denomination, meetings feature a Christian undertone.

Are 12-step groups effective? Research has shown that 12-step self-help groups do, in fact, reduce substance abuse and improve psychosocial functioning for those who adhere to the 12 steps. Research also shows that AA is most effective when combined with professional treatment, the topic of the next section.[33]

Professional Treatment Programs and Services

Social workers in the substance abuse field are typically employed in professional treatment programs and services. Individuals in drug and alcohol treatment typically have a treatment plan that includes a description of the client's addiction problem, a long-term goal in relation to this problem, short-term objectives, and specific daily and weekly treatment activities. In this section, we will describe several of the most common programs, services, and activities, including the Minnesota Model approach, twelve-step facilitation, cognitive behavioral therapy, pharmacological procedures, and various forms of counseling.

One of the most widely used treatment programs is the **Minnesota model** developed in the 1940s and '50s.[34] Not to be confused with the "models of addiction" presented earlier, this is a treatment program that employs a comprehensive multidisciplinary approach guided by the disease model of addiction and based on the principles of Alcoholics Anonymous and Narcotics Anonymous. As such, it promotes recovery from alcohol and other drug addiction but it does not promise a cure. It incorporates group therapy, counseling, and lectures to promote abstinence. In this model, the term "chemical dependency" is preferred over "addiction" or "alcoholism." In any case, this treatment approach views chemical dependency as a psychological, social, physical, and spiritual disease. While in recovery, individuals are encouraged to view the process as an ongoing lifelong commitment to growth, insight, and commitment. In addition, as part of the process, individuals are encouraged to explore their spirituality consistent with AA and NA principles.

Other treatment approaches include twelve-step facilitation, cognitive behavioral therapy, motivational enhancement therapy, and the use of pharmacological procedures.[35] The twelve-step facilitation (TSF) approach is premised on Alcoholics Anonymous principles and is similar to the Minnesota Model. In fact, it encourages participation in Alcoholic Anonymous 12-step groups as part of the therapy program. The program is brief, typically lasting 12–15 sessions. In these sessions, the social worker or other helping professional (e.g., marriage and family counselor or clinical psychologist) acts as a facilitator of change by helping the client to accept the need for abstinence from alcohol or other drugs and to participate regularly in 12-step groups.

Cognitive behavioral therapy (CBT), which was discussed in detail in Chapter 9, is based on social learning theory, as previously described. This type of therapy, which is used with cocaine addicts, for example, is usually provided by social workers or related professionals on an individual basis, but can be used in groups as well. This brief treatment, usually delivered in 12–16 sessions over 12 weeks, promotes relapse prevention by teaching specific skills and techniques to the individual to prevent relapse. Social workers assist the individual in identifying emotions and avoiding situations that lead to drug use, while at the same time drawing upon client strengths and resources that promote positive coping behaviors and change regarding the addiction.[36]

Pharmacological procedures use medications to treat the addiction. For instance, individuals in detoxification programs are frequently given medications, such as certain medications used as part of opioid detoxification treatment. Detoxification procedures may occur in inpatient hospital settings or in outpatient programs. In any case, they require careful medical supervision. Usually, medications are combined with other treatment methods when addressing alcohol and other drug addiction.

Social workers in the substance abuse field also participate in several types of counseling activities with clients. As described earlier, treatment plans for individuals in drop-in drug and alcohol treatment typically include specific daily and weekly treatment activities. These treatment activities may include individual, group, and family counseling. Often, group counseling is the primary component of client treatment, whether in inpatient or outpatient treatment programs. Group counseling may incorporate many different elements, including education, confrontation, and information sharing regarding coping methods, problem solving, or assertiveness training. The focus for both individual and group counseling tends to be the present and future rather than the past.

Family counseling, as stated, is also part of some treatment programs today.[37] Alcoholism and drug addiction can cause serious marital and other family problems, ultimately leading to divorce and family breakup. Hence, the involvement of the entire family system is considered prudent and effective treatment. In this case, social workers providing family counseling tend to emphasize education of the family regarding the disease and the family's role in the disease and recovery process. Family behavioral patterns can contribute to or mitigate excessive drinking and drug use. Of course, when clients have family members or friends who are also addicted, they may have to change their relationships in order to save themselves. Social workers providing individual, group, and family counseling help clients to clarify these issues, explore options, and reach decisions on the best courses of action. In so doing, an individual client may also take part in vocational educational planning, financial planning, or nutrition educational programs as a way to break the lifestyle patterns in which they are currently trapped.

Moreover, vocational, educational, and financial services may also be a part of an aftercare plan for the individual. **Aftercare** is the stage of intervention that follows formal addiction treatment. Aftercare may include many of the same services and supports an individual took part in during formal treatment. For this reason, aftercare is sometimes referred to as "continuing care." Individual and family counseling may be part of aftercare; 12-step support groups are typically included; and vocational, financial, and nutritional education may be incorporated. Sometimes the individual is referred to a social worker or other mental health counselor during the aftercare program to provide support during the process.[38] Where does all this activity take place? In the next section, we described the various facilities in which substance abuse treatment is delivered.

Treatment Facilities

In America, over a million people a day receive treatment for alcohol or other drug addiction in a variety of facilities.[39] The vast majority of treatment takes place in outpatient treatment facilities. Of these facilities, about 60% are private nonprofit agencies, 26% are for-profit agencies, and state and local governments provide about 11% of services. Over half of these services are a part of managed care networks.

As you know, treatment programs typically have three stages: formal treatment, aftercare, and ongoing recovery. Formal treatment may take place in a variety of settings, including therapeutic communities, inpatient and residential facilities, hospitals, and freestanding treatment centers such as mental health centers.

"Therapeutic communities" are residential programs typically used to treat drug addiction. They feature a highly structured daily routine and normally use a system of rewards and punishments for client behavior. Groups are used to confront the addicts when they regress and to allow the addicts to confess their mistakes. These facilities also promote self-reflection, hence the long-term nature and isolation of most therapeutic communities. Therapeutic communities, however, are typically the treatment of last resort for alcohol and drug addicts.

Inpatient and residential treatment programs are usually found in hospitals. These programs offer supervised detoxification. Often, detoxification includes medication. If the program is offered in a non-hospital setting, then medication is not typically used, relying instead on more socially based detoxification methods. Residential and inpatient treatment usually lasts 28 days and features 24-hour supervision, highly structured daily schedules, and total immersion in treatment, without the day-to-day stresses of everyday life. Such programs can be costly, and client regression after leaving treatment programs is often a problem.

Partial hospitalization and day treatment programs take place in hospitals or other freestanding treatment facilities. In contrast to inpatient or residential treatment, the client spends the day in a treatment facility and nights at home. This offers the chance for the addict to apply skills and coping mechanisms learned in the day treatment program within the home environment. It also helps the client to identify barriers to abstinence in their home and family life.

At the same time, spending evenings and nights at home presents an opportunity for the individual to re-abuse alcohol or other drugs. This regression is more likely to occur if family or friends are using or abusing alcohol or other drugs. Therefore, the opportunities for progress in applying new skills and knowledge in the home environment may, in fact, produce a setback for the addict.

Outpatient and intensive outpatient programs are freestanding, community-based treatment programs. Many are found in mental health centers. Intensive outpatient programs are normally held three to four evenings per week. Sessions usually last two to four hours. In contrast, regular outpatient treatment programs meet less frequently, usually one or two evenings a week for one to two hours per session. In these programs, clients get support while continuing to go to school or work during the day. Consequently, the need to work or attend school does not prevent the individual from obtaining services that are accessible in the community.

Needle Exchange Programs

Needle exchange programs have been developed across the U.S. to reduce the incidence of HIV and hepatitis. Advocates claim that needle exchange programs reduce disease spread without increasing drug use. More specifically, needle exchange programs reduce these blood-borne diseases by allowing people who continue to inject themselves with drugs to use new, sterile syringes each time. As of 2007, there were close to 200 needle exchange programs in operation

---

When you're home by yourself you're behind enemy lines.
—Anonymous

Critical Thinking Question
Social workers in the substance abuse field practice in multiple treatment settings with various intervention techniques. Which type of intervention program would you find most rewarding and why?

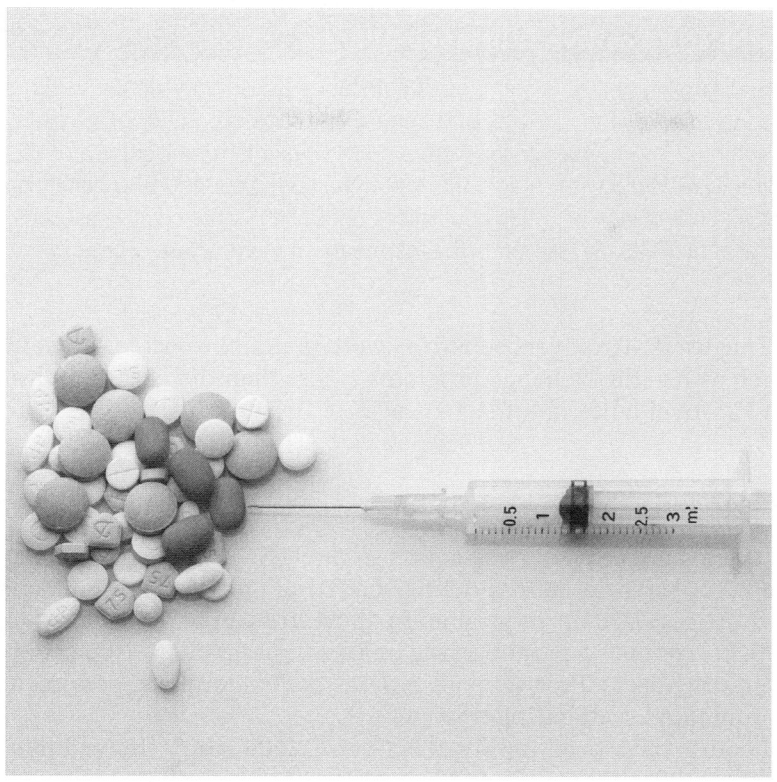

across the U.S. In fact, many programs now operate in multiple locations, including mobile van routes. These services deliver risk-reduction supplies, such as new syringes, directly to agreed-upon locations of drug users, including their residences. Many needle exchange programs allow individuals to exchange needles on behalf of other persons. These are called secondary exchanges.

The programs are typically funded with a combination of public and private funds. However, close to 75% of total funding comes from state and local governments. There is a federal law that prohibits using federal funding to support needle exchange programs. As funding has increased over the years, exchange programs have been able to offer a more comprehensive array of services to intravenous drug users and to the communities in which they live. Not only do these programs provide prevention supplies, such as alcohol pads, bleach, and clean syringes, many also provide on-site medical screenings, referrals, and education. The medical screenings and related services include HIV and hepatitis testing and counseling, hepatitis vaccinations, sexually transmitted disease (STD) screenings, and tuberculosis screenings. Referrals are also part of this comprehensive programming, including referrals to substance abuse treatment. Educational services focus on issues such as HIV/AIDS prevention, hepatitis A, B, and C prevention, STD prevention, safe injection practices, and male and female condom use.

By helping to prevent the spread of the blood-borne diseases, this comprehensive, community-based approach helps not only the intravenous drug users, but also the communities in which they live. As public support for new exchange programs has increased over the years, the programs have begun to offer services such as testing, vaccinations, and general medical care to the communities in which they are located. Thus, the whole community benefits—not

> **Research Informed Practice with HIV-Positive Substance Abusers**
>
> In 2008, social worker Starr A. Wood published the results of her study of healthcare services for HIV-positive substance abusers in rural settings. She found that rural consumers in North Carolina were faced with several barriers to obtaining services, including lack of transportation, long distances to medical facilities, a shortage of substance abuse and mental health services, and community stigma.
>
> If you were a social worker in rural North Carolina, how might this research inform your efforts to better serve this population? Specifically, what creative services could you help organize to overcome these service barriers?[41]

just the drug users. Taxpayers benefit as well, in that the cost for preventive programs such as needle exchange programs is less than the cost of treating a person with HIV over a lifetime.[40]

Drug Courts

In 1996, there were only 12 drug courts in the U.S. Today, there are 2,016 drug courts in 1,100 counties across the nation. **Drug Courts** combine law enforcement and drug treatment programs. In short, they give offenders a choice of going to prison or taking part in a drug treatment program. Most participants are nonviolent drug users. Program participants have rigorous supervision and are held accountable for attending treatment.

Drug courts have been highly effective. A 2005 study showed that 70% of drug court participants complete the program, and on average, only 17% reoffend. This contrasts with drug offenders who serve prison sentences in place of treatment. These offenders reoffend, on average, at a rate of 66%. Not only is the mandated treatment more effective at reducing recidivism, it is also less costly. The same study showed that the average annual cost for a person in court-mandated treatment is $3,500. This compares to an average annual cost of imprisonment ranging from $13,000 to $44,000 per person.

Given this treatment effectiveness and cost-efficiency, drug courts and mandated treatment are expected to grow in the future. About 120,000 people currently are involved with drug courts yearly, but there are many more who could benefit from treatment. As of 2007, the state of Missouri had 108 drug courts. New York had 62 drug courts—one in each county. The state of Florida has 109 drug courts with plans for more.

Currently, drug courts are funded by federal and state government as well as by private philanthropy. With drug courts, the drug abuser has a choice between incarceration and treatment. Thousands are choosing treatment, with great results—and at a reduced cost to taxpayers. So what started as an alternative project in 1989 in Miami to address an increase in the crack cocaine problem is now being used in many states across the U.S.[42]

Future Challenges in Drug Treatment: Dual Diagnosis

Treatment programs based on 12-step group participation, needle exchange programs, and drug courts represent positive developments for those afflicted by alcohol and other drug addictions. They are also helpful resources for social workers considering or entering the drug abuse treatment field. A challenge for social workers entering the field involves **dual diagnosis** and the treatment of coexisting disorders. Increasingly, it is found that individuals

> **Social Work Stories: Interview with Licensed Drug and Alcohol Counselor**
>
> Brian Miller is a licensed certified social worker (LICSW) in the state of New Hampshire. He is also a licensed alcohol and drug counselor (LADC) in the state. His work experience includes private practice, consulting, and teaching. He sees several issues facing social work in relation to substance abuse treatment and prevention.
>
> Brian states that "recent studies have focused on the lack of sufficient education in substance abuse issues in social work graduate schools, as well as a lack of professional training in the field to prepare social workers to address substance abuse assessment, intervention, and treatment of their clients. This is in spite of a high prevalence of co-occurring disorders in the people we treat."
>
> Brian also feels there is a shortage of social workers in the field of substance abuse treatment. "As a group, social workers seem to self-select out of the substance abuse arena, for many reasons, including: low pay, absence of 'social worker' in job title, competition for positions from other disciplines, lack of social work internships in the substance abuse field, and state requirements for licensing."
>
> Part of this shortage, Brian feels, may also be due to a philosophical chasm. "Social workers' value of client self-determination often seems to be confused when discussing interventions as a goal to treatment. This discussion just came up in my Addictions class [which Brian teaches at the University of New Hampshire], and there was heated debate regarding the 'mandating' or 'coercing' of clients to alcohol and drug treatment."
>
> According to Brian, all of these concerns raise the need for further attention to: (1) including substance abuse (and coexisting disorders) education in social work undergraduate and graduate programs; (2) developing social work internships in substance abuse settings; and (3) revisiting social work values as they relate to working with mandated client populations.[44]

with drug addictions also have other mental disorders. Sometimes these people are characterized as having "coexisting disorders," "co-occurring disorders," or "comorbidity." As a result, they require a **Dual Diagnosis**, which, by definition, is an identification of coexisting disorders. Diagnosis is made difficult for social workers and other professionals due to the overlapping symptoms of many disorders. To illustrate, studies have shown that about one-third of individuals with psychiatric disorders also have a history of chemical abuse. Further, about half of drug and alcohol abusers exhibit symptoms associated with other mental disorders. For instance, cocaine addiction is often associated with major depression. Alcohol and panic disorders often occur together in the same individual. What is more, alcoholics often exhibit conduct disorders or antisocial personalities. In contrast, females with drinking problems often have anxiety or other affective disorders. Teenagers with substance abuse issues often have attention deficit or hyperactivity disorders.

These dual diagnoses complicate treatment plan development for social workers and other helping professionals. As just discussed, clients with coexisting disorders are often difficult to diagnose accurately. Yet accurately diagnosing one disorder, but not the other, may undermine treatment. A social worker must assess both disorders accurately in order to help an individual. And even if both disorders are identified, the professional may be trained to treat one disorder but not the other. In fact, programs sometime offer treatment for one or the other disorder, but not both. And to further complicate matters, drug treatment programs historically have viewed other mental disorders associated with drug addiction as secondary to the primary addiction problem. For these reasons, programs at times will not accept patients with dual diagnoses, considering them inappropriate for treatment. To better prepare themselves, social workers who wish to work in drug treatment programs will want to gain additional education regarding other mental disorders associated with drug addiction.[43]

Critical Thinking Question

Social workers typically advocate for policies and programs aimed at preventing substance abuse, but not everyone feels our society can afford to pay for prevention. What arguments would you make to justify funding prevention programs?

Substance Abuse Prevention

Social workers and other health professionals work to prevent people from developing serious alcohol or other drug addictions. These prevention efforts are often targeted to adolescents and/or to the parents of adolescents. Prevention programs can take place in various settings, including the family, schools, or the entire community. Social workers involved in prevention efforts perform a variety of roles. They may serve as educators, drug counselors, group facilitators, case managers, community organizers, or as policy analysts and advocates.[45]

Social workers who address substance abuse prevention focus on the so-called **gateway drugs**—drugs that may eventually lead to more serious and dangerous drug experimentation. Tobacco, alcohol, prescription medications, and marijuana are gateway drugs. Adolescents who use and abuse gateway drugs often move on to more lethal drugs such as cocaine, crack, heroin, barbiturates, tranquilizers, or LSD. Furthermore, adolescent drug and alcohol abuse can result in drinking and driving, unprotected sex, interpersonal violence, property destruction, school failure, lifestyle changes (e.g., drug dealing and related criminal activity), and poor family relationships.[46]

Other social and economic costs of drug abuse include morbidity costs and mortality costs. **Morbidity costs** refer to the value of reduced or lost work productivity that results from drug abuse, while **mortality costs** refer to the projected future losses to society in worker productivity caused by premature deaths.[47]

For these reasons, social workers and other health professionals stress the importance of prevention programs. Our current prevention programming in the U.S. has experienced mixed results. These programs have suffered from inadequate funds that prevent thorough implementation of programs as designed. Program evaluation efforts have been limited by several issues, including lack of uniform agreement on the definition of substance abuse or even the definition of adolescence. In addition, evaluative survey research has been problematic, given its reliance on self-reporting by teenagers and the difficulty of measuring cultural differences among respondents. Further, the surveys tend to underrepresent certain adolescent groups, such as school dropouts and GLBTQ adolescents. These surveys also tend to underrepresent adolescents living in isolated regions of the U.S., such as Appalachia or Indian reservations.

Based on the best available data, however, certain prevention programs have shown better results than others. Certain well-known prevention programs, including DARE and Just Say No have received mixed results. DARE, for example, uses community police officers in the schools to promote knowledge, attitudes, and skills among adolescents to prevent drug and alcohol experimentation. However, DARE has been criticized for not targeting all significant causal factors of adolescent alcohol and drug use.

Other programs that incorporate resistance and broader social skills training have shown greater promise in preventing substance abuse. "Resistance skills training" involves behavioral rehearsal and role-playing, extended practice homework, and the utilization of older peer leaders. "Social skills training" consists of classroom discussion as well as cognitive behavioral skills training. Cognitive behavioral skills training, in turn, involves instruction, demonstrations, practice, feedback, and reinforcement for adolescents in ways that encourage them to avoid alcohol and other drugs.[48]

Examples of successful prevention programs include Project Star, the Life Skills Training Program, the Adolescent Alcohol Prevention Trial, Strengthening Families Program, and Reconnecting Youth. Project Star uses school-based programs, mass media, parent involvement, community organization, and health policy changes to target the entire community population. The Life Skills

> **Research Informed Practice: Substance Abuse at Your College**
>
> Is substance abuse a problem at your college or university? If so, what does your school do to address the problem? Are these interventions effective? What can be changed? Are alcohol and other drug abuse taken seriously by your school? What are your school's policies regarding substance abuse? Are these policies strictly enforced? Research the answers to these questions as they relate to you and your institution by polling 25 students not taking this course with you. Bring your findings to class to compare with those of other students. What conclusions can the class draw about your school's stance on substance abuse?

Training Program also focuses on a broad population, but is carried out primarily in the classroom. It teaches personal and social skills along with drug resistance skills. The Adolescent Alcohol Prevention Trial also focuses on a broad population and is set in the classroom. This intervention uses resistance skills training and normative education to counteract the negative influences of social pressures and role modeling. The Strengthening Families program is more selective in that it focuses on family work involving substance-abusing parents. Children in the Strengthening Families program are considered at risk because of their parents' active substance abuse. The program promotes parenting and other family skills on the part of substance-abusing parents in order to reduce the risk to their children. And finally, Reconnecting Youth targets youth who are actively exhibiting multiple problem behaviors, which might include substance abuse, depression, and suicidal ideation. The program uses social supports and life skills training in school settings to address these problematic behaviors.[49]

In summary, the prevention programs that have been most successful tend to be more comprehensive (i.e., they don't focus on a single strategy). They have multiple components involving individuals, their families, peers, schools, communities, the media, and employment. The media can be used in these programs to educate the public and raise public support for prevention programming, while reinforcing the progress of prevention efforts in the community.

Ideally, these programs focus on broad populations but can be adapted to target specific subpopulations such as high-risk youth. They should also be sensitive enough to address specific needs related to gender, ethnicity, socioeconomic status, youth developmental stage, and type of drugs being abused. To be successful, prevention programs should also include needs assessments, program evaluations, and continual communication with the community at large.[59]

SUMMARY

Substance abuse has historically been a serious social problem in the U.S. It continues to be a serious social problem today. Tobacco, alcohol, and marijuana are considered gateway drugs that may lead to use and abuse of more dangerous substances, such as methamphetamine. The problem of substance abuse has demanded a response by the U.S. social welfare system in the form of a wide range of services. These include therapeutic communities, inpatient and residential treatment, outpatient and intensive outpatient programs, needle exchange programs, and drug courts. Alcoholics Anonymous and other 12-step groups are an important part of this treatment system. Helping clients suffering from drug addiction is made more difficult when an individual exhibits both a drug addiction and another mental health disorder, resulting in overlapping symptoms. Requirements for effective treatment of co-occurring mental health and substance use issues pose a real challenge for social workers and their colleagues in the treatment field.

12 CHAPTER REVIEW

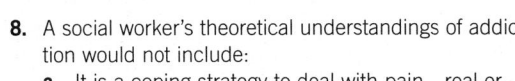

Log onto **MySocialWorkLab** to access a wealth of case studies, videos, and assessment. (*If you did not receive an access code to **MySocialWorkLab** with this text and wish to purchase access online, please visit www.mysocialworklab.com.*)

PRACTICE TEST
The following questions will test your knowledge of the content found within this chapter. For additional assessment, including licensing-exam type questions on applying chapter content to practice, visit **MySocialWorkLab**.

1. Common signs of substance abuse do *not* include:
   a. Taking greater quantities of the substance than intended
   b. Social or psychological problems associated with use
   c. High grades in school or significant job promotions
   d. Preoccupation with substance use

2. The most frequently abused substance in the U.S. is:
   a. Alcohol
   b. Tobacco
   c. Marijuana
   d. Opiates

3. Social workers are most interested in further research into which element listed below relating to substance use?
   a. Smoking prevention and cessation programs
   b. Substance use on college campuses
   c. Drinking and driving programs
   d. DARE programs

4. Excessive alcohol use is considered the _____ leading preventable cause of death in the U.S.:
   a. First
   b. Second
   c. Third
   d. Fourth

5. Arrests on college campuses involve alcohol use/misuse _____:
   a. 82% of the time
   b. 28% of the time
   c. 53% of the time
   d. Infrequently

6. Use of "crystal meth" has been linked to:
   a. Increases in HIV and AIDS
   b. Increased risk of addiction
   c. Increased health issues
   d. Increased creativity

7. Social workers consider addiction a(n) _____:
   a. Disease with biopsychosocial implications
   b. Lack of will power on the part of the addict
   c. Problem that would be cured by longer jail sentences
   d. Inevitable side effect of modern society

8. A social worker's theoretical understandings of addiction would not include:
   a. It is a coping strategy to deal with pain—real or psychic
   b. It is a genetic predisposition
   c. It is part of one's psychological makeup
   d. It is a character weakness

9. Social workers in substance treatment practice:
   a. Individuals with addictions
   b. Individuals and families
   c. Groups, but not individuals
   d. Families only

10. As part of their practice, social workers often work with individuals who carry a mental health diagnosis as well as substance abuse issues. These clients are considered to have _____:
    a. Dual diagnosis
    b. Character disorders
    c. Trauma disorders
    d. Multiple occurring phenomenon.

Log onto **MySocialWorkLab** once you have completed the Practice Test above to access additional study tools and assessment.

Answers

Key: 1) c 2) b 3) b 4) c 5) a 6) d 7) a 8) d 9) b 10) a

13

Crime and Social Work Intervention

OUTLINE CHAPTER

Defining Crime 292
Categories of Criminal Behavior

Theories of Crime and Criminal Behavior 293

Trends in Crime and Incarceration 294
Racism, Crime, and Incarceration

The Adult Criminal Justice System 296
Law Enforcement
Courts
Corrections

Youth Offenders and Juvenile Crime 299
Juvenile Justice System
Juvenile and Family Court
Recent Developments and Trends
Prevention and Diversion Programs
Restorative Justice and Juvenile Justice
Girls and Juvenile Justice

Social Work and Criminal Justice 303
Correctional Social Workers and Services to Inmates
Post-Release and Rehabilitation Services
Probation and Parole
Criminal Justice Reform

Crime Prevention 310
Reducing Recidivism
Crime Prevention Programs

Interprofessional Collaboration 312

Summary 314

Practice Test 316

 MySocialWorkLab 316

Core Competencies in this Chapter (Check marks indicate which competencies are covered in depth)									
✓	Professional Identity	✓	Ethical Practice		Critical Thinking		Diversity in Practice	✓	Human Rights & Justice
✓	Research Based Practice	✓	Human Behavior	✓	Policy Practice	✓	Practice Contexts		Engage, Assess, Intervene, Evaluate

DEFINING CRIME

Several groups of people involved with the U.S. justice system are served by social workers. This intervention may involve youth offenders, for example, but may also include parents, married couples, children, and older adults. In this chapter, we discuss crime, its relation to racism, the U.S. justice system, and the specific populations assisted by social workers and related professionals.

A **Crime** occurs when a person behaves in a way that has been defined by the government either to be prohibited by law or to involve failure to act where there is a legal responsibility to do so. Crime generally involves "an intentional act or omission in violation of criminal law . . . committed without defense or justification."[1] Both state and federal laws define criminal behavior and specify corresponding consequences. Some activities (e.g., murder, robbery, and burglary) have been considered criminal since the first civilizations began to record legal codes. Other actions, such as domestic violence and driving under the influence of drugs or alcohol, were added to the list of criminal offenses during the 20th century with increased public awareness of the devastating consequences of allowing such behavior to go unchecked. Technology has also influenced crime, with the widespread use of computers providing new opportunities for white-collar crime and cybercrime.[2]

Forensic means pertaining to or connected to courts of law. Forensic social work practice includes a wide range of activities related to criminal or civil law, expanding from its original role in traditional social history, concentrating on preparation for pre- and post-sentence evaluations, to include child protection, child-custody issues in separation, divorce, neglect, and termination of parental rights cases, juvenile and adult services, corrections and mandated treatment, and elder protection. Some areas can be controversial areas of practice, especially in regarding sex offenders. For example, social work ethics encourage evaluations that stress rehabilitation and restitution as alternatives to incarceration. Sometimes these goals conflict with legal ethics. Social workers may be called upon to advocate for clients who do not have attorneys. To do so, forensic social workers must be familiar with laws and legal responsibilities on a variety of issues such as parental rights, guardianship, custody, mediation, and mitigation. Knowledge of how to use and read legal materials, due process requirements and equal protection under law, ethics, privacy, confidentiality, and recordkeeping are essential.[3]

Categories of Criminal Behavior

- **Violation:** A crime that may result in monetary fines but cannot lead to incarceration except in cases of flagrant, multiple violations. Examples may include traffic citations and parking tickets.
- **Misdemeanor:** A crime, less serious than a felony, punishable by no more than one year in jail. Common misdemeanors include petty theft of articles worth less than a certain amount, first-time drunk driving, and leaving the scene of an accident.[4]
- **Felony:** A serious crime (e.g., extortion, kidnapping, or robbery), usually punishable by a prison term of more than one year. In many states, felonies are separated into more and less serious categories that may be referred to as "class A" or "class B." Penalties for a class A felony range from 7½ to 15 years or more in prison; penalties for a class B felony are generally 3½–7 years.[5]

> **Capital Offense**: The most serious category of crime (e.g., murder or treason), punishable by sentences up to life in jail or execution.

THEORIES OF CRIME AND CRIMINAL BEHAVIOR

Over the years, many theorists have attempted to develop a theory of criminal behavior. **Social learning theory** is perhaps the dominant theory of crime today. Basically, social learning theory asserts that the people an individual associates with have a large impact on whether or not that person will engage in crime. This occurs, in part, because associates affect the individual's beliefs, reinforcements, or punishments. An individual doesn't have to be in direct contact with others to learn from them; for example, an individual may learn to engage in violence from observing criminal acts in the media.[6]

Another theory often used in the study of crime is **strain theory**, which suggests that when individuals experience strain or stress, they may engage in crime to reduce or escape from the tension they are experiencing. This theory tends to focus on failure to achieve three related goals: money, status/respect, and—for adolescents—autonomy from adults. Crime has been linked to child abuse and neglect, criminal victimization, physical punishment by parents, negative relations with parents, teachers, peers, school, and a wide range of other stressful life events, including the divorce or separation of a parent, parental unemployment, and changing schools. Factors that may influence the effect of strain on criminal behavior include poor coping skills, limited financial and personal resources, and a lack of conventional social supports (e.g., family and friends).[7]

A third theory, **control theory**, seeks to understand why people *do not* engage in criminal behavior. According to control theory, three major restraints to criminal behavior exist: (1) when others are directly controlling the person's behavior; (2) when the person has a lot to lose by engaging in crime; and (3) when the person tries to control his or her own behavior. If left to rely solely on internal controls, individuals may not stop to consider the long-term consequences of their behavior and simply focus on the immediate, short-term benefits or pleasures of criminal acts.[8]

Labeling theory, a fourth theory of crime, proposes that labeling individuals as criminals results in difficulties in obtaining legitimate employment and reduced contact with noncriminal individuals, and eventually encourages criminal behaviors. Recent research has found that informal labeling appears to have a greater effect on subsequent crime than official labeling. This suggests that if an individual believes that others see him or her as delinquent or as a troublemaker, the individual is more likely to act in accord with this perception.[9]

Social disorganization theory explains community differences in crime rates by identifying the characteristics of communities with high crime rates: large population, widespread economic deprivation, high in multiunit housing (e.g., apartments), high in residential mobility (i.e., people frequently move into and out of the community), and high in family disruption (e.g., high rates of divorce and single-parent families). Social disorganization theorists believe these kinds of things affect community residents' willingness to exercise effective social control. This theory suggests that the number of at-risk communities has increased since the 1960s, often in inner-city areas populated largely by minority groups, due to several factors, including: (1) the decline in manufacturing

The greatest crimes are caused by excess and not by necessity.

—Aristotle

Critical Thinking Question

Social workers might reach differing conclusions about a client's criminal behavior depending on the theoretical model applied. Think about an adolescent shoplifting in a department store. How do different theories explain this behavior?

jobs in central city areas; (2) the migration of many working-class and middle-class African Americans to more affluent communities; and (3) governmental policies that have contributed to the increased concentration of poverty.[10]

Critical theories, a group of theories that take a particular perspective, look to explain group differences in crime rates in terms of the larger social environment, focusing on a variety of factors, particularly group differences in power. **Marxist theories**, for example, argue that those who own the means of production (e.g., factories, businesses) have the greatest power and use this power for their own advantage, criminalizing the behaviors of lower-class persons but ignoring the harmful actions of business and industry (e.g., pollution, unsafe working conditions). Another critical theory, **institutional anomie theory**, suggests that a high crime rate stems partly from the emphasis placed on the "American Dream." Everyone is encouraged to strive for monetary success, but little emphasis is placed on the legitimate means to achieve that success, encouraging attempts to obtain money through illegitimate channels or crime. **Feminist theories**, which are also critical theories, focus on gender differences in crime that result in large measure from differences in social learning and control for males and females.[11]

While all of these theoretical frameworks are useful, current theories should take into account various systems levels that impinge upon the individual (i.e., take a systems approach) by including individual traits, the immediate social environment, the larger social environment, and situational factors that may help to explain crime in different groups and among different types of offenders.[12]

TRENDS IN CRIME AND INCARCERATION

Serious violent crime levels, including homicide, rape, robbery, and assault, have declined dramatically since 1993.[13] Changes in the U.S. age structure have affected crime rates, including murder rates, which fell 8% between 1980 and 1995.[14] Numerous studies have demonstrated a sharp rise in criminal involvement with the onset of adolescence, followed by a steady decline with age beginning after adolescence.[15] Sharply increasing incarceration rates coupled with these changes have also contributed to a reduction in overall crime rates in recent years.[16] The number of male adults in the correctional population increased by two-thirds from 1986 to 1997, while the number of incarcerated females doubled during that period. Today, female incarceration rates continue to grow faster than males' rates. By way of perspective, this means almost 5% of the adult males and 1% of the adult females in the U.S. were under some form of correctional supervision in 1997. Prisoners convicted of violent offenses make up over half of the prison population. The U.S. reinstated the death penalty in 1976, although a number of states have maintained a moratorium on its use. Forty-two inmates were executed in 2007, 11 fewer than in 2006.[17] Counter to the downward trend in crime rates overall is a pattern of increasing juvenile crime and gun violence that has been attributed, in large part, to the introduction of crack cocaine and the resulting struggle for control over its distribution during a period of strong anti-drug law enforcement starting in 1986.[18] With the growing crack trade needing literally hundreds of thousands of "workers," and many adult drug dealers in prison or jail, a significant number of African American males aged 15 to 19 were pulled into the crack trade and armed, leading to sharp increases in juvenile gun deaths, particularly among this young group of African Americans.[19]

Racism, Crime, and Incarceration

The impression that crime is a problem disproportionately attributable to African Americans is not a new one. In fact, it dates as far back as the early days of slavery in the U.S.[20] The Department of Justice estimates that one black man in three will go to jail at some point during his life—more than five times the rate for white men. The disparity between black and white incarceration rates appears to stem from real differences in criminal behavior. For example, the Department of Justice reports that in 2002 blacks were seven times more likely than whites to commit murder. Facts like these, taken out of context, tend to fuel long-held prejudices.[21] As movements for abolition and civil rights ended the institutions of slavery, lynching, and segregation, explicit racial discrimination has been removed from the language of U.S. laws. Despite this, concerns have grown over the development of more indirect mechanisms for perpetuating de facto or "color-blind racism," where people of color, especially African Americans, are subject to unequal protection under the laws and excessive surveillance (i.e., **racial profiling**) in the name of crime control.[22] Approximately 50% of all prisoners are black, whereas 30% are white, and 17% Latino. Between 1990 and 2006, the number of white and Latino inmates increased at an equal average annual rate, whereas the number black inmates increased at a slower pace, perhaps signaling improved system efforts to provide more equal protection.[23]

The greater society's tolerance of inequality, the more extreme the scale of punishment utilized.
—Leslie W. Wilkins, Leslie and Ken Pease

For every 100,000 Americans, there are 699 individuals in prison; this is the highest incarceration rate in the world.[24] There is also no dispute that the poor and people of color, particularly African Americans, are dramatically overrepresented at every level of the criminal justice system. The overwhelming majority of those in prisons and jails were unemployed or employed in the minimum-wage service sector at the time of their commitment offenses. Also, these individuals generally have a high school education or less and often suffer from concurrent substance abuse issues.[25]

As noted earlier, women represent the fastest growing sector of the prison population. While the adult male prison population has tripled in the past 20 years, the number of women incarcerated has increased tenfold during the same time span. These prisoners are overwhelmingly women of color. African American women are three times more likely than Latinas and six times more likely than white women to be in prison. More than 60% of women in prison are serving time for nonviolent offenses, especially drug-related offenses.[26]

The current increase in incarceration rates is accompanied by legislation that further limits the political and economic opportunities for convicted felons and former inmates. Forty-eight states do not permit prison inmates to vote, 32 states disenfranchise felons on parole, and 28 states prohibit probationers from voting. Twenty-five states bar felons from ever holding public office, 33 states place a lifetime ban on gun ownership for convicted felons, and all states require driver's license suspension for convicted drug felons. States have also increased the occupational bans for convicted felons, prohibiting them from teaching, child care and related work with children, or law enforcement. Many employers and, more recently, volunteer agencies are requiring criminal background checks as part of the job application process. Drug felons are permanently barred from receiving public assistance such as Temporary Assistance for Needy Families (TANF), Medicaid, food stamps, or Supplemental Security Income, as well as federal financial aid for education.

Critical Thinking Question

Every group has basic human rights. Data indicate that some groups are more likely to be accused of committing crimes than others. Is this just? How might this trend be reversed?

They are also permanently barred from public housing, and a growing number of private rental properties now screen for convicted felons. A felony conviction by anyone in the household is grounds for eviction from public housing.[27]

THE ADULT CRIMINAL JUSTICE SYSTEM

The flowchart shown in Figure 13.1 of the events in the criminal justice system updates the original chart prepared by the President's Commission on Law Enforcement and the Administration of Justice in 1967. This chart summarizes the most common events in the criminal and juvenile justice systems, including entry into the criminal justice system, prosecution and pretrial services, adjudication, sentencing and sanctions, and corrections.

There is no single criminal justice system in this country. The U.S. justice system evolved from English common law into a complex series of procedures and decisions. We apprehend, try, and punish offenders by means of a loose confederation of agencies at all levels of government. Our justice system is based on the premise that crimes against an individual are crimes against the State; individuals who commit crimes are dealt with as though they have victimized *all* of society. Recently, there has been increased attention to the victims of crime, which has resulted in more services to help such victims. Criminal cases may be handled differently in different states or **jurisdictions**, but court decisions are based on the due process guarantees of the U.S. Constitution. Each year, the U.S. spends more than $146 billion dollars on the criminal justice system, including police, the judiciary and court systems, and corrections. More than $50 billion of this is spent directly on corrections, primarily a state government activity.[28]

Law Enforcement

The responsibility to respond to most crime rests with state and local governments. Police protection is primarily a function of cities and towns. Law enforcement agencies learn about crime from the reports of victims or other citizens, from discovery by police officers in the field, from informants, or from investigative and intelligence work. Once it has been established that a crime has been committed, a suspect must be identified and arrested for the case to move forward in the system. According to the FBI, most reported crimes go unsolved, even in the face of an extensive investigation.

For the middle class, the police protect property, give directions, and help old ladies. For the urban poor, the police are those who arrest you.

—Michael Harrington

Courts

After an arrest, a suspect charged with a crime must be taken before a judge or magistrate without unnecessary delay. The suspect is informed of the charges against him or her and a determination is made as to whether there is "probable cause" to detain the individual. Based on available information about the individual's residence, employment, family ties, criminal history and indication of substance use, the judge also makes a decision about whether to release the individual pending trial. In many jurisdictions, a preliminary hearing may follow the suspect's initial appearance before the court. The main function of this hearing is to discover whether there is probable cause to believe that the suspect committed a crime. If the judge does not find probable cause, the case is dismissed. If probable cause is found, or the individual waives his or her right to a preliminary hearing, the case may be bound over to a grand jury. If the grand

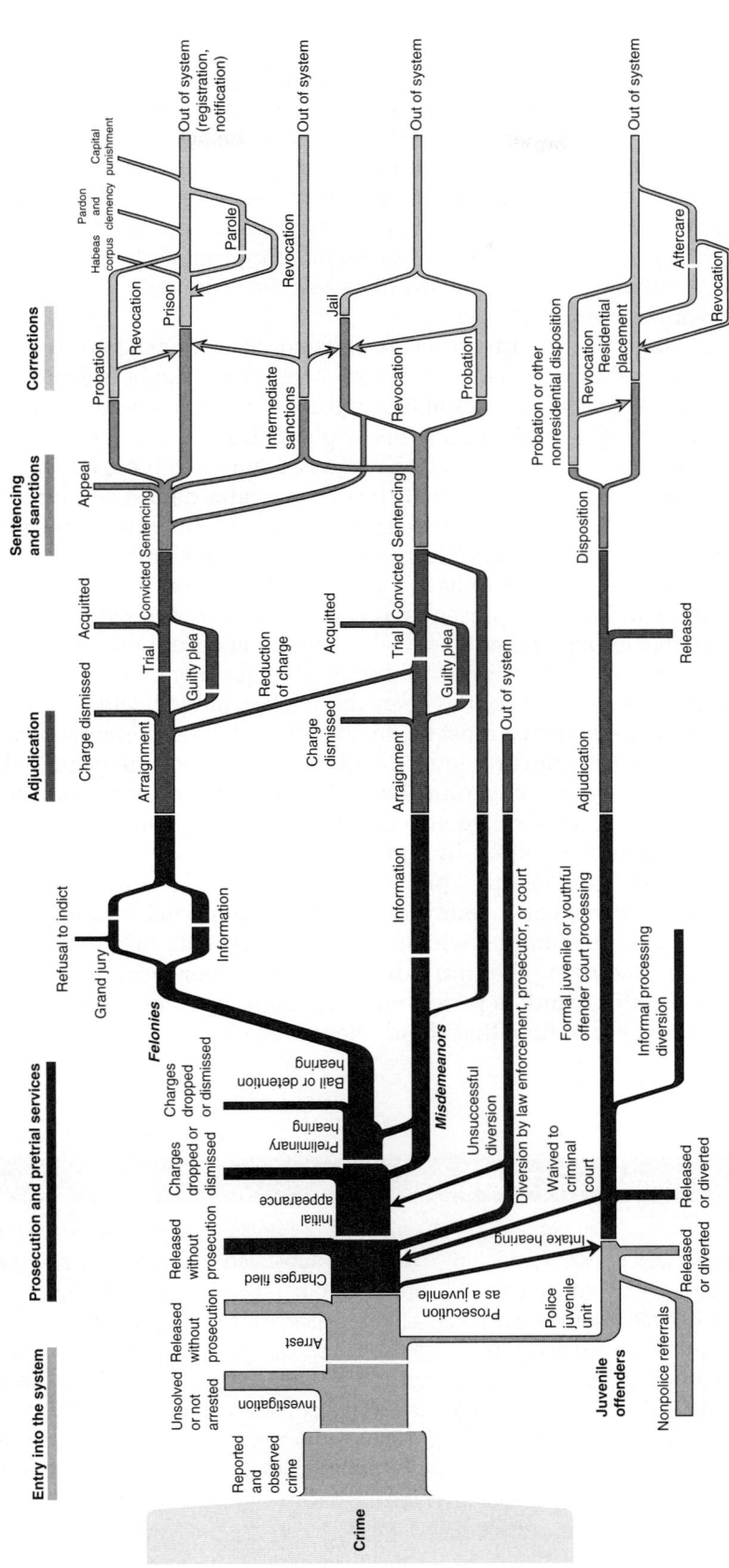

Figure 13.1

Criminal Justice System

Source: Adapted from The challenge of crime in a free society. President's Commission on Law Enforcement and Administration of Justice, 1967. This revision, a result of the Symposium on the 30th Anniversary of the President's Commission was prepared by the Bureau of Justice Statistics in 1997.

jury finds sufficient evidence, it submits an indictment, a written statement of the essential facts of the offense charged against the individual. At this point, if the individual is not in custody, law enforcement agencies will seek to arrest suspects named in the indictment. With increasing demands on our correctional system, some individuals, usually those without a prior criminal record, may be eligible for diversion from prosecution by complying with a special program such as drug or mental health treatment. Successfully completing required programs may result in the filing or dropping of charges and/or clearing the individual's criminal record in cases where the defendant had to plead guilty prior to entering diversion.

Once an indictment has been filed with the trial court, the individual is scheduled for arraignment, where he or she is again informed of the charges, advised of criminal defendants' rights, and asked to enter a plea to the charges. The individual may plead guilty or plead "nolo contendere" (i.e., accepts penalty without admitting guilt). If the court accepts this plea, no trial is held and the offender is sentenced at that time or at a later date. The individual may plead not guilty or not guilty by reason of insanity, in which case a trial date is set. Persons accused of serious crimes are guaranteed a trial by jury, but may chose to waive this right and have a judge hear the case. In either process, the prosecution and defense present evidence by questioning witnesses, while the judge decides issues of law. The trial results in acquittal or conviction on the original charges and/or lesser included offenses. Persons who are convicted may appeal to a higher court. Once convicted, a judge decides the sentence, unless by law the sentence must be decided by jury. A sentencing hearing may occur, at which the court reviews the circumstances of the crime, often relying on pre-sentence investigations by probation agencies or expert witnesses. Judges may have a wide range of sentencing options, from the death penalty down through incarceration in a prison, alternative incarcerations such as house arrests or "boot camps," probation that allows the convicted person to stay out of jail under specific conditions, or restrictions such as substance abuse testing or treatment and fines, which are usually given for minor offenses, and/or restitution, requiring the individual to pay compensation to the victim. Laws in some states mandate prison terms for certain offenses; these often include the exact length of time that should be served.

Case Study: The Mental Health–Law Interface

When I first met Harold, he was shuffling out from the back ward of a psychiatric hospital in Florida. I tried to speak to him, but he had a difficult time focusing his eyes or even realizing I was speaking to him—he had been medicated with his usual dose of antipsychotic medications, enough to make most of us fall asleep. As I studied his case, I discovered he had been admitted for pretrial evaluation on suspicion he had thrown a rock at the local schoolhouse. That was in 1919; it was now 1975—he had never returned to court. He claimed he was innocent. His denials were interpreted by treating personnel as evidence of pervasive mental illness and he was therefore subjected to a variety of treatments including shock therapy, psychosurgery and major psychiatric medication. After tapering from his medications, Harold was carefully examined and there was no evidence of severe mental illness found. We ultimately returned him to court for disposition of his case and were able to place him in a nursing home. It reminds me of how complicated the interface between the mental health and legal systems can be and how easy it was to fall in the cracks years ago—thank goodness it's harder for that to happen today.

Corrections

Corrections is primarily a function of state governments. The U.S. adult criminal justice system includes more than 3,300 jails, more than 1,500 state prisons, and 100 federal prisons, almost 300 of which are privately run.[29] Individuals sentenced to incarceration usually serve time in a local jail or a state prison. Those sentenced to less than one year generally go to jail; those sentenced to more than one year may go to prisons with varying levels of custody or to a community correctional facility. Prisoners may become eligible for parole—conditional release from prison—before their full sentence has been served (e.g., after serving a specific portion of the sentence. Parole boards or other authorities make parole decisions. These boards also have the power to revoke parole or to discharge a parolee altogether. Individuals may choose or be required to serve out their full sentences prior to release (i.e., expiration of term). Those sentenced under "determinate" sentencing laws are generally not eligible for parole.[30]

YOUTH OFFENDERS AND JUVENILE CRIME

According to FBI statistics, juveniles accounted for 19% of all arrests, 14% of all murder arrests, and 17% of all violent crime arrests in 1997. Although violent crime arrests have declined since then, the number of arrests has risen in many categories.[31] In a development that causes significant concern for social workers, a 1999 survey showed that some 5.9% of U.S. high school students surveyed said that they had carried a gun in the 30 days prior to the survey and that 18% of high school students regularly carry a knife, razor, firearm, or other weapon. Nine percent report taking weapons to school. A growing body of research exists showing that media portrayals of violence play a role in this issue.[32]

Juvenile Justice System

According to the federal government, a "juvenile" is a person who has committed a criminal act but has not yet reached his or her 21st birthday. In corrections, the terms juvenile, juvenile offender, juvenile resident, student, and resident are used interchangeably. Under most circumstances, juveniles may not be placed in adult correctional facilities. Moreover, federal law limits the release of information regarding juveniles. Juvenile court proceedings are sealed. Under federal rules, juveniles who have been sentenced as adults may be housed in an institution until they reach 18 years or age or, if sentenced as a juvenile, until they reach 21 years.[33]

Contemporary attempts to reform the juvenile justice system focus on two primary concerns: (1) due process protections that may not provide adequate safeguards for young offenders; and (2) insufficient consequences for young offenders who commit adult-like offenses, leading to recent legislative changes designed to "get tough" by shifting options from treatment to more of a punishment orientation, a politically popular position for at least the past 20 years. Placement in detention facilities remains the "program of choice" for juvenile offenders "despite the rehabilitative paradigm's symbolic goal to protect youths."[34] Support for a merger of the adult and juvenile criminal systems by get-tough advocates has expanded the scope of transfer provisions or waivers that bring juveniles into the adult criminal system.[35] Social workers employed in the juvenile justice system can work toward appropriate options for youths convicted of crimes.[36]

Juvenile and Family Court

Family law interacts with the criminal justice system in several ways. For instance, juvenile cases often begin in family court. Parental rights and obligations can be complicated by criminal convictions and prison sentences.[37] Judges, referees, commissioners, masters, and other juvenile and family law professionals assigned to the family court system confront a variety of issues, including child abuse and neglect, adoption and foster care, juvenile delinquency, family violence, victims of juvenile offenders, alcohol and drug abuse, termination of parental rights, custody and visitation, and minority issues.[38]

Recent Developments and Trends

In recent years, four-fifths of the states (approximately 40 states) have made a regular practice of housing children, even those who committed nonviolent crimes, in adult jails. Studies show consistently that those children were considerably more likely to become serious, violent criminals than children handled through the juvenile justice system. Even when not housed in adult facilities, most children taken into custody are committed to large and unruly children's prisons that resemble adult prisons. Some states (e.g., Missouri) have abandoned such facilities in favor of small, community-based centers that emphasize therapy rather than punishment. When possible, children are kept near their homes so their parents can participate in rehabilitation that includes extensive family therapy. Case managers typically provide oversight and coordinate care. Oversight does not end with the juvenile's release. The case managers follow their charges closely for many months and often help with job placement, therapy referrals, school issues, and drug or alcohol treatment. After completing the program, Missouri officials say, only about 10% of children are recommitted to the system by the juvenile courts.[39]

Prevention and Diversion Programs

Traditional violence prevention interventions have used a **deficit model approach** targeting young people most at risk for delinquent or violent behavior and working to change specific behaviors or characteristics, such as failing at school or abusing drugs. **Youth development** is a violence prevention model that shifts the focus from problems, and instead emphasizes identifying, recognizing, and then building upon youth strengths. Many adults may blame youth for the society's problems, including violence, and believe that young people are uninterested, irresponsible, and dangerous, contributing to their feelings of low self-worth, hopelessness about the future, and disconnection from adults. The underlying premise of the youth development approach is based on the belief that youth are valued assets and can contribute to family, school, and community life.[40] This is especially critical today as people bemoan the loss of a sense of community and neighborhood, and the comfort of being among others who know and care about them.[41]

Youth development occurs in the context of family, community, and country. Young people's maturation process is influenced by their surroundings and affected by relationships with key people, including parents, teachers, and peers. Every individual has unique skills and abilities, and each matures at a different pace. Developmental activities can be tailored to meet the needs of young people who are in disadvantaged circumstances so that they receive the resources necessary to address the limitations in their life circumstances. One of the greatest challenges facing youth development programs is getting adults to rethink some basic cultural assumptions. These programs emphasize cooperation, coordination, and funding to support redevelopment of entire communities rather than specific, focused programs, thus combining prevention, early intervention, community development, and youth empowerment strategies. Youth development requires organizational and community collaboration to ensure that systems that value and support young people are operating. Key components of positive youth development include providing youth with safe and supportive environments, fostering relationships between young people and caring adults who can mentor and guide them, providing youth with opportunities to identify and pursue their interests, and developing knowledge and skills in a variety of areas while providing opportunities for youth to show they care about others and promoting healthy lifestyles.[42]

Restorative Justice and Juvenile Justice

Another development in juvenile justice has been the evolution of restorative justice. Although restorative justice is not a new concept, it grew in popularity during the 1990s with the evolution of the victims' rights movement and with frustrations over the perceived deficits in the traditional juvenile

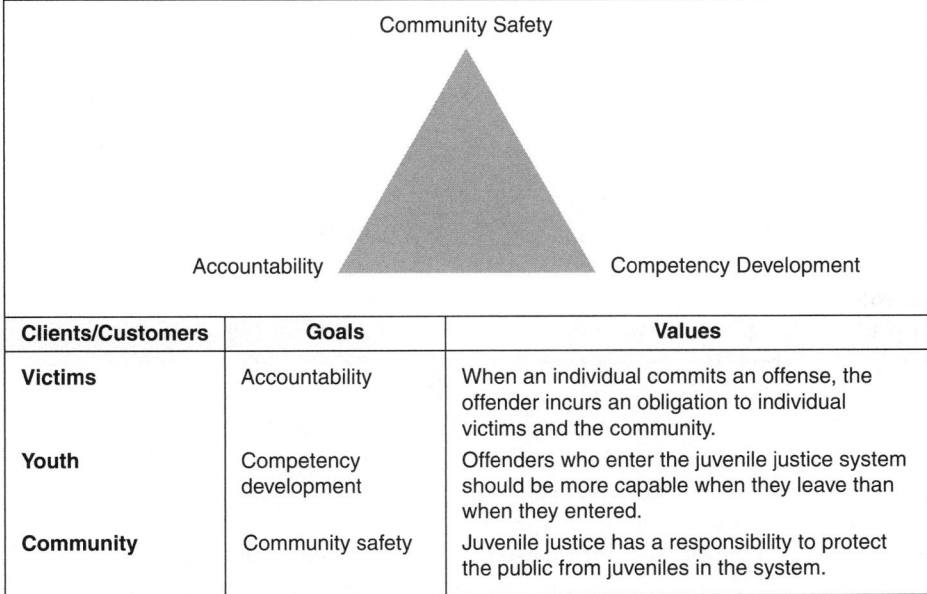

Figure 13.2
Restorative Justice
Source: www.ojjdp.ncjrs.org/pubs/implementing/balanced.html, retrieved August 2009.

justice system. While retributive justice is focused on public vengeance, deterrence, and punishment through an adversarial process, restorative justice is concerned with repairing the harm done to victims and the community through a process of negotiation, mediation, victim empowerment, and reparation. Part of restorative justice is a balanced approach that promotes maximum involvement of the victim, the offender, and the community in the justice process and allows juvenile justice systems and agencies to better protect the community by ensuring accountability of the offender and the system. Through offenders repairing the harm they caused and rebuilding relationships in the community, offenders are encouraged to become competent and productive citizens. The concept of restorative justice can help guide courts in the appropriate and equitable use of meaningful sanctions to ensure that offenders make amends to victims and the community as well as providing a connection point among disparate practices and programs such as restitution, victim services, community service, victim-offender mediation, and dispute resolution.[43]

While originally focused on the juvenile justice system, the concept of restorative justice has been adopted by the adult criminal justice system as well. Restorative justice practices have been effectively used in all 50 states and at the federal level as a component of criminal sentences and juvenile adjudications involving diversion, probation, and parole. A common and popular practical application is community service. Community service holds offenders accountable for the harm they have caused, allows victims a voice in recommending the type of community service performed, and provides communities with opportunities to improve their quality of life, while helping offenders develop new skills through supervised work activities. Examples of community service include public work programs that beautify a community's environment, such as park and roadside clean-up efforts or graffiti removal. They might also follow the example the Department of Community Corrections in Deschutes County, Oregon, where adult and juvenile offenders have participated in a number of human service and public works tasks, including the construction of a homeless shelter and domestic abuse crisis center.[44]

Girls and Juvenile Justice

According to the Office of Juvenile Justice, most of the young women in the system first come into contact with the juvenile justice system for a **status**

Research Informed Practice with Juveniles in the School Setting

Research by Ron Avi Astor et al. (*Children & Schools 27* [2005], pp. 17–32) examined school safety interventions. The research was timely, given the multiple recent school shootings occurring in the U.S. The researchers concluded that the most effective school interventions were programs that raised awareness and responsibility for school violence among students, parents, and teachers. In fact, the best programs involve teachers, students, and parents in the school system to plan, implement, and maintain the programs. Good programs include clear guidelines and procedures to be followed by all school groups for handling violent situations.

How could this research inform your efforts as a social worker to reduce violence and crime in community schools? Specifically, what roles and tasks should social workers perform?

Crime and Social Work Intervention

offense—a violation of law that applies only to juveniles (e.g., running away, truancy, liquor law violations, curfew violations).⁴⁵ Abused girls are twice as likely as non-abused girls to enter the juvenile justice system. Further, these girls may end up in the justice system as a result of attempting to avoid their abusers, running away, or fighting back. Researchers and social workers alike continue to be concerned about the criminalization of their behaviors.⁴⁶ Although girls in the juvenile justice system currently constitute a minority, the numbers are rising. Recent media attention has focused on girls as aggressors. Research suggests that girls are detained more often than boys and are more likely to be committed for minor offenses. Programs and facilities are most often designed for boys and fail to take into account gender-specific factors that contribute to girls' involvement.⁴⁷ Custody rates for black girls are typically more than three times what they are for white girls.⁴⁸

SOCIAL WORK AND CRIMINAL JUSTICE

Correctional Social Workers and Services to Inmates

The U.S. imprisons a larger proportion of its population than any other industrialized nation, and an increasing percentage of incarcerated individuals are female. The NASW would argue that, even if only from an economic standpoint, we should be concerned about the overwhelming growth of imprisonment and begin looking at ways to reduce incarceration and recidivism rates. The cost of incarcerating offenders is escalating and putting an increasing strain on federal, state, and municipal budgets. Many institutions are overcrowded and understaffed. Recidivism rates are high, further exacerbating societal problems. Clearly, some changes must be made within the correctional system to curtail these ever-increasing numbers, and the social work profession can play a key role in addressing many of these issues. The

correctional system evolved in this country to meet several social functions, including social control, protection of the public, retribution, and rehabilitation. In recent years, the correctional system's focus has shifted more toward punishment than rehabilitation. By its very nature, a system focused on social control, protection, and retribution can lead to policies that promote discrimination and social injustice and may negatively affect the social reintegration of those who serve time and are ready for release into society. Without proper resources, people serving time are at risk of unemployment, homelessness, lack of social support, discrimination, and recidivism after release. In turn, their families, communities, and society as a whole are affected.[49]

> *What is eliminated in prison is choice. Until choice can be freely exercised and caring behavior encouraged, there can be no meaningful change.*
>
> —Fay Honey Knopp et al.

Historically, many social workers have found positions in the detention and corrections field. Incarceration deserves social workers' attention because offenders need counseling, treatment, and education as they serve their time. Moreover, the incarcerated person's family is affected by economic burdens, stigma, emotional distress, and increased risk of their children committing crimes. With a growing population of incarcerated individuals, social workers can play an role as advocates and treatment providers for these vulnerable populations.[50] Several specific areas would appear to fall into the social work domain: assuring safe and humane environments that protect the public, providing cost-effective services that are responsive to the needs of the community, addressing substance abuse and mental health issues within the criminal justice system, and addressing the biopsychosocial needs of incarcerated individuals.[51] Jails and prisons have become receiving facilities for a host of disguised health, welfare, and social problems. The numbers of inmates who test positive for Human Immunodeficiency Virus (HIV) and Acquired Immunodeficiency Syndrome (AIDS) are on the rise. Dismantling psychiatric hospitals and fragmentation of the community mental health system have resulted in shifting the care of people with chronic mental illnesses from psychiatric facilities to correctional institutions.[52]

Social workers may assume many roles in the correctional system. Involvement in a criminal episode frequently occurs following the use of drugs or alcohol. Social workers with training and experience in addictions can provide valuable input and leadership in planning, developing, and implementing rehabilitation and drug treatment programs. Social workers who are knowledgeable about health care issues are an important resource in providing prevention and education programs as well as support services for incarcerated people with HIV/AIDS and other health conditions, as well as those battling chronic or terminal illnesses. The special health care concerns of aging prisoners, in particular, need to be addressed.

Among the consequences of state mental hospital deinstitutionalization in the early 1970s was the release of thousands of individuals with severe mental illness into community settings. Today, a substantial number of incarcerated individuals have diagnosed mental health problems or undiagnosed disorders that are not being treated. Social workers have a role in providing diagnosis and facilitating appropriate care for these individuals.

Prisoners' inability to be involved in the daily lives of their children and other loved ones is a source of great psychological stress and pain. Common everyday living problems, such as the death of a parent or child, divorce, or chronic illness, are intensified when incarceration disrupts natural support

> **Demonstrating Knowledge, Values, and Skills**
>
> Engage your class in a debate about whether or not individuals with a mental illness should be incarcerated when they commit a crime rather than being sent to treatment facility. Divide the class in half, with one side defending the notion that everyone who commits a crime should be incarcerated no matter their mental status. Keep in mind that this is the norm in the justice and law enforcement system. The other half of the class should debate the belief that individuals with mental illness who commit a crime need mental health services and rather than (or in addition to) incarceration. Prior to the debate, investigate current regulations for arresting an individual with a suspected mental illness. For further information on this topic, refer to P. Earley, *Crazy: A Father's Search Through America's Mental Health Madness* (New York: G. P. Putman, 2006).

systems and family functioning. Studies show that incarcerated individuals who maintain strong family and friendship ties during imprisonment and assume responsible marital and parental roles upon release have lower recidivism rates. The current trend of moving prisoners to other states due to overcrowding further cuts off family continuity and connectedness. Social workers have the knowledge and skills to develop and advocate for key family programs, as well as to provide supportive services to individual inmates during their incarceration. Female prisoners present a special range of situations needing intervention, such as pregnancy, responsibility for minor children, or history of physical or sexual abuse. Because jails tend to be designed for male populations, increased stress is likely for women. Social workers can assist the correctional system to more effectively manage issues related to the increasing number of women being incarcerated.[53]

Critical Thinking Question
Social workers often promote juvenile justice that is tailored to age group developmental needs. Brainstorm strategies for promoting appropriate options for juveniles charged with committing serious crimes.

The County Department of Correction's Programs Division in Santa Clara, California, sponsors a model corrections program. This program delivers services that include substance abuse, anger management, personal health issues, literacy and education, and job skills, and covers a large number of recipients including the inmate population, community-based organizations, and the community at large. Social workers play a large role in service delivery, including educational, treatment and vocational classes, departmental services and support, community services, alternative custody programming, inmate supervision and case management, provider contracts, and performance assessments and reviews. In addition to therapeutic supports, social workers may also be asked to contribute to legal evaluation processes within the system and make recommendations for follow-up services.[55]

One innovative development, the Artemis Program—named for the ancient Greek goddess known as a huntress and a protector of the young—addresses substance abuse for female inmates who are pregnant and/or mothers of young children. Attendees are made aware of substance abuse and its possible effects on pregnancy and motherhood. With a core of daily substance abuse prevention classes, Artemis also offers classes that teach the women health and parenting skills, spirituality and meditation, and how to access community resources upon release. One of the classes these young women take is called Parents and Children Together (P.A.C.T.), which consists of parenting classes and weekly visits for incarcerated mothers and their children. Each week, the mothers set up a playroom in the facility, making each child's visit to the facility a positive and enjoyable experience.[55]

> **Research Informed Practice**
>
> Contact your local correctional facility or state penal institution to determine if they have a social worker on staff. If so, arrange an interview to discuss this social worker's roles. What issues are prevalent in their setting? Compare and contrast with national or state data. Next, arrange an interview with a social worker at a local mental health center to discuss how decreasing resources affect their approach to clients and whether incarceration of mentally ill individuals is a local concern. Compare and contrast attitudes and opinions from the correctional and mental health social workers. Note consistencies and differences.

Post-Release and Rehabilitation Services

Although inmates are incarcerated for a variety of offenses, incarcerated offenders typically have several characteristics in common, such as a low level of educational attainment, a lack of vocational skills, and higher than average rates of unemployment. Studies indicate a significant portion of inmates have disabilities, including mental retardation, learning disabilities, chemical dependency, mental illness, and various physical disabilities. These inmates need services that are not being met currently. Overcrowded conditions in many prisons can lead to disabled individuals being integrated into the regular prison population with little or no accommodation for their disabilities. For inmates with disabilities, a disability often serves as an additional barrier to inmates successfully transitioning into post-release environments and can increase recidivism. Minimal opportunities to take responsibility, make decisions, and structure time productively tend to encourage both deep hostility and institutionalized passivity in convicts, qualities that will not contribute to their reintegration into life on the outside. Without appropriate rehabilitation services, incarcerated offenders will continue to be unprepared for community transitions, competitive employment, or to use outside support services effectively.[56]

Prisons can offer inmates opportunities to increase knowledge and improve work skills, treat addictions, and provide a general understanding of what they will need to reenter community life successfully. The incarceration period should be viewed as an opportunity to build skills and prepare for future job placement. Vocational training and/or work release programs have proven effective in reducing recidivism and increasing job readiness. Graduates of substance abuse treatment programs are less likely to be rearrested, to commit a drug-related offense, to continue drug use, or to receive a parole violation. Further, effective halfway house and pre-release programs also reduce recidivism.

One positive solution would be developing a collaborative model between vocational rehabilitation and the correctional system designed to assist inmates in their transition to post-release environments. The shared goals of a collaboration model increase the likelihood of rehabilitative services delivery. Academic programs are another means by which inmates can be prepared to function in society upon release from prison. Such programs may offer basic remedial help in reading, writing, and math or provide access to educational opportunities such as the General Educational Development (GED) test and/or college degrees. Academic programs can be responsive to current curriculum trends such as technology, microcomputers, and cultural diversity.

Prisons can also offer workshops to enhance job skills, work behavior, and social skills.[57]

Probation and Parole

Probation is a term applied to adult offenders that courts place on community supervision instead of incarceration. In some jurisdictions, probation is linked with diversion programs that address the underlying causes of the criminal behavior (e.g., mental health issues, substance use, limited education). **Parole** is a term used for adults conditionally released to community supervision, whether by parole board decision or by mandatory conditional release after serving a prison term. They are subject to being returned to jail or prison for rule violations or other offenses. The sheer volume of inmates being released from federal, state, and county prisons is now being recognized as a public safety issue.[58] At the end of 2006, over 5 million adult men and women were under federal, state, or local probation or parole jurisdiction; this group has been increasing at an average annually of 2.2% since 1995. Among offenders on probation, 49% had been convicted of committing a felony, 49% a misdemeanor, and 2% other infractions. Nearly three-quarters of probationers were supervised for a nonviolent offense, including more than a quarter for drug law violation and a sixth for driving while intoxicated. Nearly all parolees (94%) had been sentenced to prison for longer than one year. Women made up about 24% of the nation's probationers and 12% of the parolees. Approximately 55% of the adults on probation were white, 29% were black, and 13% were Latino. Forty-one percent of parolees were white, 39% were black, and 18%, Latino. Of the 2.2 million probationers who exited supervision during 2006, nearly 6 in 10 completed their full-term sentences or were released early, and about one in five was reincarcerated. This percentage has remained relatively stable since 1998.[59]

Current recidivism research indicates that more than two-thirds of released offenders will be rearrested within three years of their release.[60] Almost two-thirds of those were rearrested within the first year post-incarceration. In 2003, only 7% of the offenders were involved with transitional facilities and community release programs prior to their release into the community. Offenders involved in transitional services were eligible because they had earned a minimum-custody risk level in the prison system. Inmates at the highest risk for re-offending often do not receive treatment prior to their release from custody and are released into their communities after their sentence has been served, with no aftercare supervision or treatment.[61]

There are four phases of offender reentry, beginning with the offender's time in prison. The phases of reentry should be linked together in a continuum-of-care model for recidivism to be effectively reduced. As part of that continuum, the step-down phase plays an important role in terms of assessing the offender's current risk/need level, orienting the released prisoner to treatment and community standards, and developing master treatment plans. A critical component of an effective reentry model is a seamless "continuum of care," with information about the offender's progress being transmitted through each stage of reentry.[62]

Ideally, the rehabilitation process is initiated when the inmate enters the criminal justice system and continues throughout all phases of reentry. A standardized and validated risk and needs assessment instrument should be administered soon after an inmate's arrival at the institution. After the offender's current risk and needs are determined, an initial continuum-of-care plan should be designed. Inmates should be encouraged through a system of clearly defined sanctions and rewards to participate in the plan. The next recommended phase of reentry includes a "step-down" process in a secure setting in which prisoners are provided an orientation to treatment with an emphasis on the cognitive-behavioral treatment of criminal thinking. Prisoners are exposed to a modified therapeutic community that prepares them for their reentry by rewarding prosocial behavior and extinguishing antisocial behavior. During the step-down phase, prisoners are referred to as "residents" to denote their reentry status and to move them away from identifying themselves as prisoners. This step-down assessment and treatment occurs in a secure setting so that offenders are not prematurely exposed to the challenges of the outside world before they are ready and gives the staff an opportunity to observe prisoners over a period of time, not just in interviews. Program exercises become "dress rehearsals" for reentering offenders so that they can role-play new skills before being released into the community. Dress rehearsals can also differentiate those at high risk for failure during the community release phase from offenders who will be successful. Higher-risk offenders often have their step-down process extended.[63] After completion of the step-down phase, prisoners move into the "community reintegration" phase, with the continuum-of-care plan developed earlier in the process as a guide to needed aftercare services. Prisoners are transferred to halfway houses and monitored as a final phase prior to release back into their communities. Prisoners are provided with an orientation to the obstacles they will face before they are exposed to them. Not preparing prisoners for the stresses in the community increases the likelihood their transition will not prove successful.[64]

The Community Orientation and Reintegration Program in Pennsylvania represents an alternative approach to facilitating prisoners' transition from the prison environment to their home community. The first phase of the program is completed in the prison during the several weeks prior to discharge and addresses the critical issues of parole responsibilities, employment preparation, vocational evaluation, personal finances, substance abuse education, Alcoholics Anonymous/Narcotics Anonymous meetings, housing, family and parenting, mental health, life skills, antisocial attitudes, and community (give-back) services. The program's second phase includes two weeks of programming in one of the community corrections centers, which prepares the inmate for a gradual return to family and community during the four- to six-week period. Inmates with mental illness are closely supervised for years and are provided mental health services that are often better to those they received prior to their incarceration.[65]

Not all prisoners are available for step-down programs. A growing number of prisoners simply opt to serve their full sentences in order to gain unconditional release. In Pennsylvania, the Department of Corrections collaborated with other agencies, including the Office of Mental Health and the Pennsylvania Board of Probation and Parole, to develop reentry protocols for inmates with mental illness and co-occurring disorders. Interdisciplinary mental health treatment teams (made up of the facility's chief psychologist, psychiatrist, healthcare administrator, unit management staff, drug and alcohol treatment specialist, and a custody staff representative) meet at least 12 months prior to the inmate's release, and again six months prior to release, to conduct continuity-of-care planning. The protocol outlines procedures for obtaining a release of

> ### Social Work Stories: Working in a Transition Program
>
> Sherry Wilcox, APRN, LICSW, LADAC, began her career as a psychiatric nurse in a community hospital and also had experience working with disturbed children before returning to graduate school to study social work and become a licensed alcohol and drug counselor. "I discovered, not too surprisingly, that mental illnesses and substance abuse issues often existed side-by-side and I wanted to learn more." For the past 18 years she has worked at New Hampshire Hospital, a state run facility for mentally ill adults, where she currently heads the Restorative Partial Hospital segment of their transitional housing program.
>
> "About 75% of the participants have serious legal issues, ranging from being found incompetent to stand trial to being found not guilty by reason of insanity (NGRI) to having faced a wide range of criminal charges secondary to their mental illness," says Sherry. "It was the increased clinical emphasis and greater opportunity to work with groups as well as individuals that really caught my interest. I wanted to move away from medicine and the 'illness model.' Our program has gotten much busier over the past few years as changes in commitment laws have evolved to afford greater protections for the civil rights of incarcerated mentally ill people, especially those housed in prisons where they receive little or no treatment."
>
> For Sherry, the most rewarding part of her job is forming relationships with the people in her program and helping them to change to meet their goals. She enjoys the variety of working with this population in this setting and also values the degree of autonomy to be creative and to apply a range of skills to the situations she and her staff encounter. Bureaucracy and pressures from limited budgets and time, coupled with high demands for services, present the most difficult issues for Sherry.
>
> Sherry says she uses the 20-minute commute to and from work to gear up and decompress each day. Self-care is an important element of her practice and she gets strenuous exercise several times a week. In addition, she maintains an active family schedule and finds time for her personal pleasures, like "getting outside frequently and reading trashy novels. It is very important to keep good boundaries and do something different with your time away from work."
>
> Sherry encourages people entering the field to keep in mind that this is "not just a job. Follow your skills and interests, develop new ones and try everything—the broader your experience, the better. There is no limit to what you can do in this field if you set your mind to it."

information from the inmate, contacting community MH/MR resources in the prisoner's community, completing applications for various benefits to which the individual might be entitled (for example, medical assistance, veterans benefits, TANF, and Supplemental Security Income), arranging civil commitments for clients who meet involuntary commitment criteria, notifying law enforcement authorities regarding the release of inmates who were considered dangerous (but not committable), and providing mentally ill prisoners with a 30-day supply of medication.[66]

Criminal Justice Reform

In 2001, in a speech to the Minnesota Women Lawyers group, then U.S. Supreme Court Justice Sandra Day O'Connor stated, "If statistics are any indication, the system may well be allowing some innocent defendants to be executed. . . . Serious questions are being raised about whether the death penalty is being fairly administered in this country." Since the reinstatement of the death penalty in the 1970s, more than 100 people have been wrongfully convicted and sentenced to death in the United States, and more than 120 people have been exonerated from death row. In a comprehensive study of capital trials, nearly seven of every ten death sentences handed down by state courts from 1973 to 1995 were overturned due to "serious, reversible error," including incompetent defense counsel, suppression of exculpatory evidence, false confessions, racial manipulation of the jury, and faulty jury instructions.[67] In practice, only some criminal defendants actually receive the effective assistance of counsel. Although most wealthy and some indigent defendants receive effective representation, many indigent defendants and almost all of the working poor do not. Providing access to competent counsel with the time and resources to meaningfully try these cases is one way to enhance the fairness and reliability of our criminal justice system.[68]

Many Americans continue to believe that our criminal justice system has few significant systemic problems. Overall, they believe the costs of improving the system outweigh the marginal benefits gained by freeing a few more innocent persons. Social workers may advocate for their clients who find themselves in need of counsel and work collaboratively to ensure the best outcomes. Social work's core value of social justice is an important consideration in the delivery of services to this population.[69]

CRIME PREVENTION

Reducing Recidivism

Fostering an individual's transition from prison life to mainstream society can be challenging, especially when working with young offenders. However, recent studies have shown that intervention supported through post-release supervision is most effective at reducing recidivism. Many ex-offenders leave prison with no job prospects and no money, support system, or adequate housing. Consequently, they are at risk of re-offending when they return to their neighborhoods. Effective support services and opportunities for rehabilitation can increase the chances of a successful return to a productive life for offenders.

For ex-offenders, reentry is critical to success. **Reentry** is defined as the return of a released or paroled offender to their community. This prisoner reentry is more successful when it is planned, coordinated, and *structured*, and when the community makes a strong commitment to providing opportunities for success. Communities can form local partnerships to help develop the continuum of services that successful reentry requires. Most sources agree that reentry programs that closely monitor offenders upon release, and that provide ongoing treatment programs to ex-offenders in the community, show the highest success rates. Although there is little research on the effectiveness of parole, it is now known that supervision alone has not been found to reduce recidivism. Furthermore, incarceration for parole violations that do not involve a new crime can be counterproductive and may even reduce an offender's chances for successful reentry. Alternative sanctions must be developed. The ability to adequately monitor, case-manage, and provide counseling to parolees is critical to maintaining accountability within the system and to helping offenders meet set goals.

Although this may be regarded by some as being "soft" on offenders, the likely alternative is to repeatedly warehouse individuals and thereby lose any opportunity to make them productive members of the community workforce, earning their own way and supporting their own families.[70] The majority of inmates leave prison with no savings, no immediate entitlement to unemployment benefits, and few job prospects. In addition, inmates typically have little assistance in seeking employment, accessing treatment, and reconnecting with their families. Recent studies have indicated that the moment of release from prison presents an inmate with many barriers, both immediately upon release and during the first few days on the street. These barriers include having appropriate identification, adequate transportation, arranging for housing, employment, and assistance with family reunification. Even the time of day that an inmate is released can make it difficult to connect with family members, treatment providers, and community resources, making the first hours of release critical to an inmate's success. Making social workers available to help manage these transitions may afford a positive resource for inmates and their families.[71]

As stated earlier, approximately 95% of all incarcerated offenders will eventually reenter their home communities. Reentry is experienced by prisoners who are released under the supervised conditions of parole as well as those who are released with no supervision. The goal for both groups is to change behaviors that impede their community success, and to prevent them from committing new crimes. The combination of pre-release preparations coupled with follow-up on the outside (via parole, nonprofit community organizations, faith institutions, family, or friends) might reduce the risk of recidivism or drug relapse and improve the odds of successful reintegration after release. In-prison programs that are both cost-effective and beneficial in preparing inmates for life on the outside include those designed to change the offender's thinking with cognitive skills development, drug and/or mental health treatment, educational programming, vocational training, work (including preemployment and job-readiness skills), job development and job placement assistance, referral to community-based programs, and coordination of continuing treatment and supervision upon release. The effectiveness of these efforts relies upon partnerships among multiple government agencies and the families of offenders. This collaboration can improve outcomes by establishing a continuum of care, reducing duplication of services, and sharing costs among participating agencies and organizations. The central component of prisoner reentry is the family, on which many ex-offenders rely for a place of residence, financial assistance, and emotional support.[72]

Crime Prevention Programs

There are a variety of crime prevention programs and strategies that use specific approaches to anticipate, recognize, appraise, and address crime and/or the factors contributing to crime. Crime prevention may be targeted at different levels, including the individual, community, family, or particular types of locations. Usually, individual-level crime prevention refers to preventing someone from ever committing a crime. These types of crime prevention programs typically target risk factors. The term "crime prevention" is sometimes used in reference to programs that are designed to prevent individuals from committing subsequent crimes (i.e., recidivism). Crime prevention programs or strategies focused on the community may target changes in the community infrastructure, culture, or physical nature in order to reduce crime, such as neighborhood watches and community policing. Finally, "hot spot" policing and similar programs are an example of "place-oriented" crime prevention programs/strategies.[73] The actions of community members are extremely important in preventing crime. Law enforcement agencies can help community members to make sure that homes are secure and that people follow simple precautions to be safe, as well as working with law enforcement to be watchful for the safety of others.[75]

INTERPROFESSIONAL COLLABORATION

Critical Thinking Question

Social science literature provides the opportunity to learn about positive youth development programs. Do a database search and examine one program in detail to see if the program values and supports youth.

For more than a century, social services have been a key part of corrections, and serving crime victims and offenders has been a major social work emphasis. Correctional and social work agencies have long served the same target groups, with varying degrees of success. Studies have suggested that social work–criminal justice partnerships represent a commonsense notion; yet they are, at the same time, a major paradigm shift. Still, to achieve greater and more consistent results, it is clear that human services agencies and correctional institutions must collaborate more effectively in the future.[75]

The number of returning prisoners is on the rise, the needs of inmates and those being released are greater than before, and many jail programs have retained fewer rehabilitation services. As early as the 1920s, writers were discussing development of a social work, education, and corrections "continuum of services." Collaboration, in this case, is both a process and an outcome, in which stakeholders work together to address conflicts that cannot be effectively managed by any single agency alone. Social work's concept of a social systems approach to practice lends itself well to such a collaborative model.[76] **Multi-Agency collaboration** provides the necessary range of services often required to address the serious implications of common issues such as domestic violence and substance abuse. In recent years, more attention has been directed toward improving interagency cooperation.[77] Collaboration attempts to move past old patterns of competitiveness and divisiveness that promoted lack of cooperation within and between agencies and establish a process in which common goals are pursued in mutually beneficial ways. Multiple agencies share power, authority, and accountability. They show mutual respect for each of the other participating agencies.[78]

An example of this type of collaboration can be taken from Fresno County, California, where the number of domestic violence–related calls for assistance was almost double the state average. The community quickly recognized that any single agency was unable to effectively deal this type of problem. A partnership was arranged among community members, the sheriff's office, and a local university to address issues and barriers impeding successful transition from incarceration to the community for domestic violence and substance abuse offenders. Assessment of existing jail programs found them fragmented: inmate assessments rarely conducted; gaps or duplication in services due to lack of communication; and transitional services lacking.[79] The focus was to develop of a community-based response, offering educational services including vocational training, substance abuse classes, batterer's intervention services, anger/conflict management, parenting classes, health education, personal awareness, support groups, and pre-release employment assistance. All of these services would be coordinated through a social work practitioner and social work student interns acting as the liaison to community-based organizations, the educational/vocational community, and the Department of

Health and Human Services. Adopting a case management approach meant several key aspects needed to be addressed to avoid barriers to developing and implementing actions.[80] Task conflict is an expected part of **interprofessional collaboration**. Each agency naturally comes to the table with its own agendas and lack of knowledge about other professionals' roles and procedures. Shared decision making and effective group processing may be new territory for professionals accustomed to top-down decision-making styles. The process requires individuals to be problem centered rather than discipline or individual centered. Agencies need to establish clear communication channels to clarify the resources available and the roles played by each agency, as well as being committed to being flexible throughout the process of establishing and implementing action plans. The process of communicating about issues requiring clarification and identifying alternative solutions stimulated cohesiveness and knowledge to apply to future conflicts.[81]

Problem-solving strategies such as separating people from the problem; focusing on interests, not positions; recognizing that stakeholders' interests may be common or different at the outset, but are changeable over time; establishing options needed for mutual gain; using objective criteria and realistic goals at all stages; sharing leadership, authority, responsibility and resources whenever possible; and involving key players at every level went a long way toward enhancing collaborative efforts.[82] Several standard procedures developed, including developing realistic time frames, recruiting and cross-training staff and interns, collecting data, monitoring practices and document results, using data to drive reassessment of needs and services, identifying problems based on assessment, analyzing information about inmates, criminal statistics, detention programs, and community resources to design and implement strategies "outside the box," and constantly evaluating effectiveness.[83] The community collaborative was able to serve cooperative and promising prisoners as well as difficult-to-reach and dangerous individuals who previously had gone unserved by the system. Collaboration allowed a major realignment in the way services are provided to continue to promote healthy and safe communities.[84]

Social workers also frequently collaborate with the court system, participating as **fact witnesses**, having firsthand knowledge of the individual or situation in question, or as **expert witnesses**, called on by the court to express an interpretive opinion about the facts of a case. For a witness to qualify as expert, the court must determine that he or she has sufficient skill, knowledge, or experience in a field relevant to the case and in procedures for evaluating the case. Social workers often serve as experts in a specialty area of relevance to the case; areas of expertise commonly called for in courts include child welfare, childhood victimization, mental retardation and other developmental disabilities, mental health, deprivation, or discrimination. The role of the social worker as expert witness is to present a reliable and complete portrait of the individual on trial, informing the judge and/or jury about the individual's social history and social functioning and the social context of the crime. The social worker interprets this information, using social research and theory, to increase his or her understanding of the individual's behavior. Particular issues that may be relevant include the age of the individual or the existence of emotional or mental concerns, chronic maltreatment during childhood, remorse for the behavior, capacity for rehabilitation in prison, post-traumatic stress disorder from military service, intoxication and chemical dependency, organic brain damage, previous employment, and efforts to be a good parent and spouse. Other expert witnesses are likely to have expertise in psychology (for personality, behavioral, and intellectual assessments), neurology, pharmacology (for addiction assessments), and special education (for learning disability and mental retardation assessments). Each expert prepares an independent report, usually relying on the social history as an essential foundation for the evaluation. Social workers must be cautious in defining the limits of their expertise. Early in the consultation with attorneys and others, social workers should clarify what a social worker is and does, what the worker's area of expertise is, and how the expertise may be relevant to the needs of a given case. They should also be clear on the roles played by others.[85]

SUMMARY

Although there have been many attempts to explain criminal behavior, theories are still evolving and no one understands definitively why people commit crimes. While certain types of criminal behavior, especially violent crimes, have declined in the U.S. in recent years, crimes involving drugs are increasing. Given the political popularity of "getting tough on crime" over the last few decades, U.S. court systems mandate the longest prison sentences in the world.

Historically, social workers have filled the majority of clinical positions in the court system and corrections process. Forensic social work today involves a wide range of activities, including being an "expert witness" in child protection and domestic abuse, child-custody issues in cases of separation, divorce, neglect, termination of parental rights, juvenile and adult services, corrections and mandated treatment, and elder protection.

There are major differences in the criminal justice system for adults and juveniles, but in each system, social workers are relied on to provide decision-making support as well as individual and family services to those who come in contact with the system. Discrimination in the criminal justice system continues to present major challenges for social workers as a disproportionate number of people of color are incarcerated every year. In addition, the number of women incarcerated is rising at an accelerated rate, resulting in a range of special concerns that need attention. Becoming culturally competent is an important aspect of forensic activities.

Since a significant number of inmates have disabilities such as mental retardation, learning disabilities, chemical dependency, mental illness, or various physical disabilities, incarcerated individuals need social work services to address their counseling, treatment, and education needs during the time served in jail or prison. Dismantling of psychiatric hospitals and fragmentation of the community mental health system have accelerated the trend toward dealing with people with chronic mental illnesses by placing them in correctional settings. Social workers can play a key role in providing diagnosis and facilitating appropriate care for these individuals as well as providing expertise and leadership in the planning, development, and implementation of rehabilitation and drug treatment programs, disease prevention and health education programs, and addressing the concerns of aging prisoners. Since the incarcerated person's family is affected by economic burdens, stigma, and emotional distress, there is a role for social workers in family support as well. Social workers will play an increasing role as advocates and treatment providers for these vulnerable populations.

What to do with inmates once they have completed their sentences, given societal stigma and functional limitations placed on former inmates, is a formidable concern. Recidivism studies indicate that our current practices are not achieving their desired outcomes in the continuum of services that is necessary to address rehabilitation. The number of returning inmates is on the rise at the same time that many jail programs have retained fewer rehabilitation services. Finally, social workers play an active role in planning and implementation of probation and parole support systems. The social systems approach that is so important to social work practice lends itself well to working the interconnections among social work, education, and corrections.

13 CHAPTER REVIEW

Log onto **MySocialWorkLab** to access a wealth of case studies, videos, and assessment. (*If you did not receive an access code to MySocialWorkLab with this text and wish to purchase access online, please visit www.mysocialworklab.com.*)

PRACTICE TEST The following questions will test your knowledge of the content found within this chapter. For additional assessment, including licensing-exam type questions on applying chapter content to practice, visit **MySocialWorkLab**.

1. There are many theories attempting to explain criminal behavior. These theories:
   a. Have demonstrated validity and reliability
   b. Are open to serious debate
   c. Explain some, but not all, situations
   d. Influence the structure of the criminal justice system

2. Which factor does *not* describe the typical inmate in U.S. prisons?
   a. Poor
   b. Undereducated
   c. Possesses strong social connections to positive role models
   d. Is involved in substance use/abuse

3. Mandatory sentences in the U.S. have *not* resulted in:
   a. A sharp increase in the number of individuals in prisons
   b. A reduction in recidivism
   c. The longest prison sentences in the world
   d. The highest percentage of the population incarcerated in the world

4. Convicted felons often that find state and federal laws prevent them from certain activities once they are released. These do not include:
   a. Getting certain categories of jobs
   b. Obtaining a driver's license
   c. Voting
   d. Pursuing higher education

5. Which is *not* part of the criminal justice system?
   a. Probate courts
   b. District and superior courts.
   c. Law enforcement agencies.
   d. Prisons

6. Which is not a "status offense," that is, an offense that applies only to juveniles?
   a. Running away
   b. Truancy
   c. Robbery
   d. Curfew violations

7. Racial discrimination plays:
   a. A major role in our criminal justice system
   b. A minor role in our criminal justice system
   c. No role in our criminal justice system
   d. A well-managed role in our criminal justice system

8. The *intended* focus of our prison system is:
   a. Punishment
   b. Rehabilitation
   c. Protecting the safety of the general public
   d. Providing employment for a large number of workers

9. Which is *not* a usual activity for social workers in criminal justice settings?
   a. Work with individual inmates
   b. Provide expert testimony in court
   c. Provide family counseling and support
   d. Conduct community education programs

10. Inmates in prisons would *not* benefit from:
    a. Educational classes and remedial education
    b. Substance abuse and mental health treatment
    c. Less contact with their families
    d. Job skills training

Log onto **MySocialWorkLab** once you have completed the Practice Test above to access additional study tools and assessment.

Answers

Key: 1) b 2) c 3) b 4) d 5) a 6) c 7) a 8) b 9) b 10) c

14

Aging and Gerontological Social Work

CHAPTER OUTLINE

Who Are Older Americans? 318
Young-Old, Old-Old, and Oldest-Old
The Graying of America

Social and Economic Challenges 319
Ageism
Declines in Private Pensions
Health Care and Prescription Drugs
Transportation Alternatives
Remaining at Home

Elder Abuse 324

Life Cycle Challenges 325
Loss and Grief
Death and Dying
Finding Meaning in Later Life

Services for Older Americans 328
Social Security
Medicare
In-Home Care and Assistance Services
Residential Care and Assisted Living
Senior Centers
Hospice Care

Advocacy and Collaboration for Older Americans 332

Summary 334

Practice Test 335

MySocialWorkLab 335

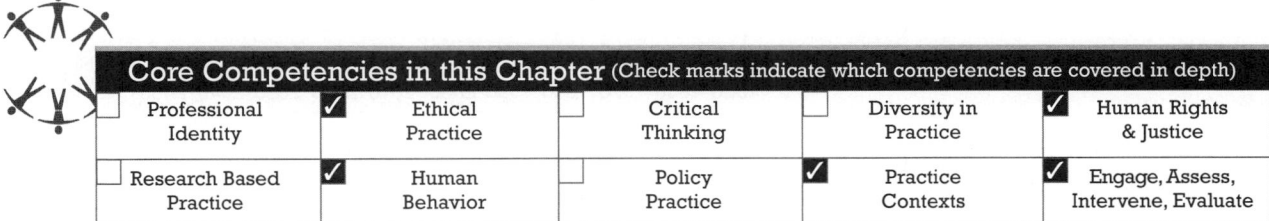

As we grow old, the beauty steals inward.
—Bronson Alcott

Critical Thinking Question

By 2050, people in the U.S. age 65 and older will constitute 21% of the population, almost doubling since 2006 as a percentage of the U.S. population. What services will need to be increased for these older Americans? What new services will be needed?

According to the National Association of Social Workers, 75% of social work professionals have older adults (age 55 and older) in their caseloads. Nearly one-quarter (24%) of social workers indicate that older adults constitute at least 50% of their caseloads. The National Institutes of Health predicts that the United States will need 60,000 to 70,000 social workers to serve this aging population, indicating an increased demand in the future for professionally trained social workers.[1] For these reasons, this chapter takes a closer look at the characteristics of these older Americans, the specific challenges they face, and the services provided by social workers and their colleagues.

WHO ARE OLDER AMERICANS?

In the U.S., and throughout the world, people 65 years of age and over represent the fastest-growing population (see Figure 14.1). In fact, this group is growing at a faster rate than the total U.S. population! As of 2006, there were 37.3 million people 65 and older, comprising 12% of the U.S. population.[2] By 2050, the group will constitute 21% of the population. In short, the U.S. population is graying. However, the development and availability of services for older Americans has lagged behind these changes in the American population.

Young-Old, Old-Old, and Oldest-Old

Average life spans are increasing with individuals who live to age 65 projected to live another 18 years. In fact, 85-year old women can expect to live seven more years.[3] One's chronological age, however, is not an accurate predictor of how young or old one feels, whether biologically, psychologically, functionally, or socially.[4] A better way to judge how old a person feels is to compare his or her physical and mental health to that of people in the same age group. Yet, for the most part, U.S. society still measures old age in terms of chronological years, with 65 being the commonly accepted definition of the beginning of older adulthood. This definition dates back to 1930, when 65 became the age at which an American could start receiving Social Security benefits.[5] Based on a chronological

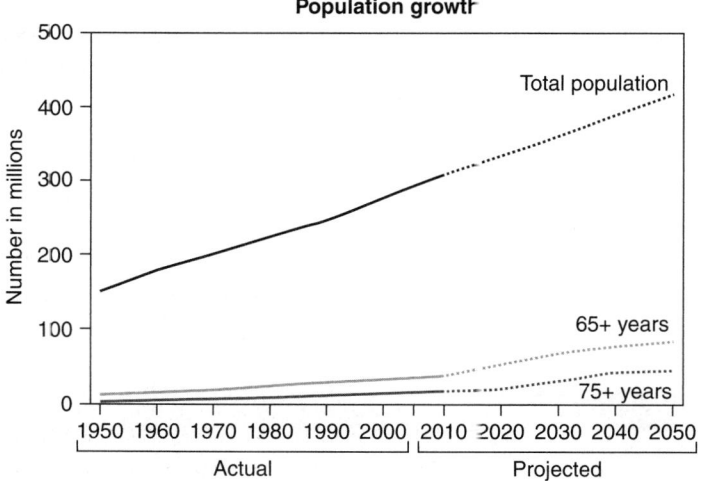

Figure 14.1
U.S. Population Growth
Source: Centers of Disease Control and Prevention, National Center for Health Statistics, Health, United States, 2007, Fig. 1 Data from the U.S. Census Bureau.

definition, older adulthood can be broken down into three categories. The **young-old** category refers to people between the ages of 65 and 74 years of age. The **old-old** category refers to those between the ages of 75 and 84 years, while the **oldest-old** category pertains to those age 85 years and older.[6]

Today, those in the first category, the young-old, typically live quite independently with little difficulty. Those in the second category, the old-old, generally have only begun to experience age-related declines in their cognitive, physical, and health status. It is the oldest-old who experience the greatest deterioration in these areas of their health, and therefore require the most services. It is this last group that is the fastest-growing population in North America and represents the greatest challenge for social welfare policy and services. For example, an estimated 4.5 million Americans now suffer from Alzheimer's disease, and virtually all people in the oldest-old category will require long-term care assistance at some point. Because of this decline in independence and functioning, the oldest-old are at increased risk of suffering from depression, isolation, and abuse. What is more, members of this group often have great difficulty asking for help and, when they do, actually receiving help, due to limitations in the availability of services as well as personal finances.[7]

The Graying of America

Researchers project that by 2030, the number of older adults in America will be over 70 million people, with 9 million of these over age 85.[9] This is what the media refers to as the "graying of America." There are many factors that contribute to these changing demographics. Advancements in medicine and technology have virtually ended the threat of infectious diseases in the U.S., resulting in lower mortality rates from infancy through adulthood. Other factors that contribute to longer life expectancy include improved sanitation, living conditions, working conditions, and nutrition.[10] Furthermore, the surge in U.S. births between 1946 and 1964, better known as the baby boom, produced a sizable cohort that is now reaching older adulthood. Continuing immigration to America of people of all ages, including older adults, is also increasing the number of older adults living in America today.[11] To complicate matters, personal factors such as gender, marital status, ethnicity, geographic residence, lifestyle, and heredity influence longevity.[12] For example, women typically seek medical care more regularly than men in America. They are also less violent, are exposed to fewer environmental hazards, and have greater social support networks.[13] Race and ethnicity are also factors. In fact, white Americans tend to live longer than members of any minority groups, due to the influences of poverty, education, and poor living conditions on people's longevity. In any case, older Americans today are living longer, in part, because they are more active, healthier, and better educated regarding their health than ever before.[14]

> **Did You Know?**
>
> Seventy-seven million people in the U.S. are known as "baby boomers," which represents 27% of the population. Baby boomers are Americans born between 1946 and 1964. In 2011, the first group of baby boomers will reach age 65. Given this population trend, there will be an increased need for social work services.[8]

SOCIAL AND ECONOMIC CHALLENGES

Ageism

American society markets itself as a youthful society. Middle-aged and older Americans are bombarded with commercials from corporate America encouraging them to think young, look young, and feel young. What is more, corporations

> **Demonstrating Knowledge, Values, and Skills: Working With Older Hispanic Clients**
>
> The older Hispanic population is predicted to grow faster than any other minority group. This group is expected to increase from 2 million in 2003 to 15 million in 2050. By 2028, the number of older Hispanic adults will surpass the number of older African Americans.[15]
>
> Make a list of the ways in which this trend might influence your preparation for a career in social work. Consider its impact on casework, group work, community organization, and policy advocacy. Consider which courses you should take. Now pair up with another student and compare notes.

There is only one solution if old age is not to be an absurd parody of our former life ... go on pursuing ends that give our existence a meaning.
—Simone de Beauvoir

have products that will facilitate this miracle if only the individual will purchase the product immediately. Older adults are considered past their prime, no longer able to work, a healthcare burden, and uneducated concerning the latest information and technology. Consequently, older adults in America face "ageism." **Ageism** is defined as discrimination based upon a person's age.

This wasn't always the case. Throughout history, individuals reaching old age were honored and considered valuable because of the relative wisdom that often accompanies longevity. Older adults typically trained younger individuals in everything from hunting and cooking to occupations such as candle-making, barrel-making, sewing, and printing.[16] Today, younger Americans rarely pursue the same occupations as their parents, and in any case, usually do not depend on their parents to learn a trade or profession. Instead, they gain higher education and occupational training through public and private education. Even information about areas such as sex education is often obtained in school, whereas this used to be the responsibility of older adults in the family.

This reduction in meaningful roles and public esteem presents older Americans with many challenges and issues. For example, older adults in America have difficulty preserving a sense of purpose and dignity in their lives, due to pressures to retire from the workforce coupled with losses in their physical, psychological, and social lives.[17] The media often betrays older adults in America as unattractive, useless, grumpy, incompetent, senile, and resource-draining. Consequently, younger Americans often fear aging and do everything they can to prevent or try to prevent this most natural of processes. Women are particularly threatened by aging in the U.S. due to the emphasis on beauty as a criterion of female value. These stereotypes lead to feelings of disempowerment and low self-worth for older Americans. Consequently, aging is now viewed as an individual and social problem that can be, and should be, cured or prevented. As a result, Americans purchase billions of dollars in goods and services that promote a healthier lifestyle. These products and services are promoted as a means to everlasting youth, or at least extended youth. As such, they help ward off the so-called "golden years," which are anything but golden from the perspective of most American advertising.[18]

Declines in Private Pensions

The decline in private pensions represents another challenge facing older Americans. Older Americans receive income from a variety of sources. Providing they are healthy enough, many work part time to earn a little money each week. Most over 65 years of age are eligible for government retirement benefits, and many have employer pension programs. Furthermore, some have personal savings and assets such as savings accounts and stocks. For those with pension benefits, on average, their pensions account for one-fifth of their total income. Nearly two-thirds of the most affluent older Americans—that is, those in the upper 20th percentile—received pension benefits in 2002; however, only 8% of the poorest older Americans—those in the bottom 20th percentile—received pension benefits from employers in 2002.[19]

Employer pension plans are essentially deferred compensation for labor, enabling workers to save a portion of their earnings over time with deferred income tax liability. This allows them to accumulate a larger retirement fund. Because many early pension plans failed to pay out funds to retired workers during severe economic downturns, the government passed the Employees Retirement Income Security Act in 1974, which ensures that workers receive benefits from their retirement plans.[20] Because of this legislation, the number of workers covered by employer pension plans shot up to 50% in the mid-1970s, from only 25% in 1950. This act also changed the nature of employer benefit plans. Prior to the act, employer pension plans were "defined benefit plans," in which both the employer and employee made regular deposits based on a fixed percentage, which were then collected during retirement. Today, however, most employers use a "defined contribution plan." This type of pension plan asks both employer and employee to make a contribution based on previously negotiated percentages from both employer and employee (the percentages from employer and employee don't have to be equal). This money is then invested in financial markets to produce a larger return to the employee upon retirement. The most popular of these defined contribution plans is the 401(k) plan, which makes contributions to a retirement account voluntary for the employee.[21]

The problem for many current workers, however, is that employer pension plans are becoming a luxury. This is because, since the 1970s, the percentage of workers with employer pension plans has stopped growing. In order to be competitive in the global economy, employers increasingly prefer workers with hourly wages and no pension or health benefits. Women are particularly vulnerable, as men are more likely to have jobs with employer pension benefits than women.[22] In any case, only a small percentage of older adults in America have substantial savings and investments. In contrast, about 80% of retired Americans live on incomes that are less than 50% of their pre-retirement annual incomes. Consequently, older Americans often postpone retirement or return to the workforce after reaching age 65.[23]

Health Care and Prescription Drugs

As people reach older adulthood, the frequency of their living with a least one chronic condition or disability increases substantially. In fact, 80% of older adults in the U.S. have at least one chronic condition or disability, including respiratory diseases, digestive diseases, circulatory diseases, arthritis, cataracts, osteoporosis, and hearing impairments. They also suffer more frequently from cognitive impairments such as memory defects, personality changes, disorientation, and loss of bodily functions. Further, older adults in America constitute about 13% of the population, yet use about 50% of hospital days.[24]

Fortunately today, medical care and prescription drugs can slow the rate of decline in the older Americans' health. Because of this, older adults are living longer despite chronic illnesses. The problem, however, is that many older Americans don't have access to affordable health care. For those who do, their health care represents a huge cost to society. Healthcare costs for Americans 65

The [character] of a country can be seen simply in how it treats its old people.

—The Bratzlaver

and older are three to five times greater than for other adults.[25] Most of these costs are attributable to chronic diseases. Those without adequate health care tend to have poorer health and shorter lives. Although nearly all older adults receive Medicare in America, its limited benefits cover only about 55% of their expenses. As a result, older adults in America spend twice as much for health care out of pocket than Americans under age 65. In fact, people over 65 represent 50% of U.S. healthcare spending.[26] The typical older adult in America uses at least four prescription drugs with a median cost of close to $700 a month. Yet only 17% of this cost is covered by private insurance.[27] Drug therapies for cancer and other life-threatening conditions can run as high as $20,000–$40,000 a month without health insurance.[28] Until health care is significantly reformed in America, the cost of health care for older Americans will continue to be a problem, taking a larger percentage of their expendable income.[29]

Transportation Alternatives

Transportation is a significant contributor to personal independence and community integration for older adults.[30] One in four drivers will be over 65 years of age by the year 2030. This reflects both the importance of transportation for older Americans and the graying of America, as previously discussed. Eighty-nine percent of men and 64% of women over age 74 continue to drive on U.S. highways.[31] At the same time, one in seven of all fatal motor vehicle accidents in 2002 involved an elderly driver. We can expect this rate to increase as the percentage of older adults increases in coming years. Consequently, many older Americans give up driving due to significant declines in their physical, visual, and cognitive functioning—this despite the fact that it is so important to their independence in the community.[32]

Older Americans, therefore, need alternative transportation—alternatives to driving themselves. An alternative source of transportation means increased mobility, vitality, and social engagement for them, while protecting society from the increased risk of fatal motor vehicle accidents involving the elderly. Yet only 5% of adults over age 50 even consider public transportation for their regular mode of transportation. This is due, in part, to the inaccessibility of public transportation in many parts of the U.S., especially in rural and suburban areas.[33]

Creative options for senior transportation are beginning to emerge due to the increased demand by elders for such services. Medicabs and Dial-A-Ride programs provide individualized door-to-door transportation services to older

---

Case Study: Living Alone at Age 94

Mrs. Brown is a 94-year old woman living by herself in a small rural community in Kansas. Her husband died several years ago. She is proud of her longevity and independence. Being a former schoolteacher, she has seen her students grow up and have children and grandchildren. She seemingly knows everyone in town.

Mrs. Brown's home is located in a wooded area at the edge of the city. To remain independent, she regularly drives into town to shop for food and get medical care. She also sees her friends along the way. As she has aged, she has become increasingly concerned about driving her car. Her reflexes and eyesight are not as good as they used to be. Consequently, she fears getting into an accident; she particularly fears hitting one of the young children on her street. Yet there is no public transportation in her community. Everyone has a car or truck, it seems. Giving up driving her car would mean the end of her independence.

If you were her social worker, how could you assist her? What services are available in your community?

Americans for a nominal fee. Further, governments are now contracting with local transportation companies to offer reduced fares on buses, taxis, trains, and even airplanes. And grants are now being allocated to private nonprofit agencies to provide senior transportation in urban and rural areas.[34]

Remaining at Home

Social workers serving older adults at times assist healthy, active clients; at other times, they may support older adults who are ill, even terminally ill. In doing such work, social workers can be found in settings that range from adult day care centers and nursing homes to hospitals and public agencies. Social workers link seniors with needed services.[35] Yet, despite stereotypes, 95% of older adults live in their own homes after they retire.[36] Of these people, 70% own their homes, 20% rent, and 5% live in congregate facilities that provide cooking, cleaning, shopping, and other services.[37] It is when frailty and other common problems become unmanageable that older Americans typically resort to institutional care. In fact, about one in three Americans over the age of 85 lives in institutional care.

Fortunately, many options to institutional care are now emerging to meet the needs of our growing elder population. In-home support services are allowing many to live independently and to avoid institutional care. Such services include homemaker services, adult foster care, visiting nurse services, Meals on Wheels, and hospice care. There are also more retirement villages, apartment complexes, and mobile home parks geared to the needs of the elderly.

Older Americans have a great need for a support system to help them remain in their homes after they become frail. Seventy-five percent of older Americans who live in assisted living facilities pay for it through personal or family assets. On average, they spend from $1,000 to $3,000 a month on such housing.[38] Unfortunately, most older Americans cannot afford this. About 30% of older Americans live in housing that is substandard and deteriorating, while about 1 million of the elderly suffering from chronic conditions live in housing that lacks support services, which puts them at increased risk of injury and additional health problems.[39]

The poorest of older Americans resort to public housing, which provides virtually no services, or nursing homes. About 3% of older Americans live in federally assisted housing; but this housing is extremely difficult to access. A 2006 AARP study found there are ten elderly applicants for every one vacant unit in federally assisted housing. These low-income seniors typically wait one or more years for federal housing assistance. This is due, in part, to budget cuts in these programs and the declining number of affordable housing units.[40] At present, most older Americans rely on some sort of family support to make

---

Research Informed Practice

The Cost of Housing

Find the classified section of your Sunday newspaper. Note the cost of buying a home in your community. Note the cost of renting a house or apartment. Determine where the most affordable apartments are located in your community. Are they located in the best neighborhoods? Are the neighborhoods safe from crime? Are they near a hospital? Do they have convenient public transportation? If you were an adult in your late seventies, would you want to live in these neighborhoods? How do you think others would feel about this prospect?

up for inadequate formal services in the U.S. social welfare system. The problem now is that this responsibility often becomes increasingly stressful for family caregivers. Family members providing informal care typically spend more than four hours per day providing this unpaid support.[41]

ELDER ABUSE

Social workers working with older adults and their families assist with decisions on assisted living arrangements, facilitate caregiver support groups, or help families with planning a loved one's long-term care.[42] However, the inadequacy of formal support services for frail older Americans has contributed significantly to a growing problem of "elder abuse."[43] The stress, financial hardship, and loss of leisure time can become overwhelming to family members who provide support to their elderly relatives.[44] When these needy family members suffer from severe mental and physical impairments, the distress can be even greater for family caregivers. Consequently, some of them begin to neglect their caregiver responsibilities or lash out in anger and resentment against their older family members, which can lead to reports of abuse and neglect.[45]

America began to recognize elder abuse and neglect as a growing national social problem in the 1980s. Reports of elder abuse rose from 117,000 in 1986 to 472,813 in 2000. Even so, the incidence of elder abuse and neglect may be much higher than these reports suggest.[46] Victims of elder abuse and neglect often have limited ability or desire to report the abuse, given their mental and physical frailties and their emotional attachments to their family caregivers. In some cases, they may fear increased abuse or abandonment if they do report the abuse or neglect—much like partners in domestic violence situations. Research suggests that the great majority of victims are females over age 80. What is more, almost half of family abusers are the adult children of their victims.[47]

Elder abuse and neglect can take place in formal institutions of care as well—institutions such as assisted living facilities or nursing homes. At times, elderly clients are pushed, grabbed, shouted and yelled at, and otherwise mistreated by institutional staff.[48] This occurs for reasons similar to those found in family abuse and neglect: caregivers suffer much stress due to the mental, physical, and behavioral problems presented by the frail elderly.

Different sources categorize **elder abuse** in slightly different ways. Generally, there are four categories: physical violence, psychological abuse, material abuse, and neglect. **Physical violence** includes the previously described pushing, grabbing, and shouting, as well as sexual assault. **Psychological abuse** includes yelling, name-calling, intimidation, and humiliation. It also includes promoting isolation or anguish. **Material abuse** pertains to the exploitation of the financial and other personal resources of the elderly adult. **Elder neglect** refers more to abandoning older adults who cannot properly take care of themselves. This can include failing to provide or meet basic needs such as food.[49] Elder neglect can be difficult to identify due to the frequency of self-inflicted neglect by elders who refuse to eat or move. In any case, American social welfare policy must address the increasing need for resources and support to facilitate caregiving services for America's growing older population.[50]

LIFECYCLE CHALLENGES

Loss and Grief

Social workers can assist seniors with feelings of loneliness, anxiety, and depression through direct counseling, special healthcare referrals, or even education on better nutrition.[51] Yet, as adults age, they inevitably experience loss in their lives. Decreased beauty, health, sensory and mental sharpness, mobility, and overall functioning accompany biological aging for everyone. As a result, many older adults find it hard to continue doing activities that they love or that are important in some way in their lives, activities such as reading, sexual intimacy, or driving. These activities were once taken for granted; as adults age, these activities often can't be done without assistance. This can be incredibly frustrating for older adults who take pride in their independence.

In addition to these biological losses, elder Americans suffer several losses when they retire. These include occupational status and income losses as well as losses of coworker friendships. Moreover, old age is a time when individuals regularly lose close friends and family members. The losses are especially poignant when the deceased is the elder's spouse or partner. These losses bring isolation for older Americans.[52]

Consequently, older Americans tend to go through relatively frequent periods of grief and bereavement. **Grief** is the emotional response to loss, while **bereavement** refers to a long-term process of adjusting to loss. Grief often involves feelings of disbelief, confusion, numbness, sorrow, anger, and guilt.[53] Individuals experiencing a significant loss may feel abandoned, lonely, depressed, or even relieved. During the bereavement stage, people often blame others or themselves, especially around the sudden death of a family member, friend, or close coworker. At other times, individuals may get obsessive over the events that led up to the loss. Sometimes, people coping with loss feel hopeless or depersonalized. Others lose interest in activities that they normally enjoy.

Older adults cope successfully with grief and bereavement with the support of social workers, other health and human service professionals, and informal caregivers. Providing such support for the growing U.S. elder population continues to be a challenge for American social welfare policy.

Research Informed Practice with Asian Elders

Ada Mui and Suk-Young Kang did a study (*Social Work 51* (2006), pp. 243–254) of six groups of Asian immigrant elders in the U.S. They found acculturation stress to be related to a perceived cultural gap between the older Asian immigrants and their adult children. This acculturation stress was associated with high levels of depression among the older immigrants. Depression among this group was also predicted by such factors as stressful life events, perceived poor health, and the level of assistance received from their adult children.

How could this research inform your efforts as a social worker to assist older Asian immigrants? Specifically, what might you do with this information if you worked with this group in a community senior center?

Death and Dying

In general, Americans tend to avoid thoughts and discussions regarding death. However, this is difficult for older Americans to do, given that the vast majority of people who die each day are over 60 years of age. Consequently, older Americans must deal with the issues of death and dying much more frequently than younger people.

Fortunately, older Americans tend to fear death less than younger Americans do. In part, this is because older Americans believe they have had their time and, thus, are much more accepting of their own mortality. Elders with strong religious beliefs tend to be less anxious about the topic of death than are other people.[55] In fact, older Americans are much more concerned about the process of dying and what it means to their loved ones than they are about death itself. They worry about their increased dependence and the impact it may have on their family members. They also tend to fear extended suffering and poor health along the way. If elders have dependent children or a disabled spouse or even unaccomplished life goals, they are apt to show more anxiety about their own death than they would otherwise.[56]

Elder Americans also worry about where they will die. Elders who are institutionalized or believe that they will die in an institution tend to be more anxious than those who live in their own communities.[57] This is because most older Americans want to die at home with dignity, in the company of their loved ones. Yet the majority of older Americans, in fact, die in large, unfamiliar, relatively impersonal hospitals, nursing homes, or other long-term care institutions.[58] This happens because family members and others believe the institutions are better equipped to handle medical emergencies and to provide palliative care.

However, what patients gain in terms of their physical care, they lose in their emotional care. Medical personnel often withdraw emotionally from dying patients as a way to shield themselves, the patients, and patient family members from difficult death-related discussions. In the process, the elder can be left feeling abandoned and humiliated, with the accompanying loss of dignity.[59] In the past, it was common for medical staff and family members to make decisions about dying patients without full knowledge of the patient's final wishes.[60] Fortunately, this led to a movement in health care for better communication among families, patients, and medical staff. Better communication about death has created another role for social workers and other types of counselors to facilitate the communication. In the process, social workers are able to help dying patients and their families better deal with the concept and reality of death. Often, this type of work takes place through hospice services and home-based palliative care—services that tend to emphasize "death with dignity" for the dying patients. Not only do hospice and related services deal with the dying patients' physical needs, they also deal with social, emotional, and spiritual needs of patients and their families.

Critical Thinking Question

Social workers are knowledgeable about the way social systems can promote individual well-being. Can there be "well-being" even for a terminally ill person? If so, what would it look like? What supports might be involved?

Social Work Stories: Working with Terminally Ill Clients

Writer Mitch Albom talks about his relationship with a dying man named Morrie:

I wondered what regrets he had once he knew his death was imminent. Did he lament lost friends? Would he have done much differently? Selfishly, I wondered if I were in his shoes, would I be consumed with sad thoughts of all that I had missed? Would I regret the secrets I had kept hidden?[54]

As a result, patients and families are better able to find meaning and dignity in death.[61]

Home-based hospice services make sense from a social welfare perspective as well. Not only do patients and families prefer them, but these services are more cost-efficient and effective than institutionalized care. About 40% of Medicare costs are attributable to patients who are in the last 30 days of their life. Further, the financial cost of institution-based care is much higher than home-based care for dying people.[62]

Yet many Americans don't use home-based hospice care. There are several reasons for this, including normal feelings of denial regarding the impending death of the individual, as well as inadequate referral services and community education regarding hospice services. But social workers and other healthcare professionals, as well as family and patient advocates, must advocate for increased use of home-based hospice and related services so that older Americans can be assured of a death with dignity.

Finding Meaning in Later Life

Today, more and more older Americans participating in the workforce are engaged in volunteerism and other social activities—decades after the age of retirement![63] With the right social and economic policies, this generation of older Americans, without a doubt, has the capacity to continue living in meaningful and productive ways. In so doing, not only will elder Americans maintain a sense of competence, self-worth, and dignity after retirement, but society will benefit from their skills, knowledge, and productivity. Policies and programs that allow elders to maintain their independence will reduce the costs to society of supporting a growing aging population, one that has been undervalued and underutilized.

In any case, elder adults often remain engaged in some type of work after retirement. Workforce participation meets not only their financial needs, but also their social and emotional needs. Elders can maintain a feeling of usefulness and gain opportunities to pass on their wisdom to younger coworkers.[64] Elder Americans who take on part-time work after retirement or engage in meaningful volunteering increase their feelings of self-worth while minimizing the negative effects of occupational role loss. Meaningful community involvement such as this reinforces social ties for older Americans, while promoting intellectual and mental creativity. Again, not only does the individual benefit, but society does as well.

Many factors contribute to a happy and meaningful old age, including good health and nutrition, financial security, regular exercise, and adaptive coping styles. Furthermore, strong ties to family, friends, and neighbors can increase health and happiness for older Americans. For example, the grandparenting role in these family networks can promote happiness, pride, and meaning for older Americans. Studies have shown that people with few social contacts are more likely to be institutionalized, have greater need, and a higher mortality rate.[65]

Older adults also benefit from strong religious and spiritual connections in their lives. Religious organizations provide a sense of group identity as well as numerous services and opportunities for socialization. Spiritual faith can provide and enhance individual coping skills with which to face the challenges of aging. Foremost among these skills is the ability to discern meaning out of life and death.[66]

Those who have reached that stage in sweetness and love, who can change their winter into a gentle, Indian summer, have come as victors through the ordeal of life.

—Sir Arthur Conan Doyle

Critical Thinking Question

Social workers assist older adults to find meaning in their lives. If you were working with someone in their nineties in a nursing home, how might you help this person to find meaning from their life story?

Chapter 14

SERVICES FOR OLDER AMERICANS

Social Security

Social Security, originally passed in 1935 by the Franklin D. Roosevelt Administration, is the cornerstone of the American social welfare system. As discussed in earlier chapters, it is a social insurance program for retired and disabled workers.[67] Roughly 90% of older Americans receive Social Security benefits. These benefits are based upon the amount of money the worker paid into the program before retirement. In 2003, the average monthly benefit for a retired worker in the United States was $895 and $452 for the spouse of the worker.[68] For 20% of older Americans, Social Security is now their sole source of income. For two-thirds of seniors, Social Security represents more than half of their income. For seniors in the lowest 40% income bracket, it represents over 80% of their income. Some $577 billion in Social Security benefits was paid out to 49.4 million recipients in 2007. Taxing current workers is the means for paying the majority of these benefits, which represents a potential social problem as the ratio of retired workers to current workers increases.[69]

Medicare

Medicare, as you know from Chapter 8, was established in 1965 as part of the Great Society program of President Lyndon Johnson.[70] Medicare is a social insurance program that assists senior citizens in paying for the cost of acute healthcare needs. These needs include hospital and physician-related services. Over 90% of older Americans who receive Social Security benefits also receive their hospital insurance through **Part A of the Medicare program**.[71] After a deductible of $992, Part A of Medicare pays for the first 60 days of hospitalization. Recipients then pay a daily coinsurance of $248 for days 61 through 90, and $496 for days 91 through 150. However, subsequent medical costs are not covered for beneficiaries.[72]

In addition, Part A covers hospice care for terminally ill patients and may cover up to 20 days in a skilled nursing facility. It also offers partial coverage of in-home rehabilitation services for up to 100 days after hospitalization. Part A does not cover long-term custodial care. Medicare beneficiaries may buy medical insurance through **Part B of the Medicare Program**. This insurance is a supplemental insurance that covers physician services, outpatient services, and ambulatory care (but not long-term custodial care). According to the American Association of Retired Persons (now known simply as AARP), in 2007 Medicare beneficiaries enrolled in Part B pay a monthly premium of $93.50, a $131 annual deductible, and a 20% coinsurance for most services.[73] Medicare began offering **Part D**, an optional prescription drug benefit for elders, under the administration of George W. Bush in 2006. The program has had numerous problems in its conception and implementation, but AARP records that subscribers may save up to $1,200 annually on drug costs.[74]

In 2005, $336 billion was spent on Medicare services. This compares to $37billion in 1980. Clearly, it's a critically needed service for older Americans. Yet the gap between healthcare costs and what Medicare will cover continues to rise. Medicare covers less than 50% of older Americans' medical bills. Furthermore, it offers little help for seniors paying for in-home or assisted living facility services.[75] As indicated earlier, a glaring weakness in the Medicare program is its inadequate coverage of long-term care for senior Americans.

Supplemental Security Income, better known as SSI, and Medicaid, a healthcare program for the poor, help to address some of this gap in long-term care coverage. For example, Medicaid covers about 40% of our nation's total long-term care costs. A weakness in Medicaid coverage, though, is that seniors typically access Medicaid only after healthcare catastrophes and after coinsurance payments have drained away their assets.[76] In any case, American social welfare policy must better meet the challenge of long-term care for its growing elder population in the 21st century.[77]

In-Home Care and Assistance Services

Most older adults receive informal assistance to stay in their own home. Fortunately, though, there has been an increase in formal in-home care and assistance services in recent years. Today, visiting nurse services, homemaker services, Meals on Wheels, adult day care, and adult foster care are available to help elders remain in their homes with the assistance of families. When family members and other informal caregivers are not present, older adults can use these services to receive help with tasks such as meal preparation, transportation, dressing and bathing, laundry, and cleaning. For example, adult day care services provide employed relatives and informal caregivers with respite, while ensuring consistent care and supervision for the older adult. In addition, the majority of day care services provide older adults with nutritious meals, medication services, and social opportunities with peers. The problem for most elders, however, is that over 50% of all in-home formal assistance services are paid for out of pocket by patients and their families. Furthermore, day care services can be quite costly, thereby excluding most low-income elders.[78]

Residential Care and Assisted Living

Sometimes older adults choose to move out of their homes in order to get the support they need. For many, this involves informal support from relatives with whom they choose to live. For others, there are more formal programs such as residential care and assisted living. These services offer a range of support to older adults, depending on the income and level of support the individual requires. For example, some elders move into "retirement hotels," which typically provide the senior with a single room and housekeeping services. Others choose "adult congregate living facilities," which offer the elder a modest apartment with safety features. Larger congregate living facilities may also provide services such as meals, transportation, housekeeping, and social programs.[79]

If the senior citizen requires more support services than typically offered in segregated living environments, then he or she may choose an **assisted living facility**. These facilities enable elders with minor impairments to continue to live relatively independently. Assisted living facilities offer residents three communal meals a day, housekeeping, medication monitoring, personal care, transportation to medical appointments, and social opportunities.[80]

For more affluent senior citizens, "retirement communities" may be the best option. These communities are enclosed facilities that typically provide residents with such services as exercise classes, a swimming pool, tennis courts, and even golf courses. More recently, retirement communities have begun offering services such as massage therapy, movies, beauty salons, investment counseling, educational seminars, reading groups, tai chi, and gourmet dining. Most assisted living facilities offer spiritual services on-site. Obviously, these are luxuries that low-income elders cannot afford. For instance, entrance fees for these retirement communities are often over $100,000, and 90% of assisted living accommodations are paid for out of pocket by the older adult and their family.[81]

Finally, many elders live in nursing homes. Many do so because nursing homes are more affordable than other alternatives. Others do so because their worsening disability cannot be adequately addressed utilizing other options. **nursing homes** are residential facilities that provide continuous care to frail and impaired elders. A typical nursing home staff includes registered nurses and other trained staff members who provide 24-hour medical supervision. Nursing homes also provide rehabilitation and other therapeutic services to elders.[82] This is in addition to basic services such as help with feeding, toileting, dressing, and mobility.

A problem for many elders living in nursing homes, however, is service quality. The quality of care can be less than optimal due to rising healthcare costs, tight budget constraints, and poorly trained staff. In the past, nursing homes have been associated with elder abuse and neglect. In addition, nursing home residents may have limited access to physicians. An additional problem is that the institutional culture of many nursing homes stresses adherence to daily routines by elders over their physical, psychological, and emotional needs on any given day.[83] Despite these limitations, millions of Americans throughout the U.S. live in nursing homes as part of the overall system of care or older Americans.

Senior Centers

Senior centers are at the heart of community-based support networks for older adults. These are community facilities or programs that offer many benefits, including a warm and friendly place to socialize with peers. Additionally, senior centers typically offer recreational programs, adult day care, volunteer opportunities, educational classes, counseling and support groups, information and referrals, and, at times, advocacy. They may also hold dinners, raffles, and games, such as bingo. Furthermore, centers often sponsor day trips that get seniors out of their communities to explore scenic areas of the country or to visit major resorts. As a result, seniors are able to remain active and integrated in the community, while not becoming isolated in those communities.

The problem in terms of social welfare policy and services is that senior centers are not designed to serve older adults with major disabilities. In addition, they often lack adequate transportation by which seniors can easily access the centers. Given the sprawling suburban communities in the U.S., lack of transportation can be a barrier for seniors wishing to use community-based senior centers. Consequently, senior centers tend to be utilized by older adults who are relatively independent and live close to the centers.[84]

Hospice Care

Hospice care is an increasingly significant resource in senior service systems. Hospice helps dying patients by providing support to the patients and their families—support not only for their physical needs, but also for their social, emotional, and spiritual needs. The hospice concept was developed in the 1960s by a London nurse who recognized the need for her terminally ill patients

Aging and Gerontological Social Work

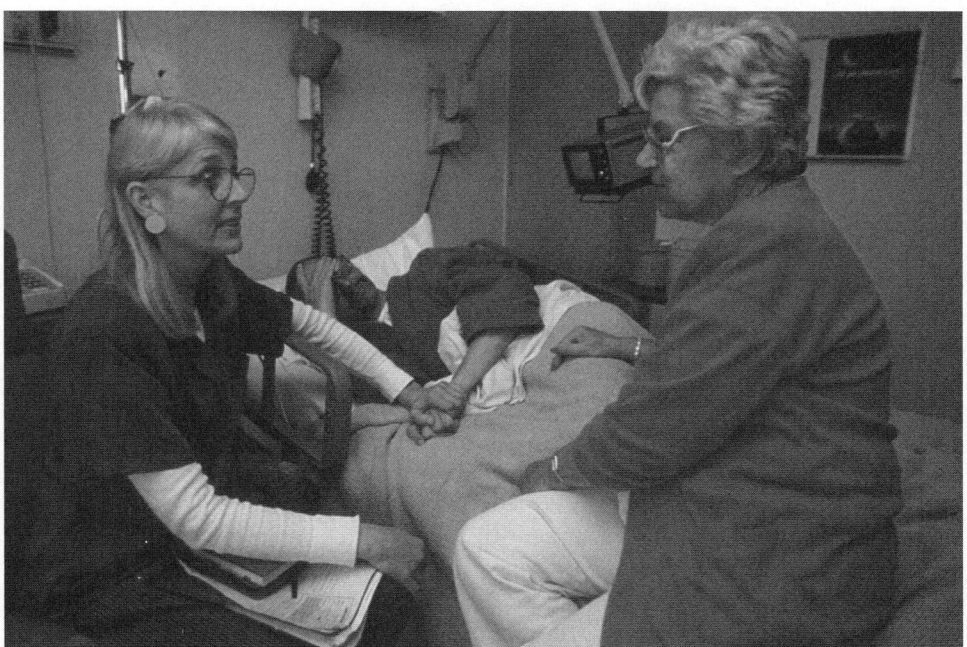

in the hospital to develop more positive attitudes toward death as a way to make dying more comfortable and dignified. Like many programs in the American social welfare system, the hospice concept was imported from Great Britain to serve Americans.[85]

Because of its philosophy of making death personable and dignified, hospice services do not attempt to prolong life. Instead, hospice services stress making the patient's dying days as meaningful and significant as possible.

Social Work Stories: The Hospice Social Worker

Hospice medical care is a relatively new source of job opportunities for master's-level, licensed social workers. Edie McCaddin-Bower has been a social worker at Seacoast Hospice in Exeter, New Hampshire, since 1994. She earned her bachelor of arts in social services from the University of New Hampshire and her master's in social work from the University of Michigan. Edie likes being a hospice social worker for many reasons. Social workers in hospice programs collaborate with an interdisciplinary team of professionals, including physicians, nurses, pastoral counselors, and home healthcare staff. Together, this team plans and carries out each patient's care.

Edie particularly enjoys helping individuals who are terminally ill, because "death is a transition everyone will go through." Edie also looks forward to listening to individuals and their loved ones share the stories of their lives. Remembering and reminiscing about special moments in the dying person's life is healthy for all of the involved people. It is part of making meaning out of the dying person's life.

What is more, Edie says that she frequently observes growth in people—even in the final days and moments of their lives. For many, this growth involves coming to terms with their mortality. For others, it may be learning to say "I love you" for the first time to a family member. "A daughter came to me one time and told me that her father had never said 'I love you' to her." When Edie asked the father about this, he responded, "She knows I love her." "But have you ever told her directly?" asked Edie. The father could not remember. In his last days, he made sure to tell his daughter that he loved her.[88]

Emphasis is on the quality of life remaining and not on futile attempts to prolong life in impersonal, dehumanizing, and alienating hospital atmospheres. Hospice encourages patients and family members to talk about death as a way to review their lives and relationships and to provide closure and meaning to those relationships and life in general.[86]

To achieve these objectives, hospice services typically involve a team of professionals, including social workers, physicians, nurses, spiritual caregivers, and trained volunteers. This interdisciplinary team collaborates to provide 24-hour care and support to patients and their families. Furthermore, hospice strives to maintain quality family contact with dying patients so that, when the time comes, his/her loved ones and familiar settings can surround the dying patient.

Hospice normally serves older adults and other patients who have a prognosis of death within weeks or months. And since 1983, Medicare, Medicaid, and several private insurance policies have covered hospice care, making it more accessible to older Americans. Even so, most hospice agencies have to supplement these funding streams with grants and charitable donations. In so doing, hospice aims to provide its services without regard to ability to pay. The future challenge for social workers and other professionals involved in hospice care is to continue providing services without requiring tests of financial means. Further, the role of social workers in hospice multidisciplinary teams needs to be better defined throughout the country. This includes training for social workers and other professionals working on issues such as patient advanced directives, informed consent, and self-determination.[87]

Critical Thinking Question

Social work is a value-based profession. Based upon what you now know about this profession, in what ways does hospice care reflect the values of social work?

ADVOCACY AND COLLABORATION FOR OLDER AMERICANS

Advocacy for the elderly in America has grown considerably since 1965. Historically, Americans have always considered the elderly to be deserving of social welfare services, given the decline in physical and mental abilities that accompany aging. This historical compassion, along with the growing numbers of older Americans, has made senior citizens in the United States one of the most politically powerful societal groups. The Older Americans Act of 1965 was passed during the Lyndon Johnson Administration.[89] This act established a system of **Area Agencies on Aging** to develop, coordinate, and, in some cases, deliver services for older Americans. Today, over 600 Area Agencies on Aging, as well as other national service organizations, serve Americans aged 60 and over. These services include **Meals on Wheels** programs and the **Foster Grandparent program**. Meals on Wheels delivers hot meals to senior citizens in their homes throughout America; the Foster Grandparent program links older adults with volunteer opportunities in their communities in order to provide seniors with opportunities for socialization and to make meaningful contributions to their neighborhoods.[90]

The Administration on Aging funds two national resource centers and several state programs that provide professionals in the public with training, technical assistance, and information on the prevention of elder abuse and neglect.[91] What is more, a long-term care ombudsman program is available in all federally funded facilities to protect long-term care residence who report abuse and other violations of their rights. All 50 states provide adult protective services for reporting and investigating elder abuse. The goal of adult protective services is to preserve the freedom and safety of older Americans with minimal life disruption. To achieve this goal, adult protective services typically offer a range of community and in-home resources to victims and abusers to reduce the probability of future abuse and prevent the senior from having to be put in institutional care.[92]

Many of the previously described programs and services have been developed, in part, because of the advocacy efforts of the **American Association of Retired Persons** (AARP). This nonprofit advocacy organization has 40 million members and offices in all 50 states. Since 1958, AARP has lobbied national and state policymakers on social problems and issues affecting senior citizens. What is more, it pursues legal action to protect older Americans' rights.[93]

In addition to this advocacy, AARP provides a variety of member services. These services include voter education, healthcare and prescription drug discount programs, travel opportunities, a library on social gerontology, a credit union, radio programs, and a monthly magazine. As such, AARP has become the leading advocacy organization for senior citizens in the U.S.[94]

AARP is joined in its advocacy efforts by the "Gray Panthers," a group established in 1970 by six women protesting their own mandatory retirements. Since then, the Gray Panthers have established a history of speaking out against age discrimination on behalf of millions of older adults in the United States. To do this, the Gray Panthers have established 85 local chapters around the country and report a membership of 70,000 seniors. The group is known for its aggressive advocacy tactics—including demonstrations, rallies, letter-writing campaigns, federal legal action, telephone campaigns, public forums, petition drives, massive education programs, and consciousness-raising groups. In addition to mandatory retirement laws, the targets of its advocacy have been such social issues as national health care, nursing home reform, affordable housing, lower prescription drug prices, elder abuse prevention, and economic security.[95]

As baby boomers reach retirement, social workers and other professions will need to collaborate with organizations such as AARP and the Gray Panthers in continuing to push for better social welfare insurance and services for older Americans. Americans are living longer and healthier; the nation must utilize the knowledge, skills, and potential contributions of its millions of older citizens. These seniors can be either part of the problem or part of the solution to aging with dignity in the U.S. All age groups will benefit in the process!

Demonstrating Knowledge, Values, and Skills

Think of an older adult that you know. Imagine that he or she has recently been released from the hospital and is coming to you for services. Create a treatment plan for this person using eldercare services and resources. Include what the client's main goal is for coming to see you for assistance. Be sure to incorporate the status of his or her housing, current mode of transportation, health status, healthcare providers, and other community programs in which the elderly person is connected or interested.

Are these resources readily available in your community and how do they play a part in your client's goal? Why is it important to consider your client's community resources (i.e., environment) as well as his or her personal resources?

SUMMARY

In the U.S., and throughout the world, people over 65 years of age represent the fastest-growing population. During the 20th century, the number of older Americans increased tenfold. At the start of the 21st century, this group reached almost 34 million people, comprising 13% of the U.S. population. These older adults face many challenges as they age, including physical violence, psychological abuse, material abuse, elder neglect, grief, and bereavement. To help elders cope with these issues, the U.S. provides Social Security, Medicare, Supplemental Security Income, Medicaid, residential care and assisted living, in-home care and assistance services, senior centers, and hospice care, among other programs. Yet this is not enough. Social workers and groups, such as AARP and the Gray Panthers, must continue to advocate for a society that treats older Americans with respect and dignity.

14 CHAPTER REVIEW

Succeed with **mysocialworklab**

Log onto **MySocialWorkLab** to access a wealth of case studies, videos, and assessment. (*If you did not receive an access code to **MySocialWorkLab** with this text and wish to purchase access online, please visit www.mysocialworklab.com.*)

PRACTICE TEST
The following questions will test your knowledge of the content found within this chapter. For additional assessment, including licensing-exam type questions on applying chapter content to practice, visit **MySocialWorkLab**.

Ethical Practice

1. According to NASW, _____ percent of social workers report they have older adults on their caseloads:
   a. 50%
   b. 75%
   c. 35%
   d. 10%

2. The surge in birthrates in the U.S. between 1946 and 1964 resulted in a generation referred to as:
   a. Baby boomers
   b. Generation X
   c. Generation Y
   d. The Truman cohort

Practice Contexts

3. Longer life in the U.S. is likely not related to:
   a. More people receiving better medical care
   b. More people involved in improved nutrition
   c. More people enjoying improved living / working conditions
   d. More people avoiding at-risk behaviors

4. Health insurance for most older Americans is provided through:
   a. Medicaid
   b. Medicare
   c. Private insurance
   d. Social security

Engage Assess Intervene Evaluate

5. The so-called "graying of America" can be seen in the fact that the fastest growing segment of American population is:
   a. Young-old (65–74 years old)
   b. Old-old (75–84 years old)
   c. Oldest-old (85 years old and older)
   d. Late adult (55–64 years old)

6. Most older adults receive the majority of needed services:
   a. In a nursing home
   b. In their own home
   c. In an assisted living facility
   d. In a hospital or rehabilitation center

7. Which of the following is *not* a social service program designed to support older adults?
   a. Meals on Wheels.
   b. Senior centers and adult day care
   c. WIC
   d. SSI

Engage Assess Intervene Evaluate

8. Which is *not* a challenge many older adults face as they age?
   a. Neglect
   b. Ageism
   c. Grief and bereavement
   d. Enhanced earning potential

Human Rights & Justice

9. One organization that advocates on behalf of older adults is:
   a. AARP
   b. GOP
   c. NAACP
   d. ACLU

10. Hospice care does not provide older adults and others who are dying with:
    a. An alternative to dying in a hospital
    b. Palliative (comfort) care as they die
    c. Death with dignity
    d. Crisis care and treatment

Log onto **MySocialWorkLab** once you have completed the Practice Test above to access additional study tools and assessment.

Answers

Key: 1) b 2) a 3) d 4) b 5) c 6) b 7) c 8) d 9) a 10) d

15

Globalization and International Social Work

CHAPTER OUTLINE

The Global Economy 337
Globalization Defined
A Brief History of Globalization
The Political Foundation of Globalization

Positive Aspects of Globalization 339
China and Globalization

The Negative Aspects of Globalization 342
The Clash of Civilizations
Unemployment and Economic Inequality
Case Study: Wal-Mart and the Power of Global Corporations
Loss of Cultural Identity

Loss of Indigenous Economies
Loss of Corporate Social Accountability
The Weakening of Democracy

The Future: Collaboration and International Social work 349
International Social Work and the Importance of Social Work Values

Summary 353

Practice Test 354

 MySocialWorkLab 354

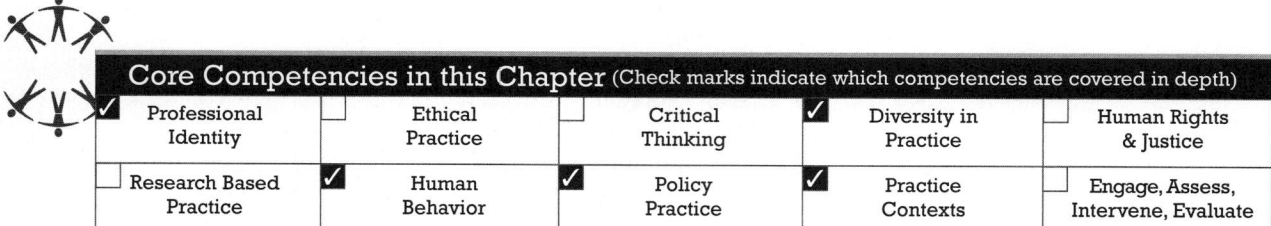

Core Competencies in this Chapter (Check marks indicate which competencies are covered in depth)					
✓ Professional Identity	☐ Ethical Practice	☐ Critical Thinking	✓ Diversity in Practice	☐ Human Rights & Justice	
☐ Research Based Practice	✓ Human Behavior	✓ Policy Practice	✓ Practice Contexts	☐ Engage, Assess, Intervene, Evaluate	

THE GLOBAL ECONOMY

An area of increasing involvement for the profession of social work is the globalization of economic, political, and social institutions. Recent developments in globalization impact the work of social workers, whether their employment is in the United States or in foreign countries. Consequently, this chapter examines historical trends in globalization, the positive and negative influences it is producing for people around the world, and the roles that social workers play in the international arena.

Globalization Defined

Globalization, as defined earlier in this book, is "the integration of markets, nation-states, and technology to a degree never witnessed before."[2] The technologies that make a global economy possible include computerization, digitization, satellite communications, fiber optics, and the Internet. These technologies, as previously stated, are allowing corporations to create a global market for their goods and services, a market that increasingly reaches across national borders, defense systems, and cultures.

Did You Know?

Although American corporations have blasted off in the application of Internet technology, the research that led to the development of the Internet was done in the U.S. government sector, not the business sector, as you might expect.[3] Despite laissez-faire rhetoric about government staying out of the way, the Internet is a good example of the way in which the public sector contributes to the private sectors, both for-profit and nonprofit, in the U.S. Ultimately, it's a partnership for social welfare!

A Brief History of Globalization

There have been three eras of globalization.[4] The first era was roughly 1492 to 1800. Globalization during this era was driven by nations changing to global economies. During this epic transition, foreign trade became more important in creating employment and national wealth. Under the "mercantilist" policies that were in place during the transition from feudalism to capitalism, the wealth of a nation-state was measured by the amount of gold and silver obtained through a favorable balance of trade. The basic economic unit was

Social Work Stories: Violence and Poverty

Author Amartya Sen discusses violence and extreme poverty:

I was playing one afternoon—I must have been around ten or so—in the garden in our family home in the city of Dhaka, now the capital of Bangladesh, when a man came through the gate screaming pitifully and bleeding profusely; he had been knifed in the back. Those were the days of communal riots (with Hindus and Muslims killing each other), which preceded the independence and partitioning of India and Pakistan. The knifed man, called Kader Mia, was a Muslim daily laborer who had come for work in a neighboring house—for a tiny reward—and had been knifed on the street by some communal thugs in our largely Hindu area. As I gave him water while also crying for help from adults in the house, and moments later, as he was rushed to the hospital by my father, Kader Mia went on telling that his wife had told him not to go into a hostile area in such troubled times. But Kader Mia had to go out in search of work and a bit of earning because his family had nothing to eat. The penalty . . . turned out to be death, which occurred later on in the hospital. . . . The experience was devastating for me. . . . But more immediately, it also pointed to the remarkable fact that . . . extreme poverty . . . can make a person a helpless prey. . . .[1]

the state, in contrast to the individual under capitalism. The larger the balance of trade, the greater was the nation's independence and power. Thus, the development of colonies overseas became increasingly important as sources of gold, silver, and tradable commodities, as places such as England and France became strong national entities. This transition was facilitated by wind, muscle, and machine power—that is, by sailing vessels, horses, human labor, and, later, the steam engine.[5]

The second era of globalization spanned the two centuries between 1800 and 2000, approximately. Corporations going global spurred globalization during this second. The transition this time was facilitated by hardware. More specifically, this second surge in globalization resulted from improvements in transportation and telecommunications.[6]

This era of globalization first witnessed the industrialization of America. For example, in the decade of the 1880s, the value of manufacturing output in the U.S. almost doubled, growing from about $5 billion to $9 billion. By 1900, the U.S. was the undisputed industrial power of the world.[7] Between 1875, when Andrew Carnegie opened his new "million-dollar" steel mill, and 1890, U.S. steel production increased 50-fold. America's ability to ship raw materials and finished products accelerated. In addition, by 1916, businessmen such as Cornelius Vanderbilt, E. H. Harriman, and Leland Stanford had built 254,000 miles of railroads, a national transportation system that represented one-third of the world's total railroad system.[8] Now American labor, raw materials, food, and other products could be more rapidly transported by sea or land. At the same time, John D. Rockefeller's Standard Oil Company, one of the world's first multinational corporations, began to supply 90% of the oil used in the U.S. and 80% of the world's supply.[9]

As America entered the 20th century, the growth in use of automobiles, electricity, radio, as well as telephones, televisions, and computers later in the century powered this second globalization phase. Automobiles, once a luxury for rich Americans, now gave industrial workers and farmers much greater mobility. Electricity put an end to much of the backbreaking work in the American home. Electric refrigerators, irons, stoves, and washing machines eventually became widespread.[10] On the farm, electric tools such as saws, pumps, and grinders made farmers more productive. By 1922, radios were common sources of news and entertainment for American families; by the 1940s, telephones became common in American households. Later, in the 1950s, radio was joined by television as a popular source of family entertainment. And finally, by the 1990s, personal computers revolutionized the home and workplace.[11]

The third and latest era in globalization started around the year 2000. Individuals going global drive this third phase. Now, the underlying technology change is software.[12] That is, the technologies that make this latest phase possible include not only computerization, but digitization, satellite communications, fiber optics, and the Internet. These technologies are allowing individuals to create a global market for their goods and services. This means that anyone with a personal computer and an Internet provider can start his or her own business, with the ability to reach individual consumers in countries all over the world. Witness the success of Amazon.com, eBay, Google, YouTube, MySpace, and Twitter.

The Political Foundation of Globalization

The political foundation of the current global economy can be traced, in part, to the Great Depression and World War II.[13] U.S. policy planners wanted to rebuild war-torn Europe, while preventing another Great Depression from happening in the future. To this end, policy planners from an elite private nonprofit group called the Council on Foreign Affairs, collaborating with planners from the federal State Department, provided President Franklin Roosevelt with a policy proposal for creating a postwar global economy. Specifically, the group's recommendations called for the creation of an institutional framework for an open global economy. Combined with similar proposals from other sources such as the U.S. Department of the Treasury, this policy planning was agreed to by the representatives of several Western nations at an international meeting at Bretton Woods, New Hampshire, in 1944.[14] The global plan led to the establishment of the **International Monetary Fund** (IMF) and the **World Bank**. The International Monetary Fund became responsible for facilitating world trade by maintaining stability and liquidity in national currencies around the globe. In addition, the World Bank was charged with the mission of promoting capital investments in developing countries.[15] As the Cold War developed, these global economic policy plans also became a means to counter the Soviet Union and the spread of communism around the world.[16]

During the 1980s, Reagan Administration policies facilitated a series of corporate acquisitions, mergers, and downsizing. It was said to be the largest corporate restructuring in U.S. history, with over 25,000 such deals during the Reagan presidency.[17] What looked to the average observer to be a corporate sector out of control in pursuit of profit was really to a large extent the redesign of the American economic sector.[18] The objective was to position American corporations for success in the new global economy. Then in 1994, during the Clinton Administration, Congress passed legislation that approved the establishment of the **World Trade Organization**.[19] This organization's purpose is to facilitate world trade, in large part by serving as an arbitrator in trade disputes between various nations around the world. These policy decisions by the World Trade Organization are binding, enforceable through trade sanctions on uncooperative countries. Thus the age of the **Multinational**, the **transnational**, and the **global corporation** is upon us, for better or for worse.[20]

POSITIVE ASPECTS OF GLOBALIZATION

The promise of a global economy based on free market principles is a rise in living standards worldwide. Supporters of globalization maintain that capitalism is a tool for creating wealth. Therefore, to the extent that countries throughout the world develop modern free market economies, billions of people around the globe will be lifted out of poverty. What data supports this assertion? Proponents of globalization say to look at world history:

> The move from universal poverty to varying degrees of prosperity has happened rapidly in the span of human history. Two hundred years ago the idea that we could potentially achieve the end of extreme poverty would have been unimaginable. Just about everybody was poor, with the exception of a very small minority of rulers and large landowners. Life was as difficult in much of Europe as it was in India or China. Our great-great-grandparents were, with very few exceptions, most likely poor and living on a farm.[21]

The argument for globalization states that the spread of free market economies, accelerated by technological breakthroughs in agriculture and industry in the mid-1700s, eventually created unprecedented prosperity in whole regions of

Once poverty is gone, we'll need to build museums to display its horror to future generations.
—Muhammad Yunus

the world, including Western Europe, the U.S., Canada, Japan, and Australia.²² Thus, world prosperity has been on the rise for 200 years—but at different rates in different regions of the world.

"**First World**" nations, such as Great Britain and the U.S., were the first to develop free market capitalist economies and are commonly known as the rich nations of the world. "**Second World**" nations refer to former non-market nations with centrally planned economies and state ownership of the means of production, nations such Russia and China.²³ These nations, although industrialized, only recently began the conversion to free market economies. The fall of the Berlin Wall in 1989 and the collapse of the Soviet Union in 1991 mark important dates in this transition. At their peak, these second world nations consisted of about 30 countries and one-third of the world's population. Virtually all of these nations are now transitioning to free market economies with the goal of full integration into the global economy. Why? The most fundamental reason is that their centrally planned economies were not producing the standard of living and level of prosperity of the free market nations in the first world. Modern advances in telecommunications prevented the totalitarian governments of second world nations from continuing to hide this fact from their citizens. Radio, television, and, more recently, the Internet have, therefore, mobilized this newest phase of globalization.

And finally, there is the "**Third World**". This term originally referred to former colonial nations emerging from imperial domination, who upon gaining independence chose not to be part of the first world capitalist nations or the second world communist bloc. Instead, they nurtured indigenous economies with the aim of independence and self-sufficiency—literally, a "third way."²⁴

Today, this group of nations is often thought of as the poor nations of the world, many found in sub-Saharan Africa and South Asia.²⁵ Global economists point out that these countries have remained poor, in part, because they have closed themselves off from the global economy and from the technological innovations that lead to progress and prosperity. They have not forced their national businesses to compete on a global scale, but have protected them with tariffs and subsidies. Consequently, these nations have supported inefficient local businesses that produce relatively high-cost products, products that can't be sold to a world market. The outcome was increasing national debt, government corruption, and national poverty.

Critical Thinking Question

International social work concerns itself with social welfare in "third world" nations. In what ways can social workers help people coping with the transition to a free market economy in former third world nations?

The solution, according to globalization experts, is for such countries to adopt free market economies. The transition will be painful at first. History shows that such transitions often involve violent clashes and value changes impacting gender roles, families, religion, and communities. But the long-term benefit may be more rapid rises in national prosperity and an end to extreme poverty.²⁶

China and Globalization

China is also transitioning to a free market economy.³² Like India, China is a former non-market, government-planned economy that was stricken by enormous poverty. Its communist government, backed by a huge military, controlled the production of goods and services for the nation. In the process, Chinese producers were subsidized by the government and protected from world competition. New ideas and technologies as well as old ideologies concerning private property and individual profit were considered a threat by the Chinese government. The result was a huge but underdeveloped labor force, most of which toiled in poverty.

[A] person stands in the great space of possibility . . . with an unfettered imagination for what can be.

—Rosamund Stone Zander and Benjamin Zander

Although poverty continues to be a problem, the transition to a free market has been sudden and dramatic. Beginning in the early 1990s, the Chinese government

Case Study: India

One case example is India.[27] Before the latest phase in globalization took hold, India was one of many government-controlled economies in the world. Such economies were commonly called command economies or centrally planned economies. Hence, India was a non-market nation, a national economy without the economic efficiencies that market economies enjoy. For example, in typical non-market economies, the price of goods and services to consumers was not based on supply and demand; manufacturers had little incentive to keep the costs of producing goods and services at a minimum. Further, non-market economies limit individual profit, thereby offering limited incentives for individual initiative and creativity in the workplace.

Instead, the government planned the economy for the nation. It decided how many different products to make and at what price to sell the products to consumers. As a result, such economies were considered over-planned and over-controlled, slow to innovate, slow to adopt new technologies, mistrustful of new ideas and information, and inattentive to consumer preferences. The result was massive poverty and a shortage of consumer goods throughout such nations.

India suffered from these economic ailments also. The nation was cut off from world trade by its government. There was a chronic shortage of food products. A large percentage of the country's population suffered from hunger. For more affluent citizens, it took months to buy a computer or an automobile. By 1991, the nation as a whole was on the verge of bankruptcy. Its national economic growth rate was close to zero.[28]

Consequently, India started the transition to a free market economy. The government gave up much control of the economy. Government subsidies to industry were cut. Tariff and trade restrictions were eliminated. Inflation was brought under control. Indian industry was galvanized and started to boom. The national economy started to grow.

As the 21st century began, India became a leading world economy. Farmers brought their crops to market as they had for centuries; however, the price they were paid was not set by local markets, but by world markets. Today, food crops are not the only product of India. India produces about 30% of the world's software engineers.[29] By 2007, the quality of its business schools was ranked eighth in the world.[30] American corporations have outsourced many telecommunications and other service jobs to a well-educated and relatively inexpensive Indian labor force. Today, when you call a credit card call center to check on your balance and someone says, "My name is Sarah; how may I help you?" Sarah may very well be a service professional in India (with the made up name, "Sarah.") In fact, India is becoming more prominent globally in many areas, including medicine and film. Globalization seems to be having a positive impact on India.

---

opened its national borders to foreign business investors, resulting in billions of dollars of investments in China. This meant that close to one-quarter of the world's population entered the global economy during this period. Today, many young people who grew up on rural farms are moving to urban areas of China to take jobs in manufacturing and services. This represents a human migration of epic proportions. These young adults are finding that they can earn 30 times the income they previously earned. Already, opening the Chinese nation to world trade has lifted over 300 million Chinese out of poverty. China now has free trade zones where businesses can manufacture and export products without government trade tariffs, which raise the cost of productions. Hence, these Chinese businesses can sell their products all over the world. Given its communist past, this is a remarkable change for the Chinese population.[33]

One of the most prominent corporations in the Chinese economy is none other than Wal-Mart, the giant American retailer. In 2004, Wal-Mart imported $18 billion

Did You Know?

India and China are examples of the **"Asian Model" of Globalization**.[31] Governments in these nations are now relying more on a free market economy than previously, but remain more involved in the economy than many Western governments. Perhaps reflecting a healthy skepticism regarding capitalism, these governments in former non-market nations aim to carefully develop and guide their market economies, hoping to avoid the irregularities and injustices of Western capitalist countries.

> **Did You Know?**
>
> Did you know that 80% of the world's future economic growth is expected to take place in urban areas? Today, more of the world's population resides in urban areas than rural areas. This is a recent development.[34]

of products made in China. This represented 10% of the goods imported into the United States from China that year.[35] Consequently, many products now purchased by American consumers are made in China by a relatively inexpensive labor force. American consumers get less costly products, while Chinese laborers get better-paying jobs.[36]

And Wal-Mart is not the only American company interested in doing business with China; many American companies have opened manufacturing and retail businesses in China. Thus, the growing importance of China in the world economy will continue in the first half of the 21st century. Economist Joseph Stiglitz, discussing globalization, wrote:

> Opening up to international trade has helped many countries grow far more quickly than they would otherwise have done. . . . Export-led growth was the centerpiece of the industrial policy that enriched much of Asia and left millions of people there far better off. Because of globalization many people in the world now live longer than before and their standard of living is far better. People in the West may regard low-paying jobs at Nike as exploitation, but for many people in the developing world, working in a factory is a far better option than staying down on the farm and growing rice.[37]

THE NEGATIVE ASPECTS OF GLOBALIZATION

Part of the problem is that globalization does not consist just of economic institutions. Many other things, even diseases such as AIDS, have been globalized. Environmental problems such as global warming have been globalized. Crime, in the form of prostitution and sexual slavery, has spread across the globe. Violence against women and children is globally pervasive. Terrorism reaches all corners of the earth.[38]

The Clash of Civilizations

What happens when people from other parts of the world value tradition more than innovation? What happens when these people respect authority more than individualism, when they want security even more than freedom, when they value cooperation more than competition, when their notion of what constitutes wealth differs from that of the U.S. and of the Western capitalist nations? Further, what happens when people from other civilizations maintain different values in terms of the relation between men and women, children and parents, the young and the elderly, life and death?

> **Research Informed Practice**
>
> The promise of globalization is an integrated free-market economic system that will raise the standard of living of all nations, developed and developing. Why then are students, union members, and environmentalists, among others, protesting globalization? Why do these protesters, beginning in Seattle, Washington, in 1999, continue to demonstrate at meetings of the World Trade Organization?
>
> Go to the Internet and use Google to collect information about the World Trade Organization. Note its history, purpose, and current leadership. Also note the various demonstrations against the WTO by activist groups around the world. Are their voices being heard in newspaper articles, on YouTube, and on other Internet sites?

A **civilization** is a broad cultural grouping. Civilizations consist of people with common self-identity in terms of their histories, languages, traditions, institutions, and religions. Furthermore, civilizations consist of one or more nations. For example, Western civilization consists of the North American nations, including the U.S., as well as European nations such as England and France. Other major civilizations include Islamic, Confucianism, Hindu, Latin American, Japanese, Slavic-Orthodox, and some would add African.[39]

Many fear that one of the major negative aspects of globalization is that it is producing and exacerbating conflicts between different world civilizations, that because of increased interaction and communication among people all over the world using new technologies such as the Internet, e-mail, television, and satellite radio, people are becoming more conscious and defensive about their cultures. Globalization may produce wealth, but it also produces tension. It is an epic event, with billions of relatively powerless people caught in the transition, while some resist the transition altogether.

Some leaders from Western nations assume that Western values are universal values, but are they? When American presidents talk of spreading freedom and democracy throughout the world, aren't they stating just this: that everyone should have the values of Western nations? How should people from other civilizations feel and react to such proclamations by Western leaders?

Their response will vary, but some will react violently. The terrorist attacks in the U.S. on September 11, 2001, were the most dramatic evidence of this. In 1993, author Samuel Huntington predicted that, in the future, major wars would be fought, not between nations, but rather between civilizations. These conflicts would be of two types, the first being wars between civilizations bordering one another geographically, such as the conflict between Muslim Pakistan and Hindu India. The second type, he predicted, will be macro wars among civilizations competing for power and control over international institutions. The current war on terrorism between the U.S. and Muslim civilization, as represented by the followers of Osama bin Laden, is the preeminent example. To the extent that corporations spreading globally diminish the nation-state as a source of identity for people, religion as practiced in distinct civilizations is expected to fill the void. Witness the rise of religious fundamentalism, not only in Muslim civilizations, but in Western nations such as the U.S. as well. The spread of capitalism globally is destined to conflict with different religious values and beliefs. This conflict is likely to be greater when the profit motive of capitalism collides with the beliefs of the world's great religions.

Demonstrating Knowledge, Values, and Skills: September 11th and the Threat of Increased Terrorism

On September 11, 2001, Islamic terrorists hijacked four U.S. commercial airplanes, one of which crashed in Pennsylvania, one hit the Pentagon building in Washington, D.C., and two toppled the World Trade Center towers in New York City. Thousands of people were killed in the attack.

To what extent is globalization a factor in the attack? In other words, to what extent does September 11th represent a clash of cultures? What policy changes should be made to address the threat of increased terrorism? Are there changes in social welfare policy that should be made? What role can social workers play?

To prevent such conflict, non-Western civilizations are attempting to modernize without "Westernizing." That is, they're trying to develop highly sophisticated economic, military, and political institutions while maintaining indigenous social institutions.[40] But will they be able to do so, when Western corporate advertising can be transmitted into the homes of people all over the world through television, radio, and the Internet—and when traditional governments are relatively powerless to prevent this communication? If so, is a world culture of Big Macs, MTV, and Star Wars inevitable, and is this a good thing?[41]

Unemployment and Economic Inequality

Some experts fear that globalization is creating a two-tiered employment system, a system that creates a relatively few good jobs while creating many low-paying jobs for the majority of the world's population. The remaining groups will be left unemployed.[42]

How does this happen? Critics contend that corporations are hiring core personnel with relatively high salaries, full benefits, and comfortable working conditions. These employees typically are engaged in finance, marketing, or technology. While providing these high-paid jobs for a small number of employees, corporations are increasingly manufacturing their products with a second tier of people. This second tier of employment is often part-time or temporary. In any case, these workers receive low wages and few benefits. Thus, while the U.S. economy is a world leader in many ways, social workers will inevitably face the challenge of addressing the problematic aspects of globalization as vulnerable populations such as children, minorities, and single mothers deal with the vast technical and economic changes ahead.

Critical Thinking Question

The technical and economic changes related to globalization are problematic for vulnerable populations such as children, minorities, and single mothers. Has anyone in your family or community been negatively impacted by globalization?

Case Study: Wal-Mart and the Power of Global Corporations

Wal-Mart is the largest retail chain in the world and in many ways exemplifies the new global economy. It has surpassed competitors such as Sears, K-Mart, and Target, by far. The company started by Sam Walton in Arkansas has grown to become a major economic force. It has achieved this with a simple philosophy: Offer consumers a good product at the lowest possible price. And it does so relentlessly. As a result, Wal-Mart saves American shoppers thousands of dollars each year. In doing so, Wal-Mart employs thousands of workers and helps to keep inflation rates low in the countries in which it operates. It

Did You Know?

Did you know that, according to one study, a typical family saves an average of 27% on groceries bought at Wal-Mart? This translates into one week of groceries free every month.[44]

also creates more sales for certain types of businesses such as restaurants in the immediate vicinity of its stores.[43]

Yet Wal-Mart has many critics. Some of this criticism concerns the way it allegedly treats its employees. The giant retailer has been accused of forcing workers to work overtime without pay.[45] The company has been accused of paying women less than men and providing women with fewer promotions.[46] Critics also contend that Wal-Mart's treatment of workers in its foreign plants resembles conditions of the 1800s in the United States. Wal-Mart is not the only company facing such charges. Reebok, The Gap, Nike, and even Walt Disney have been the targets of similar charges. In any case, according to critics, at least some of the foreign plants making products for Wal-Mart are "sweat shops." Workers in these plants make products that are sold legally in stores such as Wal-Mart, but under conditions that would be illegal in the U.S.[47] These plants allegedly ask workers to work long days, roughly 8 a.m. to 10 p.m., seven days per week with only ten days off per year for vacation. While at sewing tables, these critics charge that workers are not permitted to talk to one another or to drink water; workers are only permitted to use a restroom at times designated by management.

In addition, critics say that Wal-Mart's claims of job creation are exaggerated. Research has shown that, five years after the opening of a new Wal-Mart store in the U.S., the net job growth in the surrounding area is only about 30 jobs. The company has grown so large that it can force into bankruptcy many of the small businesses that historically lined the main streets of small American towns. Quaint little towns can become boarded-up eyesores. Families who have owned these businesses for generations have to lay off workers and find themselves unemployed. Small-town culture is destroyed. In short, Wal-Mart has minimal positive influence on job growth. Some people find jobs because of Wal-Mart, while others lose their jobs because of Wal-Mart.

Wal-Mart is not just a threat to small businesses, however. The company has become so dominant in selling to consumers that it can force other major companies that supply it with products to change their manufacturing processes in an effort to lower manufacturing costs. Lower manufacturing costs translate into lower product costs for Wal-Mart shoppers. If companies refuse, Wal-Mart has the economic strength to put the company out of business by refusing to carry their products in Wal-Mart stores. When Wal-Mart has forced other local stores out of business, manufacturers have few alternatives to reach consumers. To lower costs, these manufacturing companies, many with a long history in the United States, may be forced to close American manufacturing plants and open new plants in low-wage, low-regulation countries such as China.[48] (It should be noted again that many large, global corporations—not just Wal-Mart—can be accused of these practices to various degrees.)

Loss of Cultural Identity

Globalization also seeks to create a single market for goods and services. In so doing, it threatens local communities in terms of local values, culture, and history and results in loss of **cultural identity.** In other words, the threat is that American economic, political, and social values will extinguish, to a great extent, cultural diversity and self-determination around the world.

Take Canada, for example. Canada has a long history of national sovereignty. It is highly industrialized and one of the major economies in the world. Yet a growing problem for Canadians is loss of their culture and traditions due to the increasingly pervasive U.S. media. Strictly American traditions and values are

> **Demonstrating Knowledge, Values, and Skills: Globalization and Poverty**
>
> Critics of globalization argue that global capitalism is making an individual's "net worth" the only measure of an individual's value as a person.
>
> Do you agree? If true, does this violate the values of the social work profession, given its belief in the dignity and worth of every individual? Yet how much dignity and worth is there in poverty? To the extent that globalization ends poverty, isn't this pursuit consistent with social work values?

steadily encroaching on those of Canada through U.S. television, films, magazines, newspapers, and Internet sites. Is Canada the 51st state in the U.S. or a proud and sovereign nation? Add the increased flow of consumer goods and products across borders between the U.S. and Canada due to the North American Free Trade Agreement (NAFTA) and it becomes hard to tell.

The impact of globalization on third world nations is even more drastic. For people in many local communities in third world countries, globalization feels less like a new world order and more like a new world disorder. Their centuries-old way of life has changed drastically, much like the experience of Native Americans in the face of Western European immigration, westward expansion, and settlement.[49] In any case, globalization makes it more difficult to preserve traditional community and the values inherent in that community.

Loss of Indigenous Economies

Critics of globalization also maintain that globalization is ruining centuries-old **Indigenous Economies** around the world. They claim that world financial institutions such as the World Bank promote global corporate interests at the expense of local economies. Take small farmers in local communities, for example. These farmers, who once grew crops for local consumption, now are going bankrupt, many forced to migrate to urban areas, where they become the cheap labor supply for corporate-controlled factories.[50]

Why is this happening? In part, it is because the **terms of trade** favor powerful industrial nations.[51] For example, first world nations—in the name of free trade and globalization—have pressured third world countries to eliminate trade barriers. International lenders make this one of the conditions—referred to as **conditionality**—for making loans to third world nations.[52] However, these more developed Western nations have not completely eliminated their own trade barriers. For example, the U.S. continues to subsidize its own farmers, thus making it difficult for farmers in poor third world countries to compete in the world market.[53] Consequently, developing countries in the third world can't export their food products and earn export income.

Jamaica is one of many examples.[54] Local farmers, who have farmed their land for generations, are forced out of business because they cannot sell their food crops locally at a price lower than those of giant agribusinesses from around the world. Think about this scenario: Giant multinational corporations can raise, transport, and sell potatoes, bananas, and milk to a consumer in Jamaica at a cost lower than the local Jamaican farmer next door to the consumer can. The result: The local farmer cannot make a profit and is forced into more debt and, eventually, bankruptcy.

India, an illustration of the positive effects of globalization, is also an example of the negative effects of conditionality. Critics claim that there is a high rate of suicide among Indian farmers—due in part to globalization.[55] As

Globalization and International Social Work

> **Demonstrating Knowledge, Values, and Skills: Class Discussion**
>
> But is the fact that the Jamaican dairy farmer is forced out of business necessarily a negative occurrence for Jamaicans, in general? If the Jamaican farmer cannot supply Jamaican citizens with milk more inexpensively than multinational corporations, then shouldn't the farmer do something more useful to society? Don't poor Jamaican children and other consumers benefit from cheaper milk?

a requirement for making loans to Indian farmers, the World Bank forces these farmers to use the pesticides and hybrid seeds from multinational corporations. These hybrid seeds may not be as good as indigenous seed, often contributing to crop failure. What is more, in order to get the same benefit, these farmers have to buy and use ever greater amounts of the pesticides sold by the corporations. The result is that farmers need more loans, increasing their debt. The farmer sees no way out of this negative cycle. Some give up their farms and move to urban areas to find factory work. Others commit suicide.[56]

Loss of Corporate Social Accountability

Opponents of globalization fear the loss of corporate social accountability in the future. They warn that when government is local, while economies are global, multinational corporations and world financial institutions operate with little public accountability.[57] In other words, when multinational corporations operate globally outside of local accountability, their management is not held responsible for the social costs of their own policies. These policies include contracting out production to sweatshops that pay minimal wages, the use of technologies that displace thousands of workers, the clear-cutting of forests, and the dumping of toxic wastes. These costs of producing company products are primarily social and therefore borne by average citizens.

Critical Thinking Question
Many believe corporate management should be held responsible for the social costs (global warming, urban blight, etc.) of production. What policies could social workers formulate and advocate in order to hold corporations accountable for their actions?

Critics also fear that corporations that try to be socially responsible will find themselves at a disadvantage as they compete with less ethical companies. Socially responsible companies pay wages on which their employees can live. Such companies provide decent working conditions, health care, and other benefits. These companies are environmentally conscious and pay their fair share of taxes. And they give back to their communities through charitable donations and volunteerism. But what happens when all corporations do not operate by the same ethical standards?

Globalization opponents warn that responsible corporations that assume the social costs of their operations will be forced out of business by those that do not. Why? Because less responsible corporations will be able to sell their products at less cost to consumers, the vast majority of whom are too financially strapped to bypass the lower-priced products.

The Weakening of Democracy

Globalization's opponents contend that the greater the political power of multinational corporations, the less the political power of average citizens, and therefore the less meaningful democracy becomes. Historically, democratic government has limited and regulated the excesses of wealthy business owners and corporate management. Witness the efforts of presidents such as Theodore Roosevelt to regulate the unprecedented power of corporate monopolies, including Standard Oil. Witness the government reforms instituted by

President Franklin Roosevelt to control market speculation (the Securities and Exchange Commission) and protect the investments of ordinary citizens (the Federal Deposit Insurance Corporation).[58]

In a global economy, what institutions provide such safeguards for the public, for average citizens of the world, for populations at risk? Women? Children? Frail older people? As previously stated, global economic institutions have been established, including the International Monetary Fund (IMF) and the World Bank. The International Monetary Fund became responsible for maintaining global economic stability. It does so by maintaining stability and liquidity in national currencies around the globe. In addition, the World Bank was charged with the mission of promoting capital investments, first to reconstruct Europe after World War II, and later to promote economic development in third world countries and former communist nations.[59] The IMF increasingly has become involved in development in these countries also, although this was not its original mission.[60] Later, in the 1990s, the World Trade Organization was established to govern trade relations among nations.

The problem is that these global economic institutions are not very democratic. They are not directly accountable to average citizens of the world. The IMF, for example, is a public institution funded by taxpayers around the world. Yet average taxpayers have no voice in its policies. Instead, it reports to governments throughout the world through the central banks and ministries of finance in these nations. Furthermore, the major economic powers, particularly the United States, control the IMF. Voting takes place among nations, but it is not one nation–one vote. Rather, there is a complicated historical voting procedure based on the relative economic power of participating nations in 1944, when the IMF was conceptualized. Only the United States has veto power in the IMF.[61]

The heads of the World Bank and IMF are selected, not by any popular vote, but behind closed doors. Also, based on history and tacit agreement, the leader of the IMF is always a European, while the leader of the World Bank is always an American. These global economic leaders typically have relatively little knowledge of the intricacies of third world economies and conditions. Yet the World Bank and IMF exert strong influence over the welfare of citizens in these nations through the conditions they set for economic development loans. Critics claim that third world countries, in order to secure loans, are forced to prematurely open their fledgling industries up to foreign competition, before they are strong enough to meet the challenge. Consequently, the industries fail and need more loans. When the IMF, for example, imposes mistaken policies on tiny and frail economic institutions in third world countries, it can create social and political instability, resulting in much suffering for average citizens. With little democratic recourse, people at times have demonstrated and rioted. Again, vulnerable citizens often become the victims of such violence.[62]

Demonstrating Knowledge, Values, and Skills: Globalization

Supporters of globalization claim that "developing nations" or "emerging market nations" have to better institutionalize the concept of private property—that without this reform, the citizens of these countries cannot obtain loans to buy homes and start small businesses.[63] Critics of global capitalism claim that "private property" is simply one person controlling what many other people also need. This includes land, water, clean air, food, and shelter.

What do you think? Is this perspective too cynical? Is it fundamentally correct?[64]

THE FUTURE: COLLABORATION AND INTERNATIONAL SOCIAL WORK

International Social Work and the Importance of Social Work Values

In the past, American social workers have worked with government and through government to help protect vulnerable citizens from unscrupulous corporations and market economy injustices. As historian Paul Kennedy, author of *Preparing for the Twenty-First Century*, reminds us: "The rational market, by its very nature, is not concerned with social justice and fairness."[65] This is why professional social work will continue to be important in the future for populations at risk. To meet this challenge, the social work profession will become more internationally focused. **International social work** can be defined as "international professional action and the capacity for international action by the social work profession and its members."[66]

More specifically, international social work advocates for human rights, social justice, and social development; it promotes social work as a profession, using best practices and collaboration among social workers and their organizations.[67]

As the world increasingly becomes a global economy, there will be many opportunities for the profession of social work to play a significant role. As stated, the profession's values of respect for diversity, self-determination, and individual dignity will need to become pervasive world values to minimize conflict among the various civilizations of the world. Social workers can play a significant role in helping corporations, nongovernmental organizations, and governments to respect diversity in the workplace and in the communities they serve. Similarly, social workers can help those in these institutions become more culturally competent.[68] We believe the chances for this are good, given the self-interest of the business world in serving diverse cultures in a world market. A prerequisite for this will be increased cultural competency, not only among social workers and other helping professionals, but also among business leaders and their employees. American social workers have over 100 years of experience working with diverse populations, starting with the waves of immigrants who came to the U.S. during the late 1800s and early 1900s. Now, as business extends itself across the earth, this experience of the social work profession can and should be used.

A second major global opportunity for the profession of social work is the fight against poverty. Again, social workers have been fighting poverty for over 100 years in the U.S., and with success. Thanks to various programs for which social workers have advocated, many U.S. groups have found their way out of poverty. Social welfare programs such as Social Security, Medicare, Medicaid, SSI, the Earned Income Tax Credit, Head Start, and Food Stamps have been successful in preventing, mitigating, and, in some cases, ending poverty for vulnerable groups. These groups include children, older adults, and people with disabilities. As third world countries around the globe make the transition to modern economic systems and international trade, economic experts claim there is a real possibility of ending extreme poverty in the world by 2025.[69] It won't be easy. Poor countries will have to go through difficult transition periods and devote more resources to reducing poverty and less to warfare and government corruption. International social workers can help facilitate this transition.

Did You Know?

Here is how the ICSW describes its work:

The International Council on Social Welfare (ICSW) was founded in Paris in 1928. It is a non-governmental organisation which represents national and local organisations in more than 70 countries throughout the world. Membership also includes major international organizations.... Our member organisations represent tens of thousands of community organisations that work directly with people in poverty, hardship or distress. Our members are independent organisations working in their own communities rather than branches of organisations based in other countries. Many have been established by people who are themselves experiencing hardship.... Within their own communities, our network of organisations provides help for a wide range of people who are poor, ill, disabled, unemployed, frail or oppressed. They help young people, older people, families, indigenous peoples, migrants, refugees and others who are experiencing special hardship or vulnerability.[70]

Furthermore, to fight world poverty and other world social problems, social workers must do more of what they already do. Currently, the National Association of Social Workers (NASW) has several groups working on international issues, including the Department of Human Rights and International Affairs and the International Committee. NASW participates each year in Social Work Day at the United Nations in New York City and is a member of the United Nations Association's Council of Organizations in Washington, D.C. Social workers also work on international issues through the International Federation of Social Workers (IFSW), the International Association of Schools of Social Work, and the International Council on Social Welfare (ICSW).

Social workers will do even more internationally in the future. To achieve social and economic justice, The International Monetary Fund (IMF) and World Bank will be required to become more effective in their roles. This will consist of working more collaboratively with the United Nations and other international aid agencies. These U.N. agencies include the Food and Agriculture Organization (FAO), which helps to fight hunger through policy analysis and other technical assistance. They also include the United Nations Development Program (UNDP). This agency plays many roles, such as fighting poverty and improving health and education in third world countries. Another U.N. agency is the United Nations Human Settlements Program (UN-HABITAT). This agency promotes socially and environmentally sustainable communities. Its ultimate goal is to provide adequate shelter for all people of the world.

Social workers may also get involved with the United Nations Population Fund (UNFPA), which helps nations around the world with family planning, by establishing population and reproductive health programs.

The United Nations Children's Fund (UNICEF), the World Food Program (WFP), and the World Health Organization (WHO) provide other opportunities for social workers interested in fighting poverty internationally. UNICEF promotes child welfare through educational, health, and child protection programs. The World Food Program fights hunger throughout the world by helping to feed millions of people in over 80 countries. These recipients include most of the world's refugees. And finally, the World Health Organization offers technical assistance to countries related to health services.[71] This includes helping less developed countries to invest in public health and disease control.

As the world becomes increasingly one community, social workers can revitalize their historic roles in community organization by helping U.N. and other

Poverty is not romantic.
—Paul Collier

international aid agencies such as the Red Cross to cooperate and collaborate in their efforts to help the poor. Many of the world's problems cannot be solved just at the local level. Rather, they need regional, national, and even global cooperation among various stakeholder agencies to truly solve problems such as poverty and hunger. Social workers can play a role in facilitating such collaboration at all systemic levels.

Social workers can also play a meaningful role in international philanthropy.[72] Rich countries in the first world need to commit more money and resources than they are currently doing to end world disease and poverty.[73] These efforts have to be more than token efforts that grab much media attention but have little effect in less developed (so called third world) countries. Many U.S. social workers with jobs in administration and organizational development have experience raising money and volunteers for private nonprofit organizations such as United Way and its many affiliates in the U.S. This expertise can be translated to international aid agencies in the fight against hunger, disease, violence, and poverty worldwide. Further, it will increasingly utilize the Internet and other modern technologies (see fundraising-related Web sites such as globalgiving.com, charitynavigator.org, give.org, and kiva.org).

Globalization is creating vast wealth on an unprecedented scale around the world. Experts believe that the rich have a responsibility and the capability to end extreme poverty throughout the world by 2025.[74] Many believe that doing so will help to reduce war, terrorism, and other violence around the world. Doing so will also help to stabilize governments around the world. In short, these efforts will help to ensure an optimal environment in which to do business. Therefore, it is in the self-interest of the world's rich nations and wealthy individuals to donate more money and time to international charitable work. With today's research and technologies, global industries can operate profitably in less developed countries, environments once considered too harsh in which to do business. Therefore, some economists claim that ending extreme poverty is a realistic goal in the near future. Rich countries and wealthy individuals of the world can facilitate this in a very real and immediate way through donations of time and money. Social workers involved in charitable giving and volunteerism have an opportunity to help achieve this goal.[75]

Social workers also have a role to play in ending terrorism. What should be done to fight terrorism? In part, we must fight poverty, ignorance, and intolerance. These are among the goals of social work in an international context. Many of social work's values are America's better values: respect for diversity, service to others, empowering people to help themselves and to become more independent. Social workers engaged in work internationally will increasingly emphasize these values to counter those that focus on the more narrow-minded values that result in stereotypes, oppression, fear, hate, and terrorism. To this end, social workers will play a vital role in the 21st century.

Is a career in international social work for you? Do you like travel, languages, and different cultures? Here is what NASW has to say:

A country's political social order crumbles and the world watches a human consequence of the turmoil—children abandoned in primitive

Professional Identity

Critical Thinking Question

There are many roles that social workers can play in doing international social work, including promoting collaboration, cultural awareness, human rights, and philanthropy. In what ways might you like to be involved as a social worker?

Did You Know?

The United States armed forces actively recruit social work graduates for positions working with combat veterans and their families. For example, the Army Care Manager Program was established in 2003 with the goal of enhancing mental health services for veterans and their family members. The program is administered by the Behavioral Health Division of the Army Medical Command located at Fort Sam Houston in Texas. Sixty-six civilian clinical social workers are employed internationally at 33 Army Power Platform installations.[76]

orphanages. Humanitarian relief organizations move in to help improve conditions. Social workers are engaged to help. Some train orphanage staff in basic child development, including children's attachment and separation fears, the need for creative playtime, colorful paint and pictures on the walls, better diet, more hygienic care. Life begins to improve for the children.

Other social workers help draft standards for children's institutions including child-staff rations, recommended activities, and staff education and training. Still others work with government agencies organizing foster care services and family services and counseling. The new services will help families stay together and offer alternatives to placing children in orphanages in the future.

The functions of international social work are nearly as diverse as the people served. On one level, the work involves direct services in refugee programs, relief efforts. Inter-country adoptions and development, health care, and education. But another aspect involves advancing the efforts of national governments, intergovernmental organizations, and voluntary agencies to enhance social welfare policy, technical assistance, research, and information exchange.

Social workers manage programs, train others, help develop service delivery systems train in developing countries, and much more.

International organizations such as the United Nations and its International Children's Emergency Fund (UNICEF) employ social workers in both urban and rural projects. The World Health Organization (WHO) works on several fronts—acquired immune deficiency syndrome, drug addiction, famine—that include social work services. And the International Committee of the Red Cross performs vital disaster relief services, often with the aid of social workers.

For those practicing in this exciting field, language abilities and a desire to travel are a must as is an appreciation of other cultures. With our growing comprehension of the interdependence of nations, there is expanding potential in international social work— definitely a world worth exploring.[77]

Demonstrating Knowledge, Values, and Skills

Break up into small groups and discuss the following topics: *How has war affected each person's life? Specifically, how has the Iraq War impacted each group member's life? Does anyone in your group have family or loved ones who were involved in the war? How has this affected them? With more military veterans coming back from the Iraq War, what services are needed? How does the U.S. government support these services and programs? Is this support adequate, in your opinion? What role does social work play?* Support each other in the group and allow each person to express his or her views about war and to share experiences and stories.

SUMMARY

The globalization of capitalism represents an epic event in world history. It holds the promise of ending extreme poverty around the world. Yet it also threatens the cultural integrity of various non-Western civilizations throughout the world. Moreover, globalization threatens traditional blue-collar and other low-skilled jobs in the U.S. With unemployment and poverty come many related social problems such as substandard public education, substance abuse, domestic violence, and homelessness. For these reasons, social workers are concerned about globalization. And for these reasons, the profession of social work undoubtedly will become more internationally focused in the future.

15 CHAPTER REVIEW

Succeed with mysocialworklab

Log onto **MySocialWorkLab** to access a wealth of case studies, videos, and assessment. (*If you did not receive an access code to MySocialWorkLab with this text and wish to purchase access online, please visit www.mysocialworklab.com.*)

PRACTICE TEST The following questions will test your knowledge of the content found within this chapter. For additional assessment, including licensing-exam type questions on applying chapter content to practice, visit **MySocialWorkLab**.

Practice Contexts

1. "Globalization" can best be defined as:
   a. The integration of markets, nation-states, and technology
   b. The spread of disease worldwide
   c. The spread of telecommunications worldwide
   d. The integration of democracy and capitalism worldwide

2. As originally conceived, the International Monetary Fund became responsible for:
   a. Creating national currencies such as the euro
   b. Maintaining stability and liquidity in national currencies around the globe
   c. Promoting capital investments in developing countries
   d. Making micro-loans to small, impoverished business entrepreneurs

3. The World Trade Organization's purpose is to facilitate world trade, in large part by:
   a. Promoting capital investments in developing countries
   b. Serving as a communication vehicle among nations
   c. Making micro-loans to small, impoverished business entrepreneurs
   d. Serving as an arbitrator in trade disputes between various nations around the world

4. First world nations, such as Great Britain and the U.S., were the first to:
   a. Develop civilizations
   b. Develop free market capitalist economies
   c. Develop international trade
   d. Develop basic human rights

5. The "Asian model" of globalization refers to:
   a. International trade agreements only among Asian nations
   b. A smaller, more localized version of capitalism
   c. Governments relying more on a free market economy, but remaining more involved in the economy than many Western governments
   d. High-technology corporations based in Asian nations such as Japan, India, and China

Diversity in Practice

6. A _____ is a broad cultural grouping consisting of people with common self-identity in terms of their histories, languages, traditions, institutions, and religions:
   a. Race
   b. Nation
   c. Continent
   d. Civilization

7. _____ is a term that refers to "international organizations using social work methods or personnel."
   a. Plagiarism
   b. Accreditation
   c. Social service globalization
   d. International social work

8. The International Council on Social Welfare (ICSW) was founded in:
   a. Paris
   b. New York
   c. London
   d. Boston

9. The _____ offers technical assistance to less developed countries to invest in public health and disease control:
   a. World Bank
   b. World Health Organization
   c. World Food Program
   d. United Nations Children's Fund

10. Social workers assist the _____, which specializes in disaster relief services:
    a. World Bank
    b. World Health Organization
    c. International Committee of the Red Cross
    d. United Nations Children's Fund

Log onto **MySocialWorkLab** once you have completed the Practice Test above to access additional study tools and assessment.

Answers

Key: 1) a 2) b 3) d 4) b 5) c 6) d 7) d 8) a 9) b 10) c

16

Social Work, Policy, and Advocacy

CHAPTER OUTLINE

Social Workers Engaged in Policy Practice 356
Various Approaches to Problem Definition

The Social Worker as Advocate 358

Social and Economic Justice 360
Diversity, Oppression, and Human Rights

Stakeholders, Collaboration, and Political Strategy 361
Policy Research
Major Stakeholders
The Strengths Perspective and Policy Advocacy

Policy Windows of Opportunity
Collaboration and Political Strategy in Policy Advocacy
Social Workers and Policy Debate
Internet Advocacy

Social Workers and Advocacy Success 370

Summary 372

Practice Test 373

 MySocialWorkLab 373

Core Competencies in this Chapter (Check marks indicate which competencies are covered in depth)				
✓ Professional Identity	☐ Ethical Practice	☐ Critical Thinking	☐ Diversity in Practice	✓ Human Rights & Justice
☐ Research Based Practice	☐ Human Behavior	✓ Policy Practice	✓ Practice Contexts	☐ Engage, Assess, Intervene, Evaluate

355

Chapter 16

SOCIAL WORKERS ENGAGED IN POLICY PRACTICE

The final chapter in this text takes a closer look at social work, policy, and advocacy. This is because social work practice often involves policy. Policies impact the many social programs, benefits, and services of the U.S. social welfare system. Policy also provides the context in which social workers carry out their roles and responsibilities.

More specifically, **policy practice** in social work, by definition, involves the formulation, enactment, implementation, and assessment of social welfare policies. Usually the policy under examination is an organizational policy affecting the agency in which the social worker is employed. In this case, the social worker may become involved in revising agency policies or formulating new agency policies. Sometimes the policy involves legislation addressing a social problem that impacts agency clients. In this instance, social workers frequently contribute information on behalf of their agency and clients to legislative policymakers in state capitols and in Washington, D.C., our nation's capital. Social workers share their specialized knowledge on many social problems, from child neglect to elder abuse. This information is typically provided by social workers at public hearings. In fact, many social workers are asked by policymakers to help write specific bills before the bill goes to hearing. In this way, social workers assist in developing new legislation resulting in programs, services, or benefits for client populations.

Other social workers are engaged in policy practice while employed as policy analysts or planners. Such positions are frequently located in government at the national, state, county, and city levels. These positions can also be found in private nonprofit organizations such as advocacy organizations headquartered in Washington, D.C. The Child Welfare League of America, the Children's Defense Fund, and the American Association of Retired Persons (now AARP) are examples. Social workers in these positions do analysis that results in research reports, issue papers, fact sheets, and chart books.

Still other social workers who hope to have a greater impact on social welfare policy run for public office. Social workers serve in Congress and in state legislatures, while many others have been elected to county/borough, city/municipal, and school board positions. Social worker and U.S. Senator Barbara Mikulski from Maryland is one prominent example.

Similarly, social workers become involved in policy practice by working on the campaign of someone running for public office. As previously indicated, the candidate may be running for mayor of a city, governor of a state, U.S. Congress, or any number of other public offices. Social workers in these campaigns frequently research and write brief "position papers" on various social problems. Position papers serve to educate political candidates about individual social problems and help the candidate develop a position or stand on one or more issues related to the problem. If elected, these lawmakers often invite social workers to serve on committees or on their staff to continue their policy analysis.

Various Approaches to Problem Definition

Social workers get involved with policy in order to better address social problems of concern to them and various client populations. Consequently, they know it is important to thoroughly define the problem.[1] Social workers do this because they know they must have a thorough grasp of the social problem and related key issues before researching possible problem solutions. In doing so, they find it helpful to think about different approaches to problem definition that can be utilized depending on the situation.[2] In other words, consistent with social work values and ethics, social workers choose the method most useful in achieving their intervention goals.

One approach to problem definition is the **functional approach**.[3] According to this approach, a social problem is any condition that upsets the smooth functioning of society. An obvious example would be the problem of terrorism in America, particularly after the September 11, 2001, airplane crashes into the World Trade Center towers in New York City and the Pentagon in Washington, D.C.[4] Street crime is another example. Both can make people fearful of going about their normal daily routines.

A second way to define a problem is the **normative approach**.[5] The normative method stresses that a social problem is any condition that deviates from accepted societal norms. An illustration of such a condition would be the child sexual abuse scandal in the Catholic Church, a problem that began to receive widespread public attention in 2002.[6] Child sexual abuse violates society's norms, and the fact that some Catholic priests have carried out such abuse makes the whole problem even more shocking to average Americans.

A third approach to problem definition is the **objective approach**, which maintains that a social problem is recognized when the quantitative indicators of a problem become indisputably large over time.[7] For instance, about a quarter of the total American labor force was unemployed at the height of the Great Depression.[8] No reasonable observer could dispute that the country was in economic crisis and that something drastic had to be done. Thus, Roosevelt was able to push through his New Deal legislation.

The **subjective approach** to defining social problems is a fourth method that should be considered by policy developers.[9] In this approach, the quantitative evidence has been available for a considerable amount of time; it is the public's perception of the data that changes. To illustrate, domestic violence was once considered a personal matter, a private family issue. Today, in contrast, domestic violence is considered a social problem that requires public attention.[10]

The social worker may also want to look at the selected problem and key issue in terms of **value conflict**.[11] This approach to problem definition argues that social problems are created when groups have conflicting values. A good example is the "pro-life" versus "pro-choice" debate around abortion in America. Given the passion associated with the values of both groups, it is not a problem likely to be "solved" in the near future.

A sixth and final approach to problem definition is the **claims-making approach**. This approach uses social construction theory to argue that problem definition is, in fact, "the activities of individuals or groups making assertions of grievances and claims with respect to some putative condition."[12] In short, humans construct social problems. Therefore, it is the process of constructing social problems that is the focus in the claims-making approach. Problem definition becomes an outcome of negotiation among competing groups.

In any case, a rigorous examination of the social problem and its key dimensions may benefit from the distinct insights derived from each of these approaches to problem definition. And while each perspective can provide a unique contribution to problem definition, the six approaches are not necessarily mutually exclusive. There is overlap among them. The "value conflict"

> **Case Study: Social Justice and the Civil Rights Movement of the 1960s**
>
> To illustrate the "claims-making" approach to problem definition, consider the evolution of African American segregation from a (supposedly) natural condition to an intolerable social injustice.[13] One of Martin Luther King's organizing strategies in the civil rights movement of the 1960s was to make the segregation of African Americans problematic for Southern business and political leaders. To this end, King and other civil rights organizers persuaded the African American community of Montgomery, Alabama, to stop riding city buses until laws regarding segregated bus seating were abolished. In a second civil rights campaign, King and others organized a boycott of businesses in Birmingham, Alabama. The boycotts continued in each case until negotiation between civil rights leaders and Southern segregationists resulted in an end to racial segregation.

approach, for instance, is inherent in the "claims-making" approach. All incorporate the "objective" approach to some extent.

Furthermore, various approaches to problem definition may be useful in organizing partnerships among special interest groups to pass and implement proposed legislation. That is, social workers engaged in policy development may solicit the support of individual stakeholder groups through selection of one or more of the six approaches to problem definition. Some groups are motivated by statistical information that quantifies the problem and its key aspects. The social worker, in this case, may want to emphasize the "objective" approach. Other potential supporters are more motivated by their values concerning the problem. They don't need statistics; they just know what they believe to be important in the matter. For these groups, an approach such as the "value conflict" approach to problem definition may be more effective. In short, the way a social problem is defined can assist in generating support for policy proposals.

THE SOCIAL WORKER AS ADVOCATE

A significant aspect of professional social work involves **advocacy**. For social workers, advocacy means promoting the rights of client populations, whether those "clients" are individuals, groups, or communities. With respect to policy, there are various ways that social workers advocate for (or against) the enactment of new policy to better meet the needs of clients. Perhaps the

> **Research Informed Practice with Neglected Children**
>
> Edleson, Gassman-Pines, and Hill published their qualitative research (*Social Work 51* [2006], pp. 167–173) on a policy mistake made by the Minnesota legislature. The legislature amended the state's definition of child neglect in 1999 to include a child's "exposure to family violence." The change resulted in a dramatic increase in the number of domestic violence exposure reports, reports that had to be investigated by state child protection workers. However, there were not enough funding, services, or trained legal personnel to handle this large increase in cases. Most counties in the state were overwhelmed. Consequently, the change in the definition of the child neglect was repealed after only one year.
>
> How might this research inform your efforts as a social worker engaged in policy advocacy? What does it tell you about problem definition? What does it tell you about the implementation stage of policy development?

proposed policy in the form of a legislative bill focuses on a certain client population such as people with disabilities. Perhaps the policy recommendation pertains to an organizational policy such as equal benefit policies for same-sex domestic partners. In any case, a social worker may not only present facts and information regarding policy alternatives to policy decision makers, the social worker may be in a position to advocate for a specific policy proposal and against other proposals.

There are several advocacy roles that social workers can play.[14] One is simply as a communicator. That is, social workers involved in policy advocacy may communicate the details of social problems and new policy alternatives to professional colleagues and fellow community members. Such discourse furthers awareness and concern as a first step in building support for progressive changes.

A second advocacy role for social workers might be found in the context of an association's lobbying campaign. In such a campaign, a social worker may play the role of a paid lobbyist. In so doing, they may contact government officials on behalf of the association to provide information and their recommendations regarding a specific policy issue. Telephone calls, fax messages, e-mail, and letters to elected politicians are typical means of communication.

A third role for social work professionals is as a persuader. To provide one illustration, social workers advocating for new policy can influence the opinion of the general public on a policy issue using their professional position and expertise. Letters written to the editors of major newspapers informing readers about the proposed policy and issue, for example, are a way to educate and persuade the community.

In addition, social workers serve as a witness in advocating for specific policy recommendations. They may take part in a congressional or other public hearing on the key policy issue. The setting may be a hearing on welfare reform before a congressional committee in Washington, a state appropriations hearing regarding annual health and human service spending, or a hearing before a city or town council on its health and human services budget. In each case, social workers can bring to the public forum their firsthand knowledge of the specific needs of various populations.

Social workers also play the role of activist for a policy recommendation. In this role, the social worker takes planned, concrete action to produce social change on behalf of clients. These actions may include participating in an organized demonstration, march, sit-in, or boycott to draw attention to the social problem and new policy alternatives.

Furthermore, let's not forget that social workers can take an active role as a political campaigner, whether working for a political party or candidate or running for office themselves. Social workers often work behind the scenes gathering information to help candidates develop positions and recommendations on specific policy issues. However, there is no reason why a professional social worker couldn't be elected president of the United States. A former community organizer, Barack Obama, already has!

And finally, as part of a political strategy to get a specific policy proposal passed, social workers may play the role of collaborator. For example, social workers can organize or participate in a coalition to address a specific social problem and promote specific policy recommendations. As the previous chapters in this book illustrate, U.S. history shows many examples of advocates, including social workers, networking through various voluntary associations to promote social reform, whether it was abolition, women's suffrage, civil rights, or mental health parity.

Critical Thinking Question

There are several advocacy roles that social workers involved in policy practice can play, including communicator, lobbyist, activist, and campaigner. Given your personality and interests, in which role(s) would you feel comfortable?

Chapter 16

SOCIAL AND ECONOMIC JUSTICE

Social workers, as discussed in the previous section, often perform the advocate role in policy practice. This may mean advocating for a proposed policy within the agency in which the social worker is employed. The new policy may impact employees of the agency or it may affect the clients of the agency. At other times, social workers advocate for proposed policy at the city or county level—new policy that would address social problems in local neighborhoods, for example. Still other social workers advocate for new policy in the form of legislative bills before state legislatures and Congress.

Social and economic justice is of fundamental importance to the social work profession; therefore, social workers prioritize social and economic justice when formulating and advocating for new policy. In order to do this, social workers need to have a conception of what "justice" means to them.

Three major contemporary philosophies of social justice are libertarianism, utilitarianism, and egalitarianism.[15] The **libertarian** view holds that individual liberty is primary and that individuals must be free from coercion by the government or other entities, including coercion to part with property they have acquired legally.[16] Thus, a "just society" from the libertarian viewpoint is one in which individuals are essentially free from intrusion of any kind from government or other bodies. In the libertarian view, programs such as public assistance and affirmative action are problematic because they impede on individual self-determination and rights to property in an attempt to redistribute property, power, or other resources among citizens. Although libertarianism is focused on individual rights, utilitarianism is focused on the concept of the "greatest good."[17] In the **utilitarian** view, a just society is one that achieves the greatest good for the greatest number. This is not as simple as it sounds, however, as what constitutes the "greatest good" for a given society is open for debate. Finally, **egalitarianism**, a philosophy developed by John Rawls (1971), holds that both an equality of liberties and an equality of opportunity must be present in a just society.[18] Furthermore, inequalities in power, property, and other resources may exist only if they work to the benefit of a society's most disenfranchised members. The redistribution of resources—such as wealth, power, and access—is therefore an essential component of social justice in the egalitarian view.

[M]ore than eight million people around the world die each year because they are too poor to stay alive.
—Jeffrey D. Sachs

The social work profession draws upon each of these philosophies in its understanding of social justice and professional ethics; however, egalitarianism is the philosophy most consistent with social work's overall mission and core values. Thus, from a social work perspective, **social and economic justice** pertain to a society in which all individuals in the society have "equal economic, political, and social rights and opportunities," a society in which discrimination, oppression, and inequalities that prevent people from meeting their basic human needs do not exist.[19] As social workers, a core part of our work is to ensure that society moves closer to this state of justice.

Critical Thinking Question

In what ways could the United States move closer to a society in which discrimination, oppression, and inequality do not exist?

Diversity, Oppression, and Human Rights

In order to further social and economic justice, variables such as gender and race need to be important considerations in policy advocacy. Not only must current policies and programs be reviewed in terms of how they impact populations subject to oppression; social workers feel that the very definition of a social problem needs to be critically examined in terms of its influence on these groups. For example, does the way in which the problem is defined actually blame women or minorities for their unmet needs? Did these populations participate in defining the problem? Do policymakers hear their voices? Any definition of a social problem should be reviewed with these considerations in mind. Before finalizing and advocating for a policy recommendation, social workers return to the identified social problem to evaluate it in these terms.

Similarly, in an effort to better address existing social problems, social workers critique new policy proposals in terms of human rights and each proposal's influence on historically oppressed groups. Given the discrimination and oppression of women historically in the United States and around the world, for example, any policy proposal should be critiqued regarding its potential influence on women. That is, the basic human rights and needs of women (including the right to an education, to vote in a democracy, to marriage equality, etc.) should be considered when formulating the policy recommendation. In this case, the "gender variable" becomes an important variable in the policy analysis.

More specifically, the following five questions could be considered when developing policy recommendations that may affect women:[20] Does the proposed policy materially improve the lives of women? Does it build self-respect for women? Does the recommendation empower women? In addition, does the proposed recommendation educate women politically? And finally, will the policy recommendation weaken patriarchal control of institutions, thereby giving women more of a voice in society's institutions such as business and government?

Social workers ask similar questions to critique policy proposals in terms of their potential influence on other vulnerable populations, such as children and older adults. The major point here is that social workers play the role of advocate, in part, so that existing policies and proposed policies maximize social and economic justice for diverse and vulnerable populations.

STAKEHOLDERS, COLLABORATION, AND POLITICAL STRATEGY

Policy Research

In developing and advocating for social policy, social workers must collect a great deal of information. There are a number of sources of such information. Writings by political scientists, sociologists, social workers, and historians in various professional journals are one such source. Government Web sites are a second source. For instance, the Library of Congress maintains a Web site called "Thomas," as in Thomas Jefferson.[21] This Web site contains much information on current and past legislation. Social work advocates can search for specific legislation on a policy issue by typing key words, as in other Internet-based searches. The Web site also includes the *Congressional Record*, which contains the text of bills and other documents. The *Congressional Record* provides information on any action taken on a given day on a specific bill as well as a record of remarks made by various participants in the policymaking process. Furthermore, the Thomas Web site offers committee reports, historical documents, and information on your congressional representatives.

State governments are also helpful.[22] Individual states maintain a legislative Web site accessible to policy analysts and other interested parties. Similar to the federal government's Web site, state Web sites offer information on recent bills introduced in their respective state legislatures. This information typically includes the names of sponsors of the bill, committees, the last hearing date for the bill, and the outcome of recent hearings on the bill. Legislative information on specific bills often includes both a summary of the bill as well as the full text of the bill.

Professional organizations, such as the National Association of Social Workers (NASW), are an additional source of legislative information.[23] The NASW maintains a Web site that includes an advocacy link for social workers concerned with policy issues. This advocacy link includes the key issues on which the NASW will focus in the current congressional session. It also includes more in-depth NASW position papers on each key issue. The NASW's individual position papers, like most position papers, describe the background of the key issue and what action the organization supports regarding the issue. The Web site then assists you to take action by contacting key policymakers through various means, including e-mail messages, printed letters, and YouTube video advocacy messages.

Major Stakeholders

Another major research activity for social workers engaged in policy advocacy is to identify major stakeholders involved with the new policy proposal.[24] This is sometimes called a "stakeholder analysis." With respect to policy advocacy, a **stakeholder** by definition is any individual or group that can affect or be affected by proposed or existing legislation. Let's use advocacy at the state and national level to illustrate. Obviously, many groups will be affected by a new social policy; therefore, it is important to identify the most influential stakeholders in relation to the key policy issue. Some stakeholders have more power than others, and some stakeholders will have more interest than others in the identified issue. Some stakeholder groups, including social work clientele, may be more impacted by a specific policy proposal than are other stakeholder groups. In addition to populations whose needs will be addressed by the new legislation, major stakeholders typically include congressional or state legislative leaders, the chairpersons of pertinent committees and subcommittees, government agencies, and usually, taxpayers.

At this point, social workers often find it helpful to obtain organizational charts of decision-making bodies involved with the selected policy issue. In addition, an outline of the policymaking process is often developed. For example, on the national level, the social work advocate needs to determine which congressional committees would hear a bill on the selected issue, which subcommittees might be involved with the bill, who are the chairpersons of these committees and subcommittees, and so forth.

Identifying major stakeholders will enable the social work advocate to understand which influential groups and individuals will be involved in the policy development process. In so doing, the social work advocate typically ascertains whether or not each major stakeholder is likely to support or oppose the proposed legislation. Strong support among major stakeholders will increase the probability that the new legislation passes and that sufficient resources will be available to implement the policy adequately.

This is the "political viability" criterion. With this criterion, the social worker attempts to answer the question: Would a majority of the most powerful and influential stakeholders support the proposed legislation?

Social work advocates evaluate "power" in several ways. One way is to estimate for each stakeholder group the amount of resources available to it, resources such as money, information (including research on the key issue), volunteers, and political connections. Money will greatly determine the group's ability to make political contributions and mount an effective campaign in opposition to or support of a policy proposal. The number of volunteers will be closely associated with the membership size of the stakeholder group. Obviously, the larger the group's membership is, the greater its ability to recruit volunteers in a campaign to support or oppose the policy proposal. For these reasons, one way to estimate the power of a stakeholder group is to examine the amount of resources available to the group.

A second and related way that social work advocates measure power is to estimate the ability of a group to mobilize its resources. In calculating this, the social worker should look at the internal cohesion of the group. That is, how much solidarity is there within the membership of the group? Also, is there a virtual consensus within the group on the policy recommendation? Furthermore, just how effective is the leadership of the stakeholder group? Is there a nationally known leader with many political contacts in Congress? Is the leader generally regarded as an expert on the policy issue? Is the leader able to galvanize the group's membership in a campaign in support of or opposition to the policy recommendation? Social advocates address all of these questions.

Finally, another indicator of the stakeholder group's power is its access to key policy decision makers. Do the members of the stakeholder group, particularly its leadership, have direct access to key decision makers? Do they have an opportunity to meet one-on-one with key decision makers regarding various policy issues? Do policy decision makers ask them regularly for information and opinions on various policy issues? Social work advocates, when analyzing the overall power and influence of each major stakeholder group, examine all of these dimensions of power. It is this influence with key decision makers that is of utmost importance in getting new policies passed.

Critical Thinking Question
Social work advocates evaluate "power" in several ways. What sources of power do college students possess to influence their university or state social welfare policies?

The Strengths Perspective and Policy Advocacy

Social workers involved in policy practice try to utilize the strengths of client populations.[25] Policy planning from a "strengths perspective" might proceed as follows.

1. Identify basic needs and barriers to meeting those needs.
2. Negotiate with client groups (regarding step #1).
3. Identify ways that barriers are currently overcome.
4. Identify opportunities and resources required.
5. Formulate policy.
6. Negotiate consensus on policy goals.
7. Design programs.
8. Implement programs.
9. Evaluate program outcomes.

First of all, the social worker would initially identify the basic needs of a client group and the barriers this group faces in meeting those needs. A second step, closely related to the first, is to involve that client group in a negotiation regarding these needs and barriers. In other words, client populations should be included in any formal and conclusive identification of their basic needs and of the barriers to meeting those needs.

A third step in the policy formulation process would be the identification of ways barriers are currently overcome by clients and the programs that serve them. This step would also involve clients, perhaps sharing stories of ways in which they have overcome barriers to need fulfillment. This third step would then lead to a fourth step, which is the identification of opportunities and resources required for people to meet their basic needs.

Only after these first four steps have been completed is the social worker ready to formulate a policy proposal—the fifth step. In developing this policy proposal, policy goals would be established through a negotiated consensus with relevant stakeholders, including policymakers and client groups. Once policy goals are established (the sixth step), then the seventh step would be to design programming to achieve these policy goals. The eighth and ninth steps, respectively, would be to implement these programs, and then, finally, evaluate the outcome of the implemented programs. This final step would involve clients in the evaluation of the program as well.

The strengths perspective has an ethical value to professional social workers involved with policy work. In particular, using a strengths perspective in policy practice can result in a more inclusive approach to policy development. This is because, when client populations are viewed as having strengths, they are more likely to be included in policy formulation. A more active involvement for those impacted by these policies can be empowering. In addition, any time a strengths perspective is used, there is a greater possibility that negative labeling of clients will be avoided and individual dignity respected.

Policy Windows of Opportunity

Social workers involved with policy advocacy know that there are "windows of opportunity" for getting new policies enacted.[26] Taking advantage of these opportunities involves agenda building, problem recognition, available solutions, and the right socio-political environment. **Agenda building** can be defined as the process of developing a list of problems or other subjects that one or more people intend to address at some point in the immediate future.

With respect to agenda building and legislative advocacy, social workers distinguish between government agendas and decision agendas in policymaking. **Government agendas** are defined as general public agendas that contain problems and potential solutions that have been introduced in the policymaking arena at some point in time. In other words, these problems and/or solutions have been "floated" in the policymaking arena to gauge how important or attractive they may be to decision makers. They now are beginning to receive serious attention by policymakers. However, no serious action has been taken on either an individual problem or an individual solution by policymakers. An illustration would be the many years that the sponsors of the first national health insurance bills spent attempting to get serious hearings before Congress. Dating back to the 1940s, Medicare was a solution that was well known to policymakers, yet really did not get serious attention until the late 1950s and early 1960s.[27]

In contrast to the general government agenda, the **decision agenda**, by definition, is located within the general government agenda and contains problems and solutions ready, or close to ready, for authoritative action by policymakers.[28] The decision agenda, therefore, contains specific bills nearing a vote by policymakers during a given legislative session. To use national health insurance as an illustration, the Forand health insurance bill was introduced and rejected in 1959, the Kerrs-Mills health insurance bill introduced and passed in 1960, and the Medicare bill introduced and passed in 1965 as part of the Great Society legislation.[29] More recently, President Obama introduced and passed healthcare reform during his administration. All are examples of legislative proposals that made it to the decision agenda!

The challenge for social workers involved in policy advocacy is to get the problem of interest to them from the general government agenda to the more immediate decision agenda. Techniques used by social work advocates to push a specific problem from the general government agenda to the decision agenda include using the media to educate the public about the problem. In this way, pressure may be put on elected officials to take action on the social problem. A second technique is to organize a coalition of people who are concerned about the problem. An example might be the organizing of a coalition of child care professionals and advocates to bring attention to the problem of inadequate child care in a given state. Similarly, organizing demonstrations, rallies, and/or marches concerning the problem is a third technique. An example is the 1987 demonstration in Washington, D.C., during the first Bush Administration for increased federal funding to address the AIDS epidemic.[30]

Another way to move a problem onto the decision agenda of policymakers is to support a political candidate for office who will champion the cause. At various times, people running for office will identify themselves with an issue such as education and, as a result, commit themselves to taking action on a given problem if elected to office.

In addition, the social work advocate might present the problem as a crisis that will get worse if no action is taken. An example, again, is the AIDS epidemic in the early 1980s. And finally, framing the problem in a way that lends itself to available solutions may encourage policymakers to take action. President George H. W. Bush's use of the "available" U.S. military after the end of the Cold War to fight a "War on Drugs" is one illustration.[31]

To take advantage of an opportunity to pass new policies, social workers must be knowledgeable about possible solutions to the social problem of interest. By "solutions," we mean the various policy mechanisms (such as sanctions, administrative strategies, program designs, and treatment methodologies) currently in use. If they are not in use, they are at least known to academics, social work practitioners, and policymakers. Solutions, therefore, include those potential problem-solving initiatives currently receiving attention by policymakers as part of the general government policy agenda.

Again, the challenge for social work advocates is to get a preferred solution coupled with an identified problem on the decision agenda of policymakers during a given legislative session. Social workers considering the feasibility of a given policy proposal often forecast the various techniques for doing this. First of all, they could present their preferred solution as the most feasible solution to an existing social problem. It may be most feasible technically (in terms of current research), financially, ideologically, and/or administratively. To provide an illustration, the administration of President George W. Bush, which took office in 2001, advocated increased federal funding of "faith-based" organizations (meaning religious organizations) to address a variety of social problems.[32] Given his religious convictions, President Bush clearly took office with this as a preferred solution to many human service problems.

> **Social Work Stories: Taking a Stand for Equal Rights**
>
> Many women believed the right to vote to be a solution to women's oppression. Witness Alice Paul. Alice Paul was a strong women's rights advocate working for the passage of the 19th Amendment and also authoring and lobbying for the Equal Rights Amendment (ERA) until her death in 1977. Paul's activities in the suffrage movement included participating in various forms of advocacy, including protest marches and parades, rallies and demonstrations, congressional lobbying, visits to the White House, and public meetings.
>
> Paul also coordinated picketing of the White House, for which she was arrested and sentenced to seven months in jail. While in jail, Paul went on hunger strikes that resulted in daily force-feedings by jail staff intended to coerce compliance. She was allowed no visitors, denied access to her lawyer, and was not allowed to receive mail. The door was removed from her cell, the windows were covered, and she was awakened every hour throughout the night with a bright light. The tactics and techniques that Paul used, as well as the treatment that she endured, demonstrate her lifelong quest for women's rights.[33]

Another technique is to run for office with a desired solution to a major public problem as the centerpiece of the campaign. An illustration of this technique would be the campaign of millionaire and fiscal conservative Steve Forbes for president in 1996, presenting the "flat tax" as the solution to an unfair and overly complicated U.S. tax system.

Social work advocates must also examine the socio-political environment in which policy is developed. They do this in order to determine whether or not there is sufficient support for new policy proposals. For Congress and state legislatures, the "socio-political environment" consists of public opinion, constituent support, campaign donors, advocacy groups, lobbyists, the media, and powerful political leaders (e.g., committee chairs). For other types of public organizations, such as the Department of Health and Human Services at the national level, the socio-political environment consists of legislative guidelines, administrative regulations, taxpayer views, client feedback, and the views of elected officials. Private nonprofit organizations must consider items such as funding opportunities and guidelines, professional ethics, court rulings (such as the rulings on the tax-exempt status on nonprofit organizations), advocacy groups, client demands, and community support.

Windows of opportunity for new policy occur when existing problems, available solutions, and political support converge at some point in time.[34] Social work advocates must recognize and take advantage of these opportunities. To illustrate using the history of Medicare, the problem was inadequate health care coverage for U.S. residents. The solution presented, at least for older Americans, was Medicare. However, no major legislation was passed until the problem and the solution converged in 1965 with the political support of President Lyndon Johnson, the chair of the House Ways and Means Committee, Wilbur Mills, and many supportive advocacy groups.[35]

Collaboration and Political Strategy in Policy Advocacy

Social workers collaborate with others at many levels to change and develop new policies. As stated in previous chapters, this collaboration could be with coworkers in an interdisciplinary team (interprofessional collaboration) to change agency policies; it could be with other community agencies to change community policies (interagency collaboration). At the state and national

> **Case Study: National Coalition for the Homeless**
>
> An example of an ongoing national coalition is the National Coalition for the Homeless, which maintains a Web site at http://www.nationalhomeless.org. This coalition works to end homelessness through grassroots organizing, public education, policy advocacy, ethical assistance, and partnerships. Its Web site offers fact sheets, alerts to upcoming legislative activities, tips on communicating with Congress, forums, and personal stories of homelessness. One of the coalition's major advocacy successes was the Stewart B. McKinney Homeless Assistance Act of 1987![37]

levels, social work advocates are frequently asked to assist in developing a political advocacy strategy for passing policy proposals. The target of the strategy would be the policy decision maker, such as Congress on the national level or a state legislature on the state level. In terms of advocacy goals, the most fundamental goal would be to have the decision maker pass the policy recommendation. To do this, policy advocates frequently need to develop a political strategy involving partnerships with other policy proposal supporters. In this instance, the partnership may take the form of a coalition of major stakeholders identified as supportive. **Coalitions**, by definition, are usually temporary partnerships organized for a specific and time-limited purpose.[36] Such would be the case in organizing solely for the purpose of passing a piece of legislation. Some groups do continue to work together on a more long-term basis under the name of a coalition (see the case study below). Once organized, the coalition members can employ numerous advocacy tactics to influence policy decision makers.

The history of American social welfare shows that those who are successful in promoting social change are also those who have collaborated with like-minded groups. Therefore, social work advocates continually seek allies to pass progressive policy.

To illustrate, let's once again look at state and national legislation. In defining the social problem and key issues on which to focus, social work advocates ask: Which groups define the social problem in a comparable way? Which groups agree in identifying key aspects of the social problem? These are potential allies in organizing coalitions and/or associations to better address the issue.

In terms of examining the legislative history of the social problem, what committees and departments were involved in passing prior legislation related to the problem? Who were some of the important individuals on these committees and in these departments? Are these people still working in the same positions? If they are, social work advocates know that these are potential supporters in the attempt to formulate and pass new social policy. What client populations were affected by prior legislation? Do these client populations have advocacy groups? If so, these advocacy groups are potential supporters in passing new social policy.

With respect to examining past research on the social problem, which organizations were involved in conducting the research? How was the research applied and which groups benefited from the research? These are potential allies in policy advocacy.

And as previously discussed in identifying major stakeholders in the proposed policy, which stakeholders are probable supporters of the new legislation? Which of these likely supporters have the most interest in the proposed policy? Which have the most power and influence in the policymaking process?

Which will be affected most by new social policy that better addresses the social problem?

Finally, which groups are the biggest proponents of solutions of interest to the social work advocate? This is not to say that the social worker necessarily has a solution already picked out to address the social issue; however, based on their prior experience, several potential solutions may be of interest to the social worker and his or her employer. Therefore, other proponents of certain programming and treatment methodologies are potential allies and coalition partners.

Social Workers and Policy Debate

Some social work policy advocates may find themselves not only in the role of communicator, but also in the roles of lobbyist and persuader. In such cases, knowledge of debate tactics as they relate to policy communication may be helpful.

In the case of competing policy proposals, policy advocates need to offer their policy recommendation as an alternative to other, less desirable policy options. In so doing, the communicator needs to point out important distinctions between their recommendation and competing recommendations. The strengths of the policy proposal should be highlighted, while the weaknesses of other policy alternatives are identified.

Potential weaknesses in alternative policy options include those pertaining to problem definition. For instance, does the alternative policy recommendation clearly define the values, assumptions, and factors associated with the problem? Second, are there flaws in the research methodology of alternative policy proposals? For example, are there biases in survey instruments used to collect information in alternative policy proposals? Should a random sample have been used in collecting information? Do competing proposals rely too heavily on anecdotal evidence? These and other potential flaws can be pointed out when advocating for a specific proposal and against other policy proposals.

Third, the choice of criteria used in competing policy proposals can be critiqued. Perhaps competing proposals rely too heavily on financial criteria. Perhaps they don't rely enough on more technical criteria such as program effectiveness. Maybe competing policy proposals fail to examine potential unanticipated consequences of the proposal on certain populations. Maybe alternative proposals are vague in terms of their implementation planning. In these and other ways, social workers advocating for a specific policy recommendation may make the strongest case when communicating to policy decision makers and the public in general.

Demonstrating Knowledge, Values, and Skills

As a class exercise, students should divide up into two or more teams. Pick a social problem and have each group formulate a more precise problem statement, values and assumptions underlying the problem statement, and a policy recommendation that better addresses the problem than do current policies.

Then have the student teams present their policy analysis, stating why they feel it is the best policy alternative when compared to competing policy proposals.

Which students were most persuasive? What tactics did they use to make their case?

Internet Advocacy

Internet advocacy is another political strategy that every social worker can employ. Today, organizations, including health and human services, develop Web sites that provide crucial information about the mission and programs of the agency to the public. Visitors to the Web site can be informed in much greater detail about the services, client populations, finances, leaders, and staff of an agency than through typical agency brochures. Interested Internet visitors can find out the latest news about an organization, upcoming events, and past accomplishments.

[W]e may decide that access to the Internet is a basic human right.
—Thomas L. Friedman

Once informed and interested in the mission of the organization, an Internet user may decide to get more involved in the activities of the organization, including those dealing with policy advocacy.[38] If an organization is mounting a campaign to get a policy recommendation passed, the agency can provide Internet supporters with ways to make a financial donation to the cause and to contact crucial decision makers and other stakeholders involved with the policy recommendation. Most advocacy organizations will provide their supporters with a prewritten letter urging decision makers to take a specific action on the issue and then allow the supporter to e-mail the message directly from the Web site. In addition, agencies can provide chat areas and links with likeminded agencies (perhaps part of a coalition) right on their Web site.

Although this option may be soon replaced to a significant degree by Twitter, the new real-time, online communication service, another communication vehicle for supporters is the use of a "listserv" that allows supporters to exchange e-mail regarding the policy proposal, the decision-making process, and other related activities.[39] Furthermore, the agency Web site can be used to allow policy advocates a chance to ask questions and provide feedback to agency leaders and staff regarding the policy recommendation and advocacy campaign. As previously stated, most advocacy agencies allow their supporters an opportunity to send e-mails directly from the agency's Web site in

Critical Thinking Question

The Internet and other new technologies are increasingly used in policy practice. Can you think of a way to use your laptop computer or cell phone to advocate for a policy change at your college?

support of or opposition to a policy proposal.[40] Printed copies of such e-mails also can be collected by the agency and presented in hard copy later to policy decision makers to emphasize support for the policy proposal.

Agencies may also choose to provide campaign material on their Web site that can be printed by supporters in trying to get a policy recommendation passed. Such material may be used for posters, fliers, brochures, anecdotal stories, or fact sheets during the advocacy process.[41] Agencies in support of a policy proposal also are increasingly employing the latest in Internet animation, sound, and video such as YouTube to create advocacy messages.

Some agencies such as the NASW also provide an "online tool kit" for supporters who want to start campaigns or other initiatives.[42] In the case of a campaign to support a policy recommendation, the tool kit may be used to help organize efforts at the state and local level. Tool kits can show supporters how to raise money, write press releases, create public service announcements, and communicate with state and local policymakers. This would include, of course, ways to use the Internet in such advocacy efforts. Environmental and human rights activists have used Internet advocacy successfully in the past. These agencies include the Rain Forest Activist Network and Amnesty International. Social work associations like NASW and various political action groups such as MoveOn.org and MomsRising.org are now doing the same.

Did You Know?

Did you know that Twitter, a service that broadcasts brief messages over the Internet or by text message in real time, turned out to be a critical tool used by millions of Iranians to protest the questionable results of the 2009 presidential election in that country? Twitter helped protesters in their advocacy efforts because it is highly mobile, fast, free, public, and read on many high-tech devices.

MomsRising, for instance, is a grassroots membership organization that advocates for family economic security. It uses its Web site to provide a national soapbox for mothers to discuss issues, policies, and services involving families. And these moms are tech savvy! Their Web site allows members to participate in national and state advocacy campaigns by employing e-mail, blogs, Twitter "tweets," videos, and more. And all of this can be done from the living rooms of their homes and apartments!

SOCIAL WORKERS AND ADVOCACY SUCCESS

> Justice is the first virtue of social institutions, as truth is of systems of thought. A theory however elegant and economical must be rejected or revised if it is untrue; likewise laws and institutions no matter how efficient and well-arranged must be reformed or abolished if they are unjust.[43]
>
> —John Rawls

The American market economy produces a relatively high standard of living. Yet, when change is needed, government and voluntary associations often play leading roles in the effort. In fact, the history of American social welfare is filled with successful collaborative efforts at social reform. Social workers at times have been leaders in these reform movements. At other times, they have been called upon to implement programs and services as a result of new social legislation. In any case, don't let the cynicism of some critics fool you. As a social worker, you can make a difference!

The foremothers of social work were successful in many advocacy efforts. Dorothea Dix, one of the first great social advocates, was certainly a success in establishing state services for the mentally ill.[44] Using their excellent communication skills, women such as Lucretia Mott, Lucy Stone, Susan B. Anthony, and Elizabeth Cady Stanton during the 1800s contributed significantly to the abolition movement.[45] Many of the same women fought for women's suffrage and were ultimately successful in gaining the right to vote.

The driving force behind much social reform during the Progressive Era was the grassroots advocacy of women. The General Federation of Women's Clubs was a national advocacy network, starting at the local community level, which was very influential in passing many of the reforms of the Progressive Era. The National Congress of Mothers was another advocacy organization heavily involved in reform efforts during the Progressive Era.[46] Depending on the specific issue, at various times, these organizations partnered in coalitions with other reform groups, including progressive business associations, trade unions, farm groups, urban political machines, and the emerging social work profession.

Social workers Jane Addams, Grace Abbott, Edith Abbott, and other settlement house workers were successful in their efforts to improve the quality of life for immigrants in inner-city neighborhoods.[47] And they did so by personally witnessing the growing social need and stressing social cooperation among business, government, and voluntary associations to address this need.

Like the settlement houses, charity organization societies also stressed community collaboration in addressing social problems. Led by professionals such as social worker Mary Richmond, many of these organizations later evolved into community chests and ultimately the United Way system, a nationwide partnership between business and nonprofit health and human service organizations.[48]

Workers' Compensation and, later, Social Security and Unemployment Compensation, created during the New Deal have been a success.[49] Settlement house workers Eleanor Roosevelt, Harry Hopkins, and Frances Perkins were top advisors to President Franklin Roosevelt during the creation of the New Deal programs.[50] Eleanor Roosevelt was one of the great campaigners and advocates in American history!

The programs of the Great Society, despite continuing criticism, have been successful in many ways. The Food Stamp Program has helped the poor obtain critical food supplies.[51] Medicare, despite issues of cost control, has provided many older Americans with needed health care, while keeping them from falling into poverty.[52] Community health centers, also established during the Great Society, provide accessible services in low-income communities.[53] Poor children have benefited from the early educational support of Head Start, a Great Society program that increases the likelihood of future high school graduation and employment.[54] And the Civil Rights Acts of 1964 and 1965 ended segregation in the South and led the way to the election of the first black man as president of the United States, Barack Obama.[55]

The point is that many social programs, although perhaps not perfect, perhaps not completely solving the various problems they address, have, in fact, been successful, providing needed services and support to millions of Americans. Contemporary social workers and students studying to be social workers should be proud of these successes. American social welfare is the result of a cooperative effort,- a collaboration - among various institutions, groups, and individuals to further national well-being. To the extent that this collaboration at times has needed to be coerced, American social welfare reflects a rich heritage of advocacy that can be built upon by today's social workers. The next successful social reform movement involving social workers might address current issues involving Social Security , health care, or homelessness. It might

Research Informed Practice

One of the most important roles of a social worker is to act as an advocate. The NASW identifies ways to be an advocate on its national Web site, www.socialworkers.org. Look for "Advocacy" and click on "Legislative Advocacy Network." *Which issues are currently top priorities for social workers? What is NASW doing to advocate for these issues?* Learn how you can take action on the federal issues important to social workers by contacting your members of Congress through the Legislative Advocacy Network.

Poverty exists because we've built our philosophical framework on assumptions that underestimate human capacities.

—Muhammad Yunus

---

address international issues related to globalization and international poverty. It might address any number of concerns. Whatever the cause, social advocacy will continue, and hopefully, social workers will play a lead role in the effort.

In so doing, let a vision of social justice guide the profession of social work, a vision based on respect for diversity, individual dignity, self-determination, human rights, and empowerment. Every graduate, upon leaving social work education, should have a personal and professional vision of social justice to guide his or her future activities as a social worker. Without this social vision, social work becomes a profession without passion, a profession without power!

SUMMARY

Social workers engage in advocacy in order to promote social and economic justice. This could mean advocating for a proposed policy within the agency in which the social worker is employed. The new policy may impact employees of the agency (e.g., better health care) or it may affect the clients of the agency (e.g., stricter client confidentiality procedures). At other times, social workers advocate for proposed policy at the city or county level, promoting new policy that would address social problems in local neighborhoods, for instance. Still other social workers advocate for new policy in the form of legislative bills before state legislatures and Congress. When doing so, social workers may play one of several advocacy roles, including that of a witness, collaborator, lobbyist, or activist. Furthermore, social workers have a long history of successful advocacy. These successes include child labor laws, maternal and child health services, Social Security , unemployment compensation, food stamps, housing assistance, early childhood education, and civil rights legislation. These laws, policies, programs, and services have helped millions of people to lead healthy, productive lives. If you agree, perhaps a career in social work would be right for you!

16 CHAPTER REVIEW

Succeed with MySocialWorkLab

Log onto **MySocialWorkLab** to access a wealth of case studies, videos, and assessment. (*If you did not receive an access code to* **MySocialWorkLab** *with this text and wish to purchase access online, please visit www.mysocialworklab.com.*)

PRACTICE TEST
The following questions will test your knowledge of the content found within this chapter. For additional assessment, including licensing-exam type questions on applying chapter content to practice, visit **MySocialWorkLab**.

Policy Practice

1. _____ in social work involves the formulation, enactment, implementation, and assessment of social welfare policies:
   a. Case management
   b. Research methods
   c. Administration
   d. Policy practice

2. The _____ approach to problem definition maintains that a social problem is recognized when the quantitative indicators of a problem become indisputably large over time:
   a. Functional
   b. Normative
   c. Objective
   d. Subjective

3. An advocacy role in which the social worker takes planned, concrete action to produce social change on behalf of clients is called:
   a. Lobbyist
   b. Activist
   c. Campaigner
   d. Witness

4. A "just society" from this viewpoint is one in which individuals are essentially free from intrusion of any kind from government or other bodies:
   a. Marxist
   b. Libertarian
   c. Utilitarian
   d. Egalitarian

5. A just society is one that achieves the greatest good for the greatest number according to this viewpoint:
   a. Marxist
   b. Libertarian
   c. Utilitarian
   d. Egalitarian

Professional Identity

6. Which of the following philosophies is most consistent with social work's overall mission and core values?
   a. Egalitarianism
   b. Utilitarianism
   c. Libertarianism
   d. Marxism

7. The Library of Congress maintains a legislative Web site called:
   a. George
   b. Benjamin
   c. John
   d. Thomas

8. With respect to policy practice, a _____ is any individual or group that can affect or be affected by proposed or existing legislation:
   a. Lobbyist
   b. Stakeholder
   c. Caucus
   d. Participant

9. _____ for new policy occur when existing problems, available solutions, and political support converge at some point in time:
   a. Windows of opportunity
   b. Strategies
   c. Agendas
   d. None of the above

10. _____ are usually temporary partnerships organized for a specific and time-limited purpose.
    a. Coalitions
    b. Networks
    c. Associations
    d. Task forces

Log onto **MySocialWorkLab** once you have completed the Practice Test above to access additional study tools and assessment.

Answers

Key: 1) d 2) c 3) b 4) b 5) c 6) a 7) d 8) b 9) a 10) a

Notes

Chapter 1

1. Craig Winston LeCroy, *The Call To Social Work* (Thousand Oaks, CA: Sage, 2002), pp. 35–36.
2. Ibid., p. 43.
3. National Association of Social Workers (NASW), *Code of Ethics*, retrieved February 17, 2010, from www.naswdc.org/pubs/code/code.asp.
4. International Federation of Social Workers, "Ethics in Social Work, Statement of Principles," retrieved February 17, 2010, from www.ifsw.org/publications/4.4.pub.html.
5. Council on Social Work Education (CSWE), *2008 Educational Policy and Accreditation Standards* (Alexandria, VA: Council on Social Work Education, Inc., 2008), p. 1.
6. Ibid., p. 3.
7. Charles Zastrow, *Introduction to Social Work and Social Welfare: Empowering People*, 8th ed. (Belmont, CA: Brooks/Cole, 2004), pp. 77–79.
8. Ibid., p. 50.
9. Loretta Schwartz-Nobel, *Growing Up Empty: How Federal Policies Are Starving America's Children* (New York: Harper Collins, 2002), pp. 124–125.
10. Mary E. Woods and Florence Hollis, *Casework: A Psychosocial Therapy* (Boston: McGraw-Hill, 2002), p. 39.
11. Karla Krogsrud Miley, Michael O'Melia, and Brenda DuBois, *Generalist Social Work Practice: An Empowering Approach*, 5th ed. (Boston, MA: Pearson Education, Inc., 2007), p. 364.
12. Vincent Guilamo-Ramos, Patricia Dittus, James Jaccard, Margaret Johansson, Alida Bouris, and Neifi Acosta, "Parenting Practices among Dominican and Puerto Rican Mothers," *Social Work* 52(1) (2007), pp. 17–27.
13. Miley, O'Melia, and DuBois, pp. 39–45; Zastrow, p. 53.
14. John Poulin, *Collaborative Social Work: Strengths-Based Generalist Practice* (Belmont, CA: Thomson Learning, Inc., 2000), pp. 343–344.
15. Miley, O'Melia, and DuBois, pp. 10, 227, 353–358.
16. NASW, *General Fact Sheets: Social Work Profession*, retrieved February 17, 2010, from www.naswdc.org.
17. See Bruce S. Jansson, *Becoming an Effective Policy Advocate: From Policy Practice to Social Justice* (Belmont, CA: Brooks/Cole, 2007).
18. L. Parrott, *Social Work and Social Care* (London: Taylor & Francis Books, 2001), p. 56.
19. NASW, *General Fact Sheets: Social Work Profession*, retrieved February 17, 2010, from www.naswdc.org.
20. Zastrow, p. 55.
21. Beulah Compton, Burt Galoway, and Barry Cournoyer, *Social Work Processes*, 7th ed. (Belmont, CA: Brooks/Cole, 2005), pp. 24–38.
22. Marianne R. Woodside and Tricia McClam, *An Introduction to Human Services*, 5th ed. (Belmont, CA: Thomson Brooks/Cole, 2006), pp. 206–210.
23. Jerry Marx, 2008, personal interview with Lorrie Marx Addams.
24. Gianna Kelfala, 2006, personal interview with Emily Sawka.
25. Schwartz-Nobel, p. 153.
26. NASW, *Code of Ethics*, retrieved February 17, 2010, from www.naswdc.org/pubs/code/code.asp.
27. Ibid.
28. Poulin, pp. 21–23.
29. Frederic G. Reamer, *The Foundations of Social Work Knowledge* (New York: Columbia University Press, 1994), pp. 204–220.
30. NASW, *Code of Ethics*, retrieved February 17, 2010, from www.naswdc.org/pubs/code/code.asp.
31. Ibid.
32. Studs Terkel, *Working: People Talk About What They Do All Day and How They Feel About What They Do* (New York: The New Press, 2004), pp. 7–9.
33. Miley, O'Melia, and DuBois, pp. 66–71, 81–84.
34. Lawrence Shulman, *The Skills of Helping Individuals, Families, Groups, and Communities*, 4th ed. (Itasca, IL: F. E. Peacock Publishers, Inc., 1999), pp. 120–121.
35. George A. Appleby, Edgar Colon, and Julia Hamilton, *Diversity, Oppression, and Social Functioning: Person-in-Environment Assessment and Intervention* (Boston, MA: Allyn & Bacon, 2001), pp. 241–242.
36. Miley, O'Melia, and DuBois, pp. 232–237.
37. R. Bush, "An Examination of Five Essential Competencies for Empowerment Practice," *Journal for Baccalaureate Social Work* 9(2) (2004), pp. 47–62.
38. Ibid., pp. 53–56, 61.
39. Reamer, p. 266.
40. Schwartz-Nobel, pp. 139–140.
41. Appleby, Colon, and Hamilton, pp. 43–44.
42. Schwartz-Nobel, p. 22
43. Poulin, pp. 7–8.
44. Miley, O'Melia, and DuBois, pp. 85–93.
45. Ibid., pp. 95–102.
46. Ibid., pp. 249–253, 400–407.
47. Barbara Enrenreich, *Nickel and Dimed: On (Not) Getting by in America* (New York: Holt, 2001), pp. 59–60.
48. CSWE, *2007 Survey of Social Work Programs, Research Brief*, retrieved May 27, 2008, from www.cswe.org.
49. University of New Hampshire Social Work Department Self-Study, January 2002, pp. 211–252.
50. Bureau of Labor Statistics, *Occupational Outlook Handbook, 2008–09 Edition*, retrieved June 4, 2009, from http://www.bls.gov/oco/ocos060.htm.
51. Margaret Gibelman, "The Search for Identity: Defining Social Work—Past, Present, Future," *Social Work*, 44(4) (1999), pp. 298–310.
52. Bureau of Labor Statistics, *Occupational Outlook Handbook, 2010–11 Edition*, retrieved March 18, 2010, from http://www.bls.gov/oco/ocos060.htm#outlook.
53. NASW, *General Fact Sheets: Social Work Profession*, retrieved February 17, 2010, from www.naswdc.org.

Quotes

David K. Shipler, *The Working Poor: Invisible in America*, (New York: Vintage/Random House, 2005), p. 9.

Gail Collins, *When Everything Changed: The Amazing Journey of American Women from 1960 to the Present* (New York: Little, Brown, and Co., 2009), p. 337.

Jeffrey D. Sachs, *The End of Poverty: Economic Possibilities for Our Time* (New York: Penguin, 2009), p. 347.

Chapter 2

1. Council on Social Work Education (CSWE), *2008 Educational Policy and Accreditation Standards* (Alexandria, VA: Council on Social Work Education, Inc., 2008), p. 9.
2. Katherine van Wormer, *Introduction to Social Welfare and Social Work: The U.S. in Global Perspective* (Belmont, CA: Thomson Learning, Inc., 2006), pp. 262–264.
3. Ibid., pp. 281–283.
4. Ibid.
5. Robin Karr-Morse and Meredith S. Wiley, *Ghosts from the Nursery: Tracing the Roots of Violence* (New York: Atlantic Monthly Press, 1997), p. 24.
6. Ibid., p. 22.
7. Ibid., p. 29.
8. Ibid., p. 22.
9. Ibid., p. 44.
10. Ibid., p. 80.
11. Erik H. Erikson, *Childhood and Society* (New York: Norton, 1993).
12. William Cairn, *Theories of Development: Concepts and Applications*, 4th ed. (Upper Saddle River, NJ: Prentice Hall, 2000), p. 277.
13. Ibid., pp. 110–139.
14. Jose B. Ashford, Craig Winston LeCroy, and Kathy L. Lortie, *Human Behavior and the Social Environment: A Multidimensional Perspective* (Belmont, CA: Brooks/Cole, 2001), pp. 75–76.
15. Ibid., p. 113.
16. Ibid., p. 112.
17. John S. Darcy and John F. Travers, *Human Development Across the Lifespan*, 6th ed. (Boston, MA: McGraw-Hill, 2006), pp. 43–45.
18. Ibid.
19. Ibid.
20. Ibid.
21. Ibid.
22. Abraham Maslow, *Motivation and Personality*, 3rd ed. (New York: HarperCollins, 1987).
23. Van Wormer, pp. 285–286.
24. Urie Bronfenbrenner, "Toward an Experimental Ecology of Human Development," *American Psychologist 32* (1977), pp. 513–531.
25. Van Wormer, p. 296.
26. Janean E. Dilworth-Bart and Colleen F. Moore, "Mercy Mercy Me: Social Injustice and the Prevention of Environmental Pollutant Exposures Among Ethnic Minority and Poor Children," *Child Development 77*(2) (March/April 2006), pp. 247–265.
27. Ibid., p. 248.
28. George L. Engle, "The Clinical Application of the Biopsychosocial Model," *American Journal of Psychiatry 137* (1980), pp. 535–544.
29. Carel B. Germain and Alex Gitterman, "Ecological Perspectives," in Richard L. Edwards (Ed.), *Encyclopedia of Social Work*, 19th ed. (Washington, DC: NASW Press, 1995), pp. 818–823.
30. Ibid.
31. Ibid., p. 817.
32. Ibid.
33. Ibid.
34. Ibid.
35. Ibid., p. 818.
36. Ibid.
37. Ibid., p. 819.
38. Dennis Saleebey, *The Strengths Approach in Social Work Practice*, 4th ed. (Boston, MA: Pearson, 2006).
39. Ibid., pp. 1–22.
40. Ibid.
41. Dennis Salleebey, "Strengths-Based Patrice," in Richard L. Edwards and J. G. Hopps (Eds.), *Encyclopedia of Social Work*, 19th ed. (2003 Supplement) (Washington, DC: NASW Press, 2003), p. 154.

Quotes

Margaret Mead, "Meade's Maxim," in John Peers (Comp.), *1001 Logical Laws* (Garden City, NY: Doubleday, 1979), p. 155.

Jane Addams, *Peace and Bread in Time of War* (New York: McMillian, 1922), p. 133.

Michael Harrington, *The Other America: Poverty in the United States* (New York: Macmillan, 1962), Appendix 1.

Brooks Atkinson, *Once Around the Sun* (New York: Harcourt, Brace, 1951), 24 August.

Chapter 3

1. Beulah R. Compton, Burt Galaway, and Barry R. Cournoyer, *Social Work Processes*, 7th ed. (Belmont, CA: Brooks/Cole, 2005), pp. 4–5.
2. Katherine van Wormer, *Introduction to Social Welfare and Social Work: The U.S. in Global Perspective* (Belmont, CA: Thomson Learning, Inc., 2006), pp. 12–13; Barker, p. 408.
3. John M. Romanyshyn and Annie L. Romanyshyn, *Social Welfare: Charity to Justice* (New York: Random House, 1971), as cited in M. Siporin, *Introduction to Social Work Practice* (New York: Macmillan Publishing Co., Inc., 1975), p. 4.
4. Bill Clinton, *Giving: How Each of Us Can Change the World* (New York: Knopf, 2007), pp. 3–12, 185–203; Jeffrey D. Sachs, *The End of Poverty: Economic Possibilities for Our Time* (New York: Penguin, 2005), pp. 226, 266; Lester M. Salamon, *The State of Nonprofit America* (Washington, DC: Brookings Institution Press, 2002), pp. 3–52.
5. Adam Smith, *The Wealth of Nations* (with Introduction by Alan B. Krueger) (New York: Bantam, 2003).
6. Sachs, p. 327.
7. Neil Heilbroner and Lester Thurow, *Economics Explained: Everything You Need to Know About How the Economy Works and Where It's Going* (New York: Touchstone, 1998), pp. 11–20.
8. David A. Moss, *A Concise Guide to Macroeconomics: What Managers, Executives, and Students Need to Know* (Boston: Harvard Business School Press, 2007), p. 11; Heilbroner and Thurow, p. 14.
9. Moss, p. 11; Heilbroner and Thurow, pp. 14–20.
10. Heilbroner and Thurow, p. 24.
11. Ibid.
12. Thomas L. Friedman, *The Lexus and the Olive Tree* (New York: Anchor Books, 2000), p. 9.

13. Ibid.
14. Jacob S. Hacker, *The Great Risk Shift: The New Economic Insecurity and the Decline of the American Dream* (New York: Oxford University Press, 2008), pp. 63–64.
15. Moss, p. 29; Organisation for Economic Co-operation and Development (OECD), *Economic Survey of the United States, May 2000*, retrieved January 10, 2001, from www.oecd.org.
16. Ibid.
17. Aileen McCabe, "China to Knock Off Japan as World's Second Largest Economy," *The Vancouver Sun*, January 21, 2010, retrieved February 18, 2010, from www.vancouversun.com; OECD, p. 10.
18. Moss, pp. 63–64; Matt Miller, *The 2% Solution: Fixing America's Problems in Ways That Liberals and Conservatives Can Love* (New York: Public Affairs, 2003), pp. 4–7, 11–13.
19. Tim Harper, *The U.S. Constitution: A Plain-English Guide to the Document That Defines the American Way of Life* (New York: Penguin, 2007), p. 19; Stephen J. Wayne, G. Calvin Mackenzie, David M. O'Brien, and Richard L. Cole, *The Politics of American Government: Foundations, Participation, and Institutions* (New York: St. Martin's, 1995), pp. 413–414.
20. Harper, pp. 21–22.
21. Children's Defense Fund, *2000 Congressional Workbook: Basic Process and Issue Primer* (Washington, DC: Author, 2000), p. 27.
22. Wayne et al., p. 416.
23. Ibid., pp. 416–417.
24. U.S. House of Representatives, *Leadership*, retrieved February 18, 2010, from www.house.gov/house/orgs_pub_hse_ldr_wwwshtml; Wayne et al., pp. 420–422.
25. U.S. Senate, *Leadership*, retrieved February 18, 2010, from www.senate.gov/pagelayout/senators/a_three_sections_with_teasers/leadership.htm; Wayne et al., pp. 422–423.
26. Wayne et al., p. 428.
27. Ibid., pp. 431–448.
28. Clinton, p. 9; Salamon, 2002, p. 4; Michael O'Neill, *The Third America: The Emergence of the Nonprofit Sector in the United States* (San Francisco, CA: Jossey-Bass, 1989), p. 7.
29. Salamon, 2002, p. 7; O'Neill, p. 2.
30. Salamon, 2002, p. 7; O'Neill, p. 4.
31. Salamon, 2002, pp. 7, 524; O'Neill, p. 4.
32. See Giving USA Foundation, *Giving USA 2007: The Annual Report on Philanthropy for the Year 2006* (Glenview, IL: Giving USA Foundation, 2007).
33. Ibid.
34. Ibid.
35. Bruce S. Jansson, *American Social Welfare Policies—Past, Present, and Future* (Belmont, CA: Thomson Brooks/Cole, 2005), pp. 85–86, 237, 296–297; O'Neill, pp. 16–17.
36. Lester M. Salamon, *Partners in Public Service: Government-Nonprofit Relations in the Modern Welfare State* (Baltimore, MD: Johns Hopkins University Press, 1995), pp. 84–85.
37. Heilbroner and Thurow, p. 57
38. Ibid., p. 79; Brian Snowdon and Howard R. Vane, *Modern Macroeconomics: Its Origins, Development, and Current State* (Northhampton, MA: Edward Elgar, 2005), pp. 1–3.
39. Heilbroner and Thurow, pp. 71–80.
40. Ibid., pp. 177–178; CoinNews, *Current CPI and Inflation Rate*, retrieved February 18, 2010, from www.usinflationcalculator.com; Google, *Unemployment Rate*, retrieved February 18, 2010, from www.google.com/publicdata.

Quotes

Muhammad Yunus, *Creating a World Without Poverty: Small Business and the Future of Capitalism* (New York: Public Affairs, 2007), p. 5.

John F. Kennedy, *Profiles in Courage: Decisive Moments in the Lives of Celebrated Americans* (New York: Harper and Brothers, 1956), p. 224.

Thomas L. Friedman, *The Lexus and the Olive Tree: Understanding Globalization* (New York: Farrar, Straus, and Giroux, 2000), p. 447.

Chapter 4

1. Armando Morales and Bradford Sheafor, *Social Work: A Profession of Many Faces*, 5th ed. (Boston, MA: Allyn and Bacon, 1989), p. 9; Council on Social Work Education (2008), *Educational Policy and Accreditation Standards*, retrieved February 21, 2010, from www.cswe.org/File.aspx?id=13780.
2. Morales and Sheafor, pp. 222–224
3. Karla K. Miley, Michael O'Melia, and Brenda L. DuBois, *Generalist Social Work Practice: An Empowering Approach*, 5th ed. (Boston: Pearson Education, 2007), pp. 16–21; Brenda L. DuBois and Karla K. Miley, *Social Work: An Empowering Profession*, 5th ed. (Boston, MA: Pearson Education, 2005), p. 227.
4. Miley, O'Melia, and DuBois, pp. 16–21; DuBois and Miley, p. 229.
5. Linda May Grobman, *More Days in the Lives of Social Workers* (Harrisburg, PA: White Hat Communications, 2005), pp. 205–209.
6. John Poulin, *Collaborative Social Work* (Belmont, CA: Thomson Learning, 2000), pp. 34–38.
7. Miley, O'Melia, and DuBois, pp. 107–113.
8. DuBois and Miley, pp. 201–202; Miley, O'Melia, and DuBois, pp. 34–36, 47–49.
9. DuBois and Miley, pp. 202–203.
10. Ibid.
11. National Association of Social Workers (NASW) (2008), *Code of Ethics*, retrieved February 21, 2010, from www.naswdc.org/pubs/code/code.asp.
12. Poulin, pp. 16–17.
13. Miley, O'Melia, and DuBois, pp. 138–146.
14. Morales and Sheafor, pp. 197–198.
15. Ibid.
16. NASW (2008), *Code of Ethics*, retrieved February 21, 2010, from www.naswdc.org/pubs/code/code.asp.
17. *Webster's New World College Dictionary*, 4th ed. (Foster City, CA: IDG Books Worldwide, 2001), p. 471.
18. Miley, O'Melia, and DuBois, pp. 142–152; Morales and Sheafor, pp. 250–251.
19. Morales and Sheafor, pp. 250–251.
20. Poulin, pp. 40–42.
21. Charles Zastrow, *Introduction to Social Work and Social Welfare: Empowering People* 8th ed. (Belmont, CA: Thomson Brooks/Cole, 2004), p. 74.
22. Lambert Maguire, *Clinical Social Work: Beyond Generalist Practice with Individuals, Groups, and Families* (Pacific Grove, CA: Brooks/Cole Publishing Company, 2002), pp. 299–305.
23. Ibid.
24. Ibid.
25. Miley, O'Melia, and DuBois, pp. 34–39.

26. Zastrow, p. 74.
27. Poulin, pp. 65–74.
28. Ibid.
29. Ibid., pp. 84–93.
30. Ibid., pp. 94–95.
31. Ibid., pp. 94–97
32. Dennis Saleebey, *The Strengths Perspective in Social Work Practice,* 4th ed. (Boston: Pearson Education, 2006), pp. 249–255.
33. Bridget Freisthler, Emily Bruce, and Barbara Needell, "Understanding the Geospatial Relationship of Neighborhood Characteristics and Rates of Maltreatment for Black, Hispanic, and White Children," *Social Work 52*(1) (2007), pp. 7–15.
34. NASW (2008), *Code of Ethics*, retrieved February 21, 2010, from www.naswdc.org/pubs/code/code.asp.
35. Zastrow, p. 74.
36. Maguire, pp. 85–86.
37. Ibid.
38. Miley, O'Melia, and DuBois, pp. 146–152.
39. Ibid., pp. 95–98, 140–151.
40. Maguire, pp. 105–106.
41. NASW (2008), *Code of Ethics*, retrieved February 21, 2010, from www.naswdc.org/pubs/code/code.asp.
42. Maguire, pp. 45–46; 82–83.
43. Ibid., pp. 82–83.
44. Ibid., p. 81
45. Ibid., pp. 45–46; 50–52.
46. Ibid., p. 52
47. DuBois and Miley, pp. 125–131.
48. O. William Farley, Larry Lorenzo Smith, and Scott W. Boyle, *Introduction to Social Work*, 11th ed. (Boston: Allyn & Bacon, 2009), pp. 371–373.
49. Grobman, 2005, p. 211.
50. Maguire, pp. 163–162.
51. Ibid., pp. 147–156.
52. NASW (2008), *Code of Ethics*, retrieved February 21, 2010, from www.naswdc.org/pubs/code/code.asp.
53. DuBois and Miley, pp. 125–131.
54. Zastrow, pp. 99–101; DuBois and Miley, pp. 125–131.
55. Zastrow, pp. 75–77; Maguire, pp. 88–89.
56. DuBois and Miley, pp. 221–222.
57. Allen Rubin and Earl Babbie, *Research Methods for Social Work*, 5th ed. (Belmont, CA: Thomson Brooks/Cole, 2005), pp. 182–198; Poulin, pp. 143–148.
58. Poulin, pp. 148–157.
59. Rubin and Babbie, pp. 365–392; Miley, O'Melia, and DuBois, pp. 415–420, 425–433.
60. NASW (2008), *Code of Ethics*, retrieved February 21, 2010, from www.naswdc.org/pubs/code/code.asp.
61. Poulin, pp. 197–198.
62. Miley, O'Melia, and DuBois, pp. 438–448.
63. Poulin, pp. 198–199.
64. Ibid., pp. 199–202.
65. Maguire, pp. 30–36; Miley, O'Melia, and DuBois, pp. 457–462.

Quotes

Barack Obama (July 12, 2006), Presentation to Campus Progress Annual Conference, Washington, DC, retrieved February 2, 2010, from http://www.asksam.com/ebooks/releases.asp?file=Obama-Speeches.ask&dn=Campus%20Progress%20Annual%20Conference.

Maya Angelou, quoted in Donna Brown Agins, *Maya Angelou: "Diversity Makes for a Rich Tapestry"* (Berkeley Heights, NJ: Enslow Publishers, 2006).

Henry David Thoreau, *Walden* (Cambridge: The University Press, 1910).

Chapter 5

1. Council on Social Work Education, *2008 Educational Policy and Accreditation Standards* (Alexandria, VA: Council on Social Work Education, Inc., 2008), pp. 4–5.
2. Audry Smedley, *Race in North America: Origin and Evolution of a Worldview* (Boulder, CO: Westview Press, 1993).
3. John Scott and Jordan Marshall (Eds.), *Dictionary of Sociology* (New York: Oxford University Press, 2005), p. 543.
4. Smedley, pp. 303–304.
5. See Cornell West, *Race Matters* (New York: Vintage Books, 1994).
6. Smedley, p. 30.
7. Dareld Wing Sue, *Multicultural Social Work Practice* (Hoboken, NJ: Wiley Interscience, 2006), p. 17.
8. Scott and Marshall, p. 166.
9. M. Edward Ransford, "Two Higherarchies," in Maurianne Adams, Warren Blumenfeld, Rosie Castañeda, Heather W. Hackman, Madeline L. Peters, and Ximena Zúñiga (Eds.), *Readings for Diversity and Social Justice* (New York, NY: Routledge, 2000), p. 412.
10. Donna Langston, "Tired of Playing Monopoly?" in Maurianne Adams, Warren Blumenfeld, Rosie Castañeda, Heather W. Hackman, Madeline L. Peters, and Ximena Zúñiga (Eds.), *Readings for Diversity and Social Justice* (New York: Routledge, 2000), p. 398.
11. See Alfred Kinsey et al., *Sexual Behavior and the Human Male* (Bloomington, IN: Indiana University Press, 1948).
12. U.S. Social Security Administration, "What We Mean by Disability," retrieved October 23, 2006, from http://www.ssa.gov/dibplan/dqualify4.htm.
13. Scott and Marshall, p. 158.
14. National Association of Social Workers (NASW) (2008), *Code of Ethics*, retrieved June 3, 2008, from http://www.socialworkers.org/pubs/Code/code.asp.
15. U.S. Census Bureau, 2005 American Community Survey, retrieved from http://factfinder.census.gov.
16. Frank Hobbs and Nicole Stoops, *Demographic Trends in the 20th Century.* U.S. Census Bureau, Census 2000 Special Reports, Series CENSR-4 (Washington, DC: U.S. Government Printing Office, 2002), p. 56.
17. Ibid, p. 71.
18. Ibid, p. 75.
19. U.S. Census Bureau, *Dynamic Population Profile*, retrieved September 12, 2006, from http://www.census.gov/population/pop-profile/dynamic/RACEHO.pdf.
20. U.S. Department of Homeland Security, Office of Immigration Statistics, *2004 Yearbook of Immigration Statistics*, retrieved September 12, 2006, from http://www.census.gov/compendia/statab/tables/06s0005.xls.
21. U.S. Census Bureau, *June Current Population Survey, Selected Years 1994–2004*, retrieved June 16, 2009, from http://www.census.gov/population/socdemo/fertility/tabH7.csv.
22. Ibid.
23. Beth Hess, Elizabeth W. Markson, and Peter J. Stein, "Racial and Ethnic Minorities: An Overview," in Paula S. Rothenberg (Ed.), *Race, Class and Gender in the United*

States: An Integrated Study, 5th ed. (New York: Worth Publishers, 2000), p. 325.
24. Christine Lesiak (Producer), In the White Man's Image (Alexandria, VA: PBS Video, 1991).
25. Derald Wing Sue and David Sue, Counseling the Culturally Diverse: Theory and Practice, 4th ed. (New York: John Wiley and Sons, 2003), p. 275.
26. M. Annette Jaimes and Theresa Halsey, "American Indian Women: At the Center of Indigenous Resistance in North America," in M. Annette Jaimes (Ed.), The State of Native America: Genocide, Colonization and Resistance (Boston, MA: South End Press, 1993), pp. 311–344.
27. Substance Abuse and Mental Health Services Administration, Results from the 2008 National Survey on Drug Use and Health: National Findings (NSDUH Series H-36, HHS Publication No. SMA 09-4434) (Rockville, MD: Office of Applied Studies, 2009).
28. W. J. Frank, R. S. Moore, and G.M. Ames, "Historical and Cultural Roots of Drinking Problems Among American Indians," American Journal of Public Health 90 (2000), pp. 344–351.
29. White Bison, retrieved February 15, 2010, from http://www.whitebison.org/about-white-bison/about-white-bison.htm.
30. White Bison, retrieved February 15, 2010, from http://www.whitebison.org/wellbriety-movement/story-wellbriety-movement.htm.
31. Don Coyhis and Richard Simonelli, "Rebuilding Native American Communities," Child Welfare 85(2) (March/April 2005), pp. 323–336.
32. Encore Careers, "The Purpose Prize," retrieved February 15, 2010, from http://www.encore.org/prize/nominate?ref=candidatepage.cfm?candidateid=5017.
33. Jesse D. McKinnon and Claudette E. Bennett, We the People: Blacks in the U.S. (Census 2000 Special Report) _(Washington, DC: U.S. Census Bureau, 2005), p. 1.
34. Centers for Disease Control, National Center for Health Statistics, National Vital Statistics System, Deaths, Percent of Total Deaths, and Death Rates for the 15 Leading Causes of Death in 5-Year Age Groups, by Race and Sex: United States, 1999–2003, retrieved June 18, 2009, from http://www.cdc.gov/nchs/datawh/statab/unpubd/mortabs/lcwk1_10.htm.
35. Sue and Sue, p. 293.
36. Roberto Ramirez, We the People: Hispanics in the United States (Census 2000 Special Reports) (Washington, DC: U.S. Census Bureau, 2004), p. 1.
37. Ibid., pp. 2–3.
38. Ibid., p. 10.
39. Sue and Sue, p. 355.
40. Ramirez, pp. 1–20.
41. Ibid., pp. 14–16.
42. Hess, Markson, and Stein, p. 330.
43. Ibid.
44. Sue and Sue p. 327.
45. R. L. Sell, J. A. Wells, and D. Wypij, "The Prevalence of Homosexual Behavior and Attraction in the United States, the United Kingdom and France: Results of National Population-Based Samples," Archives of Sexual Behavior 24(3) (June 1995), pp. 235–248.
46. Rothenberg, p. 71.
47. Human Rights Campaign, State-Wide Anti-Discrimination Laws and Policies, retrieved November 12, 2006, from http://www.hrc.org/Template.cfm?Section=Your_Community&Template=/ContentManagement/ContentDisplay.cfm&ContentID=14821.
48. Human Rights Campaign, Statewide Hate-Crime Laws, retrieved November 12, 2006, from http://www.hrc.org/Template.cfm?Section=Your_Community&Template=/ContentManagement/ContentDisplay.cfm&ContentID=19445.
49. Human Rights Campaign. Statewide Prohibitions on Marriage for Same-Sex Couples, retrieved November 12, 2006, from http://www.hrc.org/Template.cfm?Section=Your_Community&Template=/ContentManagement/ContentDisplay.cfm&ContentID=19449.
50. Human Rights Campaign, Relationship Recognition in the US., retrieved November 12, 2006, from http://www.hrc.org/Template.cfm?Section=Your_Community&Template=/ContentManagement/ContentDisplay.cfm&ContentID=16305.
51. NASW (June 28, 2004), Same Sex Marriage Position Statement, retrieved November 12, 2006, from http://www.socialworkers.org/diversity/lgb/062804.asp.
52. U. Boehmer, "Twenty Years of Public Health Research: Inclusion of Lesbian, Gay, Bisexual, and Transgender Populations," American Journal of Public Health 92(7) (2002), pp. 1125–1130.
53. The Medical Foundation, Health Concerns of the Gay, Lesbian, Bisexual, and Transgender Community, 2nd ed., retrieved June 17, 2009, from http://www.glbthealth.org/documents/HealthConcerns.pdf.
54. Ibid.; Sue and Sue, p. 382.
55. Jay P. Paul, Joseph Catania, Lance Pollack, Judith Moskowitz, Jesse Canchola, Thomas Mills, Diane Binson, and Ron Stall, "Suicide Attempts Among Gay and Bisexual Men: Lifetime Prevalence and Antecedents," American Journal of Public Health 92 (2002), p. 1338.
56. Qi Wang, Disability and American Families: 2000 (Census 2000 Special Reports) (Washington, DC: U.S. Census Bureau, 2005), p. 3.
57. U.S. Department of Justice, ADA Legal Documents, Public Law 101-336, retrieved November 11, 2006, from www.usdoj.gov/crt/ada/pubs/ada.txt.
58. Ibid.
59. Rosie Castañeda and Madeline Peters, "Ableism," in Maurianne Adams, Warren Blumenfeld, Rosie Castañeda, Heather W. Hackman, Madeline L. Peters, and Ximena Zúñiga (Eds.), Readings for Diversity and Social Justice (New York: Routledge. 2000), p. 320.
60. Ibid.
61. Ibid., p. 11.
62. Ibid.
63. Ibid., p. 3.
64. Ibid., p. 12.
65. Willie V. Ryan, "The Disability Rights Movement," in Maurianne Adams, Warren Blumenfeld, Rosie Castañeda, Heather W. Hackman, Madeline L. Peters, and Ximena Zúñiga (Eds.), Readings for Diversity and Social Justice. (New York: Routledge, 2000), p. 326.
66. Iris Marion Young, "Five Faces of Oppression," in Maurianne Adams, Warren Blumenfeld, Rosie Castañeda, Heather W. Hackman, Madeline L. Peters, and Ximena Zúñiga (Eds.), Readings for Diversity and Social Justice (New York: Routledge, 2000), p. 37.
67. Ibid.

68. Jean Baker Miller, *Towards a New Psychology of Women*, 2nd ed. (Boston, MA: Beacon Press, 1986), p. 3.
69. Ibid.
70. Ibid., pp. 6–9.
71. Ibid., p. 10.
72. Dareld Wing Sue *Multicultural Social Work Practice* (Hoboken, NJ: Wiley Interscience, 2006), p. 16.
73. Beverly Daniel Tatum, *"Why Are All the Black Kids Sitting Together in the Cafeteria" and Other Conversations About Race* (New York: Basic Books, 1997), p. 21.
74. Ibid.
75. Miller, p. 116.
76. Ibid.
77. Tatum, p. 7.
78. Langston, p. 400.
79. Heather Hackman, "Sexism," in Maurianne Adams, Warren Blumenfeld, Rosie Castañeda, Heather W. Hackman, Madeline L. Peters, and Ximena Zúñiga (Eds.), *Readings for Diversity and Social Justice* (New York: Routledge, 2000), pp. 199–200.
80. Marilyn Frey, "Oppression," in Paula S. Rothenberg (Ed.), *Race, Class and Gender in the United States*, 5th ed. (New York: Worth Publishers, 2001), p. 141.
81. Warren J. Blumenfeld and Diane Raymond, "Prejudice and Descrimination," in Maurianne Adams, Warren Blumenfeld, Rosie Castañeda, Heather W. Hackman, Madeline L. Peters, and Ximena Zúñiga (Eds.), *Readings for Diversity and Social Justice* (New York: Routledge, 2000), p. 25.
82. Castañeda and Peters, p. 320.
83. NASW (2007), *Code of Ethics*, retrieved June 17, 2009, from www.naswdc.org/pubs/code/code.asp
84. Dennis Saleebey, *The Strengths Based Approach in Social Work Practice* (White Plains, NY: Longman, 1992), p. 12; Dennis Saleebey, *The Strengths Perspective in Social Work Practice,* 4th ed. (Boston: Pearson Education, 2006), pp. 14–15.
85. Saleebey, 1992, p. 3; Saleebey, 2006, pp. 1–2, 18.
86. Saleebey, 1992, p. 4; Saleeby, 2006, pp. 4–5, 12.
87. Saleebey, 1992, pp. 1–27.
88. Ibid., p. 6.
89. Dennis Saleebey, "Strengths-Based Practice," in Richard L. Edwards and J. G. Hopps (Eds.), *Encyclopedia of Social Work*, 19th ed. (2003 Supplement) (Washington, DC: NASW Press, 2003), p. 154.

Quotes

Margaret Mead, *Sex and Temperament in Three Primitive Societies* (New York: HarperCollins, 2001) p. 300.
William Hazlitt, "On Prejudice," *Sketches and Essays*, 1839.
Lord Acton, letter to Bishop Mandell Creighton, April 5, 1887.
Marilyn Frey, "Oppression," in L. Richards, V. Taylor, and N. Whittier (Eds.), *Feminist Frontiers IV* (New York: McGraw Hill, 1997), p. 8.

Chapter 6

1. Ralph Dolgoff and Donald Feldstein, *Understanding Social Welfare: The Search for Social Justice*, 7th ed. (Boston, MA: Pearson, 2007), pp. 64–65; Howard Zinn, *A People's History of the United States: 1492–Present* (New York: HarperPerennial, 2005), p. 49; Walter I. Trattner, *From Poor Law to Welfare State: A History of Social Welfare in America*, 6th ed. (New York: The Free Press, 1999), pp. 30–32.
2. Dolgoff and Feldstein, pp. 62–66; Phyllis J. Day, *A New History of Social Welfare*, 5th ed. (Boston: Pearson, 2006), pp. 144–149. See also Michael B. Katz, *In the Shadow of the Poorhouse: A Social History of Welfare in America*, 10th ed. (New York: Basic Books, 1996), p. 11.
3. Katz, p. 14.
4. Dolgoff and Feldstein, pp. 44–56, 61–65.
5. Trattner, pp. 22–23.
6. Dolgoff and Feldstein, pp. 62–66.
7. Zinn, pp. 88–89; Trattner, p. 24.
8. Michael O'Neill, *The Third America: The Emergence of the Nonprofit Sector in the United States* (San Francisco: Jossey-Bass, 1989), p. 20.
9. Trattner, p. 17.
10. Dolgoff and Feldstein, pp. 61–64; Trattner, p. 35.
11. Howard Jacob Karger and David Stoesz, *American Social Welfare Policy: A Pluralist Approach*, 5th ed. (Boston, MA: Pearson, 2008), pp. 39–41; Trattner, p. 35.
12. O'Neill, p. 30.
13. Ibid., pp. 29–30.
14. Paul Johnson, *A History of the American People* (New York: HarperPerennial, 1999), pp. 43–44.
15. Karger and Stoesz, p. 40.
16. Trattner, pp. 36–38.
17. Karger and Stoesz, p. 40; Day, pp. 144–149; Trattner, p. 36.
18. Jean Strouse, *Morgan: American Financier* (New York: HarperPerennial, 2000), p. 24.
19. Zinn, p. 225; Strouse, pp. 73–74.
20. Zinn, pp. 227–228.
21. Ibid., p. 240.
22. Matthew Josephson, *The Robber Barons* (New York: Harcourt Brace, 1962), p. 362.
23. Ibid., pp. 362–363.
24. Katz, pp. 23–24.
25. Ibid., p. 23.
26. Katz, pp. 22–25; Bruce S. Jansson, *The Reluctant Welfare State: American Social Welfare Policies-Past, Present, and Future* (Belmont, CA: Thomson Brooks/Cole, 2005), pp. 72–75.
27. Jansson, pp. 72–75.
28. David Wagner, *The Poorhouse: America's Forgotten Institution* (Lanham, MD: Rowland and Littlefield, 2005), p. 39; Katz, pp. 26–36.
29. Jansson, pp. 75–79.
30. Ibid.
31. James Leiby, *A History of Social Welfare and Social Work in the United States* (New York: Columbia University Press, 1978), p.112; Trattner, p. 93.
32. Emma Brace, *The Life of Charles Loring Brace: Chiefly Told in His Own Letters* (New York: Charles Scribner's Sons, 1894), pp. 1, 8, 34, 154.
33. Leiby, p. 78.
34. Trattner, p. 90.
35. Leiby, p. 114; Trattner, p. 92.
36. Trattner, p. 94.
37. Jansson, p. 157; Trattner, p. 93.
38. Jansson, p. 157.
39. Leiby, p. 114.
40. Trattner, p. 93.
41. Leiby, p. 115.
42. Jansson, p. 157.
43. Leiby, p. 114.
44. Katz, pp. 79, 83–85.

45. Jansson, p. 157.
46. Ibid., p. 158.
47. Leiby, p. 137.
48. Zinn, pp. 253–295; R. D. Putnam, *Bowling Alone* (New York: Simon and Schuster, 2001), pp. 384–385, 368, 395.
49. Paul F. Boller, Jr., *Presidential Campaigns* (New York: Oxford University Press, 1985), pp. 191–192.
50. James T. Patterson, *America's Struggle Against Poverty in the Twentieth Century* (Cambridge, MA: Harvard University Press, 2000), pp. 10–11.
51. Jane Addams, *Twenty Years at Hull-House* (New York: Penguin Putnam, 1961), p. 65.
52. Ibid., p. 194.
53. Ibid., p. 187.
54. Zinn, p. 327.
55. Ibid., p. 325.
56. Jansson, p. 128.
57. Ibid., p. 135; Theda Skocpol, *Protecting Soldiers and Mothers: The Political Origins of Social Policy in the United States* (Cambridge, MA: Harvard University,1995), p. 266.
58. Skocpol, pp. 262, 266–267.
59. Jansson, p. 135.
60. Zinn, p. 322.
61. Jansson, p. 158; Ron Chernow, *Titan: The Life of John D. Rockefeller, Sr.* (New York: Vintage Books, 1999), pp. 98–99.
62. Skocpol, pp. 290–293.
63. Jansson, pp. 137.
64. Putnam, pp. 386–387.
65. Skocpol, pp. 318, 329, 332–333; Putnam, p. 386.
66. Leiby, p. 127; Katz, p. 164.
67. Leiby, pp. 128–129.
68. Ibid., p. 128; Harold B. Hunting, *Lillian Wald: Crusading Nurse* (Freeport, NY: Books for Libraries Press, 1945), p. 13; Clare Coss (Ed.), *Lillian D. Wald: Progressive Activist* (New York: The Feminist Press, 1989), p. xv.
69. Trattner, p. 175.
70. Ibid., p. 171.
71. Addams, p. 138.
72. Ibid., p. 70.
73. Ibid., pp. 87–90, 98–99.
74. Trattner, p. 171.
75. Addams, pp. 198–199.
76. Dorothy Rose Blumberg, *Florence Kelley: The Making of a Social Pioneer* (New York: Augustus M. Kelley, 1966), pp. 171–174; Skocpol, pp. 383, 404; Trattner, pp. 179–181.
77. Coss, p. xvi.
78. Trattner, p. 182.
79. Jansson, pp. 132–133.
80. Leiby, pp. 171–173.
81. Ibid., pp. 114–115, 172–174.
82. Ibid., p. 173.
83. Jansson, p. 218.
84. Leiby, p. 171.
85. Johnson, p. 718.
86. Jansson, pp. 166–168.
87. Patterson, p. 38.
88. Ibid.
89. Katz, p. 214.
90. Patterson, p. 41.
91. Katz, p. 214.
92. Ibid., pp. 223–224.
93. Ibid., p. 224.
94. Katz, p. 214.
95. Leiby, p. 104.
96. Ibid., pp. 184–188.
97. Frances Perkins, *The Roosevelt I Knew* (New York: The Viking Press, 1946), p. 37.
98. Boller, p. 234.
99. Jansson, p. 197.
100. John H. Ehrenreich, *The Altruistic Imagination: A History of Social Work and Social Policy in the United States* (Ithaca, NY: Cornell University Press, 1985), p. 107.
101. Jansson, pp. 197, 202.
102. Ibid., pp. 205–206.
103. Doris Kearns Goodwin, *No Ordinary Time* (New York: Touchstone, 1995), p. 87.
104. Jansson, p. 208.
105. Ehrenreich, pp. 64–65; Trattner, pp. 255–262.
106. Jansson, p. 218.
107. Ehrenreich, p. 78.
108. Goodwin, pp. 96, 365, 381.
109. Leiby, p. 224; Goodwin, pp. 87, 106–107, 212, 257.
110. George Martin, *Madam Secretary Frances Perkins* (Boston: Houghton Mifflin, 1976), pp. 3–4.
111. Ibid., pp. 60–63, 72–74.
112. Ibid., p. 205.
113. Trattner, pp. 285, 296–297.
114. Zinn, pp. 393–394.
115. Goodwin, p. 163; Trattner, p. 282.
116. Trattner, p. 282.
117. Goodwin, pp. 162–163.
118. Trattner, p. 295.
119. Ehrenreich, p. 156; David Remnick, The Bridge: The Life And Rise Of Barack Obama (New York: Alfred A. Knopf, 2010), p. 198.
120. Jansson, pp. 245–246.
121. Jansson, p. 246.
122. Joseph A. Califano, Jr., *The Triumph and Tragedy of Lyndon Johnson: The White House Years* (College Station: Texas A&M University Press, 2000), p. 58.
123. Jansson, pp. 247–248.
124. Ibid., pp. 248–249.
125. Ibid., pp.249–250.
126. Jansson, p. 252; Trattner, pp. 330–331; Leiby, p. 325.
127. Leiby, pp. 314–315.
128. Ehrenreich, pp. 169–175.
129. Edward D. Berkowitz, *America's Welfare State: From Roosevelt to Reagan* (Baltimore, MD: Johns Hopkins University Press, 1991), p. 118.
130. David Halberstam, *The Powers That Be* (New York: Dell, 2000), p. 788.
131. Califano, p. 341.
132. Trattner, pp. 349–351.
133. Trattner, p. 349; Jansson, pp. 273–275.
134. Jansson, pp. 275–285; Trattner, pp. 349–351.
135. Trattner, p. 348.
136. Jansson, pp. 275–285.
137. Trattner, p. 348.
138. Jansson, pp . 275–285.
139. Trattner, p. 350.
140. Day, pp. 363–373; Jansson, pp. 275–285.
141. Jansson, pp. 275–288.
142. Halberstam, pp. 190, 846–847.
143. Zinn, p. 504.
144. Ibid., pp. 504–514.

145. Harriet Sigerman, *Biographical Supplement and Index* (Nancy F. Cott [Ed.], *The Young Oxford History of Women in the United States*, Vol. 2) (New York: Oxford University Press, 1995), p. 73; Kay Mills, *This Little Light of Mine: The Life of Fannie Lou Hamer* (New York: Dutton/Penguin Books, 1993), pp. 12, 248–249.
146. Mills, pp. 36–37, 50–51, 57–58.
147. Ibid., p. 318.
148. Sigerman, p. 37; Reba Carruth and Vivian Jenkins Nelson, *Shirley Chisholm: Woman of Complexity, Conscience, and Compassion* (Frank P. LeVeness and Jane P. Sweeney [Eds.], *Women Leaders in Contemporary U.S. Politics*) (Boulder, CO: Reinner, 1987), pp. 11, 13, 16.
149. Sigerman, p. 37.
150. Ehrenreich, p. 190.
151. Ibid., pp. 195–197.
152. Ibid., pp. 201–203.
153. Ibid., pp. 204–205.
154. Jansson, pp. 291–293.
155. Wagner, p. 135.
156. Day, pp. 390–398; Lou Cannon, *President Reagan: The Role Of A Lifetime* (New York: PublicAffairs, 2000), p. 6.
157. Bruce S. Jansson, *Becoming an Effective Policy Advocate: From Policy Practice to Social Justice*, 5th ed. (Belmont, CA: Thomson Brooks/Cole, 2008), pp. 24–25; Day, pp. 394–398.
158. Day, pp. 390–398; Jansson, 2005, p. 310; Cannon, p. 223.
159. Day, pp. 398–410; Wagner, pp. 135–136.
160. Jansson, 2005, pp. 316–325.
161. Ibid.
162. Jansson, 2005, pp. 337–338.
163. Diana M. DiNitto, *Social Welfare: Politics and Public Policy*, 6th ed. (Boston, MA: Pearson, 2007), p. 62.
164. Jansson, 2005, pp. 382–383.
165. Day, p. 450; Jansson, 2005, p. 394; George Stephanopoulos, *All Too Human: A Political Education* (Boston: Back Bay Books, 2000), p. 420.
166. Day, p. 450.
167. Jansson, 2005, pp. 363–365, 397.
168. Ibid., p. 342.
169. Ehrenreich, pp. 207–208.
170. See Joe Klein, *The Natural: The Misunderstood Presidency of Bill Clinton* (New York: Random House, 2002) and Bill Clinton, *My Life* (New York: Knopf, 2004).
171. Jerry D. Marx and Fleur A. Hopper, "Faith-based vs. Fact-based Social Policy: The Case of Teen Pregnancy Prevention." *Social Work* 50(3) (2005), pp. 280–282.
172. Sasha Issenberg, "$787 b stimulus bill approved," retrieved March 22, 2010, from www.Boston.com/news/nation/Washington/articles/2009/02/14/$787b_stimulus_bill_approved/; Matt Viser and Susan Milligan, "Historic OK on Health," retrieved March 22, 2010, from www.boston.com/news/nation/washington/articles/2010/03/22/historic_ok_on_health/.

Quotes

Eleanor Roosevelt, *The Autobiography of Eleanor Roosevelt* (Cambridge, MA: Da Capo Press, 1992), p. 278.
David K. Shipler, *The Working Poor: Invisible in America*. New York: Vintage/Random House, 2005), p. 11.
Barak Obama, 2009, Speech to a Joint Session of Congress, September 9, 2009.

Chapter 7

1. Carmen DeNavas-Walt, Bernadette D. Proctor, and Jessica C. Smith, *Income, Poverty, and Health Insurance Coverage in the United States: 2007* (U.S. Census Bureau, Current Population Reports, P60-235) (Washington, DC: U.S. Government Printing Office, 2008), p. 12.
2. Ibid, p. 14.
3. National Center for Health Statistics, *Health, United States, 1998, with Socioeconomic Status and Health Chartbook*. (Hyattsville, MD: U.S. Department of Health and Human Services, 1998), p. 54.
4. Greg J. Duncan, W. Jean Yeung, Jeanne Brooks-Gunn, and Judith R. Smith, "How Much Does Childhood Poverty Affect the Life Chances of Children?" *American Sociological Review* 63(3) (1998), pp. 406–423.
5. Council on Social Work Education, *Educational and Policy Accreditation Standards* (Washington, DC: Council on Social Work Education, 2001).
6. Diana M. DiNitto, *Social Welfare: Politics and Public Policy*, 5th ed. (Boston, MA: Allyn & Bacon, 2000), p. 67.
7. U.S. Census Bureau, "How the Census Bureau Measures Poverty (Official Measure)," retrieved June 17, 2006, from: http://www.census.gov/hhes/www/poverty/povdef.html.
8. James Lin and Jared Bernstein, "What We Need to Get By: A Basic Standard of Living Costs $48,778, and Nearly a Third of Families Fall Short," Economic Policy Institute Briefing Paper #228, retrieved June 23, 2009, from: http://www.epi.org/publications/entry/bp224.
9. Dana Millbank, "Old Flaws Undermine New Poverty-Level Data," *Wall Street Journal* (October 5, 1995), pp. B1, 8.
10. University of Wisconsin, Institute for Research on Poverty, "Improving Measurement of American Poverty," *Focus* 19(2) (Spring 1998), p. 2, retrieved June 10, 2006, from http://www.ssc.wisc.edu/irp/focus/foc192.pdf.
11. Douglas J. Besharov and Peter Germanis, "Reconsidering the Federal Poverty Measure," retrieved June 10, 2006, from http://www.welfareacademy.org/pubs/poverty/povmeasure.description.pdf.
12. Constance F. Citro and Robert T. Michael (Eds.), *Measuring Poverty: A New Approach* (Washington, DC: National Academy Press, 1995).
13. Ibid.
14. Ibid.
15. U.S. Census Bureau, "Income, Poverty, and Health Insurance Coverage in the United States: 2004," p. 11, retrieved June 1, 2006, from http://www.census.gov/prod/2005pubs/p60–229.pdf.
16. Ibid. p. 7.
17. Ibid, p. 11.
18. DeNavas-Walt, Proctor, and Smith.
19. Ibid.
20. Ibid.
21. Signe-Mary McKernan and Caroline Ratcliffe, *Events That Trigger Poverty Entries and Exits* (Washington, DC: Urban Institute Press, December 2002), p. 22.
22. Hilary W. Hoynes, Marianne E. Page, and Ann Huff Stevens, "Poverty in America: Trends and Explanations," *Journal of Economic Perspectives* 20(1) (Winter 2006), p. 64.
23. DeNavas-Walt, Proctor, and Smith.
24. Ibid.

25. George Acs, Katherine Ross Phillips, and Daniel McKenzie, "Playing by the Rules but Losing the Game: America's Working Poor," in Richard Kazis and Marc Miller (Eds.), *Low-Wage Workers in the New Economy* (Washington, DC: Urban Institute Press, 2000), pp. 21–44.
26. Ibid.; DeNavas-Walt, Proctor, and Smith.
27. Acs, Phillips and McKenzie
28. Ibid.
29. Ibid.
30. Ibid.
31. Ibid.
32. Timothy Smeeding, "Public Policy, Economic Inequality and Poverty: The United States in Comparative Perspective" *Social Science Quarterly* 86 (2005), p. 977.
33. Ibid.
34. Hoynes, Page, and Stevens, p. 64.
35. Ibid.
36. Smeeding, p. 980
37. Marjorie E. Starrels, Sally Bould, and Leon J. Nicholas, "The Feminization of Poverty in the United States: Gender, Race, Ethnicity and Family Factors," *Journal of Family Issues* 15(4) (1994), p. 590.
38. Ibid. pp. 592–593.
39. U.S. Census Bureau, *Current Population Survey 2005*, Annual Social and Economic Supplement, retrieved July 26, 2006, from http://pubdb3.census.gov/macro/032005/pov/new14_000.htm.
40. Michael B. Katz, *The Undeserving Poor: From the War on Poverty to the War on Welfare* (New York: Pantheon Books, 1989), p. 17.
41. Ibid., p. 18.
42. Ibid., p. 17.
43. Ibid., p. 19.
44. Edward Banfield, *The Unheavenly City Revisited* (Boston: Little Brown, 1974), p. 235.
45. Ibid.
46. Bruce S. Jansson, *The Reluctant Welfare State: American Social Welfare Policies—Past, Present, and Future*, 4th ed. (Belmont, CA: Wadsworth/Thomson Learning, 2001), pp. 194, 199; Sar A. Levitan, Garth L. Mangum, and Stephen L. Mangum, *Programs in Aid of the Poor* (Baltimore: Johns Hopkins University Press, 1998), p. 58.
47. Neil Gilbert, Harry Specht, and Paul Terrell, *Dimensions of Social Policy*, 3rd ed. (Englewood Cliffs, NJ: Prentice Hall, 1993), pp. 71–72.
48. Social Security Administration, *Budget*, retrieved June 18, 2008, from www.ssa.gov/budget/FactCard2009.pdf; Social Security Administration, "2002 OASDI Trustees Report: Overview," retrieved August 18, 2002, from http://www.ssa.gov/OACT/TR/TR02/II_highlights.html; Levitan, Mangum, and Mangum, pp. 58–63; Jansson, p. 282.
49. Jansson, p. 282.
50. Levitan, Mangum, and Mangum, p. 61; Social Security Administration, "A Snapshot," retrieved August 16, 2002, from http://www.ssa.gov/pubs/10006.html.
51. Levitan, Mangum, and Mangum, p. 61; Linda P. Anderson, Paul A. Sundet, and Irma Harrington, *The Social Welfare System in the United States: A Social Worker's Guide to Public Benefits Programs* (Boston: Allyn & Bacon, 2000), p. 27; Social Security Administration, "A Snapshot," 2002.
52. Levitan, Mangum, and Mangum, pp. 63–64.
53. Ibid., pp. 93–95; U.S. Department of Labor Employment and Training Administration, "Unemployment Insurance Fact Sheet," retrieved August 19, 2002, from http://workforcesecurity.doleta.gov/unemploy/uifactsheet.asp; Mike Miller, U.S. Department of Labor Employment and Training Administration, Office of Workforce Security, personal communication, August 20, 2002.
54. Theda Skocpol, *Protecting Soldiers and Mothers: The Political Origins of Social Policy in the United States* (Cambridge, MA: Harvard University), pp. 290–293.
55. Frank Kimball, Maine State Department of Professional and Financial Regulation, Bureau of Insurance, personal communication, August 21, 2002; Levitan, Mangum, and Mangum, pp. 96–98.
56. Gilbert, Specht, and Terrell, pp. 71–72.
57. Children's Defense Fund, "Summary of the New Welfare Legislation," retrieved August 27, 1997, from http://www.childrensdefensefund.org/welfarelaw.html; U.S. Department of Health and Human Services, Administration for Children and Families, "ACF Overview: Discretionary Spending," retrieved August 18, 2002, from http://www.acf.dhhs.gov/programs/olab/budget/Press03.htm.; U.S. Department of Health and Human Services, Administration for Children and Families, Office of Family Assistance, personal communication, August 22, 2002.
58. Children's Defense Fund, 1997; U.S. Department of Health and Human Services, Administration for Children and Families, "ACF Overview: Discretionary Spending," 2002.
59. Children's Defense Fund, 1997; U.S. Department of Health and Human Services, Administration for Children and Families, Office of Family Assistance, personal communication, 2002.
60. Jansson, p. 279; Walter I. Trattner, *From Poor Law to Welfare State: A History of Social Welfare in America*, 6th ed. (New York: The Free Press, 1999), p. 348; Social Security Administration, "A Snapshot," 2002.
61. Levitan, Mangum, and Mangum, pp. 85–87; Social Security Administration, "A Snapshot," 2002; Social Security Administration, "Executive Summary," retrieved August 18, 2002, from http://www.ssa.gov/OACT/SSIR/SSI02/exec_sum.html.
62. Levitan, Mangum, and Mangum, p. 87; Social Security Administration, "Executive Summary," 2002.
63. Levitan, Mangum, and Mangum, p. 88; Urban Institute, "State General Assistance Programs 1998," retrieved August 18, 2002, from http://newfederalism.urban.org/html/ga_programs/ga_full.html; Steven G. Anderson, Anthony P. Halter, and Brian M. Gryzlak, "Changing Safety Net of Last Resort: Downsizing General Assistance for Employable Adults," *Social Work* 47(3) (2002), pp. 249–258.
64. Children's Defense Fund, 1997; Ram A. Cnaan and Stephanie C. Boddie, "Charitable Choice and Faith-Based Welfare: A Call for Social Work," *Social Work* 47(3) (2002), pp. 224–235.
65. Michael B. Katz, *In the Shadow of the Poorhouse*, 10th ed. (New York: Basic Books, 1996), pp. 290–292, 310.
66. Levitan, Mangum, and Mangum, pp. 131–133; U.S. Department of Agriculture, "About FSP—Introduction," retrieved August 16, 2002, from http://www.fns.usda.gov/fsp/MENU/ABOUT/ABOUT.HTM; U.S. Department of Agriculture, "Fact Sheet on Food Stamp Resources, Income, and Benefits," retrieved August 16, 2002, from http://www.fns.usda.gov/fsp/MENU/APPS/BENEFITS/fsResBenEli.htm; U.S. Department of Agriculture, "Food and Nutrition Service Programs," retrieved August 26,

Notes

2002, from http://www.fns.usda.gov/fns/MENU/PROGRAMS.htm
67. U.S. Department of Agriculture, Food and Nutrition Service, "Food Stamp Participation and Costs," retrieved February 29, 2008, from http://www.fns.usda.gov/pd/fssummar.htm.
68. Children's Defense Fund, 1997; U.S. Department of Agriculture, "About FSP—Introduction," 2002.
69. Children's Defense Fund, *The Special Supplemental Food Program for Women, Infants, and Children (WIC)* (November 2005), retrieved February 29, 2008, from http://www.childrensdefense.org/site/DocServer/wic.pdf?docID=529.
70. U.S. Department of Agriculture, Food and Nutrition Service, "WIC Program Participation and Costs," retrieved February 29, 2008, from http://www.fns.usda.gov/pd/wisummary.htm.
71. U.S. Department of House and Urban Development, *FY2007 HUD Budget Summary*, retrieved February 29, 2008, from http://www.hud.gov/about/budget/fy07/fy07budget.pdf.
72. Jansson, pp. 210–211; Levitan, Mangum, and Mangum, pp. 122–124.
73. Levitan, Mangu, and Mangum, pp. 125–127; David Thigpen, "The Long Way Home," *Time* (5 August 2002), p. 42; Bret Ladine, "Housing Trust Funds Gaining Momentum," *Boston Globe* (19 August 2002), pp. A1, A4, retrieved August 19, 2002, from http://www.boston.com/dailyglobe2/231/nation/Housing_trust_funds_gaining_momentumP.shtml; Department of Housing and Urban Development, "Housing Choice Vouchers Fact Sheet," retrieved August 19, 2002, from http://www.hud.gov/offices/pih/programs/hcv/about/fact_sheet.cfm.
74. David Shumaker, "Field Guide to Housing Trust Funds" (National Association of Realtors), retrieved February 29, 2008, from http://www.realtor.org/libweb.nsf/pages/fg322.
75. National Low Income Housing Coalition, "National Affordable Housing Trust Fund Act Introduced in Senate" (Press Release, December 19, 2007), retrieved February 29, 2008, from http://www.nlihc.org/detail/article.cfm?article_id=4784&id=61.
76. Levitan, Mangum, and Mangum, p. 126.
77. Habitat for Humanity International, "A Brief Introduction to Habitat for Humanity International," retrieved November 14, 2001, from http://www.habitat.org/how/tour/1.html; Habitat for Humanity International, "Habitat for Humanity Fact Sheet," retrieved November 14, 2001, from http://www.habitat.org/how/factsheet.html.
78. Habitat for Humanity, "Habitat for Humanity Fact Sheet," retrieved February 29, 2008, from http://www.habitat.org/how/factsheet.aspx.
79. National Coalition for the Homeless, "How Many People Experience Homelessness? NCH Fact Sheet #2," retrieved November 15, 2001, from http://www.nationalhomeless.org.
80. National Law Center on Poverty and Homelessness, "2007 Annual Report," p. 6, retrieved January 14, 2009, from http://www.nlchp.org/content/pubs/2007_Annual_Report2.pdf.
81. Levitan, Mangum, and Mangum, pp. 171–172.
82. Ibid., pp. 150–151, 154–156, 161–170.
83. Ibid., pp. 137, 176–177.
84. Amy Corria and Katie VonDeLinde, *Integrating Anti-Poverty Work into Domestic Violence Advocacy: Iowa's Experience* (Building Comprehensive Solutions to Domestic Violence, publication #17) (Harrisburg, PA: National Resource Center on Domestic Violence, 2002).
85. Ibid, p. 1.
86. Ibid., p. 4.
87. Ibid.
88. Council on Social Work Education, *Educational and Policy Accreditation Standards* (Washington, DC: Council on Social Work Education, 2008).

Quotes

Michael Harrington, *The Other America: Poverty in the United States* (New York: Macmillan, 1962).
Franklin Delano Roosevelt, Second Inaugural Address, January 20, 1937.
Barbara Ehrenreich, *Nickel and Dimed: On (Not) Getting By in America* (New York: Henry Holt and Company, 2001), p. 221.
Brooks Atkinson, *Once Around the Sun* (New York: Harcourt, Brace, 1951), 24 August.

Chapter 8

1. U.S. Department of Labor, Bureau of Labor Statistics, *Occupational Outlook Handbook, 2010–11 Edition, Social Workers*, retrieved February 1, 2010, from http://www.bls.gov/oco/ocos060.htm.
2. Ibid.
3. Ibid.; U.S. Administration on Aging, *A Statistical Profile Of Older Americans aged 65+* (Washington, DC: U.S. Department of Health and Human Services, 2004).
4. Centers for Disease Control and Prevention, *Heart Disease* (Atlanta, GA: Department of Health and Human Services, Centers for Disease Control and Prevention, 2007), retrieved February 23, 2008, from http://www.cdc.gov/heartdisease/index.htm.
5. J. Beder, *Hospital Social Work: The Interface of Medicine and Caring* (New York: Routledge, 2006).
6. Ibid.
7. Ibid.
8. National Cancer Institute, *Cancer Health Disparities: Questions and Answers, National Cancer Institute Factsheet* (Bethesda, MD: National Cancer Institute, National Institutes of Health, 2007), retrieved February 20, 2008, from http://www.cancer.gov/cancertopics/factsheet/cancer-health-disparities.
9. Oncology Social Workers Organization, *Oncology Social Workers Serving People with Cancer and Their Families Worldwide* (n.d.), retrieved February, 20, 2008, from http://www.aosw.org/docs/OSW-Broch1.pdf.
10. Ibid.
11. Centers for Disease Control and Prevention, *Overweight and Obesity* (Atlanta, GA: Department of Health and Human Services, Centers for Disease Control, Division of Nutrition, Physical Activity and Obesity, National Center for Chronic Disease Prevention and Health Promotion, 2007), retrieved February 1, 2010, from http://www.cdc.gov/nccdphp/dnpa/obesity/index.htm.
12. National Institutes of Health, *First Federal Obesity Clinical Guidelines Released, NIH New Release* (Bethesda, MD: National Institutes of Health, National Heart, Lung and Blood Institute, 1998), retrieved February 2, 2010, from http://www.nhlbi.nih.gov/new/press/oberel4f.htm.
13. A. Adachi-Mejia, M. Longacre, J. Givson, M. Beach, L. Titus-Ernstoff, and M. Dalton, "Children with a TV in

Their Bedroom at Higher Risk for Being Overweight," *International Journal of Obesity* 31 (2007), pp. 644–651.
14. M. Seipel, "Social Burden of Obesity on U.S. Adults," *Journal of Health and Social Work* 20 (2005), p. 6.
15. E. Rothblum, "The Stigma of Women's Weight: Social and Economic Realities," *Feminism and Psychology* 124 (1992), pp. 61–73.
16. Seipel.
17. L. Lanningham-Foster, T. Jensen, R. Foster, A. Redmond, B. Walker, D. Heinz, and J. Levine, "Energy Expenditure of Sedentary Screen Time Compared with Active Screen Time for Children," *Pediatrics* 118 (2006), pp. e1831–e1835.
18. M. Gard and J. Wright, *The Obesity Epidemic: Science, Morality and Ideology* (London: Routledge, 2005), p. 117.
19. American Academy of Allergy, Asthma and Immunology, *Asthma Statistics* (Milwaukee, WI: Author, n.d.), retrieved February 1, 2010, from http://www.aaaai.org/media/resources/media_kit/asthma_statistics.stm.
20. D. Parker-Oliver "Asthma Management: A Role for Social Work," *Health and Social Work* 30 (2005), pp. 167–170.
21. Centers for Disease Control and Prevention, *A Glance at the HIV/AIDS Epidemic* (Atlanta, GA: Department of Health and Human Services, Centers for Disease Control and Prevention, 2007), retrieved February 1, 2010, from http://www.cdc.gov/hiv/resources/factsheets/At-A-Glance.htm.
22. J. Schroeder, C. Latkin, D. Hoover, A. Knowlton, J. Zenilman, S. Strathdee, and D. Celentano, "Social Factors Related to Antiretroviral Therapy Use in Injection Drug Users," *AIDS and Behavior* 5 (2001), pp. 363–369; J. Serovich, P. Brucker, and J. Kimberley, "Barriers to Social Support for Persons Living with HIV/AIDS," *AIDS Care* 12 (2000), pp. 651–662.
23. J. Dunn, S. Steginga, S. Occhipinti, and K. Wilson, "Evaluation of a Peer Support Program for Women with Breast Cancer: Lessons for Practitioners," *Journal of Applied & Community Psychology* 9 (1999), pp. 13–22.
24. P. Marino, J. Simoni, and L. Solverstein, "Peer Support to Promote Medication Adherence Among People Living with HIV/AIDS: The Benefits to Peers," *Social Work in Healthcare* 45 (2007), pp. 67–80.
25. G. Herek, J. Capitanio, and K. Widaman, "HIV-Related Stigma and Knowledge in the United States: Prevalence and Trends, 1991–1999," *American Journal of Public Health* 92 (2002), pp. 371–376; M. Lekas, K. Siegal, and E. Schrimshaw, "Continuities and Discontinuities in the Experiences of Felt and Enacted Stigma Among Women with HIV/AIDS," *Qualitative Health Research* 16 (2006), pp. 1165–1190.
26. Ibid.
27. Ibid., p. 61.
28. L. Akinbami, *Asthma Prevalence, Healthcare Use and Mortality: United States, 2003–2005.* (Hyattsville, MD: National Center for Health Statistics, 2007).
29. Ibid.
30. National Association of Social Workers (NASW) (2007), *Code of Ethics*, retrieved February 1, 2010, from www.naswdc.org/pubs/code/code.asp.
31. The American Foundation, *American Medicine*, Vol. 2 (New York: The American Foundation 1937).
32. D. Hirschfield, *The Lost Reform: The Campaign for Compulsory Health Insurance in the United States from 1932 to 1943.* (Cambridge, MA: Harvard University Press, 1970).
33. The Kaiser Family Foundation, *Total Number of Medicare Beneficiaries, 2008,* retrieved February 1, 2010, from http://www.statehealthfacts.org/comparemaptable.jsp?ind=290&cat=6.
34. The Kaiser Family Foundation, "The Medicaid Program at a Glance, March 2007," retrieved February 1, 2010, from http:/www.kff.org/Medicaid/7235.cfm.
35. Kaiser Commission on Medicaid and the Uninsured, *Kaiser Family Foundation and Urban Institute Estimates: Birth Data: NGA, MCH Update,* May 19, 2008, retrieved June 5, 2008, from http://facts.kff.org/chart.aspx?ch=464.
36. K. Call, M. Davern, and L. Blewett, "Estimates of Health Insurance Coverage: Comparing State Surveys with the Current Population Survey," *Health Affairs* 26 (2007), pp. 269–278.
37. D. Rowland, *Healthcare: Squeezing the Middle Class with More Costs and Less Coverage,* Testimony before the U.S. House of Representatives Ways and Means Committee, "Economic Challenges Facing Middle Class Families," 110th Congress, 1026 (January 31, 2007), retrieved February 25, 2008, from http://www.kff.org/uninsured/upload/7612.pdf.
38. Department of Health and Human Services, *Children's Health Insurance Program Reauthorization Act (CHIPRA) of 2009, Overview* (Washington, DC: U.S. Department for Health and Human Services, Centers for Medicare and Medicaid Services, 2009), retrieved February 1, 2010, from http://www.cms.hhs.gov/CHIPRA/.
39. C. Denavas-Walt, B. Proctor, and J. Smith, *Income, Poverty and Health Insurance Coverage in the United States: 2006* (U.S. Census Bureau, Current Population Reports, P60-233) (Washington, DC: U.S. Government Printing Office, 2007).
40. S. Gorin, "The Unraveling of Managed Care: Recent Trends and Implications," *Health and Social Work* 28 (2003), p. 241.
41. D. Mechanic, *The Truth About Healthcare: Why Reform Is Not Working in America* (New Brunswick, NJ: Rutgers University Press, 2006).
42. K. Terry, *RX for Healthcare Reform* (Nashville, TN: Vanderbilt University Press, 2007).
43. Ibid., p. 29.
44. M. Evans, "Will It Last? Hospital Profits Hit an All-Time High in 2003," *Modern Healthcare* 35 (2005), pp. 8–9; M. Evans, "Hospitals' Profitable Year," *Modern Healthcare* 43 (2006), pp. 8–9.
45. Terry.
46. R. Seifert and M. Rukavina, "Bankruptcy Is the Tip of a Medical-Debt Iceberg," *Health Affairs Journal* 25 (2006), pp. w89–w92.
47. Denavas-Walt, Proctor, and Smith.
48. Ibid.
49. D. Oswald, J. Bodurtha, J. Willis, and M. Moore, "Underinsurance and Key Health Outcomes for Children with Special Healthcare Needs," *Pediatrics* 119 (2007), p. e341.
50. Seifert and Rukavina.
51. Ibid.
52. Terry.
53. Ibid., p. 143.
54. M. Openshaw, "The Economics of Prescription Drug Prices, Government Intervention and the Importation of Drugs from Canada," *Nursing Economics* 23 (2005), p. 308.
55. Ibid.

56. R. Daly, "Prescription Drug Costs Increases Far Outpace U.S. Inflation Rate," *Psychiatric News 40* (2007), p. 12; American Association of Retired Persons, "AARP: Prices of Common Brand-Name Medicines Rose an Average of 7.4 Percent Last Year," *International Herald Tribune* (March 4, 2008); M. Chisholm, J. Turner, and J. DiPiro, "Medicare-Approved Drug Discount Cards and Prescription Drug Prices," *American Journal of Health-Systems Pharmacists 52* (2005), p. 1482.
57. CBS News/New York Times, CBS News/New York Times Poll, U.S. Healthcare Politics, February 23–27, 2007, for release March 1, 2007, p. 1, retrieved March 3, 2008, from http://www.cbsnews.com/stories/2007/03/01/opinion/polls/printable2528357.shtml.
58. Ibid.
59. V. Fuchs, "What Are the Prospects for Enduring Comprehensive Healthcare Reform?" *Health Affairs 26* (2007), p. 1542.
60. J. Gruber, "The Massachusetts Healthcare Revolution: A Local Start for Universal Access," *Hastings Center Report 36* (2006), pp. 14–19.
61. Ibid., p. 15.
62. Gruber.
63. Ibid., p. 15.
64. J. Nyman, "Is 'Moral Hazard' Inefficient? The Policy Implications of a New Theory," *Health Affairs 23* (2004), pp. 195–199.
65. DirigoHealth, "Affordable High Quality Healthcare for All Maine People" (n.d.), retrieved February 22, 2008, from http://www.dirigohealth.maine.gov/dhlp01.html.
66. "Health Care" (2010), retrieved February 1, 2010, from http://www.maine.gov/governor/baldacci/policy/health_care.html
67. "Health Care: The President's Proposal for Health Reform," retrieved February 23, 2010, from http://www.whitehouse.gov/Issues/health-Care.
68. The Patient Protection and Affordable Care Act, retrieved March 22, 2010, from http://dpc.senate.gov/dpcdoc-sen_health_care_bill.cfm.
69. Ibid.
70. D. K. Goodwin, "As Big as Social Security," retrieved March 22, 2010, from http://www.thedailybeast.com/blogs-and-stories/2010-03-22/as-big-as-social-security/.
71. R. Barker, *The Social Work Dictionary*, 5th ed. (Washington, DC: NASW Press, 2003).
72. P. Hookey, "Social Work in Primary Healthcare Settings," in N. Bracht (Ed.), *Social Work in Healthcare: A Guide to Professional Practice* (Binghamton, NY: Haworth, 1978), pp. 211–223.
73. G. Krell and G. Rosenberg, "Predicting Patterns of Social Work Staffing in Hospital Settings," in K. Davidson and S. Clarke (Eds.), *Social Work in Healthcare*, Part II (Binghamton, NY: Haworth, 1990), pp. 617–640.
74. Beder.
75. H. Geiger, "Community-Orientated Primary Care: A Path to Community Development," *American Journal of Public Health 92* (2002), pp. 1713–1716.
76. Ibid., p. 1714.
77. K. Davis and C. Schoen, *Health and the War on Poverty: A Ten-Year Appraisal* (Washington, DC: The Brookings Institute, 1978), pp. 104–105.
78. D. Hawkins and S. Rosenbaum, "Health Centers at 40: Implications for Future Public Policy," *Journal of Ambulatory Care Management 28* (2005), pp. 357–365.
79. Ibid.
80. D. Reese and M. Raymer, "Relationships Between Social Work Involvement and Hospice Outcomes: Results of the National Hospice Social Work Survey," *Social Work 49* (2004), pp. 415–422.
81. Ibid.
82. R. Moroney, "Public Health Services," in R. Edwards (Ed.), *Encyclopedia of Social Work*, 19th ed. (Washington, DC: NASW Press, 1995), pp. 1967–1973.
83. V. Marshall and M. Altpeter, "Cultivating Social Work Leadership in Health Promotion and Aging: Strategies for Active Aging Interventions," *Health and Social Work 30* (2005), pp. 135–144.
84. Centers for Disease Control and Prevention, *The Changing Epidemic: How Is CDC Responding?* (Atlanta, GA: Department of Health and Human Services, Centers for Disease Control and Prevention, 2006), retrieved February 27, 2008, from http://www.cdc.gov/hiv/resources/reports/hiv3rddecade/chapter3.htm#prevention_program.
85. Centers for Disease Control and Prevention, "Annual Smoking-Attributable Mortality, Years of Potential Life Lost and Economic Costs—United States, 1995–1999," *Morbidity and Mortality Weekly Report 51* (2002), pp. 300–303.
86. T. Novotny and G. Giovino, "Tobacco Use," in R. Brownson, P. Remington, and J. Davis (Eds.), *Chronic Disease Epidemiology and Control* (Washington, DC: American Public Health Association, 1998).
87. Ibid.
88. A. Hyland and C. Higbee, "One Year After the Hawaii Smokefree Law" (Report prepared for the Hawaii State Department of Health) (Buffalo, NY: Department of Health Behavior, Roswell Park Cancer Center, 2008).
89. Centers for Disease Control and Prevention, *National Diabetes Fact Sheet: General Information and National Estimates on Diabetes in the United States, 2005* (Atlanta, GA: U.S. Department of Health and Human Services, Centers for Disease Control and Prevention, 2005).
90. Ibid.
91. Foundation for Healthy Communities, "Keene Kids 'Take 10!' to Prevent Type 2 Diabetes," Community Headlines, Foundation for Healthy Communities Newsletter, November 17, 2004 (Concord, NH: Foundation for Healthy Communities), retrieved February 28, 2008, from http://www.healthynh.com/fhc/communityhealth/Headlines.php.
92. Ibid.
93. Ibid.
94. Ibid.
95. Ibid.
96. Beder, p. 5.
97. Ibid.
98. L. Cowles, *Social Work in the Health Field* (Binghamton, NY: Haworth, 2000).
99. Beder.
100. Daniel W. L. Lai and Shirley B. Chau, "Effects of Service Barriers on Health Status of Older Chinese Immigrants in Canada," *Social Work 52*(3) (July 2007), pp. 261–268.

Quotes

Gloria Steinem, *Revolution from Within: A Book of Self-Esteem* (Boston, MA: Little, Brown, 1992), p. 26.

J. Lewis, "Marian Wright Edelman Quotes" (2010), retrieved from http://womenshistory.about.com/od/quotes/a/marian_edelman.htm.

Chapter 9

1. National Institute of Mental Health (NIMH), "The Numbers Count: Mental Disorders in America," retrieved January 18, 2008, from http://www.nimh.nih.gov/health/publications/the-numbers-count-mental-disorders-in-america.shtml.
2. Ibid.
3. Ibid.
4. Ibid.
5. T. L. Mark, K. R. Levit, R. M. Coffey, D. R. McKusick, H. J. Harwood, E. C. King et al., *National Expenditures for Mental Health Services and Substance Abuse Treatment, 1993–2003* (SAMHSA Publication No. SMA 07-4227) (Rockville, MD: Substance Abuse and Mental Health Services Administration, 2007).
6. National Association of Social Workers (NASW), retrieved January 10, 2008, from www.naswdc.org.
7. NASW Center for Workforce Studies, *Licensed Social Workers in the United States, 2004* (Washington, DC: NASW Center for Workforce Studies, 2006), p. 4.
8. David Mechanic, "Mental Health and Mental Illness: Definitions and Perspectives," in Allan Horwitz and Teresa Scheid (Eds.), *A Handbook for the Study of Mental Health: Social Contexts, Theories and Systems* (New York: Cambridge University Press, 1999), pp. 22–27.
9. Clifford Whittingham Beers, *A Mind That Found Itself* (New York: Longmans, 1909), p. 169.
10. G. N. Grob, *The Mad Among Us* (Cambridge, MA: Harvard Univeristy Press), p. 58.
11. NIMH, "About NIMH," retrieved February 3, 2008, from www.nimh.nih.gov/about.
12. Ibid.
13. Sheldon Preskorn, "Mental Disorders Are Medical Disorders," in William Barbour (Ed.), *Mental Illness: Opposing Viewpoints* (San Diego, CA: Greenhaven Press, 1995), pp. 29–36.
14. Ibid.
15. National Alliance for the Mentally Ill, "About Mental Illness," retrieved February 13, 2008, from http://www.nami.org/Content/NavigationMenu/Inform_Yourself/About_Mental_Illness/About_Mental_Illness.htm.
16. Erick H. Turner, Annette M. Matthews, Eftihia Linardatos, Robert A. Tell, and Robert Rosenthal, "Selective Publication of Antidepressant Trials and Its Influence on Apparent Efficacy," *New England Journal of Medicine* 358(3) (2008), pp. 252–260; Benedict Carey, "Antidepressant Studies Unpublished," *New York Times* (January 17, 2008).
17. Turner, Matthews, Linardatos, Tell and Rosenthal; Carey
18. David Mechanic, "Mental Health Policy at the Millennium: Challenges and opportunities," in *Mental Health, United States, 2000* (Rockville, MD: U.S. Department of Health & Human Services, Substance Abuse & Mental Health Administration, 2000), pp. 53–63.
19. Mechanic, 1999, p. 25.
20. Ibid., p. 24.
21. Christopher Peterson, "Psychological Approaches to Mental Illness," in Allan Horwitz and Teresa Scheid (Eds.), *A Handbook for the Study of Mental Health: Social Contexts, Theories and Systems* (New York: Cambridge University Press, 1999), p. 104.
22. Ibid., p. 106.
23. Ibid., p. 107.
24. Ibid., p. 108.
25. Ibid., p. 109.
26. Ibid., p. 110.
27. Ibid., p. 104.
28. Ibid., p. 112.
29. Ibid., p. 115.
30. Ibid., p. 116.
31. Thomas Scheff, *Being Mentally Ill* (New York: Aldine, 1984), p. 30.
32. Peggy A. Thoits, "Sociological Approaches to Mental Illness," in Allan Horwitz and Teresa Scheid (Eds.), *A Handbook for the Study of Mental Health: Social Contexts, Theories and Systems* (New York: Cambridge University Press, 1999), pp. 121–138.
33. Scheff, pp. 30–31.
34. Thoits, p. 136.
35. Thomas Szasz, "The Myth of Mental Illness," *American Psychologist* 15 (1960), reprinted in Richard Vatz and Lee Weinberg *Thomas Szasz: Primary Values and Major Contentions* (Buffalo, NY: Prometheus Books, 1983), pp. 113–118.
36. Thomas Szasz, *Second Sin* (Garden City, NY: Anchor Press, 1973).
37. Szasz, "Myth of Mental Illness," p. 114.
38. Ibid., p. 113.
39. Mitchell Wilson, "DSM-III and the Transformation of American Psychiatry: A History," *American Journal of Psychiatry* 150(3) (March 1993), pp. 399–410.
40. Ibid.
41. Ibid.
42. DSM Prelude Project, retrieved February 4, 2008, from http://dsm5.org/timeline.cfm.
43. Herb Kutchins and Stuart Kirk, *Making Us Crazy* (New York: Free Press, 1997), pp. 12–13.
44. Lisa Cosgrove, Sheldon Krimsky, and Manisha Vijayaraghavan, "Financial Ties Between DSM-IV Panel Members and the Pharmaceutical Industry," *Psychotherapy & Psychosomatics* 75(3) (April 2006), pp. 154–160.
45. Ibid.
46. American Psychiatric Association. (2000). *Diagnostic and statistical manual of mental disorders* (4th ed., text revision). Washington, DC: Author..
47. NIMH, "The Numbers Count."
48. Ibid.
49. Ibid.
50. APA, p. 157.
51. NIMH, "The Numbers Count."
52. APA, p. 312.
53. NIMH, "The Numbers Count."
54. Ibid.
55. APA, p. 356.
56. Ibid., p. 362.
57. NIMH, "The Numbers Count."
58. Ibid.
59. Sally Satel, "Mind over Manual" (Op-Ed), *New York Times* (September 13, 2007).
60. NIMH, "The Numbers Count."
61. APA, p. 476.
62. Ibid., p. 468.
63. Ibid., p. 547.
64. Ibid., p. 581.
65. NIMH, "The Numbers Count."
66. Ibid.
67. APA, p. 589.

68. Ibid., p. 594.
69. Ibid., p. 787.
70. NIMH, "The Numbers Count."
71. APA, p. 685.
72. Ronald C. Kessler and Shanyang Zhao, "The Prevalence of Mental Illness," in Allan Horwitz and Teresa Scheid (Eds.), *A Handbook for the Study of Mental Health: Social Contexts, Theories and Systems* (New York: Cambridge University Press, 1999), p. 76.
73. APA, p. 704.
74. Ibid., pp. 899–903.
75. Dareld Wing Sue, *Multicultural Social Work Practice* (Hoboken, NJ: Wiley Interscience, 2006), pp. 204–205.
76. Mary E. Woods and Howard Robinson, "Psychosocial Theory and Social Work Treatment," in Francis Turner (Ed.), *Social Work Treatment: Interlocking Theoretical Approaches* (New York: Free Press, 1996), pp. 557–558.
77. Ibid., pp. 555–556.
78. Alfred Kadushin and Goldie Kadushin, *The Social Work Interview: A Guide for Human Service Professionals*, 4th ed. (New York: Columbia University Press, 1997), p. 100.
79. Ibid., pp. 102–103.
80. Ibid., pp. 103–127.
81. Ibid., pp. 100–101.
82. Mary E. Woods and Florence Hollis, *Casework: A Psychosocial Therapy*, 5th ed. (Boston, MA: McGraw Hill, 2000), pp. 545–550.
83. Karen Krist-Ashman, *Introduction to Social Work and Social Welfare: Critical Thinking Perspectives* (Pacific Grove, CA: Brooks-Cole, 2003), p. 387.
84. Michael P. Nichols and Richard C. Schwartz, *The Essentials of Family Therapy*, 2nd ed. (Boston, MA: Pearson, 2005), p. 59.
85. Ibid., p. 5.
86. Graham Thornicroft, *Shunned: Discrimination Against People with Mental Illness* (London, UK: Oxford University Press, 2006), p. 73.
87. Sue R. Noe, "Discrimination Against Individuals with Mental Illness," *Journal of Rehabilitation 63* (January–March, 1997), pp. 20-26.
88. Thornicroft, p. 75.
89. Sue, p. 241.
90. Ibid.
91. Michael Lindsey, Wynne S. Korr, Marina Broitman, Lee Bone, Alan Green, and Philip J. Leaf, "Help-Seeking Behaviors and Depression Among African American Adolescent Boys," *Social Work 51*(1) (January 2006), pp. 49–56.
92. Krist-Ashman, p. 363.
93. Center for an Accessible Society, "Supreme Court Upholds ADA 'Integration Mandate' in *Olmstead* decision," retrieved February 24, 2008, from http://www.accessiblesociety.org/topics/ada/olmsteadoverview.htm.
94. Mechanic, 2000, pp. 53–63.
95. Ibid.
96. Ibid., p. 54.
97. Ibid.
98. NASW Center for Workforce Studies, *Licensed Social Workers in Behavioral Health, 2004* (Washington, DC: NASW Center for Workforce Studies, March 2006), p. 1.
99. Jeffery A. Cohen, "Managed Care and the Evolving Role of the Clinical Social Worker in Mental Health," *Social Work, 48*(1) (January 2003), pp. 34–43.
100. U.S. Department of Health and Human Services, *Mental Health: Culture, Race, and Ethnicity—A Supplement to Mental Health: A Report of the Surgeon General* (Rockville, MD: U.S. Department of Health and Human Services, Substance Abuse and Mental Health Services Administration, Center for Mental Health Services, 2001), p. 5.
101. Ibid.
102. Ibid., p. 64.
103. Ibid., p. 68.
104. Ibid., pp. 160–167.
105. Cohen, p. 35.
106. Mechanic, 2000, pp. 53–63.
107. Ibid.
108. Ibid.; Cohen, p. 35.
109. Mechanic, 2000, pp. 53–63.
110. Cohen, p. 35.
111. Mechanic, 2000, pp. 53–63.
112. Substance Abuse and Mental Health Services Administration, "Evidenced-Based Practices: Shaping Mental Health Services Towards Recovery: Assertive Community Treatment," retrieved February 24, 2008, from http://mentalhealth.samhsa.gov/cmhs/communitysupport/toolkits/community/ACTpractinfo.asp.
113. Andrew Kent and Tom Burns, "Setting Up an Assertive Community Treatment Service," *Advances in Psychiatric Treatment 2* (1996), pp. 143–150.
114. Ibid.
115. NIMH, "The Numbers Count."

Quotes

William Menninger, quoted in "Neglect Is Noted in Mental Health," *New York Times* (November 22, 1957).
Barbara Ehrenreich, *Fear of Falling: The Inner Life of the Middle Class* (New York: Pantheon, 1989), p. 1.
Judith Jordan, "Relational Learning in Psychotherapy Consultation ad Supervision," in Maureen Walker and Wendy B. Rosen (Eds.), *How Connections Heal: Stories from Relational Cultural Therapy* (New York: Guilford Press, 2004), p. 22.
Lewis Mumford, quoted in Carey Winfrey, "Lewis Mumford Remembers," *New York Times* (July 6, 1977).

Chapter 10

1. P. Scommegna, *Increased Cohabitation Changing Children's Family Settings* (Research on Today's Issues No. 13) (Washington, DC: Demographic and Behavioral Sciences Branch, Center for Population Research, National Institute of Child Health and Human Development, National Institutes of Health, 2002), p. 1.
2. J. Pawelski, E. Perrin, J. Foy, C. Allen, J. Crawford, M. Del Monte, M. Kaufman, J. Klein, K. Smith, S. Springer, J. Tanner, and D. Vickers, "The Effects of Marriage, Civil Unions and Domestic Partnership Laws on the Health and Well-Being of Children," *Pediatrics 118* (2006), pp. 349–364.
3. C. Osborne and S. McLanahan, *Partnership Instability and Child Wellbeing* (Working paper No. 2004-16-FF, Fragile Families and Child Wellbeing Study, Center for Research on Child Wellbeing), retrieved January 30, 2008, from http://crcw.princeton.edu/publications/publications.asp.
4. B. Carter and M. McGoldrick, *The Changing Family Life Cycle: A Framework for Family Therapy*, 3rd ed. (Boston: Allyn & Bacon, 2005), pp. 1–2.

5. S. Braver, J. Shapiro, and M. Goodman, "The Consequences of Divorce for Parents," in M. Fine and J. Harvey (Eds.), *Handbook of Divorce and Relationship Dissolution* (Mahwah, NJ: Erlbaum, 2005).
6. G. Bowen, L. Desimone, and J. McKay, "Poverty and the Single Mother Family: A Macroeconomic Perspective," *Marriage and Family Review 20* (1995), p. 117.
7. M. Emick and B. Hayslip, "Custodial Grandparenting: Stresses, Coping Skills and Relationships with Grandchildren," *International Journal of Aging and Human Development 48* (1999), pp. 35–62; B. Hayslip, R. Shore, C. Henderson, and P. Lambert, "Custodial Grandparenting and the Impact of Grandchildren with Problems on Role Satisfaction and Role Meaning," *Journal of Gerontology: Social Sciences 53B* (1998), pp. S164–S173.
8. M. Campa and J. Eckenrode, "Pathways to Intergenerational Adolescent Childbearing in a High-Risk Sample," *Journal of Marriage and Family 68* (2006), pp. 558–572; J. Corcoran, "Ecological Factors Associated with Adolescent Pregnancy: A Review of the Literature," *Adolescence 34* (1999), pp. 603–619; B. Ellis et al., "Does Father Absence Place Daughters at Special Risk for Early Sexual Activity and Teenage Pregnancy?" *Child Development 74* (2003), pp. 801–821.
9. M. Durose, C. Harlow, P. Langan, M. Motivans, R. Rantala, and E. Smith, *Family Violence Statistics* (Report No. NCJ-207846) (Washington, DC: U.S. Department of Justice, Office of Justice Programs, Bureau of Justice Statistics, 2005), p. 4.
10. A. Maher, D. Zillmer, S. Hadley, and L. Luedtke, "Addressing Family Violence: A Professional Imperative," *Orthopaedic Nursing 21* (2002), pp. 10–15.
11. National Criminal Justice Reference Service, *Family Violence: Facts and Figures, 2007*, retrieved February 1, 2010, from http://www.ncjrs.gov/spotlight/family_violence/facts.html.
12. Durose et al.
13. Ibid.
14. H. Bragg, *Child Protection in Families Experiencing Domestic Violence* (Washington, DC: U.S. Department of Health and Human Services, Administration for Children and Families, Administration on Children, Youth and Families, Children's Bureau, and Office on Child Abuse and Neglect, 2003), pp. 29–30.
15. J. Campbell et al., "Intimate Partner Violence and Physical Health Consequences," *Archives of Internal Medicine 162* (2002), p. 1156.
16. Centers for Disease Control and Prevention, "Youth Risk Behavior Surveillance—United States," *Morbidity and Mortality Weekly Report 55* (2005), retrieved February 1, 2010, from http://www.cdc.gov/HealthyYouth/yrbs/index.htm.
17. Child Welfare Information Gateway, *Defining Child Abuse and Neglect: Definitions in Federal Law, 12/7/07*, retrieved February 1, 2010, from http://www.childwelfare.gov/can/defining/federal.cfm.
18. Child Welfare Information Gateway, *Defining Child Abuse and Neglect: State Definitions of Child Abuse and Neglect, 1/28/10*, retrieved February 1, 2010, from http://www.childwelfare.gov/can/defining/state.cfm.
19. U.S. Department of Health and Human Services, Administration on Children, Youth and Families, *Child Maltreatment* (Washington, DC: U.S. Government Printing Office, 2007).
20. Ibid.
21. National Association of Social Workers (NASW) (2007), *Code of Ethics*, retrieved February 1, 2010, from www.naswdc.org/pubs/code/code.asp.
22. D. Finkelhor, "Epidemiological Factors in the Clinical Identification of Child Sexual Abuse," *Child Abuse and Neglect 17* (1993), pp. 67–70.
23. M. Abramovitz, "Women in a Bind: The Decline of Marriage, Market and the State," in C. Broussard and A. Joseph (Eds.), *Family Poverty in Diverse Contexts* (2009), pp.36-47 (New York: Routledge).
24. J. Bernstein and I. Shapiro, *Nine Years of Neglect: Federal Minimum Wage Remains Unchanged for Ninth Straight Year, Falls to Lowest Level in More Than Half a Century* (Center on Budget and Policy Priorities, Economic Policy Institute, 2006), retrieved February 1, 2010, from http://www.cbpp.org/8-31-06mw.htm.
25. Abramovitz.
26. P. Pecora, J. Whittaker, A. Maluccio, R. Barth, and R. Plotnick, *The Child Welfare Challenge* (New York: Aldine De Gruyter, 2000), p. 296.
27. R. McRoy, "Expedited Permanency: Implications for African-American Children and Families," *Virginia Journal of Social Policy and the Law 12* (2005), p. 477.
28. U.S. Department of Health and Human Services, Administration for Children and Families, Administration of Children, Youth and Families, Children's Services Bureau, *AFCARS Report* No. 9 (Washington, DC: U.S. Government Printing Office, 2005).
29. U.S. Department of Health and Human Services, Administration on Children, Youth and Families, *Child Maltreatment 2003* (Washington, DC: U.S. Government Printing Office, 2005).
30. P. Placek, "National Adoption Data," in T. Atwood (Ed.), *Adoption Factbook IV* (Sterling, VA: National Council for Adoption, 2007).
31. U.S. Department of Health and Human Services, *The AFCARS Report: Preliminary FY 2003 Estimates as of April 2005* (Washington, DC: Author, 2005).
32. J. Demick, "Challenging the Common Myths About Adoption," *Brown University Child and Adolescent Behavior Letter 23*(8) (2007), p. 8.
33. Parents Anonymous (2007), retrieved February 1, 2010, from http://www.parentsanonymous.org/paIndex10.html.
34. Head Start Program Factsheet, *FY-2007 Program Statistics* (2008), retrieved February 1, 2010, from http://www.acf.hhs.gov/programs/ohs/about/fy2008.html.
35. K. Gorey, "Early childhood Education: A Meta-Analytic Affirmation of the Short- and Long-Term Benefits of Educational Opportunity," *School Psychology Quarterly 16*(2001), pp. 9–10.
36. Ibid.
37. R. Caputo, "Head Start, Other Preschool Programs and Life Success in a Youth Cohort," *Sociology and Social Welfare 30* (2003), pp. 105–126.
38. Ibid, p. 122.
39. M. Weist, M. Ambrose, and C. Lewis, "Expanded School Mental Health: Collaborative Community-School Example," *Children and Schools 28* (2006), p. 45.
40. U.S. Department of Education, National Center for Education Statistics, *Characteristics of the 100 Largest Public Elementary and Secondary School Districts in the United States: 2000–01* (NCES 20022351) (Washington, DC: Author, 2002), p. 55.

41. R. Constable and D. Lee, *Social Work with Families* (Chicago: Lyceum Books, 2004), p. 8.
42. J. Katz, *The Macho Paradox: Why Some Men Hurt Women and How All Men Can Help,* (Naperville, IL: Sourcebooks, 2006).
43. A. Garwick, K. Rhodes, M. Peterson-Hickey, and W. Hellerstedt, "Native Teen Voices: Adolescent Pregnancy Prevention Recommendation," *Journal of Adolescent Health 42* (2008), pp. 81–88.

Quotes

Barbara Bush, Speech before the Republican National Convention, August 19, 1992, Houston, TX.

J. Bernard, *The Future of Marriage* (New Haven, CT: Yale University Press, 1982), p. 5.

J. Lewis, "Marian Wright Edelman Quotes" (2010), retrieved from http://womenshistory.about.com/od/quotes/a/marian_edelman.htm.

Chapter 11

1. John T. Pardeck, *Social Work After the Americans with Disabilities Act* (Westport, CT: Auburn House, 1998), p. 95.
2. P. Jaeger and C. Bowman, *Understanding Disability: Inclusion, Access, Diversity, and Civil Rights* (Westport, CT: Greenwood Publishing Group, 2005), pp. 3–7.
3. G. May and M. Raske, *Ending Disability Discrimination: Strategies for Social Workers* (Boston, MA: Pearson, Allyn & Bacon, 2005), p. 16.
4. Brenda DuBois and Karla K. Miley, *Social Work: The Empowering Profession*, 5th ed. (Boston, MA: Allyn & Bacon, 2005) pp. 333–334.
5. D.B.Carr, 1998, cited in A. Chandra, T. Barrett, and D. Paul, "A Brief review of Worker Disability with a Call for a Consumer Perspective," *Hospital Topics 81*(4) (2003), pp. 30–35.
6. Jaeger and Bowman, pp. 17–23.
7. DuBois and Miley, pp. 333–334.
8. Pardeck, p. 95.
9. D. Goode, *Quality of Life for Persons with Disabilities: A Review and Synthesis of the Literature* (Washington, DC: American Association on Mental Retardation, 1997), pp. 81–82.
10. DuBois and Miley, pp. 339–342.
11. Goode, pp. 81–82.
12. DuBois and Miley, pp. 339–342
13. S. Dziegielewski, 2004, as cited in M. Egan and G. Kadushin, *Social Work Practice in Community -Based Healthcare* (Philadelphia: Haworth Press, 2007), pp. 277–278.
14. DuBois and Miley, pp. 339–342.
15. S. Parrish and Z. Lutwick, "A Critical Analysis of the Emerging Crisis in Long-Term Care for People with Developmental Disabilities," *Social Work 50*(4) (2005), pp. 346–349.
16. Ibid.
17. Ibid.
18. N. R. Hooyman and J. Gonyea, 1995, as cited in Parrish and Lutwick, pp 346–349.
19. May and Raske, pp. 5–17.
20. C. Horejsi, "Developmental Disabilities: Opportunities for Social Workers," *Social Work 24*(1) (1979), pp. 40-43.
21. Parrish and Lutwick, pp. 351–352.
22. K. Deweaver and N. Kropf, "Persons with Mental Retardation: A Forgotten Minority in Education," *Journal of Social Work Education 28*(1) (1992), pp. 36–46.
23. H. Grossman, *Classification in Mental Retardation* (Washington, DC: American Association on Mental Deficiency, 1983), p. 1.
24. American Association on Mental Retardation (AAMR), *Mental Retardation: Definition, Classification, and Systems of Supports*, 10th ed. (Washington, DC: AAMR, 2002).
25. National Association of Social Workers (NASW), *Social Work Speaks: National Association of Social Workers Policy Statements, 2000–2003*, 5th ed. (Washington, DC: NASW Press, 2003) p. 246.
26. Horejsi, pp 40–43.
27. NASW, p. 247.
28. M. Holosko and P. Taylor (Eds.), *Social Work Practice in Health Care Settings*, rev. ed. (Toronto, Ontario: Canadian Scholars' Press, 1992), pp. 555–562.
29. Ibid.
30. H. Golding, E. Bass, A. Percy, and M. Goldberg, "Understanding Recent Estimates of PTSD and TBI from Operations Iraqi Freedom and Enduring Freedom," *Journal of Rehabilitation Research and Development 46*(5) (2009), retrieved from http://www.rehab.research.va.gov/jour/09/46/5/pdf/golding.pdf.
31. Holosko and Taylor, pp. 555–562.
32. J. Beder, *Hospital Social Work* (New York: Routledge, 2006), pp. 111–113.
33. Ibid., pp. 113–116.
34. LD Online (2002), *The ABC's of LD* (Washington, DC: WETA), retrieved from http://www.ldonline.org.
35. Ibid.
36. National Joint Committee on Learning Disabilities (NJCLD) (2006), *Learning Disabilities and Young Children: Identification and Intervention*, retrieved from http://www.ldonline.org.
37. Ibid.
38. S. Dhooper, *Social Work in Health Care the 21st Century* (Belmont, CA: Sage, 1997), p. 85.
39. National Center for Learning Disabilities (NCLD), *LD at a Glance* (New York: NCLD, 2001), retrieved from www.id.org.
40. NJCLD, 2006.
41. LD Online.
42. Beder, pp. 109–110.
43. Ibid.
44. DuBois and Miley.
45. Ibid.
46. Ibid.
47. ALS Association (2004), *About ALS*, retrieved June 23, 2008, from www.alsa.org.
48. Ibid.
49. Jaeger and Bowman.
50. Ibid.
51. Ibid.
52. Ibid.
53. Ibid.
54. Ibid.
55. Ibid.
56. *Buck v. Bell*, 1927, as cited in Jaeger and Bowman, p. 207.
57. Parrish and Lutwick, pp. 345–354.
58. Jaeger and Bowman.
59. Ibid.
60. L. Fort Cowles, *Social Work in the Health Field: A Care Perspective* (Philadelphia: Haworth Press, 2003), pp. 203–206.

61. Office of Special Education Programs, *IDEA Regulations: Individualized Education Program (IEP)* (Washington, DC: U.S. Department of Education, 2000), pp. 2–3, retrieved June 23, 2008, from http://idea.ed.gov.
62. Pardeck, p. 95.
63. May and Raske, pp. 48–50.
64. Ibid., pp. 47–48.
65. Retrieved from http://www.perkinscoie.com/news/pubs_detail aspx?publication=1808&op=updates.
66. Jaeger and Bowman, pp. 39–43.
67. T. Honeycutt, "Program and Benefit Paths to the Social Security Disability Insurance Program," *Journal of Vocational Rehabilitation* 21(2) (2004), pp. 83–94, retrieved April 20, 2007, from the Academic Search Premier database.
68. SSA Office of Disability and Income Security Programs, SSA Office of Disability and Income Security Programs, *Social Security: 2006 Red Book: A Summary Guide to Employment Support for Individuals with Disabilities Under the Social Security Disability Insurance and Supplemental Security Income Programs* (Publication No. 64-030), retrieved June 23, 2008, from http://www.socialsecurity.gov/redbook/eng/redbook.pdf.
69. Holosko and Taylor, pp. 467–470.
70. Honeycutt, pp. 83–94.
71. Ibid.
72. Ibid.
73. Holmes, 2002, as cited in A. Chandra, T. Barrett, and D. Paul, "A Brief Review of Worker Disability with a Call for a Consumer Perspective," *Hospital Topics* 81(4) (2003), pp. 30–35, retrieved April 21, 2007, from the MEDLINE database.
74. Beder, p. 109.
75. American Heart Association, 2004, as cited in Beder, pp. 109–110.
76. Holosko and Taylor, pp. 467–470.
77. Ibid.
78. Ibid.
79. Ibid.
80. Ibid.
81. Dziegielewski, cited in Egan and Kadushin, pp. 267–268.
82. Ibid.
83. Fort Cowles, pp. 267–268.
84. Dziegielewski, cited in Egan and Kadushin, pp. 267–268.
85. Dhooper, p. 85.
86. Dziegielewski, cited in Egan and Kadushin, pp. 267–268.
87. Ibid.
88. Ibid.
89. Parrish and Lutwick, p. 352.
90. National Dissemination Center for Children with Disabilities, *NICHCY Connections . . . to Resources on IDEA 2004* (Washington, DC: Academy for Educational Development, 2006), retrieved June 23, 2008, from www.nichcy.org/new.htm.
91. E. Fossey and E. Fossey, "Effective Interdisciplinary Teamwork: An Occupational Therapy Perspective." *Australasian Psychiatry* 9(3) (2001), pp. 232–235, retrieved April 21, 2007, from the Academic Search Premier database.
92. Dziegielewski, cited in Egan and Kadushin, pp. 350–362.
93. Goode, pp. 81–82.
94. Ibid.
95. S. Altshuler and S. Kopels, "Advocating in Schools for Children with Disabilities: What's New with IDEA?" *Social Work* 48(3) (2003), p. 329.
96. Jaeger and Bowman, pp. 34–38.
97. DuBois and Miley, pp. 396–397.
98. Ibid.
99. Ibid.
100. Altshuler and Kopels, pp. 320–328.
101. Parrish and Lutwick, pp. 346–349.
102. Ibid.

Quotes

Thomas Szasz, "Personal Conduct," *The Untamed Tongue: A Dissenting Dictionary* (Chicago: Open Court, 1990).

Albert Einstein, retrieved from http://lucarinfo.com/inspire/deinstein.html.

Special Olympics Athlete's Oath, retrieved February 14, 2010, from www.specialolympics.org.

Jean Vanier, retrieved February 13, 2010, from http://www.quotesdaddy.com/author/Jean+Vanier.

Chapter 12

1. Gary L. Fisher and Thomas C. Harrison, *Substance Abuse: Information for School Counselors, Social Workers, Therapists, and Counselors*, 4th ed. (New York: Pearson, 2009), p. 14.
2. Ibid., pp. 14–15.
3. Ibid.
4. Ibid., p. 14.
5. Centers for Disease Control (CDC), "Current Smoking," retrieved July 2, 2009, from http://www.cdc.gov/nchs/data/nhis/earlyrelease/200812_08.pdf; American Cancer Society, Cigarette Smoking," retrieved July 2, 2009, from http://www.cancer.org/docroot/PED/content/PED_10_2X_Cigarette_Smoking.asp?sitearea=PED.
6. Ibid.
7. CDC, "Faststats—Alcohol Use," retrieved July 2, 2009, from http://www.cdc.gov/nchs/fastats/alcohol.htm.
8. National Institute on Alcohol Abuse and Alcoholism, "FAQ for the General Public," retrieved July 2, 2009, from http://www.niaaa.nih.gov/FAQs/General-English/default.htm.
9. CDC, "Faststats – Alcohol Use"; Fisher and Harrison, p. 15.
10. Kim Painter, "Time to Toast Sober Reality," *USA Today* (17 December 2007), p. 9D.
11. Caroline Knapp, *Drinking: A Love Story* (New York: Delta, 1996), Prologue.
12. American Council for Drug Education, "Basic Facts About Drugs: Marijuana," retrieved July 2, 2009, from http://www.acde.org/common/Marijana.htm.
13. "Pediatricians Call for R Rating for Movies Depicting Smoking," *Alcoholism and Drug Abuse Weekly* (May 28, 2007), p. 6; "NIDA Finds Extraordinary Results in Early Trials of Nicotine Vaccine," *Alcoholism and Drug Abuse Weekly* (May 28, 2007), pp. 6–7.
14. Painter, p. 9D.
15. Donna Leinwand, "College Drug Use, Binge Drinking Rise" *USA Today* (March 15, 2007), p. 3A; Painter, p. 9D.
16. Beth Sussman, "Friday Classes Limit Student Drinking on Thursday," *USA Today* (June 27, 2007), p. 6D.
17. "Would an Age 18 Minimum Curb Alcohol Abuse?" *USA Today* (November 26, 2007), p. 12A.
18. Christopher Palmeri, "Hands Up and Back Away from the Brownies," *Business Week* (August 13, 2007), p. 9.
19. "Breaking Bonds of Addiction," *USA Today* (April 18, 2002), p. 8D; Sarah Childress, "Crystal Handcuffs," *Newsweek* (May 16, 2005), retrieved February 10, 2008, from Academic Search Premier, http://web.ebscohost.com; Andrew Murr and Sarah Childress, "A New Menace

Notes

on Rez," *Newsweek* (September 27, 2004), retrieved January 10, 2008, from Academic Search Premier, http://web.ebscohost.com; Partnership for a Drug-Free America, "Crystal Meth," retrieved July 3, 2009, from http://www.drugfree.org/portal/drug_guide/crystal_meth/; U.S. Department of Health and Human Services, SAMSHA, Office of Applied Studies, "State Variations in Nonmedical Use of Prescription Psychotherapeutic Drugs," retrieved July 6, 2009, from http://oas.samhsa.gov/prescription/Ch7.htm#7.6.

20. Pat Mail, "Drugs: The Longest US War." *Nation's Health 36*(7) (2006), retrieved February 11, 2008, from Academic Search Premier, http://web.ebscohost.com.libproxy.unh.edu/; Donya C. Arias, "High Rate of Incarcerated Black Men Devastating to Family Health," *Nation's Health 37*(2) (2007), retrieved February 11, 2008, from Academic Search Premier, http://web.ebscohost.com; Marc Maurer, David L. Weimer, and Philip Heymann, "A Better War on Drugs," *Issues in Science and Technology 23*(2) (2007), retrieved February 11, 2008, from Academic Search Premier, http://web.ebscohost.com.
21. Patt Denning, Jeannie Little, and Adina Glickman, *Over the Influence: The Harm Reduction Guide for Managing Drugs and Alcohol* (New York: Guilford Press, 2004), pp. 5–8; Fisher and Harrison, pp. 37–49.
22. Frederick Rotgers, Jon Morgenstern, and Scott T. Walters, *Treating Substance Abuse: Theory and Technique*, 2nd ed. (New York: Guilford Press, 2003), pp. 10–11; Fisher and Harrison, pp. 46-49.
23. Fisher and Harrison, pp. 37–38.
24. Ibid.
25. Ibid.
26. U.S. Department of Health and Human Services, SAMSHA, Office of Applied Studies, "Results from the 2007 National Survey on Drug Use and Health: National Findings," retrieved July 7, 2009, from http://oas.samhsa.gov/nsduh/2k7nsduh/2k7results.cfm#2.10.
27. U.S. Department of Health and Human Services, SAMSHA, Office of Applied Studies, "Results from the 2007 National Survey on Drug Use and Health: National Findings," retrieved July 7, 2009, from http://oas.samhsa.gov/nsduh/2k7nsduh/2k7results.cfm#2.14.
28. Fisher and Harrison, pp. 38-39.
29. Rotgers, Morgenstern, and Walters, pp. 10–11; Fisher and Harrison, p. 39–41; Denning, Little, and Glickman, pp. 5–8.
30. Fisher and Harrison, pp. 183–184.
31. Alcoholics Anonymous, "Information On AA," retrieved July 9, 2009, from http://www.aa.org/lang/en/subpage.cfm?page=1.
32. Al-Anon, *One Day at a Time in Al-Anon* (New York: Al-Anon Family Group Headquarters, Inc., 1992), p. 367.
33. Fisher and Harrison, p. 189.
34. National Institute on Drug Abuse, "Approaches to Drug Abuse Counseling," retrieved July 9, 2009, from http://www.drugabuse.gov/ADAC/ADAC11.html.
35. Fisher and Harrision, p. 137; National Institute on Drug Abuse, "Approaches to Drug Abuse Counseling," retrieved July 10, 2009, from http://www.drugabuse.gov/adac/adac10.html.
36. National Institute on Drug Abuse, "A Cognitive Behavioral Approach: Treating Cocaine Addiction," retrieved July 10, 2009, from http://www.drugabuse.gov/TXManuals/CBT/CBT1.html.
37. Barbara S. McCrady, Elizabeth E. Epstein, and Rene D. Sell, "Theoretical Bases of Family Approaches to Substance Abuse Treatment," in Frederick Rotgers, Jon Morgenstern, and Scott T. Walters, *Treating Substance Abuse: Theory and Technique*, 2nd ed. (New York: Guilford Press, 2003), pp. 112–139; William Fals-Stewart, Timothy J. O'Farrell, and Gary R. Birchler, "Family Therapy Techniques," in Frederick Rotgers, Jon Morgenstern, and Scott T. Walters, *Treating Substance Abuse: Theory and Technique*, 2nd ed. (New York: Guilford Press, 2003), pp. 140–165; Fisher and Harrison, pp. 140–141.
38. Fisher and Harrison, p. 144.
39. Charles Zastrow, *Introduction to Social Work and Social Welfare: Empowering People*, 8th ed. (Belmont CA: Thomson Brooks/Cole, 2004), pp. 291–297; Fisher and Harrison, pp. 144–146.
40. "Texas Senate Approves Needle Exchange," *Alcoholism and Drug Abuse Weekly* (May 7, 2007), p. 7; "Needle Exchange Faces Budget Cuts," *Alcoholism and Drug Abuse Weekly* (March 26, 2007), p. 7; "Syringe Exchange Programs—United States," *Morbidity and Mortality Weekly Report* (November 9, 2007), pp. 1164–1167.
41. Starr A. Wood, "Health Care Services for HIV-Positive Substance Abusers in a Rural Setting," *Social Work in Health Care 47* (2008), pp. 108–121.
42. Barry R. McCaffrey, "Expand Drug Courts Through Public-Private Partnerships," *USA Today* (January 3, 2008), p. 12A, retrieved February 11, 2008, from Academic Search Premier, http://web.ebscohost.com; David Unze, "More Places Turning to Drug Courts," *USA Today* (December 21, 2007), p. 3A, retrieved February 11, 2008, from Academic Search Premier, http://web.ebscohost.com; "Arizona Launches 10-Point Strategy for Methamphetamine," *Alcoholism and Drug Weekly 19*(20) (May 21, 2007), pp. 1, 5, 6.
43. Fisher and Harrison, pp. 154–155.
44. Jerry D. Marx, 2008, personal interview with Brian Miller.
45. David Skiba, Jacquelyn Monroe, and John S. Wodarski, "Adolescent Substance Use: Reviewing the Effectiveness of Prevention Strategies," *Social Work 49* (2004), pp. 343–353.
46. Ibid., p. 349.
47. Ibid., p. 345.
48. Ibid., p. 347.
49. Ibid., p. 349.
50. Ibid., p. 347.

Quotes

P. J. O'Rourke, "Studying for Our Drug Test," *Give War a Chance* (New York: Atlantic Monthly Press, 1992).

C. Aaron McNeece and Diana M. DiNitto, *Chemical Dependency: A Systems Approach*, 3rd ed. (Boston, MA: Allyn & Bacon, 2004).

Alcoholics Anonymous, *The Big Book*, retrieved February 15, 2010, from http://www.notable-quotes.com/a/alcoholism_quotes.html.

Anonymous individual on recovery, retrieved February 15, 2010, from http://www.cyberrecovery.net/forums/showthread.php?t=3559.

Chapter 13

1. P. W. Tappan, *Crime, Justice and Correction* (New York: McGraw-Hill Co., 1960), retrieved from http://www.nolo.com/definition.cfm/term/D82E9E8C-BB95-4F9A-97E134E302E0D7C2.

2. Electronic Law Library, retrieved January 15, 2008, from http://www.lectlaw.com/def/c330.htm.
3. J. O'Neill, "Forensic Field Broader Than Most Think" (National Association of Social Workers, 2003), retrieved April 5, 2008.
4. Electronic Law Library.
5. Ibid.
6. Law Library, "American Law and Legal Information," retrieved January 15, 2008, from http://law.jrank.org/pages/815/Crime-Causation-Sociological-Theories-.html.
7. Ibid.
8. Ibid.
9. Ibid.
10. Ibid.
11. Ibid.
12. Ibid.
13. Retrieved from http://www.whitehouse.gov/fsbr/crime.html.
14. S. D. Levitt, "The Limited Role of Changing Age Structure in Explaining Aggregate Crime Rates," *Criminology 37*(3) (1999), pp. 581–597.
15. J. J. Donohue, "Understanding the Time Path of Crime," *Journal of Criminal Law and Criminology 88*(4) (1998), p. 1437.
16. Ibid.
17. U.S. Department of Justice, Office of Justice Programs, Bureau of Justice Statistics, "Crime and Justice Electronic Facts," retrieved from http://www.ojp.gov/bjs/gcorpop.htm.
18. Donohue, p. 1439.
19. A. Blumstein, "Youth Violence, Guns and the Illicit-Drug Industry," *Journal of Criminal Law and Criminology 86*(1) (1995), pp. 26–36.
20. K. Welch, "Black Criminal Stereotypes and Racial Profiling," *Journal of Contemporary Criminal Justice 23*(3) (2007), p. 276.
21. *Economist*, *376*(8438) (August 6, 2005), p. 20.
22. R. Brewer and N. Heitzeg, "The Racialization of Crime and Punishment, Criminal Justice, Color-Blind Racism, and the Political Economy of the Prison Industrial Complex," *American Behavioral Scientist 51*(5) (January 2008), pp. 625–626.
23. Bureau of Justice Statistics, 2004.
24. Ibid.
25. U.S. Department of Justice, Office of Justice Programs, Bureau of Justice Statistics, "Crime and Justice Electronic Facts, retrieved from http://www.ojp.gov/bjs/gcorpop.htm.
26. Bureau of Justice Statistics, 2004.
27. Brewer and Heitzeg, pp. 627–628.
28. Bureau of Justice Statistics, 2004.
29. Brewer and Heitzeg, p. 637.
30. U.S. Department of Justice, Office of Justice Programs, Bureau of Justice Statistics, retrieved January 15, 2008, from: http://www.ojp.gov/bjs/pub/pdf/cjsflowco.pdf.
31. U.S. Department of Justice, Federal Bureau of Investigation, "Crime in the United States, 1996," in U.S. Department of Justice, Office of Justice Programs, Office of Juvenile Justice and Delinquency Prevention, *Juvenile Justice Bulletin* (NCJ 167578, November 1997).
32. "Children, Violence and the Media: A Report for Parents and Policy Makers," *Congressional Digest* (November 1999), pp. 266–267.
33. Federal Bureau of Prisons, retrieved February 2, 2008, from http://www.bop.gov/locations/cc/ccc_faqs.jsp.
34. S. M. Coupet, "What to Do with the Sheep in Wolf's Clothing: The Role of Rhetoric and Reality About Youth Offenders in the Constructive Dismantling of the Juvenile Justice System," *Pennsylvania Law Review 148*(4), pp. 1303–1304.
35. Ibid.
36. *Social Work Speaks*, 7th ed. (NASW Policy Statements, 2006–2009), pp. 67–70.
37. K. Strutin, "Criminal Justice Resources: Juvenile Law and Family Court Resources, 2006," retrieved January 31, 2008, from http://www.llrx.com/features/juvenilelaw.htm.
38. "About the National Council of Juvenile and Family Court Judges," retrieved January 31, 2008, from http://www.ncjfcj.org/content/view/15/75/.
39. "The Right Model for Juvenile Justice," *New York Times* (October 28, 2007).
40. National Clearinghouse on Families and Youth, *Report of the Analysis of Federal Youth Development Programming* (November 1999).
41. "Reconnecting Youth & Community: A Youth Development Approach," retrieved January 31, 2008, from http://www.ncfy.com/publications/reconnect/approach.htm.
42. National Youth Violence Prevention Resource Center, "Youth Development as a Violence Intervention Model."
43. Retrieved August 2009 from www.ojjdp.ncjrs.org/pubs/implementing/balanced.html.
44. U.S. Department of Justice, National Institute on Justice (December 2007).
45. Leslie Acoca, "Investing in Girls: A 21st Century Strategy," *Juvenile Justice, 6*(1) (1999), p. 5.
46. *Girls' Coalition Newsletter 10*(1) (Fall 2002/ Winter 2003).
47. Ibid.
48. Howard Snyder and Melissa Sickmund, *Juvenile Offenders and Victims: 1999 National Report* (Washington, DC: Office of Juvenile Justice and Delinquency Prevention).
49. *Social Work Speaks*, 7th ed. (NASW Policy Statements, 2006–2009), pp. 67–70.
50. Ibid.
51. Ibid.
52. Ibid.
53. Ibid.
54. County of Santa Clara Web site, retrieved February 4, 2008, from http://www.sccgov.org/portal/site/scc/article.
55. Ibid.
56. Dina McDaniel, retrieved from Bureau of Prisons Inmate Home Page: "Inmate Matters," 1992, retrieved February 2, 2008, from http://www.bop.gov/inmate_programs/index.jsp#.
57. Ibid.
58. J. Petersilia, "Meeting the Challenge of Prisoner Reentry," *Journal of Community Corrections 13*(1) (2003), p. 29.
59. Bureau of Justice Statistics, 2007.
60. Ibid.
61. Petersilia, p. 29.
62. R. Fretz, "Step Down Programs: The Missing Link in Successful Inmate Reentry," *Corrections Today 67*(2) (2005), p. 102.
63. Ibid.
64. Ibid.
65. L. Couturier, F. Maue, and C. McVey, "Releasing Inmates with Mental Illness and Co-Occurring Disorders into the Community," *Corrections Today 67*(2) (2005), pp. 82–85.
66. Ibid.
67. "The Justice Project," retrieved February 9, 2008, from http://www.thejusticeproject.org/.

68. Ibid.
69. R. Uphoff, *Wisconsin Law Review*. "Convicting the Innocent: Aberration or Systemic Issue?" *Wisconsin Law Review*, Volume 2006, #2.
70. J.A. Beck and Robert Shumsky, 1997 A Comparison of Retained and Appointed Counsel in Cases of Capital Murder, retrieved from http://www.springerlink.com/content/p02quw2x172755g4/..
71. R. K. Warren, 2007 "Evidence -based Practices and State Sentencing Policy: Ten Policy Initiatives to Reduce Recidivism" 82 Indiana Law Journal 1307.
72. Ibid.
73. Bureau of Justice Assistance, Center for Program Evaluation, retrieved February 9, 2008, from http://www.ojp.usdoj.gov/BJA/evaluation/psi_cp/.
74. "Crime Prevention," retrieved February 9, 2008, from http://www.ojp.usdoj.gov/BJA/topics/crime_prevention.html
75. J. Brown, P. Unsinger, and H. More, *Law Enforcement and Social Welfare: The Emergency Response* (Springfield, IL: Charles Thomas, 1990).
76. I. Cannon, *On the Social Frontier of Medicine: Pioneering in Medical Social Service* (Cambridge, MA, Harvard University Press, 1923).
77. Brown, Unsinger, and More.
78. Inter-Professional Collaboration Training Project, *Modules for Inter-Professional Collaboration Program* (Fresno: California State University, 1997).
79. R. Palacio, "The Social Conditions of Children and Youth in the San Joaquin Valley" (Working Paper No. 3) (Fresno: Central California Center for Health and Human Services, California State University, 2001).
80. Ibid.
81. M. A. Lowe, J. Parks, and C. Tilkes, "Using Inter-Professional Collaboration to Restructure Detention Program Delivery," *Corrections Today* 65(2) (2003), pp. 70–73.
82. J. Graham and K. Barter, "Families in Society," *Journal of Contemporary Human Services* 80(1) (1999), pp. 6–13.
83. Lowe, Parks, and Tilkes.
84. Ibid.
85. A. B. Andrews, "Social Work Expert Testimony Regarding Mitigation in Capital Sentencing Proceedings," *Social Work* 36(5) (1991), pp. 440–445.

Quotes

Aristotle, *Politics*, (Benjamin Jowett, Trans., 1885), 2.7.
Leslie W. Wilkins and Ken Pease, quoted in Marc Mauer, *Race to Incarcerate* (New York: New Press, 1999), p. 39.
Michael Harrington, *The Other America: Poverty in the United States* (New York: Macmillan, 1962).
Fay Honey Knopp et al., *Instead of Prisons* (Syracuse, NY: Prison Research Education Action Project, 1976), p. 9.

Chapter 14

1. National Association of Social Workers (NASW), *Facts About Social Work and Aging*, retrieved February 21, 2010, from http://www.socialworkers.org/pressroom/swm2006/facts2.asp.
2. National Center for Health Statistics (NASW), *Health, United States, 2008 with Chartbook* (Hyattsville, MD: Author, 2009), retrieved June 26, 2009, from http://www.cdc.gov/nchs/fastats/older_americans.htm; About.com, *Census Offers Statistics on Older Americans*, retrieved June 28, 2008, from http://usgovinfo.about.com.
3. NASW, *Facts About Social Work and Aging*, retrieved February 21, 2010, from http://www.socialworkers.org/pressroom/swm2006/facts2.asp.
4. Joan T. Erber, *Aging and Older Adulthood* (Belmont, CA: Thomson Wadsworth, 2005), pp. 9–15.
5. Ibid.
6. Ibid.
7. Ada Mui and Suk-Young Kang, "Acculturation Stress and Depression Among Asian Immigrant Elders," *Social Work* 51(3) (2006), pp. 243–254; James Thorson, *Aging in a Changing Society*, 2nd ed. (Philadelphia, PA: Taylor & Francis, 2000); pp. 3–5; Erber, p. 419.
8. NASW, *Facts About Social Work and Aging*, retrieved February 21, 2010, from http://www.socialworkers.org/pressroom/swm2006/facts2.asp.
9. Robert L. Clark, Richard V. Burkhauser, Marilyn Moon, and Joseph F. Quinn, *The Economics of an Aging Society* (Malden, MA: Blackwell Publishing, Ltd., 2004), pp. 11–31.
10. Lewis R. Aiken, *Aging and Later Life: Growing Old in Modern Society* (Springfield, IL: Charles C. Thomas Publisher, Ltd., 2001), pp. 3–16.
11. Clark et al., pp. 11–31.
12. Aiken, pp. 3–16.
13. Ibid.
14. Nancy R. Hooyman and H. Asuman Kiyak, *Social Gerontology: A Multidisciplinary Perspective*, 7th ed. (New York: Pearson, 2005), pp. 142–151; Aiken, pp. 3–16.
15. National Association of Social Workers (NASW), *Facts About Social Work and Aging*, retrieved February 21, 2010, from http://www.socialworkers.org/pressroom/swm2006/facts2.asp.
16. Charles Zastrow, *Introduction to Social Work and Social Welfare: An Empowering Approach.* (Belmont, CA: Thomson Brooks/Cole Publishing Co., 2004), pp. 474–501.
17. Hooyman and Kiyak, pp. 65–100; Zastrow, pp. 474–501.
18. Not that the media is totally misleading. See Laura Katz Olson, *The Not-So-Golden Years: Caregiving, the Frail Elderly, and the Long-Term Care Establishment* (New York: Rowman and Littlefield Publishers, 2003).
19. Clark et al., pp. 38–48; 137–156.
20. Ibid., pp. 154–156.
21. Ibid., pp. 138–145.
22. See The New Strategist Editors, *Older Americans: A Changing Marker* (Ithaca, NY: Strategist Publications, 2004).
23. Zastrow, pp. 474–501.
24. Aiken, pp. 52–75.
25. Centers for Disease Control and Prevention and the Merck Company Foundation, *The State of Aging and Health in America 2007* (Whitehouse Station, NJ: The Merck Company Foundation), retrieved April 13, 2007, from http://www.cdc.gov/aging.
26. AARP, *Bulletin Today*, retrieved June 28, 2008, from http://aarp.org; Aiken, pp. 52–75.
27. Marty Davis and Johnnie Prather (Eds.), "Brand-Name Drug Prices Climb Again in 2006, *AARP Watchdog Report* 4(2), retrieved April 13, 2007, from http://.assets.aarp.org/www.aarp.org_/cs/elec/watchdog_march_2007.pdf.
28. Ibid.
29. Victor R. Fuchs, "Health Care for the Elderly: How Much? Who Will Pay for It?" *Health Affairs* 18(1) (2007), pp. 11–21.

30. Aiken, pp. 262–264; see also Elizabeth Vierck and Kris Hodges, *Aging: Lifestyles, Work, and Money* (Westport, CT: Greenwood Press, 2005).
31. Aiken, pp. 262–264.
32. Kathleen McInnis-Dittrich, *Social Work with Elders: A Biopsychosocial Approach to Assessment and Intervention*, 2nd ed. (New York: Pearson, 2005), pp. 30–41; Hooyman and Kiyak, pp. 109–139, 164–182; Aiken, pp. 262–264.
33. Thorson, p. 51.
34. Aiken, pp. 262–264.
35. NASW, *Facts About Social Work and Aging*, retrieved February 21, 2010, from http://www.socialworkers.org/pressroom/swm2006/facts2.asp.
36. Erber, pp. 392–395.
37. Aiken, pp. 259–260; Erber, pp. 392–402.
38. Ibid.
39. Aiken, pp. 259–260; Olson, pp. 102–119.
40. Olson, pp. 102–119.
41. National Alliance for Caregiving, *Caregiving in the United States* (Bethesda, MD: Metlife Foundation), retrieved April 14, 2007, from http://www.caregiving.org/data/04execsumm.pdf.
42. NASW, *Facts About Social Work and Aging*, retrieved February 21, 2010, from http://www.socialworkers.org/pressroom/swm2006/facts2.asp.
43. L. Renee Bergeron, "Self-Determination and Elder Abuse: Do We Know Enough?" *Journal of Gerontological Social Work 46*(3/4) (2006), pp. 81–102.
44. Ibid.
45. Ibid.
46. Aiken, pp. 286–290.
47. Ibid.
48. Olson, pp. 108–119; Catherine Hawes, *Elder Abuse in Residential Long-Term Care Facilities: What Is Known About the Prevalence, Causes, and Prevention*, testimony before the U.S. Senate Committee on Finance, June 12, 2002.
49. Aiken, pp. 286–290; Erber, pp. 363–367.
50. Olson, pp. 68–71.
51. NASW, *Facts About Social Work and Aging*, retrieved February 21, 2010, from http://www.socialworkers.org/pressroom/swm2006/facts2.asp.
52. Erber, pp. 459–466.
53. Ibid.
54. Mitch Albom, *Tuesdays with Morrie* (New York: Doubleday, 1997), p. 64.
55. Erber, pp. 454–456.
56. Zastrow, pp. 491–493; Erber, pp. 454–456.
57. Erber, pp. 454–456.
58. Aiken, pp. 304–329.
59. Ibid.
60. Zastrow, pp. 491–493.
61. Aiken, pp. 304–329.
62. Erber, pp. 118–119, 458.
63. See Nancy Morrow-Howell, Melinda Carden, and Michael Sherraden, *Volunteerism, Philanthropy, and Service*, in Lenard W. Kaye (Ed.), *Perspectives on Productive Aging: Social Work with the New Aged* (Washington, DC: NASW Press, 2005), pp. 83–106.
64. Ibid.
65. Ibid., p. 87.
66. James W. Ellor, *Spiritual and Religious Growth*, in Lenard W. Kaye (Ed.), *Perspectives on Productive Aging: Social Work with the New Aged* (Washington, DC: NASW Press, 2005), pp. 149–162.
67. Bruce S. Jansson, *The Reluctant Welfare State: American Social Welfare Policies—Past, Present, and Future*, 5th ed. (Belmont, CA: Thomson Brooks/Cole, 2005), pp. 197–202.
68. Social Security Administration, *Budget*, retrieved June 18, 2008, from www.ssa.gov/budget/FactCard2009.pdf.
69. Clark et al., pp. 38–43.
70. Jansson, pp. 247–249.
71. Erber, p. 118; Clark et al., pp. 280–284.
72. AARP, *AARP Member Resources* (Washington, DC), retrieved April 20, 2007, from http://www.aarp.org.
73. Ibid.
74. Ibid.
75. Cynthia Moniz and Stephen Gorin, *Health and Healthcare Policy: A Social Work Perspective* (Boston, MA: Allyn & Bacon, 2003).
76. Erber, p. 119.
77. Katz Olson, pp. 45–47.
78. Erber, pp. 392–401.
79. Ibid.
80. Ibid.
81. Aiken, pp. 258–259.
82. Thorson, pp. 269–273.
83. Aiken, pp. 259–260; Thorson, pp. 269–273.
84. Kaye, p. 42; Thorson, pp. 382–393.
85. Zastrow, pp. 474–501.
86. Ibid.
87. Ibid.
88. Jerry D. Marx, personal interview with Edie McCaddin-Bower on May 17, 2008.
89. Jansson, p. 338.
90. U.S. Administration on Aging, *Celebrate Long-Term Living: Annual Report 2005* (Washington, DC: U.S. Department of Health and Human Services, 2005).
91. Ibid.
92. National Center on Elder Abuse, *Adult Protective Services* (Washington, DC: U.S. Administration on Aging, Department of Health and Human Services), retrieved April 16, 2007, from http://www.elderabusecenter.org/.
93. AARP, *AARP History*, retrieved February 22, 2010, from www.aarp.org/aarp/About_AARP/.
94. Ibid.
95. Gray Panthers, *Gray Panthers: Age and Youth in Action* (Washington, DC: The Gray Panthers), retrieved April 8, 2007, from http://www.graypanthers.org.

Quotes

Bronson Alcott, in Ralph Waldo Emerson, journal, 1845, undated.

Simone de Beauvoir, "Conclusion," *Coming of Age* (Patrick O'Brian, Trans.), 1970/1973.

The Bratzlaver.

Sir Arthur Conan Doyle, *The Brown Hand*, retrieved February 15, 2010, from http://www.litquotes.com/quote_topic_resp.php?QuoteType=Aging&Amazon=Aging.

Chapter 15

1. Amartyra Sen, *Development as Freedom* (New York: Anchor Books, 2000), p. 8.
2. Thomas L. Friedman, *The Lexus and the Olive Tree: Understanding Globalization* (New York: Anchor Books, 2006), p. 9.
3. Ibid., p. 63.
4. Thomas L. Friedman, *The World Is Flat* (New York: Picador, 2007), pp. 9–11.

5. Ibid.
6. Ibid.
7. Bruce S. Jansson, *The Reluctant Welfare State: American Social Welfare Policies—Past, Present and Future,* 5th ed. (Belmont, CA: Wadsworth/Thomson Learning, 2005), pp. 112–113; Ron Chernow, *Titan: The Life of John D. Rockefeller, Sr.* (New York: Vintage Books, 2004), pp. 98–99; Steven Rosefielde, *Comparative Economic Systems: Culture, Wealth, and Power* (Malden, MA: Blackwell, 2002), p. 82.
8. Jansson, pp. 112–118.
9. Ibid.
10. Jansson, pp. 166–168
11. Ibid.
12. Friedman, 2007, pp. 9–11.
13. Jansson, p. 420.
14. Friedman, 2006, p. 59.
15. Jansson, p. 420.
16. Friedman, 2006, pp. 8–9.
17. Jansson, pp. 317–318; Lou Cannon, *President Reagan: The Role of a Lifetime* (New York: Public Affairs, 2000), p. 8.
18. Friedman, 2006, p. 59.
19. Jansson, p. 420.
20. Rosefielde, pp. 182–191.
21. Jeffrey D. Sachs, *The End of Poverty: Economic Possibilities for Our Time* (New York: Penguin, 2005), p. 26.
22. Ibid., p. 31.
23. Ibid., p. 47.
24. Ibid., p. 47.
25. Ibid., p. 49.
26. See Samuel P. Huntington. *The Clash of Civilizations and the Remaking of World Order* (New York: Simon & Schuster, 1996).
27. Sachs, pp. 170–187; *Commanding Heights: The Battle for the World Economy,* on Disc 3 of *The New Rules of the Game* (DVD) (Boston, MA: Height Productions and WGBH, 2003).
28. *Commanding New Heights.*
29. Ibid.
30. Barbara Kiviat, "Getting to the Top," *Time* 170(22) (November 26, 2007), p. 61.
31. Joseph Stiglitz, *Globalization and Its Discontents,* (New York: Norton, 2003), p. 10.
32. Sachs, pp. 148–169.
33. *Commanding Heights*; Robert Reich, *Supercapitalism: The Transformation of Business, Democracy, and Everyday Life* (New York: Knopf, 2007), p. 4.
34. Steven Johnson, *The Ghost Map* (New York: the Penguin Group, 2006), p. 231.
35. Charles Fishman, *The Wal-Mart Effect: How the World's Most Powerful Company Really Works—And How It's Transforming the American Economy* (New York: Penguin, 2006), p. 103.
36. Greg Spotts, *Wal-Mart: The High Cost of a Low Price* (documentary film) (New York: The Disinformation Company, 2005).
37. Stiglitz, p. 4.
38. Friedman, 2006, pp. 327–364.
39. Huntington, pp. 40–48.
40. Ibid., pp. 74–78.
41. Friedman, 2006, pp. 296–301.
42. Jansson, pp. 479–481.
43. Fishman, pp. 4–9, 151.
44. Ibid., p. 151.
45. Spotts.
46. "Wal-Mart Fails to Halt Suit," *Boston Globe*, December 12, 2007, p. C4.
47. Fishman, pp. 183–184.
48. Ibid., pp. 9–12, 145.
49. Benjamin Barger, *Community Values and Globalization* (CBS Audio, 2003); Jansson, pp. 49–55, 92–98.
50. See Noam Chomsky et al., *Monkeywrenching the New World Order: Global Capitalism and Its Discontents* (Oakland, CA: AK Press, 2001).
51. Stiglitz, p. 7.
52. Ibid., p. 9.
53. Ibid., pp. 6–7.
54. Stephanie Black, *Life and Debt* (video recording) (New York: New York Video, 2001).
55. See Chomsky et al.
56. Ibid.
57. See Korten, 1995; Christopher Lasch, *The Revolt of the Elites and the Betrayal of Democracy* (New York, Norton, 1995).
58. Jansson, pp. 166–187.
59. Stiglitz, p. 11; Korten, p. 136.
60. Stiglitz, p. 11.
61. Ibid., p. 12.
62. Ibid., pp. 18–20.
63. *Commanding Heights.*
64. See Chomsky et al.
65. Paul Kennedy, *Preparing for the Twenty-First Century* (New York: Vintage, 1994), p. 56.
66. Lynne M. Healy, *International Social Work: Professional Action in an Interdependent World,* 2nd ed. (New York: Oxford University Press, 2008), p. 10.
67. International Federation of Social Workers (IFSW), retrieved January 4, 2008, from www.icsw.org.
68. Michal E. Mor Barak, "The Inclusive Workplace: An Ecosystems Approach to Diversity Management," *Social Work* 45(4) (2000), pp. 339–352.
69. Sachs, p. 266.
70. International Council on Social Welfare, *Our Members,* retrieved February 22, 2010, from www.icsw.org/intro/ourmembe.htm.
71. Sachs, p. 286.
72. See Bill Clinton, *Giving: How Each of Us Can Change the World* (New York: Knopf, 2007).
73. Sachs, 2005, pp. 288–289.
74. Ibid.
75. Ibid.
76. Jill J. Henderson, "U.S. Army Social Work Care Manager Program: An Initial Program Analysis," *Military Medicine* 172 (2007), pp. 533–538.
77. National Association of Social Workers (NASW), *International Social Work,* retrieved January 4, 2008, from www.socialworkers.org.

Quotes

Muhammad Yunus, *Creating a World Without Poverty: Small Business and the Future of Capitalism* (New York: Public Affairs, 2007), p. 223.

Rosamund Stone Zander and Benjamin Zander, *The Art of Possibility* (London: Penguin Books, 2002), p. 19.

Paul Collier, *The Bottom Billion: Why the Poorest Countries Are Failing and What Can Be Done About It* (New York: Oxford University Press USA, 2007), p. 191.

Chapter 16

1. Diana M. DiNitto, *Social Welfare: Politics and Public Policy*, 6th ed. (Boston: Pearson Education, 2007), pp. 5–19; Bruce S. Jansson, *Becoming an Effective Policy Advocate: From Policy Practice to Social Justice*, 5th ed. (Belmont, CA: Thomson Brooks/Cole, 2008), pp. 216–252.
2. Jansson, pp. 220–222, 248–252; Nancy M. Henley, "Women as a Social Problem: Conceptual and Practical Issues in Defining Social Problems," in Edward Seidman and Julian Rappaport (Eds.), *Redefining Social Problems* (New York: Plenum Press, 1986), pp. 65–79.
3. Ibid.
4. Associated Press, "Antiterrorism Efforts Are Faulted," *New York Times* (November 29, 2007), p. 28, retrieved June 30, 2008, from EBSCOHOST, Academic Search Premier, http://web.ebscohost.com.
5. Henley, p. 70.
6. Ian Fisher, Laurie Goodstein, Neela Banerjee, Abby Goodnough, and Katie Zezima, "Benedict Meets with the Victims of Sexual Abuse," *New York Times* (April 18, 2008), p. 1, retrieved June 30, 2008, from EBSCOHOST, Academic Search Premier, http://web.ebscohost.com.
7. Henley, p. 71.
8. Bruce S. Jansson, *The Reluctant Welfare State: American Social Welfare Policies—Past, Present and Future*, 5th ed. (Belmont, CA: Wadsworth/Thomson Learning, 2005), pp. 168–187.
9. Henley, pp. 71–72.
10. Anuj Chopra, "Indian Women Tap New Protection Against Domestic Violence," *Christian Science Monitor* 99(70) (March 8, 2007), p. 12, retrieved June 30, 2008, from EBSCOHOST, Academic Search Premier, http://web.ebscohost.com.
11. Henley, pp. 72–73.
12. Ibid., p. 73.
13. Jansson, 2005, pp. 236–242.
14. Jansson, 2008, pp. 343–478; Margaret Dietz Domanski, "Prototypes of Social Work Political Participation: An Empirical Model," *Social Work* 43(2) (1998), pp. 156–167.
15. Ralph Dolgoff and Donald Feldstein, *Understanding Social Welfare: A Search for Social Justice*, 7th ed. (Boston: Pearson Education, 2007), pp. 152–153; Howard J. Karger and David Stoecz, *American Social Welfare Policy: A Pluralist Approach*, 5th (Boston: Pearson Education, 2008), p. 18.
16. Dolgoff and Feldstein, p. 152; Karger and Stoecz, p. 18.
17. Dolgoff and Feldstein, pp. 152–153.
18. Ibid., p. 153; John Rawls, *A Theory of Justice* (Cambridge, MA: Belknap Press, 1971).
19. National Association of Social Workers (NASW), *Social Justice*, retrieved June 26, 2009, from http://www.socialworkers.org/pressroom/features/issue/peace.asp; Dolgoff and Feldstein, pp. 11–12.
20. Jan L. Hagan and Liane V. Davis, "Working with Women: Building a Policy and Practice Agenda," *Social Work* 37(6) (1992), pp. 495–502.
21. Library of Congress, *Thomas*, retrieved from February 17, 2010, from http://thomas.loc.gov.
22. For example, see http://www.nh.gov/.
23. NASW, *Legislative Advocacy Network*, retrieved February 17, 2010, from http://www.socialworkers.org/advocacy/default.asp.
24. Jansson, 2008, pp. 111–152, 258–260.
25. Dennis Saleebey, *The Strengths Perspective in Social Work Practice*, 4th ed. (Boston: Pearson, 2006); Rosemary Kennedy Chapin, "Social Policy Development: The Strengths Perspective," *Social Work* 40(4) (1995), pp. 506–513.
26. Jansson, 2008, pp. 185–213.
27. Jansson, 2005, pp. 247–249.
28. DiNitto, pp. 5–19; Jansson, 2008, pp. 185–213.
29. Jansson, 2005, pp. 247–249.
30. Ibid., pp. 333–335.
31. Ibid., pp. 326–330, 333–335.
32. "Taxpayers Can't Fight Plan Allowing Federal Funds for Religious Charities, *USA Today* (June 26, 2007), p. 2a, retrieved June 30, 2008, from EBSCOHOST, Academic Search Premier, http://web.ebscohost.com.
33. S. Hawranick, J. M. Doris, and R. Daugherty, R., "Alice Paul: Activist, Advocate, and One of Ours," *Affilia* 23 (2008), p. 2; J. H. Baker, J. H., *Sisters: The Lives of America's Suffragists* (New York: Hill and Wang, 2005).
34. Jansson, 2008, pp. 390–405; John W. Kingdon, *Agendas, Alternatives, and Public Policies* (New York: HarperCollins, 1984), p. 152, 174, 187.
35. Jansson, 2005, pp. 247–249.
36. Karen S. Haynes and James S. Mickelson, *Affecting Change: Social Workers in the Political Arena* (Boston: Allyn & Bacon, 2003), pp. 122–123.
37. National Coalition for the Homeless, "About NCH," retrieved February 17, 2010, from http://www.nationalhomeless.org/.
38. NASW, *Legislative Advocacy Network*, retrieved February 17, 2010, from http://www.socialworkers.org/advocacy/default.asp.
39. See NASW's Media Listserve, retrieved February 17 2010 from http://www.socialworkers.org/pressroom/media/mediaListserve.asp#.
40. NASW, *Legislative Advocacy Network*.
41. Ibid.
42. Ibid.
43. Rawls, p. 3.
44. Jansson, 2005, pp. 75–81.
45. Phyllis F. Day, *A New History of Social Welfare*, 5th ed. (Boston: Pearson Education, 2006), pp. 196–199, 221–224, 271–272; Jansson, 2005, pp. 99–111; 144–152.
46. Day, pp. 256–276; Jansson, 2005, pp. 124–156.
47. Day, pp. 229–232; Jansson, 2005, pp. 124–156.
48. Day, pp. 225–228; Jansson, 2005, p. 218.
49. Day, pp. 293–302; DiNitto, pp. 39–45; Jansson, 2005, pp. 197–202.
50. Day, pp. 292–293; Jansson, 2005, pp. 218–220.
51. Jansson, 2005, pp. 245–252; Day, pp. 335–352.
52. Ibid.
53. Ibid.
54. Ibid.
55. Joseph A. Califano, Jr., *The Triumph and Tragedy of Lyndon Johnson: The White House Years* (College Station: Texas A&M University Press, 2000), p. 58; Jansson, 2005, pp. 245–252.

Quotes

Jeffrey D. Sachs, *The End of Poverty: Economic Possibilities for Our Time* (New York: Penguin, 2005), p. 1.

Thomas L. Friedman, *The Lexus and the Olive Tree: Understanding Globalization* (New York: Farrar, Straus, and Giroux, 2000), p. 449.

Muhammad Yunus, *Creating a World Without Poverty: Small Business and the Future of Capitalism*. New York: Public Affairs, 2007), p. 5.

Text Credits

Chapter 1

From "A Meaningful Path" by Michael Pesce et al. from THE CALL TO SOCIAL WORK: LIFE STORIES by Craig Winston LeCroy. (Sage Publications, 2002). Copyright © 2002 by Sage Publications, Inc. Reprinted by permission.

From "A Passion for Justice" by Hannah Freese et al. from THE CALL TO SOCIAL WORK: LIFE STORIES by Craig Winston LeCroy. (Sage Publications, 2002). Copyright © 2002 by Sage Publications, Inc. Reprinted by permission.

Excerpts from NASW Code of Ethics from the preamble and page 4 as found on http://www.socialworkers.org/pibs/code/code/asp. Copyrighted material reprinted with permission from the National Association of Social Workers, Inc.

Source: http://www.ifsw.org/f38000138.html

Council on Social Work Education, From "2008 Educational Policy and Accreditation Standards" (Alexandria, VA: Council on Social Work Education, Inc., 2008), p. 1. http://www.cswe.org/File.aspx?id=13780. Reprinted by permission.

Excerpts from pp. 22, 124-125, 139-140, 153 in GROWING UP EMPTY by Loretta Schwartz-Nobel. Copyright © 2002 by Loretta Schwartz-Nobel. Reprinted by permission of HarperCollins Publishers and the author.

"Jobs for Unskilled Workers" from the book Nickel and Dimed: On (Not) Getting By in America by Barbara Ehrenreich. Copyright © 2001 by Barbara Ehrenreich. Reprinted by arrangement with Henry Holt and Company, LLC. and International Creative Management, Inc.

Chapter 2

Based on Bronfenbrenner's ecological model.

Excerpts from NASW Code of Ethics from the preamble and page 4 as found on http:www.socialworkers.org/pibs/code/code/asp. Copyrighted material reprinted with permission from the National Association of Social Workers, Inc.

The Council on Social Work Education outlines the areas of focus for HBSE courses footnote 3, Source:" 2008 Educaitonal Policy and Accreditation Standards" Alexandria, VA Council on Social Work Education,Inc., 2008) p. 9. Reprinted by permission.

Print use only credit: Figure of Erickson's Stages of Personality Development from CHILDHOOD AND SOCIETY by Erik H. Erickson. Copyright © 1950, © 1963 by W.W. Norton & Company, Inc., renewed © 1978, 1991 by Erik H. Erickson. Used by permission of W.W. Norton & Company, Inc. and The Hogarth Press c/o The Random House Group Ltd.

From Van Wormer. Introduction to Social Welfare and Social Work, I/e. Copyright © 2006 Wadsworth, a part of Cengage Learniing, Inc. Reproduced by permission. www.cengage.com/permissions

Chapter 3

From SOCIAL WELFARE: CHARITY TO JUSTICE by John M. Romanyshyn and Annie L. Romanyshyn (Random House, 1971).

Thomas L. Friedman, THE LEXUS AND THE OLIVE TREE (New York: Farrar Straus & Giroux, LLC, 1999), p. 9.

Copyright © 2007 LexisNexis, a division of Reed Elsevier Inc. All rights reserved. LexisNexis and the Knowledge Burst logo are registered trademarks of Reed Elsevier Properties Inc. and are used with the permission of LexisNexis.

Chapter 4

Reprinted with permission from the publisher of More Days in the Lives of Social Workers by Linda May Grobman. Copyright © 2005. Reprinted by permission of White Hat Communications.

Excerpts from NASW Code of Ethics from the preamble and page 4 as found on http:www.socialworkers.org/pibs/code/code/asp. Copyrighted material reprinted with permission from the National Association of Social Workers, Inc.

Webster's New World College Dictionary, 4th ed. Copyright © 2000 by John Wiley & Sons, Inc. Reproduced with permission of John Wiley & Sons, Inc.

Excerpts from NASW Code of Ethics from the preamble and page 4 as found on http:www.socialworkers.org/pibs/code/code/asp. Copyrighted material reprinted with permission from the National Association of Social Workers, Inc.

Reprinted with permission from the publisher of More Days in the Lives of Social Workers by Linda May Grobman. Copyright © 2005. Reprinted by permission of White Hat Communications.

Excerpts from NASW Code of Ethics from the preamble and page 4 as found on http:www.socialworkers.org/pibs/code/code/asp. Copyrighted material reprinted with permission from the National Association of Social Workers, Inc.

Chapter 5

Excerpts from NASW Code of Ethics from the preamble and page 4 as found on http:www.socialworkers.org/pibs/code/code/asp. Copyrighted material reprinted with permission from the National Association of Social Workers, Inc.

Same Sex Marriage Position Statement. June 28, 2004. http://www.socialworkers.org/diversity/lgb/062804.asp?print=1. Copyrighted material reprinted with permission from the National Association of Social Workers, Inc.

From Toward a New Psychology of Women by Jean Baker Miller, published by Beacon Press. Copyright © 1986 by Beacon Press. Reproduced with permission of Beacon Press via Copyright Clearance Center and by permission of the agent, Sheil Land Associates Ltd.

From Why Are All the Black Kids Sitting Together in the Cafeteria? by Beverly Daniel Tatum. Copyright © 2003 by Beverly Tatum. Reprinted by permission of Basic Books, a member of the Perseus Books Group.

From Readings for Diversity and Social Justice: An Anthology on Racism, Sexism, Classism, Anti-Semitism, Heterosexism, and Ableism by Heather Hackman. Copyright © 2000 by Taylor&Franics Group LLC. Books. Reproduced by permission of the publisher via Copyright Clearance Center.

Used courtesy of Teaching Tolerance. All rights reserved. www.tolerance.org

Excerpts from NASW Code of Ethics from the preamble and page 4 as found on http:www.socialworkers.org/pibs/code/code/asp. Copyrighted material reprinted with permission from the National Association of Social Workers, Inc.

Chapter 7

Source: Matthew Fellowes, "From Poverty, Opportunity: Putting the Market to Work for Lower Income Families," (Washington, DC: Brookings Institution, July 2006). pp. 6–7. Reprinted by permission.

Text adapted from "Integrating Anti-Poverty Work into Domestic Violence Advocacy: Iowa's Experience" by Amy Coreia and Katie M. Ciroba VonDeLinde from Building Comprehensive Solutions to Domestic Violence, Publication # 17 (National Resource Center on Domestic Violence).

Chapter 8

Michael M.O. Seipel. From "Social Burden of Obesity on U.S. Adults," Journal of Health and Social Work vol. 20, issue 2 (2005). Reprinted by permission of the publisher, Taylor & Francis, Ltd. http://www.informaworld.com).

Excerpts from NASW Code of Ethics from the preamble and page 4 as found on http://www.socialworkers.org/pibs/code/code/asp. Copyrighted material reprinted with permission from the National Association of Social Workers, Inc.

D. Oswald, J. Bodurtha, J. Willis & M.Moore. "Underinsurance and Key Health Outcomes for Children With Special Healthcare Needs," Pediatrics, 119, pp. 341–347 (2007).

Copyrighted and published by Project HOPE/Health Affairs as Victor Fuchs, "What are the Prospects for Enduring Comprehensive Healthcare Reform?" Health Affairs 26, no. 6, pp. 1542–1544 (2007) p. 1542.

From V. Marshall & M. Altpeter. "Cultivating Social Work Leadership in Health Promotion and Aging: Strategies for Active Aging Interventions", Health and Social Work 30, pp. 135–144 (2005). Copyrighted material reprinted with permission from the National Association of Social Workers, Inc.

Chapter 9

Reprinted with permission from the Diagnostic and Statistical Manual of Mental Disorders. Text Revision, Fourth Edition, copyright © 2000. American Psychiatric Association.

Chapter 10

Excerpts from NASW Code of Ethics from the preamble and page 4 as found on http://www.socialworkers.org/pibs/code/code/asp. Copyrighted material reprinted with permission from the National Association of Social Workers, Inc.

From SOCIAL WORK WITH FAMILIES by Robert Constable and Daniel B. Lee (Lyceum Books 2004). Reprinted by permission of the publisher.

Chapter 12

From Drinking: A Love Story by Caroline Knapp, copyright © 1995 by Caroline Knapp. Used by permission of Dial Press/Dell Publishing, a division of Random House, Inc.

Courtesy of Brian Miller.

Chapter 15

From Sen Amartya, Development as Freedom. Copyright © 1999 by Amartya Sen. First published by Alfred A. Knopf, a division of Random House, Inc.

"The Spread of Economic Prosperity" from THE END OF POVERTY by Jeffrey D. Sachs, copyright © 2005 by Jeffrey D. Sachs. Used by permission of The Penguin Press, a division of Penguin Group (USA) Inc. and Penguin Books Ltd.

print only credit: From GLOBALIZATION AND ITS DISCONTENTS by Joseph E.Stiglitz. Copyright © 2002 by Joseph E.Stiglitz. Used by permisison of W.W. Norton & Company, Inc. and Allen Lane, Penguin Books Ltd. SEE COMMENT FOR ELECTRONIC CREDIT

Source: The International Council on Social Welfare. Our Members. http://www.icsw.org/intro/ourmembe.htm

Excerpts from International Social Work as found on http://www.socialworkers.org/pubs/choices/choices2.asp. Copyrighted material reprinted with permission from the National Association of Social Workers, Inc.

Chapter 16

Reprinted by permission of the publisher from A Theory of Justice by John Rawls, p. 3. Cambridge, Mass: The Belknap Press of Harvard University Press, Copyright © 1971, 1999 by the President and Fellows of Harvard College.

Photo Credits

Chapter 1
Tony Freeman/PhotoEdit, Inc. p. 1; Ariel Skelley/Corbis, p. 8

Chapter 2
Tony Freeman/PhotoEdit, Inc. 28; Nick Ut/AP Photo, p. 41

Chapter 3
Martin H. Simon/Corbis, p. 49; Jim Commentucci/Syracuse Newspapers/The Image Works, p. 59

Chapter 4
Bob Daemmrich/The Image Works, p. 62; Peter Byron/PhotoEdit, Inc. p. 78

Chapter 5
Tom&Dee Ann McCarthy/Corbis, p. 86; Michael Newman/PhotoEdit, Inc. p. 103

Chapter 6
Bettmann/Corbis, p. 114; Bettmann/Corbis, p. 126

Chapter 7
Mario Tama/Getty Images, p. 139; David M. Grossman/The Image Works, p. 161

Chapter 8
Ed Kashi/Corbis, p. 165; Michael A. Keller/Corbis, p. 183

Chapter 9
Morgan David de Lossy/Corbis, p. 188; Esbin-Anderson/The Image Works, p. 208

Chapter 10
Bob Daemmrich/The Image Works, p. 214; Paul Costello, p. 233

Chapter 11
Don Emmert/AFP/Getty Images, p. 233; Michael Newman/PhotoEdit, Inc. p. 264

Chapter 12
Indexopen, p. 268; Harry Choi/TongRo/Corbis, p. 285

Chapter 13
Christina Barany/Getty Images, p. 291; Sean Cayton/The Image Works, p. 304

Chapter 14
David Sacks, p. 315; Alamy, p. 329

Chapter 15
Alamy, p. 334; Sean Adair/Corbis, p. 340

Chapter 16
Jeff Greenberg/PhotoEdit, Inc., p. 353; Michael Newman/PhotoEdit, Inc., p. 367

Index

AAP. *See* American Academy of Pediatrics
AARP. *See* American Association of Retired Persons
Abbott, Edith, 371
Abbott, Grace, 371
Ableism, 108–109
Absolute poverty, 140–141
ACOA. *See* Adult children of alcoholics
ACT. *See* Assertive Community Treatment
Activism, American, 51
"Activist" role, 4
Acton, John Dalberg, 100
ADA. *See* Americans with Disabilities Act
Adaptation, 45
ADD. *See* Attention Deficit Disorder
Addams, Jane, 31, 120, 122–123, 371
ADHD. *See* Attention Deficit Hyperactivity Disorder
Administration careers, 9–10
Adolescent-mother pair study, 6. *See also* Children
Adolescent pregnancy, 94, 157, 172–173, 183, 233–234, 240, 270
Adoption, 2, 25, 231–232
Adoption and Safe Families Act (1997) (ASFA), 231
Adult children of alcoholics (ACOA), 280
Adult protective services, 6, 50
Advocacy
  "advocate" role, 4, 78, 185, 358–359, 372
  for gerontology services, 332–333
  social advocacy of women, 121–123, 370–371
  for social and economic justice, 360–361
  strengths-based approach to policy advocacy, 363–364
Advocates for Healthy Youth (AFHY), 185
Afghanistan, war in, 210, 343, 351. *See also* Veterans
AFHY. *See* Advocates for Healthy Youth
African Americans, 89, 105, 144–145, 206, 271
  Civil Rights Acts, 371
  civil rights movement, 92–93, 129–130, 133, 295–296, 358
  incarceration rates, 277, 294–296
  poverty by education level/race/gender, 150
African immigrants, 93

Aftercare, 283–285
Ageism, 319–320. *See also* Gerontological services
Agency level
  field practicum at, 22, 24–25
  interagency collaboration, 9, 162, 185–186, 211, 265
Agenda building, 364
AIDS/HIV. *See* Human Immunodeficiency Virus
Al-Anon (family members of substance abusers), 280
Alaskan Native peoples, 145, 271
Alateen (family members of substance abusers), 280
Alborn, Mitch, 326
Albuquerque, New Mexico, 71
Alcoholics Anonymous (AA), 4, 91, 280–282. *See also* Wellbriety Movement
Alcoholism, 154, 272, 287
  AA, 4, 91, 280–282
  driving under the influence, 273–274
  fetal alcohol syndrome, 270–271
Alcott, Bronson, 318
ALS. *See* Amyotrophic lateral sclerosis
Altpeter, M., 184
Alzheimer's disease, 183, 196
AMA. *See* American Medical Association
American Academy of Pediatrics (AAP), 273
American Association of Retired Persons (AARP), 323, 328, 333–334
American Medical Association (AMA), 280
American Psychiatric Association (APA), 194
American Recovery and Reinvestment Act (2009), 178–179
American Red Cross, 4, 51, 351
Americans with Disabilities Act (ADA), 97, 108–109, 135, 258
  2008 amendment to, 255
Amnesia, 196
Amnesty International, 370
Amok culture-bound syndrome, 200
Amyotrophic lateral sclerosis (ALS), 251–252
Angelou, Maya, 66
Anglicans, 116
Annapolis, Maryland, 4
Anorexia, 198
Anthony, Susan B., 371
Antidepressant medication, 191

Anti-immigration sentiment, 94
Anti-Pauper Movement, 117–118
Antisocial personality disorder, 199
Anxiety/arousal levels, 33. *See also* Stress
Anxiety disorders, 197
APA. *See* American Psychiatric Association
Area Agencies on Aging, 332
Aristotle, 293
Army Care Manager Program, 351
Artemis Program, 305
ASDs. *See* Autism Spectrum Disorders
ASFA. *See* Adoption and Safe Families Act
Asian Americans, 89, 94–95, 144–145, 325
  poverty by education level/race/gender, 150
  tobacco usage, 271
"Asian Model" of globalization, 341
Assertive Community Treatment (ACT), 211
Assessment, of data, 68–73, 79–80, 202
Assimilation, 91
Assisted living facility, 329–330
Asthma, 169
Astor, Ron Avi, 303
Atkinson, Brooks, 154
Attention Deficit Disorder (ADD), 196
Attention Deficit Hyperactivity Disorder (ADHD), 196, 250
Autism Spectrum Disorders (ASDs), 196
Autonomy *v.* shame and doubt stage, 34
Avoidant personality disorder, 199

Baby boomers, 319
Baccalaureate degree in social work (BSW), 22, 24–25, 189
Baldacci, John, 179
Banfield, Edward, 153
Baptists, 116
Baylor University Hospital, 171
Beers, Clifford, 190, 204
Behavior regression, 81
Bell, Alexander Graham, 253
Bell hooks. *See* Watkins, Gloria Jean
Bereavement, 325
Bernard, Jesse, 220
Bertalanffy, Ludwig von, 42
BIA. *See* Bureau of Indian Affairs
Bicameral legislature, 55
Big Brothers, 51
Big Sisters, 51
Binge drinking, 273–274

Binge-eating disorder, 198
Biological domain, 32–33
Biopsychosocial model, 29, 31–32, 278
Birthrates, 89
Blaming the victim, disability perspective, 243
Blended families, 221
Blind spots, 101
Block grants, 131, 135, 157
BLS. *See* Bureau of Labor Statistics
Bodurtha, J., 176
Boise, Idaho, 110
Borderline personality disorder, 199
Boston, Massachusetts, 115, 116
Boundaries, 69
Boys Clubs, 51
Brain, 31, 249–250
   neuronal "pruning," 32–33
   stroke impacting, 251–252
   substance abuse impacting, 32
"Broker" role, 4
Bronfenbrenner, Urie, 37–39
Bronx, New York City, 6
Brown v. Board of Education (1954), 92
BSW. *See* Baccalaureate degree in social work
Bulimia, 198
Bureau of Indian Affairs (BIA), 91
Bureau of Labor Statistics (BLS), 25, 166
Bush, Barbara, 216
Bush, G. H. W., 135, 159, 365
Bush, G. W., 136–137, 159, 160, 236, 365

Cabot, Richard, 166
Calvin, John, 115
Calvinism, 115
Cambodian Americans, 94–95, 95
Canada, 345–346
Canadian Patent Medicines Prices Review Board, 177
Cancer, 167–168, 272–273
CAP. *See* Community Action Program
Capitalism, 51–53
Capital offense, 293
Caputo, R., 236
Cardiovascular disease (CVD), 166–167
Careers, in social work, 5–11, 25
Caribbean Americans, 93, 94
Carter, Betty, 217–219
Carter, Jimmy, 134
Carter and McGoldrick's family life cycle stages, 217–219
CASA. *See* National Center on Addiction and Substance Abuse
Case management, 5, 6, 9, 30, 134, 201, 261
Catholics, 116, 357
CBT. *See* Cognitive behavioral therapy
CDC. *See* Centers for Disease Control
Centers for Disease Control (CDC), 170, 183, 184, 272–273
Charcot, Jean-Martin, 252
Charitable giving programs, 51, 118–119, 123–124
   spiritual salvation linked to, 117

Charleston, South Carolina, 115
Chau, Shirley B., 185
Child abuse, 91, 132, 225–228, 239, 357
Child Abuse Prevention Act (1974), 132
Child care, 2, 25, 51, 131, 135, 157, 229–230, 254, 332
   costs, 227–228
   issues/failure to address, 133
Child Care and Development Block Grant (1990), 131, 135, 157
Child protective services, 6, 29, 50, 228–229
Children. *See also* Disability; Family; Parenting; Pregnancy; Substance abuse
   adoption, 2, 25, 231–232
   Advocates for Healthy Youth, 185
   Alateen, 280
   child, couple, and family therapy, 237–238
   child abuse, 91, 132, 225–228, 239, 357
   Child Welfare League of America, 10
   CHIP, 174, 178
   CHIPRA, 174
   custody of, 30, 219–221
   depression study, 206
   Elementary and Secondary Education Act, 130
   Erikson's stages of development, 33–34, 36
   fetal alcohol syndrome, 270–271
   foster care, 2, 25, 229–230, 332
   Foster Grandparent program, 332
   Head Start program, 29, 163, 235, 236
   high school completion, 234, 271
   Juvenile Justice and Delinquency Act, 132
   Medicaid for, 172–173
   mental disorders diagnosed/infancy through adolescence, 195
   minimum drinking age, 274
   niche concept applied to, 45
   obese, 168–169, 257
   Piaget's cognitive stages, 34–36
   poverty trend, 144–145
   smoking cigarettes, 271
   substance abuse, 272–274
   Vygotsky on, 35–36
   WIC, 159, 234
   youth incarceration rate, 294–296
   youth offenders and juvenile crime, 299–303
   youth suicide, 91, 94, 219, 222, 227
Children's Defense fund, 10
Children's Health Insurance Program (CHIP), 174, 178
Children's Health Insurance Program Reauthorization Act (CHIPRA), 174
Child Welfare League of America, 10
China, 340–342
Chinese Americans, 94–95, 185, 278
CHIP. *See* Children's Health Insurance Program
CHIPRA. *See* Children's Health Insurance Program Reauthorization Act

Chisholm, Shirley, 133
Christianity, 40, 105, 115–116, 117, 357
   Bush, G. W., "faith-based" policies, 137, 365
   Habitat for Humanity, 160–161
Cigarettes. *See* Smoking
City services, 69
Civic Ventures, 91
Civilization, 343
Civil Rights Acts (1964 and 1965), 371
Civil rights movements, 40. *See also* Discrimination; Oppression
   African American, 92–93, 129–130, 133, 295–296, 358
   disabilities, 97, 108–109, 135, 255, 258
   GLBTQ, 45, 89, 95–97, 195, 215–217, 223, 232
   impact on professional social work, 134
   indigenous peoples, 91–92
   racism, crime, and incarceration v., 295–296
   for social and economic justice, 3, 109–111, 132, 171, 360, 361–370
   women, 117, 121–123, 132–134, 366, 370–371
Civil unions, 96–97, 217
Civil War, U. S., 92
Claims-Making Approach, to problem definition, 357
Class advocacy, 78. *See also* Social class
Classism, 105–106
Client outcome assessment, 79–80
Client-worker relationship, establishment of, 202–203
Clinical psychology, 12
Clinical social worker, 189, 200–201
Clinton, Bill, 96, 135–137, 159
Clinton, Hillary, 137
Cloud, Jennifer M., 254
Coalition building, 78
Coalitions, 367
Cocaine, 270
CODA (co-dependents anonymous), 280
Cognitive-behavioral model, of mental disorder, 192
Cognitive behavioral therapy (CBT), 282
Cognitive development, 34–35
Cognitive disabilities, 248–252
Cognitive disorders, 196
Cognitive stages, Piaget's, 34–36
Cohabit, 217
Colbert, Jean-Baptiste, 53
Collaboration, interprofessional, 9
   Assertive Community Treatment, 211
   for criminal justice, 312–314
   for domestic violence, 162
   for gerontology services, 332–333
   for international social work, 349–352
   occupational, physical, and speech therapists, 265
   social workers and healthcare professionals, 185–186

Collins, Gail, 7
Colonialism, 115–116, 340
  "colonially induced despair," 91–92
Colorado Springs, Colorado, 91
Columbus, Ohio, 261
Community, 8–9, 130, 181–182
  Assertive Community Treatment, 211
  concept of, 46
  generalist social work with, 77–78
  Housing and Community Development Act, 160
Community Action Program (CAP), 130
Community assessment, 70–72
Community health clinic (CHC), 181–182
Community Orientation and Reintegration Program, Pennsylvania, 308
Community re-entry
  outpatient clinics, 6, 283–285, 289
  for TBI, 249–250
Competence, 45, 65–66, 80, 89
Computerization, 54
Concrete operations, 35
Conditionality, 346–347
Conflict management, 258
Congressional Record, 362–363
Conservative values, 51–53
Consumer Price Index for All Urban Consumers (CPI-U), 141–143
Control Theory, 293
Coping, 45
Core values, of social work, 14–15
Corporations, 51, 53, 208, 257, 337, 339
  loss of social accountability, 347
Corrections, 299
  services for inmates, 303–309
Council on Social Work Education (CSWE), 24
  2008 Educational Policy and Accreditation Standards, 3
Counseling/counselor, 5, 12–13, 81, 137, 208, 211, 228, 258–259, 265, 330
  addiction, 278, 282–283
  addiction aftercare, 283–285
  brain injury, 249–250
  couples, 238–239
  death and dying, 326, 331
  disabilities, 245
  domestic violence, 234–235
  family, 180–181
  financial investment, 329
  group, 167, 180
  HIV, 183, 285
  interview with drug and alcohol counselor, 287
  loss and grief, 325
  mental health, 201
  play therapy technique, 238
County Department of Correction's Programs Division, Santa Clara, 305
Courts system, 296–298
Coyhis, Don, 91
CPI-U. *See* Consumer Price Index for All Urban Consumers

Crazy: A Father's Search Through America's Mental Health Madness (Earley), 305
Crime, 292
  adult criminal justice system, 296–299
  categories of criminal behavior, 292–293
  criminal justice, 303–310
  criminal justice system, 296–298
  interprofessional collaboration for preventing/reducing, 312–314
  post-release and rehabilitation services, 306–307
  prevention, 310–312
  theories of criminal behavior, 293–294
  trends in, and incarceration, 294–296
  youth offenders/juvenile crime, 299–303
Crime Bill (1994), 136
Criminal justice reform, 309–310
Criminal justice system, 296–298
Crisis intervention, 25
Crystal methamphetamine, 275
CSWE. *See* Council on Social Work Education
Cultural commonality, 66
Cultural competency, 65–66, 89
Cultural identity, 345–346
Cultural level, 38, 45–46
Cultural matrix, 88
Cultural/social blind spots, 101
Cultural specificity, 66
Culture, 88, 208
  -bound syndromes, 200
Culture of poverty, 152–154
CVD. *See* Cardiovascular disease

Dartmouth Medical School, 168
Data, collection and assessment, 68–73, 79–80, 202
Day care center, 2, 51
Death penalty, 309–310
de Beauvoir, Simone, 320
Decision agenda, 364–365
Defense mechanism, 12, 192
Defense of Marriage Act (DOMA), 96–97
Deficit-based model, 45–46
Deficit Model Approach, 300
Deinstitutionalization, 206
Dementia, 196
Demick, J., 231
Democracy. *See also* Civil rights movements
  globalization's impact on, 347–348
  local, 9
  women's right to vote, 133, 366
Department of Agriculture, U. S. (DOA), 141, 159
Dependent personality disorder, 199
Depression, 97, 191, 197, 202, 206
  biological component, 32–33
Deprivation, 140
Developmental disabilities, 245–248, 261
Developmental models, of mental disorder, 191–192

DFWP. *See* Drug Free Workplace
Diabetes, 93, 185, 251
Diagnostic and Statistical Manual of Mental Disorders (DSM), 194–195
  categories of mental disorders, 196
Dialysis patients, 6
Digitization, 54
DiNitto, Diana M., 273
Dirigo Health Reform Act (2003), 179
Disability, 25, 88, 98
  ableism v., 108–109
  civil rights movement, 97, 108–109, 135, 255, 258
  cognitive, 248–252
  current social response to, 254–255
  developmental, 245–248
  disabling illness: stroke, ALS, 251–252
  Education for All Handicapped Act, 132, 250
  history of social response to, 252–254
  in-home services, 261–263
  Integrated Disability Management Programs, 258
  Medicaid for people with, 172–173
  NASW ethical standard, 89
  physical, 243–245
  poverty and, 153
  publicly funded services, 256–258
  rehabilitation and vocational services, 259–260
  residential services, 260–261
  Social Security assistance, 155
  special education, 263–265
Disability paradigm, 244
Disabling illness, 251–252
Disaster relief, 25
Discrimination, 77, 89, 92–99. *See also* Civil rights movements
  classism, 105–106
  feminization of poverty, 151–153
  mental disorders, 204
  poverty from exploitation and, 150–151
Disease. *See also* Human Immunodeficiency Virus
  disabling illness, 251–252
  ethnic groups v., 92–94
  likelihood of illness among minority groups, 170–171
Disease model, of substance abuse, 280
Diversity. *See* Human diversity
Divorce, 219–220
Dix, Dorothea, 370
DOA. *See* Department of Agriculture, U. S.
DOMA. *See* Defense of Marriage Act
Domestic violence, 25, 91, 94, 132, 223–224, 276
  counseling, 234–235
  inter-professional collaboration v., 162
Dominant culture, 88
Domination, subordination and, 99–100
Doyle, Arthur Conan, 327

Index

Driving under the influence, 273–274
Drug addiction, 269. *See also* Substance abuse
Drug courts, 286
Drug Free Workplace (DFWP), 258
DSM. *See* Diagnostic and Statistical Manual of Mental Disorders
Dual diagnosis, drug abuse and, 286–287
Dukakis, Michael, 135

EAP. *See* Employee Assistance Program
Earley, P., 305
Eating disorders, 25, 198, 207
Economic inequality, 147–148, 153, 360–361
Economic institutions, 51–54, 59–60
Ecosystem, 43–45
"Ecosystems perspective," 11
Ecstasy, 270
Edelman, Marian Wright, 171, 230
2008 Educational Policy and Accreditation Standards, 3
Education for All Handicapped Children Act (1975), 132, 250
EEOC. *See* Equal Employment Opportunity Commission
Egalitarian philosophy, 360
Ego integrity *v.* despair stage, 34
Ehrenreich, Barbara, 149, 194
Ehrenreich, John, 133
Einstein, Albert, 250
Elderly, 25, 89, 131, 228, 253. *See also* Gerontological services
  Alzheimer's disease, 183, 196
  Area Agencies on Aging, 332
  neglect of, 223–224
  niche concept applied to, 45
  nursing homes, 51, 172–173, 254, 323–324, 326–327, 330, 333
  Old Age, Survivors, and Disability Insurance (OASDI), 155
  poverty trend for, 144–145
  private pensions, 320–321
  risk of stroke, 251
Elementary and Secondary Education Act (1965), 130
Elizabethan Poor Law Act (England/1601), 115, 137, 252
Emergency room (ER), 261
Emotional abuse, child, 225
Emotional intelligence, 32, 106–107
Emotional status, 70
Empathy, 65
Employee assistance, 4, 25, 156, 256–257, 258, 345, 371
  EAP, 51, 208, 257
  EEOC, 227
Employee Assistance Program (EAP), 51, 208, 257
Employment. *See also* Unemployment
  after-tax income/by group, 149
  American Recovery and Reinvestment Act, 178–179
  disability and, 259–260
  family un-friendly workplace, 227–228
  low market demand, 153
  minimum wage, 147–148
  parents' place of, 38
  payroll taxes, 155
  two-tiered employment system, 54
  vocational counseling, 13, 259–260
"Enabler" role, 4
End-stage disease, 172
Engagement process, 66–67
English language, 89, 208
Entry drugs, 270, 288
Environmental toxins, 41–42
Equal Employment Opportunity Commission (EEOC), 227
Equal Rights Amendment (ERA), 133, 366
Equilibrium, between people and environment, 5, 11, 12, 42
ER. *See* Emergency room
ERA. *See* Equal Rights Amendment
Erikson, Erik, 33–34, 36
Esteem, 36–37, 45
Ethics
  areas of competency, 45, 65–66, 80, 89
  for-profit adoption, 232
  human relationships, 67
  individual dignity and worth, 66
  Judeo-Christian tradition, 40
  in local democracy, 9
  NASW ethical standard, 89
  oppressed/vulnerable persons, 108–109
  poverty/discrimination issues, 77
  prosperity linked to morality, 117
  socioeconomic aspects of illness, 170–171
Ethnicity/ethnic group, 87, 278
  disease *v.*, 92–94
  fertility rate *v.*, 89
  NASW ethical standard, 89
  smoking per, 271
Ethnocentrism, 104–105
European Americans, 89, 95, 110, 144–145, 208
  child abuse, 226
  partner abuse, 224
  poverty by education level/race/gender, 150
European welfare states, 52
Evaluation, 78–80, 203
Evidence-based treatment, in mental health services, 210
Executive branch, 54
Expert witnesses, 313

Factors of production, 53
Fact witnesses, 313
Fair Minimum Wage Act (2007), 147
"Faith-based" policies, 137, 365
Faith-based services, 4
Family, 6–7. *See also* Children; Gerontological services; Parenting; Substance abuse
  adolescent pregnancy, 94, 157, 172–173, 183, 233–234, 240, 270
  adoption, 2, 25, 231–232
  aftercare for substance abuse, 283–285
  alternative education programs, 237–238
  in Bronfenbrenner's scheme, 37–39
  challenges facing, 219–227
  changes in functions of, 216
  child, couple, and family therapy, 237–238
  child abuse, 91, 132, 225–228, 239, 357
  child care costs, 227–228
  child protective services, 6, 29, 50, 228–229
  couples counseling, 238–239
  custodial grandparent families, 220–221
  demographic changes, 215
  developmental disability care by, 247
  diverse forms of, 216–217
  divorce, 219–220
  domestic violence services, 25, 91, 94, 132, 162, 234–235, 276
  elder abuse, 324–325
  family leave, 133, 136, 254, 257, 258
  family planning services, 25, 132, 234
  generalist social work with, 75–76
  Head Start and Early Head Start, 29, 163, 235, 236
  life cycle stages, 217–219
  Medicaid for, 172–173
  mental disorder intervention, 204–205
  nuclear, 216
  out-of-home placement/foster care, 2, 25, 229–230, 332
  partner abuse, 223–224, 276
  poverty *v.* changing family structure, 151–152
  removal *v.* reunification debate, 230–231
  same-sex marriages, 96–97, 217
  school social work, 236–237
  services in educational settings, 235
  services to batterers, 235
  services to survivors, 234–235
  single-parent, 219–221
  strength/resiliency of, 70
  TBI care by, 249–250
  therapy, 238–239
  un-friendly workplace for, 227–228
  violence, 222–224
  violence prevention, 239
Family and Medical Leave Act (FMLA), 133, 136, 254, 257, 258
Family assessment, 69–70
Family leave, 133, 136, 254, 257, 258
Family life cycle stages, 217–219
Family planning, 25, 132, 234. *See also* Women
Family Planning Services and Population Act (1974), 132
Farewell get-together, 83

Federal Deposit and Insurance Corporation, 53, 348
Federal minimum wage, 147–148
Federal Poverty Thresholds, 141
Feedback, concept of, 42
Fee-for-Service plan, 173
Fellowes, Matt, 151
Felony, 292
Feminist theories/views, 34, 106–107
 of criminal behavior, 294
Feminization of poverty, 151–153
Fetal alcohol syndrome, 270–271
Fiber optics, 54
Field practicum, 22, 24–25
Filipino Americans, 94–95
Financial abuse, 223–224
Financial referral, 258
Finkelhor, David, 226–227
First Amendment, 116
First World nations, 340
Fisher, L., 278
Fishing communities, 41
Flashbacks, 197
FMLA. *See* Family and Medical Leave Act
Food and Agriculture Organization (FAO), 350
Food budgets, U. S. D. A., 141
Food Stamp Program, 4, 131, 158–159, 234
Ford, Gerald, 134
Forensic social work, 292
Formal operations, 35
Foster care, 2, 25, 229–230, 332
Foster Grandparent program, 332
Fragmentation, healthcare, 174–175
Fram, 237
Free market philosophy, 53, 339–340
Freese, Hannah, 2
Freud, Sigmund, 33, 134, 192, 201
Friedman, Thomas, 369
Frye, Marilyn, 105
Functional Approach, to problem definition, 357

GAD. *See* Generalized Anxiety Disorder
Galton, Francis, 253
Gard, M., 168–169
Gateway drugs, 270, 288
Gay, Lesbian, Bisexual, Transgender, and Queer/Questioning (GLBTQ), 89, 95–97, 195
 families, 215–217, 223, 232
 niche concept applied to, 45
Gehrig, Lou, 252
Gender identity, 88–89
Gender identity disorder (GID), 198
General Assistance, 157–158
General Federation of Women's Clubs, 371
Generalist social work practice, 63
 data collection and assessment, 68–73, 79–80, 202
 evaluation, 78–80
 with families, 75–76
 with groups, 76–77
 with individuals, 74–75
 intervention, 73–74
 with organizations and communities, 77–78
 termination, 80–83, 203
Generalized Anxiety Disorder (GAD), 197
Generativity *v.* stagnation stage, 34
Genetic endowment, 12
 biological domain, 32–33
Gerontological services, 25. *See also* Elderly
 advocacy and collaboration for, 332–333
 ageism, 319–320
 declines in private pensions, 320–321
 elder abuse, 324
 hospice, 330–332
 in-home care and assistance services, 329
 life cycle challenges, 325–327
 Medicare for, 328–329
 prescription drugs, 321–322
 remaining at home, 323–324
 residential care and assisted living, 329–330
 senior centers, 330
 social security, 328
 transportation alternatives, 322–323
 who are older Americans?, 318
Ghosts from the Nursery (Karr-Morse and Wiley), 32
Ghost sickness, culture-bound syndrome, 200
GID. *See* Gender identity disorder
Girls Clubs, 51
Girl Scouts of America, 4
GLBTQ people. *See* Gay, Lesbian, Bisexual, Transgender, and Queer/Questioning
Global Corporations, 339
Globalization, 31, 53–54, 89
 China and, 340–342
 future, 349–352
 history, 337–338
 negative aspects of, 342–348
 political foundation of, 338–339
 positive aspects of, 339–342
Global positive sense, of oneself, 45
Global warming, 41, 347
Goodwin, Doris Kearns, 179
Gore, Al, 136
Gorey, K., 236
Government agendas, 364
Grandparent-as-custodian families, 220–221
Gray Panthers, 333–334
Great Depression, 52–53, 124–125, 171, 338
Grief, 325
Group assessment, 70
Groups/group work, 7–8
 after-tax income/by group, 149
 generalist social work with, 76–77

 poverty rates among, 144–145
 school peer group, 38
 support groups, 4, 204, 232, 258, 280–282
Gruber, Jonathan, 177
Guilamo-Ramos, Vincent, 6

Habitat concept, 45
Habitat for Humanity, 4, 160–161
Hackman, W., 106–107
Hamer, Fannie Lou, 133
Harrington, Michael, 37, 133, 140, 296
Harrison, Thomas C., 278
Hate-motivated crime, 97
Hawaii, 184
Hazlitt, William, 89
HBSE. *See* Human Behavior and Social Environment
Head injury, 249–250
Head Start program, 29, 163, 235
 Improving Head Start for School Readiness Act, 236
Healthcare, 25, 135. *See also specific groups*
 fragmentation, 174–175
 services, 171
 "wellness program," 257–258
Health insurance, 136, 163
 as controversial, 171
 for family of four, 178
 innovations/proposals for, 177–180, 367
 mental health parity, 205, 276
 National Healthcare System, 178–180
 Obama's healthcare reform, 137
 prescription drugs, 176–177
 private and managed care, 173–175
 un-covered middle class, 176
 uninsured and underinsured, 175
Health Maintenance Act (1973), 132, 172
Health Maintenance Organization (HMO), 174
Health Savings Account (HSA), 178
Heart disease, 93, 166–167
 diabetes and, 185
 risk of stroke, 251
Heroin, 270
Hetereosexism, 107
Heterosexual-homosexual scale, 89. *See also* Gay, Lesbian, Bisexual, Transgender, and Queer/Questioning
Hierarchy of Needs, 36–37
High school, completion of, 234, 271
Hill-Burton Act, 253–254
History
 of globalization, 337–338
 of social response to disabilities, 252–254
History, of social work
 almshouses, 115–116
 Anti-Pauper Movement, 117–118
 Bush, G. H. W., impact on, 135
 Bush, G. W., impact, 136–137

Index

business charitable contributions, 123–124
Clinton, B., impact on, 135–136
development of charities, 118–119
Great Depression, 52–53, 124–125, 171, 338
health services and, 171–172
Johnson's Great Society, 129–131, 365, 371
Nixon's social welfare partnership, 131–132
Obama's impact, 137
Progressive Era, 119–120, 371
Reagan's New Federalism, 134–135
role of philanthropy, 117
role of religion and First Amendment, 116
Roosevelt's New Deal, 125–129
Settlement Houses, 121–123, 370–371
sociopolitical context v. casework, 134
women's movement of 1960s and 1970s, 132–134
Histrionic personality disorder, 199
HIV. See Human Immunodeficiency Virus
HMO. See Health Maintenance Organization
Hollywood films, negative influence from, 273, 279, 320
Homelessness, 4, 25, 161, 207, 367
case managers for, 6
Homeostasis, 42
Homophobia, 107
Homosexual, 88–89, 195. See also Gay, Lesbian, Bisexual, Transgender, and Queer/Questioning
Hopkins, Harry, 371
Hospice, 25, 182, 330–332
Hospitals, 6, 51, 166, 171, 181
Household Food Consumption Survey (1955), 141
House of Representatives, 55
Housing Act (1990), 160
Housing and Community Development Act, 160
Housing and Urban Development (HUD), 159
Housing assistance, 25
Housing Choice Voucher Program, 160
HSA. See Health Savings Account
HUD. See Housing and Urban Development
Human Behavior and Social Environment (HBSE), 23
biological domain, 32–33
biopsychosocial model, 31–32
CSWE on course content, 30
psychological domain, 33–37
social domain, 37–39
spiritual and physical domains, 40–42
Human capital, 149–150, 153
Human diversity, 87–89
cultural competency and, 65–66, 89
learning to work across, 110
organizing principles of, 98–103

social justice and, 360–361
in United States, 90–98
Human Immunodeficiency Virus (HIV)
Medicaid for, 172–173
minority groups, 92–93
national AIDS prevention, 183
needle exchange programs, 285
services, 25
stigma of, 170
Humanistic approach, 36–37, 193
Human rights and justice, 360–370. See also Civil rights movements; Social justice
restorative justice, 301–302
Huntington Beach, California, 41

ICADV. See Iowa Coalition Against Domestic Violence
ICF/MR. See Intermediate Care Facilities/Mentally Retarded
ICSW. See International Council on Social Welfare
IDEA. See Individuals with Disabilities Education Act
Identity
identity v. role confusion stage, 34
individual/group/universal, 100–101
self-actualization, 36–37
sexual and gender identity disorders, 198
Ideology
conservative, 51–53
liberal, 51–53
radical left, 52
IDM. See Integrated Disability Management Programs
IFSW. See International Federation of Social Workers
IMF. See International Monetary Fund
Immigration/immigrants, 89, 93–95, 105, 117, 145
Improving Head Start for School Readiness Act (2007), 236
Impulsivity, 33
Incarceration, 277, 294–296. See also Crime
Incest, 225–227
Income groups, after taxes, 149
India, 341, 346–347
Indian Self-Determination and Educational Assistance Act, 91
Indigenous peoples, 90, 92, 110, 144–145, 271
Medicine Wheel 12-Steps, 91
terms of trade and conditionality, 346–347
Individual level, 5–6, 45–46
generalist social work at, 74–75
Individual Service Plan (ISP), 245–247
Individuals with Disabilities Education Act (IDEA), 250
Industrialization, 117–124
Industry v. inferiority stage, 34
Infectious disease, 12
HIV, 25, 92–93, 170, 172–173, 183, 285

Inhalants, 270
In-home care and assistance
for disabilities, 261–263
for elderly, 329
Initiative v. guilt stage, 34
Institutional Anomie Theory, 294
Integrated Disability Management Programs (IDM), 258
Intercountry adoptions, 231–232
Intermediate Care Facilities/Mentally Retarded (ICF/MR), 247
International Council on Social Welfare (ICSW), 350
International Federation of Social Workers (IFSW), 350
"social work" concept, 3
International Monetary Fund (IMF), 339, 348, 350
conditionality, 346–347
International social work, 349–352
Internet, 337–338, 369–370
Internet, invention of, 337
Intimacy v. isolation stage, 34
Intoxication, 269
Iowa Coalition Against Domestic Violence (ICADV), 162
Iraq, mental health v. war in, 210, 343, 351. See also Veterans
Isolation, 200, 254
ISP. See Individual Service Plan

Jamaica, 346–347
Japan, 54
Japanese Americans, 94–95
Jefferson, Thomas, 116, 361
Jersey City, New Jersey, 29
Jewish Americans, 40, 278
"Jim Crow" laws, 92
Job Training and Partnership Act, 135
Johnson, Lyndon, 52, 129, 131, 365, 367
War on Poverty, 130, 181–182
Johnson's Great Society, 129–131, 365, 371
Jordan, Judith, 200
Judeo-Christian tradition, 40
Judicial branch, 54
Jurisdictions, 296
Just society, 360
Juvenile and family court, 300
Juvenile Justice and Delinquency Act (1974), 132
Juvenile justice system, 299–300

Kang, Suk-Young, 325
Karr-Morse, Robin, 32
Katz, Jackson, 239
Katz, Jonathan, 115
Keene, New Hampshire, 185
Keller, Helen, 253
Kennedy, Edward, 179
Kennedy, John F., 206
Kennedy, Paul, 349
Kerrs-Mills health insurance bill, 365
King, Martin Luther, Jr., 92, 129, 133, 358
Kinsey, Alfred, 88–89

Kinsey Scale of Sexual Orientation, 89
Kirk, Stuart, 195
Knapp, Caroline, 272
Knopp, Fay Honey, 304
Knowledge, 3
Korean Americans, 94–95
Kutchins, Herb, 195

Labeling Theory, 193–194, 293
Lafayette, Louisiana, 202
Lai, Daniel W. L., 185
Laissez-faire philosophy, 53, 337
Langston, Donna, 88
Language acquisition, 32–33
Laotian Americans, 95
Latino/as, 93, 94, 144–145, 150, 271
Law enforcement, 296
Least restrictive environment, 206
Legal referral, 258
Legal system. *See also* Crime; *specific court case or law*
    "Jim Crow" laws, 92
    law enforcement, 296
    mental health system interface with, 298
Legislative branch, 54
Lewis, Oscar, 152–153
Liberals' values, 51–53
Libertarian philosophy, 360
Library of Congress, 361
Licensed social worker (LICSW), 287
LICSW. *See* Licensed social worker
Life cycle stages
    Carter and McGoldrick's family, 217–219
    challenges for elderly, 325–327
    individual, 69–70
    Marshall and Altpeter health strategies, 184
Life stressors, 33, 45
Lifestyle changes, 167, 182–183, 257, 258
Lindsey, Michael, 206
Lobbying, 359, 366, 368, 372
Long-term disability (LTD), 257
Love/belonging, 36–37
Lower class, 88, 110
Low market demand, 153
LSD, 270
LTD. *See* Long-term disability

Macro level, 4, 140, 236
    environmental triggers of asthma, 169
    mental disorder intervention, 205–208
    overweight children activities, 169
Magnetic resonance imaging (MRI), 32
Maine State Healthcare Program, 179
Majority Leader, 55
Mal de ojo (evil eye) culture-bound syndrome, 200
Managed care
    health insurance, 173–175
    mental health services, 209
Marginalized community, 41
Marijuana, 270, 272, 275
Marital counseling, 238–239

Marital status, 89
Market economy, 12. *See also* Globalization
    capitalism, 51–53
    liberal v. conservative views, 51–53
Market system, 53
Marshall, V., 184
Marx, Karl, 294
Marxist theories, of criminal behavior, 294
Maslow, Abraham, 36–37
Maslow's Hierarchy of Needs, 36–37
Massachusetts General Hospital, 166
Masters degree in social work (MSW), 189, 207, 228, 236
Materialist perspective, on disability, 243–244
"Maximum feasible participation," 130
Mayo Clinic, 169
McCaddin-Bower, Edie, 331
McGoldrick, Monica, 217–219
McNeece, C. Aaron, 273
Mead, Margaret, 87
Meals on Wheels, 332
"Mediator" role, 4
Medicaid, 4, 130–131, 137, 234
    developmental disabilities services, 247
    expanded coverage, 179
    for selected populations, 172–173
Medical debt, 175
Medical model, 190
Medical perspective, on disability, 243
Medical setting, 180–185
Medicare, 4, 130–131, 135, 172–173, 364–365
    Parts A, B, and D, 328–329
Medicare Prescription Drug Improvement and Modernization Act (2003), 172–173
Medicine Wheel 12-Steps, 91
Menninger, William, 189
Mental disorders, 195–200
    medical model of, 190–191
    NGRI, 309
    substance abuse concurrent with, 276
Mental health system/services
    agency profile, 207
    counseling, 13
    insurance coverage, 136, 276
    least restrictive environment, 206
    legal system interface with, 298
    macro level intervention, 205–208
    mental health agency profile, 207
    micro level, 200
    parity, 205
    SAMHSA, 11, 91
Mental illness
    biological component, 32–33
    conceptualizations of, 189–194
    diagnosis, 12
    poverty v., 154
    Westernization of, 200
Mental retardation (cognitive disability), 248

Mentoring, 234
Metabolic disorders, 12
Mezzo level, 4, 140
    mental disorder intervention, 203–205
Micro level, 4, 140
Middle class, 88, 296
    health insurance coverage, 176
Miller, Brian, 287
Miller-Cribbs, 237
Mills, Wilbur, 367
A Mind That Found Itself (Beers), 190, 204
Minimum drinking age, 274
Minimum wage, 147–148
Minority groups, 15, 89, 93. *See also specific group*
    diabetes and, 185
    HIV/AIDS among, 92–93
    likelihood of illness among, 170–171
    as stakeholders, 360–361
    unemployment rates, 92–93
Minority Leader, 55
Misdemeanor, 292
Mixed economy, 52
Model, 29. *See also specific field*
Mohican Nation, 91
MomsRising.org, 370
Mood disorders, 197
Morbidity costs, 288
Mortality costs, 288
Mothers, at home, 7
Mothers Against Drunk Driving, 4
Mothers Anonymous, 233
Mott, Lucretia, 371
MoveOn.org, 370
MRI. *See* Magnetic resonance imaging
MSW. *See* Masters degree in social work
Mui, Ada, 325
Multidimensional view, 31–32
Multinational organizations, 339
Mumford, Lewis, 208

NA. *See* Narcotics Anonymous
NAFTA. *See* North American Free Trade Agreement
Narcissistic personality disorder, 199
Narcotics Anonymous (NA), 280
NASW. *See* National Association of Social Workers
National Affordable Housing Trust Fund Act (2007), 160
National Association of Social Workers (NASW), 89, 318, 350, 362, 370
    Code of Ethics, 3, 16–17
    on growth of incarceration rates, 303
    on mental health field, 208
    on right to marry, 96–97
    on service areas, 25
    on "social work," 3
    on ways to advocate, 372
National Center on Addiction and Substance Abuse (CASA), 273
National Coalition for the Homeless, 161, 367
National Congress of Mothers, 371

National Federation of Societies for Clinical Social Work (est. 1971), 136
National Institutes of Health (NIH), 11, 318
National Institutes of Medicine, 105
National Institutes of Mental Health (NIMH), 189
National Law Center on Homelessness and Poverty, 161
National Welfare Rights Organization (est. 1967), 133–134
Native Hawaiian and Pacific Islanders, 144–145
Nature v. nurture debate, 32–33
Needle exchange programs, 285
Neighborhood crime watch, 9
Neighborhood development, 25
Nervios culture-bound syndrome, 200
Neurochemistry, 32–33. See also Brain
New Deal, 125–129, 371
New Federalism, 134–135
New York City, 115, 158, 344
NGRI. See Not guilty by reason of insanity
Niche concept, 45
Nicotine, 269–270. See also Smoking
Nike, 342
NIMH. See National Institutes of Mental Health
Nixon, Richard, 131–132, 173
No Child Left Behind Act (2001), 237
Nonprofit agencies, 4, 50, 116, 118
Noradrenalin, 33
"Normal," 110
Normative Approach, to problem definition, 357
North American Free Trade Agreement (NAFTA), 346
Not guilty by reason of insanity (NGRI), 309
Nuclear family, 216
Nursing homes, 51, 172–173, 254, 323–324, 326–327, 330, 333

OASDI. See Old Age, Survivors, and Disability Insurance
Obama, Barack, 65, 371
 American Recovery and Reinvestment Act, 178–179
 healthcare reform, 137, 365
Obesity, 168–169, 257
The Obesity Epidemic, Science, Morality and Ideology (Gard and Wright), 168–169
Objective Approach, to problem definition, 357
Obsessive-compulsive personality disorder (OCD), 199
 substance abuse concurrent with, 276
OCD. See Obsessive-compulsive personality disorder
O'Connor, Sandra Day, 309
Old Age, Survivors, and Disability Insurance (OASDI), 155
Oldest-old category, 319

Old-old category, 319
Olmstead v. L. C., 206
Omnibus Budget Reconciliation Acts (1981 and 1982), 135
Oncology social workers, 167
Oppression, 93–94. See also Civil rights movements; Discrimination; *specific group*
 "colonially induced despair," 91–92
 ethics toward vulnerable persons, 108–109
 living experience of, 104–109
 poverty from discrimination/exploitation, 150–153
 power and, 102–103
 social justice v., 360–361
Organization assessment, 70–72
Organizations and communities, 8–9, 130, 181–182
 Assertive Community Treatment, 211
 concept of community, 46
 generalist social work with, 77–78
 Housing and Community Development Act, 160
O'Rourke, P. J., 269
Orshansky, Mollie, 141
OSHA/Safety Programs, 258
Oswald, D., 176
The Other America (Harrington), 140
Outpatient clinics, 6, 283–285, 289

PA. See Parents Anonymous
Pacific Islanders, 144–145
PACT. See Parents and Children Together
Pain relievers, 270
Paranoid personality disorder, 199
Parenting, 233, 305. See also Children
 in Bronfenbrenner's model, 38
 education and support for, 25, 30, 232
 involvement in substance abuse prevention, 288–289
 single-parent family, 219–221
 support services, 25, 30, 232
 "War on Drugs" impact on, 277
Parents and Children Together (PACT), 305
Parents Anonymous (PA), 233
Parish, Susan, 254
Parks, Rosa, 129
Parole, 307
Partner abuse, 223–224, 276
"Party system," 55
Patient Protection and Affordable Care Act (2010), 174, 179
Paul, Alice, 366
Payroll taxes, 155
PCP, as entry drug, 270
Pease, Ken, 295
Pease, Leslie, 295
Peer group, 38
Perkins, Frances, 371
Personality development, 33–34
Personality disorder, 199. See also *specific disorder*

Personal Responsibility and Work Opportunities Act (PRWOA), 136, 158, 228
Pesce, Michael, 2
Pharmaceuticals/pharmaceutical companies, 194, 283
 health insurance covering, 176–177
 Medicare Prescription Drug Improvement and Modernization Act, 172–173
 prescription drugs for elderly, 321–322
 psychotropic medication, 191
Philadelphia, Pennsylvania, 115, 116
Philanthropy, early history, 117
Physical abuse
 adult, 223–224
 child, 225
Physical disabilities, 97, 243–245
Piaget, Jean, 34–36
Point-of-service plan (POS), 174
Police protection, 296
Policy analysis, 25
Policy practice, 10–11, 356
Policy research, 361–362
Policy windows of opportunity, 364, 366
Political context, 38
Political institutions, 51, 54–57
Poor Law Act (1601), 115, 137, 252
Poor relief, 115, 116
Portland, Main, 13
POS. See Point-of-service plan
Postmodernist perspective, on disability, 244
Post-Traumatic Stress Disorder (PTSD), 197, 210, 276
Poverty, 77, 94, 117, 337, 372. See also Food; Medicaid; Publicly funded services
 causes of, 52–53, 145–154
 children in, 144–145
 culture of, 152–154
 demographic trends, 144–145
 disability and, 153
 discrimination/ethics issues, 77
 domestic violence and, 162
 by education level/race/gender, 150
 environmental toxins and, 41–42
 federal thresholds/guidelines, 141–142
 feminization of, 151–153
 Harrington on, 37
 homelessness, 4, 6, 25, 161, 207, 367
 introduction to, 140
 medical debt, 175
 mental illness and, 154
 niche concept applied to, 45
 numbers in millions, 143–145
 in poor v. rich country, 3
 problems/alternatives to current federal thresholds, 142–143
 variables associated with, 153
 wage inequality, 147–148, 152–153
War on Poverty, 130, 181–182
 youth tobacco usage and, 271

Poverty Guidelines, 141–142
Power, oppression and, 102–103
PPO. *See* Preferred Provider Organization
Preferred Provider Organization (PPO), 174
Pregnancy
  adolescent, 94, 157, 172–173, 183, 233–234, 240, 270
  Medicaid for, 172–173
  smoking during, 270
Prejudice, 99, 105. *See also* Discrimination
Preoperational thought, 35
Preparing for the Twenty-First Century (Kennedy, P.), 349
Prescription drugs. *See* Pharmaceuticals/pharmaceutical companies
Prevention, 50, 70, 91
  adolescent pregnancy, 240
  child abuse, 132
  crime, 310–311
  family violence, 239
  HIV, 183
  needle exchange programs as, 285
  poverty, 118
  substance abuse programs as, 288–289
  tobacco usage, 184, 272–273
  of violence against women, 132, 224, 239, 276
  of youth crime/violence, 300–301
Private insurance and managed care, 174–175
  Fee-for-Service plan, 173
Private pensions, 320–321
Probation, 307
Process *v.* result, 31
Progressive Era, 119–120, 371
Protestant Social Gospel movement, 40
"Pruning" (neuronal), 32–33
PRWOA. *See* Personal Responsibility and Work Opportunities Act
Psychiatric facility, 6
Psychiatry, 12
Psychodynamic theories, of mental disorder, 192
"Psychoeducational" groups, 7
Psychological abuse, 223–224
Psychological domain, 33–37
Psychological models, of addiction, 279
Psychology, 12
Psychotherapy, 136, 137, 201–203
Psychotropic medication, 191
PTSD. *See* Post-Traumatic Stress Disorder
Public assistance programs, 295–296
Public Housing Program, 4, 159
Publicly funded services, 154–158
  for disabilities, 256–258
Public sector, partnered with private sector, 337
Puerto Ricans, 171

Puritans, 116, 117
Purpose, 3

Quakers, 116
"Queer," 97

Race, 87. *See also specific group*
  NASW ethical standard, 89
  poverty by education level/gender and, 150
  tobacco usage, 271
Racial profiling, 295
Racism, 25, 93, 94. *See also* Civil rights movements
  environmental toxins and, 41–42
  hazardous to health, 105
  in institutions, 12
  "Jim Crow" laws, 92
  living experience of, 104
  racial profiling, 295
Radical left, 52
Rain Forest Activist Network, 370
Rawls, John, 370
R&D. *See* Research and development
Reagan, Ronald, 95, 134–135, 159
  Tax Reform Act, 160–161
Reagan's New Federalism, 134–135
RealCare Baby, 240
Reasonable accommodation, 255
Recidivism, 303–305, 307, 310–311
Reciprocal relationship, 31
  ecosystems, 43–45
Red Cross, 4, 51, 351
Regression, in client behavior, 81
Rehabilitation, 132, 258, 261. *See also* Substance abuse
  counseling, 13, 91
  post-release from prison, 306–307
  substance abuse treatment facilities, 283–285
  traumatic brain injury care, 249–250
  vocational services for disabilities, 259–260
Rehabilitation Act (1973), 132
Relatedness, 45
Relative poverty, 141
Reliability, 79
Research and development (R&D), 6, 24–25, 176
Residential care
  for disabilities, 260–261
  for elderly, 329–330
Residential treatment programs, 207
Resources, connecting clients to, 82
Respite care, 182
Restorative justice, 301–302
Revenue sharing, 131
Richmond, Mary, 371
Risk management, 258
Robertson, Pat, 106–107
Roe v Wade, 133
Romanyshyn, L., 50
Romanyshyn, M., 50
Roosevelt, Eleanor, 371

Roosevelt, Franklin D., 52, 125–129, 143, 348, 371

Sachs, Jeffrey D., 360
Safety, in Hierarchy of Needs, 36
Salvation Army, 4
Same-sex marriages, 96–97, 217
SAMHSA. *See* Substance Abuse and Mental Health Services Administration
Sanction, 3
Sanitation, 171
Satellite communications, 54
S-CHIP. *See* State Children's Health Insurance Program
Schizoid personality disorder, 199
Schizophrenia, 32, 196, 207
Schizotypal personality disorder, 199
School alternative programs, 25
School safety intervention, 303–304
SEC. *See* Securities and Exchange Commission
Second World nations, 340
Section 8 Program, 159
Securities and Exchange Commission (SEC), 53
Sedatives, 270
Seipel, M., 168
Self-actualization, 36–37
Self-determination, 91, 206
Self-direction, 45
Self-help, 64–65, 233, 280–282
Sen, Amartya, 337
Senate, 55
Senior centers, 330
Sensori-motor intelligence, 35
Serenity Prayer, 282
Serotonin, 33
Service barriers, 185
SES. *See* Socioeconomic status
Settlement Houses, 121–123, 370–371
Sexism, 106–107
Sexual abuse, child, 225–227, 357
Sexual Assault Support Services, 14
Sexually transmitted diseases (STDs), 285
Sexual orientation, 88–89
Sexual violence, 14, 224, 225–227
Shared residence, 261
Shepard, Matthew, 97
Shipler, David, 3, 130
Short-term disability (STD), 257
Shunned (Thornnicroft), 204
"Silent majority," 132
Sinclair, U., 120
Single-mother households, 217, 220, 230
Single-parent family, 219–221
Single system design, 80
Skills, 3
Slavery, 92
Smedley, Biran D., 87
Smith, Bob, 281

Smoking, 183–184, 257
  by gender/race/ethnicity/education, 271
  preventing youth from, 272–273
  preventing youth smoking, 272–273
  risk of stroke, 251
  as substance abuse, 269–270
Social class, 78, 88, 110, 176, 178
  classism, 105–106
Social Disorganization Theory, 293–294
Social domain, 37–39
Social environment. *See* Human behavior and social environment
Social groups, 98–99
Social institutions, 57–59
  quality of life *v.*, 51
Social justice, 3, 109–111, 132, 171, 360
  stakeholders, collaboration, and political strategy, 361–370
Social labeling theory, 193–194, 293
Social learning theory, 74, 279, 293
Socially marginalized community, 41
Social perspective, on disability, 243
Social phobia, 276
Social response, to disability, 254–255
Social Security, 4, 171–172, 328
  assistance for disabilities, 155
Social Security Act (1935), 126, 253–254
  Title XX, 132
Social Security Administration, 88, 131
Social Security Disability Insurance (SSDI), 256
Social welfare system, U. S., 131–134, 350
  Great Depression and creation of, 124–129
  policy and services, 23
  reform, 158
  social welfare concept, 50
  social work related to, 4–5
  welfare-to-work programs, 258
Sociocultural models, of addiction, 278
Socioeconomic status (SES), 170–171
Sociology, 12
Sociopolitical context, 134
Speaker of the House, 55
Special education, for disabilities, 263–265
Special Revenue Sharing, 131
Spiritual and physical domains, 40–42
SSDI. *See* Social Security Disability Insurance
SSI. *See* Supplemental Security Income
St. Vincent de Paul Village, San Diego, 14
Stakeholders, 362
Standardized scales, for client progress, 79–80
Stanton, Elizabeth Cady, 371
State Children's Health Insurance Program (S-CHIP), 163. *See also* Children's Health Insurance Program
State minimum wage, 147–148
Status offense, 302–303
STD. *See* Short-term disability
STDs. *See* Sexually transmitted diseases

Steinham, Gloria, 170
Stereotyping, 320
Stewart B. McKinney Homeless Assistance Act (1987), 161, 367
Stiglitz, Joseph, 342
Stigma
  disabilities, 244
  family member incarceration, 277
  HIV, 170
Stimulants, 270
Stone, Lucy, 271
Stonewall Riot (1969), 96
Strain Theory, 293
Strengths-based approach, 29, 45–46, 109–110, 245
  policy advocacy and, 363–364
Stress
  anxiety/arousal levels, 33
  coping concept, 45
  environmental toxins, 41
  management, 258
  substance abuse and, 276
Stroke, 251–252
Subjective Approach, to problem definition, 357
Subordination, domination and, 99–100
Substance abuse, 7, 25, 97, 154, 207, 269–271
  biopsychosocial model of addiction, 278
  brain function *v.*, 32
  crystal methamphetamine, 275
  disease model, 280
  driving under the influence, 273–274
  drug courts, 286
  Drug Free Workplace, 258
  dual diagnosis, 286–287
  entry drugs of abuse, 270, 288
  federal "War on Drugs," 277
  marijuana debate, 270, 272, 275
  needle exchange programs, 285
  Parents and Children Together *v.*, 305
  preventing youth smoking, 272–273
  prevention, 287–289
  professional treatment programs, 282–283
  psychological models of addiction, 279
  risk of stroke, 251
  SAMHSA, 11, 91
  sociocultural models of addiction, 278
  symptoms and solutions, 276
  treatment facilities, 283–285
  Twelve-Step Support Groups, 280–282
  youth drugs and alcohol, 273–274
Substance Abuse: Information for School Counselors, Social Workers, Therapists, and Counselors (Fisher and Harrison), 278
Substance Abuse and Mental Health Services Administration (SAMHSA), 11, 91
Sue, David Wing, 93
Suicide, 97
  youth, 91, 94, 219, 222, 227

Supplemental Security Income (SSI), 157, 256
Support groups, 4, 204, 232, 258, 280–282
Systems theory, 11, 37–39, 42–46
Szasz, Thomas, 193–194, 244

TANF. *See* Temporary Assistance to Needy Families
Tatum, Beverly Daniel, 100–101
Tax Reform Act (1986), 160–161
TBI. *See* Traumatic brain injury
"Teacher" role, 4, 11
Temporary Assistance to Needy Families (TANF), 4, 136, 146, 149, 156–157, 159, 228, 230, 234
  drug felons barred from receiving, 295
Termination, 80–83, 203
Terms of trade, 346–347
Terry, K., 175
Thai Americans, 94–95
Therapy groups, 203–204
Third World nations, 340
Thomas Web site, 361
Thoreau, Henry David, 78
Thornnicroft, Graham, 204
Tobacco. *See* Smoking
Tranquilizers, 270
Transactional approach, 31–32
Transnational organizations, 339
Transportation alternatives, 322–323
Traumatic brain injury (TBI), 249–250
Traumatic experiences, 12
Tree planting, 9
Tribal courts, 91–92
Trust *v.* mistrust stage, 34
Twelve-Step Support Groups, 280–282
21st Century Community Learning Centers, 237
Twitter, 370
Two-tiered employment system, 54

Unconscious, concept of, 192
Underinsured, 175
UNDP. *See* United Nations Development Program
Unemployment. *See also* Employment
  as cause of poverty, 146
  globalization *v.*, 344
  insurance for, 4, 155–156
  rates of, 54, 92–93, 94
UNFPA. *See* United Nations Population Fund
UN-HABITAT. *See* United Nations Human Settlements Program
Uninsured, individuals and families, 175
United Nations Development Program (UNDP), 350
United Nations Human Settlements Program (UN-HABITAT), 350
United Nations Population Fund (UNFPA), 350
United Way of America, 4, 10, 51, 371
Upper class, 88

Upper-middle class, 88
Urbanization, 12, 342, 347
　CPI-U, 141–143
　health services, 171
　HUD, 159
　industrialization, 117–124
Utilitarian philosophy, 360

Validity, 79
Value Conflict, 357
Values, 3, 14–15, 51. *See also* Ethics
　international social work, 349–352
Values-based profession, 14–22
Van Horn, 237
Veterans, 58, 166, 253, 255, 275, 351–352
　mental health services for, 210
Violation, 292
Virtue, 370. *See also* Values
Visibility, 89
VISTA. *See* Volunteers in Service to America
Vocational services, 13, 259–260
Volunteers in Service to America (VISTA), 130
Vygotsky, Leo, 35–36

Wage inequality, 147–148, 152–153
Wal-Mart, 341–342, 344–345
War on Drugs, 277
War on Poverty, 130, 181–182
War on Terrorism, 343–344
Watkins, Gloria Jean (bell hooks), 107
Welfare-to-work programs, 258. *See also* Social welfare system, U. S.
Well-being, societal, 59–60
Wellbriety Movement, 91
"Wellness program," 257–258
West, Cornell, 87
Westernization, 88
　globalization and, 342–348
　of mental illness, 200
WFP. *See* World Food Program
Whips, 55

White Americans, 89, 95, 110, 144–145, 208, 271
　child abuse, 226
　partner abuse, 224
　poverty by education level/race/gender, 150
White Bison, 91
WHO. *See* World Health Organization
Wholeness, 42
WIC nutrition program. *See* Women, Infants, and Children nutrition program
Wilcox, Sherry, 309
Wiley, Meredith S., 32
Wilkins, Leslie W., 295
Willis, J., 176
Wilson, Bob, 281
Windows of opportunity, policy, 364, 366
Women, 6, 97, 106–107, 198, 370. *See also* Women's movement
　child abuse victims, 226, 227
　in democracy, 133, 366
　family planning, 25, 132, 234
　fertility rate v. ethnic group, 89
　gender identity, 88–89
　GID, 198
　girls and juvenile justice, 302–303
　Great Society impacting, 130, 371
　incarceration rates, 295–296, 305
　Mothers Against Drunk Driving, 4
　mothers at home, 7
　National Congress of Mothers, 371
　Nixon's affirmative action for, 132
　poverty among, 150–153
　pregnancy, 94, 157, 172–173, 183, 233–234, 240, 270
　single-mother households, 217, 220, 230
　as stakeholders, 360–361
　tobacco usage, 271
　violence against, 132, 224, 239, 276
　WIC, 159, 234
Women, Infants, and Children (WIC) nutrition program, 159, 234

Women's movement
　19th century/Women's Rights Movement, 117
　1960s and 1970s, 132–134
　African American, 133
　Equal Rights Amendment, 133, 366
　feminist theories/views, 34, 106–107, 294
　impact on professional social work, 134
　National Women's Trade Union League, 122
　social advocacy of women/Settlement Houses, 121–123, 370–371
Wood, Starr A., 286
Workers' compensation, 4, 156, 256–257, 371
Workhouses, 115–116
Working class, 88, 178
Working poor, 4, 7, 146–147, 295–296
Workplace
　family un-friendly, 227–228
　substance abuse/violence in, 276
World Bank, 339, 346–347
World Food Program (WFP), 350
World Health Organization (WHO), 350
World Trade Organization (WTO), 339, 343, 348
World Wars, 253, 338–339, 348
Wormer, Van, 40, 50
Wright, J., 168–169
WTO. *See* World Trade Organization

Xenophobia, 94–95, 105

YMCA, 4
Young-old category, 319
Youth Development, violence prevention model, 300–301
Yunus, Muhammad, 54, 339, 372

Zander, Benjamin, 340
Zander, Rosamund Stone, 340
Zar culture-bound syndrome, 200